THE PRIVATE SIDE OF TRANSFORMING OUR WORLD – UN SUSTAINABLE DEVELOPMENT GOALS 2030 AND THE ROLE OF PRIVATE INTERNATIONAL LAW

INTERSENTIA | ONLINE

An open access online version of this book is also available,
thanks to financing by the Max Planck Institute for
Comparative and International Private Law.
Visit www.intersentiaonline.com for more information.

THE PRIVATE SIDE OF TRANSFORMING OUR WORLD

UN Sustainable Development Goals 2030 and the Role of Private International Law

Edited by
Ralf MICHAELS
Verónica RUIZ ABOU-NIGM
Hans VAN LOON

Project Coordinator
Samuel ZEH

INTERSENTIA

Cambridge – Antwerp – Chicago

Intersentia Ltd
8 Wellington Mews
Wellington Street | Cambridge
CB1 1HW | United Kingdom
Tel: +44 1223 736 170
Email: mail@intersentia.co.uk
www.intersentia.com | www.intersentia.co.uk

Distribution for the UK and
Rest of the World (incl. Eastern Europe)
NBN International
1 Deltic Avenue, Rooksley
Milton Keynes MK13 8LD
United Kingdom
Tel: +44 1752 202 301 | Fax: +44 1752 202 331
Email: orders@nbninternational.com

Distribution for Europe
Lefebvre Sarrut Belgium NV
Hoogstraat 139/6
1000 Brussels
Belgium
Tel: +32 (0)800 39 067
Email: mail@intersentia.be

Distribution for the USA and Canada
Independent Publishers Group
Order Department
814 North Franklin Street
Chicago, IL 60610
USA
Tel: +1 800 888 4741 (toll free) | Fax: +1 312 337 5985
Email: orders@ipgbook.com

The Private Side of Transforming our World – UN Sustainable Development Goals 2030 and the Role of Private International Law

ISBN 978-1-83970-166-5
D/2021/7849/141
NUR 822

British Library Cataloguing in Publication Data. A catalogue record for this book is available from the British Library.

PREFACE

The seeds for this project were shared between the editors at the beautiful gardens of the Peace Palace in The Hague in the spring of 2018. The 'decade of action' was close and we were puzzled by the complete absence of any reference to the role of private international law in our emerging global society, not only in the UN 2030 Agenda but also in other specific soft law instruments adopted under the auspices of the UN, like the Global Compacts for Migration and for Refugees. How could we make visible the hidden private international law potential, its underutilised methodologies; how could we expose it, reconstruct it, transform it? Some things were clear. It needed collaborative scholarship, courageous, creative, bold. It needed perspectives from all corners of our world. It needed an inter-generational approach. Other issues were more fluid, particularly in terms of disciplinary boundaries, and much of what you will read in these chapters benefits from private and public international law dialogues, interdisciplinary and transdisciplinary insights, and diverse conceptualisations of private international law.

A call for papers inviting scholars to examine the relationship between the SDGs and private international law – one for each Goal – found an enthusiastic response, resulting in over 130 proposals from around the world. Selecting the 17 papers was one of the most difficult parts of this journey. We decided in favour of breadth of perspectives and approaches across regions and across generations. Some contributors are private international law experts, others come from neighbouring fields. Some are researchers, others teachers, others law reformers. All found the project was challenging and at times daunting – not least because most of the work was undertaken during a global pandemic.

The chapters in the book demonstrate the role that private international law plays, and the role it could play, for each of the SDGs. Written by a diverse group of scholars, with different disciplinary backgrounds, different home countries, and different ideological and methodological inclinations, they create a multifaceted picture that is not coherent and therefore promising: taken together, the chapters show the multiple roles private international law can play for the SDGs.

We are most grateful to everyone who joined us on this collaborative journey. To the many scholars who engaged with the call, and to the committed authors who contributed to shape this scholarship through several iterations of their chapters. To the publishers, for their support throughout this process. Special thanks go to the project coordinator, Samuel Zeh, of the Hamburg Max Planck Institute.

CONTENTS

LIST OF CONTRIBUTORS

Eduardo Álvarez-Armas
Senior Lecturer in Commercial Law, Brunel University London, United Kingdom; Collaborateur scientifique, Université catholique de Louvain, Belgium

Vivienne Bath
Professor of Chinese & International Business Law, Associate Director – International, Centre for Asian and Pacific Law, University of Sydney, Australia

Gülüm Bayraktaroğlu-Özçelik
Associate Professor of Private International Law, Bilkent University, Bilkent, Ankara, Turkey

Klaus D. Beiter
Associate Professor, North-West University, Potchefstroom, South Africa; Affiliated Research Fellow, Max Planck Institute for Innovation and Competition, Munich, Germany

Sabine Corneloup
Professor of Private Law, University Paris II Panthéon-Assas, France

Klaas Hendrik Eller
Assistant Professor for European Private Law, University of Amsterdam, Amsterdam Center for Transformative Private Law (ACT), The Netherlands

Nikitas E. Hatzimihail
Associate Professor, University of Cyprus, Cyprus

Thalia Kruger
Professor of Private International Law, University of Antwerp, Belgium; Honorary Research Associate, University of Cape Town, South Africa

Ulla Liukkunen
Professor of Labour Law and Private International Law, University of Helsinki; Director of the Finnish Center of Chinese Law and Chinese Legal Culture, Finland

Benyam Dawit Mezmur
Professor of Law, University of the Western Cape, South Africa

Ralf Michaels
Director, Max Planck Institute for Comparative and International Private Law, Hamburg, Germany; Chair in Global Law, Queen Mary University London, United Kingdom; Professor of Law, Hamburg University, Germany

Richard Frimpong Oppong
Professor of Law, California Western School of Law, San Diego, United States of America; Fellow of the Ghana Academy of Arts and Sciences

Fabricio B. Pasquot Polido
Professor of Private International Law, Comparative Law and Technologies and Head of Centre for Transnational and Comparative Legal Studies, Universidade Federal de Minas Gerais, Brazil

Verónica Ruiz Abou-Nigm
Senior Lecturer in International Private Law, University of Edinburgh, United Kingdom

Jay Sanderson
Professor and Head of the School of Law and Society, University of the Sunshine Coast, Australia

Tajudeen Sanni
One Ocean Hub funded Research Fellow, Chair in Law of the Sea and Development in Africa, Institute for Coastal and Marine Research, Nelson Mandela University, South Africa

Geneviève Saumier
Peter M. Laing Q.C. Professor of Law, McGill University, Canada

Anabela Susana de Sousa Gonçalves
Associate Professor, University of Minho, Portugal

Drossos Stamboulakis
Lecturer, Monash University, Australia

Jeannette M.E. Tramhel
Senior Legal Officer, Department of International Law, Secretariat for Legal Affairs, Organization of American States

Hans van Loon
Member of the *Institut de droit international*; Former Secretary General, Hague Conference on Private International Law, The Hague

Jinske Verhellen
Professor of Private International Law, Ghent University, Belgium

INTRODUCTION

The Private Side of Transforming our World – UN Sustainable Development Goals 2030 and the Role of Private International Law

Ralf Michaels, Verónica Ruiz Abou-Nigm and Hans van Loon

Our world is in a deep dual crisis – deeper yet than the crisis emerging from the COVID-19 pandemic. The social part of that crisis has been known for a long time: poverty, combined with ills like maltreatment of women and children and others, and inequality. The traditional response has been to enhance economic development, and that has yielded some success of the last half-century: extreme poverty has declined worldwide. Still, much remains to be done.

Unfortunately, the social problems worldwide – poverty and inequality – are accompanied by a threefold planetary crisis of climate change, nature loss, and pollution. Temperatures are rising at unprecedented speed; biodiversity is quickly declining, with uncertain consequences for all of us, and pollution has emerged as a global threat, already taking millions of lives each year, and getting worse. Many now suggest that the Earth has entered a new stage in its development, the 'Anthropocene'.[1]

The ensuing conundrum for the world is considerable. On the one hand, we want to spur development to reduce poverty and inequality. On the other hand, we know that economic development, with its usage of carbon fuels and land resources, has devastating effects on the planet. We must then achieve economic development in the Global South that is sustainable. And we must, in addition, change ways in the Global North, which creates most of the negative impacts.

This is the dual crisis addressed by the 17 Sustainable Development Goals 2030 (SDGs). Although not beyond criticism, the SDGs have enlivened a worldwide debate on efforts to achieve both development and sustainability. One tool is, unsurprisingly, law, and indeed respect for the rule of law itself is included in the SDGs as a 'transversal goal'. The implications for law have been abundantly researched. Most of that research, however, focuses on public law, either international[2] or domestic.[3] Some research also looks at

---

1 Will Steffen, Åsa Persson, Lisa Deutsch, Jan Zalasiewicz, Mark Williams, Katherine Richardson, Carole Crumley, et al, 'The Anthropocene: From Global Change to Planetary Stewardship' (2011) 40(7) Ambio 739–761. For implications for law, see, e.g., Jedediah Purdy, *After Nature: A Politics for the Anthropocene* (Harvard University Press 2015).

2 See, e.g., Winfried Huck, *Sustainable Development Goals* (Beck 2021); Duncan French and Louis Kotzé, *Sustainable Development Goals – Law, Theory and Implementation* (Edward Elgar Publishing 2018); Markus Kaltenborn, Markus Krajewski and Heike Kuhn, *Sustainable Development Goals and Human Rights* (Springer 2020); Inga Winkler and Carmel Williams, *The Sustainable Development Goals and Human Rights: A Critical Early Review* (Routledge 2018).

3 E.g. Winfried Huck and Claudia Kurkin, 'Die UN-Sustainable Development Goals (SDGs) im transnationalen Mehrebenensystem' (2018) 78 Heidelberg Journal of International Law 375; ASviS, *Italy and the Sustainable Development Goals* (2020) <https://asvis.it/public/asvis2/files/Rapporto_ASviS/Rapporto_ASviS_2020/Report_ASviS_2020_ENG_final.pdf> accessed 6 July 2021.

private law.[4] Absent from such research is, however, private international law. That is a significant lacuna. Private international law can no longer (if it ever could) be viewed as a 'merely technical' device to resolve conflicts of law based on formal criteria. Rather, private international law is a core element of transnational regulation. It can therefore foster or hinder sustainable development too.

1. THE UN SUSTAINABLE DEVELOPMENT GOALS 2030

1.1. ORIGIN AND NATURE

On 25 September 2015, the United Nations General Assembly unanimously adopted the Resolution 'Transforming Our World: the 2030 Agenda for Sustainable Development'.[5] The core of the Resolution consists of 17 Sustainable Development Goals (SDGs) with 169 associated targets, and many more indicators. In this focus on development, the SDGs build on the earlier UN Millennium Development Goals (MDGs) adopted in 2000,[6] and explicitly both incorporate and continue the MDGs' development priorities: eradicate poverty, improve basic human health, and enhance food security, educational opportunities and gender equality.

However, they go further in an important way. Unlike the MDGs, the SDGs focus not only on development but also add, equally importantly, sustainability. Therefore, the SDGs are of a 'dual nature'. While pursuing 'development', this aim is fundamentally qualified by 'sustainability': their overarching purpose is to transform societies in the direction of sustainability. The SDGs add a large number of new goals to the MDGs, including many aimed at 'protect[ing] the planet from degradation, including through sustainable consumption and production, sustainably managing its natural resources and taking urgent action

4 Axel Halfmeier, 'Nachhaltiges Privatrecht' (2016) 216 Archiv für civilistische Praxis 717; Bram Akkermans and Gijs van Dijck (eds), *Sustainability and Private Law* (Boom 2019); Jan-Erik Schirmer, 'Nachhaltigkeit in den Privatrechten Europas' (2021) 26 Zeitschrift für Europäisches Privatrecht 35; see also Cristina Poncibò, 'The Contractualisation of Environmental Sustainability' (2016) 12 European Review of Contract Law 335; Beate Sjåfjell and Benjamin Richardson (eds), *The Future of Company Law and Sustainability* (CUP 2015).

5 UN General Assembly, 'Transforming Our World: the 2030 Agenda for Sustainable Development', UN Doc A/RES/70/1 (21 October 2015) <https://sdgs.un.org/2030agenda> accessed 6 July 2021.

6 World Health Organization, 'Millennium Development Goals (MDGs)' (19 February 2018) <https://www.who.int/news-room/fact-sheets/detail/millennium-development-goals-(mdgs)> accessed 6 July 2021.

on climate change'.[7] Human activity has become a dominant force on our planet, with unanticipated adverse consequences for the Earth's life-support systems, risking exceeding, and indeed already exceeding, what is called 'planetary boundaries',[8] with potentially irreversible catastrophic effects for future generations and ecosystems.

The dual focus has a consequence: the SDGs cover the whole world more explicitly than did the MDGs. Whereas the MDGs were centred on issues of particular importance to developing countries, the SDGs were conceived as universally applicable to all countries and 'highlight challenges that require substantial behavioural changes on the part of the residents of developed countries as well as efforts to improve the circumstances of those living in developing countries'.[9] Underlying the SDGs 2030 is, then, an understanding of interconnectedness, and an understanding of responsibility of the Global North for the Global South that goes beyond mere wealth redistribution. Life in the Global North has created unsustainable damages to the planet. This creates a dual task – to achieve sustainability in the Global North, and to enable and spur development in the rest of the world that is also sustainable.

Each of the 17 SDGs addresses a specific issue or range of issues, and fixes governance goals and specific detailed targets to resolve them, generally within specific timeframes (usually by 2030, sometimes by 2025 or 2020). The Goals and targets are supported by indicators, which at the regional and national levels are to be developed by UN Member States, and at the global level are established by a global indicator framework,[10] reviewed on an annual basis, with a comprehensive review every five years.[11] Monitoring and revision of the Goals, targets and indicators are entrusted to the High-level Political Forum on Sustainable Development, under the auspices of the UN Economic and Social Council.[12]

Some SDGs are obviously interconnected in terms of common or related global issues, as well as ways to deal with them. Unfortunately, while the SDGs contain cross-references to each other, they are essentially self-standing

---

7 Preamble to the SDGs, p 2.

8 Stockholm Resilience Center, 'Planetary boundaries' <https://www.stockholmresilience.org/research/planetary-boundaries.html> accessed 6 July 2021.

9 Oran Young, Arild Underdal, Norichika Kanie and Rakhyun Kim, 'Goal setting in the Anthropocene: The Ultimate Challenge of Planetary Stewardship' in Norichika Kanie and Frank Biermann, *Governing through Goals* (MIT Press 2017) 54.

10 See UN General Assembly Resolution on Work of the Statistical Commission pertaining to the 2030 Agenda for Sustainable Development, Annex, UN Doc A/RES/71/313 (10 July 2017).

11 See <https://unstats.un.org/sdgs/> accessed 6 July 2021.

12 See High-Level Political Forum, Sustainable Development Knowledge Platform (2020) <https://sustainabledevelopment.un.org/hlpf/2020> accessed 6 July 2021.

and 'do not speak to each other'. They also lack a hierarchal order. Other interconnections appear when it is acknowledged that the full realisation of Goals 1–15 requires the promotion of all the targets of Goal 16, as well as of Goal 17. The latter two may therefore be considered 'transversal' and 'instrumental' Goals. Agenda 2030 is meant to be indivisible, that is, pursuing the targets in relation of one of the SDGs should not negatively affect the progressive achievement of targets in relation to the other SDGs. Beyond these interconnections, many SDGs are connected to a variety of other global and regional governance instruments, from which, on the one hand, they derive context and meaning, and to the realisation of which, on the other, they may give a boost.

1.2. GOAL-SETTING AND RULEMAKING AS GOVERNANCE STRATEGIES

The SDGs are not legally binding, no more than the UN Resolution on which they are based. They articulate aspirations, and set out procedures to achieve them, with benchmarks to measure and assess progression towards accomplishment. This is a governance strategy that differs from traditional rulemaking, which is rather aimed at enabling and regulating human behaviour by defining – directly or, as in the case of private international law, primarily indirectly – rights and obligations through norms that usually remain in place until they are replaced by new ones.

The aspirational nature of the SDGs allows them to encompass an exceptionally 'broad and universal policy agenda'[13] while seeking moral, theoretical and practical support for their achievement from a variety of actors, and through an array of disciplines including, but by no means only, law. Their non-legally binding nature enables them to account for and adapt to differing levels of development and uneven capabilities between states. Moreover, and importantly, while '[g]overnments have the primary responsibility for follow-up and review',[14] the 'journey [towards the realisation of the SDGs] will involve Governments as well as parliaments, the United Nations system and other international institutions, local authorities, indigenous peoples, civil society, business and the private sector, the scientific and academic community – and all people'.[15]

---

13 Introduction to the SDGs, para 18, p 6.

14 Para 47, p 11.

15 Para 52, p 12.

This is why the SDGs are typified as a 'polycentric'[16] or 'multilevel' governance model balancing top-down and bottom-up approaches.[17] Indeed, the notion of responsible business conduct or corporate social responsibility – for human rights violations, environmental degradation and governance shortcomings down corporations' global value chains – continues to spread and intensify around the globe. Therefore, businesses, and the private sector, along with public authorities, are becoming key actors for the realisation of the SDGs. The same goes for local and indigenous communities, non-governmental organisations and other private persons.

Indicator-driven, target-setting governance has a strong quantitative slant to it. But much of the work to be done requires *qualitative* changes, not least in human behaviour. Norm promotion and rulemaking, therefore, remain crucially needed as complementary or implementing strategies to achieve SDGs' governance objectives. This appears from several targets themselves, which refer, directly or indirectly, to binding international multilateral treaties or institutions which they seek to embrace and reinforce.

1.3. STRENGTHS AND WEAKNESSES OF THE SDGs GOVERNANCE MODEL

The SDGs are not undisputed. Academic critique varies widely: it extends from questioning the very ability of the SDGs to adequately address 'the scale and urgency of the unfolding planetary catastrophe', stating that they 'offer no real possibility of global, climate or social justice for current or future generations'.[18] Such questioning stretches from expressions of doubts and regrets about certain aspects, to suggestions to further strengthen the Goals through indicators and commitments. They have even been said to be, 'in their present guise, … rhetorically ambitious but simultaneously destructive.'[19] And their

16 Takahiro Yamada, 'Corporate Water Stewardship: Lessons for Goal-based Hybrid Governance' in Norichika Kanie and Frank Biermann, *Governing through Goals* (MIT Press 2017) 189.

17 Joyeeta Gupta and Måns Nilsson, 'Toward a Multi-level Action Framework for Sustainable Development Goals' Norichika Kanie and Frank Biermann, *Governing through Goals* (MIT Press 2017) 278.

18 Sam Adelman, 'The Sustainable Development Goals, anthropocentrism and neoliberalism', in Duncan French and Louis Kotzé, *Sustainable Development Goals* (Edward Elgar Publishing 2018) 39.

19 Louis Kotzé, 'The Sustainable Development Goals: an existential critique alongside three new-millennial analytical paradigms' in Duncan French and Louis Kotzé, *Sustainable Development Goals* (Edward Elgar Publishing 2018) 65.

ambition has not yet been matched by full success, as the UN Secretary-General has recently pointed out.[20]

Indeed, the SDGs are certainly not free from shortcomings. While measurability is at their core so as to enable achievements to be assessed and compared, many of the targets remain open-ended or vague, leaving room for normative debate and weak implementation.[21] Furthermore, the SDGs lack a robust institutional monitoring framework.[22] As a result, oversight of implementation at the global level also is left largely open-ended. More specifically, the SDGs have been criticised, for example, for paying little attention to the rights and vulnerabilities of indigenous peoples.[23]

Tensions between potentially clashing targets and differing prioritisations may lead to setbacks and jeopardise the universality of the Agenda. A key objection concerns the unresolved opposition concealed in the SDGs' dual nature: the tension between development and sustainability. How can economic growth as a necessary condition for eradicating poverty, ending hunger, providing water and sanitation, and improving education and health, on the one hand, be reconciled with respect for ecosystems, on the other, which may require the reverse: less economic expansion?

Obviously, economic growth at the cost of human dignity and health, natural systems and the world's climate is incompatible with *sustainable* development. While Target 8.4 includes the call to 'decouple economic growth from environmental degradation', other SDGs call for economic growth without further qualification (Targets 2.a, 10.6, 17.5). One would also have wished for a stronger encouragement than Target 12.c, addressed to 'developed' countries in particular, to introduce fossil fuel reforms, including the reduction of fossil fuel subsidies. These are among the very first measures, one would think, to take to ease the transition to non-fossil-fuel

---

20 See United Nations, The Sustainable Development Goals Report 2020 (2020) <https://unstats.un.org/sdgs/report/2020/The-Sustainable-Development-Goals-Report-2020.pdf> accessed 6 July 2021, which, as UN Secretary-General Guterres points out in his foreword, shows that even 'before the COVID-19 pandemic, progress remained uneven and we were not on track to meet the Goals by 2030 … Now, due to COVID-19, an unprecedented health, economic and social crisis is threatening lives and livelihoods, making the achievement of Goals even more challenging.'

21 Several chapters in Noha Shawki (ed) *International norms, normative change, and the UN Sustainable Development Goals* (Lexington Books 2016) shed light on the normative controversies during the negotiation process, including on the 'transversal' SDGs 16 and 17.

22 However, other agencies have accepted (co-)responsibility for certain SDG indicators. For example, as noted by Benyam Dawit Mezmur (SDG 1), UNICEF has accepted (co-)responsibility for a number of child-focused SDG indicators.

23 Lynda Collins, 'Sustainable Development Goals and human rights: challenges and opportunities' in Duncan French and Louis Kotzé, *Sustainable Development Goals* (Edward Elgar Publishing 2018) 87.

energy production.[24] Targets 10.1 (on reducing inequality) and 17.19 (on developing alternative measurements instead of GDP), both to be achieved by 2030, could be interpreted as leaving these fundamental objectives to post-2030 generations.[25]

That said, whatever reservations one may have, the SDGs are (unlike the MDGs) the outcome of a broad consultation and negotiation process; they have attracted wide attention and mobilised world-wide support; and they constitute a roadmap for the current decade, the most authoritative and comprehensive global guide[26] humanity has ever had. The SDGs, in contrast with binding treaties, are not addressed to states only but appeal to all, including the private sector and civil society. Moreover, and perhaps paradoxically, they have become a focal point for comprehensive thinking about the world's future, a primary unifying narrative, activating everyone's sense of joint responsibility, inviting and empowering us all to set our sights high.

The goal-setting governance structure of the SDGs provides a pathway; its objectives can and should be advanced in time and impact as awareness of Agenda 2030 increases. Law can and should play a significant role. Courts have already granted legal standing to individuals and NGOs seeking to represent future generations, and have interpreted the law as requiring intergenerational equity.[27] In another development, constitutions, laws and courts in a number of countries have granted legal personhood or standing to rivers and other non-human parts of nature, and even to Earth itself 'as a collective subject of public interest'.[28] Ideas are being proposed to ground the principle of

---

24 See Assia Elgouacem, 'Designing fossil fuel subsidy reforms in OECD and G20 countries: A robust sequential approach methodology', OECD Environment Working Paper No 168 (21 October 2020) <https://www.oecd-ilibrary.org/environment/designing-fossil-fuel-subsidies-reforms-in-oecd-and-g20-countries_d888f461-en> accessed 6 July 2021.

25 See Open Letter to the UN, signed by Chomsky, Pogge, Klein ... (29 September 2015) <http://www.globalsocialjustice.eu/index.php/articles/1053-open-letter-to-the-un-signed-by-chomsky-pogge-klein> accessed 6 July 2021.

26 Or in the words of UN Secretary-General Guterrez, also referring to the COVID- 19 epidemic: 'a path that brings health to all, revives economies, brings people in from the margins of society and builds long-term resilience, sustainability, opportunity and peace'. Secretary-General's opening remarks at Sustainable Development Goals Moment [as delivered] (18 September 2020) <https://www.un.org/sg/en/content/sg/statement/2020-09-18/secretary-generals-opening-remarks-sustainable-development-goals-moment-delivered> accessed 6 July 2021.

27 Oran Young, Arild Underdal, Norichika Kanie and Rakhyun Kim, 'Goal setting in the Anthropocene: The Ultimate Challenge of Planetary Stewardship' in Norichika Kanie and Frank Biermann, *Governing through Goals* (MIT Press 2017) 66. In its order of 24 March 2021, the German Constitutional Court placed strong emphasis on this aspect, see <https://www.bundesverfassungsgericht.de/SharedDocs/Entscheidungen/DE/2021/03/rs20210324_1bvr265618.html>.

28 See the Bolivian *Ley de Derechos de la Madre Tierra*, December 2010, Art 5, <https://www.bivica.org/files/tierra-derechos-ley.pdf> accessed 6 July 2021. See, generally, Tiffany Challe,

sustainability in a basic global norm – a sustainability *Grundnorm* – parallel to the protection of human rights.[29]

2. SDGs AND PRIVATE INTERNATIONAL LAW

The SDGs are ambitious, and it will take enormous efforts on multiple levels to achieve them. It is therefore striking, given the multilevel governance model, that nearly all instruments and institutions mentioned throughout the targets belong to the realm of public international law. There is a near-complete absence of any reference to the role of *private*, including commercial, law, and the role it plays via *private international law* in our global economy and emerging world society. This is a significant gap. Most transactions, most investments, most destruction of our environment, happen not through public but through private action, and are governed not exclusively by public law but also, perhaps predominantly, by private law. Private law, therefore, has an important role to play in the quest for sustainability, and this is increasingly being recognised.[30] What remains under the radar, so far, is private international law.

The SDGs seem to have a blind spot for what is in fact already a relevant governance tool for their achievement and has potential to become even more pertinent thereto. We see an important, constructive role for private international law as an indispensable part of the global legal architecture. It is needed to turn the SDGs into reality, to reduce the tension between development and sustainability, and to reinforce the human rights component of the SDGs in cross-border situations, in short: to do its part to strengthen the SDGs' plan of action. This requires a two-step, or a two-stage, approach. The first step is to bring to the surface the hidden – 'forgotten' by the SDGs framework – role private international law plays in enabling and regulating cross-border conduct affecting the life and well-being of human beings, the ecosystems, and the planet as a whole. The second step is to explore, for each of the SDGs, how private international law could, or should, be reformed to better respond to the wide range of economic, social and environmental challenges which the SDGs attempt to address.

'The Rights of Nature – Can an Ecosystem Bear Legal Rights?', Climate Law Blog (22 April 2021) <http://blogs.law.columbia.edu/climatechange/2021/04/22/the-rights-of-nature-can-an-ecosystem-bear-legal-rights/> accessed 6 July 2021.

29 See Norichika Kanie and Frank Biermann, *Governing through Goals* (MIT Press 2017) passim, in particular 67–70.

30 Axel Halfmeier, 'Nachhaltiges Privatrecht' (2016) 216 Archiv für civilistische Praxis 717; Bram Akkermans and Gijs van Dijck (eds), *Sustainability and Private Law* (Boom 2019); Jan-Erik Schirmer, 'Nachhaltigkeit in den Privatrechten Europas' (2021) 26 Zeitschrift für Europäisches Privatrecht 35; see also Cristina Poncibò, 'The Contractualisation of Environmental Sustainability' (2016) 12 European Review of Contract Law 335; Beate Sjåfjell and Benjamin Richardson (eds), *The Future of Company Law and Sustainability* (CUP 2015).

2.1. WHAT IS PRIVATE INTERNATIONAL LAW?

What is private international law? Private international law is the discipline that addresses problems arising from private interactions that are connected to more than one legal system. Narrowly understood, private international law contains three areas. The first is (adjudicatory, or judicial) jurisdiction: which courts and authorities have jurisdiction in matters of international private relationships, and how jurisdictional conflicts are resolved. The second is choice of law: which law, or which laws, applies to those relationships. The third field is recognition and enforcement of judgments: whether and under what conditions the courts of one jurisdiction will give effect to foreign decisions and official acts of another. More broadly understood, private international law also contains uniform transnational private law (like the United Nations Convention on Contracts for the International Sale of Goods[31]).

The name 'international' is a bit of a misnomer. Private international law rules are, traditionally and formally, domestic law: each country has its own, and differences among the private international law rules of different countries create significant difficulties.[32] Early hopes of deriving private international law rules from (customary) public international law never materialised: traditional public international law has little to say about private international law, human rights now play a somewhat bigger role. However, for a long time there have been projects to unify private international laws. In the European Union, much private international law has been 'federalised' – moved to the European level. Globally, many rules on private international law are the subject of international treaties and conventions, most importantly under the leadership of the Hague Conference on Private International Law (HCCH).

2.2. IMPLICIT INTERPLAY WITH THE SDGs

Although private international law is not mentioned explicitly, even a cursory stroll through the SDGs demonstrates their implicit interplay with private international law. For example, the SDGs set out goals regarding personal status and family relations: '[b]y 2030, provide legal identity for all, including birth registration' (Target 16.9), or '[e]liminate … forced marriage' (Target 5.3), both well-known themes of private international law in cross-border scenarios.

31 United Nations Convention on Contracts for the International Sale of Goods (CISG) (Vienna, 1980).

32 This is of course a simplification. For the view that private international law 'effects an international ordering of regulatory authority in private law, structured by international principles of justice, pluralism and subsidiarity', see Alex Mills, *The Confluence of Public and Private International Law* (CUP 2009).

Moreover, they focus on trade and thereby invoke *contract law* in multiple ways. On the one hand, they encourage freedom of contract when they call to 'correct and prevent trade restrictions and distortions in world agricultural markets' (Target 2.b) or 'promote the development, transfer, dissemination and diffusion of environmentally sound technologies to developing countries on favourable terms ... as mutually agreed' (Target 17.7). On the other hand, they insist on restrictions, for example the 'immediate and effective' eradication of forced labour, 'modern slavery' and child trafficking (Targets 8.7, 16.2), as well as the goals to 'by 2030 significantly reduce illicit financial and arms flows' (Target 16.4); 'substantially reduce corruption and bribery in all their forms' (Target 16.5).

The SDGs also assume a role for *tort law*, or law of delict, including its application to cross-border situations, for example to fulfil goals regarding environmental protection and climate change.

Other targets concern cross-border *civil litigation*. Thus, the call to 'ensure equal access to justice for all' (Target 16.3) has traditionally been confined to equal treatment within one legal system. But as a global goal, it invokes global equality: for instance, the ability for European victims of the Volkswagen diesel scandal to access courts like US victims, or providing recourse to compensation for Latin Americans victims of oil pollution on a similar level to those in Alaska. All of this has multiple implications in the sphere of cross-border civil procedure: the admissibility of global class actions and public interest actions, judicial jurisdiction, recognition and enforcement of judgments concerning corporate social and environmental responsibility, and so on.

Finally, the SDGs have an institutional component. SDG 16 calls, among other things, for 'strong institutions' and it encourages cooperation. What come into focus here, from a private international law perspective, are institutions like the Hague Conference on Private International Law and its Hague Conventions, as well as other instruments of cooperation and institutionalisation in the private international law realm.

2.3. CHALLENGES FOR PRIVATE INTERNATIONAL LAW

One task is to make the implicit role of private international law explicit – to demonstrate concretely in what ways private international law already exists with regard to the SDGs. Another is, however, to assess how well existing private international law already performs its role for the SDGs, and how capable it is of doing so. Here, the discipline runs into three challenges, but we see the beginnings of responses.

First, countries around the world differ regarding the stance of private international law in their legal systems: there are differences between the civil law and common law traditions; some countries, like the United States, have methods of their own; some countries are more 'internationalists' than others; and many countries have borrowed private international law methodologies and techniques from other countries, other regions, and other legal traditions, with differing degrees of success. In some countries, institutions may lack the power, and sometimes also the sophistication, to accept the idea that they could apply another law than their own, or that private parties could themselves designate a foreign court or a foreign law for their transactions, let alone their family relationships.[33] At the same time, such a country may well be exposed to private international law's impact, for example when it engages in a foreign investment contract with a foreign multinational company. That company may require, as one of the conditions of the contract, acceptance of the exclusive jurisdiction of a forum in its home country or of an international arbitral tribunal, and/or of the applicability of the law of its home country or a third state. Since unfamiliarity with private international law will generally go hand in hand with a fragile legal infrastructure and a weak economic bargaining position, the host country will often be unable to resist such conditions. This predicament is relevant to several SDGs.

Second, private international law remains, very often, domestic. Following the formation of the nation-state in the 19th century, private international law mostly developed as a domestic law methodology to deal with situations with a 'foreign element'. Especially in Europe and the United States, private international lawyers anchored the discipline in their national legal order, projecting its conceptions and values onto the international plane. Only rarely was the inverse true, as was the case when several Latin American countries adopted agreed conceptions and values at the international level[34] by first adopting the Montevideo Treaties.[35] Conversely, public international lawyers showed little interest in how private relations, economic activity and legal ordering of these relations and activity affected global affairs. Even though the late 19th century already saw the birth of initiatives aiming at international harmonisation of private international law embodied in multilateral treaties – instruments of public international law – this picture started to change, except for Latin America, in a meaningful way only after World War II. Increasing internationalisation came under pressure later,

---

33 Cf for an illustrative anecdote, Georges Droz, 'Regards sur le droit international privé comparé', Cours général, Hague Academy of International Law, Recueil des cours, vol 299 (1991-IV), 25.

34 So much so that 'divorce' as a legal category in private international law was regulated in the Montevideo Treaties even though at the time of adoption of the Treaties none of the signatories provided for divorce in their national legal systems (Ruben Santos Belandro in Cecilia Fresnedo de Aguirre and Gonzalo Lorenzo Idiarte (eds), *Jornadas 130 Aniversario Tratados de Montevideo 1889* (FCU 2019) 66).

35 Margarita Argúas, 'The Montevideo Treaties of 1889 and 1940 and their Influence on the Unification of Private International Law in South America' in Maarten Bos (ed), *The Present State of International Law and Other Essays* (Kluwer Press 1973) 345.

due to three countervailing but interrelated developments: increased diversity through the increasingly active role of countries in the Global South, growing unilateralism in the United States, and in between these two, the increasing regionalisation of EU private international law, leading to more integration internally and more isolation externally. New opportunities for communication, travel, investment, production and marketing across all regions and continents have caused a huge expansion of the range, intensity, velocity and impact of private relationships and transactions. As a result, legal doctrine, case law and legislation are gradually shifting from an essentially domestic, and sometimes regional perspective, to a more transnational, indeed global, perspective. These perspectives are not geared towards top-down universalism but focus on the horizontal interactions between normative orders, including, but not reserved to, interactions between national legal systems.

Third, private international law was long viewed as a purely technical and formal discipline with no political relevance and no regulatory potential, a discipline that presumes equivalence of legal systems. In this regard, private international law's strength is also its weakness. Its strength is its focus on private relationships. It has developed refined techniques to allocate issues to legal orders and laws, and to facilitate communication and cooperation between authorities and courts. It has found methods to favour desirable and necessary substantive outcomes. Yet its focus on the private sphere has often led the discipline to lose sight of the larger – political, social, economic, cultural, but also public (international) law – context in which private and commercial relationships develop, and, as a result, of its own effect on the international ordering of legal authority in private law – its hidden governance role.[36]

2.4. RECOGNISING THE TRANSFORMATIVE POTENTIAL OF PRIVATE INTERNATIONAL LAW

If it were true that private international law had no regulatory effect and no governance role, the discipline would be of no use to foundationally regulatory issues like the SDGs, and it would have nothing to say about the emerging North–South tensions. Fortunately, we know that this is not an accurate description.[37] Private international law has a dual regulatory potential.

[36] See, generally, Alex Mills, *The Confluence of Public and Private International Law* (CUP 2009). See also Verónica Ruiz Abou-Nigm et al (eds), *Linkages and Boundaries in Private and Public International Law* (Hart 2018).

[37] Horatia Muir Watt, 'Private International Law: Beyond the Schism' (2011) 2 Transnational Legal Theory 347; Ralf Michaels, 'Towards a Private International Law for Regulatory Conflicts?' (2017) 59 Japanese Yearbook of International Law 175; Hans van Loon, 'The Global Horizon of Private International Law' (2015) 380 Recueil des cours 9.

First, private international law rules can be used to deal with regulatory laws.[38] Second, like other laws, it has regulatory effects on its own: it participates in the designation of winners and losers; it sets incentives that can lead to better or worse conduct.[39]

Agenda 2030 calls on *all* the planet's actors to make their contribution to the realisation of its Goals. Through the lens of law, the world is a patchwork of legal orders and systems in constant flux governing human activity. Therefore, ways must be found to connect and mediate between those orders and systems to make them serve the SDGs. Private international law has an important role to play in this regard.

It is helpful to distinguish here between private international law's two roles regarding human conduct: its *regulatory* and its *enabling* function. Its rules and their underlying policies regarding vulnerable and weaker parties offer an example of its well-established *regulatory* function. For example, in cross-border situations, children and the elderly are particularly vulnerable, and need protection. A number of Hague, EU and Inter-American private international law instruments offer such protection. In respect of children, this private international legal framework is intimately connected with that of the 1989 United Nations Convention on the Rights of the Child, including its implementation across the world. Private international law also regulates protection of persons in an economically weaker position than their counterparties in specific transactions, such as employees and consumers, which is often aggravated in cross-border scenarios. Special rules have also been developed to protect persons from transnational environmental damage.

Outside of such situations, private international law generally has an *enabling* role, facilitating cross-border relations and transactions. As noted already, contemporary private international law tends to increase the freedom of parties in international situations to transcend the boundaries of their legal orders and systems, enabling them to choose a competent court or arbitral tribunal (party autonomy). The Hague Conventions on administrative and judicial cooperation and EU, Inter-American and Mercosur instruments have facilitated the circulation across borders of public documents, service of process, taking of evidence, access to justice, and the recognition and enforcement of foreign judgments.

---

38 See, e.g., Annelise Riles, 'Managing Regulatory Arbitrage: A Conflict of Laws Approach' (2014) 47 Cornell Journal of International Law 63; Mathias Lehmann, 'Regulation, global governance and private international law: squaring the triangle' (2020) 16 Journal of Private International Law 1.

39 Robert Wai, 'Transnational Liftoff and Juridical Touchdown: The Regulatory Function of Private International Law in an Era of Globalization' (2002) 40 Columbia Journal of Transnational Law 209; Jacco Bomhoff and Anne Meuwese, 'The Meta-regulation of Transnational Private Regulation' (2011) 38 Journal of Law and Society 138.

The distinction between the enabling and regulatory roles of private international law is not clear-cut. The same set of rules that enables one party, under certain conditions, to pursue her rights against another party, may, if she is successful, prevent that other party from effectuating her rights. Conversely, if those conditions are not met, this will enable the other party to pursue her goal.[40]

More generally, enabling private international law rules are subject to open-ended corrective rules. These rules may apply *ex ante*, i.e. as 'overriding mandatory norms', which apply in the country of the court addressed, irrespective of that country's choice of law rules (in some legal systems such norms may even derive from the law of a third state). Or they may apply *ex post*, when the result of applying a foreign law or enforcing a foreign judgment in the case at hand would jeopardise that country's public policy. However, both overriding mandatory rules and the public policy exception are fluid notions, without predictable regulatory outcomes.

3. SOME GENERAL FINDINGS RESULTING FROM THE PROJECT

3.1. PRIVATE INTERNATIONAL LAW ROLES IN THE REALISATION OF AGENDA 2030

Three main findings emerge from the ground-breaking research conducted in this project. First, all authors agree that private international law has a part to play in the realisation of Agenda 2030. Second, many chapters highlight, and deplore, the underutilisation of, or even disregard for, private international law by the SDGs governance framework. More broadly, they lament the blind spot as regards the function of private law and private international law in global instruments relevant to the SDGs: too much emphasis on interstate relations, liabilities and remedies; too little on access to justice and remedies for private actors. Third, many authors express their conviction that there is an urgent need for private international law to become (far) more aware of and engaged in the realisation of the SDGs, and, to that end, reorient itself towards these Goals, and if necessary re-conceptualise itself.

---

40 Similarly, where private international law rules make party autonomy subject to certain conditions, the parties' freedom is to that extent also regulated, thereby perhaps enabling others to pursue their interests. And private international law instruments establishing cross-border cooperation between authorities to enable, for example, the service of process or the taking of evidence on behalf of the plaintiff also offer protection to the defendant or witnesses.

While all authors share the view that private international law is relevant to the realisation of the SDGs, several contributors remind us that this role has its limits. *Richard Frimpong Oppong (SDG 6)*, when suggesting private international law reform, points out that to reverse the current trend towards declining water and sanitation services in a number of African countries 'substantial investments in water supply and sanitation facilities and infrastructure … should be at the top of the list of all governments, especially governments in developing countries where the need is often most pressing'. More generally, 'the issues involved in achieving SDG 6 are too complex and multifaceted to be resolved through traditional private international law methodologies, and adversarial litigation or international arbitration'. Likewise, *Geneviève Saumier (SDG 12)*, when suggesting several improvements to private international law, highlights the critical importance of attitudinal changes that are necessary to reduce 'unsustainable consumption and production [patterns which] result from human activities [and which, therefore,] largely escape the reach of law'. This, she argues, applies even more strongly to the consumption than to the production side.

Indeed, regarding *production* patterns, there is a manifest ongoing development both at the global and the regional level towards strengthening responsible business conduct. At the UN, a General Assembly working group is preparing an 'international legally binding instrument on transnational corporations and other business enterprises with respect to human rights'.[41] The latest August 2020 draft contains several provisions dealing with private international law.[42] In the European Union (following important initiatives at the national level),[43] the Commission is working towards an instrument to impose due diligence obligations on companies. Ahead of the Commission's proposals, the European Parliament on 10 March 2021 adopted a draft Directive obliging EU Member States to 'lay down rules to ensure that undertakings carry out

41 Based on UN General Assembly Resolution on elaboration of an international legally binding instrument on transnational corporations and other business enterprises with respect to human rights, UN Doc A/HRC/RES/26/9 (14 July 2014).

42 See Legally Binding Instrument to Regulate, in International Human Rights Law, the Activities of Transnational Corporations and Other Business Enterprises, OEIGWG Chairmanship Second Revised Draft (6 August 2020) Arts 9–12 <https://www.ohchr.org/Documents/HRBodies/HRCouncil/WGTransCorp/Session6/OEIGWG_Chair-Rapporteur_second_revised_draft_LBI_on_TNCs_and_OBEs_with_respect_to_Human_Rights.pdf> accessed 6 July 2021. See also the Report on the sixth session of the WG, UN Doc A/HRC/46/73 (14 January 2021).

43 Above all, the 2017 French *Loi sur le devoir de vigilance*. In June 2021, the German Bundestag passed a law on corporate social responsibility in supply chains, *Gesetz über die unternehmerischen Sorgfaltspflichten in Lieferketten*; see <https://www.csr-in-deutschland.de/EN/Business-Human-Rights/Supply-Chain-Act/supply-chain-act.html;jsessionid=9F61D2EB0229E04899F47D97CCF2535F> accessed 6 July 2021. Contrary to the French act, however, the German draft does not plan to sanction infringements by civil (tortious) liability towards victims.

effective due diligence with respect to potential or actual adverse impacts on human rights, the environment and good governance in their operations and business relationships'. This proposal also contains a provision on private international law.[44]

Moreover, recent judicial decisions in particular in the United Kingdom and the Netherlands relating to private international law tend to reinforce the transnational responsibility of corporations for human rights violations and damage to the environment.[45]

On the *consumption* side, there is, as *Geneviève Saumier (SDG 12)* points out, still 'no indication that legislatures are moving toward imposing obligations directly on consumers to behave in ways that are consistent with SDG 12'. However, there is some hope, she argues, that through private international law consumers may, indirectly, push for sustainable production, including through reformed jurisdictional and procedural rules and increased opportunities 'to hold [multinationals] to account regarding the use of eco-labels through courts'. *Jeannette M.E. Tramhel (SDG 2)* also offers ideas on how private voluntary standards relating to agricultural products could be given international recognition (as 'ECOTERMS') to encourage a shift towards more sustainable consumption and thereby create demand for more sustainably produced foods.

3.2. THE UNDERUTILISATION OF AND DISREGARD FOR PRIVATE INTERNATIONAL LAW

Several chapters note the lack of use made of, or disregard for, private international law, not only by the SDGs but more generally in international governance instruments. *Ulla Liukkunen (SDG 8)* regrets that the International Labour Organization, in its regulatory activity, has not focused on questions of private international law relating to labour contracts and labour market issues. As a result, the task of regulating these questions falls on regional or national private international law initiatives, where much work remains to be done. The protection offered by national private international law regimes for individual employment contracts varies and often does not reach posted workers who are

---

44 See European Parliament resolution of 10 March 2021 with recommendations to the Commission on corporate due diligence and corporate accountability, 2020/2129(INL) (10 March 2021) Arts 4(1) and 20 <https://www.europarl.europa.eu/doceo/document/TA-9-2021-0073_EN.html> accessed 6 July 2021.

45 *Vedanta Resources plc and Another v Lungowe and Others* [2019] UKSC 20, and *Okpabi and Others v Royal Dutch Shell plc and Another* [2021] UKSC 3; Hague Court of Appeal 29 January 2021, *Four Nigerian Farmers and Milieudefensie v Shell*, ECLI:NL:GHDHA:2021:132, ECLI:NL:GHDHA:2021:133, and ECLI:NL:GHDHA:2021:134; Hague District Court 26 May 2021, *Milieudefensie et al v RDS*, ECLI:NL:RBDHA:2021:5337.

only temporarily working in another country, nor forms of work that are not based on employment contracts. The EU's revised Posted Workers Directive[46] establishes a fragile balance between the promotion of free movement of services and the need for minimum protection of posted workers – between economic and social objectives. Likewise, *Tajudeen Sanni (SDG 14)* emphasises the private (international) law deficit in the protection of local communities who depend for their livelihood on sustainable use of the oceans, seas and marine resources, the regulation of which falls exclusively on states and public law, with no access to justice for these local communities. Both the 1982 United Nations Convention on Law of the Sea (UNCLOS) and the 1992 Convention on Biological Diversity (CBD) lack 'specific mechanisms that aid private actions to tackle infractions on the marine space at a transboundary level'.

Private international law, in the words of *Nikitas E. Hatzimihail (SDG 7)* 'can help expedite the international flows of information, financial, technological and material resources needed in order to make energy access both truly universal and truly sustainable'. Harmonised private international law rules increase this potential. Yet, as *Sabine Corneloup and Jinske Verhellen (SDG 16)* observe in relation to issues of legal identity, although an array of private international law instruments is available, they remain under-exploited. Indeed, the underutilisation of private international law around the globe can be ascribed, in large part, to the fact that the principal vehicle for private international law unification is the multilateral treaty. Multilateral treaties, or conventions, have the great merit of establishing uniform binding rules that can have a real impact on cross-border relationships and transactions. But their weakness is that, however much based on agreement or even consensus among the negotiating states, they nevertheless must pass the subsequent test of national constitutional procedures for their acceptance by each state. As a result, it often takes decades before they reach a meaningful number of participating states.

This is one of the reasons why soft law private international law instruments are gaining popularity. And just as the SDGs, although not binding, may have significant transformative potential, such soft law instruments, by meeting constitutional requirements, may have direct impact.[47] Soft law may also be a technique to refine and develop existing binding private international law rules. *Gülüm Bayraktaroğlu-Özçelik (SDG 5)*, for example, argues that soft law could

---

46 Directive 2018/957/EU of the European Parliament and of the Council of 28 June 2018 amending Directive 96/71/EC concerning the posting of workers in the framework of the provision of services.

47 UNCITRAL and UNIDROIT have made wide use of non-binding model laws, rules, legal and legislative guides and recommendations. By contrast, soft law produced by the Hague Conference generally supplements binding conventions. The 2015 Hague Principles on Choice of Law in International Commercial Contracts are a notable exception.

be used to identify where, in different fields of private international law, gender equality is still deficient. She advocates a role for the Hague Conference to provide, as a strategic project, soft law principles to help national legislators, administrative officials and judges achieve gender equality and empowerment of women and girls in cross-border situations. In the context of *SDG 6*, *Richard Frimpong Oppong* also argues that the 'facilitative role of private international law could be enhanced by embracing soft law as part of the applicable law'.

That said, binding unified private international law rules generally result in higher levels of certainty and predictability. They are even indispensable for establishing reciprocal obligations between states on jurisdiction, recognition and enforcement, and administrative and judicial cooperation. It is no surprise, therefore, that binding regulations remain the preferred private international law instrument of the European Union – with a tremendous advantage over Hague Conference, UNIDROIT and UNCITRAL conventions: once adopted, they apply directly within the EU Member States.

3.3. THE NEED FOR PRIVATE INTERNATIONAL LAW TO ENGAGE MORE VIGOROUSLY IN THE ATTAINMENT OF THE SDGs

Beyond the idea of promoting existing (and future) private international law more effectively, several chapters highlight the need for greater *engagement* of private international law in the attainment of the SDGs. This may require the distinction between private international law rules (the normative sphere) and private international law as a field of knowledge (the disciplinary sphere). Sustainability and development are themes that private international law has not traditionally paid much attention to, neither in the normative nor in the disciplinary spheres. However, this engagement is emerging in the disciplinary sphere, and there are signs that it is already reaching the normative realm. *Jeannette M.E. Tramhel (SDG 2)*, for example, notes in the work of UNCITRAL, UNIDROIT, FAO and OAS a shift in focus from the 'Big Ag' actors in the global agri-food sector to micro, small and medium-sized enterprises. This has resulted in a range of innovative legislative and other texts to assist such enterprises by reducing legal impediments and improving their access to credit, simplified business formation and other legal tools.

3.3.1. Challenges as a Result of the Development of New Technologies

As a general observation, *Fabricio B. Pasquot Polido (SDG 17)* notes that, in the context of the 'development, transfer, dissemination and diffusion of environmentally sound technologies', chiefly to the Global South, private international law should become more alert to and respectful of the SDGs in its dealings with intellectual property rights, international licensing, transfer of technology, research and development agreements, and joint ventures.

In relation to SDG 3, *Anabela Susana de Sousa Gonçalves* notes the promising development of information and communication technology, such as international e-health platforms and apps. She shows how these digital tools have already increased access to specialised medical care from developed countries for healthcare providers and patients in developing countries. The challenge for private international law now is to provide clarity, security and protection to weaker parties regarding the contractual arrangements involved. Private international law should also address the tort issues resulting from medical malpractice in ICT healthcare and the insurance questions concerning the risks resulting from these activities. Another challenge is the protection of personal health data in transnational digital settings. In the absence of a global legal framework regarding data protection, she recommends the two private international law techniques used in the EU General Data Protection Regulation: giving extraterritorial effect to its rules on the transfer of data and enabling enforcement of data protection laws against companies not established in, but with certain connections to, the EU. On the other hand, regarding medically assisted procreation, with its 'reproductive tourism effects', she endorses the global harmonisation of private international law rules, work which is ongoing by the Hague Conference.

The global use of ICT also plays an important role in the rapid integration of big cities into the global economy, and globalisation at large, discussed by *Klaas Hendrik Eller (SDG 11).* Digital platforms such as those of Airbnb and Yelp are transforming city economics, the destinations and mobility of tourists, and the composition of neighbourhoods. Property or usage rights 'are dissolved as a service, thereby often bypassing public regulations … Ultimately, alleged discrimination and localised disputes between guests and hosts are absorbed by algorithmic governance and online dispute mechanisms.' And like Airbnb engages in a 'servicification' of 'home', WeWork does so for the workplace. There is an urgent need for harmonised regulation of the contractual freedom and dispute resolution facilitated by digitisation.

3.3.2. Party Autonomy and its Limits: Recognising the SDGs Interests of Host Countries and their Citizens

Klaus D. Beiter (SDG 4) demonstrates that in the context of transnational education contracts, party autonomy – regarding both choice of court and choice of law – has enabled foreign companies to disregard human rights norms, including those pertaining to education, in the host state where they are active. He forcefully contends that this is unacceptable and requires limits to be set on party autonomy. Similarly, *Vivienne Bath (SDG 9)* argues that, in the context of transnational infrastructure projects, sustainable development should guide private international law, where needed overriding party autonomy. When enforcing their claims, foreign companies should recognise the responsibility of the host state to its citizens and domestic stakeholders in relation to infrastructure projects, and respect the SDG interests of the host state embodied in its laws. *Drossos Stamboulakis and Jay Sanderson (SDG 15)* likewise stress that private international law should highlight 'its potential global governance role in promoting or facilitating private action geared at environmental protection and sustainability, rather than its apparently neutral basis, commonly undergirded in a trade context by deference to party autonomy.'

Indeed, from the perspective of sustainability, party autonomy is somewhat suspicious. If party autonomy is a way for parties to create additional wealth that can be distributed among them, chances are this creation comes with negative externalities. Private international law prevents such negative externalities only incompletely, for example by restricting negative third-party effects of any variation by the parties of the law to be applied in choice of law agreements (see e.g., Art 2(3) of the Hague Principles on Choice of Law in International Commercial Contracts[48] preserves pre-existing rights of a third party in case of a change in applicable law).

The research conducted substantiates the necessary contention of party autonomy in fields beyond the more traditional spheres commonly examined by private international law scholars; many chapters in this book move above and beyond screening and mapping across the breadth of the SDGs providing insights in contexts that have not been scrutinised from a private international law perspective before.

3.3.3. Responsible Business Conduct

Many chapters welcome the ongoing global, regional and national legislative initiatives and recent private international law judgments that tend to reinforce the transnational responsibility of corporations for human rights violations and damage to the environment referred to above (section 3.1). This reinforcement of corporate social responsibility (CSR) has many implications for private international law: it affects rules on jurisdiction, the law applicable to contracts and torts (including the correcting mechanisms of overriding mandatory rules and public policy), and the enforcement of judgments, all of which may need to be revisited to see whether they are still 'fit for purpose'.

Beyond these ongoing developments, *Thalia Kruger (SDG 10)* advocates a more holistic view on corporations to capture multinational group structures. This may call into question the traditional prohibition on 'lifting the corporate veil'.

48 Approved on 19 March 2015.

Private international law would thus have to rethink the *lex societatis*, the law applicable to companies. *Vivienne Bath (SDG 9)* argues for civil litigation reforms to enable consolidation of multiple disputes relating to the same development project, as a much-needed contribution to making such projects more sustainable. Moreover, the participation of domestic stakeholders from the host state in such proceedings should be considered. Obviously, the 'long-arm' extension of the jurisdiction of the court over the consolidated dispute would then require new forms of cooperation between courts and arbitral tribunals.

3.3.4. *Private International Law, the Environment and Climate Change*

In their discussion of SDG 15, 'Life on land', *Drossos Stamboulakis and Jay Sanderson* note the lack of success of harmonisation efforts in relation to environmental damage, both at the global level in the context of the Hague Conference and, with the exception of the EU, at the regional level. They note that 'traditional private international law approaches offer little integration of sustainability concerns'. SDG 15, therefore, should provoke a reconceptualisation of how regulatory private international law rules on jurisdiction, applicable law and enforcement of judgments could play a greater governance role 'geared at environmental protection and sustainability ... rather than its apparently neutral basis, commonly undergirded in a trade context by deference to party autonomy'.

Regarding, more specifically, global warming, *Eduardo Álvarez-Armas (SDG 13)* takes a more optimistic stance. He sees an important role for tort-based private international climate change litigation. Beyond its compensation and/injunctive relief potential, such litigation could have a deterrent function regarding greenhouse gas emissions, and thus prevent future climate-related damage.

3.3.5. *Overcoming the Public/Private Divide*

As *Sabine Corneloup and Jinske Verhellen (SDG 16)* point out, effectively addressing legal identity issues – also discussed by *Benyam Dawit Mezmur (SDG 1)* and *Gülüm Bayraktaroğlu-Özçelik (SDG 5)* – requires private international law to adopt an integrative approach that does not eschew its possible implications in the realm of public law. Currently, in the migration context, private international law tends to be instrumentalised for public migration law purposes, with double standards (migrants/non-migrants) in terms of the effect given to status and relationships established abroad as a result. This is neither fair nor sustainable. Private international law should determine questions relating to the law applicable to, and the recognition of, that status and those relationships, and migration law should, in principle, follow suit, not the other way round. Moreover, the techniques developed by the Hague Conference for direct judicial and administrative cross-border cooperation could be applied and further developed in order to fill the global governance gaps relating to migration.

Offhand rejection of such ideas simply because they touch on public law is short-sighted.

3.3.6. *Furthering Sustainability via Overriding Mandatory Rules and Public Policy?*

Many contributors to this book propose creative solutions to make private international law more fit for purpose in relation to sustainable development. For example, regarding *jurisdiction*, they propose to facilitate access to the courts, not frustrated by the use of *forum non conveniens*; and to provide for concentration of jurisdiction in complex litigation on infrastructure projects. More broadly regarding access to justice they suggest broader scope for (cross-border) class actions and public interest actions. Regarding *applicable law* they propose giving alleged victims of violations of human rights and environmental damage the option to choose one or more laws in addition to the law of the place of the injury or damage. Regarding *foreign decisions and public acts*, promoting their effective circulation by basing their recognition and enforcement on predictable, agreed criteria, not unduly hampered by outdated sovereignty concerns seems plausible. Moreover, as *Fabricio B. Pasquot Polido (SDG 17)* suggests, existing and planned private international law rules could be routinely submitted to impact assessments.

Combined with the strong suggestion to make wider, global use of existing international instruments, these proposals portray a more robust governance role for private international law, including in the context of the SDGs. Pending the realisation of these aspirations, however, many chapters advocate a stronger role for overriding mandatory rules and the public policy exception in order to achieve SDGs objectives, in particular by limiting unbounded party autonomy. Still, so far overriding mandatory rules and public policy are primarily thought of as exceptional mechanisms to protect rules that are considered vital by countries in terms of their *national* interests. This suggests that a reconceptualisation of these methods may be needed to allow them to give effect to *global sustainable development* needs.[49]

---

[49] The Declaration made by the Government of Uruguay to the CIDIP II conference in 1976, on 'The scope of public order', available at <http://www.oas.org/juridico/english/sigs/b-45.html> accessed 6 July 2021, could be considered as a model for such a redefinition: 'the approved formula conveys an exceptional authorization to the various States Parties to declare in a nondiscretionary and well-founded manner that the precepts of foreign law are inapplicable whenever these concretely and in a serious and open manner offend the standards and principles essential to the international public order on which each individual state bases its legal individuality.'

This would not be entirely untrodden territory. Already several Hague Children's Conventions make the application of the public policy exception subject to the qualifier 'taking into account the best interests of the child'.[50] This implies that, under certain circumstances, even vital domestic interests normally protected by public policy may have to give way to the global imperative of safeguarding human rights. With regard to overriding mandatory rules, it is noteworthy that the proposal for a Directive on corporate due diligence and corporate accountability adopted by the European Parliament on 10 March 2021 contains a special rule on private international law, according to which '[EU] Member States shall ensure that relevant provisions of this Directive are considered overriding mandatory provisions in line with Article 16 [of the Rome II Regulation ("Overriding mandatory provisions")]'.

Clearly, in the context of our topic, a qualifier of public policy like 'taking into account the imperatives of sustainable development' would not be enough, nor would 'imperatives of sustainable development' be sufficient as an overriding mandatory rule. Yet, as further work goes on to give legal substance and precision to norms of sustainable development, including perhaps the idea of a basic norm of sustainability (section 1.3 above), this may give impetus to further thinking about an enhanced role for overriding mandatory rules and a more targeted use of the public policy exception in adapting private international law to the needs of sustainable development.

4. FUTURE AGENDAS

The project provides a beginning, not a conclusion. It offers rich and diverse insights for developing future research and policy agendas around private international law, sustainability and development, both in general and in relation to specific objectives and targets. It is also possible to find avenues for cooperation between academia and law and policymakers, including in the sense of multi-stakeholder partnerships promoted by SDG 17.

In addition to the processes associated with innovative and transformative multi-stakeholder partnerships examined in the final chapter, several chapters in this book signal pathways for public–private partnerships in sectors where they are currently under-exploited. Collaborative endeavours involving the private sector in the promotion of the SDGs may also include less formalised 'joint initiatives between private, philanthropic and public sector actors aimed

[50] See Art 24 1993 Adoption Convention; Arts 22 and 23(2)(d) 1996 Child Protection Convention; followed by Art 23(a) Brussels II *bis* Regulation.

at achieving the public good'.[51] They may operate at any level from global to local.

For instance, as also argued by *Jeannette M.E. Tramhel (SDG 2)*, the need to engage the private sector more effectively in the agri-business sector is considered to offer a mechanism to leverage knowledge from the private sector, together with much-needed financing, to help modernise and spread benefits across to small farmers. In particular, joint ventures and community-supported agriculture offer 'complementary ways to rethink the political economy of food chains'.[52]

Another context where public–private partnerships could have extensive impact is that of remittances, which is discussed by *Thalia Kruger* in relation to SDG 10. This is an issue that has already received considerable attention in international fora, including the UN and the Hague Conference,[53] albeit without yet reaching full fruition. Finding solutions that allow remittances at reasonable costs while protecting against risks such as money laundering would benefit from partnerships between regulators and banks.[54]

Nevertheless, multi-stakeholder partnerships[55] present their own challenges, including from a private international law perspective. These come to the surface, for instance, in the context of urban governance, where a range of examples of less traditional multi-stakeholder partnerships – which raise very interesting questions from a (private international law) regulatory perspective – are examined by *Klaas Hendrik Eller* in relation to SDG 11. More prominently, in connection with SDG 16, *Sabine Corneloup and Jinske Verhellen* provide several examples to illustrate that a wide range of public–private partnerships in the field of legal identity raise concerns from the perspective of sustainability and development. In turn, private international law techniques are at times[56]

---

51 See Susan L Robertson et al, 'An Introduction to Public Private Partnerships and Education Governance' in Susan L Robertson et al (eds), *Public Private Partnerships in Education: New Actors and Modes of Governance in a Globalizing World* (Edward Elgar 2012) 6–7.

52 Marlo Rankin et al, 'Public–private partnerships for agri-business development – A review of international experiences' (FAO, 2016).

53 See Permanent Bureau of the Hague Conference on Private International Law, 'Some Reflections on the Utility of Applying Certain Techniques for International Co-operation Developed by the Hague Conference on Private International Law to Issues of International Migration', Preliminary Document No 8 of March 2006 for the attention of the Special Commission of April 2006 on General Affairs and Policy of the Conference, 7–8, Meeting of April 2006 <https://www.hcch.net/en/governance/council-on-general-affairs/archive> accessed 6 July 2021.

54 See Louis De Koker, Supriya Singh and Jonathan Capal, 'Closure of Bank Accounts of Remittance Service Providers: Global Challenges and Community Perspectives in Australia' (2017) 36 University of Queensland Law Journal 119.

55 See United Nations Department of Economic and Social Affairs (UN DESA), *The SDG Partnership Guidebook* (version of 1 January 2020).

56 See discussions in relation to SDGs 4, 6 and 9 in the respective chapters.

used as necessary safeguards in normative frameworks for multi-stakeholder partnerships, allowing for the articulation of sustainability and development in relation to the objectives of the partnership itself, and for balance between private and public interests in pursuit of the SDGs.

Moreover, the importance of further empirical research for aspiring to transformative outcomes should be emphasised. The need for further assessment of the impact of private international law in the lives of individuals, companies and countries in their private transnational relationships is mentioned in several chapters. The SDGs' methodology of goals, targets and indicators promotes an empirical lens, engaging with quantitative as well as qualitative aspects.

Internalising the centrality of empirical research seems inherently connected to the grassroots transformation that many of the chapters in this book speak about. This comes to the fore both when examining policy objectives that are beyond the 'traditional' contexts scrutinised in the field, such as when looking into the activities of private education providers in the Global South in relation to SDG 4, and when reconstructing 'typical' private international law considerations, such as issues around birth registration in relation to SDG 16. Cooperation in obtaining, sharing and disseminating data is a crucial endeavour which, in turn, private international law mechanisms should strive to facilitate. SDG 17 invites innovative thinking in terms of collaboration and cooperation towards these global goals.

Rethinking, re-conceptualising and re-configuring is considered necessary for private international law to contribute to the transformation of our world. Several factors appear essential to these transformative processes: cross-sector collaboration, participatory approaches, inclusive regulatory models, promotion of fundamental rights, and endorsement of substantive outcomes (geared towards sustainability).

In some instances, this reconfiguration relates to spatial considerations. That is the case in relation to sustainable urban transformations. *Klaas Hendrik Eller*, in his chapter, explains that SDG 11 portrays cities as pivotal sites for sustainable futures, and while private law paves the way for the delocalisation of urban social relations, 'implies reaching beyond the category of 'space' and retracing how legally mediated non-spatialised processes manifest themselves inside the city walls.'

In other scenarios, reconceptualisation is sought in relation to the utilisation and interpretation of existing rules and doctrines, with a sustainability-endorsing approach. This is proposed by *Geneviève Saumier* in relation to sustainable consumption and production patterns in SDG 12.

Further transformative power could manifest through procedural 'revolutions', such as the proposed private international climate change litigation (PICCL), as discussed by *Eduardo Álvarez-Armas (SDG 13)*.

More generally, and transversally to the UN Agenda 2030, rethinking is necessary to balance competing and potentially conflicting values inherent in coupling development with sustainability: accommodating these, *Drossos Stamboulakis and Jay Sanderson (SDG 15)* state, 'requires a reconceptualisation of private international law: highlighting its potential global governance role in promoting or facilitating private action geared at environmental protection and sustainability, rather than its apparently neutral basis, commonly undergirded in a trade context by deference to party autonomy.' As proposed by *Richard Frimpong Oppong (SDG 6)*, '[t]his facilitative role of private international law could be enhanced by embracing soft law as part of the applicable law, encouraging the localisation of international contracts through using choice-of-law and jurisdiction agreements, and developing local legal expertise, including the capacity of courts in the Global South to handle transnational claims.'

Finally, at this point, we dare to advance an idea that is directly inspired by the goal-setting approach of the SDGs. We also believe that it finds support in various chapters of this book. Most, if not all, of the Hague Conference, UNIDROIT and UNCITRAL multilateral treaties serve one or more purposes of the SDGs. This, in fact, should make their acceptance by states a priority. Therefore, would it not be conceivable for these organisations to borrow the goal-setting technique from Agenda 2030? The policymaking bodies of these organisations could establish a list – or several lists, according to varying needs of different states – prioritising conventions, and, for each one, define a reasonable schedule for their submission for approval by national legislatures. This could take the form of, or be a constitutive part of, a private international law indicators framework. The goal-setting would not entail an obligation of result, but of effort. It would be completed by a reporting mechanism on progress made. In this way, the hard work of negotiating multilateral treaties on private international law could be made far more impactful, thus significantly supporting the goals of Agenda 2030.

All in all, the research shows that for private international law to commit to the global objectives of the UN 2030 Agenda, more is necessary than mapping existing methodologies and techniques. There is a need to reconceptualise disciplinary objectives profoundly, and to reinvigorate the individual-enabling dynamics ('leaving no-one behind') that are core to both private international law and the SDGs. Future research agendas should contribute towards reviving marginalised understandings of its methodology, revealing inequalities hidden under its technicalities, and embracing transformation.

This book underscores the need for private international lawyers to be aware of, and engage with, the larger political, social, economic, cultural and public (international) law context of their daily work on cross-border private law relationships and transactions. And it demonstrates, we hope, that, to explore this larger context, the SDGs framework provides inspiring guidance.

SDG 1: NO POVERTY

Benyam Dawit MEZMUR

Goal 1: End poverty in all its forms everywhere

1.1 By 2030, eradicate extreme poverty for all people everywhere, currently measured as people living on less than $1.25 a day

1.2 By 2030, reduce at least by half the proportion of men, women and children of all ages living in poverty in all its dimensions according to national definitions

1.3 Implement nationally appropriate social protection systems and measures for all, including floors, and by 2030 achieve substantial coverage of the poor and the vulnerable

1.4 By 2030, ensure that all men and women, in particular the poor and the vulnerable, have equal rights to economic resources, as well as access to basic services, ownership and control over land and other forms of property, inheritance, natural resources, appropriate new technology and financial services, including microfinance

1.5 By 2030, build the resilience of the poor and those in vulnerable situations and reduce their exposure and vulnerability to climate-related extreme events and other economic, social and environmental shocks and disasters

1.a Ensure significant mobilization of resources from a variety of sources, including through enhanced development cooperation, in order to provide adequate and predictable means for developing countries, in particular least developed countries, to implement programmes and policies to end poverty in all its dimensions

1.b Create sound policy frameworks at the national, regional and international levels, based on pro-poor and gender-sensitive development strategies, to support accelerated investment in poverty eradication actions

1. INTRODUCTION

The international community made a bold step in adopting the Sustainable Development Goals (SDGs). The most ambitious aspect of the SDGs is probably Goal 1 on ending poverty. In the Millennium Development Goals (MDGs) era, poverty did not get a separate goal and was lumped with the goal on hunger.

Because poverty is multidimensional and often intergenerational, one of the most effective ways of ending extreme poverty by 2030 is to end child poverty. After all, poverty affects children disproportionately, and in fact there is evidence that one out of five children live in extreme poverty.[1] The cost of not addressing it during childhood is devastating, because children experience poverty in 'different ways than adults and are almost certain to miss out on a good start in life'.[2] Part of the optimism to address child poverty urgently also emanates from the understanding that child poverty is an enabler for other child rights violations, such as exploitation and abuse, deprivation of a family environment, dropping out of school, or being recruited as a child soldier or for the purposes of trafficking. In the context of COVID-19, there are already predictions that poverty might deepen in some corners of the world.[3] In fact, as a result of the

1 Report of the Secretary-General on SDG Progress 2019, Special Edition <https://sustainabledevelopment.un.org/content/documents/24978Report_of_the_SG_on_SDG_Progress_2019.pdf> accessed 12 July 2021.

2 UNICEF and the World Bank Group, 'Ending Extreme Poverty: A Focus on Children' (2 October 2016) <https://www.unicef.org/media/49996/file/Ending_Extreme_Poverty_A_Focus_on_Children_Oct_2016.pdf> accessed 12 July 2021.

3 An estimated 150 million more people have been pushed into extreme poverty, disproportionately affecting women and children AFP 'World Bank chief warns extreme poverty could surge by 100 mln' (21 August 2020) <https://www.bangkokpost.com/world/1972219/world-bank-chief-warns-extreme-poverty-could-surge-by-100m> accessed 12 July 2021; World Bank, 'COVID-19 to Add as Many as 150 Million Extreme Poor by 2021'

effect of diversion of resources created by COVID-19 away from child health and education, children are, among others, missing out on life-saving vaccines, facing increased stress and mental health issues, and dealing with limited access to free and compulsory primary education.[4]

The link between the SDGs and international human rights law has now been made clearer than in the previous context of the MDGs. For example, the International Covenant on Economic, Social and Cultural Rights (ICESCR) has been described as 'a fundamental pillar of the 2030 Agenda'.[5] The common objective between the SDGs and the ICESCR lies in the coordinated efforts to lift everyone out of poverty.

There is also a general sense of shared optimism by many scholars and practitioners alike (including organisations) that both the Convention on the Rights of the Child (CRC) (and its relevant optional protocols) and, in the context of Africa (where the largest number of children living in poverty exist), the African Charter on the Rights and Welfare of the Child (ACRWC) would benefit significantly from the implementation of the SDGs. There is an increasingly abundant literature, including academic literature, that draws a parallel between the provisions of international human rights instruments, including the CRC and ACRWC, and the SDGs and their respective targets. In fact, given the close link between the SDGs and children, UNICEF has been made responsible for eight global SDG indicators and co-custodian for a further 11,[6] and supports countries in generating, analysing and using data for these indicators for all their citizens.[7]

Of course, the implementation of the CRC and ACRWC depends a lot on different aspects of international law that go beyond human rights law. For example, international labour law, and international criminal law play an important role. However, it is not only public international law that is of relevance to the implementation of the CRC and the ACRWC. Among other things, private international law plays a role, for example in respect of abduction,

---

(7 October 2020) <https://www.worldbank.org/en/news/press-release/2020/10/07/covid-19-to-add-as-many-as-150-million-extreme-poor-by-2021> accessed 12 July 2021.

4 See, for example, Vera Clemens et al 'Potential effects of "social" distancing measures and school lockdown on child and adolescent mental health' (23 May 2020) 29 European Child & Adolescent Psychiatry 739–742 <https://link.springer.com/article/10.1007/s00787-020-01549-w.> accessed 14 July 2021; Xiao Zhou 'Managing psychological distress in children and adolescents following the COVID-19 epidemic: A cooperative approach' (2020) 12 Psychological Trauma: Theory, Research, Practice, and Policy S76–S78 <https://doi.apa.org/fulltext/2020-43039-001.html> accessed 12 July 2021.

5 Committee on Economic, Social and Cultural Rights, 'The Pledge to Leave No One Behind: The International Covenant on Economic, Social and Cultural Rights and the 2030 Agenda for Sustainable Development. Statement by the Committee on Economic, Social and Cultural Rights', UN Doc E/C.12/2019/1 (5 April 2019) para 4.

6 UNICEF, 'Using data to achieve the Sustainable Development Goals (SDGs) for children' <https://data.unicef.org/children-sustainable-development-goals/> accessed 12 July 2021.

7 ibid.

intercountry adoption, family environment, age determination, child marriages, and so forth. Despite this reality, and the link between the CRC and the SDGs, most of the academic as well as non-academic literature on the implementation of the SDGs – and SDG 1 on ending poverty is no exception – hardly recognise the important role that private international law can and should play.

With this as a backdrop, it is not common to associate issues pertaining to child poverty and children on the move with private international law. After all, issues pertaining to refugees, asylum seekers and migration are predominantly the preserve of public international law. This chapter intends to look at SDG 1 on poverty and interrogate some of the limited, albeit important, roles that private international law can play to prevent and address the poverty of children on the move.

There are a few private international law instruments that are of relevance to children and their rights. Prime amongst these are the 1993 Hague Convention on the Protection of Children and Co-operation in Respect of Intercountry Adoption, the 1980 Convention on the Civil Aspects of Child Abduction, the 1996 Hague Convention on Jurisdiction, Applicable Law, Recognition, Enforcement and Cooperation in Respect of Parental Responsibility and Measures for the Protection of Children, and the 2007 Hague Child and Family Support Convention.[8] Among other things, some of these instruments 'emphasize international co-operation, the principle of mutual benefit and international law',[9] which are of course relevant for addressing poverty, including child poverty, in all its forms.

With a view to complying with the space limit, this chapter should inevitably benefit from a manageable scope. In this regard, a logical geographical focus of the content of a contribution of this nature often gravitates towards one of two continents – Africa or Asia. This chapter focuses on the former – among other reasons because, as data from 2016 has shown, children living in extreme poverty are concentrated in Sub-Saharan Africa, which has both the highest rates of children living in extreme poverty (around 49 per cent), and the largest share of the world's extremely poor children (around 51 per cent).[10] In addition, it is worth mentioning that the term 'children on the move' is used in this chapter loosely and covers refugees and asylum seekers as well as migrants. In the instances where the context explicitly indicates, it also covers intercountry adoption, maintenance and issues relating to parental child abduction.

---

8 See the Special Sections on Adoption, Child Abduction, Child Protection, and Child Support at the Hague Conference (HCCH) website: <https://www.hcch.net/en/home> accessed 12 July 2021.

9 Kenneth Asamoa Acheampong, 'Sustainable Development Goals, Stateless Individuals and Inclusive Education' (2017) 25 University of Botswana Law Journal 30, 32.

10 UNICEF and the World Bank Group, 'Ending Extreme Poverty: A Focus on Children' (2 October 2016) <https://www.unicef.org/publications/files/Ending_Extreme_Poverty_A_Focus_on_Children_Oct_2016.pdf>, 3 accessed 12 July 2021.

In reaching its conclusions, this chapter proceeds as follows. After this introduction, section 2 makes an attempt to provide some background to the MDGs, highlight some of the relevant lessons learned from the MDGs' implementation, and proffer some takeaways. Section 3 looks into SDGs and international law, with a focus on SDG 1 on ending extreme poverty, especially child poverty. This section zooms in on some of the issues pertaining to child poverty in the context of Africa that private international law can address. Section 4, which is the crux of the chapter, starts by offering a general exposé of some of the issues that private international law can contribute to with a view to addressing the poverty of children on the move. It then proceeds to discuss three specific issues – birth registration, child marriage and intercountry adoption – and demonstrate a few scenarios where private international law can aid in preventing or addressing child poverty, and can facilitate the implementation of SDG 1. In section 5, the chapter offers brief concluding remarks.

2. THE MDGs AND POVERTY

For 15 years, from 2000 to 2015, the MDGs guided international development policy and practice. It would be accurate to say that they have, to a certain extent, also informed development law.[11] Composed of a hierarchy, the MDGs had eight goals. While the vision of the Millennium Declaration included, among other things, human rights, democracy and good governance, the MDGs did not explicitly incorporate these aspects As Nanda described it, this was a 'glaring omission' that 'had been lost in translation', which ultimately led to adverse consequences.[12]

There are a number of reasons that are advanced to explain the success, but also shortcomings, of the MDGs.[13] In respect of the former, a few of the arguments are: the solid international political legitimacy provided by the source of the MDGs, the Millennium Declaration, approved by 189 states; the fact that a number of international and regional institutions supported the implementation, monitoring and evaluations of the MGDs; and the focus of the MDGs on a fairly manageable, limited number of targets. One of the forms of progress that was achieved through the MDGs is also the direct reference to

11 See, for example, Maya Fehling, Brett D Nelson and Sridhar Venkatapuram, 'Limitations of the Millennium Development Goals: a literature review' (2013) 8(10) Global Public Health 1109–1122.

12 Ved P Nanda, 'The Journey from the Millennium Development Goals to the Sustainable Development Goals' (2016) 44 Denver Journal of International Law and Policy 389, 393.

13 See, for example, Maya Fehling, Brett D Nelson and Sridhar Venkatapuram, 'Limitations of the Millennium Development Goals: a literature review' (2013) 8(10) Global Public Health 1109–1122.

concrete human conditions with which people could empathise, rather than the abstract term 'poverty', which was open to interpretation.[14]

There is also a long list of arguments making the case about some of the main shortcomings of the MDGs.[15] The fact that the MDGs did not incorporate the core human rights standards or explicitly address inequality are two examples.[16] The selection of the Goals was also criticised as being less participatory. Moreover, while the MDGs were intended to be global in nature, the Goals and their respective targets did not adequately cover issues of relevance for the developed world.[17] In this respect, it has been highlighted that, despite the presence of poverty in high- and middle-income countries, the MDGs did not address this issue.[18] In addition, progress has been reported as being uneven, leaving a number of groups that should have been prioritised for development in limbo.

In relation to poverty, the MDGs had the intention of addressing it as a core issue. In fact, one of the initial statements of the Millennium Declaration reads: 'We will spare no effort to free our fellow men, women and children from the abject and dehumanizing conditions of extreme poverty, to which more than a billion of them are currently subjected'.[19] Therefore, SDG 1 aimed to '[e]radicate extreme poverty and hunger'. Target 1.A planned to 'halve, between 1990 and 2015, the proportion of people whose income is less than $1 a day'.[20]

Fortunately, Target 1.A, which aimed to reduce by half the proportion of people living in extreme poverty, was achieved in 2010, five years ahead

---

14 Sakiko Fukuda-Parr and David Hulme, 'International Dynamics and the "End of Poverty": Understanding the Millennium Development Goals' (2011) 17(1) Global Governance 17, 23.

15 See ibid 26, indicating in part that '[t]he NGO networks were also critical of the content … of the MDGs because: (1) important goals, especially reproductive health goals, were excluded; (2) the goals and targets were not ambitious enough, especially for countries that had already achieved them; (3) the Goal 8 partnership goals and targets were weak and lacked quantitative targets; and (4) systemic reforms of global governance structures and policies were excluded'.

16 Gillian MacNaughton and Diane F Frey, 'Decent Work, Human Rights and the Sustainable Development Goals' (2016) 47(2) Georgetown Journal of International Law 607, 611.

17 Report of the Secretary-General on SDG Progress Report of the Secretary-General on SDG Progress 2019, Special Edition <https://sustainabledevelopment.un.org/content/documents/24978Report_of_the_SG_on_SDG_Progress_2019.pdf> accessed 12 July 2021.

18 ibid.

19 UN General Assembly, Millennium Declaration: Resolution adopted by the General Assembly, UN Doc A/55/L.2 (5 September 2000) para 11 <https://www.ohchr.org/EN/ProfessionalInterest/Pages/Millennium.aspx> accessed 12 July 2021.

20 Target 1.B aimed at achieving 'full and productive employment and decent work for all, including women and young people', while Target 1.C aimed to 'halve, between 1990 and 2015, the proportion of people who suffer from hunger'.

of schedule.[21] In the 25 years that preceded the end date of the MDGs, more than 1 billion people have been lifted out of extreme poverty.[22] In 2015, the then UN Secretary-General Ban Ki Moon said that the 'global mobilization behind the Millennium Development Goals has produced the most successful anti-poverty movement in history'.[23] It has also been argued that the main reason why the first goal of the MDGs is to reduce the proportion of people living in extreme income poverty is 'to make it clear that the shift from a focus on national development to global poverty reduction did not suggest that economic growth, based on globalization, was to be marginalized'[24] and to ensure continuity with previous commitments to deal with mass poverty.[25]

However, a number of human rights scholars have also found Target 1.A to be regressive and, in fact, non-compliant with the human rights obligations of states.[26] For example, a strong argument has been made that, on the basis of the ICESCR, states parties have the obligation to recognise 'the fundamental right of everyone to be free from hunger'.[27] Linked to Target 1.A is, among others, Target 7.c, which aimed to halve the proportion of persons without sustainable access to safe drinking water, but did not address the obligation under international human rights law that the water should be affordable.[28] It has also been contended that, unlike the SDGs, the MDGs failed to incorporate the opportunities for, and the role of, decent work as an important component of poverty eradication. While there was an effort to remedy this shortcoming in 2007, through an addition of a new decent work target, it was somehow considered to be too little too late.[29]

There were also concerns that MDG 1 focused on the symptoms, but not the causes, of poverty. Moreover, the unevenness of the recorded progress

21 The World Bank, 'Remarkable Declines in Global Poverty, But Major Challenges Remain' (17 April 2013) <https://www.worldbank.org/en/news/press-release/2013/04/17/remarkable-declines-in-global-poverty-but-major-challenges-remain> accessed 12 July 2021.

22 <https://www.un.org/millenniumgoals/poverty.shtml> accessed 12 July 2021.

23 UN, 'The Millennium Development Goals Report 2015' <https://www.un.org/millenniumgoals/2015_MDG_Report/pdf/MDG%202015%20rev%20(July%201).pdf> accessed 14 July 2021.

24 Sakiko Fukuda-Parr and David Hulme, 'International Dynamics and the "End of Poverty": Understanding the Millennium Development Goals' (2011) 17(1) Global Governance 17, 30.

25 ibid.

26 Thomas Pogge, 'The First United Nations Millennium Development Goal: A cause for celebration' (2010) 5(3) Journal of Human Development 377.

27 To take the necessary action to mitigate and alleviate hunger as provided for in Art 11(2) of the ICESCR.

28 Mac Darrow, 'The Millennium Development Goals: Milestones or Millstones? Human Rights Priorities for the Post-2015 Development Agenda' (2012) 15 Yale Human Rights and Development Law Journal 55.

29 Gillian MacNaughton and Diane F Frey, 'Decent Work, Human Rights and the Sustainable Development Goals' (2016) 47(2) Georgetown Journal of International Law 607, 612. It is also provided that '[t]he new decent work goal and targets adopted in September 2015 mean that "decent work for all" is finally a central feature of the global plan to eliminate poverty.'

was disconcerting, especially as the world's poor remain overwhelmingly concentrated in some parts of the world. In 2011, nearly 60 per cent of the world's one billion extremely poor people lived in just five countries: India, Nigeria, China, Bangladesh and the Democratic Republic of the Congo.[30] The decline in extreme poverty was also mainly because of progress in two countries – China and India – with sub-Saharan Africa still suffering from a highly concentrated level of extreme poverty (more than 40 per cent of the population) in 2015.[31] It was also predicted that extreme poverty would rise in Western Asia between 2011 and 2015,[32] underscoring some of the shortcomings of the Goals and their implementations.

3. THE SDGs AND CHILD POVERTY

3.1. BACKGROUND TO THE SDGs

It is reasonable that there appears to be significant consensus that the SDGs and their respective targets did not emerge from, and were inserted into, an international law vacuum, but that they are actually grounded in aspects of international law.[33] In this respect, public international law occupies a largely dominant space.

The UN Charter, the Universal Declaration of Human Rights (UDHR) and the nine core UN human rights instruments, which include the ICESCR and CRC, have informed the SDGs.[34] After all, the Member States of the UN stressed in the SDGs' Declaration: 'We reaffirm the importance of the Universal Declaration of Human Rights, as well as other international instruments relating to human rights and international law.'[35]

As mentioned above, one of the lessons of the MDGs is that while a number of targets were met, they were met in an uneven manner – and there is an argument that the 'spirit of the MDGs was not found', raising the vexing question of what

---

30 UN, 'The Millennium Development Goals Report 2015', 15 <https://www.un.org/millenniumgoals/2015_MDG_Report/pdf/MDG%202015%20rev%20(July%201).pdf> accessed 14 July 2021.

31 ibid.

32 ibid.

33 Rakhyun E Kim, 'The Nexus between International Law and the Sustainable Development Goals' (2016) 25(1) Review of European, Comparative & International Environmental Law 15, 15.

34 See the International Covenant on Civil and Political Rights (adopted 16 December 1966, entered into force 23 March 1976) 999 UNTS 171; the International Covenant on Economic, Social and Cultural Rights (adopted 16 December 1966, entered into force 3 January 1976) 993 UNTS 3; and the UN Declaration on the Right to Development, 1986.

35 See UN General Assembly, 'Transforming Our World: the 2030 Agenda for Sustainable Development', UN Doc A/RES/70/1 (21 October 2015) para 19.

the role of international law should be in order to truly integrate the SDGs and targets and achieve the intended long-term sustainable development.[36] This role could, and even should, be used to bring relevant international law institutions out of their comfort zones and settled mandates, and to have them join hands to pursue a common goal of achieving the SDGs. Indeed, as the norm internalisation of the MDGs took place, a significant amount of mobilisation among and within organisations took hold, including national governments, private corporations, municipalities, UN agencies, international financial institutions, etc.[37] However, the extent to which organisations that are involved in international law, let alone private international law, are part of this movement is quite minimal.

Leaving no one behind, and reaching those who are furthest behind first, has important implications for addressing poverty.[38] A good number of groups of persons who are at risk of being left behind are explicitly mentioned in Agenda 2030. Paragraph 23 of the General Assembly Resolution reads in its relevant part that:

> People who are vulnerable must be empowered. Those whose needs are reflected in the Agenda include all children, youth, persons with disabilities (of whom more than 80 per cent live in poverty), people living with HIV/AIDS, older persons, indigenous peoples, refugees and internally displaced persons and migrants.[39]

The explicit mention of these general groups who are at risk of being left out is helpful as a broad guide for identification and prioritisation in the

---

36 Rakhyun E Kim, 'The Nexus between International Law and the Sustainable Development Goals' (2016) 25(1) Review of European, Comparative & International Environmental Law 15, 15.

37 Sakiko Fukuda-Parr and David Hulme, 'International Dynamics and the "End of Poverty": Understanding the Millennium Development Goals' (2011) 17(1) Global Governance 17, 28.

38 Veronica P Arauco et al, 'Strengthening Social Justice to Address Intersecting Inequalities Post-2015' (ODI 2014) viii. There is ample evidence that shows that often development leaves the poorest behind. A recent report by the UN has underscored that 'inequality within countries is very high. While inequalities between average national incomes are large, considerable disparities are also found among people at the bottom and at the top of the income distribution across within countries … [H]igh or growing inequality not only harms people living in poverty and other disadvantaged groups, it affects the well-being of society at large.' See UN Department of Social and Economic Affairs, 'World Social Report, Inequality in a Rapidly Changing World' (2020) 20. One of the strong arguments made for using human rights principles in the implementation of the SDGs is that they assist to 'look behind the symptoms to tackle the structural causes of poverty, inequality, social injustice and environmental degradation'. Laura-Maria Craciunean, 'Looking at the Millennium Development Goals and the Sustainable Development Goals through an All Human Rights Lens' (2015) 1 Acta Universitatis Lucian Blaga 202, 207–208.

39 UN General Assembly, 'Transforming Our World: the 2030 Agenda for Sustainable Development', UN Doc A/RES/70/1 (21 October 2015) para 23.

implementation of the 2030 Agenda. However, it is important to acknowledge that the depth and urgency of action to cater for these groups also depends on the specificities of different national contexts.[40]

3.2. POVERTY

The SDG 1 targets are indeed ambitious and build significantly on their precursors under the MDGs. Currently, it is reported that, of a world population of approximately 7 billion people, 2.2 billion live in poverty.[41] What is even more concerning is that 15 per cent of the world population is at risk of multidimensional poverty which covers multiple deprivations such as poor health and lack of access to education, and a significant number of these are persons below the age of 18 or persons in vulnerable situations, such as minorities and refugees.[42] Such statistics prevail not because there are not adequate resources in the world to address multidimensional poverty, especially of children, but because of inequality.[43]

The SDG progress reports (2019 and 2020) of the UN Secretary-General portray a relatively dire picture of the current situation, as well as of the projected status by 2030, in respect of achieving SDG 1.[44] According to the 2019 report, while the percentage of the world's population living in extreme poverty declined to 10 per cent in 2015, extreme poverty is still projected to be at 6 per cent in 2030, far short of the 3 per cent target set for SDG 1. Moreover, in sub-Saharan Africa, the share of the working poor stood at an alarming 38 per cent in 2018. In addition, while the benefits of social protection systems in reducing poverty are well understood, large numbers of people (in 2016, 55 per cent of the world's population, or around 4 billion people) are not covered by any system of cash benefits or social protection, displaying significant regional disparities, with sub-Saharan Africa having the lowest rate of coverage at only 13 per cent.[45]

40 For example, it is notable that other groups, such as stateless persons, who are often overrepresented in poverty data, are not mentioned.

41 The World Bank, 'Poverty Overview' (last updated 24 September 2018) <http://www.worldbank.org/en/topic/poverty/ overview> accessed 12 July 2021.

42 ibid.

43 ibid.

44 UN, 'The Sustainable Development Goals Report 2019' <unstats.un.org/sdgs/report/2019/The-Sustainable-Development-Goals-Reports-2019.pdf> accessed 12 July 2021; UN, 'The Sustainable Development Goals Report 2020' <unstats.un.org/sdgs/report/2020/The-Sustainable-Development-Goals-Report-2020.pdf> accessed 12 July 2021.

45 Just over 30 per cent of children worldwide enjoy effective access to social protection. Almost two-thirds of children globally – mostly in Africa and Asia – are not covered. See ILO, '4 billion people worldwide are left without social protection' <https://www.ilo.org/global/about-the-ilo/newsroom/news/WCMS_601903/lang--en/index.htm> accessed 12 July 2021.

The measurement and reported progress in reducing extreme poverty is not without reproach. For example, in his departing critical report to the Human Rights Council, which he titled 'Report on the Parlous State of Poverty Eradication',[46] the Special Rapporteur for extreme poverty, Philip Alston, indicated that the mainstream narrative about the reduction of extreme poverty is not accurate, and that the reported decline is based on a flawed international poverty line created by the World Bank, which focuses on a 'standard of miserable subsistence' rather than 'an even minimally adequate standard of living'.[47] Often, law that is intended to help fight poverty and realise the right to an adequate standard of living that is beyond the 'standard of miserable subsistence' should address various issues. For example, it would attempt to revise legal and administrative rules that place a disproportionate burden on persons living in poverty in terms of accessing services; to bring down the economic, social and administrative barriers that prevent persons living in poverty from engaging in productive livelihood activities; to facilitate adequate access to resources such as land, fisheries and forests, and adequate water for subsistence farming; and to ensure that those living in poverty, in particular women, have access to basic financial services, including bank loans.[48]

Under international human rights law, the obligations of states in respect of international cooperation and assistance also play an important role in addressing poverty, and such cooperation and assistance is incorporated in the Charter of the United Nations[49] and in several international human rights treaties.[50] Some of the basic principles for the purposes of international cooperation and assistance include that the assistance provided is managed according to human rights standards, and that states should take into account poverty reduction measures in development cooperation, trade, taxation and investment.[51] Moreover, states have an obligation to avoid measures that could negatively affect the rights of persons living in poverty outside of their borders, which could require undertaking an assessment of the extraterritorial impacts of laws, policies and practices.[52]

---

46 Philip Alston, 'Report of the Special Rapporteur on Extreme Poverty and Human Rights: The Parlous State of Poverty Eradication', UN Doc A/HRC/44/40 (2 July 2020) <https://www.ohchr.org/EN/Issues/Poverty/Pages/parlous.aspx> accessed 12 July 2021.

47 ibid paras 82–85.

48 OHCHR, 'Guiding Principles on extreme poverty and human rights' (2012) 20–21 <https://www.ohchr.org/documents/publications/ohchr_extremepovertyandhumanrights_en.pdf> accessed 13 July 2021.

49 Arts 55 and 56.

50 For example, Art 4 CRC.

51 OHCHR 'Guiding Principles on extreme poverty and human rights' (2012) 33 <https://www.ohchr.org/documents/publications/ohchr_extremepovertyandhumanrights_en.pdf> accessed 13 July 2021.

52 ibid 3.

3.3. SDG 1 AND CHILD POVERTY

Given the negative and often life-long development outcome effects of poverty on children, there are legal as well as moral arguments that can be made that addressing childhood poverty should be made a priority in implementing SDG 1.[53] What such prioritisation looks like would be dependent on country contexts. The cost of not addressing child poverty during childhood could be devastating, because children experience poverty in 'different ways than adults and are almost certain to miss out on a good start in life'.[54] Moreover, the tendency to look at children, by definition persons below the age of 18, as a monolithic group for the purposes of the SDGs in general, and SDG 1 in particular, is inaccurate. For example, in regard to child poverty, the youngest children are the worst off – it is reported that 'over 20 per cent of all children below 5 in the developing world live in extremely poor households, compared with nearly 15 per cent of 15–17 year olds'.[55]

Within the UN system, the recognition of the direct link between child rights and child poverty is strong. A 2007 UN Resolution stated that:

> children living in poverty are deprived of nutrition, water and sanitation facilities, access to basic health-care services, shelter, education, participation and protection, and … while a severe lack of goods and services hurts every human being, it is most threatening and harmful to children.[56]

There are a number of common drivers of child poverty. These are found at the household level, where the background of the parents (educational level, single motherhood, etc.) plays a role; at the personal level, where children in poverty experience shame, etc., because of exclusion; at the institutional level, where children in poverty have less access to essential services; at the policy level, in the design and implementation of economic and social policies; and at

---

53 Children experience disproportionate levels of persisting global poverty, and due to their particular life-stage and phase of development suffer broad and deep consequences of growing up in poverty throughout their lives, hampering the fulfilment of all of their human rights. The large amount of dependency that children have on their parents/caregivers exacerbates their poverty capacities and opportunities to cope with and address poverty and its associated deprivations. OHCHR, 'Human rights dimension of poverty', UN Doc A/65/259 (9 August 2010) <http://www.ohchr.org/EN/Issues/Poverty/DimensionOfPoverty/Pages/Index.aspx> accessed 12 July 2021.

54 UNICEF and the World Bank Group, 'Ending Extreme Poverty: A Focus on Children' (2 October 2016) 2 <https://www.unicef.org/publications/files/Ending_Extreme_Poverty_A_Focus_on_Children_Oct_2016.pdf> accessed 12 July 2021.

55 ibid 3.

56 UN General Assembly Resolution, The Rights of the Child', UN Doc A/RES/61/146 (23 January 2007) para 46.

the environmental level because of insecurity created as a result of natural or manmade disasters and shocks.[57]

There is also a very direct link between a number of the SDGs and the provisions of the CRC. While the detailed analysis of this is the subject of a number of other studies, suffice it to mention here, as an example, that Target 1.2, which plans to 'reduce at least by half the proportion of men, women and children of all ages living in poverty in all its dimensions according to national definitions', is directly relevant for Article 6(2) of the CRC, which requires states Parties to 'ensure to the maximum extent possible the survival and development of the child'. Article 27(1) of the CRC on adequate standard of living also resonates very well with this same target.

There are multiple stubborn challenges that persist that make the realisation of children's rights difficult. Extreme poverty amongst the most marginalised children is one such critical challenge, which in some cases risks reversing progress made in previous years.[58] Despite the recorded decline in mortality rates over the last three decades, the data shows that 'children born in the poorest households are twice as likely to die, on average, as those in the richest'.[59] There is also an acknowledgement that in a global reality where the number of out-of-school children at the primary level has remained largely static since 2007, child poverty contributes to the reasons for the remaining 8 per cent of primary-school-age children who are out of school.[60] Within this category of children are a significant number of migrants, refugees and those in disaster areas, which means that targeted interventions are required to break down each group's unique and specific barriers to access.[61]

Furthermore, while understanding and measuring child poverty through the framework of multidimensional poverty is critical, such measurement does still have its own limitations. For example, there is a concern that many

---

57 Save the Children, 'Child Poverty: What drives it and what it means to children across the world' (2016) <resourcecentre.savethechildren.net/node/9684/pdf/child_poverty_report_4web_0.pdf> accessed 12 July 2021.

58 UNICEF, 'For Every Child, Every Right: The Convention on the Rights of the Child at Crossroads' (November 2019) 2 <https://www.unicef.org/media/62371/file/Convention-rights-child-at-crossroads-2019.pdf> accessed 12 July 2021. While often the focus of child poverty discourse is on low- and middle-income countries, it does not mean that there are no children living in poverty in comparatively rich countries. These group of children are often characterised as being victims of a result of economic instability and austerity policies. See UNICEF, Save the Children et al, 'Child poverty: indicators to measure progress for the SDGs' (March 2015) <https://resourcecentre.savethechildren.net/node/9654/pdf/child_poverty_indicators_to_measure_progress_in_the_sdgs_global_coalition_to_end_child_poverty_march_2015_0.pdf> accessed 14 July 2021.

59 UNICEF, 'For Every Child, Every Right: The Convention on the Rights of the Child at Crossroads' (November 2019) 18 <https://www.unicef.org/media/62371/file/Convention-rights-child-at-crossroads-2019.pdf> accessed 12 July 2021.

60 ibid 31.

61 ibid.

measurements of child poverty focus on the rights of the child that are easily quantified – at the cost of those that are difficult or impossible to quantify.[62] This also means that intangible but important quality-related issues critical for the enjoyment of the rights of the child (for example, discrimination against refugee children, or the effect of separation from a parent on the mental health of a child) are overlooked in the measurement of child poverty.[63] There are also significant concerns about the manner in which the measurement of child poverty and the policy and legislative measures that are intended to address it are based on the household unit.[64] The focus on the household unit for the purposes of measurement means that a significant number of children who are deprived of a family environment – often those in very difficult circumstances, such as unaccompanied refugee, asylum-seeking and migrant children[65] – are overlooked.[66]

It should also be mentioned that, while there seems to be some level of understanding that poverty is expressed on the basis of household income, where the '$1.25 a day' metric provides an easy and comparable way of measuring monetary poverty for the purposes of the estimated cost of basic food basket, the measurement of child poverty is more complex.[67] This is because, firstly, children often do not earn an income and thus depend on, but do not have a say about, the income of their parents, and secondly because such a measurement presumes that household income is equitably distributed, which is not necessarily the case.[68]

On a positive note, there is strong evidence that social protection programmes are an effective tool for lifting families and children out of poverty. Such systems include conditional and unconditional cash transfers, school meal schemes, and food rations, which are intended to help families out of poverty and enable them to protect themselves from the shocks of multidimensional poverty.[69] Their effect on beneficiaries is not only short term but also long term,

---

62 See generally Save the Children, 'Child Poverty: What drives it and what it means to children across the world' (2016) <resourcecentre.savethechildren.net/node/9684/pdf/child_poverty_report_4web_0.pdf> accessed 12 July 2021.

63 ibid.

64 ibid.

65 ibid 11.

66 In fact, sometimes because of the non-alignment of migration laws and civil laws, including in respect of age determination, birth certificates, parental responsibility, etc., these groups of children would have a remote prospect of overcoming multidimensional poverty.

67 Save the Children, 'Child Poverty: What drives it and what it means to children across the world' (2016) 7 <resourcecentre.savethechildren.net/node/9684/pdf/child_poverty_report_4web_0.pdf> accessed 12 July 2021.

68 ibid.

69 UNICEF and the World Bank, 'Ending Extreme Poverty: A Focus on Children' (2 October 2016) 7 <https://www.unicef.org/publications/files/Ending_Extreme_Poverty_A_Focus_on_Children_Oct_2016.pdf> accessed 12 July 2021.

and includes improvements in respect of nutritional status as well as health outcomes. The often-highlighted large-scale intervention examples of Brazil (via the 'family allowance' programme) and Mexico (via the 'Prospera' conditional cash transfer programme) have helped to make a dent in child poverty in those countries.[70] The extent to which such social protection systems are inclusive, and benefit asylum seekers, refugees and migrants, is crucial.

4. CHILDREN ON THE MOVE, SDG 1 AND SOME REFLECTIONS ON THE ROLE OF PRIVATE INTERNATIONAL LAW

4.1. GENERAL: CHILDREN ON THE MOVE AND POVERTY

Given its centrality, SDG 1 on ending poverty is linked in various ways to a number of other Goals.[71] It is no surprise that that the SDGs identify, among others, children, refugees and internally displaced persons and migrants as vulnerable persons.[72] Some issues – namely poverty, hunger, education, health, gender equality and access to justice – are critical for millions of children on the move in Africa. In fact, children on the move and their families, before deciding on a destination in Africa, take into consideration issues such as safety, prospect of job opportunities, the presence of family members in the destination country, and humanitarian assistance, as well as ease of access to asylum procedures.[73]

Unfortunately, despite the increasing evidence that there is a direct link between migration and poverty, there is only minimal recognition both in law and practice (especially in Africa) that private international law plays an important role for ensuring that children that are on the move are protected and their best interests upheld. The opportunity for children and their families to benefit from safe, regular and orderly migration can be affected both positively

70 UNICEF, 'Children, food and nutrition: Growing in a changing world' (2019) 131 <https://www.unicef.org/media/63016/file/SOWC-2019.pdf> accessed 12 July 2021.

71 These include ending hunger (SDG 2); ensuring healthy lives and promoting well-being (SDG 3); ensuring inclusive and quality education (SDG 4); achieving gender equality and empowering all women and girls (SDG 5); ensuring sustainable water and sanitation for all (SDG 6); and strengthening the means of implementation and revitalising the Global Partnership for Sustainable Development (SDG 17).

72 Sumudu Atapattu, 'From Our Common Future to Sustainable Development Goals: Evolution of Sustainable Development under International Law' (2019) 36(2) Wisconsin International Law Journal 215, 226–227.

73 African Union and the International Organization for Migration, 'Africa Migration Report: Challenging the Narrative' (2020) https://publications.iom.int/system/files/pdf/africa-migration-report.pdf accessed 12 July 2021.

and negatively by various factors that are the subject of private international law. For example, it has been noted in general in the context of Europe that children in international migration might have their best interests compromised because of the non-alignment of tasks within Member States – between those responsible for children's protection under migration law on the one hand, and those with responsibilities to protect them under civil law on the other. In this respect, significant differences might exist in relation to: (1) cooperation mechanisms at the EU level for migration and for civil law issues; (2) the distribution of jurisdiction among Member States; (3) recognition of family relations as well as personal status laws; and (4) whether issues pertaining to care arrangements (recognition of existing ones, as well as appointment of guardians for unaccompanied minors) are dealt with as separate legal questions.[74]

The Global Compact for a Safe, Orderly and Regular Migration (2018) also acknowledges the link between poverty, SDGs, and migration. For example, with a view to minimising the adverse drivers and structural factors that compel people to leave their country of origin, states undertake to '[i]nvest in programmes that accelerate States' fulfilment of the Sustainable Development Goals with the aim of eliminating the adverse drivers and structural factors that compel people to leave their country of origin, including through poverty eradication'[75] Moreover, in order 'to accelerate the implementation of the 2030 Agenda for Sustainable Development in geographic areas from where irregular migration systematically originates due to consistent impacts of poverty',[76] the Global Compact calls on states to further increase cross-border international and regional cooperation.

The need to facilitate interstate cooperation and provide a calibrated regional approach has been highlighted as critical to addressing the human rights of children on the move in Africa.[77] This approach is supported by the CRC Committee, which has indicated that 'a comprehensive interpretation of the Conventions should lead State parties to develop … regional … cooperation in order to ensure the rights of all children in … migration'.[78]

---

74 European Parliament, 'Children on the move: A private international law perspective' (2017) <https://www.europarl.europa.eu/RegData/etudes/STUD/2017/583158/IPOL_STU(2017)583158_EN.pdf> accessed 14 July 2021. See also the chapter on SDG 16 in this volume.

75 UN General Assembly Resolution, Global Compact for Safe, Orderly and Regular Migration, UN Doc A/RES/73/195 (11 January 2019) para 18(b).

76 ibid para 39(b).

77 In this respect, the extent to which the African Union's (AU) 2018 draft revised framework policy integrates elements of the CRC could prove to be important.

78 Joint General Comment (JGC) No 3 of the Committee on the Protection of the Rights of All Migrant Workers and Members of Their Families and No 22 of the Committee on the Rights of the Child is entitled 'general principles regarding the human rights of children in the context of international migration', while the second one is Joint General Comment No 4 of the Committee on the Protection of the Rights of All Migrant Workers and Members of

The challenges children on the move face are diverse. In the context of Djibouti, for example, it has been noted that there is still an issue, within the law, of discrimination against migrant children.[79] Their lack of identity documents disqualifies them from accessing basic public services, such as healthcare and education.[80] As a result, they are denied child protection in the country in which they reside on their journey, and many are caught in a web of prostitution rings or other exploitative and illegal networks, or endure life on the streets.[81]

It has been rightly argued that 'preservation of the family environment and maintaining relations' are among seven elements that need to be taken into account when assessing what is in the best interests of the child in a particular case.[82] In fact, globalisation processes, increased migration, and the increase in the number of mixed marriages or unions and of different cross-border family disputes have made protection of children in such situations increasingly topical. International instruments that deal with different cross-border family issues include the Hague 'Children's Conventions' referred to in the introduction of this chapter. It has been rightly pointed out that 'the CRC family and the Hague family are visibly linked to one another'.[83] The increase in the number of children involved in cross-border family disputes and the need to protect their interests inevitably affect the issue of child maintenance,[84] and private international law instruments on the international recovery of child support can help address child poverty, even though the level of ratification of these instruments in Africa remains too low.

Still within the context of a family environment, the importance of the appointment of a guardian for unaccompanied children on the move could have implications for children's well-being, including child poverty. In some instances, it would be important that the appointment of a guardian in one state benefits from recognition in another state. Article 20 of the CRC, in listing

---

Their Families and No 23 of the Committee on the Rights of the Child entitled 'State obligations regarding the human rights of children in the context of international migration in countries of origin, transit, destination and return,' para 48.

79 Committee on the Rights of the Child, Concluding Observations: Djibouti, UN Doc CRC/C/DJI/CO/2 (October 2008) para 26.

80 ibid.

81 International Organization for Migration, 'Djibouti Works to Assist Street Children, Beginning with a Study on Their Needs: IOM Report' <https://www.iom.int/news/djibouti-works-assist-street-children-beginning-study-their-needs-iom-report> accessed 3 January 2021.

82 Committee on the Rights of the Child, General Comment No 14 on the right of the child to have his or her best interests taken as a primary consideration (Art 3, para 1), UN Doc CRC/C/GC/14 (29 May 2013) paras 58–70.

83 Hans van Loon, 'Protecting children across borders: the interaction between the CRC and the Hague Children's Conventions' in Ton Liefaard and Julia Sloth-Nielsen (eds), *The United Nation Convention on the Rights of the Child: taking stock after 25 years and looking ahead* (Brill/Nijhoff 2017) 33.

84 The provisions of the CRC (Art 27(4)) are explicit in this regard.

the various alternative forms of care for children deprived of their family environment, highlights in Article 20(c) that '[s]uch care could include, inter alia, foster placement, *kafalah* of Islamic law', etc.[85] It is also possible to make a *kafalah* arrangement in a contracting state to the 1996 Hague Convention, and in those instances the recognition of the *kafalah* should be guaranteed in other contracting states. If experience from the EU is of any guidance, it is important that private international law recognition rules and migration should be better coordinated with a view to ensuring that Member State allow children placed under *kafalah* the right to enter and reside on their territory unless it is against the child's best interests.[86]

With a view to making the link with SDG 1 on poverty more plausible and highlighting directly relevant scenarios for Africa, the next subsections proffer some insights into three topics. The first deals with the cross-cutting theme of age determination, the second one addresses child marriages, and the final section ventures into some of the connections between adoption and poverty.

4.2. AGE DETERMINATION AND STATUS AS A CHILD

Article 2 of the African Children's Charter offers a clear and concise definition of a child as 'every human being under 18 years'. The scope of application of the CRC and the African Children's Charter is linked to the definition of a child. Indeed, age is a criterion that can help to escape the ambiguities and contradictions of other definitions of a child, as it gives predictability regarding which rule or provision will apply to whom. The link between birth registration, nationality and migration status is well documented, and having a childhood status is important for the purposes of the various services and rights that children are entitled to, not only in the country of origin, but also in countries of transit and/or origin.

Private international law rules determine which law applies to the child's personal status. In the context of Europe, it has been argued that in 'the majority of cases, PIL rules refer to the nationality of the person at stake, but the place of the habitual residence might also be a relevant criterion, especially when

[85] *Kafalah* under Islamic law entails the acceptance of children without families in what is tantamount to a permanent form of foster care, but without the children concerned taking on the family name or enjoying the right to inherit from the family with which they are placed. See Rachel Hodgkin and Peter Newell, *Implementation Handbook for the Convention on the Rights of the Child* (UNICEF 2002) 295–296.

[86] European Parliament, 'Children on the move: A private international law perspective' (2017) <https://www.europarl.europa.eu/RegData/etudes/STUD/2017/583158/IPOL_STU(2017)583158_EN.pdf> accessed 14 July 2021. See also the chapter on SDG 16 in this volume.

the State of nationality's PIL rules (issue of renvoi) come into play'.[87] Thus, in some cases a person who is 18 or 19 years old could still be considered a child, depending on the law that applies to him or her.[88] From the point of view of addressing childhood poverty in respect of SDG 1, the reverse is more relevant, whereby in some instances a person who is 16 or 17, or a child bride (because of the concept of emancipation), might be considered to be an adult, and miss out on child-specific protection measures, including the appointment of legal guardians and benefits from child grants, opportunities and rights, depending on the law that applies to him or her.

Usually states establish a number of practices for assessing the age of a young person in the instances where documentation that establishes age is either not available or its validity is questioned. These practices, medical or otherwise, do have a margin of error of at least two years. Given the absence of a procedure that is 100 per cent accurate for the purposes of age determination, it is recommended that a combination of methods (medical, social, interviews, etc.) should be used. Intrusive age determination processes should be avoided, or at least be minimised.

In the instances where the authenticity of a document providing proof of age is questioned, cooperation between the authorities that issued the document and those questioning its authenticity is critical. Moreover, within the European Union, and with a view to upholding the best interests of a child, the findings of an age assessment process in a Member State should be recognised and accepted not only by the various authorities within the Member State that undertook the assessment, but also by the authorities of other Member States.[89]

Birth certificates are the most common method for proving age. However, on the African continent, only 55 per cent of children below the age of five in

87 ibid.

88 ibid 34.

89 ibid 38. On age assessment generally see also Joint General Comment (JCG) No 4 (2017) of the Committee on the Protection of the Rights of All Migrant Workers and Members of Their Families and No 23 (2017) of the Committee on the Rights of the Child on state obligations regarding the human rights of children in the context of international migration in countries of origin, transit, destination and return, point 4: 'To make an informed estimate of age, States should undertake a comprehensive assessment of the child's physical and psychological development, conducted by specialist paediatricians or other professionals who are skilled in combining different aspects of development. Such assessments should be carried out in a prompt, child-friendly, gender-sensitive and culturally appropriate manner, including interviews of children and, as appropriate, accompanying adults, in a language the child understands. Documents that are available should be considered genuine unless there is proof to the contrary, and statements by children and their parents or relatives must be considered. The benefit of the doubt should be given to the individual being assessed. States should refrain from using medical methods based on, inter alia, bone and dental exam analysis, which may be inaccurate, with wide margins of error, and can also be traumatic and lead to unnecessary legal processes. States should ensure that their determinations can be reviewed or appealed to a suitable independent body.'

Africa have a birth certificate.[90] For children on the move, especially those that come from rural areas or from marginalised communities, or move as a result of calamities such as conflict or climate-change-induced disasters, not having one's birth registered or not having a birth certificate is often the rule rather than the exception. Often children and their families that are on the move might find themselves in poverty, and the costs associated with birth registration can be insurmountable for children born into poverty. This is all more so where costs for activities such as transport, verification of documents from countries of origin, or penalties for late registrations are associated with birth registration systems.

Some jurisdictions have established a (late) birth registration system that is decentralised and involves the local courts.[91] While it is not considered good practice to require families to provide prior documentation as a condition for registration, especially in the instances where such documentation is difficult or impossible to obtain, in the instances it is a requirement, private international law can play an important role. For children on the move, especially those that were born in the country of either origin or transit and whose parents are trying to get the birth registered in a country of destination, different complex rules, including those pertaining to private international law, might be at play. Scenarios in this respect could range from those that register all births, to those that only register births that took place on their territory, those that register a birth if one of the child's putative legal parents is a national of the registering state, and those that register the birth of a child abroad at their embassies/consulates, where they exist.[92]

Cooperation between various authorities, some of which could also be facilitated through harmonisation of private international law, is not always a cost-neutral exercise for the well-being of children on the move. For example, one of the concerns of migrant families relating to having the birth of their children registered in countries of destination is the possibility that data-sharing between health service providers or civil servants responsible for registration and immigration enforcement authorities could lead to their arrest, detention and/or deportation.

Finally, legal identity, including birth registration, is part of the SDGs as Target 16.9, which includes strategies to reach all children without

---

90 Even the development of the necessary legal frameworks, and their subsequent implementation, is still in its infancy in a number of countries in the region. For example, Ethiopia's Proclamation No 760/2012 on Registration of Vital Events and National Identity Card Proclamation, amended by Proclamation No 1049/2017, is only a few years old.

91 For example in Togo.

92 See HCCH, 'A study of legal parentage and the issues arising from international surrogacy arrangements' (2014) <https://assets.hcch.net/docs/bb90cfd2-a66a-4fe4-a05b-55f33b009cfc.pdf> accessed 12 July 2021.

discrimination.[93] As a result, facilitating birth registration for children on the move is not only relevant for addressing child poverty, but is in fact a target in its own right. As far as the former is concerned, however, the recognition of the status of childhood – which could often mean appointment of guardians, access to education and healthcare, no detention, and opportunities to benefit from child-specific social protection services, such as child support grants – is critical to addressing multidimensional poverty, and the role private international law can play in this regard should be considered closely.[94]

4.3. CHILD MARRIAGE

The CRC does not prohibit child marriage explicitly.[95] However, a number of its provisions have been interpreted as prohibiting the practice.[96] Often, in relation to African countries, recommendations have been made to states to remove exceptions that allow marriages below the age of 18 not only on the basis of the CRC, but also based on the provisions of the African Children's Charter.[97] Despite this, in some African jurisdictions (and elsewhere too) the possibility is provided for children below 18 to be allowed to marry based on legitimate exceptional grounds – for example, based on parental/judicial consent when such a marriage is considered to be in the best interests of the child.

The high presence of child marriages in the two least developed corners of the word – sub-Saharan Africa and Southeast Asia – is one indication of the close link between child marriage and poverty.[98] Families facilitate child

---

93 The absence of a birth certificate makes the children more vulnerable to trafficking, sale, child labour and illegal adoption. Migrant children without birth registration or without a birth certificate are especially vulnerable to exploitation and abuse, particularly if they are in an irregular situation. See further the chapter on SDG 16 in this volume.

94 See also the chapter on SDG 16 in this volume, section 3.2.2.

95 The CEDAW, on the other hand, explicitly prohibits the practice of early marriages under Art 16(2), though it does not provide the minimum age for marriage. See also the chapter on SDG 5 in this volume, section 4.2.

96 These provisions include Art 24(3), which requires states to 'take … measures with a view to abolishing traditional practices', and Art 2(1), which prohibits discrimination on the basis of sex. Child marriage is also closely linked with the definition of a child. See Sharon Detrick, *A commentary on the United Convention of the Rights of the Child* (Martinus Nijhoff 1999) 58–59; Geraldine Van Bueren, *The international law on the rights of the child* (Martinus Nijhoff 1995) 36–37.

97 In the context of Guinea, despite the prohibition of child marriages in its Penal Code (2016), the Committee asked the state party 'to expeditiously amend its legislation to remove all exceptions that allow marriage under the age of 18 years, in line with the Convention and the … Charter'. Committee on the Rights of the Child, Concluding Observations: Guinea, UN Doc CRC/C/GIN/CO/3-6 (February 2019) para 16.

98 UNICEF, 'Child marriage and the law: Technical note for the Global Programme to End Child Marriage' (2020) 1 <https://www.unicef.org/media/86311/file/Child-marriage-the-law-2020.pdf> accessed 13 July 2021.

marriages with a view to securing a better future for the child bride and her family, and often make such a decision as the best option out of a menu of poor choices. Child marriages are also undertaken in the interest of the family, often where girls are perceived as a burden on household expenses. Such decisions are made despite the fact that evidence shows that 'girls who marry young are more likely to be poor and remain poor'.[99]

There is also a link between children on the move and child marriage. The notion of so-called 'temporary' or 'tourist marriages'[100] is one example of this.[101] Since the problem of child marriages may be exacerbated as a result of a humanitarian crisis, there is a possibility of children on the move being married off not only in the country of origin, but also in the country of transit, and then arriving at the country of destination, raising complex legal questions that, among others, private international law assists to address. In the few jurisdictions that automatically accord adult status to child brides, it could mean that these child brides would lose the protection they should benefit from as child migrants.[102] In this respect, the story of a 14-year-old asylum-seeking girl from Syria in Norway who had an 18-month-old child and was again pregnant, and the decision by the Norwegian authorities to investigate filing charges against her adult husband, triggered debate;[103] similar incidents are not unheard of in the context of Africa. Suggestions have been made to develop guidelines on how to handle individual cases of migrant/asylum-seeking brides and their adult husbands.[104] The automatic refusal to accept the effects of such marriages could have severe legal consequences for children on the move, as, for example, it would mean no family reunification visa or residence permits, the need to appoint guardians, etc.[105]

---

99 ibid.

100 See Joint General Comment (JGC) No 3 of the Committee on the Protection of the Rights of All Migrant Workers and Members of Their Families, para 24.

101 In the context of Egypt, the CRC Committee has expressed its deep concern 'at "tourist"/ "temporary" marriages'. Committee on the Rights of the Child, Concluding Observations: Egypt, Un Doc CRC/C/EGY/CO/3-4 (July 2011) para 70.

102 These benefits could include access to education, appointment of guardians, protection against detention, and any social protection programmes (such as child support grants) that could be available to children and can address multidimensional poverty.

103 See 'Child brides pose new challenge in ongoing refugee crisis' *Newsinenglish Norway* (4 December 2015) <https://www.newsinenglish.no/2015/12/04/child-brides-pose-new-challenge-in-ongoing-refugee-crisis/> accessed 12 July 2021.

104 See Emma Batha, 'Norway to ban child marriages as it seeks to set a global example', *Reuters* (22 May 2018) <https://www.reuters.com/article/us-norway-childmarriage-lawmaking/norway-to-ban-child-marriage-as-it-seeks-to-set-a-global-example-idUSKCN1IN29D> accessed 12 July 2021.

105 See, for example, European Parliament, 'Children on the move: A private international law perspective' (2017) 37 <https://www.europarl.europa.eu/RegData/etudes/STUD/2017/583158/IPOL_STU(2017)583158_EN.pdf> accessed 14 July 2021.

From the point of view of multidimensional poverty, child marriage affects access to education and health services, complicates children's development, and could even contribute to child mortality, as well as abuse, sexual exploitation and economic exploitation. Child brides that are on the move are in general exposed to these challenges more, especially if they are unaccompanied, have their children with them, etc. Therefore a blanket non-recognition of such child marriage arrangements in the context of international migration might fail to comply with the best interests of a child. The assessment of such arrangements to determine best interests could possibly also be informed by the legislative framework that could have permitted the child marriage, including if it is done through parental consent or through the authorisation of judicial bodies, which could raise questions of recognition as well as cooperation.

Here too, the fact that ending child marriage is envisaged as a goal within the SDGs (both Target 5.3, which aims to end child marriage by 2030, and SDG 16 on ending violence against children) should also inform the discussion on the implications of the instances where child marriage is recognised/accommodated, with a view to upholding the best interests of the child (the child bride and/or the children from the child marriage, if any), so as to address multidimensional poverty. This potential tension – namely between ending child marriage on the one hand, and on the other recognising it in exceptional circumstances, especially in the context of children on the move, at times with the assistance of private international law – would benefit from additional research in its own right. Given the three different approaches to ensuring that the minimum age of marriage is enforced in Africa – namely that some countries criminalise, others ban or invalidate, and yet others just provide the minimum age at 18 (with no express ban or criminalisation)[106] – means that there is a lack of harmonisation, leaving much room for private international law to address.

4.4. INTERCOUNTRY ADOPTION

As mentioned above, a number of countries on the African continent experience high levels of HIV/AIDS, conflict, and more importantly poverty, which in turn has led to a large number of children being deprived of their family environment. After all, apart from state actions such as deportation and imprisonment, the use of the word 'deprived' in Article 20(1) of the CRC and Article 25(1) of the ACRWC encompasses other scenarios, such as poverty

[106] See UNICEF, 'Child marriage and the law: Technical note for the Global Programme to End Child Marriage' (2020) 1 <https://www.unicef.org/media/86311/file/Child-marriage-the-law-2020.pdf> accessed 14 July 2021.

and illness,[107] that could deprive a child of a meaningful family environment. Abandonment and displacement (which could also be because of poverty) are other common reasons that prevent children from being able to grow up in their family environment.

Private international law, in particular the 1993 Hague Convention on Intercountry Adoption, plays a very important role in adoptions, and there is a direct as well as indirect link between poverty and intercountry adoption. Some scholars have written about cross-cultural concerns in intercountry adoption, including the link between intercountry adoption and poverty.[108] Poverty, especially multidimensional poverty, is one of the main factors that severely limits the capacity of African families to take care of their children. Therefore, drawing the line between termination of parental rights and responsibilities, abandonment and voluntary relinquishment, on the one hand, and poverty, on the other, as potential grounds for adoptability is not always easy. In addition, many children taken away from their original families come from homes where parental neglect is sometimes barely distinguishable from the effects of dire poverty.

Poverty alone as a ground for adoptability is considered not to be in accordance with the provisions of the CRC,[109] and the CRC Committee has continued to raise serious concerns about the fact that children living in poverty are over-represented among children separated from their parents, in both developed and developing countries.[110] The UN Guidelines for the Appropriate Use and Conditions of Alternative Care for Children evinces a similar position.[111] Thus, when poverty is the main reason why parental responsibility is terminated

107 In this regard, there is merit in pointing out that Art 23(4) of the Convention on the Rights of Persons with Disabilities, adopted in December 2006, states that '[i]n no case shall a child be separated from parents on the basis of a disability of either the child or one or both of the parents'.

108 See for example Elizabeth Bartholet, 'Where Do Black Children Belong? The Politics of Race Matching in Adoption' (1999) 139(5) University of Pennsylvania Law Review 1163; Fiona Bowie (ed), *Cross-Cultural Approaches to Adoption* (Routledge 2004).

109 See Committee on the Rights of the Child, Concluding Observations: Nepal, UN Doc CRC/C/15/Add.261 (September 2005) para 54(c). If poverty is to find its way into the legal books as a ground for the determination of the adoptability of a child at all, some precautionary measures need to be taken. This is partly because the existence of the possibility of declaring the adoptability of a child solely on the basis of poverty is prone to a high level of abuse. For instance, agencies arranging adoption placements could easily secure consent of parents by using financial inducement and invoke poverty as a ground for the adoptability of a child. This way, the use of poverty as a ground for adoptability also makes a loophole that compromises the requirement that consent be fully informed and be given free from either duress or financial inducement.

110 See Committee on the Rights of the Child, 'Day of General Discussion: Children Without Parental Care', UN Doc CRC/C/153 (17 March 2006) para 658.

111 See UN, 'Guidelines for the Alternative Care of Children' (2010) para 15, which provides that '[f]inancial and material poverty, or conditions directly and uniquely imputable to such

or abandonment or relinquishment is chosen, the rule requiring family preservation dictates that families should be offered support in keeping their children. This may take the form of the creation of domestic social services to aid children in poverty-stricken birth families. Indeed, such services would fit neatly into the interventions aimed at achieving SDG 1.

A number of complex questions need a response in the rare instances where a country decides to consider poverty as a valid ground for establishing the adoptability of a child. In this respect, for example, on what/whose standards is poverty in this respect to be assessed? Should the inability to care for the child be demonstrated by using local standards when the parent is destitute and cannot provide the child with the nourishment and shelter necessary for subsistence consistent with the standards of the child's place of residence?[112] Should such an assessment of poverty look at multidimensional poverty? In addition, how should standards like 'persistent failure to maintain' a child (as found, for example, in the Kenyan Children Act) be linked to poverty and be interpreted for the purpose of determining the adoptability of a child? Are there also potential roles to be played by anti-poverty interventions so that eligible/interested individuals who would like to adopt may not be disqualified by virtue of their poverty (including financial status)? Could this mean that a prospective adopter could adopt a child on a very meagre income and then go and apply for a child support grant?

Moreover, it has also been reported that, with globalisation, the shortage of adoptable children in many corners of the world, increasing poverty in Africa, and accompanying weak institutional law-enforcement capacity of state institutions, there are instances where caregivers are involved in selling children and other similar activities, which are often a manifestation of extreme poverty.[113] Hogbacka is of the view that 'in the context of deprivation ... consent is so severely restricted as to be no real choice'.[114] An important

poverty, should never be the only justification for the removal of a child from parental care, for receiving a child into alternative care, or for preventing his/her reintegration, but should be seen as a signal for the need to provide appropriate support to the family'.

112 See Katherine Sohr, 'Difficulties in Implementing the Hague Convention on the Protection of Children and Co-Operation in Respect of Intercountry Adoption: A Criticism of the Proposed Ortega's Law and an Advocacy for Moderate Adoption Reform in Guatemala' (2006) 18(2) Pace International Law Review 559, 565.

113 David M Smolin, 'Child Laundering as Exploitation: Applying Anti-Trafficking Norms to Intercountry Adoption Under the Coming Hague Regime' (2007) 32:001 Vermont Law Review 43. Also see Benyam D Mezmur, 'The Sins of the "Saviours": Child Trafficking in the Context of Intercountry Adoption in Africa', (Hague Conference on Private International Law 2010); Barbara Stark, 'When Genealogy Matters: Intercountry Adoption, International Human Rights, and Global Neoliberalism' (2017) 51 Vanderbilt Journal of Transnational Law 159.

114 Riita Hogbacka, 'Intercountry Adoption, Countries of Origin, and Biological Families', ISS Working Paper No. 598 of the International Institute of Social Studies in the Hague

element of free consent is to ensure that consent is not induced by payment or compensation,[115] as well as by undue influence or fraud, which poverty could increase the risk of for families of origin.[116] Therefore, the instances where poverty might lead to irregular/illegal activities in the context of adoption, constituting not only a violation of established private international law rules and practices, but also a contravention of criminal law provisions, are real. Private international law provides some guidance on how to prevent financial inducement, including on how costs associated with medical or legal documentation and travel should be regulated by states.[117]

5. CONCLUDING REMARKS

The SDG on poverty is very ambitious. It builds on some of the experiences from the MDGs, and its relevance for child poverty is immense. Given the fact that poverty is multidimensional and often intergenerational, it is acknowledged that one of the most effective ways of ending extreme poverty by 2030 is to end child poverty.

There are various types of partnerships, including inter- and intra-disciplinary ones, that should inform and assist in, among other things, policy coherence, collection of disaggregated data, mobilisation and efficient management of resources, multi-sectoral collaboration, and institutional collaboration, in the global effort to achieve the SDGs. In this respect, there is an abundance of research showing the importance of a number of aspects of public international law, especially international human rights law, and assessing the connection that this field of international law has in conceptualisation, implementation and evaluation. The focus of this literature has gone beyond focusing on the national sphere, and further assesses, for example, the obligations of states to avoid measures that could negatively affect the rights of persons living in poverty outside of their borders, which could require undertaking an assessment of the extraterritorial impacts of laws, policies and practices.

However, less attention has been given to the role of private international law. One of the key lessons on addressing child poverty from the era of the

(2014) 1, 12 <http://repub.eur.nl/pub/77406> accessed 12 July 2021. This, however, should not be understood to necessarily mean that children of poor parents should not be adopted simply because their parents cannot give consent, but that poverty should not be the determining factor.

115 Art 4(c)(3) of the 1993 Hague Convention on Intercountry Adoption.

116 A similar position has been taken by the CRC Committee.

117 HCCH, 'The Implementation and Operation of the 1993 Hague Intercountry Adoption Convention: Guide to Good Practice' (2008) Guide No 1, 34 <https://assets.hcch.net/docs/bb168262-1696-4e7f-acf3-fbbd85504af6.pdf> accessed 14 July 2021.

MDGs is the appreciation that past progress is no guarantee of continued progress, and that the increasing emergence of poverty-accelerating factors – such as displacement – can and do reverse progress. In this respect, it is critical to try to assess the role of different aspects of international law, including private international law. The above discussions (which can even be described as 'tinkering at the edges') of the three topics considered – age determination, child marriage and intercountry adoption – show that there exists multiple cross-border-related aspects of child poverty that are of interest to private international law that policymakers, academicians and practitioners should pay attention to.

SDG 2: ZERO HUNGER

Jeannette M.E. Tramhel

Goal 2: End hunger, achieve food security and improved nutrition and promote sustainable agriculture

2.1 By 2030, end hunger and ensure access by all people, in particular the poor and people in vulnerable situations, including infants, to safe, nutritious and sufficient food all year round

2.2 By 2030, end all forms of malnutrition, including achieving, by 2025, the internationally agreed targets on stunting and wasting in children under 5 years of age, and address the nutritional needs of adolescent girls, pregnant and lactating women and older persons

2.3 By 2030, double the agricultural productivity and incomes of small-scale food producers, in particular women, indigenous peoples, family farmers, pastoralists and fishers, including through secure and equal access to land, other productive resources and inputs, knowledge, financial services, markets and opportunities for value addition and non-farm employment

2.4 By 2030, ensure sustainable food production systems and implement resilient agricultural practices that increase productivity and production, that help maintain ecosystems, that strengthen capacity for adaptation to climate change, extreme weather, drought, flooding and other disasters and that progressively improve land and soil quality

2.5 By 2020, maintain the genetic diversity of seeds, cultivated plants and farmed and domesticated animals and their related wild species, including through soundly managed and diversified seed and plant banks at the national, regional and international levels, and promote access to and fair and equitable sharing of benefits arising from the utilization of genetic resources and associated traditional knowledge, as internationally agreed

2.a Increase investment, including through enhanced international cooperation, in rural infrastructure, agricultural research and extension services, technology development and plant and livestock gene banks in order to enhance agricultural productive capacity in developing countries, in particular least developed countries

2.b Correct and prevent trade restrictions and distortions in world agricultural markets, including through the parallel elimination of all forms of agricultural export subsidies and all export measures with equivalent effect, in accordance with the mandate of the Doha Development Round

2.c Adopt measures to ensure the proper functioning of food commodity markets and their derivatives and facilitate timely access to market information, including on food reserves, in order to help limit extreme food price volatility

1. INTRODUCTION

The 2030 Agenda for Sustainable Development, of which the 17 Sustainable Development Goals (SDGs) constitute the core, has potentially significant impact for future generations and the direction of the global food system. This chapter considers how private international law – used here in a broad sense – can be used towards the actualisation of SDG 2 'to end hunger, achieve food security and improved nutrition and promote sustainable agriculture.'

Section 1 provides context and a deconstruction of SDG 2 in relation to the right to food. Section 2 considers private international law as relevant to SDG 2, both under the traditional conflict-of-laws approach and under a more expanded interpretation. Section 3 examines legal instruments in subject areas with importance for smallholders, namely access to credit and simplified business registration, and those designed specifically for the agricultural sector, concerning contract farming and land investment contracts. Section 4 considers topics that could be further developed, such as private standards, and ways that private international law might be better engaged in the necessary shift towards a more sustainable global agri-food system. The chapter concludes with some reflections on recent changes in the focus of and approach to harmonisation within the field, and the growing recognition of the unrealised potential of private international law in contributing towards actualisation of many of the goals and aspirations articulated by public international law instruments.

1.1. CONTEXT

The current global population of 7.7 billion is projected to reach 9.7 billion by 2050.[1] It has been estimated that this will require an increase in food production of over 60 per cent, taking into account shifts in diet towards more livestock-based foods.[2] At the same time, roughly one-third of food produced is lost or wasted.[3] Adding to the complexity are the impacts of global warming on agricultural production, even as that production simultaneously contributes towards at least one-fifth of global emissions.[4] The challenge to

---

1 UN, Department of Economic and Social Affairs, 'World Population Prospects 2019: Highlights' (2019).

2 N Alexandratos and J Bruinsma, 'World agriculture towards 2030/2050: the 2012 revision', ESA Working Paper No 12-03, Food and Agriculture Organization of the United Nations (FAO) (2012).

3 FAO, 'Global food losses and food waste – Extent, causes and prevention' (2011).

4 FAO et al, 'The State of Food And Agriculture. Climate Change, Agriculture and Food Security' (2016) 5.

reduce emissions and simultaneously increase food production will require a radical transformation of the global food system and substantial shifts in consumption patterns.[5] Thus, efforts to end hunger, achieve food security and improved nutrition must be contemporaneous with promoting sustainable agriculture.

Before plunging ahead into analysis, it would be prudent to acknowledge the elephant in the room, which might be introduced with the following commentary:

> The industrial food system that has come to dominate in developed urban areas of the globe is a textbook case of market breakdown. What we have is an increasingly dominant global food system that produces abundantly, but whose products are increasingly out of reach to significant proportions of the global population, and which inexorably makes those who can afford its food sick, due to a combination of chronic diseases that are directly linked to consuming what the food industry finds the most profitable to produce and to promote. This is the classic case when government intervention is called for … This is a result of concentrated food monopolies that increasingly have more power than governments; they can dictate to governments what governments should do.[6]

Unsurprisingly, not everyone would agree. The dialogue around agri-food systems has become quite polarised. Some, whose position is voiced in the quotation above, consider the industrial agri-food system or 'Big Ag' as a primary cause behind global hunger;[7] others consider it to be the cure.[8] This polarisation is evident in debates over international agricultural trade,[9]

---

5 The Lancet Commission, 'Food in The Anthropocene: the EAT-Lancet Commission on Healthy Diets From Sustainable Food Systems. Summary Report' (2 February 2019) 393 (10170) The Lancet 447.

6 R Salvador, Member of the International Panel of Experts on Sustainable Food Systems (IPES-Food), 'Food Security as a Challenge in Post COVID-19, Virtual Forum', Transcript of remarks made 22 June 2020, Organization of American States (OAS), Secretariat for Legal Affairs <http://www.oas.org/en/sla/virtual_forum_Challenges_Food_Security.asp> accessed 12 July 2021.

7 See, for example, C Nair, 'The pandemic is just another sign of our broken food system', *World Economic Forum* (29 April 2020) <https://www.weforum.org/agenda/2020/04/how-to-feed-the-world-in-2050/> accessed 12 July 2021.

8 See, for example, 'How to Feed the Planet: The Global Food Supply Chain is Passing a Severe Test', *The Economist* (9 May 2020). Described as a 'capitalist miracle,' it is noted therein that 'the global supply of food has nearly tripled since 1970, as the population has doubled to 7.7bn. At the same time, the number of people who have too little to eat has fallen from 36% of the population to 11%'.

9 World Trade Organization (WTO), 'UN Rapporteur and WTO Head debate the impact of trade on hunger' (WTO, 11 May 2009) <https://www.wto.org/english/forums_e/debates_e/debate14_summary_e.htm> accessed 12 July 2021.

nutrition and wellness,[10] and definitions of sustainable agriculture.[11] It is also apparent in practice; co-existing with the sophisticated and complex industrial agri-food system is another reality, that of smallholder agriculture,[12] as an estimated 500 million smallholder farms in the developing world support almost two billion people.[13]

Within that context, as the COVID-19 pandemic began to unfold in early 2020, it revealed vulnerabilities and weaknesses in the current agri-food system at global, regional and local levels, particularly in supply chains, and calls were made to keep these 'functioning well.'[14] The pandemic has brought to the forefront debates and divisions over policy approaches towards achieving global food security and the actualisation of SDG 2. Unfortunately, the most recent projections indicate that the world is currently *not* on track to meet Zero Hunger by 2030 and that the pandemic threatens to push millions more into severe food insecurity.[15]

For these reasons it was considered advisable, prior to embarking on an analysis of private international law mechanisms, to recognise the difficulty of such an exercise 'in the abstract' absent any kind of acknowledgement of the elephant in the room. Should private international law remain aloof from policy debates? Should its mechanisms and instruments be viewed as no more than neutral tools, mere soldiers following the chain of command in a war on hunger? At a minimum, recognition that there are fundamental differences in opinion over the *means* by which to achieve SDG 2 can provide some context for a discussion as to the possible application of private international law towards that end.

---

10 A Jacobs and M Richtel, 'How Big Business Got Brazil Hooked on Junk Food', *New York Times* (16 September 2017) <https://www.nytimes.com/interactive/2017/09/16/health/brazil-obesity-nestle.html> accessed 12 July 2021. Some executives of multinational food companies quoted therein maintain that 'their products have helped alleviate hunger [and] provided crucial nutrients'.

11 See section 1.3.4, *infra*.

12 Smallholders are defined as 'small-scale farmers, pastoralists, forest keepers, fishers who manage areas from less than one hectare to 10 hectares.' FAO, 'Smallholders and Family Farmers Factsheet' <http://www.fao.org/fileadmin/templates/nr/sustainability_pathways/docs/Factsheet_SMALLHOLDERS.pdf> accessed 12 July 2021.

13 It is estimated that smallholder farms produce about 80 per cent of the food consumed in Asia and sub-Saharan Africa. Committee on World Food Security, High Level Panel of Experts (HLPE), 'Investing in smallholder agriculture for food security' <http://www.fao.org/fileadmin/user_upload/hlpe/hlpe_documents/HLPE_Reports/HLPE-Report-6_Investing_in_smallholder_agriculture.pdf> accessed 12 July 2021.

14 FAO, IFAD, WFP and the World Bank on the occasion of the Extraordinary G20 Agricultural Minister's Meeting, 'Joint Statement on COVID-19 Impacts on Food Security and Nutrition' (21 April 2020) <https://www.worldbank.org/en/news/statement/2020/04/21/joint-statement-on-covid-19-impacts-on-food-security-and-nutrition> accessed 12 July 2021.

15 FAO et al, 'The State of Food Security and Nutrition in the World 2020: Transforming food systems for affordable healthy diets' (2020) (SOFI Report 2020).

At first glance it might appear that private international law, whether under a conflict-of-laws approach or the more expanded interpretation used in this chapter, is of primary significance for 'Big Ag' actors in the global agri-food sector. This is changing, however, both in terms of the application of some instruments (see section 4.1, *infra*, on access to credit), and in the methodologies used in their development. In the past, perhaps the discourse had not been as open to hearing the range of voices – those of women, indigenous peoples, smallholders and other marginalised groups – whose particular vulnerabilities the SDGs are primarily intended to address. What is encouraging, as illustrated in this chapter, is that the dialogue is responding, albeit slowly, to the need for greater inclusivity in the range of stakeholder groups affected by these instruments and this, in turn, can improve their effectiveness in addressing and regulating the very mechanisms that can be used as levers to actualise the SDGs and broader goals. Perhaps this offers a glimmer of hope for private international law 'beyond the schism.'[16]

1.2. SDG 2 AND THE RIGHT TO FOOD

Underpinning the goals set out in SDG 2 is the right to food (RTF). Unlike SDG 2, however, the RTF *does* correspond with certain legal obligations and responsibilities on the part of states, as has been recognised in numerous international law instruments.[17] Its articulation has evolved over time from the initial concept in the 1948 Universal Declaration of Human Rights, which recognises the RTF as part of the right to an adequate standard of living.[18] It was further elaborated in the 1966 International Covenant on Economic, Social and Cultural Rights (ICESCR), which recognises the right to adequate food and, more specifically, the right to be free from hunger.[19] The basis for state obligations derives from Article 2 of the ICESCR, which requires states to take steps 'with a view to achieving progressively the full realization of the rights recognized'.[20] During the 1996 World Food Summit, states requested

---

16 H Muir Watt, 'Private International Law Beyond the Schism' (2011) 2 Transnational Legal Theory 347.

17 UN Committee on Economic, Social, and Cultural Rights, General Comment 12. The right to adequate food (Art 11), UN Doc E/C.12/1999/5 (1999).

18 'Everyone has the right to a standard of living adequate for the health and well-being of himself and of his family, including food, …' UN General Assembly, Universal Declaration of Human Rights, UN Doc A/RES/217(III) A (1948), GAOR 3rd Session Part I 71, Art 25.

19 UN General Assembly, International Covenant on Economic, Social and Cultural Rights, UN Doc A/RES/21/2200 (1966) 993 UNTS 3, Art 11.

20 ibid Art 2(1).

'a better definition of the rights relating to food in Article 11 [of the ICESCR]'.[21] In response, General Comment No 12 outlines different levels of obligations; it notes that more immediate and urgent steps may be needed to ensure the fundamental right to freedom from hunger and malnutrition (para 1), while the right to adequate food will have to be realised progressively (para 6). The right to be free from hunger is the only right described as fundamental[22] and is therefore argued to be absolute, in contrast to the right to adequate food, which is more limited.[23] Thus, these two *rights* directly correspond to and underpin the *goals* as expressed in SDG 2.

In the course of this progressive development, in 2000 the UN Commission on Human Rights (UNHRC) established the mandate of the Special Rapporteur on the RTF in order 'to respond fully to the necessity for an integrated and coordinated approach in the promotion and protection of the right to food.'[24] Subsequently, in 2002 at the World Food Summit at which the RTF was reaffirmed, states requested practical guidelines for its implementation.[25] This resulted in the adoption of Voluntary Guidelines to Support the Progressive Realization of the Right to Adequate Food in the Context of National Food Security.[26] Accordingly, the RTF and the evolution of its interpretation have led to the development of a pragmatic instrument that can also guide states in the actualisation of SDG 2.

1.3. SDG 2: A DECONSTRUCTION

1.3.1. 'End Hunger'

Hunger is synonymous with chronic *undernourishment*, described as insufficient dietary energy consumption.[27] It is estimated that almost 9 per cent of the

---

21 UN Committee on Economic, Social, and Cultural Rights, General Comment 12. The right to adequate food (Art 11), UN Doc E/C.12/1999/5 (1999), para 2.

22 This has been noted by several authors, e.g., N Smita, 'The Right to Food: Holding Global Actors Accountable under International Law' (2006) 10 Columbia Journal of Transnational Law 691, 706.

23 A R Ganesh, 'The Right to Food and Buyer Power' (2010) 11(1) German Law Journal 1198.

24 UNHRC, 56th Session, E/CN.4RES/2000/10 (17 April 2000). The original three-year mandate has been periodically renewed.

25 FAO, 'Declaration of the World Food Summit: Five Years Later' (2002) para 10 <http://www.fao.org/docrep/MEETING/005/Y7106E/Y7106E09.htm#TopOfPage> accessed 12 July 2021.

26 FAO, 'Voluntary Guidelines to Support the Progressive Realization of the Right to Adequate Food in the Context of National Food Security', adopted by the 127th Session of the FAO Council, November 2004 (RTF Guidelines).

27 FAO et al, 'The State of Food Security and Nutrition in the World 2020: Transforming food systems for affordable healthy diets' (2020) (SOFI Report 2020), Glossary.

world's population is undernourished (690 million in 2019).[28] While the Prevalence of Undernutrition (PoU) estimates the *proportion* of those undernourished within a population, the Food Insecurity Experience Scale (FIES) measures the *severity* of the food insecurity situation in different cultural, linguistic and development contexts.[29] The global rating for 2019 indicates the prevalence of food insecurity to be 9.7 per cent severe and 25.9 per cent moderate and severe.[30] These two indicators, PoU and FIES, have been specified as the means to evaluate and monitor progress towards Target 2.1.[31]

1.3.2. 'Achieve Improved Nutrition'

Improved nutrition is achieved by addressing *malnutrition*, a condition caused by 'inadequate, unbalanced or excessive consumption and includes undernutrition (child stunting and wasting and vitamin and mineral deficiencies) as well as overweight and obesity.'[32] As of 2019, the global rate of children suffering from stunting is 21.3 per cent (one in five) and from wasting it is 6.9 per cent.[33] These two indicators, prevalence of stunting and malnutrition (by wasting or overweight), have been specified as the means to evaluate and monitor progress towards those aspects of Target 2.2.[34]

At the same time, rates of obesity continue to increase, with 13.1 per cent of all adults worldwide and 5.6 per cent of all children now considered obese.[35] Hunger and obesity can be observed often in the same countries or even the same individuals, which is described as the 'hunger–obesity paradox' or the 'double burden' of malnutrition.[36] What this illustrates is that food *availability*, the first pillar of food security, alone is not enough.

1.3.3. 'Achieve Food Security'

Food security is achieved 'when all people, at all times, have physical, social and economic access to sufficient, safe and nutritious food which meets their dietary

28 ibid 3.
29 ibid 4 and 19.
30 ibid 20, Table 3.
31 UN, Department of Economic and Social Affairs, 'Sustainable Development Goals, Targets and Indicators' <https://sdgs.un.org/goals/goal2> accessed 12 July 2021.
32 FAO et al, 'The State of Food Security and Nutrition in the World 2020: Transforming food systems for affordable healthy diets' (2020) (SOFI Report 2020), Glossary.
33 ibid 13.
34 UN, Department of Economic and Social Affairs, 'Sustainable Development Goals, Targets and Indicators' <https://sdgs.un.org/goals/goal2> accessed 12 July 2021.
35 FAO et al, 'The State of Food Security and Nutrition in the World 2020: Transforming food systems for affordable healthy diets' (2020) (SOFI Report 2020).
36 FAO et al, 'The State of Food Security and Nutrition in the World: Building Climate Resilience for Food Security and Nutrition' (2018) (SOFI Report 2018) 27.

needs and food preferences for an active and healthy life.'[37] This widely accepted definition is consistent with the RTF and its evolution as described above.[38] The reference to 'all people at all times' reflects the concept of sustainable development; as specifically noted in General Comment No 12, 'the notion of adequate food or food security, [implies] food being accessible for both present and future generations.'[39] Elaboration of the four pillars – availability, access, utilisation and stability – is also grounded in this evolution.[40]

Pillar one, availability, refers to 'the possibilities either for feeding oneself directly from productive land or other natural resources, or for well-functioning distribution, processing and market systems that can move food from the site of production to where it is needed in accordance with demand'[41] – in other words, physical availability of food through *production*, *distribution* and *exchange*.[42] Production is affected by both *biophysical* aspects (climate, geography, rainfall and temperature, as well as changes in these factors due to climate change; agricultural practices and soil management; crop and livestock selection and management) and *socio-economic* aspects (land ownership and tenure; land use designation; natural resource access and allocation; and access to financial resources). Distribution encompasses the full spectrum of the supply chain 'from farm to fork' that requires extensive physical and economic infrastructure to transport not only products to the consumer but also inputs to producers. Exchange is made possible through the international trading system, which includes institutions and specific rules for the agri-food sector (Targets 2.3–2.5, 2.a–2.c).

Pillar two, access, encompasses *physical, economic* and *social* access.[43] Physical or 'direct' access refers to food produced by oneself or one's family; economic or 'indirect' access to food is determined by disposable income, food prices and social support. The concept of access takes into consideration social aspects, such as allocation of food within the household and adequacy for all members, given that the needs of women, children or the elderly can at times be marginalised. It also incorporates human dignity, in that

---

37 FAO, 'Declaration of the World Food Summit', FAO Doc WSFS 2009/2 (16–18 November 2009).

38 See in particular UN Committee on Economic, Social, and Cultural Rights, General Comment 12. The right to adequate food (Art 11), UN Doc E/C.12/1999/5 (1999), paras 6 and 7.

39 ibid.

40 FAO, 'Declaration of the World Food Summit', FAO Doc WSFS 2009/2 (16–18 November 2009), n 1.

41 UN Committee on Economic, Social, and Cultural Rights, General Comment 12. The right to adequate food (Art 11), UN Doc E/C.12/1999/5 (1999), para 12.

42 FAO and EU, 'An Introduction to the Basic Concepts of Food Security' (EC-FAO Food Security Programme 2008) <http://www.fao.org/docrep/013/al936e/al936e00.pdf> accessed 12 July 2021.

43 UN Committee on Economic, Social, and Cultural Rights, General Comment 12. The right to adequate food (Art 11), UN Doc E/C.12/1999/5 (1999), para 13.

access should be possible without resort to begging, theft or scavenging[44] (Target 2.1).

Pillar three, utilisation, encapsulates consumption and metabolism of food, which encompasses safety, metabolic limitations and choice. Food safety is concerned with the supply chain, handling and preparation. Utilisation includes consideration of malnutrition resulting from nutrient deficiencies, poor metabolism due to allergies or health conditions, and supplementary fortification of foods. It also concerns food choice, which includes the option of culturally appropriate foods[45] (Targets 2.1–2.2).

Pillar four, stability, is largely dependent upon the first three pillars over time.[46] Chronic food insecurity refers to long-term and persistent lack of adequate food, whereas transitory food insecurity can occur periodically because of environmental factors (floods or droughts), social instability (war or political upheaval) or changes in economic circumstances (unemployment), or, as the world has just witnessed, collapse in supply chains due to a pandemic.

Given the complexity and range of issues that extend beyond agriculture and include health, education, transport and trade policy, among others, an overarching and cross-sectoral approach to developing effective policy is essential. Accordingly, states have been encouraged by the UN Committee on World Food Security 'to develop stable and long-term national food security and nutrition strategies'[47] that can serve to guide this process.

1.3.4. 'Promote Sustainable Agriculture'

Interpretation of what constitutes 'sustainable' agriculture continues to unfold. As defined by the Food and Agriculture Organization of the United Nations (FAO), it is 'the management and conservation of the natural resource base, and the orientation of technological and institutional change in such a manner as to ensure the attainment and continued satisfaction of human needs

---

44 UN Commission on Human Rights, 'The right to food: Report by the Special Rapporteur on the Right to Food', Mr Jean Ziegler, UN Doc E/CN.4/2001/53 (7 February 2001) paras 14 and 18. See also UN Committee on Economic, Social, and Cultural Rights, General Comment 12. The right to adequate food (Art 11), UN Doc E/C.12/1999/5 (1999), para 4.

45 FAO and EU, 'An Introduction to the Basic Concepts of Food Security' (EC-FAO Food Security Programme 2008) <http://www.fao.org/docrep/013/al936e/al936e00.pdf> accessed 12 July 2021. See also UN Committee on Economic, Social, and Cultural Rights, General Comment 12. The right to adequate food (Art 11), UN Doc E/C.12/1999/5 (1999), paras 8–11.

46 ibid.

47 Committee on Food Security (CFS), 'Principles for Responsible Investment in Agriculture and Food Systems', endorsed by the CFS at its 41st Session on 15 October 2014 (RAI Principles), Principle 35.

for present and future generations. [It] conserves land, water, plant and animal genetic resources, is environmentally non-degrading, technically appropriate, economically viable and socially acceptable.'[48] Most definitions tend to be complex and yet rather general,[49] some equate a definition with the goal,[50] and some might raise more questions than answers.[51] Definitions tend towards either an 'ecocentric' approach that emphasises low levels of growth of human development and organic and biodynamic farming techniques, together with changes in consumption patterns, or a 'technocentric' approach that includes a variety of strategies but with a focus on biotechnology as the best way to meet increasing demands.[52]

More recently, there seems to be less emphasis on sustainable agriculture per se with discussions turning towards sustainable food systems. A recent example is the European Union's Farm to Fork Strategy,[53] which includes a lengthy description of sustainable food production and 10 specific actions in order to achieve it.[54] This may be indicative of the most pragmatic approach – a gradual transition.

Apart from definitions, valuable and relevant guidance can be gleaned from other sources; key among these are the Voluntary Guidelines on the Responsible Governance of Tenure of Land, Fisheries and Forests in the Context of National Food Security (VGGT)[55] and the Principles for Responsible Investment in Agriculture and Food Systems (RAI Principles)[56] endorsed by the Committee on World Food Security (discussed in section 3.4, *infra*).

---

48 FAO, 'Report of the FAO Council, 94th Session' cited in FAO, 'Building a Common Vision for Sustainable Food and Agriculture: Principles and Approaches' (2014) 12.

49 For example, see U.S. Code, Title 7, Section 3103 (19). See also Union of Concerned Scientists, 'What is sustainable agriculture?' <https://www.ucsusa.org/resources/what-sustainable-agriculture> accessed 12 July 2021.

50 University of California Davis, Sustainable Agriculture Research and Education Program, 'What is sustainable agriculture?' <https://sarep.ucdavis.edu/sustainable-ag> accessed 12 July 2021.

51 For example, this definition might prompt one to ask how sustainable agriculture differs from the 'modern' agriculture it is said to complement. Western Sustainable Agriculture Research and Education, 'What is sustainable agriculture?' <https://western.sare.org/about/what-is-sustainable-agriculture/> accessed 12 July 2021.

52 G M Robinson, 'Towards Sustainable Agriculture: Current Debates' (July 2009) 3(5) Geography Compass 1757.

53 European Commission, 'A Farm to Fork Strategy for a fair, healthy and environmentally-friendly food system', COM(2020)381 (20 May 2020), see section 2.1.

54 ibid section 2.1 'Ensuring sustainable food production'.

55 CFS, 'Voluntary Guidelines on the Responsible Governance of Tenure of Land, Fisheries and Forests in the Context of National Food Security', endorsed by the CFS at its 38th (Special) Session on 11 May 2012 (VGGT).

56 Committee on Food Security (CFS), 'Principles for Responsible Investment in Agriculture and Food Systems', endorsed by the CFS at its 41st Session on 15 October 2014 (RAI Principles).

Space constraints permit only a nod to urban agriculture, the importance of which is increasingly recognised; enabling food production in urban and peri-urban areas in closer proximity to growing urban populations is an essential consideration in the design of sustainable food systems.

While Targets 2.1 and 2.2 are more specific to ending hunger and improving nutrition, Targets 2.3–2.5 and 2.a–2.c are more closely associated with achieving food security and promoting sustainable agriculture. Nonetheless, as progress towards any of these targets will contribute towards actualisation of SDG 2, it cannot be over-emphasised that to realise these 'integrated and indivisible' global goals requires an interdisciplinary and holistic approach. The next section will consider how private international law can be used in this endeavour.

2. PRIVATE INTERNATIONAL LAW AND SDG 2

2.1. A 'CONFLICT-OF-LAWS' APPROACH

Some of the insights derived from the analyses of conflict-of-laws cases examined in relation to other SDGs could be equally applicable to SDG 2. Consider as an example SDG 6 on water management, for which 'the traditional private international law framework is limited and arguably ill-equipped' for reasons that include the 'complex network of elements, interest, actors and legal regimes and the unsuitability of the substance-neutrality of the choice-of-law methodology for resolving water conflicts.'[57] This limitation is illustrated in *Vedanta Resources plc and Konkola Copper Mines plc v Lungowe*[58] concerning jurisdiction and mentioned here for two reasons. First, the case underscores the 'integrated and indivisible' nature of the SDGs, given that water management is also essential for agriculture. Secondly, the emphasis of the case could have been food production or, rather than a mining operation, the defendant companies could have been engaged in industrial agriculture and discharged toxic pesticides that caused harm to the claimant's food source. Analyses across the classic trilogy of conflict-of-laws issues in relation to any one of the SDGs might very well have broader application.

57 See section 3 in the chapter on SDG 6 in this volume.

58 [2019] UKSC 20. The claimants alleged that the Nchanga Copper Mine in the Republic of Zambia repeatedly discharged toxic chemicals into their local watercourses, polluting the only source of water for drinking and *crop irrigation* (emphasis added to stress relevance of the case not only for SDG 6 but also for SDG 2). For a full discussion of the case, see section 5.2 in the chapter on SDG 6 in this volume.

2.1.1. *Jurisdiction*

Limitations of the traditional approach are also evidenced when confronting the challenges that have ensued from the global agri-food system as demonstrated in *Achuko v Absa Bank Ltd and Others.*[59] Two South African banks had prearranged non-competitive corn and soybean futures trades on the Chicago Board of Trade in breach of US law. Achuko claimed that this conduct infringed South Africa's Constitution, section 27(1)(b), according to which everyone has the right to have access to sufficient food, and argued that it would compromise the price of food, especially maize meal, and thereby create a risk for food security. While acknowledging territoriality as the traditional basis for jurisdiction, the court explained that this principle includes a subjective aspect, which recognises the power of the state to enact laws that govern conduct within its territory, and an objective aspect, which recognises the power of the state to enact laws that concern conduct taking place outside of its borders the effects of which take place within its borders. The issue was not whether the conduct was unlawful under the law of the United States but rather whether the conduct and its consequences infringed rights conferred by the South African Constitution. Accordingly, the court found that the question did fall within its jurisdiction and reasoned that if the effects of conduct undertaken abroad occurred in South Africa and those effects gave rise to an infringement of the guaranteed rights, the infringement was no less significant because the effects had their origin abroad; however, the applicant had failed to prove any such infringement or threat thereof. While the case has broad relevance for SDG 2, it is particularly significant for international agricultural trade and food commodity markets (Targets 2.b and 2.c).

Harmonised rules to reduce the risk of parallel litigation in different states would be welcomed by international businesses, including those in the agri-food sector. An important development in this regard is the Hague Conference on Private International Law (HCCH) 2005 Choice of Court Convention; by promoting party autonomy regarding adjudicatory jurisdiction, it facilitates transaction planning in cross-border cases.[60] More recently, the focus of HCCH has returned to the topic of jurisdiction, currently under discussion by an experts group.[61]

---

59 *Achuko v Absa Bank Ltd and Others* [2019] ZAGPJHC 264, [2020] (1) SA 533 (GJ). See also *American Banana Co v United Fruit Co*, 213 U.S. 347 (1909).

60 The Hague Convention of 30 June 2005 on Choice of Court Agreements (concluded 30 June 2005, entered into force 1 October 2015) <https://assets.hcch.net/docs/510bc238-7318-47ed-9ed5-e0972510d98b.pdf> accessed 12 July 2021.

61 HCCH, 'Jurisdiction Project' <https://www.hcch.net/en/projects/legislative-projects/jurisdiction-project> accessed 12 July 2021.

2.1.2. *Applicable Law*

Clarity in the applicable law reduces legal uncertainty also, particularly in regard to international commercial contracts, and thereby contributes towards a more conducive business environment. While some work products clarify choice-of-law rules, others promote development of uniform law. In the first category, two recent developments are noteworthy. In 2015, the HCCH Principles on Choice of Law in International Commercial Contracts were approved.[62] This instrument encourages adherence to the principle of party autonomy and illustrates how a choice-of-law regime that gives effect to the principle may be constructed.[63] In 2019, the Guide on the Law Applicable to International Commercial Contracts in the Americas (OAS Contracts Guide) was approved.[64] While it, too, encourages recognition of party autonomy, given that adherence to this principle is unclear in several states within the region, it also provides clarity on applicable law rules in the absence of effective choice.[65] An example from the second category is the Tripartite Legal Guide to Uniform Legal Instruments in the area of International Commercial Contracts (with a focus on sales).[66] A joint initiative of the United Nations Commission on International Trade Law (UNCITRAL), the International Institute for the Unification of Private Law (UNIDROIT) and HCCH, it seeks to promote 'adoption, application and uniform interpretation' of instruments developed by these three organisations.[67]

The relevance for SDG 2 is twofold. First, all three of these endeavours strengthen the basic principle of party autonomy and advance the development of uniform law in the area of international commercial contracts. Moreover, the principle serves as an important foundation for other private international law initiatives, particularly those designed for the agricultural sector concerning contract farming and land investment contracts (see sections 3.3 and 3.4, *infra*). Secondly, these initiatives have also helped to confirm and clarify important limitations on party autonomy. For example, consumer and employment contracts are generally excluded from the scope, as is the case

62 HCCH, 'Principles on Choice of Law in International Commercial Contracts' (approved 19 March 2015) <https://assets.hcch.net/docs/5da3ed47-f54d-4c43-aaef-5eafc7c1f2a1.pdf> accessed 12 July 2021, (HCCH Principles).

63 ibid. See Introduction, para I.5.

64 Organization of American States (OAS) and Inter-American Juridical Committee (IAJC), 'Guide on the Law Applicable to International Commercial Contracts in the Americas', OAS/Ser.Q, CJI/RES. 249 (XCIV-0/19) (21 February 2019).

65 ibid. See Purpose and Objectives, paras 8 and 9.

66 HCCH, Permanent Bureau, 'Development of the Legal Guide to Uniform Legal Instruments in the Area of International Commercial Contracts (with a focus on sales)', Prel Doc 16 (January 2020) <https://assets.hcch.net/docs/dcb33143-5373-4446-a6ae-487d92d5e294.pdf> accessed 12 July 2021.

67 ibid para 5.

in the aforementioned HCCH Principles and OAS Contracts Guide.[68] This is because many states have enacted legislation to protect parties that are presumed to hold weaker bargaining positions, specifically consumers and workers. In addition, these initiatives emphasise that a choice of law cannot override mandatory public policies.[69] This restriction has been described as having two facets: 'the provisions of the law of the forum shall necessarily be applied when they are mandatory requirements' and 'application of the law designated may be only be excluded when it is manifestly contrary to the public order of the forum.'[70] In this way, contracting parties are precluded from a choice of law that would override human rights, environmental standards and other public policy-driven provisions of the law of the forum.

2.1.3. Recognition and Enforcement of Judgments

The HCCH 2019 Convention on the Recognition and Enforcement of Foreign Judgments in Civil and Commercial Matters is intended to promote access to justice and multilateral trade and investment through judicial cooperation and a uniform set of core rules.[71] A common aspect of instruments on this subject is that although the *substantive* legal issues are addressed, the *procedure* for the actualisation of recognition and enforcement is delegated to the domestic law of each state.[72] Given that domestic procedures frequently also pose obstacles, an initiative is underway at the Inter-American Juridical Committee that would build on the aforementioned HCCH Convention to consider how states might

68 HCCH, 'Principles on Choice of Law in International Commercial Contracts' (approved 19 March 2015) <https://assets.hcch.net/docs/5da3ed47-f54d-4c43-aaef-5eafc7c1f2a1.pdf> accessed 12 July 2021 (HCCH Principles, Art 1.1; Organization of American States (OAS) and Inter-American Juridical Committee (IAJC), 'Guide on the Law Applicable to International Commercial Contracts in the Americas', OAS/Ser.Q, CJI/RES. 249 (XCIV-0/19) (21 February 2019), Recommendation 5.1.

69 HCCH, 'Principles on Choice of Law in International Commercial Contracts' (approved 19 March 2015) <https://assets.hcch.net/docs/5da3ed47-f54d-4c43-aaef-5eafc7c1f2a1.pdf> accessed 12 July 2021 (HCCH Principles), Art 11; Organization of American States (OAS) and Inter-American Juridical Committee (IAJC), 'Guide on the Law Applicable to International Commercial Contracts in the Americas', OAS/Ser.Q, CJI/RES. 249 (XCIV-0/19) (21 February 2019), Recommendation 17.

70 The Inter-American Convention on the Law Applicable to International Contracts (Mexico Convention) (adopted 17 March 1994, entered into force 15 December 1996) OAS Treaty Series No 78 (1996) Arts 11 and 18, respectively. See also Organization of American States (OAS) and Inter-American Juridical Committee (IAJC), 'Guide on the Law Applicable to International Commercial Contracts in the Americas', OAS/Ser.Q, CJI/RES. 249 (XCIV-0/19) (21 February 2019), para 478.

71 The Hague Convention of 2 July 2019 on the Recognition and Enforcement of Foreign Judgments in Civil or Commercial Matters (concluded 2 July 2019, not yet in force) <https://assets.hcch.net/docs/806e290e-bbd8-413d-b15e-8e3e1bf1496d.pdf> accessed 12 July 2021.

72 ibid Art 14.

simplify internal procedures for the recognition and enforcement of foreign judgments.[73]

These recent developments in the classic trilogy provide greater clarity in the law and contribute towards an improved international business environment, and consequently for global agri-business. Other developments with more direct and potentially more significant implications for SDG 2 fall within the more expanded interpretation of the field.

2.2. PRIVATE INTERNATIONAL LAW IN THE BROADER SENSE

Economic and other functions enabled by the domestic legal framework can be significantly enhanced when national laws (including conflict-of-laws rules) are harmonised with those of other states. Recognising the value of such harmonisation, certain international entities were established for that purpose, namely, UNCITRAL, UNIDROIT and HCCH. Regional organisations that work in this field include the Organization of American States (OAS), Organization for the Harmonization of Business Laws in Africa (OHADA), and the Organization for the Harmonization of Business Law in the Caribbean (OHADAC), among others. Valuable contributions are also made by international non-governmental organisations such as the International Chamber of Commerce (ICC), the work products of which are widely used and often incorporated by reference into legal instruments.[74]

To facilitate international trade and commerce, for example, these organisations address legal issues inherent in a variety of topics that include international sale of goods, transport, electronic commerce, procurement and infrastructure development, international payments, security interests and alternative dispute settlement.[75] Codifying international rules in these areas of the law improves the 'legal lubricant' that enables the machinery of international commerce to operate; as such, these advances are as relevant to the agri-food sector as any other.

Given that food availability is a function of production, distribution and exchange, this requires not only physical infrastructure, but also economic infrastructure which, in turn, requires the necessary legal framework to enable these transactions by means of contract, bills of lading, letters of credit, etc. and, more recently, by electronic means. Thus, many of the private international law

---

73 OAS and IAJC, 'Domestic Procedures for the Recognition and Enforcement of Foreign Judgments: Recommendations', OEA/Ser.Q, CJI/doc.611/20 (30 June 2020).

74 ICC, 'INCOTERMS 2020', frequently incorporated by reference into international commercial contracts. <https://iccwbo.org/resources-for-business/incoterms-rules/incoterms-2020/> accessed 12 July 2021.

75 UNCITRAL, 'Texts and Status' <https://uncitral.un.org/en/texts> accessed 12 July 2021.

instruments that have been developed in these areas are relevant to the first pillar of food security – *availability*.

As evidenced by the COVID-19 pandemic, disruptions in supply chains can have a devastating impact on food security. In this regard, the UNIDROIT Principles of International Commercial Contracts[76] have been identified as a resource in the event of contractual disruptions.[77] For example, as to whether COVID-19 may be invoked as an excuse for non-performance, parties might refer to these for interpretation of 'force majeure' (Art 7.1.7) or 'hardship' (Arts 6.2.2–6.2.4). Along a similar line and in regard to COVID-19 and frustration of international contracts, it has been recommended that states, judges and arbitrators take into account the OAS Contracts Guide to promote party autonomy and uphold choice of law, and allow recourse to instruments such as the UNIDROIT Principles, among others.[78] These exemplify contributions of private international law towards maintaining free flow in international trade and commerce and thereby strengthening pillar four – *stability*.

If that were all, it would seem that to the extent private international law facilitates greater and more efficient international trade in the agri-food sector, its contribution is largely in terms of ensuring food availability and 'more of the same'. The lack of express connection with any of the particular targets of SDG 2 does seem odd, given the mammoth power of global agri-business that could be harnessed in the service of ending hunger. Is there possibly an elephant lurking in the background? Could this be revealed as the 'schism' identified by Watt to explain why 'states have been complicit in the development of the informal empire that now threatens to overwhelm them'?[79]

More recently, however, a different perspective is being taken: UNCITRAL Working Group I has been looking specifically at reducing legal obstacles faced by micro, small and medium-sized enterprises (MSMEs);[80] UNIDROIT has been coordinating with the FAO and the International Fund for Agricultural Development (IFAD), which has resulted in a number of jointly produced instruments;[81] and at the OAS, work on warehouse receipts was initiated

76 UNIDROIT, 'Principles of International Commercial Contracts' (4th ed, 2016).

77 UNIDROIT, 'Note of the Secretariat on the UNIDROIT Principles of International Commercial Contracts and the COVID-19 Health Crisis' <https://www.unidroit.org/english/news/2020/200721-principles-covid19-note/note-e.pdf> accessed 12 July 2021.

78 Instituto Hispano Luso Americano Derecho Internacional, 'COVID-19 and Frustration of International Contracts. IHLADI Recommendations' <http://ihladi.net/wp-content/uploads/2020/07/COVID-19-and-frustration-of-international-contracts.pdf> accessed 12 July 2021.

79 H Muir Watt, 'Private International Law Beyond the Schism' (2011) 2 Transnational Legal Theory 347, 382.

80 UNCITRAL, 'Working Group I: Micro, Small and Medium-sized Enterprises' <https://uncitral.un.org/en/working_groups/1/msmes> accessed 12 July 2021.

81 UNIDROIT, 'Private Law Aspects of Agricultural Finance' (2010) C.D. (89) 7 Add. 4; UNIDROIT Colloquium, 'Promoting Investment in Agricultural Production: Private Law Aspects' (November 2011).

out of concern over lack of credit in the agricultural sector, particularly for smallholders.[82] Perhaps indicative of a new approach, several these initiatives are relevant to specific targets of SDG 2 as discussed below.

3. PRIVATE INTERNATIONAL LAW AND SDG 2: SPECIFIC APPLICATIONS

3.1. ACCESS TO CREDIT

Access to credit is important across all sectors of the economy and is one of the 12 areas considered by the World Bank in its 'Doing Business' reports concerning regulations that enhance (or constrain) business activity.[83] While important for all businesses, large and small, access to credit is particularly difficult for MSMEs, which is why it is included in Target 2.3 in relation to SDG 2 and in Target 8.3 in relation to SDG 8 (see section 3.2, *infra*).

In many parts of the world, lenders still prefer traditional forms of collateral, i.e. land and high-value equipment. MSMEs without such assets are either unable to access credit at all, or only in 'unsecured' form at very high rates of interest.[84] Moreover, in times of crisis, MSMEs without credit may have no choice other than to liquidate business assets, such as equipment, inventory, seedstock or livestock. If these productive assets could instead be used as collateral, not only would this provide the necessary liquidity to respond to emergencies and opportunities during recovery and rebuilding, it would also enable MSMEs to expand and climb the value chain.

As indicated in Target 2.3, access to credit is particularly important for marginalised groups, 'in particular women'. While considerable work has been done to reduce the gender gap, financial inclusion has remained unchanged over the past decade.[85] Expanding the range of acceptable collateral to include movable assets is especially important for women, whose ownership of immovable property is frequently disproportionate to that of men. In its report on 'Enabling the Business of Agriculture', the World Bank has identified regulatory obstacles to market integration and entrepreneurship. One of the eight indicators monitors access to finance, which takes into consideration

---

82 See section 3.1.2, *infra*.

83 World Bank, 'Doing Business 2020, Overview' <https://www.doingbusiness.org/en/reports/global-reports/doing-business-2020> accessed 12 July 2021.

84 OAS, Department of International Law, 'Improving Access to Credit – A Video Explanation' <http://www.oas.org/en/sla/dil/newsletter_Access_to_Credit_Feb-2017.html> accessed 15 March 2021.

85 FAO, 'Women's access to rural finance: challenges and opportunities' (2019).

warehouse receipts (see section 3.1.2, *infra*) and inclusive finance.[86] Given the widely recognised importance of credit for agricultural development and financial inclusion, possible contributions from private international law should be considered.

3.1.1. Secured Transactions

Over the last 20 years, a number of instruments have been developed to modernise and improve the domestic laws that govern secured lending. One of the first was the Model Inter-American Law on Secured Transactions (2002) and its accompanying Model Regulatory Regulations (2009).[87] This was followed by the UNCITRAL Model Law on Secured Transactions (2016) plus a number of supplementary tools that include legislative guides and practice guides.[88] Today, states around the world are initiating reforms of their domestic legislation on the basis of these models and supplementary tools. With a modern secured transactions regime as a foundation, other lending vehicles can be added to even further expand credit availability, through assignment of receivables and factoring.[89] Greater market competition among lenders resulting from certainty in the legal rules that govern these practices, in both domestic and cross-border transactions, will lead to better terms of credit for all.

3.1.2. Warehouse Receipts

For many producers, especially those who do not own land, the harvested crop can represent their single asset of greatest value. Without credit, smallholders are often forced to sell their crops immediately upon harvest in order to pay debts and buy inputs for the next season. But harvest is typically when prices are lowest due to abundant supply. Warehouse receipts financing enables the deposit of goods with a licensed warehouse operator in exchange for a receipt that represents title to those goods; with that receipt, the depositor is able to obtain financing secured by the stored goods as collateral.[90] The importance and potential of warehouse receipts financing for the agricultural sector has been widely recognised; as noted above, warehouse receipts is one of two elements

---

86 World Bank, 'Enabling the Business of Agriculture 2019', 37 <https://eba.worldbank.org/en/eba> accessed 12 July 2021.

87 OAS, 'Model Inter-American Law on Secured Transactions', OEA/Ser.K/XXI.6, CIDIP-VI/RES.5/02 (8 February 2002).

88 UN, UNCITRAL Model Law on Secured Transactions (2016) <https://uncitral.un.org/sites/uncitral.un.org/files/media-documents/uncitral/en/19-08779_e_ebook.pdf> and <https://uncitral.un.org/en/texts/securityinterests> accessed 12 July 2021.

89 Space constraints do not permit discussion of international instruments in these areas.

90 H D Gabriel, 'Warehouse Receipts and Securitization in Agricultural Finance' (2012) 17 Uniform Law Review 369.

considered by the World Bank when evaluating access to finance.[91] But in order for the system to function well, lenders need to have confidence in both the integrity of the physical warehousing infrastructure and the underlying legal regime.

Building upon legislative guides developed by the FAO and by the World Bank,[92] in 2016 the Inter-American Juridical Committee of the OAS approved Principles for Electronic Warehouse Receipts for Agricultural Products.[93] This work helped to clarify legal uncertainties around the use of this mechanism and provided the basis for further work on a Model Law on Warehouse Receipts, which is currently under development as a joint project of UNCITRAL and UNIDROIT.[94]

Although warehouse receipts financing has significant potential to improve access to credit, it is important to bear in mind whether and how it can assist smallholders. For example, on the matter of co-mingling, while the legal issue concerns whether domestic law permits individual depositors to hold a 'pro-rata' interest in co-mingled, undifferentiated stored commodities, the pragmatic issue is resistance to co-mingling, which is often encountered among smallholders.[95] The voices brought into the discussion will have a bearing on the shape of the instrument and whether it will benefit primarily larger players in the agri-food sector or whether it will encourage progression towards Target 2.3.

3.1.3. *High-Value Equipment*

Another important instrument to mention is the Convention on International Interests in Mobile Equipment (2001)[96] and its accompanying protocols. The Cape Town Convention, as it is known, seeks to facilitate the acquisition and use of mobile equipment of high value by establishing legal rules that reflect the principles underlying asset-based financing and leasing, a legal framework for international interests in such equipment and an international registry system.[97]

---

91 World Bank, 'Enabling the Business of Agriculture 2019', 37.

92 FAO and ERBD, 'Designing Warehouse Receipt Legislation: Regulatory Options and Recent Trends' (2014); World Bank, 'A Guide to Warehouse Receipt Financing Reform: Legislative Reform' (2016).

93 OAS and IAJC, 'Electronic Warehouse Receipts for Agricultural Products', CJI/doc.505/16 rev.2 (27 September 2016).

94 UNIDROIT, 'Model Law on Warehouse Receipts, Study XXXIII' <https://www.unidroit.org/work-in-progress/model-law-on-warehouse-receipts> accessed 12 July 2021.

95 OAS and IAJC 'Electronic Warehouse Receipts for Agricultural Products', CJI/doc.505/16 rev.2 (27 September 2016).

96 UNIDROIT, Convention on International Interests in Mobile Equipment, 2307 UNTS 285 (adopted 16 November 2001) (Cape Town Convention) <https://www.unidroit.org/english/conventions/mobile-equipment/mobile-equipment.pdf> accessed 12 July 2021.

97 ibid Preamble.

The recent Protocol for Mining, Agricultural and Construction Equipment, referred to as the MAC Protocol, provides certain adaptations to meet the particular requirements of these three sectors.[98] Predicted to have an economic impact of $23 billion on GDP in developing countries every year, it is described as 'one of the most important commercial law instruments aimed at improving economic growth, food security and infrastructure.'[99]

3.1.4. *Summary on Credit*

Any efforts that help to liberalise credit for international trade and commerce in general will undoubtedly also benefit the agri-food sector. While all of the initiatives mentioned above can expand credit options for larger players, it is secured transactions law reform that has the greatest potential to improve credit for smallholders and MSMEs as envisioned in Target 2.3 for the actualisation of SDG 2. One of the prerequisites to affordable access to credit, however, is formal business registration.

3.2. SIMPLIFIED BUSINESS REGISTRATION

In many countries, formal business 'start-up' is complex, which necessitates either a certain level of skill or assistance by a third party, making the process time-consuming and costly. As a result, formal business registration is out of reach for many MSMEs, which, as a consequence, conduct their business activities in the informal sector. The figures are staggering.[100] Informal businesses either have no access to credit or must resort to informal credit, usually at high rates of interest without protection of the law.

The need for formalisation has been recognised in the SDGs; Target 8.3 encourages states 'to promote development-oriented policies that … encourage the formalization and growth of [MSMEs]'. Since 2013, UNCITRAL Working Group I has been working towards reducing the legal obstacles faced by MSMEs throughout their lifecycle.[101] This began with a focus on simplification

---

98 UNIDROIT, Protocol to the Convention on International Interests in Mobile Equipment on Matters Specific to Mining, Agricultural and Construction Equipment (adopted 22 November 2019) (MAC Protocol) <https://www.unidroit.org/english/conventions/mobile-equipment/mac-protocol-e.pdf> accessed 12 July 2021.

99 UNIDROIT, 'MAC Protocol – Economic Impact' <https://www.unidroit.org/economic-benefit> accessed 12 July 2021.

100 About 61 per cent of the world's employed are engaged in informal employment. In the agricultural sector, the figure is over 90 per cent. International Labour Organization, 'Women and Men in the Informal Economy: A Statistical Picture' Third Edition (30 April 2018).

101 UNCITRAL, 'Working Group I: Micro, Small and Medium-sized Enterprises' <https://uncitral.un.org/en/working_groups/1/msmes> accessed 12 July 2021.

of incorporation and good practices in business registration, which led to adoption of the UNCITRAL Legislative Guide on Key Principles of a Business Registry (2019).[102] This work continued with the development of and recent adoption of the UNCITRAL Legislative Guide on a Limited Liability Enterprise (2021).[103] The latter offers recommendations to states on a simplified legal form that could be used by MSMEs to facilitate their participation in the economy. Along a similar line is a regional instrument in the Americas, the Model Law on the Simplified Corporation, which OAS Member States have been invited to adopt in accordance with their domestic laws and regulatory framework.[104]

While formalisation in and of itself has many benefits for the individual and for society as a whole, its primary contribution in the context of this discussion is to enable access to formal credit for Target 2.3.

3.3. CONTRACT FARMING

The trend in recent years towards contract farming, which has occurred largely due to the shift away from open market-based procurement and towards globalised value chains, holds significant implications for SDG 2. Under this approach, a contract farming agreement (CFA) is made between producers and a buyer in advance of production. The terms usually specify price, quantity and quality of the product and a date for delivery, and may also include specific production methods and whether inputs (such as seeds, fertilisers and pesticides) and technical advice will be provided.[105]

Contract farming offers advantages and disadvantages to buyers, producers and consumers.[106] The buyer can exact more consistent supply and quality with less need to acquire land but may face higher transaction costs and risks of

---

102 UNCITRAL, 'Legislative Guide on Key Principles of a Business Registry (2019)', UNGA Res 73/197 (2018) GAOR 73rd Session Supp No 17 (A/73/17), ch IV, ss B and C <https://uncitral.un.org/sites/uncitral.un.org/files/media-documents/uncitral/en/lg_business_registry-e.pdf> accessed 12 July 2021.

103 UNCITRAL, 'Draft Legislative Guide on an UNCITRAL Limited Liability Organization', Note by the Secretariat, A/CN.9/1062 (6 April 2021) <https://undocs.org/en/A/CN.9/1062> accessed 12 July 2021. Approved by the UNCITRAL Commission at its 54th Session held 28 June – 16 July 2021 <https://uncitral.un.org/en/commission> accessed 12 July 2021.

104 OAS and IAJC, 'Project for a Model Act on Simplified Stock Corporation', CJI/RES.188 (LXXX-0/12); OAS General Assembly, 'Model Law on the Simplified Corporation', AG/RES. 2906 (XLVII-O/17).

105 FAO, 'Contract Farming Resource Center' <http://www.fao.org/in-action/contract-farming/background/en/> accessed 12 July 2021.

106 UNIDROIT, 'Selected Web and Bibliographical References on or relevant for Contract Farming Operations' <https://www.unidroit.org/community-of-practice/legal-resources/web-bibliogr-references#a20> accessed 12 July 2021.

side-selling or misuse of inputs. Producers can benefit from more stable and better incomes, access to markets, inputs, credit and technical advice but may face unequal bargaining power, dependency or lock-in, and risk of increased indebtedness. Given buyer preference for negotiating with fewer but larger and more educated producers, contract farming may exclude smallholders,[107] those with less optimal land, with fewer resources and in remote areas who are in weaker bargaining positions.[108] Specialisation in cash crops may lead to monoculture and result in loss of biodiversity.[109] While export-led contract farming contributes towards greater product diversity and (usually) lower prices for consumers abroad, when local agricultural production is diverted towards export monoculture, this may lead to less local product diversity and increased prices in traditional foods produced for local consumption.

It has been noted by De Schutter, the Special Rapporteur on the RTF at the time, that 'unless the realization of the [RTF] serves as the foundation of the current reinvestment in agriculture, the situation of the poorest farmers working on the most marginal land could be further aggravated by this process, which leads to increased competition for productive resources, and the existing dualization of the farming sector could worsen as a result.'[110] Although contract farming is generally associated with foreign investment and export-led agriculture, it can also be adopted by local actors, including public bodies.[111] Thus, whether contract farming is used to contribute towards realisation of the RTF will be very much dependent on the particular context, the specific contractual arrangements and to what extent a human-rights-based approach is adopted.[112] Accordingly, to ensure that the practice serves in the actualisation of the RTF, it has been recommended that CFAs should address certain key elements, such as long-term economic viability, support for small-scale farmers in negotiations, gender equality, environmental sustainability, and dispute settlement.[113]

Several documents offer guidance on the subject, starting with the FAO's Guiding Principles for Responsible Contract Farming Operations (2012).[114]

---

107 V Vabi Vamuloh et al, 'Achieving Sustainable Development Goals in the global food sector: A systematic literature review to examine small farmers engagement in contract farming' (2019) 2 Business Strategy and Development 276. Although noting 'increasing consensus among contract farming scholars that farmer exclusion is a rampant problem', the authors found that the literature lacks a consolidated understanding of the factors that drive smallholder participation.

108 UN General Assembly, 'The right to food. Note by the Secretary General. Interim Report of the Special Rapporteur on the RTF', UN Doc A/66/262 (4 August 2011) para 1.

109 ibid.

110 ibid.

111 ibid para 2.

112 ibid para 11.

113 ibid. See also UN General Assembly, 'Report of the Special Rapporteur on the RTF. Final Report: The transformative potential of the RTF', UN Doc A/HRC/25/57 (24 January 2014).

114 FAO, 'Guiding Principles for responsible contract farming operations' (2012).

Building on these principles, UNIDROIT, the FAO and the IFAD worked in cooperation to develop the Legal Guide on Contract Farming (2015) (CF Guide).[115] While its primary focus is the bilateral relationship between buyer and producers throughout the process from negotiation to dispute settlement, the first chapter provides an overview of the relevant domestic legal framework within which contract farming is conducted. This overview is elaborated upon in a subsequent legislative study by the FAO, 'Enabling Regulatory Frameworks for Contract Farming'.[116] Designed to assist national regulators and policymakers to evaluate the existing regulatory framework for contract farming in light of critical issues and objectives for the sector, the study includes a cautionary note that such evaluation requires careful consideration as to potential impacts upon the RTF; among the considerations identified are the following: a switch from subsistence farming to commercial agriculture may deprive producers of an important source of food; if a cash crop fails to generate enough income, farmers may be unable to cover their own food costs; and concentration on cash crop monoculture may have implications for the food security of the country as a whole.[117]

Drawing upon this guidance, a Model Agreement for Responsible Contract Farming was developed with simplified provisions 'to operationalize the principles elaborated in the Guide' and that can be adapted to the specific context and legal system.[118] By addressing some of the inequalities that disadvantage producers, it aims to create more equitable and transparent business relationships, and to thereby encourage responsible contract farming. The Model Agreement emphasises fair contracting, recognising that these kinds of relationships are frequently characterised by an imbalance of power; accordingly, it includes provisions to ensure producers receive ample time to review the contract, seek advice, and properly understand their obligations (Model Provision 1.2). The accompanying commentary notes that 'it is preferable that the person performing most of the work under the contract, often a woman, be included as a party' and buyers are encouraged to avoid exacerbating gender inequalities, notwithstanding the difficulties of culturally embedded practices. The commentary acknowledges that, in respect of exclusive output arrangements, limited exceptions can be allowed for small quantities that the producer may keep for household consumption or sale on the local market; this partially addresses the recommendation made by De Schutter that

115 UNIDROIT, FAO and IFAD, 'Legal Guide on Contract Farming' (2015).

116 T Viinikainen and C Bullon Caro, Development Law Service, FAO Legal Office, 'Enabling Regulatory Frameworks for Contract Farming', FAO Legislative Study 111 (2018).

117 ibid 39.

118 FAO and IISD, 'Model Agreement for Responsible Contract Farming. With Commentary' (2018).

farmers be allowed to use a portion of their land to grow food for their own consumption and that a certain percentage of the cash crops be sold on the local market.[119] Adherence to these recommendations can help better align CFAs with Target 2.3.

Concerning agricultural practices, it is recommended that, 'in order to promote environmentally sustainable agricultural production, [CFAs] should ideally encourage a reduction in the use of chemical fertilizers and pesticides, greater efficiency in their application and increased use of biological inputs. Technical advice and training should also focus on promoting sustainable farming practices.'[120] As to production methods that support a shift to more sustainable systems, it is suggested that such requirements be clear, preferably with reference to specific standards or annexed documents. In respect of intellectual property rights, the commentary notes that whereas the buyer may want to impose obligations or conditions to protect such rights, for example, concerning seed or plant varieties, 'producers should carefully consider and ideally seek independent legal advice … [as] such obligations can have implications for the producer's production practices, for instance the ability of the producer to save and reuse seed.'[121] Implementation of these recommendations would help CFAs become more aligned with Targets 2.4 and 2.5.

While a number of the recommendations made by the Special Rapporteur on the RTF have been incorporated into the Model CFA and although contract farming does have the potential to improve livelihoods for producers through their improved access to 'inputs, knowledge, markets and opportunities for value addition', there are no guarantees that these benefits will be enjoyed by *smallholders* or marginalised groups mentioned in Target 2.3. Moreover, even if numerous individual CFAs are in alignment with these guidance documents, without reference to the larger context such as that which might be provided by cumulative effects impact assessments or overarching policies, contract farming might undermine, rather than contribute towards, food security. Accordingly, this evidences the need to integrate contract farming as part of a broader national food security approach.

3.4. AGRICULTURAL LAND INVESTMENT CONTRACTS

Another topic with significant implications for SDG 2 is private-sector investment in agricultural land. Noting that 'more and better investment is essential for achieving food security, adequate nutrition and reducing poverty', UNIDROIT, the FAO and the IFAD have produced a Legal Guide on Agricultural

119 ibid.
120 ibid 14.
121 ibid.

Land Investment Contracts (ALIC Guide).[122] Given the complexity and challenges inherent in the process of preparing, negotiating and implementing these types of contracts in accordance with international principles,[123] the ALIC Guide was developed to provide guidance on how to improve such contracts, to 'operationalize' the international principles and standards established by the VGGT, the RAI Principles and the UN Guiding Principles on Business and Human Rights[124] and in accordance with the CF Guide and the 2016 UNIDROIT Principles of International Commercial Contracts.[125]

The focus of the ALIC Guide is on contracts between investors and governments and between investors and local communities. Instead of land sales, which are excluded, the Guide encourages alternative models of long-term agricultural investment such as leases. It covers the entire process, from the pre-contractual phase through to possible breach and termination. Several of the matters addressed in the first few chapters are relevant to the regulatory aspect of ALICs in relation to SDG 2. In Chapter 1, concerning sources of law, it is noted that whereas the domestic law of some states might not be sufficiently developed in some subject areas that intersect with ALICs (e.g. human rights, environmental regulation), the Guide might supplement these gaps. Similarly, where the domestic law falls short in respect of certain investor obligations, such as due diligence or disclosure, the ALIC could require the investor to comply with the laws of its own state or with specified international standards.[126] Chapter 2 places particular emphasis on protecting and respecting the rights of legitimate tenure right holders. Addressing issues around equal access to land by marginalised groups can help bring ALICs into greater alignment with Target 2.3. Feasibility studies and impact assessments are among the pre-contractual issues considered in Chapter 3, with references to the RAI

---

122 UNIDROIT, FAO and IFAD, 'Legal Guide on Agricultural Land Investment Contracts', Study 80B (December 2020) (ALIC Guide). Text as approved by the UNIDROIT Governing Council but subject to minor adjustments following the clearance processes of the partner organisations FAO and IFAD. <https://www.unidroit.org/english/documents/2020/study80b/s-80b-alic-draft-e.pdf> accessed 12 July 2021.

123 ibid Foreword, iii.

124 UNHRC, 'Guiding Principles on Business and Human Rights: Implementing the United Nations "Protect, Respect and Remedy" Framework', UN Doc A/HRC/17/31 (21 March 2011) (Ruggie Principles).

125 UNIDROIT, FAO and IFAD, 'Legal Guide on Agricultural Land Investment Contracts', Study 80B (December 2020) (ALIC Guide). Text as approved by the UNIDROIT Governing Council but subject to minor adjustments following the clearance processes of the partner organisations FAO and IFAD. <https://www.unidroit.org/english/documents/2020/study80b/s-80b-alic-draft-e.pdf> accessed 12 July 2021, Introduction, para 10.

126 ibid, para 1.1.

Principles and the VGGT throughout. The suggestions made here can help ALICs become more effective in reaching Target 2.4.

By integrating key elements from the VGGT and RAI Principles with the UNIDROIT Principles, the ALIC Guide has great potential for shaping the future direction of agricultural land investment contracts such that these types of investments might contribute towards reaching Target 2.a, as well as Targets 2.3–2.5, as explained above. Time will tell whether the ALIC Guide may be offered as a response to the criticism that 'no significant move has been made as yet to tame multinational corporate misconduct in respect either of environmental protection or access of local communities to agricultural land [although] the tools that might have addressed such issues belong to private international law.'[127]

3.5. LEGAL STRUCTURE FOR AGRICULTURAL ENTERPRISES

Initiatives such as the ALIC Guide serve as reminders of the need to engage the private sector more effectively in the actualisation of SDG 2. While public–private partnerships (PPPs) are commonly used in infrastructure construction projects, their use in the agri-business sector is relatively new.[128] Known as 'agri-PPPs', these arrangements offer a mechanism to leverage knowledge from the private sector together with much-needed financing 'to help modernize the agriculture sector and deliver multiple benefits that can contribute towards sustainable agricultural development that is inclusive of smallholder farmers.'[129]

Secondly, although better access to markets can lead to improved livelihoods for smallholders, contract farming is not the only option. Given the possibilities offered by farmer-controlled enterprises, joint ventures and community-supported agriculture as 'complementary ways to rethink the political economy of food chains',[130] UNIDROIT has included the topic of the legal structure of agricultural enterprises in its work programme.[131]

---

127 H Muir Watt, 'Private International Law Beyond the Schism' (2011) 2 Transnational Legal Theory 347, 382.

128 M Rankin et al, 'Public–private partnerships for agri-business development – A review of international experiences' (FAO, 2016).

129 ibid 3.

130 ibid.

131 UNIDROIT, 'Work Programme for the triennial period 2020–2022' <https://www.unidroit.org/about-unidroit/work-programme> accessed 12 July 2021.

4. ADDITIONAL TOPICS FOR CONSIDERATION

4.1. PRIVATE STANDARDS

The predominance of private standards in the food industry has implications not only for consumers, but also for producers required to meet these standards that span the supply chain from farm to fork. Although the food industry is subject to public sector regulation, the movement towards greater self-regulation and 'private food law'[132] that has accompanied the growth and transformation in global agri-food trade in recent decades has prompted emergence of a new governance structure referred to as the 'Tripartite Standards Regime', comprising standards, certification and accreditation.[133] This increased prevalence in the use of private 'voluntary' standards (PVS) (compliance with such standards being voluntary in theory and law, but perhaps not in economic reality), has been, in part, in response to consumer concerns over health and safety and growing awareness of the environmental and social aspects of food production. PVS is also a way to bridge the legal systems of different states; a business might require compliance with PVS so as to ensure it meets standards imposed by law in its own state, if the goods are produced in a state with lesser or an absence of relevant standards.

Standards necessitate certification, which requires accreditation, and all three have been moving into the purview of the private sector. PVS can be used for what is called '(supply) chain orchestration';[134] suppliers must demonstrate proof (through certification) that standards have been met and such certification is often demonstrated by a symbol or trademark. PVS for one product can be interconnected with that of another (e.g. to be certified, a chicken must be fed certified feed). The range of labels is now familiar to anyone who does any shopping – 'organic', 'free-range', 'halal' and 'vegan' are examples that indicate food production methods, concern for animal welfare, religious observance, dietary restrictions, and so forth. PVS can be that of an individual firm, or a collective national or international standard, such as GlobalGAP, discussed below.[135]

---

132 This has been described as 'food law privately made'. B van der Meulen, 'Private Food Law: The emergence of a concept' in B van der Meulen (ed), *Private Food Law: governing food chains through contract law, self-regulation, private standards, audits and certification schemes* (Wageningen Academic Publishers 2011) 32.

133 L Busch, 'Quasi-states? The unexpected rise of private food law' in B van der Meulen (ed), *Private Food Law: governing food chains through contract law, self-regulation, private standards, audits and certification schemes* (Wageningen Academic Publishers 2011) 61.

134 ibid 68.

135 S Henson and J Humphrey, 'Codex Alimentarius and private standards' in B van der Meulen (ed), *Private Food Law: governing food chains through contract law, self-regulation, private standards, audits and certification schemes* (Wageningen Academic Publishers 2011) 154.

A cornerstone of international food regulation is Codex Alimentarius, a set of international food standards, guidelines and codes of practice according to which national governments establish their own regulations and which also serves as a reference point for the World Trade Organization's Agreement on Sanitary and Phytosanitary Measures.[136] Its Commission (CAC) is the body responsible for implementation, which functions much like any other inter-governmental standard-setting body. However, private companies often develop their own standards that may go beyond these internationally legislated requirements. While private companies can thereby be seen as 'translating the rules of Codex into standards that provide sufficient guidance for implementers', authors Henson and Humphrey conclude there is limited evidence to support the contention that PVS threatens the status of Codex standards or undermines the CAC mandate to promote consumer protection and fair agri-food trade.[137] But they do point out that some aspects of the 'wake-up call' are warranted, such as concerns over timeliness and inclusiveness in the CAC standard-setting process.

Perhaps along this line is the Global Partnership for Good Agricultural Practice (GlobalGAP), which is a private-sector body that sets standards for the certification of agricultural products around the globe.[138] A GlobalGAP certificate covers all matters concerning production until the product leaves the farm gate.[139] The aim is to establish a single standard among businesses to enable access for agricultural products to major import markets. The approach is also gaining importance in domestic markets, for example KenyaGAP.[140]

PVS and initiatives such as GlobalGAP are of growing relevance for smallholders. On the one hand, stringent requirements can pose a threat that may exclude smallholders, although this might be ameliorated by group certification. On the other hand, PVS does provide a mechanism by which to introduce better and more sustainable practices.[141] In a pilot project with smallholders it

136 FAO, 'Codex Alimentarius Commission' <http://www.fao.org/fao-who-codexalimentarius/committees/cac/about/en/> accessed 12 July 2021.

137 S Henson and J Humphrey, 'Codex Alimentarius and private standards' in B van der Meulen (ed), *Private Food Law: governing food chains through contract law, self-regulation, private standards, audits and certification schemes* (Wageningen Academic Publishers 2011) 171.

138 GlobalGAP, 'What we do' <https://www.globalgap.org/uk_en/what-we-do/> accessed 12 July 2021.

139 B van der Meulen, 'The Anatomy of Private Food Law' in B van der Meulen (ed), *Private Food Law: governing food chains through contract law, self-regulation, private standards, audits and certification schemes* (Wageningen Academic Publishers 2011) 94.

140 GlobalGAP, 'Kenya-GAP successfully re-benchmarked for GlobalGAP' <https://www.globalgap.org/uk_en/media-events/news/articles/Kenya-GAP-Successfully-Re-benchmarked-for-GLOBALG.A.P.-Integrated-Farm-Assurance-Standard-Version-4/> accessed 12 July 2021.

141 M Will, 'GlobalGAP smallholder group certification: Challenge and Opportunity for smallholder inclusion into global value chains' in B van der Meulen (ed), *Private Food Law: governing food chains through contract law, self-regulation, private standards, audits and certification schemes* (Wageningen Academic Publishers 2011) 206.

was found that despite the high cost and complexity of compliance, significant impacts with regard to economic viability, environmental sustainability and social advancement were achieved.[142] Although additional data is needed before drawing conclusions, the potential here seems enormous.

4.2. MARKET CONCENTRATION

4.2.1. Option 1 for Regulating Competition: Frontal Attack

In relation to SDG 2, there is concern over whether trends towards greater market concentration can coincide with Target 2.3, which seeks to expand access to land and other resources by more participants; with Target 2.4, which seeks to ensure sustainable food production systems; with Target 2.5, which seeks to maintain genetic diversity and equitable sharing of its benefits; and with the overarching goal 'to promote sustainable agriculture'. By contrast, others maintain that it is only through 'Big Ag' and its economies of scale, which led to the large increases in agricultural production during the last century, that the needs of growing populations can be met.

Notwithstanding differing opinions about the role of multinationals in achieving global food security, it is undeniable that considerable control in the agri-food sector is held by a relatively small number of companies.[143] While supply chains connect millions of farmers at one end with millions of consumers at the other, 'the agri-business corporations occupying strategic positions in the middle are exceedingly few'.[144] For example, coffee is produced by about 25 million farmers and purchased by about 500 million consumers, yet 45 per cent of all coffee is roasted by only four firms.[145] About 90 per cent of all global trade in grain is conducted by only four agri-business companies.[146] Not only are companies within the agri-business sector highly consolidated, there is also considerable vertical integration; the main six global companies involved in the proprietary seed industry are related to or owned by the largest

142 ibid 215.

143 IPES-Food, 'Too Big to Feed: Exploring the Impacts of Mega-mergers, Consolidation and Concentration of Power in the Agri-food Sector' (2017) <http://www.ipes-food.org/_img/upload/files/Concentration_FullReport.pdf> accessed 12 July 2021.

144 De Schutter, 'Addressing Concentration in Food Supply Chains: The Role of Competition Law in Tackling the Abuse of Buyer Power', Briefing Note 03 (December 2010) <https://www.ohchr.org/Documents/Issues/Food/BN3_SRRTF_Competition_ENGLISH.pdf> accessed 12 July 2021.

145 ibid.

146 IPES-Food, Too Big to Feed: Exploring the Impacts of Mega-mergers, Consolidation and Concentration of Power in the Agri-food Sector' (2017) <http://www.ipes-food.org/_img/upload/files/Concentration_FullReport.pdf> accessed 12 July 2021.

agrichemical corporations.[147] Similar examples of market domination and concentration can be found in other sectors related to agri-business, such as production of farm machinery, shipping and transport, commodity trading, wholesale distribution and retail grocery.[148] It has been suggested that, to a large extent, it is through the denials of private international law that states have been complicit in the development of the informal empire that now threatens to overwhelm them.[149]

At the national level, competition and anti-trust laws have been in place for decades in several states but their effects on the agri-business sector have been minimal. It is hard to argue against the evidence that 'Big Ag' has provided consumers with more food at lower prices, given the primary goal of competition law is maximisation of consumer welfare.[150] By that standard, however, insufficient attention is given to the externalities of industrial agriculture and potential harms suffered by small farmers. The RTF – and consequently SDG 2 – is not only about poor consumers having access to food at an affordable price, it is also about those depending on farming for their livelihoods having sufficient incomes to allow them to purchase food.[151] Accordingly, in his final report as Special Rapporteur, De Schutter recommended use of competition law to combat excessive concentration, specifically that developed countries where dominant agri-businesses are domiciled should more actively address buyer power, whereas developing countries should impose duties or controls to prevent conduct that harms the welfare of producers.[152]

At the international level, attempts at regulation or some form of harmonisation of domestic competition laws has proven difficult. Efforts towards an international solution in the 1970s and 1980s resulted in non-binding principles on restrictive business practices.[153] In the 1990s, initiatives were

147 ibid 21. Syngenta (Switzerland), Bayer (Germany), BASF (Germany), DuPont (USA), Monsanto (USA), and Dow (USA), known as the 'Big Six', currently control both 60 per cent of the global seed market and 75 per cent of the global pesticides market.

148 ibid.

149 H Muir Watt, 'Private International Law Beyond the Schism' (2011) 2 Transnational Legal Theory 347, 382.

150 This paradox of anti-trust regulation, which permits economic concentration so long as it does not impede consumer welfare (i.e. price), is undergoing renewed scrutiny. A focus solely on price takes only the short-term view, whereas long-term interests are best promoted through a competitive process and open markets. See L M Khan, 'Amazon's Antitrust Paradox' (2017) 126(3) Yale Law Journal 564.

151 De Schutter, 'Addressing Concentration in Food Supply Chains: The Role of Competition Law in Tackling the Abuse of Buyer Power', Briefing Note 03 (December 2010) <https://www.ohchr.org/Documents/Issues/Food/BN3_SRRTF_Competition_ENGLISH.pdf> accessed 12 July 2021.

152 ibid.

153 Organisation for Economic Co-operation and Development (OECD), 'Declaration on International Investment and Multinational Enterprises', OECD Doc C(76)99/FINAL; UN, 'The Set of Multilaterally Agreed Equitable Principles and Rules for the Control of Restrictive Business Practices', UN Doc TD/RBP/CONF/10/Rev.2.

undertaken to develop a universal instrument;[154] although that did not materialise,[155] calls have been made once again to consider a possible treaty on competition.[156] The current trend, however, appears to be away from seeking harmonisation, towards coordination and cooperation among competition authorities.[157] Perhaps competition law needs to be re-conceptualised 'not only as an instrument for achieving economic efficiency, innovation, consumer welfare and/or increased national productivity, but also as a sophisticated tool to ensure distributive justice, particularly with respect to the [RTF]'[158] and the actualisation of SDG 2.

The situation raises questions as to possible contributions from private international law. One response has been to address the question of applicable law for tort actions based on unfair competition; although this does little to address the root cause, it might be further developed for global application.[159] Another suggestion would be in the form of an instrument that may be used as a new mode of governance in a global context.[160] Given that competition law rules are regarded as mandatory provisions that express public policy, in a world in which multinational agri-businesses employ strategies that are global in nature, perhaps what is needed is 'an appropriately drafted private international law instrument preserving the diverse national competition law cultures.'[161] But this would require considerable bravery in the shadow of the elephant and there is no reason to believe such efforts would not encounter the same resistance as previous attempts.

4.2.2. *Option 2 for Regulating Competition: Addressing Consequences*

Rather than a direct attack on excessive market concentration, one might consider its consequences in order to design tools that could more effectively

---

154 'Draft International Antitrust Code as a GATT-MTO-Plurilateral Trade Agreement', 64 Antitrust & Trade Reg Rep (BNA) No 1628 (19 August 1993) (Special Supp).

155 D J Gifford, 'The Draft International Antitrust Code Proposed at Munich: Good Intentions Gone Awry' (1996) 6 Minnesota Journal of Global Trade 1.

156 IPES-Food, 'Too Big to Feed: Exploring the Impacts of Mega-mergers, Consolidation and Concentration of Power in the Agri-food Sector' (2017) <http://www.ipes-food.org/_img/upload/files/Concentration_FullReport.pdf> accessed 12 July 2021.

157 J Basedow, 'International Antitrust or Competition Law' (May 2014) in R Wolfrum (ed), *The Max Planck Encyclopedia of Public International Law* (OUP 2014, online edition) (accessed 12 July 2021).

158 I Lianos and A Darr, 'Hunger Games: Connecting the Right to Food and Competition Law', CLES Research Paper Series 2/2019, Centre for Law, Economics and Society, Faculty of Laws, UCL (2019) 9.

159 Regulation (EC) No 864/2007 of the European Parliament and of the Council of 11 July 2007 on the law applicable to non-contractual obligations (Rome II) [2007] OJ L 199/40, Art 6.

160 M Danov, 'Global competition law framework: A private international law solution needed' (2016) 12(1) Journal of Private International Law 77.

161 ibid.

address the issue. As a consequence of dominant buyer power, downward price pressure forces less efficient producers to merge, cut costs or exit the market. While this may be considered beneficial if cost savings are passed onto consumers, this is not always the case.[162] Such buyer power can also be used to force compliance with PVS and, as was discussed above, this can effectively force out smallholders. Or, as in one case, downward price pressure prompted smallholders to produce even more coffee, which led to oversupply and a vicious circle that forced smallholders off their lands as coffee is typically cultivated on hilly land at high altitudes with few alternative crops.[163] Concentrated buyer power also raises concern over associated direct or indirect control over production methods that are typically heavily dependent on inputs from non-renewable resources and high levels of mechanisation. Certain factors in these production methods, such as high initial investment, can make market entry cost-prohibitive for smaller producers and possibly act as 'lock-ins' that can thwart shifts to more sustainable practices.

Given that CFAs and agricultural land investment contracts are commonly used in agri-business, the legal instruments and guides that have been discussed in this chapter should be enlisted in addressing some of the consequences of excessive market power. For example, both the CF Guide and accompanying Model CFA and the ALIC Guide recommend that provisions be included in CFAs and ALICs to encourage sustainable agricultural practices; the ALIC Guide encourages extensive consultation with a wide range of stakeholders and offers guidance on conducting various kinds of impact assessments. GlobalGAP as a private mechanism offers an avenue for group certification that might enable smallholder participation. Use of these guides and options as ways to ameliorate the negative effects of market concentration on smallholders needs further exploration.

4.3. BROADER CONSIDERATIONS

Within the domain of public international law, there are several valuable legal instruments that offer guidance for the actualisation of SDG 2. Some of these have already been mentioned, notably the VGGT, the RAI Principles, the Ruggie Principles and the RTF Guidelines, among others. Advances have also been made by the private sector, through corporate social responsibility or

162 De Schutter, 'Addressing Concentration in Food Supply Chains: The Role of Competition Law in Tackling the Abuse of Buyer Power', Briefing Note 03 (December 2010) <https://www.ohchr.org/Documents/Issues/Food/BN3_SRRTF_Competition_ENGLISH.pdf> accessed 12 July 2021. As the following example illustrates, between 1997 and 2002 farm prices for coffee beans fell by 80 per cent while retail prices for coffee fell only by 27 per cent.

163 ibid.

responsible business conduct, and growing use of corporate codes of conduct or pledges made by individual businesses.[164]

By contrast, the field of (classic) private international law seems to maintain a blind eye. The traditional conflict-of-laws approach has been criticised in that the presupposition of choice of applicable law from among several domestic laws ignores the political dynamics of the real world.[165] Agricultural production has essentially been re-mapped by the global supply chain as organised by multinational agri-business and this reshaping of the global agri-food economy has, in effect 'lifted any restraints on the extent to which foreign investment should impact upon sovereign decisions over … agriculture.'[166]

One option for redress is to revisit this traditional approach. An alternative that has been gathering momentum is emergence of uniform law, and encouragement for parties to choose a universal standard rather than between competing domestic laws. The groundwork for this is already being laid; consider the OAS Contracts Guide recommendation that states should 'recognize and clarify choice of non-state law'.[167] While this is in respect of the law applicable to international commercial contracts, therein lies the possibility to include not only the UNIDROIT Principles but also, where applicable, references to non-state law in other areas, as yet emerging and being articulated, such as by the VGGT, the RAI Principles and the RTF Guidelines, among others, and that can fill important gaps left by domestic law.

Within private international law in its broader sense, as some of the examples in this chapter indicate, a crack is emerging in the silent veneer, as evidenced by the development of instruments that no longer remain aloof from wider policy considerations. In contract farming, such considerations are thoroughly discussed in the guidance documents, while in the Model CFA direct references are made to the VGGT and RAI Principles in the accompanying commentary. Similar integration abounds in the ALIC Guide.

Such transparency and willingness to incorporate policy questions should not only be applauded, but also applied to the development of private international instruments involving other aspects of the global agri-food system. For example, perhaps distribution agreements could be examined, in light of the recent production by the OECD and FAO of Guidance for Responsible Agricultural

164 See for example, Netafim, 'Sustainable Agriculture, Business Conduct Policies' <https://www.netafim.com/en/Sustainable-agriculture/business-conduct-policies/> accessed 12 July 2021.

165 H Muir Watt, 'Private International Law Beyond the Schism' (2011) 2 Transnational Legal Theory 347, 387.

166 ibid.

167 Organization of American States (OAS) and Inter-American Juridical Committee (IAJC), 'Guide on the Law Applicable to International Commercial Contracts in the Americas', OAS/Ser.Q, CJI/RES. 249 (XCIV-0/19) (21 February 2019), Recommendation 6.1.

Supply Chains.[168] As to the suggestion that insufficient attention has been given to private rule-making, the potential role of PVS in encouraging a shift towards sustainability should be examined and maximised. For example, the designation of 'organic' food, a term first coined by the private sector, has been described as 'a success story of private regulation'.[169] Capitalising on such an approach to develop other terms could encourage not only a shift towards more sustainable agricultural production, but also towards more nutritious and sustainable food consumption and reduced food waste. Alternatively, in reverse order, efforts could begin with development of an international standard for promotion by industry. By way of example, the emerging concept of a 'sustainable diet' such as that proposed by EAT-Lancet – simultaneously also a 'nutritious diet' – could be referenced by private industry through PVS as being 'in compliance with …'[170] This could be a significant contribution; a major challenge faced by health and nutrition agencies in the public sector is the dearth of resources for informational campaigns in comparison with the deep pockets available for commercial advertising.[171] Organisations such as UNIDROIT that are involved in the development of private international instruments might consider expanding their future work programmes to include these and other aspects of the global agri-food system, similar to collaborations with the FAO, the IFAD and the WFP, perhaps in partnership with the CAC, the WHO and other entities involved with producing nutrition and other agri-food standards.

5. REFLECTIONS

Private international law instruments serve to facilitate international trade and commerce in all economic sectors, including agriculture. As the global agri-food system is currently structured, food is becoming increasing available, through the functions of production, distribution and exchange, which are largely

---

168 OECD/FAO, 'Guidance for Responsible Agricultural Supply Chains' (OECD Publishing 2016).

169 H Schmidt, 'Organic Food: A private concept's take-over by government and the continued leading role of the private sector' in B van der Meulen (ed), *Private Food Law: governing food chains through contract law, self-regulation, private standards, audits and certification schemes* (Wageningen Academic Publishers 2011) 298.

170 The Lancet Commission, 'Food in The Anthropocene: the EAT-Lancet Commission on Healthy Diets From Sustainable Food Systems. Summary Report' (2 February 2019) 393(10170) The Lancet 447.

171 A Jacobs and M Richtel, 'How Big Business Got Brazil Hooked on Junk Food', *New York Times* (16 September 2017) <https://www.nytimes.com/interactive/2017/09/16/health/brazil-obesity-nestle.html> accessed 12 July 2021. Some executives of multinational food companies quoted therein maintain that 'their products have helped alleviate hunger [and] provided crucial nutrients.'

orchestrated by a limited number of multinational corporations that serve as the connection between millions of producers and millions of consumers. But *availability* must also be accompanied by the other three pillars of *accessibility* (affordability), *utilisation* (nutrition) and *stability* to achieve food security and, as that is defined 'for all people at all times', food security can only be achieved while also promoting sustainable agriculture.

There are differences of opinion as to how this can be actualised. We live not only in a globalised world but a polarised one, in which a complex industrial agricultural network enables some to enjoy a diet where one out of every five calories consumed crosses a border and yet, at the same time, 500 million smallholders barely eke out a living. These worlds are difficult to reconcile; perhaps there would be agreement at least to consider the intention and consequences of any proposed course of action – will it help bridge or increase this divide? Will the livelihoods of smallholder farmers thereby be improved? Will they be better able to climb the value chain? Or will this contribute towards greater concentration and displacement? Does this advance the progressive realisation of the RTF?

Private international law seems far removed from these questions, which are typically within the purview of governments and policymakers. But as illustrated in this chapter, work in the field is being undertaken with a new perspective that is conscious not only of immediate impacts but also the prospective far-reaching consequences. This is evident in efforts at UNCITRAL and the OAS to reduce legal impediments of MSMEs and improve their access to credit, various initiatives on warehouse receipts financing, and the recent guides on contract farming and agricultural land investment contracts. Change is also evident in the way that private international law instruments are being developed. This chapter has illustrated the benefits of inter-agency cooperation, where UNIDROIT, the FAO and the IFAD have combined their expertise and employed extensive consultations to include not only private international law experts, but stakeholder groups across the spectrum of the agricultural sector. This approach is essential, not only in the development of new private international law instruments, but equally so in their implementation and application at the domestic level.

Using private international law to harness global agri-business in the actualisation of SDG 2 will be quite an undertaking. But just imagine the power that could be (un)leashed! In that regard, the following suggestions are offered as a way forward:

- Promote existing work products on: (1) secured transactions, including receivables finance and high-value equipment; (2) simplified business formation; (3) contract farming; and (4) agricultural land investment.

States should be encouraged to initiate the necessary domestic reforms on the basis of these model instruments and guidance documents in order to, respectively: (1) improve access to credit; (2) encourage formalisation; (3) improve access to markets and opportunities for value addition, inputs, knowledge and other productive resources; and (4) ensure secure and equal access to land while encouraging increased investment to enhance agricultural productivity (Targets 2.3 and 2.a).

- Promote support of the development of new instruments (e.g. warehouse finance) that address issues fundamental to the actualisation of SDG 2 and include in their development representation of marginalised groups so as to ensure that their voices are heard and their concerns are addressed. One of the ways private international law instruments might be more effective in this regard would be through their connection to policy instruments, such as the requirement of impact assessments as to the potential impact on human rights, specifically the RTF but also others related to gender, health and decent work, and on the environment. There may even be ways to examine competition law through the more traditional approach of conflict of laws that is yet to be explored (Target 2.3).
- Given their reliance on contract farming and agricultural land investment contracts, global agri-businesses should be engaged through those mechanisms to operationalise international norms as outlined in the VGGT, the RAI Principles and the RTF Guidelines, among others. As these types of agreements are already in use, by ensuring consistency with international standards using guidance documents such as the CF Guide, the Model CFA and the ALIC Guide, such agreements can become powerful tools for engaging smallholders and marginalised groups, improving their access to inputs, knowledge, credit and markets, and for shifting towards more sustainable agricultural practices. States should be encouraged to initiate the necessary domestic reforms to bring their domestic legislation into alignment with the recommendations of these guidance documents (Targets 2.3–2.5).
- Similarly, consideration should be given to the development of a guidance document or model agreement 'beyond the farm gate', taking into consideration the recent OECD/FAO Guidance for Responsible Agricultural Supply Chains.
- Consideration should be given as to how private international law might be used to engage the power of PVS. Efforts should be made to explore how PVS could be leveraged to develop international standards (or vice versa) for labels that might encourage a shift towards more sustainable consumption and thereby create demand for more sustainably produced foods. Perhaps as a sibling to the INCOTERMS, consideration could be given to the development of ECOTERMS, as well as standards that quantify the EAT-Lancet 'sustainable diet' and indicate 'low-waste' packaging and 'heritage

seed preservation', among others. As interpretation of the terms 'sustainable' and 'sustainable agriculture' continues to evolve, smaller steps can be taken to deconstruct and define specific aspects within the concept. This will require an interdisciplinary approach and the kinds of inter-agency collaboration that have already begun.

- As per the HCCH Principles and the OAS Contracts Guide, states should affirm their clear adherence to the principle of party autonomy and recognition of a choice of 'non-state' law, while clarifying limitations of public policy provisions that protect those with weaker bargaining power. This will enable parties and adjudicators to incorporate references to international standards in the negotiation and interpretation of international commercial contracts.
- Finally, states should be encouraged to take into consideration these instruments and guides and other contributions of private international law – in the broad sense – in relation to the development of 'stable and long-term national food security and nutrition strategies' as recommended in RAI Principle 35.

Untamed elephants cause significant damage to crops and harm to smallholders throughout the world. And yet, through better efforts using private international law initiatives, the strength and power of 'Big Ag' can and must be harnessed for the heavy lifting that will be required in making a shift towards sustainable agriculture and for the broader actualisation of SDG 2.

SDG 3: GOOD HEALTH AND WELL-BEING

Anabela Susana de Sousa Gonçalves

Goal 3: Ensure healthy lives and promote well-being for all at all ages

3.1 By 2030, reduce the global maternal mortality ratio to less than 70 per 100,000 live births

3.2 By 2030, end preventable deaths of newborns and children under 5 years of age, with all countries aiming to reduce neonatal mortality to at least as low as 12 per 1,000 live births and under-5 mortality to at least as low as 25 per 1,000 live births

3.3 By 2030, end the epidemics of AIDS, tuberculosis, malaria and neglected tropical diseases and combat hepatitis, water-borne diseases and other communicable diseases

3.4 By 2030, reduce by one third premature mortality from non-communicable diseases through prevention and treatment and promote mental health and well-being

3.5 Strengthen the prevention and treatment of substance abuse, including narcotic drug abuse and harmful use of alcohol

3.6 By 2020, halve the number of global deaths and injuries from road traffic accidents

3.7 By 2030, ensure universal access to sexual and reproductive health-care services, including for family planning, information and education, and the integration of reproductive health into national strategies and programmes

3.8 Achieve universal health coverage, including financial risk protection, access to quality essential health-care services and access to safe, effective, quality and affordable essential medicines and vaccines for all

3.9 By 2030, substantially reduce the number of deaths and illnesses from hazardous chemicals and air, water and soil pollution and contamination

3.a Strengthen the implementation of the World Health Organization Framework Convention on Tobacco Control in all countries, as appropriate

3.b Support the research and development of vaccines and medicines for the communicable and non-communicable diseases that primarily affect developing countries, provide access to affordable essential medicines and vaccines, in accordance with the Doha Declaration on the TRIPS Agreement and Public Health, which affirms the right of developing countries to use to the full the provisions in the Agreement on Trade-Related Aspects of Intellectual Property Rights regarding flexibilities to protect public health, and, in particular, provide access to medicines for all

3.c Substantially increase health financing and the recruitment, development, training and retention of the health workforce in developing countries, especially in least developed countries and small island developing States

3.d Strengthen the capacity of all countries, in particular developing countries, for early warning, risk reduction and management of national and global health risks

1. THE SUSTAINABLE DEVELOPMENT GOALS AND GOAL 3

The Sustainable Development Goals (SDGs) were adopted in 2015, following the Millennium Development Goals (MDGs), which, under the auspices of the United Nations, united the world's efforts to help the poorest countries.

Compared to the MDGs, one of the main features of the SDGs is their universality, since they depart from the awareness that sustainable development should be a goal for every country.[1] This means that sustainable development also poses challenges for all countries, although on different levels, depending on their individual situations and degrees of development. This global vision of the world's development implies a common responsibility of all countries and the commitment of public and private players.[2] Partnering the public and the private sector increases the social, economic and environmental responsibility and the impact of the actions adopted.[3]

The involvement of private stakeholders, alongside public players, in the SDGs represents an evolution from a philanthropic model to a model that uses business resources as a way to achieve sustainable development. As Lalaguna argues, 'for example, by developing new technologies, services, products or business models that address poverty, hunger, environmental protection or health, the private sector can have a multiplying effect in improving lives around the world, and in doing so improving their prospects'.[4] Therefore, there is a new background of actors that have a common mission and responsibility, from national authorities to international organisations, the business sector, civil society, individuals, philanthropists and universities.[5] All of them are involved in the commitment to creating sustainable development, in the many dimensions set out in 2015, and in global decision-making.

Sustainable development is closely connected with certain international legal principles, in particular the principle of international cooperation and the principle of international protection of human rights.[6] In the first case, sustainable development is associated with universal solidarity of all stakeholders in a global effort, while in the second case, the right to sustainable development is seen as a human right.[7] In fact, according to Article 1(1) of the Declaration on the

1 On the universal characteristic of the SDGs, see Paloma Durán y Lalaguna, 'The sustainable development goals: an introduction' in Sagrario Morán Blanco and Elena C Díaz Galán (eds), *International Society and Sustainable Development Goals* (Editorial Aranzadi 2016) 40–41.

2 ibid.

3 Irina Zapatrina, 'Sustainable Development Goals for Developing Economies and Public-Private Partnership' (2016) 11 European Procurement & Public Private Partnership Law Review 39, 39–45.

4 Paloma Durán y Lalaguna, 'The sustainable development goals: an introduction' in Sagrario Morán Blanco and Elena C Díaz Galán (eds), *International Society and Sustainable Development Goals* (Editorial Aranzadi 2016) 43.

5 ibid 35; Tonia Novitz and Margherita Pieraccinipp, 'Agenda 2030 and the Sustainable Development Goals: "Responsive, Inclusive, Participatory and Representative Decision-Making"?' in Margherita Pieraccini and Tonia Novitz (eds), *Legal Perspectives on Sustainability* (Bristol University Press 2020) 57–58.

6 About the several dimensions of sustainable development, see Cástor Miguel Díaz Barrado, 'Sustainable development goals: a principle and several dimensions' in Sagrario Morán Blanco and Elena C Díaz Galán (eds), *International Society and Sustainable Development Goals* (Editorial Aranzadi 2016) 59.

7 ibid.

Right to Development, adopted as United Nations General Assembly Resolution 41/128 of 4 December 1986, the right to enjoy economic, social, cultural and political development is stated to be an inalienable human right. This 'link between development goals and human rights is important as it transfers policy commitments by the international community into a legally enforceable set of rights for individuals'.[8]

The 2030 Agenda for Sustainable Development establishes seven SDGs and 169 targets, as a way to eradicate poverty globally and to achieve balanced sustainable development in three dimensions – social, economic and environmental[9] – in pursuit of a strategy to bring about a modern vision of human rights. SDG 3 addresses the need to promote good health and well-being as crucial to sustainable development. The 13 targets set out in SDG 3 aim to promote good health and well-being, and can be summarised into four main topics: health issues, family planning, reduction of traffic accidents, and reduction of pollution.

The following targets fall into the category dealing with *health issues*: reducing maternal mortality (Target 3.1); ending all preventable deaths under five years of age (Target 3.2); fighting communicable diseases (Target 3.3); reducing mortality from non-communicable diseases and promoting mental health (Target 3.4); preventing and treating substance abuse (Target 3.5); achieving universal health coverage (Target 3.8); and providing access to vaccines, medicines and health services, and capacity-building, in particular in developing countries (Targets 3.a–3.d). The topic of *family planning* covers universal access to sexual and reproductive care, family planning and education (Target 3.7). The category of *reduction of traffic accidents* consists of the target on reducing road injuries and deaths (Target 3.6). Finally, the topic of *pollution reduction* consists of the target on reducing illnesses and death from hazardous chemicals and pollution (Target 3.9).

Law, in its different dimensions, can be a constructive instrument for achieving SDG 3 and facing the emerging challenges that result from globalisation. Globalisation, which has in its basis private international law relations, implies mass global consumption, travel and migration, all of which enhance the possibility of the spread of diseases across borders, ecosystem degradation as a result of environmental pollution, and other global burdens that endanger

---

8 Christina Binder and Jane Alice Hofbauer, 'Good health and well-being. Ensure healthy lives and promote well-being for all at all ages' in Sagrario Morán Blanco and Elena C Díaz Galán (eds), *International Society and Sustainable Development Goals* (Editorial Aranzadi 2016) 215.

9 According to the UN General Assembly, 'Transforming Our World: The 2030 Agenda for Sustainable Development', UN Doc A/RES/70/1 (21 October 2015) <https://sustainable development.un.org/post2015/transformingourworld> accessed 1 February 2020.

global health.[10] Consequently, this chapter explores the interaction of private international law and SDG 3, through the four clusters of issues identified.

2. HEALTH ISSUES AND PRIVATE INTERNATIONAL LAW

The right to health is protected in Article 25 of the Universal Declaration of Human Rights, which states that 'everyone has the right to a standard of living adequate for the health and well-being of himself and of his family', and Article 12 of the International Covenant on Economic, Social and Cultural Rights, which establishes the right to enjoy the highest attainable standard of health. In SDG 3, the target on achieving universal health functions as an underlying principle to achieving the right to health.

2.1. E-HEALTH PLATFORMS AND APPLICATIONS

One way to achieve universal health coverage and improve healthcare, especially in less economically developed countries, would be through the development of international e-health platforms and applications that provide increased access to physicians and specialised medical care. E-health platforms and apps allow specialised medical human resources from developed countries to be closer to physicians or other healthcare professionals and patients from low- and middle-income countries. These new platforms arrived to complement, or even replace, the provision of traditional healthcare, providing a range of benefits, both to consumers (patients) and to doctors or other healthcare professionals and, consequently, promoting greater specialisation and competition in medical services. Making use of information and communication technologies (ICT) allows accessible, safe, effective, quality and affordable healthcare to reach a greater number of people and gives significant medical backup to the local healthcare workforce. These e-health platforms and applications could have an important impact on quality healthcare services in poorer countries.[11]

---

10 Lawrence O Gostin, 'Global Health Law Governance' (2008) 22 Emory International Law Review 35, 37.

11 One example is the Unjani Clinics, a social franchising initiative created in South Africa that, through an e-health portal (that includes electronic health records, patient apps, an emergency call system, among others) and tablet-based teleconsultations, allows access to quality healthcare in remote rural areas: Daniela Rudner, Lynda Toussaint and Nao Sipula, 'Unjani Nurses lead the way: How eHealth can improve access to healthcare in rural South Africa' in Thomas Christian Bächle and Alina Wernick (eds), *The Futures of eHealth, Social, Ethical and Legal Challenges* (Alexander von Humboldt Institute for Internet and

Before the COVID-19 pandemic, there was already the idea that different persistent and emerging health issues in the poorest countries could only be solved with the commitment of developed countries.[12] However, the pandemic showed that even developed countries' abilities to cope with such a crisis differ widely and made obvious the need for international cooperation and resource-sharing in the health sector. Taking into account the financial difficulties in the poorest countries, aging populations in developed countries, the economic crisis and exceptional situations such as the one caused by the pandemic COVID-19, digital tools are the fastest, safest, most economical and most effective way, of sufficient quality, to provide with citizens all relevant health information, necessary social assistance and appropriate health monitoring. In this regard, there is a growing tendency for healthcare to adapt to the needs of the modern patient, so ubiquitous ICT tools will certainly be the solution to respond to this trend.[13]

One example of an e-health platform is the Pager application, which emerged in the US in 2014 and is already expanding in Latin America, with the aim of reinventing traditional medical care.[14] It is a virtual assistance platform that operates in different countries, but with national command centres. Pager simplifies the healthcare experience and allows patients to interact with their doctor or his or her team through the platform, anytime and anywhere. With the app, users can explain their health problems to a team of specialists and be given solutions. They are also able to schedule appointments online or at home, which avoids needing to travel and spend time in hospital waiting rooms. As a result, costs are controlled and users are able to make payments digitally.[15]

Society 2019) 109–114. As stated in Niklas Trinkhaus, 'International perspectives on eHealth' in Thomas Christian Bächle and Alina Wernick (eds), *The Futures of eHealth, Social, Ethical and Legal Challenges* (Alexander von Humboldt Institute for Internet and Society 2019) 103, 105–106, the development of e-health technologies and infrastructures, through international cooperation, could be a way of achieving universal global health coverage.

12 Niklas Trinkhaus, 'International perspectives on eHealth' in Thomas Christian Bächle and Alina Wernick (eds), *The Futures of eHealth, Social, Ethical and Legal Challenges* (Alexander von Humboldt Institute for Internet and Society 2019) 103; Lawrence O Gostin, 'Global Health Law Governance' (2008) 22 Emory International Law Review 35, 35–47.

13 ibid; Verina Wild, Sarah Akgül, Katharina Eisenhut, Tereza Hendl, Bianca Jansky, Felix Machleid, Niels Nijsingh, Nicole Peter and Ela Sauerborn, 'Ethical, legal and social aspects of mHealth technologies: Navigating the field' in Thomas Christian Bächle and Alina Wernick (eds), *The Futures of eHealth, Social, Ethical and Legal Challenges* (Alexander von Humboldt Institute for Internet and Society 2019) 19–29; Irma Klünker, 'Markets for eHealth: Perspectives from innovators and entrepreneurs' in Thomas Christian Bächle and Alina Wernick (eds), *The Futures of eHealth, Social, Ethical and Legal Challenges* (Alexander von Humboldt Institute for Internet and Society 2019) 99–106; J Kelly Barnes, 'Telemedicine: a conflict of laws problem waiting to happen – how will interstate and international claims be decided?' (2006) 28(2) Houston Journal of International Law 491, 492–495.

14 Information available at <https://www.pager.com> accessed 20 November 2020.

15 See Joel Berg, 'From 8 to 50 states, Pager expands survive nationwide', *MedCity News* (2020) <https://www.medcitynews.com> accessed 15 June 2020.

Pager is a provider of information, navigation and coordination services, that gives its users access to various services in the healthcare arena, including screenings, telemedicine, prescriptions, consultations, transport to hospital units and medical offices, and monitoring of convalescence.[16] The example of Pager demonstrates that e-health platforms can be a way to promote access to health in the poorest countries and to strengthen collaborations between countries in the health sector, since it can allow patients in developing countries to consult doctors in developed countries. This is a creative and innovative approach that allows the involvement of private stakeholders and public players, access to life-saving techniques, and universal health coverage, which is considered central to SDG 3.[17]

When these e-health platforms and apps have a transnational nature, private international law instruments are the answer to establish the legal framework governing them and to settle any disputes that may arise. As regards the legal framework for transnational e-health platforms and apps, several issues can be raised: the nature of the contract concluded when patients make a medical appointment using ICT tools like the internet, telephone or SMS; whether it is a consumer contract; and the mechanisms to protect the weaker party to the contract, for example in the case of choice-of-court agreements, choice-of-law clauses, unfair terms and general contractual terms. Non-contractual obligations can also arise as a result of a tort/delict resulting from medical malpractice when using ICT, as well as private international law questions resulting from the international insurance contracts which cover the risks resulting from these ICT activities.

These questions pose challenges for private international law rules and, at the first stage, the answers will be provided by national law: conflict-of-law rules, jurisdiction rules, overriding mandatory rules, public policy mechanisms, and substantive rules.

It is also possible to find legal answers common to several countries in integrated regional areas, like the European Union, in private international law instruments and substantive rules. As private international law instruments examples, it is possible to list Regulation (EC) No 593/2008 of the European Parliament and of the Council of 17 June 2008 on the law applicable to contractual obligations (Rome I), Regulation (EC) No 864/2007 of the European Parliament and of the Council of 11 July 2007 on the law applicable to non-contractual obligations (Rome II), and Regulation No 1215/2012 of the European Parliament

16 See Jasmine Pennic, 'Pager goes international, expands virtual care model to Latin America', *Hit Consultant* (2020) <https://www.hitconsultant.net> accessed 15 June 2020.

17 Sara Bennett, Nasreen Jessani, Douglas Glandon, Mary Qiu, Kerry Scott, Ankita Meghani, Fadi El-Jardali, Daniel Maceira, Dena Javadi and Abdul Ghaffar, 'Understanding the implications of the Sustainable Development Goals for health policy and systems research: results of a research priority setting exercise' (2020) 16 Globalization and Health 5.

and of the Council of 12 December 2012 on jurisdiction and the recognition and enforcement of judgments in civil and commercial matters (Brussels I Recast). The conflict-of-law rules of Rome II Regulation will apply to determine the law applicable to medical malpractice claims brought against physicians in a telemedicine situation. Rome I Regulation will apply to determine the law that governs telemedicine contracts.

However, in the European Union, it is also possible to find substantive rules common to the several Member States that could also be useful in establishing the legal framework applicable to these transnational e-health platforms and apps. That would be the case, among other examples, for Directive 2011/24/EU of 9 March 2011 on the application of patients' rights in cross-border healthcare; Directive 2000/31/EC of 8 June 2000 on certain legal aspects of information society services, in particular electronic commerce, in the Internal Market; Directive 2002/58/EC of 12 July 2002 concerning the processing of personal data and the protection of privacy in the electronic communications sector; the Regulation (EU) No 2017/745 of 5 April 2017 on medical devices; and Directive 93/13/EEC of 5 April 1993 on unfair terms in consumer contracts. Although the scope of application of each of these legal instruments varies, they are meant to regulate the internal market of the European Union and ultimately, as far as telemedicine is concerned, protect EU patients.[18]

At a third level, it is also possible to find international legal instruments that, between the contracting states, can determine the legal framework applicable to these transnational e-health platforms and apps, like the Hague Convention of 2 July 2019 on the Recognition and Enforcement of Foreign Judgments in Civil or Commercial Matters, or the Hague Convention of 30 June 2005 on Choice of Court Agreements. For telemedicine providers, it is important to be able to predict the legal effects of telemedicine, and the prior determination of the court that has jurisdiction is an important aspect of reducing the uncertainty regarding contractual claims.

Finally, international disputes related to e-health platforms and apps can also be solved through arbitration, which is considered the best form of international dispute resolution because of its main features. In taking the dispute from the state jurisdiction and handing it over to an arbitrator, arbitration has certain advantages that make it an attractive way of solving international litigation. Looking at the difficult challenges that the COVID-19 pandemic posed for all sectors of the economy all over the world, one can see that some arbitral tribunals reacted quickly to the disruption caused by the pandemic. They adopted urgent arbitration procedures for the resolution of disputes

[18] For a more in-depth look at some of these instruments, see Vera Lúcia Raposo, 'Telemedicine: The legal framework (or the lack of it) in Europe' (2016) 12 GMS Health Technology Assessment https://www.ncbi.nlm.nih.gov/pmc/articles/PMC4987488/> accessed 19 February 2020.

arising from COVID-19, with procedures to allow for remote case management, implemented secure online communication, adopted virtual hearings, and issued protocols and guidelines to help cope with this new reality.[19] This is proof of the flexibility of arbitration in solving international disputes. The landmark instrument for the recognition and enforcement of international arbitration decisions is the United Nations Convention of 10 June 1958 on the Recognition and Enforcement of Foreign Arbitral Awards, which, at least between the contracting states, guarantees the effectiveness of arbitration agreements and the fair enforcement of contractual rights and obligations.

2.2. PROTECTION OF PERSONAL DATA

Telemedicine also poses problems as regards data protection and international transfer of data, often across jurisdictions. An example of this is the health grid,[20] which is a system that allows the management of healthcare resources and makes data available to different players in healthcare systems, such as physicians, healthcare centres, patients, citizens and researchers. The health grid is based on the sharing of data (including personal data) and information. The main objective of the health grid is to facilitate provision of healthcare services and to allow health research. To that end, it allows the sharing of resources, data, information and problem-solving strategies between individuals or institutions, forming a virtual network and enabling international cooperation.[21] Information is shared even if the data are stored in another country. In fact, 'in order to be truly effective, such grid applications must draw together huge amounts of data from disparately located computers – which implies data sharing across jurisdictions and the sharing of responsibilities by a range of different data controllers'.[22] The COVID-19 pandemic showed the importance of sharing data, namely for research purposes, which benefits developed countries and

19 Cleary Gottlieb, *International Arbitration in the Time of COVID-19: Navigating the Evolving Procedural Features and Practices of Leading Arbitral Institutions* (2020) 1–9 <https://www.clearygottlieb.com/-/media/files/alert-memos-2020/international-arbitration-in-the-time-of-covid19.pdf> accessed 1 December 2020.

20 On the concept of grid, with some examples, see Ian Foster, Carl Kesselman and Steven Tuecke, 'The anatomy of the grid: enabling scalable virtual organizations' (2001) 15(3) International Journal of High Performance Computing Applications 200, 200–222.

21 On the development of grid technologies for e-health in the European Union, see European Commission, *e-Health – making healthcare better for European citizens: An action plan for a European e-Health Area, Communication from the Commission to the Council, the European Parliament, the European Economic and Social Committee and the Committee of the Regions*, COM(2004)356, 1–26.

22 Stefaan Callens, 'The EU legal framework on e-health' in Elias Mossialos, Govin Permanand, Rita Baeten and Tamara Hervey (eds), *Health Systems Governance in Europe: The Role of European Union Law and Policy, Health Economics, Policy and Management* (CUP 2010) 580.

developing countries alike. That was clear in the development of the vaccines against the virus, which were developed in some countries, tested in others, and now will benefit all countries worldwide. As previously stated, one of the main features of the SDGs is their universality, which means that sustainable development is a goal for every country. However, depending on the situation in individual countries, the challenges will be different.

All these new technologies in e-health services and health research pose problems of data protection, and the transfer of personal data between countries is faced with the challenge that some states adopt a stricter policy of data protection and create higher barriers to the international transfer of personal data than others. This is the case in the European Union which, despite being made up of 27 Member States, has a common legal framework for all the Member States that strictly protects personal data as a fundamental right, under Article 8 of the EU Charter of Fundamental Rights. However, beyond this common legal framework, the protection of processing of personal data is also dealt with at the international level, by other legal instruments like Article 8 of the European Convention on Human Rights (ECHR), the Council of Europe's Convention 108 for the Protection of Individuals with regard to Automatic Processing of Personal Data and its Protocols,[23] the OECD's Guidelines governing the Protection of Privacy and Transborder Flows of Personal Data,[24] and the 2013 UN General Assembly Resolution 68/167 on the right to privacy in the digital age,[25] which is based on the right to privacy set in Article 12 of the Universal Declaration of Human Rights and Article 17 of the International Covenant on Civil and Political Rights. These international instruments have also inspired the national laws of several other states in creating an effective framework for the protection of personal data. Examples include the United Kingdom Data Protection Act 1998 or the Brazilian General Law of Data Protection.

Other states are more timid in the regulation of the processing of personal data. The United States is one example, where data protection is not strongly regulated, in accordance with the policy of letting the market rule itself. This self-regulation is in line with the non-constitutional protection of privacy in the United States and the conception that privacy has economic and social costs that need to be balanced against economic efficiency and security.[26] In the United States, there is no global approach to personal data, and the legal framework

---

23 See also the Council of Europe, *Guidelines on the protection of individuals with regard to the processing of personal data in a world of big data* (Directorate General of Human Rights and Rule of Law T-PD(2017)01) <https://rm.coe.int/16806ebe7a> accessed 23 November 2020.

24 OECD, *The OECD Privacy Framework* (2013) <http://www.oecd.org/sti/ieconomy/oecd_privacy_framework.pdf> accessed 23 November 2020.

25 UN General Assembly, *The right to privacy in the digital age*, UN Doc A/RES/68/167 (21 January 2013).

26 Lauren B Movius and Nathalie Krup, 'U.S. and EU Privacy Policy: Comparison of Regulatory Approaches' (2009) 3 International Journal of Communication 169, 176–177.

mixes federal and state legislation and self-regulation guidelines, sometimes in the form of best practices, in sector-specific contexts, like healthcare, education, communications, and financial services, among others.[27] Examples of federal sector-specific legislation are the Financial Services Modernization Act, the Health Insurance Portability and Accountability Act, the Controlling the Assault of Non-Solicited Pornography and Marketing Act (CAN-SPAM Act), the Fair Credit Reporting Act, the Electronic Communications Privacy Act, the Computer Fraud and Abuse Act, and the Children's Online Privacy Protection Act. Each one of these sector-specific pieces of legislation has its own definition of personal data, requirements relating the processing of data, provisions on breaches and security, targeted actions, and penalties,[28] in what can be called a patchwork system.[29] If there is no specific sectoral legislation, the data subject can only rely on tort law or contract law, depending on the situation,[30] neither of which have specific solutions for the protection of personal data, like the principle of minimisation, proportionality, purpose limitations, the requirement to notify the data subject of data collected and its purpose, the entities to which the personal data may be disclosed, guarantees regarding storage, measures to ensure lawful and fair processing, and time limits for keeping or destroying the data collected, among others. As a result, 'for millions of Americans, entrusting your personal data with a business and their data system is the reality and the personal cost of doing business', as is the misuse of these personal data.[31]

Directly or indirectly, 'unilateral national Internet regulations may affect both the Internet activities of users in other jurisdictions as well as the regulatory approach of other nations'.[32] One example is the EU's Regulation (EU) No 2016/679 on the protection of natural persons with regard to the processing of personal data and on the free movement of such data (GDPR), and its legal framework on health data, which can have extraterritorial effect, also known as regulatory spill-over.[33]

---

27 Shawn Marie Boyne, 'Data Protection in the United States' (2018) 66 American Journal of Comparative Law 299; Michael P Roch, 'Filling the void of data protection in the United States: following the European example' (1996) 12(1) Santa Clara Computer and High-Technology Law Journal 71, 88.

28 Shawn Marie Boyne, 'Data Protection in the United States' (2018) 66 American Journal of Comparative Law 299, 299–344.

29 Jana N Sloane, 'Raising data privacy standards: The United States' need for a uniform data protection regulation' (2018–2019) 12 John Marshall Law Journal 23, 24.

30 Michael P Roch, 'Filling the void of data protection in the United States: following the European example' (1996) 12(1) Santa Clara Computer and High-Technology Law Journal 71, 92–93.

31 Jana N Sloane, 'Raising data privacy standards: The United States' need for a uniform data protection regulation' (2018–2019) 12 John Marshall Law Journal 23, 24.

32 Lauren B Movius and Nathalie Krup, 'U.S. and EU Privacy Policy: Comparison of Regulatory Approaches' (2009) 3 International Journal of Communication 169, 170.

33 Expression used by Jack Goldsmith, 'Unilateral Regulation of the Internet: A Modest Defense' (2000) 11 European Journal of International Law 135, 142, referring to Directive 95/46/EC of

As far as health data is concerned, the European Union legal framework for data protection establishes a high standard of protection for data subjects in comparison with other legal systems.[34] In the GDPR, data concerning health receive enhanced protection in the field of personal data, because they are considered particularly sensitive, given the specificity of the information that they may reveal about the person. Data concerning health includes all the data that gives information about the physical and mental health of a natural person (Art 4(15)). According to the ECJ, which has adopted a broad definition, personal data covers all health-related identifying features, because it includes information on all aspects of a person's health, whether physical or mental.[35] Recital 35 of the GDPR lists a set of elements that can constitute examples of data concerning health, like the health information referred to in Directive 2011/24/EU of 9 March 2011 on the application of patients' rights in cross-border healthcare: a number or symbol assigned to a natural person to uniquely identify the natural person for health purposes; information derived from the testing or examination of a body part or bodily substance, including from genetic data and biological samples; and any information on, for example, a disease, disability, disease risk, medical history or clinical treatment. Related to data concerning health are genetic data that may result from any medical examination, such as clinical analyses of a biological sample, and may give information about a person's inherited or acquired health characteristics (Art 4(13)). Taking into consideration the specificity of data concerning health, Article 9 of the GDPR, subject to some exceptions, blocks the processing of these special categories of personal data.[36]

One of these exceptions specifically covers the processing of personal data concerning health for research purposes, which became vital during the

---

24 October 1995 on the protection of individuals with regard to the processing of personal data and on the free movement of such data, revoked by the GDPR; Lauren B Movius and Nathalie Krup, 'U.S. and EU Privacy Policy: Comparison of Regulatory Approaches' (2009) 3 International Journal of Communication 169, 171.

34 See Lee A Bygrave, 'Privacy in a Global Context – A Comparative Overview' (2004) 47 Scandinavian Studies in Law 320, 320–348; Lingjie Kong, 'Data Protection and Transborder Data Flow in the European Context' (2010) 21(2) European Journal of International Law 441, 441–456; Christopher Kuner, *Regulation of Transborder Data Flows under Data Protection and Privacy Law: Past, Present and Future*, OECD Digital Economy Papers No 187 (2011) 1–39; Dan Jerker B Svantesson, *Extraterritoriality in Data Privacy Law* (Ex Tuto Publishing 2013) 39–45.

35 Case C-101/01 *Reference to the Court under Article 234 EC by the Göta hovrätt (Sweden) for a preliminary ruling in the criminal proceedings before that court v Bodil Lindqvist* [2003] ECLI:EU:C:2003:596, para 2.

36 About the protection of personal data concerning health, see Anabela Susana de Sousa Gonçalves, 'Processing of personal data concerning health under the GDPR' in Maria Miguel Carvalho (ed), *E-Tec Yearbook, Health Law and Technology* (Research Centre of Justice and Governance/University of Minho School of Law 2019) 1–24.

COVID-19 pandemic. Article 9(2)(j) of the GDPR deals precisely with archiving purposes in the public interest, or scientific, historical, statistical research purposes, provided that the safeguards of Article 89(1) are in place, on the basis of European or national laws that should establish suitable and specific measures to safeguard the data subject's rights and shall be proportionate to the aim pursued. The GDPR recognises the importance of research in the health sector and the need to process personal data for scientific research purposes as a way to make important breakthroughs in the medical field (recital 157). Still, the GDPR should apply to the processing of such data. Member States are authorised to establish specific conditions and measures in order to guarantee the rights of the data subject, namely technical and organisational measures to respect the principle of data minimisation, taking into consideration the principles of proportionality and necessity, like pseudonymisation,[37] controlled access or managed access models to control the use of research databases, processing data in safe havens, encryption and key management.

The direct or indirect influence of the GDPR over cross-border cases is achieved in two ways: the transfer of protected data to third states, and the enforcement of data protection laws on third state companies.

2.2.1. Transfer of Protected Data to Third States

Telemedicine, the health grid, e-health platforms and health research all often involve international transfer of data. International transfer of data from the European Union to third countries is governed by Chapter V the GDPR and is only possible when the third state has an adequate/equivalent level of protection (Art 45) or the processor or controller has adopted adequate safeguards according to Article 46, except for specific situations set out in Article 49.

The importance of these rules became clear in the *Schrems II* decision of the ECJ, where the court declared invalid the Decision of the European Commission 2016/1250 on the adequacy of the protection provided by the EU-US Privacy Shield, which facilitated the transfer of data between the European Union and the United States.[38] The decision of the ECJ was based on the grounds that

---

[37] This is a process by which personal data is separated from the person and cannot be attributed to a specific person, except by the use of additional information that is kept separately. There are technical and organisational security measures to guarantee that those attributes remain separate and to ensure that a specific natural person is not identified; however, the natural person can be identified if those attributes are put together.

[38] Case C-311/18 *Data Protection Commissioner v Facebook Ireland Ltd, Maximillian Schrems, intervening parties: The United States of America, Electronic Privacy Information Centre, BSA Business Software Alliance Inc., Digitaleurope* [2020] ECLI:EU:C:2020:559. On the EU-US Privacy Shield, see Shakila Bu-Pasha, 'Cross-border issues under EU data protection law with regards to personal data protection' (2017) 26(3) Information & Communications Technology Law 213, 223–227.

United States law does not ensure a level of protection essentially equivalent to the one guaranteed by European Union law, since it permits interference with fundamental rights, without respecting the principle of proportionality.[39] If the EU-US Privacy Shield is invalid, the transfer of data between the EU and the United States under this instrument is unlawful too. Thus, the transfer of personal data from the European Union to the United States can only take place under Articles 45(3) or 46 of the GDPR. In conclusion, the GDPR's requirements of an adequate level of protection and appropriate safeguards in the international transfer of data is an example how the high standard of protection of personal data presented in the European Union legal framework may be, on the one hand, an obstacle to the international transfer of personal data concerning health. On the other hand, it can be seen as an incentive for third states to increase their levels of protection of personal data.

2.2.2. Enforcement of Data Protection Laws on Third State Companies

The GDPR has extraterritorial application, as can be concluded by analysing its conflict-of-law rule, set out in Article 3.[40] This means that the EU can enforce its data protection law against companies from third states that have some connections with the EU, even if those links are not the strongest, thus expanding the application of EU law.[41] This means that if a third state company has the connections identified in the GDPR or needs to mix European and non-European data, the regulatory spill-over of the GDPR 'encourages it to move its data processing operations to Europe … and will often encourage firms to comply with the most restrictive regulatory regime'.[42] Because of this extraterritorial application of EU data protection law, or the effects of its regulatory spill-over, the EU is accused by some

39 Case C-311/18 *Data Protection Commissioner v Facebook Ireland Ltd, Maximillian Schrems, intervening parties: The United States of America, Electronic Privacy Information Centre, BSA Business Software Alliance Inc., Digitaleurope* [2020] ECLI:EU:C:2020:559, paras 150–202.

40 For more details, see Anabela Susana de Sousa Gonçalves, 'The extraterritorial application of the EU Directive on data protection' (2015) 19 The Spanish Yearbook of International Law 195, 195–209; Anabela Susana de Sousa Gonçalves, 'Aplicação (extra)territorial do Regulamento Geral de Proteção de Dados' (2019) 2 Anuário de Direitos Humanos 1, 1–20; Dan Svantesson, 'Extraterritoriality in the Context of Data Privacy Regulation' (2012) 7(1) Masaryk Journal of Law and Technology 87, 87–95.

41 Shakila Bu-Pasha, 'Cross-border issues under EU data protection law with regards to personal data protection' (2017) 26(3) Information & Communications Technology Law 213, 218; Clare Sullivan, 'EU GDPR or APEC CBPR? A comparative analysis of the approach of the EU and APEC to cross border data transfers and protection of personal data in the IoT era' (2019) 35(4) Computer Law & Security Review 380, 383; Joshua Paul Meltzer, 'The Internet, Cross-Border Data Flows and International Trade' (2014) 2(1) Asia & the Pacific Policy Studies 90, 93; W Gregory Voss, 'Cross-Border Data Flows, the GDPR, and Data Governance' (2020) 29 Washington International Law Journal 485, 497–498.

42 Jack Goldsmith, 'Unilateral Regulation of the Internet: A Modest Defense' (2000) 11 European Journal of International Law 135, 143.

authors of legislating for the world.[43] For others, the extraterritorial jurisdictional claims are reasonable, because if states do not extend their data protection to the conduct of third parties, they will not provide effective protection for their citizens.[44] When the processing of personal data has a worldwide reach and the main seats of the major controllers, such as Facebook, Google, Amazon, Apple and Microsoft, are located outside the Union, the broad scope of the GDPR's application guarantees the fundamental right to data protection, which it aims to implement.[45] When companies progressively expand their activities, giving them a global scope, conflicts may arise between the economic interests of these companies and the national jurisdictions that try to ensure real and effective protection of personal data. In the absence of an international consensus on a minimum standard of protection of personal data, it is natural that states, or in this case the European Union, opt to amplify their personal data legal standards, attempting to cover these delocalised situations and expanding the scope of their law.

As stated before, the high legal standard of protection of personal data present in the European Union framework may be an obstacle to the international transfer of personal data concerning health and the sharing of these data for health research purposes. However, it may also be an encouragement to other states to consider the protection of personal data as a fundamental right too, as recommended by several international human rights instruments, which is an effect that cannot be overlooked as being positive.

In fact, the UN has recognised that 'quality, accessible, timely and reliable disaggregates data will be needed to help with the measurement of progress and to ensure that no one is left behind', as this is important for decision-making.[46] The Data Privacy, Ethics and Protection Guidance Note on Big Data for Achievement of the 2030 Agenda safeguards that data access, analysis and processing must be consistent with the United Nations Charter, and the processing of data is presented as a way of furthering the SDGs.[47] That is why

---

43 Lee A Bygrave, 'Privacy in a Global Context – A Comparative Overview' (2004) 47 Scandinavian Studies in Law 320, 334; Lee A Bygrave, 'Determining Applicable Law pursuant to European Data Protection Legislation' (2000) 16 Computer Law & Security Report 252, 252–257; Peter Ford, 'Implementing the EC Directive on Data Protection – an outside perspective' (2003) 9 Privacy Law and Policy Reporter 141, 141–149.

44 Dan Svantesson, 'Extraterritoriality in the Context of Data Privacy Regulation' (2012) 7(1) Masaryk Journal of Law and Technology 87, 87–95.

45 With the same opinion see Ludovic Pailler, 'L'applicabilité spatiale di Règlement Générale sur la Protection des Données (RGPD) – Commentaire de l'article 3' (2018) 3 Clunet 823, 849; Svetlana Yakovleva, 'Should Fundamental Rights to Privacy and Data Protection be a Part of the EU's International Trade 'Deals'?' (2018) 17(3) World Trade Review 477, 486.

46 UN General Assembly, 'Transforming Our World: The 2030 Agenda for Sustainable Development', UN Doc A/RES/70/1 (21 October 2015) <https://sustainabledevelopment.un.org/post2015/transformingourworld> accessed 1 February 2020.

47 United Nations Development Group, *Data privacy, ethics and protection guidance note on big data for achievement of the 2030 agenda*, 3 <https://unsdg.un.org/sites/default/files/UNDG_BigData_final_web.pdf> assessed 20 November 2020.

it is stated, specifically regarding sensitive data like health data, that 'stricter standards of data protection should be employed while obtaining, accessing, collecting, analysing or otherwise using data on vulnerable populations and persons at risk, children and young people, or any other sensitive data'.[48] In the same document some illustrations are given on how data science and analytics can contribute to sustainable development. For example, data science and analytics can contribute to SDG 3 by 'mapping the movement of mobile phone users [that] can help predict the spread of infectious diseases'.[49] The importance of sharing data for research purposes, already referred to, is another example, because it will benefit developed countries and developing countries alike, as well as vulnerable populations.

In the absence of an international/global harmonisation strategy, which is not easy because states have different economic, social, technological and political interests, the EU's GDPR shows that: (1) enhanced data protection through unification of laws of several countries in this domain is possible, and (2) this may result in, or be given (Art 3 GDPR), a spill-over effect affecting the regulatory approach of other states as well as companies in other states.

3. FAMILY PLANNING AND PRIVATE INTERNATIONAL LAW

Family planning is another cluster of the SDG 3 that can interact with private international law. The topic of family planning includes universal access to sexual and reproductive care, family planning and education (Target 3.7). As stated above, the SDGs must be related with human rights, and SDG 3 specifically with the right to health. One of the dimensions of the right to health is the right to enjoy the benefits of scientific progress and its applications, stated in Article 15 of the International Covenant on Economic, Social and Cultural Rights, and Right to the highest attainable standard of health, stated in Article 12 of the same international instrument.[50] The link between family planning, the right to enjoy the benefits of scientific progress and its applications draws attention to medically assisted procreation as a way of creating a family and a method of family planning for couples with fertility issues or couples that cannot conceive together without assistance.

48 ibid 5.

49 ibid 13.

50 Christina Binder and Jane Alice Hofbauer, 'Good health and well-being. Ensure healthy lives and promote well-being for all at all ages' in Sagrario Morán Blanco and Elena C Díaz Galán (eds), *International Society and Sustainable Development Goals* (Editorial Aranzadi 2016) 215, 217.

3.1. REGULATORY DIVERSITY REGARDING MEDICALLY ASSISTED PROCREATION

Medically assisted procreation has evolved as science has progressed, raising several ethical and legal problems. The diversity in states' regulation of access to medically assisted procreation techniques has led to reproductive tourism, where people travel to another country to have access to other reproductive techniques that are not available in their country of habitual residence.

To take one example, from a comparative perspective, there are countries that have a legal framework regarding surrogacy; others that do not have a legal framework, but accept surrogacy; and a third set of countries that forbid it.

Within the legal systems that regulate surrogacy, there are two different kinds of models regarding the establishment of parenthood: the model of legal transfer of parenthood; and the model of judicial transfer of parenthood. Countries that accept surrogacy following the model of legal transfer of parenthood have the simplest option, since the transfer of parenthood between the pregnant woman and the beneficiaries takes place directly and immediately, as a result of the law, after delivery. This is the case in Russia,[51] Ukraine,[52] Greece,[53] South Africa,[54] India,[55] and some North American states, such as North Dakota, Delaware, Illinois, Maine, Nevada, New Hampshire, Virginia and Washington.[56] A paradigmatic example of the countries that adopt the model of judicial transfer of parenthood is the United Kingdom, where the pregnant woman is considered the mother after delivery, but the beneficiaries can apply to the court for a parental order, to transfer the parenthood of the child from the pregnant woman to the beneficiary couple.[57] The model of judicial transfer of parenthood is still practiced in some North American states, such as Alabama, California, Florida, Texas and Utah.[58]

---

51 Laurence Brunet, Janeen Carruthers, Konstantina Davaki, Derek King, Claire Marzo and Julie Mccandless, *A Comparative Study on the Regime of Surrogacy in EU Member States* (Policy Department C: Citizens' Rights and Constitutional Affairs, European Parliament, Directorate General for Internal Policies 2013) 333–338.

52 ibid 10.

53 ibid 281–283.

54 ibid 339–350.

55 ibid 32, 34 and 61.

56 Alex Finkelstein, Sarah Mac Dougall, Angela Kintominas and Anya Olsen, 'Surrogacy Law and Policy in the U.S.: A National Conversation Informed by Global Lawmaking' (2016) Columbia Law School Sexuality & Gender Law Clinic 55, 55–83.

57 Amel Alghrani and Danielle Griffiths, 'The regulation of surrogacy in the United Kingdom: the case for reform' (2017) 29(2) Child and Family Law Quarterly 165, 171–173; Laurence Brunet, Janeen Carruthers, Konstantina Davaki, Derek King, Claire Marzo and Julie Mccandless, *A Comparative Study on the Regime of Surrogacy in EU Member States* (Policy Department C: Citizens' Rights and Constitutional Affairs, European Parliament, Directorate General for Internal Policies 2013) 230.

58 Alex Finkelstein, Sarah Mac Dougall, Angela Kintominas and Anya Olsen, 'Surrogacy Law and Policy in the U.S.: A National Conversation Informed by Global Lawmaking' (2016) Columbia Law School Sexuality & Gender Law Clinic 55, 55–83.

There is a second group of countries that do not regulate surrogacy: those countries neither allow nor prohibit it, creating situations where there is a legal void. This is the case for several European countries, such as the Netherlands, Belgium, Ireland, the Czech Republic, Hungary, Poland, Denmark, Finland, Sweden, Estonia, Latvia, Lithuania, Romania, Slovakia, Slovenia, Luxembourg and Cyprus.[59]

There is a third group of countries that clearly prohibit surrogacy, establishing civil and criminal sanctions for those who resort to it. Spain, France, Italy, Germany, Austria, Bulgaria, Malta are examples.[60]

In reproductive tourism, one phenomenon that has been particularly extensively discussed, taking into consideration its social impact, is international surrogacy. Because of international surrogacy, several countries are on the reproductive tourism route, and there are even international agencies dedicated to facilitating this medically assisted procreation technique.[61]

3.2. REPRODUCTIVE TOURISM

Nationals and residents of countries that have a restrictive attitude to surrogacy sometimes travel to countries that allow it. The objective is to make use of surrogacy as beneficiaries, with the intention of later recognising the child's parenthood in their countries of origin. The phenomenon of reproductive tourism poses problems for the recognition of the legal effects resulting from surrogacy carried out in another country, namely the recognition of parenthood rights established abroad. In the countries that have a restrictive attitude, recognition of parenthood rights established abroad is generally refused, through the public policy exception.[62]

Recognition of parenthood rights poses difficult human rights challenges, which have been dealt with the European Court of Human Rights (ECtHR) in several cases.[63]

---

59 Cf Laurence Brunet, Janeen Carruthers, Konstantina Davaki, Derek King, Claire Marzo and Julie Mccandless, *A Comparative Study on the Regime of Surrogacy in EU Member States* (Policy Department C: Citizens' Rights and Constitutional Affairs, European Parliament, Directorate General for Internal Policies 2013) 15–16.

60 ibid.

61 Laurence Brunet, Janeen Carruthers, Konstantina Davaki, Derek King, Claire Marzo and Julie Mccandless, *A Comparative Study on the Regime of Surrogacy in EU Member States: Executive Summary* (European Parliament, Directorate General for Internal Policies 2012) 3.

62 See Anabela Susana de Sousa Gonçalves, 'O reconhecimento da filiação constituída no estrangeiro em resultado de uma gestação de substituição' in Benedita Mac Croirie, Miriam Rocha and Sónia Moreira (eds), *Temas de Direito e Bioética, Novas questões do Direito da Saúde* (vol I, Escola de Direito da Universidade do Minho 2018) 7–32.

63 In the cases: ECHR *Mennensson v France* App no 65192/11 (26 June 2014); ECHR *Labassee v France* App no 65941/11 (26 June 2014); ECHR *Paradiso and Campanelli v Italy*

The *Mennensson* case[64] concerned the refusal of the French authorities to recognise legal parenthood, which had been established in the United States, of two children born via surrogacy to the beneficiaries, who were French nationals and resided on France.[65] In its decision, the ECtHR considered that there was a violation of the children's right to private life, because this right implies that the elements that constitute a person's identity as a human being, like legal parenthood, must be defined. In this case, the children were in a situation of legal uncertainty, since despite the establishment of legal parenthood under California law, the French court's refusal to recognise the effects of the Californian decision meant that this relationship was not recognised by the French legal order. This contradiction weakened the child's identity in the French legal system, and negatively affected the definition of their nationality (another essential element of the children's identity) and their succession rights.[66] Although the Court recognised France's prerogative in discouraging its nationals from travelling abroad to resort to surrogacy, it also stated that the lack of recognition in French law of the legal parenthood had not only effects on the parents, but above all on the children, whose respect for private life was seriously affected.[67] This situation was considered incompatible with the child's best interests, which was further aggravated by the fact that the children were actually the father's biological children, which the French state did not recognise.[68] Although acknowledging the lack of consensus between European states regarding surrogacy and the moral and ethical doubts it raises, the ECtHR considered that the states' margin of appreciation should be reduced when what is at stake is an important element of the existence or identity of an individual.[69]

The *Paradiso and Campanelli*[70] case involved an Italian couple who resorted to surrogacy in Russia, using the husband's genetic material. The couple got from the Italian Consulate in Moscow the documents that would allow them

App no 25358/12 (27 January 2015); and in ECHR *Advisory opinion concerning the recognition in domestic law of a legal parent-child relationship between a child born through a gestational surrogacy arrangement abroad and the intended mother Requested by the French Court of Cassation* [GC] App no P16-2018-001 (10 April 2019) para 35. On the case law of the ECtHR on surrogacy, see Anabela Susana de Sousa Gonçalves, 'Procriação medicamente assistida' in Paulo Pinto de Albuquerque (ed), *Comentário da Convenção Europeia dos Direitos Humanos e dos Protocolos Adicionais* (vol I, Universidade Católica Editora 2019) 646–669.

64 ECHR *Mennensson v France* App no 65192/11 (26 June 2014).

65 The *Labassee* case involves a similar situation: ECHR *Labassee v France* App no 65941/11 (26 June 2014).

66 ECHR *Mennensson v France* App no 65192/11 (26 June 2014); ECHR *Labassee v France* App no 65941/11 (26 June 2014), paras 97–98.

67 ibid paras 99–100.

68 ibid.

69 ECHR *Mennensson v France* App no 65192/11 (26 June 2014); ECHR *Labassee v France* App no 65941/11 (26 June 2014), paras 77–80. Also in ECHR *Labassee v France* App no 65941/11 (26 June 2014), paras 56–59.

70 ECHR *Paradiso and Campanelli v Italy* App no 25358/12 (27 January 2015).

to return to Italy with the child, but, once in Italy, the registration of the birth certificate was refused by the Italian authorities. Several proceedings were opened and in a DNA analysis of the child it was discovered that the beneficiary was not the child's biological father, which the Russian fertility clinic, when questioned, attributed to an error. Consequently, when the child was almost 10 months old, she was removed from the family and, first, handed over to social services and placed in a children's institution and later adopted by another couple when she was two years old. After trying to retrieve the child in the Italian courts unsuccessfully, the couple appealed to the ECtHR, alleging that the measures taken by the Italian authorities in relation to the child, which resulted in the definitive removal of the latter, had violated their right to respect for private and family life, guaranteed by Article 8 of the Convention.

After a first decision of the Second Chamber in 2015 in one direction,[71] in 2017 the Grand Chamber of the ECtHR reversed the decision.[72] The Grand Chamber considered that the Italian authorities had adequately weighed the conflicting public and private interests, with the public interest prevailing, since the prohibition of surrogacy aims to guarantee a public and ethical interest in a legislative policy that consists in protecting the children and women affected by this practice. Surrogacy raises ethical questions and the measures adopted were aimed at discouraging Italian nationals from resorting to surrogacy abroad, with the expectation of legalising the situation in Italy.[73] The ECtHR also stressed that the use of surrogacy raises sensitive ethical issues about which there is no consensus among European states.[74] Therefore, the Grand Chamber concluded that the Italian courts, having determined that the child would not suffer irreversible or irreparable damage from the separation, and while recognising the impact that the separation had on the couple's lives, considered that the Italian courts had made a balanced decision between the different interests in question, within the wide margin of appreciation that is recognised by Article 8(2) of the ECHR.[75]

Those cases show that states cannot ignore the scientific advancement that surrogacy brings,[76] because they may find themselves in an incongruous and

---

71 In which the ECtHR ruled on the applicability of the right to respect for family life, regardless of the Italian authorities' refusal to recognise filiation: ibid para 88.

72 ECHR *Paradiso and Campanelli v Italy* [GC] App no 25358/12 (24 January 2017).

73 ibid para 202.

74 ibid para 203.

75 ibid paras 204, 215.

76 And even forced the ECtHR to issue an advisory opinion requested by the French *Cour de Cassation* on the recognition in national law of filiation between a child born of surrogacy and the beneficiary mother: ECHR *Advisory opinion concerning the recognition in domestic law of a legal parent-child relationship between a child born through a gestational surrogacy arrangement abroad and the intended mother Requested by the French Court of Cassation* [GC] App no P16-2018-001 (10 April 2019), para 35.

discriminatory situation in which they do not allow their citizens to use this technique in their country in line with a restrictive policy, but are faced with the dilemma of recognising, or not, the legal effects (or certain legal effects) of parenthood resulting from surrogacies carried out abroad. For this reason, states' laws must not ignore surrogacy and must acknowledge scientific progress and its applications, and should regulate it. However, there will always be states with more permissive laws, which may open the door to the exploitation of children and women by reproductive tourism and the commercial interests involved. This reality can only be overcome by the development of broad consensus among states, which results from international instruments, such as the work being developed on surrogacy in the context of the Hague Conference.[77] Again, a private international law instrument, like the one that is been discussed in the Hague Conference, should provide a minimum common ground for the recognition of foreign judicial decisions on legal parenthood regarding surrogacy, balancing the right to family planning, the right to enjoy the benefits of scientific progress and its applications, the right to family life, and the rights of the children involved and their best interests.

4. REDUCTION OF TRAFFIC ACCIDENTS AND PRIVATE INTERNATIONAL LAW

4.1. SUSTAINABLE DEVELOPMENT AND THE REDUCTION OF TRAFFIC ACCIDENTS

The third cluster of SDG 3 that can interact with private international law is the topic of reduction of traffic accidents. Sustainable development involves private players, like companies, that should develop innovative and effective solutions, and increase energy efficiency, by replacing traditional products with other more technologically advanced solutions that reduce emissions and waste and improve operational efficiency.

One industry that recognises the importance of sustainability is the automobile industry. The automobile industry is currently progressively accepting the shared responsibility 'to provide value to society by delivering safe, secure and

[77] With the same opinion, Alfonso Luis Calvo Caravaca and Javier Carrascosa González, 'Gestación por sustitución y derecho Internacional Privado. Más allá del Tribunal Supremo y del tribunal Europeo de Derechos Humanos' (2015) 7(2) Cuadernos de Derecho Transnacional 45, 111–112; Hughes Fulchiron, 'La lutte contre le tourisme procréatif: vers un instrument de cooperation international' (2014) 2 Clunet 563, 576–578; Claire Fenton-Glynn, 'International surrogacy before the European Court of Human Rights' (2017) 13(3) Journal of Private International Law 546, 566.

sustainable mobility for all',[78] by reducing traffic fatalities through measures in the construction and innovation of vehicles that improve safety. In addition, the automobile industry is concerned with sustainable mobility by improving and reducing air pollution, developing efficient zero-emission vehicles, incorporating innovation into the vehicle manufacturing process, and reducing air pollutants, with positive impacts for health.[79]

From the perspective of innovation, the automobile industry is developing automated driving and other advanced technologies to reduce deaths and injuries from traffic accidents. Active safety and automated driving technologies to reduce deaths and injuries from traffic accidents are even presented as one of the main objectives of some automobile brands, like Toyota,[80] along with positive impacts in terms of reducing traffic congestion and atmospheric pollution. As a result, the commitment of the automobile industry to sustainability by developing active safety and automated driving technologies to reduce traffic accidents is also included in SDG 3.

4.2. PRODUCT LIABILITY

Consumer awareness in developed countries of sustainable products and the importance of public policies on sustainable development to encourage innovation, clean energy and sustainable mobility may give rise to what is called low liability law shopping by the producer.[81] This is a phenomenon in which states with a low degree of consumer protection in terms of producer responsibility are specifically sought out for testing or selling products which the producer suspects (or is certain) are not safe or, in this case, not sustainable. One example of this is the well-known case where automobile manufacturer made vehicles fitted with emissions-cheating software to pass emissions tests, deceiving its customers spread over several countries. However, the examples can be more serious and mass damages can easily arise, for example in a case where a vehicle manufacturer exports vehicles with a problem in the braking system or another safety defect to several countries. In these situations, the private international law rules about product liability gain renewed importance in correcting the attempts to profit from low liability law shopping.

---

78 According with the Nissan statement supporting the SDGs: <https://www.nissan-global.com/EN/SUSTAINABILITY/REPORT/SDGS/> accessed 20 November 2020.

79 ibid; see also the Toyota statement supporting the SDGs: <https://global.toyota/en/sustainability/sdgs/> accessed 20 November 2020.

80 Toyota statement supporting the SDGs: <https://global.toyota/en/sustainability/sdgs/> accessed 20 November 2020.

81 James J Fawcett, 'Products Liability in Private International Law: A European Perspective' (1993) 238 Collected Courses of the Hague Academy of International Law 13, 126–127.

The substantive rules about product liability are centred around consumer protection.[82] In product liability, consumer protection is essential, but so is predictability for the producer in terms of the applicable law. Albert Ehrenzweig, already in the 1960s, defended the need for a special conflict-of-law rule that considers the balance between these two types of interests.[83] This was undoubtedly the result of the development of producer responsibility around that time, initially in the United States and later in Europe.[84]

In fact, technological development has involved the mass production of products, as well as the opening of international distribution channels, which has allowed the internationalisation of the risk resulting from a possibly defective product. Therefore, added to the urgent need for consumer protection in these transnational situations, and the producer's interest in being able to foresee the applicable law (and even to consider the viability of the internationalisation of the production and distribution chain), is added the need to promote equal treatment between agents that operate or direct their activity to the same market.

By way of example, the European Union has recognised the importance of a special conflict-of-law rule in product liability that would 'meet the objectives of fairly spreading the risks inherent in a modern high-technology society, protecting consumers' health, stimulating innovation, securing undistorted competition and facilitating trade',[85] which can be found in Article 5 of the Rome II Regulation.

At the international level, there is the Hague Convention of 2 October 1973 on the Law Applicable to Products Liability. However, this Convention has not been widely ratified, mainly due to its complicated combination and hierarchy of connecting factors.[86]

---

82 Alberto Saravalle, *Responsabilità del produttore e diritto internazionale privato* (CEDAM 1991) 19, 51.

83 Albert Ehrenzweig, 'Products liability in the conflict of laws – towards a theory of enterprise liability under "foreseeable and insurable laws"' (1960) 69 Yale Law Journal 978, 978–991.

84 On the development of product liability in the United States and in Europe, see Warren Freedman, *International Products Liability* (vols 1 and 2, WS Hein & Co 1995); Alberto Saravalle, *Responsabilità del produttore e diritto internazionale privato* (CEDAM 1991) 3 et seq.

85 Recital 20 of Regulation (EC) No 864/2007 on the law applicable to non-contractual obligations (Rome II).

86 For this opinion, see, e.g. James J Fawcett, 'Products Liability in Private International Law: A European Perspective' (1993) 238 Collected Courses of the Hague Academy of International Law 13, 154–155; Alberto Saravalle, 'The law applicable to products liability: hopping off the endless merry-go-round' in Alberto Malatesta (ed), *The unification of choice of law rules on torts and other non-contractual obligations in Europe, The 'Rome II' proposal* (Cedam 2006) 107, 108; Joan C Seuba Torreblanca, 'Derecho de daños y Derecho internacional privado: algunas cuestiones sobre la legislación applicable y la Propuesta de Reglamento "Roma II"' (2005) 1 InDret 2, 11.

5. REDUCTION OF POLLUTION AND PRIVATE INTERNATIONAL LAW

5.1. ENVIRONMENTAL SUSTAINABILITY

Finally, the last cluster of the SDG 3 that can interact with private international law is the topic of pollution reduction and environmental sustainability.

The 1972 UN Stockholm Conference on the Human Environment established the right to a healthy environment and, since then, the social concerns relating ecological threats have increased. Environmental pollution has a health cost and, according to the 1978 UN Report of the World Commission on Environment and Development, 'when urban air quality deteriorates, the poor, in their more vulnerable areas, suffer more health damage than the rich, who usually live in more pristine neighbourhoods. In fact, the Climate Change 2014 Synthesis Report projects that climate change is expected to increase diseases, especially in low-income, developing countries, and to aggravate pre-existing health problems,[87] because there is a relationship between human health and the quality of the environment. Globally, wealthier nations are better placed financially and technologically to cope with the effects of possible climatic change'.[88] Environmental sustainability is not only about maintaining the diversity and quality of the world's ecosystems, but also about maintaining human life and human health.[89] The 1992 Rio de Janeiro United Nations Framework Convention on Climate Change and the 2015 Paris Agreement recognise that taking action against climate change is a way of promoting human health and sustainable development.[90] This dependence of human health and environmental factors on the reduction of pollution and a healthy environment is also recognised by the 1989 European Charter on Environment and Health of the World Health Organization. Consequently, the pollution prevention approach is an essential element of sustainability and of the right to health.

---

87 Rajendra K Pachauri and Leo Meyer (eds), *Climate Change 2014: Synthesis Report. Contribution of Working Groups I, II and III to the Fifth Assessment Report of the Intergovernmental Panel on Climate Change* (IPCC 2014) 15, 69 <https://www.ipcc.ch/site/assets/uploads/2018/02/SYR_AR5_FINAL_full.pdf> accessed 20 November 2020.

88 United Nations, *Report of the World Commission on Environment and Development: Our Common Future* <https://sustainabledevelopment.un.org/content/documents/5987our-common-future.pdf> accessed on 20 November 2020.

89 Boubaker Elleuch, Farah Bouhamed, Mabrouk Elloussaief and Madi Jaghbir, 'Environmental sustainability and pollution prevention' (2018) 25 Environmental Science and Pollution Research 18223, 18223.

90 United Nations, *Report of the Conference of the Parties on its twenty-first session, held in Paris from 30 November to 13 December 2015*, UN Doc FCCC/CP/2015/10 (29 January 2016) 15 <https://unfccc.int/resource/docs/2015/cop21/eng/10.pdf> accessed on 20 November 2020.

Pollution produces serious environmental and health impacts. Besides public policies to reduce pollution, promote the development of energy efficiency and clean sources of energy, and reduce the emissions of health-damaging air pollutants, among others, it is important that states develop a policy of environmental damage liability, on one hand to oblige the polluter to pay compensation for damage caused by harmful environmental activities, giving satisfaction to the victim that sustained the damage, and on the other hand to achieve the objective of reducing pollution by increasing the pattern of care in some potential polluting activities.

5.2. ENVIRONMENTAL LIABILITY

The liability arising from environmental pollution is multi-layered, since from environmental pollution can result different types of damage, from damage of a predominantly economic nature, to physical damage. At the same time, damage to the environment can easily end up being of an international nature. Industrial accidents or inadequate rules or carelessness when carrying out dangerous activities can pollute water, air and even land located in other countries, affecting a large number of people simultaneously, located in the same or in different states. One illustrative example is the *Land Oberösterreich against ČEZ as* case decided by the ECJ.[91] The Land Oberösterreich owned agricultural land that was located in Austria, 60 km from the Tremelin nuclear power plant, which was located in the Czech Republic and operated by the Czech company ČEZ. The Land Oberösterreich requested that ČEZ be ordered to put an end to the effects resulting from ionising radiation released by the nuclear power plant, because the levels of radiation were higher than what would result from the normal operation of a nuclear power plant. Another example is the *Handelskwekerij GJ Bier BV v Mines de Potasse d'Alsace SA* case,[92] where a group of Dutch horticulturists made a claim against a company based in France, which was accused of polluting the waters of the Rhine river with certain substances that caused damage to crops and obliged the claimants to incur additional expenses to mitigate the effects of these substances. The polluting discharges were carried out in France and the harmful results occurred in the Netherlands. Consequently, the harmful event was disconnected in space: the event occurred in France and the damage in the Netherlands. In fact, looking back over history, there are a large number of examples of accidents with catastrophic environmental effects that produced

91 Case C-343/04 *Land Oberösterreich v ČEZ as* [2006] ECLI:EU:C:2006:330.

92 Case 21-76 *Handelskwekerij GJ Bier BV v Mines de potasse d'Alsace SA* [1976] ECLI:EU:C:1976:166.

massive damage with a large number of people affected, as in the Chernobyl case or in the Bhopal case.[93]

The wide reach that environmental damage can have, crossing country borders, has led states, at an international level, to promote uniform laws, which aim to provide a unified legal response, even in very limited areas, eliminating the phenomenon of environmental dumping. This is the case of the International Convention on Civil Liability for Oil Pollution Damage of 29 September 1969, which came into force in 1975, with Protocols in 1976, 1984, 1992 and amendments in 2000; the Convention on Third Party Liability in the Field of Nuclear Energy of 29 July 1960, which entered into force on 1 April 1988, amended by a Protocol in 1964 and another in 1982; the 1997 Vienna Convention on Civil Liability for Nuclear Damage and the 1997 Convention on Supplementary Compensation for Nuclear Damage; and the Convention on Civil Liability for Damage Caused during Carriage of Dangerous Goods by Road, Rail and Inland Navigation Vessels of 10 October 1989. However, the uniformity just described only exists in specific sectors.

Therefore, in other fields, private international law may assist in the search for compensation for damage caused by harmful environmental activities, but can also play a role in deterrence and in increasing the patterns of care, with positive impacts on the reduction of pollution and on human health. The above-mentioned case law of the CJEU on conflict of jurisdictions offers an example, where the CJEU interpreted the legal provision on applicable jurisdiction in such a way that it facilitated environmental claims.[94] Another example may be found in the EU's Rome II Regulation, which has a conflict-of-law rule applicable to environmental damage, namely Article 7. As stated in the Rome II Regulation proposal, 'the point is not only to respect the victim's legitimate interests but also to establish a legislative policy that contributes to raising the general level of environmental protection, especially as the author of the environmental damage, unlike other torts or delicts, generally derives an economic benefit from his harmful activity'.[95] This is an example of a private

93 On this type of industrial accidents with mass damages, see AAVV, *La práctica internacional en matéria de responsabilidad por accidentes industriales catastróficos*, José Juste Ruiz and Tullio Scovazzi (eds) (Tirant lo Blanch 2005); Tito Ballarino, 'Questions de droit international privé et dommages catastrophiques' (1990-I) 220 Recueil des Cours de l'Academie de Droit International 200, 328 et seq; Christian von Bar, 'Environmental damage in private international law' (1997) 268 Recueil des Cours de l'Academie de Droit International 291, 303–304; Francisco Javier Zamora Cabot, 'Accidentes en massa y "forum non conveniens": el caso Bhopal' in Carlos Jiménez Piernas (ed), *La responsabilidad internacional, Aspectos de derecho internacional público y derecho internacional privado* (Édición Alicante 1990) 533, 533–564.

94 Case C-343/04 *Land Oberösterreich v ČEZ as* [2006] ECLI:EU:C:2006:330; Case 21-76 *Handelskwekerij GJ Bier BV v Mines de potasse d'Alsace SA* [1976] ECLI:EU:C:1976:166.

95 European Commission, *Proposal for a Regulation of the European Parliament and the Council on the law applicable to non-contractual obligations (Rome II)*, COM(2003) 427 final, 19.

international law conflict-of-law rule at the service of achieving environmental sustainability. What is at stake is not only the victim's legitimate interests, but also the interests of environmental legislative policy, which includes the 'polluter pays' principle as a fundamental standard,[96] compensation for damage, prevention of environmental damage, and the weighing of the benefits obtained by the tortfeasor.

6. RESULTS

The challenge of this study was to establish the relationship between private international law and SDG 3. As a result, several intersections were explored as regards health issues, family planning, traffic accidents and reduction of pollution. All of these intersections show that private international law is present in several areas of daily life and can be an instrument to achieve the 13 targets of SDG 3 and the protection of human rights that is associated with it.

At the intersection between private international law and health issues, it was explored how telemedicine and e-health platforms and applications with transnational features can contribute to universal health coverage and to improving healthcare in the poorest countries. However, they also pose legal challenges for private international law, like the nature of the contract concluded when patients make a medical appointment using ICT tools like the internet, telephone or SMS; whether it is a consumer contract; and the mechanisms in place to protect the weaker party in the contract, for example in the case of choice-of-court agreements, choice-of-law clauses, unfair terms and general contractual terms. Non-contractual obligations can also arise as a result of a tort/delict resulting from medical malpractice when using ICT, as well as private international law questions resulting from the international insurance contracts, covering risks resulting from these activities. In addition the answers given by national laws, the laws of integrated regional areas and international conventions, arbitration was presented as way of resolving international disputes related to e-health platforms and apps. Additionally, telemedicine, e-health platforms and applications pose problems of data protection, specifically for personal data concerning health and the international transfer of data, which is also relevant in research concerning health. Although these are activities that bring universal benefits, for both developing and developed countries, the transfer of personal data between countries is faced with the challenge that some states adopt a stricter

96 The 'polluter pays' principle is one of the pillars of international environmental liability and of the European Union law, as result of Art 191 of the Treaty on the Functioning of the European Union.

policy of data protection and create higher barriers to the international transfer of personal data to countries that do not have similar standards. However, the United Nations recommends that sensitive data, like health data, should have stricter standards of data protection. The increase of the standards of personal data can be achieved, failing international harmonisation of the legal framework regarding data protection, through the effects of the regulatory spill-over of the data protection law of states that have stricter standards of protection, including or through conflict-of-law rules designed to produce that effect.

The second cluster identified in SDG 3 that interacts with private international law is family planning, which includes universal access to healthcare and the right to enjoy the benefits of scientific progress and its applications. The diversity in states' regulation of access to medically assisted procreation techniques creates reproductive tourism, where people travel to another country to gain access to other reproductive techniques that are not available in their country of habitual residence. As regards international surrogacy in particular, reproductive tourism poses difficult human rights challenges. Ultimately, those challenges can only be overcome through the development of a broad consensus among states, which results from international instruments, such as the work being done on surrogacy from a private international law perspective in the context of the Hague Conference.

Another link identified between SDG 3 and private international law was in the domain of the reduction of traffic accidents. The automobile industry is currently progressively developing safe, secure and sustainable mobility for all, with the aim of reducing traffic fatalities and air pollutants, with positive impacts for health. Consumer awareness of sustainable development products in developed countries may give rise to low liability law shopping by the producer. This is a phenomenon in which states with a low degree of consumer protection in terms of producer responsibility are targeted for testing or selling products that are not safe or not entirely safe. In these situations, mass damage can easily arise, and private international law rules on product liability gain renewed importance in avoiding attempts to profit from the phenomenon of low liability law shopping.

The last cluster of the SDG 3 that can interact with private international law is the topic of pollution reduction and environmental sustainability. Pollution produces serious environmental and health impacts. As the environmental damage can easily have cross-border effects, private international law instruments concerning environmental liability can be used to achieve environmental sustainability. They can work in favour of the victim to obtain compensation for damages, and they can also be a tool to enforce options of environmental legislative policy, like the 'polluter pays' principle and the deterrence of environmental infringement behaviour.

Looking at the several matters explored, it is possible to conclude that private international law can be an instrument to achieve SDG 3, the right to enjoy economic, social, cultural and political development and, consequently, can be used as a strategy to promote a modern vision of human rights. In addition, this chapter also shows the challenges that lie ahead for private international law, in its role as a mechanism to achieve SDG3, and the need to develop new solutions.

SDG 4: QUALITY EDUCATION

Klaus D. Beiter

Goal 4: Ensure inclusive and equitable quality education and promote lifelong learning opportunities for all

4.1 By 2030, ensure that all girls and boys complete free, equitable and quality primary and secondary education leading to relevant and effective learning outcomes

4.2 By 2030, ensure that all girls and boys have access to quality early childhood development, care and pre-primary education so that they are ready for primary education

4.3 By 2030, ensure equal access for all women and men to affordable and quality technical, vocational and tertiary education, including university

4.4 By 2030, substantially increase the number of youth and adults who have relevant skills, including technical and vocational skills, for employment, decent jobs and entrepreneurship

4.5 By 2030, eliminate gender disparities in education and ensure equal access to all levels of education and vocational training for the vulnerable, including persons with disabilities, indigenous peoples and children in vulnerable situations

4.6 By 2030, ensure that all youth and a substantial proportion of adults, both men and women, achieve literacy and numeracy

4.7 By 2030, ensure that all learners acquire the knowledge and skills needed to promote sustainable development, including, among others, through education for sustainable development and sustainable lifestyles, human rights, gender equality, promotion of a culture of peace and non-violence, global citizenship and appreciation of cultural diversity and of culture's contribution to sustainable development

4.a Build and upgrade education facilities that are child, disability and gender sensitive and provide safe, non-violent, inclusive and effective learning environments for all

4.b By 2020, substantially expand globally the number of scholarships available to developing countries, in particular least developed countries, small island developing States and African countries, for enrolment in higher education, including vocational training and information and communications technology, technical, engineering and scientific programmes, in developed countries and other developing countries

4.c By 2030, substantially increase the supply of qualified teachers, including through international cooperation for teacher training in developing countries, especially least developed countries and small island developing States

1. INTRODUCTION: 'THE PRIVATE IS POLITICAL'

'The private is political' was the famous slogan of the student and feminist movements in the 1960s to query paternalism, sexism and oppression in private relations, especially within the traditional family. Its essential claim was that private relations are not a mere reflection of autonomous consensus, but frequently reproduce deeper social and political inequality. Accordingly, the slogan called for a political discourse on the 'private', to lay bare and address systemic injustice. Perhaps the slogan also has relevance in an analysis of current private international law, here in its application to the sphere of education. Perhaps private international law in this, as in other spheres, is not a mere neutral framework that allows for the fair resolution of transnational disputes between private actors. Specifically adopting a North–South perspective, private international law, in its current configuration, might disadvantage 'weaker' stakeholders in education – ministries of education, public educational institutions, students, parents or teachers – in poor countries, and favour 'stronger' stakeholders – education providers, edu-businesses, contractors and funders – with their principal places of business in rich countries.

International human rights law (IHRL) protects the right to education, for example in Articles 13 and 14 of the International Covenant on Economic, Social and Cultural Rights (ICESCR)[1] or Articles 28 and 29 of the Convention on the Rights of the Child (CRC).[2] These provisions require the regulation of education in terms of public law to enable the state to ultimately execute its educational mandate. However, private law also has a role to play in this sphere, namely whenever stakeholders in education interact on the basis of horizontal equality. Yet there has been a rapid expansion of the private education sector. The literature observes a general 'privatisation of education' taking place[3] and warns of the dangers entailed by the emergence of a 'global education industry'.[4] There has been, for example, a proliferation of private education providers, both commercial and non-commercial, in many countries. In consequence, ever more disputes in the sphere of education are subject to private law. Moreover, we live in times of globalisation. Services, including education services, are increasingly traded across borders. The WTO's General Agreement on Trade in Services (GATS) and other free trade agreements create the necessary international legal framework for this to happen. Multinational companies, such as Bridge International Academies, operate 'low-cost' private schools in countries of the developing world. Privatisation linked to globalisation means that ever more disputes in the sphere of education will have to refer to the rules of private international law.

This chapter addresses two situations. Firstly, it looks at 'typical' private law actions brought against the branch or subsidiary of a foreign private actor offering education services in a certain country (or the foreign actor itself, where services are being rendered cross-border). There could thus be a contractual or delictual claim raised by a student, parent or teacher against a school, or a claim by a government against an edu-business (but also vice versa) in the context of a public–private partnership (PPP). It should not be possible in these cases to

---

1 International Covenant on Economic, Social and Cultural Rights, 16 December 1966 (entered into force 3 January 1976) 993 UNTS 3 (ICESCR), Arts 13, 14.

2 Convention on the Rights of the Child, 20 November 1989 (entered into force 2 September 1990) 1577 UNTS 3, Arts 28, 29.

3 See Antoni Verger, Clara Fontdevila and Adrián Zancajo, *The Privatization of Education: A Political Economy of Global Education Reform* (Teachers College Press 2016).

4 See Antoni Verger, Christopher Lubienski and Gita Steiner-Khamsi (eds), *World Yearbook of Education 2016: The Global Education Industry* (Routledge 2016) or Marcelo Parreira do Amaral, Gita Steiner-Khamsi and Christiane Thompson (eds), *Researching the Global Education Industry: Commodification, the Market and Business Involvement* (Palgrave Macmillan 2019).

avoid the protective effect of minimum education standards (MES) that must regulate private actors in education, even if they are only background norms to a dispute. The avoidance of MES might thus flow from strategic choice-of-jurisdiction or -law clauses permitted by a state's law, or the reluctance or failure of a state, or its courts, to adequately rely on the private international law concepts of overriding mandatory rules or *ordre public* and to link these to MES (if formulated whatsoever). Failures – as resulting from lack of expertise, infrastructure and resources – are particularly prevalent in developing countries as the host states of foreign private actors in education.

Secondly – as the focus of the chapter – the possibility of bringing a private law action against the controlling company of an edu-business, whose subsidiary in another (especially developing) country is responsible for infringing rights in education in a more systematic manner there, in the home state of the controlling company, is examined. Traditionally, this is rather difficult. The motive here would be to target the controlling company for its own failings with regard to the activities of its subsidiaries, failings of a subsidiary that may be ascribed or imputed to it, or failings thereof to which it contributed. This can be described as an instance of 'transnational human rights litigation', this term including also 'human rights' litigation grounded in, for instance, contract or delict. Its purpose is to vindicate education as a human right. It may secure access to a sophisticated system of courts and law, achieve 'tangible' and symbolic justice, and facilitate effective enforcement. The discussion takes place in the context of the growing problem of multinational 'low-cost' private schools mushrooming in developing countries, undermining the right to education there in many ways. The case of Bridge International Academies will serve as a case in point to help structure the discussion.

SDG 4 deals with education and lifelong learning. Via its link to the right to education, SDG 4 potentially offers an opportunity to propel the development of private international law in such a way as to mend the deficiencies identified in this chapter and to achieve a greater balance in private international law in the education context. The central device employed to connect private international law to human rights will be 'the duty to protect', requiring states to protect individuals *against private actors*, the duty covering domestic and extraterritorial obligations. The focus will essentially be on commercial actors.

2. SDG 4: INCLUSIVE AND EQUITABLE QUALITY EDUCATION

SDG 4 constitutes the third global commitment of its kind to deal with lack of adequate access to education in many countries of the world. The first undertaking was that of Jomtien of 1990, calling for 'basic' education for all and laying the basis of the Education for All (EFA) movement.[5] This was followed, in 2000, by the undertaking of Dakar, complemented by Goal 2 of the UN's Millennium Development Goals (MDGs). Both notably sought the achievement of universal primary education by 2015.[6] SDG 4, envisaging 'inclusive and equitable quality education' and 'lifelong learning opportunities for all' by 2030, is much broader in scope.

In comparison with MDG 2, the formulation of SDG 4 reveals a number of advances from a human rights perspective. While MDG 2 focused solely on the completion of primary education, SDG 4 also envisages the completion of secondary education. This is in accordance with Article 13(2) of the ICESCR, which, apart from requiring primary education to be 'compulsory' and 'available free to all', also obliges states parties to make secondary education 'generally available' and 'accessible to all'.[7] This should be read in conjunction with the ILO's Minimum Age Convention of 1973, which provides for the minimum age for admission to employment to be aligned with compulsory schooling, stipulating a minimum age of not less than 15 years.[8] Hence, compulsory education that is available free to all should also constitute a priority beyond (the six years of) primary education.

Unlike MDG 2, SDG 4 expressly calls for access to early childhood care and pre-primary education to be ensured for all. Although international human rights treaties do not as a rule expressly refer to such care and education, the interpretative materials of the various human rights treaty bodies make it clear that they do form part of the right to education. The Committee on Economic, Social and Cultural Rights (CESCR), the body of independent experts supervising implementation of the ICESCR, for example, has in the past expressed concern if in a state party there is limited availability of preschool education.[9] In the literature it is also stated that 'it is important to recognise the relevance of Early Childhood Care and Education (ECCE) to the achievement of many of the ... SDGs'.[10]

---

5 World Conference on Education for All, World Declaration on Education for All and Framework for Action to Meet Basic Learning Needs, 5–9 March 1990, Jomtien, Thailand.

6 World Education Forum, Dakar Framework for Action, 26–28 April 2000, Dakar, Senegal, para 7(ii); General Assembly Resolution 55/2, United Nations Millennium Declaration, 18 September 2000, para 19, point 2.

7 International Covenant on Economic, Social and Cultural Rights, 16 December 1966 (entered into force 3 January 1976) 993 UNTS 3 (ICESCR), Art 13(2)(a), (b), respectively.

8 Convention concerning Minimum Age for Admission to Employment, 26 June 1973, ILO Convention No 138 (entered into force 19 June 1976) 1015 UNTS 297, Art 2(3).

9 UN Committee on Economic, Social and Cultural Rights (CESCR), Concluding Observations: Mexico, UN Doc E/C.12/MEX/CO/5-6 (17 April 2018), paras 65(c), 66(c).

10 John Siraj-Blatchford, 'Preface' in John Siraj-Blatchford, Cathy Mogharreban and Eunhye Park (eds), *International Research on Education for Sustainable Development in Early Childhood* (Springer 2016) v.

Similarly, unlike MDG 2, SDG 4 clearly underlines the importance of equal access for all to 'affordable' technical and vocational education and training (TVET) and tertiary education. This approximates requirements under the ICESCR to the effect that TVET and higher education be made 'accessible', in the case of higher education 'equally' on the basis of an individual's 'capacity'. The ICESCR imposes a stricter requirement of *progressively free* education, however.[11] As is often said today, higher education must be the 'engine of development' in the global knowledge society. In the context of the SDGs, there often is a special recognition of 'the responsibility that the higher education community bears in the international pursuit of sustainable development'.[12]

SDG 4 gives greater attention to considerations of equality. While MDG 2 did refer to gender parity, the overall approach of the MDGs was quantitative in nature, which could conceal the persistence of discrimination. The SDGs are permeated by the appreciation that, in fulfilling the goals, 'no person should be left behind'. SDG 4 thus mentions various typically marginalised groups that should enjoy equal access or treatment: girls and women, persons with disabilities, indigenous persons and children in vulnerable situations. There is a reference to 'inclusive' learning environments, which provides a link to a concept of substantive equality, in accordance with the demands of international human rights treaties, such as the UNESCO Convention against Discrimination in Education of 1960, requiring 'static' or systemic discrimination to be addressed effectively.[13]

Finally, unlike MDG 2, SDG 4 expressly envisages 'quality' ECCE, primary education, secondary education, TVET and higher education. The CESCR has emphasised quality education as an aspect of the right to education. Education must be 'acceptable (e.g. relevant, culturally appropriate and of good quality)'.[14] Correlating with this demand, SDG 4 mentions 'relevant' skills for employment, 'safe, non-violent, inclusive and effective' learning environments, or the supply of 'qualified' teachers. Corresponding to the educational aims prescribed by the ICESCR,[15] SDG 4 stresses the importance of 'education for sustainable

---

11 International Covenant on Economic, Social and Cultural Rights, 16 December 1966 (entered into force 3 January 1976) 993 UNTS 3 (ICESCR), Art 13(2)(b), (c) (secondary and higher education to be made progressively free).

12 International Conference on Higher Education for Sustainable Development, Nagoya Declaration on Higher Education for Sustainable Development, 9 November 2014, Nagoya, Japan, para 2.

13 (UNESCO) Convention against Discrimination in Education, 14 December 1960 (entered into force 22 May 1962) 429 UNTS 93, Art 4 ('equality of opportunity and of treatment in the matter of education').

14 CESCR, General Comment No 13: The Right to Education (Art 13 of the ICESCR), UN Doc E/C.12/1999/10 (8 December 1999), para 6(c).

15 International Covenant on Economic, Social and Cultural Rights, 16 December 1966 (entered into force 3 January 1976) 993 UNTS 3 (ICESCR), Art 13(1).

development' (ESD), as well as the furtherance of values related to human rights, gender equality, peace, global citizenship, cultural diversity, etc. Regarding ESD, this may perhaps be said to have two facets. On the one hand, it is an integral part of the right to quality education. On the other, ESD is 'an enabler of sustainable development', facilitating attainment of most other SDGs.[16] This aspect had in principle already been identified in the UN's famous Brundtland Report of 1987, which explained that education 'can enhance a society's ability to overcome poverty, increase incomes, improve health and nutrition, and reduce family size',[17] thus including issues now covered by the SDGs.

SDG 4 has been concretised by the Incheon Declaration and Framework for Action, adopted at the World Education Forum, held at Incheon, Republic of Korea in May 2015. Additionally, the implementation architecture of SDG 4 comprises a Steering Committee, periodic Global Education Meetings, and the annual, independent 'Global Education Monitoring Report'. The Steering Committee represents states, UN agencies (including UNESCO, UNICEF, the UNDP, the ILO and the World Bank), the OECD, the Global Partnership for Education, civil society and the teaching profession. UNESCO coordinates the SDG 4 process.

3. ROLES FOR PRIVATE LAW AND PRIVATE INTERNATIONAL LAW IN THE SPHERE OF EDUCATION

3.1. PRIVATE LAW IN EDUCATION

In 1954, the Supreme Court of the United States, in the landmark case of *Brown v Board of Education of Topeka*, remarked that, to ensure the crucial opportunity of education was not denied to any child, education 'is perhaps the most important function of state and local governments'.[18] This reflects the traditional vision of the state as prime provider of education. Going hand in hand with this vision, public law constitutes the main instrument for regulating education. Nevertheless, private education is also a feature of education systems. IHLR explicitly protects 'the liberty of individuals and bodies to establish and

16 See UNESCO World Conference on Education for Sustainable Development, Aichi-Nagoya Declaration on Education for Sustainable Development, 10–12 November 2014, Aichi-Nagoya, Japan, para 6 (referring to both these facets).

17 World Commission on Environment and Development, Report: 'Our Common Future', UN Doc A/42/427 (4 August 1987), ch 4, para 61.

18 *Brown et al v Board of Education of Topeka et al*, 347 U.S. 483, 493 (1954).

direct educational institutions'[19] and 'the liberty of parents … to choose for their children schools, other than those established by the public authorities'.[20] These liberties are subject to the proviso that MES, which states *must* lay down, be complied with, and further that the aims of education postulated by IHRL, notably 'the full development of the human personality', be observed by private educational institutions.[21] Private law plays an important role in regulating legal relations in the sphere of private education, as private actors 'contract' with each other. Yet private law is also relevant in public education, and public law in private education. Ultimately, whether a certain relationship qualifies as one of private or public law will often be answered differently by different legal systems. In many ways, 'the public' and 'the private' in education are 'historical and cultural constructs'.[22]

Where would one typically encounter private law in education? Let us consider two instances. The first relates to tort law. Private law may offer a delictual claim of compensation for patrimonial damage, solace for pain and suffering, or satisfaction for intentional infringement of personality rights, suffered by a student and caused by a school's or a specific teacher's conduct (even in the public school context). Where caused by a specific teacher, the school (or state) would often be liable vicariously. It is this possibility of bringing a delictual action for damages against an educational institution that holds substantial potential for bringing a private law claim against not only, but notably, a *private* actor in education, seeking redress for human rights violations committed by the latter.

The second instance relates to contract law. The legal relationship between student and educational institution could be regulated by a contract. The same is true for the employment relationship between teacher and educational institution. While contracts in both instances are generally concluded in the sphere of private education, they are increasingly (construed to have been) concluded in the sphere of public education as well. This concerns specifically, but not only, the university context. Contract law further plays an important role in the life of students (apprenticeship-TVET contracts with private employers, study loan contracts with financial institutions, transport or rental (accommodation) agreements, etc.). Similarly, schools and universities conclude contracts on a regular basis (maintenance of premises, technical support, provision of office supplies, construction work, consultancy services, etc.).

---

19 International Covenant on Economic, Social and Cultural Rights, 16 December 1966 (entered into force 3 January 1976) 993 UNTS 3 (ICESCR), Art 13(4).

20 ibid Art 13(3).

21 ibid Art 13(1), (3) and (4). On the compulsory nature of the requirement to lay down MES in these provisions, see CESCR, General Comment No 13: The Right to Education (Art 13 of the ICESCR), UN Doc E/C.12/1999/10 (8 December 1999), para 54.

22 Susan L Robertson et al, 'An Introduction to Public Private Partnerships and Education Governance' in Susan L Robertson et al (eds), *Public Private Partnerships in Education: New Actors and Modes of Governance in a Globalizing World* (Edward Elgar 2012) 4.

3.2. THE PRIVATISATION OF EDUCATION

An extensive privatisation of education has taken and is continuing to take place. Privatisation in education could neutrally be described as involving 'a transfer of assets, management, functions or responsibilities previously owned or carried out by the state to private actors'.[23] The problematic nature of such privatisation lies in the fact that it 'describes a direction of change',[24] an ongoing process entailing a continuous moving away from a division of responsibilities between 'the public' and 'the private' in education that would need to be retained for a society to remain able to guarantee free quality education to everyone. The problem lies in the sum total of acts of privatisation, structural or content-related, that ultimately jeopardise the education mission.

Privatisation in education may take various forms. Services may be contracted out. This may cover 'non-core' education services, such as maintenance of facilities, technical support or human resources functions, but also 'core' education services.[25] Hence, course design or exam paper preparation and marking could be assigned to a private company. Especially universities are eager these days to 'unbundle' academic responsibilities and outsource them to 'part-time staff'.[26] Expertise previously provided from within government departments is now provided by consultancy firms. Accountability pressures (e.g. good PISA results) entail increased reliance on consultancy services, which tend to focus on short-term solutions.[27] Whereas government departments used to play a seminal role in the development or supply of educational materials, and in securing the provision of computer equipment, educational institutions will now engage more directly with large education corporations (e.g. Pearson) and ICT companies (e.g. Microsoft), which have assumed key roles in this context. Having created long-term dependencies, facilitated by overall 'digitisation' (products being let rather than sold), these firms are not mere 'suppliers' anymore, but exercise a perpetual powerful influence on education.[28] Public schools may also contract

23 Fons Coomans and Antenor Hallo de Wolf, 'Privatisation of Education and the Right to Education' in Koen de Feyter and Felipe Gómez Isa (eds), *Privatisation and Human Rights in the Age of Globalisation* (Intersentia 2005) 241.

24 Paul Starr, 'The Meaning of Privatization' (1988) 6 Yale Law & Policy Review 6, 13.

25 Stephen J Ball and Deborah Youdell, 'Hidden Privatisation in Public Education' (Report by Education International 2008) 27.

26 See e.g. Susan Robertson and Janja Komljenovic, 'Unbundling the University and Making Higher Education Markets' in Antoni Verger, Christopher Lubienski and Gita Steiner-Khamsi (eds), *World Yearbook of Education 2016: The Global Education Industry* (Routledge 2016).

27 Antoni Verger, Christopher Lubienski and Gita Steiner-Khamsi, 'The Emergence and Structuring of the Global Education Industry: Towards an Analytical Framework' in Antoni Verger, Christopher Lubienski and Gita Steiner-Khamsi (eds), *World Yearbook of Education 2016: The Global Education Industry* (Routledge 2016) 10.

28 Similarly, see Stephen J Ball and Deborah Youdell, 'Hidden Privatisation in Public Education' (Report by Education International 2008) 28.

out the management of an institution in its entirety. Educational management organisations, such as EdisonLearning Inc. operating in the UK and the US, are for-profit entities that specialise in managing schools.[29] As any of the private actors assuming what used to be public responsibilities in the sphere of education may be – and increasingly are – foreign private actors, the potential role of private international law becomes readily apparent.

However, privatisation of education, insofar as it may implicate private international law, should be understood to also cover the following phenomena:

- To the extent that education as an essential public service is systemically provided by private providers, this is indicative of privatisation. The expert Guiding Principles on the Human Rights Obligations of States to Provide Public Education and to Regulate Private Involvement in Education (Abidjan Principles) of 2019 reiterate the position of IHRL, in terms of which private educational institutions may not 'supplant or replace' public education, but only 'supplement' it.[30] The extensive provision of 'low-cost' private education in especially developing countries by (often global) chains of for-profit schools (e.g. Bridge International Academies) must, therefore, be considered a privatisation of education.
- Privatisation must also be held to cover the situation of public educational institutions adopting the methods and practices of business. Line and performance management are becoming accepted methods of running an educational institution such as a university. Students in universities are seen as consumers of an education product that is sold – and are granted legal claims under consumer law. Public universities increasingly seek to enter foreign higher education markets.
- Finally, PPPs have become a notable feature of education systems. In a stricter sense, these are partnerships based on a contract between a government and one or more (increasingly also foreign) private actors, with the government laying down regulatory standards and providing finance, and the private actor(s) supplying a service benefiting students. In a wider sense, PPPs also encompass less formalised 'joint initiatives between private, philanthropic and public sector actors aimed at achieving the public good'.[31] PPPs entail obvious benefits for business and, it is said, also for government, which benefits from 'risk sharing' and the delivery of a 'good' product.

---

29 See Fons Coomans and Antenor Hallo de Wolf, 'Privatisation of Education and the Right to Education' in Koen de Feyter and Felipe Gómez Isa (eds), *Privatisation and Human Rights in the Age of Globalisation* (Intersentia 2005) 248–249.

30 Guiding Principles on the Human Rights Obligations of States to Provide Public Education and to Regulate Private Involvement in Education, 13 February 2019, Abidjan, Côte d'Ivoire (Abidjan Principles), Guiding Principle 48a.

31 See Susan L Robertson et al, 'An Introduction to Public Private Partnerships and Education Governance' in Susan L Robertson et al (eds), *Public Private Partnerships in Education: New*

The privatisation of education is closely related to its liberalisation, globalisation and digitisation. The *liberalisation* of education is a product of the GATS. The GATS has been described as a 'game changer' for education, transforming education 'as largely a nationally-located and governed public service, into a globally regulated tradeable economic commodity'.[32] The *globalisation* of education follows from the combined efforts of neoliberally inclined intergovernmental, state and private actors advancing largely standardised solutions to the world's education problems and proffering the global education industry as being able to help solve most of these problems. Since 2015, for instance, the OECD has been convening Global Education Industry Summits to this end. The *digitisation* of education refers to the increased use of ICT and 'edu-tech' in administering education and delivering it, including across borders. Liberalisation, globalisation and digitisation are processes that mutually reinforce each other.

3.3. 'GOOD' PRIVATE EDUCATION AND 'BAD' PRIVATISATION OF EDUCATION

Private education does fulfil a useful function. Notably not-for-profit private educational institutions may cater to linguistic or cultural minorities, marginalised religious groups, or gifted or disadvantaged students, who may be better served by interest groups fully understanding the special educational needs of those groups. Private educational institutions further often offer 'alternative' educational approaches, thereby strengthening freedom in education.[33] However, privatisation in education is of a different calibre. As a fundamental tenet of neoliberalism, extending provision by the market is supposed to lead to better quality, enhanced efficiency and increased choice.[34] Research, however, bears out that, if social disadvantagement is accounted for, private education does

---

Actors and Modes of Governance in a Globalizing World (Edward Elgar 2012) 6–7 (PPPs in a stricter and wider sense).

32 Antoni Verger and Susan L Robertson, 'The GATS Game-Changer: International Trade Regulation and the Constitution of a Global Education Marketplace' in Susan L Robertson et al (eds), *Public Private Partnerships in Education: New Actors and Modes of Governance in a Globalizing World* (Edward Elgar 2012) 104.

33 See Klaus D Beiter, *The Protection of the Right to Education by International Law: Including a Systematic Analysis of Article 13 of the International Covenant on Economic, Social and Cultural Rights* (Martinus Nijhoff Publishers 2006) 146–147, 259–260, 311, 445, 450–453, 559–560, 561–567 (state to protect and fund private education benefiting specific, often vulnerable groups), 39–41, 537 (private education contributing to freedom in education).

34 See Right to Education Project, 'Privatisation of Education: Global Trends of Human Rights Impact' (2014) <https://www.right-to-education.org/es/resource/privatisation-education-global-trends-human-rights-impact> 18–22 ((supposed) positive impacts of privatisation); Laura Day Ashley et al, 'The Role and Impact of Private Schools in Developing Countries: A Rigorous Review of the Evidence' (University of Birmingham et al 2014) 50–52 ('conclusions' on these supposed advantages).

not perform better than public education.[35] Enhanced efficiency (lower costs) in private provision further often comes at a price in conflict with human rights – standardised syllabi and teaching methods, underpaid teachers, or a curriculum that focuses on narrow economically oriented knowledge and skills.[36] Moreover, choice through privatisation means choice only for those that can pay. Privatisation always entails fees, leading to the exclusion of the most vulnerable in society.[37]

Privatisation undermines education as a public good and human right. As a public good, education should not be subject to the logic of the market. Education as a public good requires the *regulation* of education ('ensuring its framework') to be the 'exclusive' responsibility of the state. Insofar as the *provision* and *funding* of education are concerned, the state must bear an 'important', most often the 'main', responsibility.[38] In its General Comment No 13, providing guidance with regard to the interpretation of Article 13 of the ICESCR, the CESCR highlights that, as a human right, education 'in all its forms and at all levels' must be available, accessible, acceptable and adaptable.[39] This can only be guaranteed, and is best accomplished, by the state. The CESCR thus underlines that 'Article 13 regards States as having principal responsibility for the direct provision of education in most circumstances'.[40] Private actors in education must comply with MES that states are obliged to lay down.[41]

4. 'TYPICAL' PRIVATE LAW ACTIONS AGAINST A FOREIGN PRIVATE ACTOR, OVERRIDING MANDATORY RULES AND *ORDRE PUBLIC*

Privatisation, linked to liberalisation, globalisation and digitisation, means that private international law will come to play an enhanced role as transnational

35 See e.g. Donald R Baum, 'The Effectiveness and Equity of Public-Private Partnerships in Education: A Quasi-Experimental Evaluation of 17 Countries' (2018) 26(105) Education Policy Analysis Archives.

36 Laura Day Ashley et al, 'The Role and Impact of Private Schools in Developing Countries: A Rigorous Review of the Evidence' (University of Birmingham et al 2014) 52 ('lower costs were often clearly related to lower teacher salaries').

37 ibid ('findings relating to improved equity and access were overwhelmingly negative').

38 Further developing Rita Locatelli, *Reframing Education as a Public and Common Good: Enhancing Democratic Governance* (Palgrave Macmillan 2019) 99–103. See also Guiding Principles on the Human Rights Obligations of States to Provide Public Education and to Regulate Private Involvement in Education, 13 February 2019, Abidjan, Côte d'Ivoire (Abidjan Principles), preamble ('State's role as educational guarantor').

39 CESCR, General Comment No 13: The Right to Education (Art 13 of the ICESCR), UN Doc E/C.12/1999/10 (8 December 1999), para 6.

40 ibid para 48.

41 ibid para 54.

private law disputes will increase, including in the field of education. Foreign private providers may offer education products locally, whether cross-border (including through online education), by opening a local branch or by registering a local subsidiary. 'Typical' private law actions could be brought against the branch or subsidiary of a foreign private actor offering education services in a certain country, or the foreign actor itself, where services are being rendered cross-border – all these actors conveniently termed 'foreign private actor/provider' in the next paragraph. It may be pointed out that what is a *public* school, university or teacher in one state, when not acting as a bearer of state authority in another state, is largely in the same position as a *private* actor in education in that state. Disputes in this context are, therefore, amenable to the rules of private international law too.

One could imagine the following types of claims arising. A *student* could bring a claim against a foreign private provider of education who has misrepresented that its qualifications are accredited by the host state, whereas in fact they are not. It could be claimed that the education offered suffers from quality deficits. Classes or learning materials may not live up to the standard necessary to enable students to pass qualifying exams set by the host state. A student could claim that disciplinary measures or expulsion (termination of contract) did not follow standard procedures, for example by not affording the opportunity to be heard. Similarly, action could be instituted by a *teacher*, who might query non-increases in salary, or salary cuts, justified by reference to allegedly tight budgets, an institutional decision that unfavourably impacts on benefits under a social insurance scheme, or narrow prescriptions as to the dispensation of teaching, which limit professional or academic freedom. Action could also be instituted by a *government* against a foreign private actor that has assumed contractual duties in the context of a PPP in the education sector. The government could thus claim that the construction of a school by a foreign private actor reveals quality deficits (e.g. no safe water and sanitation, inadequate lighting or ventilation in classrooms, or health or security hazards on premises). In all these cases, private law claims based on breach of contract or the commission of a delict are conceivable.

In the absence of any choice-of-jurisdiction or -law clause in a contract, if any of these disputes were to land before a local court – that is, a court of the host state in which the education service is being provided by the foreign private actor – that court would frequently, in accordance with 'its' private international law rules, accept jurisdiction to hear the matter and decide it in terms of the local law. This is the result of the transaction being so closely linked to the host state. This may be exemplified by reference to European Union law.

Under the Brussels I *bis* Regulation, if one were to consider a contract between a student and an educational institution a consumer contract, jurisdiction in contractual disputes would exist for the courts of both the state in which the student as consumer is domiciled and that where the other party to the contract is domiciled. A foreign private actor in education could, of course, register a local subsidiary. The (mere) presence of a branch, whose operations are implicated, can sometimes be construed as a domicile. Online education, it seems, will not be considered offered under a consumer contract just because the provider's website is accessible in a country, if the provider does not clearly direct its professional activities to that country. As for contracts of employment (with teachers), jurisdiction exists for the courts of both the state in which the employer is domiciled (again, a branch can sometimes mean domicile) and that where the employee habitually carries out the work. In all other cases (e.g. PPP agreements), the jurisdictional link would be provided by the defendant's domicile, the place where a branch is situated or that where services were (or should have been) provided. In delictual disputes, apart from the defendant's domicile or branch location, a jurisdictional link is provided by the place where the harmful event occurred, this covering the place where the harm is suffered. In most cases, therefore, the jurisdiction of the courts of the host state is confirmed.[42]

It may be noted that US courts, in inter-state disputes concerning a contract between a student residing in one state and an educational institution physically present in another, have held that the student's residence does not suffice to establish jurisdiction. In *Siskind v Villa Foundation for Educ., Inc.*, it was required that the educational institution affirmatively seek business in that state.[43] In the internet age, this has been held to mean that mere access to online teaching will not be enough. An educational institution must specifically target citizens of another state and then knowingly enter into an ongoing business relationship with them.[44]

Concerning the applicable law, under the Rome I Regulation, addressing contractual obligations, again, if one considers a contract between a student and an educational institution a consumer contract, then the law of the state in which the student has their habitual residence will govern the contract, if the service provider is professionally active in that state or directs such activities to that state. As for contracts of employment (with teachers), the law of the state in which the employee habitually carries out the work governs the contract. In all other cases, the law governing a contract for the provision of services is the law of the state in which the service provider has its habitual residence – unless the contract is 'manifestly more closely' connected with another state, in which case

---

42 Regulation (EU) No 1215/2012 of the European Parliament and of the Council of 12 December 2012 on jurisdiction and the recognition and enforcement of judgments in civil and commercial matters [2012] OJ L 351/1, Arts 4(1), 7(1)(a), (b), (2), (5), 17(1)(c), (2), 18(1), 20(1), (2), 21(1)(a), (b)(i).

43 *Siskind v Villa Foundation for Educ., Inc.* 642 S.W.2d 434 (1982).

44 *Marten v Godwin*, 499 F.3d 290 (3d Cir. 2007); *Watiti v Walden University*, 2008 U.S. Dist. LEXIS 43217 (D.N.J. May 30, 2008); *Kloth v Southern Christian University*, 320 F. App'x 113 (3d Cir. 2008).

the law of that state will govern the contract. Most frequently, therefore, the law of the host state is implicated.[45] Under the Rome II Regulation, in the case of a delict, the law of the state of the parties' common habitual residence at the time of damage, otherwise the law of the state in which the damage occurs – unless the delict is 'manifestly more closely' connected with another state, in which case the law of that state – is applicable, again ordinarily referring to the law of the host state.[46]

Any contract alluded to above could contain a choice-of-jurisdiction clause, referring a matter to the courts of the home state of a foreign private actor in education. Such clauses in contracts between students or teachers and an educational institution are highly suspicious.[47] It is ordinarily not realistic to expect students or teachers to bring a claim in the courts of any state other than that of their domicile. As Basedow holds, a 'contractual clause that attributes exclusive jurisdiction to a court ... is incompatible with the right of access to a court if that attribution leads to a denial of justice'.[48] This might well be the case in these instances. Similarly, choice-of-jurisdiction clauses, for example in PPP agreements in the education sector, may not result in the protective effect of MES of the host state being avoided.

What if, however, the private international law rules applied by the courts of the host state do actually refer to a foreign law, or if the contract with a private actor in education contains a choice-of-law clause to this effect? What is important in these cases – as in all private law actions brought by or against private actors in education decided by the local courts – is that MES that must regulate private actors in education be directly applied or relied on as background norms, as appropriate. As pointed out, Article 13(4) of the ICESCR grants the freedom to establish and operate private educational institutions subject to the requirement that such institutions conform to MES which states are obliged to lay down. Where does one find these MES recorded in international law?

---

45 Regulation (EC) No 593/2008 of the European Parliament and of the Council of 17 June 2008 on the law applicable to contractual obligations (Rome I) [2008] OJ L 177/6, Arts 4(1)(b), (3), 6(1), 8(2).

46 Regulation (EC) No 864/2007 of the European Parliament and of the Council of 11 July 2007 on the law applicable to non-contractual obligations (Rome II) [2007] OJ L 199/40, Art 4(1), (2), (3).

47 EU law, subject to limited exceptions, forbids choice-of-jurisdiction clauses that deny the consumer or employee access to the courts of the defendant's or their own domicile: see Regulation (EU) No 1215/2012 of the European Parliament and of the Council of 12 December 2012 on jurisdiction and the recognition and enforcement of judgments in civil and commercial matters [2012] OJ L 351/1, Arts 19, 23, respectively.

48 Institute of International Law, Commission No 4, Human Rights and Private International Law, Working Document of Rapporteur Jürgen Basedow, No 11 (September 2018), Draft Resolution, Art 10(1) <https://www.idi-iil.org/app/uploads/2019/06/Commission-4-Droits-de-lhomme-et-droit-international-prive-Basedow-Travaux-La-Haye-2019.pdf>.

The Abidjan Principles of 2019 emphasise that states must 'prioritis[e] … the provision of free, quality, *public* … education',[49] inter alia in their allocation of resources for education.[50] The Principles evidently connect to the Covenant's requirement of MES.[51] They require states to 'adopt[] and enforce[] … effective regulatory measures, to ensure the realisation of the right to education where private actors are involved in the provision of education'.[52] States must impose 'public service obligations' on private actors involved in education.[53] The Principles provide for a range of topics on which MES binding on private educational institutions should be adopted. There should thus be MES concerning the governance of private educational institutions (e.g. on the registration and licensing of institutions, levels of fees, or learners' certification). Standards should address the rights of learners. Issues to be covered are, inter alia, freedom of speech, non-discrimination, curricula, learning materials and teaching methods, due process, discipline, expulsion and learning environments. There must further be standards on minimum professional qualifications of teachers, their academic freedom and labour rights.[54]

MES may also be found elsewhere. Article 13(2)(e) of the ICESCR obliges states parties to 'continuously improve … the material conditions of teaching staff'. It is against the background of this provision that one must understand the adoption of the Recommendation concerning the Status of Teachers by UNESCO and the ILO in 1966[55] and the Recommendation concerning the Status of Higher-Education Teaching Personnel by UNESCO in 1997.[56] Both applicable to public and private educational institutions, they regulate matters such as terms and conditions of employment, salaries, social security, professional or academic freedom, and conditions for effective teaching and learning (class size, teaching aids, school buildings, etc.).

How does one secure the application of MES where the courts of the host state apply a foreign law? The essential instruments of private international law that may prove crucial in this regard are the concepts of overriding mandatory rules and *ordre public*. Overriding mandatory norms are norms of a legal system

---

49 Guiding Principles on the Human Rights Obligations of States to Provide Public Education and to Regulate Private Involvement in Education, 13 February 2019, Abidjan, Côte d'Ivoire (Abidjan Principles), Guiding Principle 17 (own emphasis).
50 ibid Guiding Principle 34.
51 ibid Overarching Principle 3 (alluding to Art 13(3) and (4) of the ICESCR).
52 ibid Guiding Principle 51.
53 ibid Guiding Principles 19, 52.
54 ibid Guiding Principle 55 mentions these aspects.
55 Special Intergovernmental Conference on the Status of Teachers, UNESCO/ILO Recommendation concerning the Status of Teachers, 5 October 1966, CFS.67/VII.4/A/F/S/R (1966).
56 UNESCO General Conference, Recommendation concerning the Status of Higher-Education Teaching Personnel, 11 November 1997, UNESCO Doc 29 C/Res 11 (1997).

that are so important that they must apply, that they cannot be derogated from by contract, irrespective of which law governs a dispute. Their importance is premised on their centrality to realising a state's political, economic and social goals or their clear purpose of protecting a weaker contracting party.[57] These days, it is submitted, these aims should include a state's ambition to comply with IHRL, including the right to education, to which SDG 4, in turn, is linked. *Ordre public* is a related, but more amorphous concept. It negatively signifies that a state will not apply a foreign law to the extent that it is repugnant to fundamental principles of that state. Some overriding mandatory norms could also be described as concretised *ordre public*. The concept of *ordre public* is usually restricted to 'more fundamental' principles, often necessitating concretisation on a case-by-case basis.[58] Yet again, *ordre public* should be linked to the right to education and SDG 4. Basedow proposes that, '[i]n assessing the compatibility of the law designated by the conflict of laws rules with rules of the *ordre public* and overriding mandatory laws (imperative norms), [a] court [would have to] take into account human rights which form part of the forum's *ordre public international*, notably the principle of non-discrimination'.[59] From the above it is clear that each state, notably also developing states, must adopt MES restricting private actors in education. They must further develop the concepts of overriding mandatory norms and *ordre public* as part of their private international law, and clearly link these to human rights, including the right to education, to ensure that MES cannot be avoided by reason of the application of a foreign law. These are duties accruing to both legislatures and courts. The SDG agenda and SDG 4 should be relied on to propel this development.

The underlying rationale for the above approach must be seen to lie in the state's duty to protect. States have obligations to *respect*, *protect* and *fulfil* human rights under international human rights treaties. With regard to the right to education in Article 13 of the ICESCR, the CESCR accordingly states:

> The obligation to *respect* requires States parties to avoid measures that hinder or prevent the enjoyment of the right to education. The obligation to *protect* requires States parties to take measures that prevent third parties from interfering with the enjoyment of the

57 See Kerstin Ann-Susann Schäfer, 'Application of Mandatory Rules in the Private International Law of Contracts: A Critical Analysis of Approaches in Selected Continental and Common Law Jurisdictions, with a View to the Development of South African Law' (doctoral thesis, University of Cape Town, 2002) <https://open.uct.ac.za/handle/11427/11036> 11–12, ch 3 ('Internationally Mandatory Rules'), ch 4 ('Internationally Mandatory Rules of the *lex fori*').

58 See ibid 85–92 (on *ordre public*).

59 Institute of International Law, Commission No 4, Human Rights and Private International Law, Working Document of Rapporteur Jürgen Basedow, No 11 (September 2018), Draft Resolution, Art 14(1) <https://www.idi-iil.org/app/uploads/2019/06/Commission-4-Droits-de-lhomme-et-droit-international-prive-Basedow-Travaux-La-Haye-2019.pdf>.

> right to education. The obligation to *fulfil (facilitate)* requires States to take positive measures that enable and assist individuals and communities to enjoy the right to education. Finally, States parties have an obligation to *fulfil (provide)* the right to education.[60]

It is the state's duty to protect the right to education that assumes central importance in a discussion of the role of private actors in education. The CESCR and the ComRC (the Committee on the Rights of the Child under the CRC) have in separate General Comments on the role of business operators emphasised the state's duty to protect. Citizens need to be protected against such operators by the state regulating their operations.[61] Whenever essentially public services, including education, are provided by private providers, the latter 'should … be subject to strict regulations that impose on them so-called "public service obligations"'.[62] The UN's Guiding Principles on Business and Human Rights (UNGPs) of 2011 similarly articulate the state's duty to provide protection against human rights abuse by business enterprises.[63] States must 'exercise adequate oversight' when they contract with, or legislate for, business enterprises to provide public services.[64] The August 2020 draft of the UN Treaty on Business and Human Rights explicitly mentions the duty to protect in its preamble.[65] Regulation entails effective policies, legislation, regulations, monitoring and remedies.[66] Insofar as remedies in the

60 CESCR, General Comment No 13: The Right to Education (Art 13 of the ICESCR), UN Doc E/C.12/1999/10 (8 December 1999), para 47 (own emphases).

61 CESCR, General Comment No 24: State Obligations under the International Covenant on Economic, Social and Cultural Rights in the Context of Business Activities, UN Doc E/C.12/GC/24 (10 August 2017), paras 14–22; Committee on the Rights of the Child (ComRC), General Comment No 16: On State Obligations Regarding the Impact of Business on Children's Rights, UN Doc CRC/C/GC/16 (7 February 2013), para 28.

62 CESCR, General Comment No 24: State Obligations under the International Covenant on Economic, Social and Cultural Rights in the Context of Business Activities, UN Doc E/C.12/GC/24 (10 August 2017), para 21.

63 John Ruggie, 'Report of the Special Representative of the Secretary-General: Guiding Principles on Business and Human Rights: Implementing the United Nations "Protect, Respect and Remedy" Framework', UN Doc A/HRC/17/31 (21 March 2011) (UNGPs), Guiding Principle 1.

64 ibid Guiding Principle 5.

65 UN Human Rights Council, Open-Ended Intergovernmental Working Group, Second Revised Draft 6 August 2020, Legally Binding Instrument to Regulate, in International Human Rights Law, the Activities of Transnational Corporations and Other Business Enterprises (Draft UN Treaty), preamble, 8th recital.

66 See CESCR, General Comment No 24: State Obligations under the International Covenant on Economic, Social and Cultural Rights in the Context of Business Activities, UN Doc E/C.12/GC/24 (10 August 2017), para 14; ComRC, General Comment No 16: On State Obligations Regarding the Impact of Business on Children's Rights, UN Doc CRC/C/GC/16 (7 February 2013), para 28; John Ruggie, 'Report of the Special Representative of the Secretary-General: Guiding Principles on Business and Human Rights: Implementing the United Nations "Protect, Respect and Remedy" Framework', UN Doc A/HRC/17/31 (21 March 2011) (UNGPs), Guiding Principle 1; UN Human Rights Council, Open-Ended

context of the right to education are concerned, this entails, on the one hand, that private law (also human rights-based) remedies must be available against those private actors in education, whether local or foreign-based, violating entitlements ultimately rooted in the right to education (see next section). On the other hand, it means that 'typical' private law actions against private actors in education, whether local or foreign-based, must be decided on the basis or against the background of MES applicable in education, whatever law is applied to resolve the dispute.

However, what if the courts of another state, notably the home state of a foreign private actor in education, were to accept jurisdiction in a dispute? The courts could thus be referred to the law of the host or that of the home state. Would they, in either case, apply, or take into account, the protective MES of the host state? These standards are in the nature of rules of public law. Without addressing the legal theory in any detail here, the customary position of private international law, ultimately following from the non-intervention principle of public international law, is that a foreign *lex causae* – doctrinally or by reason of public policy – usually does not include rules of public law, alternatively, that the forum state's law, where this is applicable, will only exceptionally apply foreign overriding mandatory rules[67] (or *ordre public*) – to wit, crucial MES of the host state. From the perspective of IHRL, it would be important that the highest protective standards, if needs be those of the host state, be applicable. Lehmann very meaningfully recommends that

> conflict-of-law rules should clarify that the public aim or public law nature of regulatory rules does not stand in the way of their application in civil and commercial proceedings. … [F]oreign public policy rules should be allowed to intervene more freely into private relationships governed by another law.[68]

From the viewpoint of the home state, the ultimate justification for such an approach may again be seen to lie in the duty to protect, notably in its *extraterritorial* dimension, resting on the home state.

Intergovernmental Working Group, Second Revised Draft 6 August 2020, Legally Binding Instrument to Regulate, in International Human Rights Law, the Activities of Transnational Corporations and Other Business Enterprises (Draft UN Treaty), Arts 6, 7, 8; Maastricht Principles on Extraterritorial Obligations of States in the Area of Economic, Social and Cultural Rights (2011), Principle 24.

67 For the legal theory on both aspects, see Kerstin Ann-Susann Schäfer, 'Application of Mandatory Rules in the Private International Law of Contracts: A Critical Analysis of Approaches in Selected Continental and Common Law Jurisdictions, with a View to the Development of South African Law' (doctoral thesis, University of Cape Town, 2002) <https://open.uct.ac.za/handle/11427/11036> ch 5 ('Foreign Internationally Mandatory Rules').

68 Matthias Lehmann, 'Regulation, Global Governance and Private International Law: Squaring the Triangle' (2020) 16 Journal of Private International Law 1, 29.

5. PRIVATE LAW ACTIONS AGAINST, AND IN THE HOME STATE OF, A CONTROLLING COMPANY TO VINDICATE HUMAN RIGHTS

5.1. MULTINATIONAL 'LOW-COST' PRIVATE SCHOOLS: THE CASE OF BRIDGE INTERNATIONAL ACADEMIES

In developing countries the privatisation of education is of particular concern. Public education systems frequently reveal quality deficits and outright gaps in provision. Various governments are exiting the education sector, relying rather on private education providers, many from affluent countries, to fill the void. Many of these providers fail to live up to the requirements of the right to education. MES binding on private educational institutions may not have been set, or may not be enforced, in developing countries. Private law (also human rights-based) remedies against private providers may not be available or effective.[69] In the light of the threat *foreign* private providers pose to the right to education, the question arises whether developed countries do not bear a duty to protect learners, parents and teachers in developing countries against private providers from developed countries causing havoc to education in the Global South – not least by developing their law, including their private international law, in a way that allows for private law actions against, and in the home state of, the controlling company of an edu-business to vindicate education as a human right. It should be possible simultaneously to sue the subsidiary itself, for its own failings, in the stated home state as well. Private law actions vindicating human rights could be contractual or delictual in nature, but could also be based directly on human rights violations by private actors (the latter implicated by the envisaged UN Treaty on Business and Human Rights).[70]

Answering this question may be contextualised by addressing a topic of grave concern in developing countries, the uncontrolled establishment of so-called

---

69 These realities have been the driving force behind the adoption of the Abidjan Principles (Guiding Principles on the Human Rights Obligations of States to Provide Public Education and to Regulate Private Involvement in Education, 13 February 2019, Abidjan, Côte d'Ivoire). On the devastating consequences of the privatisation of education in Africa, Asia, or Latin America, see the wealth of resources on the website of the NGO Right to Education Initiative, at <https://www.right-to-education.org/issue-page/privatisation-education>.

70 The August 2020 draft of the UN Treaty on Business and Human Rights grants to victims of 'human rights abuses' in the context of business activities the right of access to an effective remedy: UN Human Rights Council, Open-Ended Intergovernmental Working Group, Second Revised Draft 6 August 2020, Legally Binding Instrument to Regulate, in International Human Rights Law, the Activities of Transnational Corporations and Other Business Enterprises (Draft UN Treaty), Art 4(2)(c). 'Human rights abuse' is defined as 'any harm committed by a business enterprise … that impedes the full enjoyment of internationally recognized human rights and fundamental freedoms': ibid Art 1(2). Liability for human rights abuses clearly covers the civil liability of business enterprises: ibid Art 8.

'low-cost' private schools, many by foreign education providers, undermining the right to education in these countries in various ways. The case of Bridge International Academies will be used as an example to help structure the discussion. Bridge International Academies, with its headquarters in Nairobi, Kenya, is a subsidiary company of NewGlobe Schools Inc., founded in Delaware, US. One of Bridge's activities is to operate 'low-cost' schools in developing countries, in Kenya, Nigeria, Uganda, etc. There are accordingly additional offices in Lagos and Kampala, but also in Washington, DC and London. The company had identified as lucrative 'the USD $64 billion "parent paid market" made up of the 800 million nursery and primary aged children living on less than $2 a day'.[71] Apparently, the 'cofounders wondered why no one was thinking about schools in developing countries the way Starbucks thought about coffee'.[72] The idea is to sell basic education as a uniform product at 'affordable' prices to the masses through a franchise of schools.[73] Bridge's plans are to educate 10 million children throughout Africa and Asia by 2025.[74]

Meanwhile, serious concern regarding the effects of Bridge's operations on the right to education has been noted. In Uganda, Bridge had opened and operated 63 schools without obtaining the requisite licences, disrespecting Ugandan sovereignty. In 2016, Uganda accordingly ordered the closure of all Bridge schools in the country. This ruling was confirmed by the High Court in 2018.[75] Yet there are still Bridge schools in operation in Uganda.[76] A 2016 study by Education International on Bridge schools in Kenya found major quality deficits.[77] It observed that 'over 71.5% of the teachers [are] unqualified and all teachers work between 59 and 66 hours a week with no official breaks'. Further, 'the teachers use a scripted curriculum with prepared notes and instructions that are designed [to] be used to the letter by the teacher'. In fact, teachers are

---

71 Graham Brown-Martin, 'Power, Corruption and Lies' (13 July 2016) <https://medium.com/friction-burns/power-corruption-and-lies-53b2fd2ed558>.

72 Bridge International Academies, 'Knowledge for All', Presskit (2013) 2, 5.

73 See 'Bridge v. Reality: A Study of Bridge International Academies' For-Profit Schooling in Kenya' (Education International and Kenya National Union of Teachers 2016) 7–9 (describing the business model); Curtis Riep, 'What Do We Really Know about Bridge International Academies? A Summary of Research Findings' (Education International 2019) 6–7 (commenting on the 'academy-in-a-box model').

74 Curtis Riep and Mark Machacek, 'Schooling the Poor Profitably: The Innovations and Deprivations of Bridge International Academies in Uganda' (Education International 2016) 2.

75 See *Bridge International Academies (K) Ltd v Attorney General*, High Court of Uganda, Kampala, Misc Application No 70 of 2018, 16 March 2018, para 11 ('a high level of reckless disregard').

76 On the situation in Uganda, see Curtis Riep and Mark Machacek, 'Schooling the Poor Profitably: The Innovations and Deprivations of Bridge International Academies in Uganda' (Education International 2016).

77 The findings that follow have been condensed from 'Bridge v. Reality: A Study of Bridge International Academies' For-Profit Schooling in Kenya' (Education International and Kenya National Union of Teachers 2016), especially 53–55.

to use so-called 'teacher-computers', mobile electronic devices, which instruct them what to say and do at any given moment in class. The study also finds that Bridge does not offer equitable access to education for all. Schools are mainly operated in lucrative areas of the country, there is no adequate provision for children with special needs, and fees are strictly enforced. Children with even a miniscule unpaid fee balance may be excluded. Children that do not attain 70 per cent in each subject are often advised to go to other schools instead. The study finally finds that Bridge does not offer 'affordable' primary education. While Bridge claims that school costs US$5–6 per month, the actual cost is US$20–25. Sending three children to school costs 30 per cent of a household's income rather than the 10 per cent Bridge claims. Referring inter alia to assessments by the CESCR and the African Commission on Human and Peoples' Rights, the UN Special Rapporteur on the Right to Education, in 2019, described Bridge as an 'emblematic' example of the 'worrying' nature of commercial school chains.[78]

In a case such as that of Bridge, is there not also a duty on the home state of the controlling company to require the latter to ensure that its subsidiaries operating in other, notably developing, countries comply with MES (as set by home states) and, in this way, observe the right to education in developing countries? Is there sometimes also a duty to regulate a subsidiary directly? If these questions are answered in the affirmative, must it then not also be possible to bring a human rights-vindicating private law action against the controlling company in its home state, based on direct, strict or contributory liability of the controlling company with regard to the activities of its subsidiaries? Should it further not be possible in appropriate instances to institute action against a subsidiary itself in the home state of the controlling company for its own failings? Which law should govern these cases? It is submitted that these questions can be answered in favour of extended protection by relying on the concept of the extraterritorial duty to protect from IHRL.

5.2. THE EXTRATERRITORIAL DUTY TO PROTECT

While the Permanent Court of International Justice, in the *Lotus* case of 1927, expressed the view that states have 'a wide measure of discretion … [to] extend the application of their laws and the jurisdiction of their courts to persons, property and acts outside their territory',[79] restrictions do exist. Broadly these flow from the public international law principle that no state may intervene directly or indirectly in the internal affairs of any other state. As for *prescriptive*

---

78 Koumbou Boly Barry, 'Report of the Special Rapporteur on the Right to Education: The Implementation of the Right to Education and SDG 4 in the Context of the Growth of Private Actors in Education', UN Doc A/HRC/41/37 (10 April 2019), paras 19–25.

79 *SS Lotus* (France v Turkey), 1927 PCIJ (ser A) No 10 (7 September) 19.

jurisdiction, states will usually refrain from legislating extraterritorially in the sphere of public or quasi-public law (e.g. criminal or competition law) where necessary to avoid conflicts in regulatory policies; as for *adjudicative* jurisdiction – the domain of private international law – it will be required that the case pertain to private law and reveal a sufficient nexus with the forum state.[80]

It may be asked whether IHRL *requires* the exercise of prescriptive and adjudicative extraterritorial jurisdiction as part of an extraterritorial duty to protect in appropriate cases. Based on the case law and other interpretative materials of various international human rights bodies, Augenstein and Jägers, for example, deduce a duty directly implicating the protective application of the rules of private international law not only from the right of access to justice, but also extraterritorial state obligations under various human rights of IHRL.[81] Such an approach should be supported. Principle 24 of the Maastricht Principles on Extraterritorial Obligations of States in the Area of Economic, Social and Cultural Rights of 2011, a document drafted by experts on international law, accordingly provides for an obligation of states to regulate private actors as follows:

> All States must take necessary measures to ensure that non-State actors which they are in a position to regulate, ... such as private individuals and organizations, and transnational corporations and other business enterprises, do not nullify or impair the enjoyment of economic, social and cultural rights. These include administrative, legislative, investigative, adjudicatory and other measures.[82]

The criterion that a state be 'in a position to regulate' a private actor is a normative requirement enquiring into the legitimacy of a state extraterritorially regulating a private actor – into whether there exists 'a reasonable link' between the state concerned and the private actor (or their conduct).[83] In international law, a state may regulate the conduct of its nationals abroad. Hence, where an edu-business

---

80 See Alex Mills, *The Confluence of Public and Private International Law: Justice, Pluralism and Subsidiarity in the International Constitutional Ordering of Private Law* (CUP 2009) 225–229.

81 Daniel Augenstein and Nicola Jägers, 'Judicial Remedies: The Issue of Jurisdiction' in Juan J Álvarez Rubio and Katerina Yiannibas (eds), *Human Rights in Business: Removal of Barriers to Access to Justice in the European Union* (Routledge 2017) 11–16. For an analysis from the 'access to justice' perspective, not further pursued here, in the European context, see Louwrens R Kiestra, *The Impact of the European Convention on Human Rights on Private International Law* (TMC Asser Press 2014).

82 Maastricht Principles on Extraterritorial Obligations of States in the Area of Economic, Social and Cultural Rights (2011), Principle 24. For a reproduction of, and commentary to, the Maastricht Principles, see Olivier De Schutter et al, 'Commentary to the Maastricht Principles on Extraterritorial Obligations of States in the Area of Economic, Social and Cultural Rights' (2012) 34 Human Rights Quarterly 1084.

83 Maastricht Principles on Extraterritorial Obligations of States in the Area of Economic, Social and Cultural Rights (2011), Principle 25(d) (obligation to regulate 'where there is a reasonable link').

incorporated in developed state A operates a (mere) branch in developing state B, the branch counts as a national of state A. It may be regulated by state A. It must be regulated by it to the extent that it may violate the right to education, or any other human right.[84] However, where the entity in state B is separately incorporated there, the matter is more complicated. As a proper subsidiary, the entity will now become a national of state B. Yet the effective protection of human rights may make it necessary, in certain cases at least, to lift the corporate veil of a subsidiary, to prevent abuse of a company construction to escape human rights accountability. In these instances, one may have to look at the nationality of the directors or shareholders of a subsidiary – regarding shareholders, notably that of the controlling company – to provide the necessary jurisdictional link.[85] Jurisdiction here may extend to local offices through which a subsidiary acts in third states. Jurisdiction may also arise by virtue of the fact that a company creates a threat of violation of human rights in state A, even though the harm only materialises in state B.[86] This covers cases of harm caused by cross-border delivery of education services (including online education). It could also include the case of an edu-business company in state A developing the overall business strategy or even merely providing needed capital there, but a branch, subsidiary or local office of a subsidiary in state B or C (operating for example 'low-cost' private schools there), as a 'completing' factor, actually causing violations of the right to education in state B or C. Jurisdiction then covers the controlling company and, by extension, it is submitted, also the branch, subsidiary and local office.

While the above seeks to provide a nationality-based foundation for a state to directly regulate a private actor acting abroad, there is also another approach in the case of multinational corporations, that of 'parent-based extraterritorial regulation'.[87] The exercise of extraterritorial jurisdiction here is more indirect. The underlying idea is that, as a state may, and must, regulate companies domiciled within its territory, such regulation may, and again must, be such as to require the company to ensure human rights are respected in its worldwide operations,

---

84 ibid Principle 25(b) (obligation to regulate on the ground of nationality).

85 ibid Principle 25(c) (obligation to regulate 'where the corporation, *or its parent or controlling company*, has its centre of activity, is registered or domiciled, or has its main place of business or substantial business activities, in the State concerned' (own emphasis)); Olivier De Schutter et al, 'Commentary to the Maastricht Principles on Extraterritorial Obligations of States in the Area of Economic, Social and Cultural Rights' (2012) 34 Human Rights Quarterly 1084, 1140–1141 (nationality of corporation on the basis of 'the nationality of its owners, managers, or other persons deemed to be in control of its affairs').

86 Maastricht Principles on Extraterritorial Obligations of States in the Area of Economic, Social and Cultural Rights (2011), Principle 25(a) (obligation to regulate where 'the harm or threat of harm originates or occurs on [a state's] territory').

87 See Olivier De Schutter et al, 'Commentary to the Maastricht Principles on Extraterritorial Obligations of States in the Area of Economic, Social and Cultural Rights' (2012) 34 Human Rights Quarterly 1084, 1141.

including by all its branches or subsidiaries, and the local offices of subsidiaries, wherever they operate. Whereas direct regulation seeks to regulate the actor acting abroad as such, indirect regulation aims to constrain that actor through control of the home company in its home state. Consequently, an edu-business company in state A may and must be required to ensure that a subsidiary in state B does not, for example, operate 'low-cost' private schools there that violate the right to education.

The extraterritorial duty to protect is expressly recognised by both the CESCR and the ComRC in their General Comments on business and human rights.[88] In addition, the UNGPs and the August 2020 draft of the UN Treaty on Business and Human Rights require states to provide protection against human rights abuse by third parties 'within their territory and/or jurisdiction'[89] and 'within their territory or jurisdiction',[90] respectively. In the context of the right to education, the Abidjan Principles, evidently relying on the Maastricht Principles, formulate a comprehensive duty to protect as follows:

> States must take all effective measures to ensure that private actors involved in education, which the States are in a position to regulate, do not nullify or impair the enjoyment of the right to education wherever they operate. Measures may include administrative, legislative, investigative, adjudicatory, or any other measures.[91]

An extraterritorial duty to protect, as outlined above, does not conflict with the non-intervention principle of international law. Human rights, generally, are today recognised as giving rise to obligations *erga omnes*.[92] They are seen to embody expressions of a transnational community interest. The exercise of extraterritorial jurisdiction can for that reason not readily be considered as

---

88 CESCR, General Comment No 24: State Obligations under the International Covenant on Economic, Social and Cultural Rights in the Context of Business Activities, UN Doc E/C.12/GC/24 (10 August 2017), paras 30–35; ComRC, General Comment No 16: On State Obligations Regarding the Impact of Business on Children's Rights, UN Doc CRC/C/GC/16 (7 February 2013), paras 43–46.

89 John Ruggie, 'Report of the Special Representative of the Secretary-General: Guiding Principles on Business and Human Rights: Implementing the United Nations "Protect, Respect and Remedy" Framework', UN Doc A/HRC/17/31 (21 March 2011) (UNGPs), Guiding Principle 1.

90 UN Human Rights Council, Open-Ended Intergovernmental Working Group, Second Revised Draft 6 August 2020, Legally Binding Instrument to Regulate, in International Human Rights Law, the Activities of Transnational Corporations and Other Business Enterprises (Draft UN Treaty), Arts 6(1), 8(1).

91 Guiding Principles on the Human Rights Obligations of States to Provide Public Education and to Regulate Private Involvement in Education, 13 February 2019, Abidjan, Côte d'Ivoire (Abidjan Principles), Guiding Principle 61.

92 Ian D Seiderman, *Hierarchy in International Law: The Human Rights Dimension* (Intersentia 2001) 145.

amounting to one state superimposing its values on another.[93] Moreover, it needs to be remembered that the primary duty to protect lies with the host state.[94]

5.3. PRESCRIPTIVE JURISDICTION

The August 2020 draft of the UN Treaty on Business and Human Rights obliges states parties to 'regulate effectively' the activities of business enterprises 'domiciled within their territory or jurisdiction', notably by requiring them to undertake 'human rights due diligence' (HRDD).[95] Draft Article 1 on definitions seems to imply that jurisdiction may exist where preparation or planning of business takes place in one state, but actual business operations in another, or where business conduct in one state may cause harm in another.[96] Private providers of education must be made to bear 'public service obligations' and be required to comply with MES as envisaged in the Abidjan Principles. As appropriate to the circumstance, private actors in education would have to undertake HRDD. From the perspective of the host state of a private provider (in our example, Kenya, Nigeria, Uganda), that state must lay down MES and ensure these are strictly complied with by the local actor (Bridge in Kenya, Nigeria, Uganda). From the perspective of the home state (the US), both the home company and, as appropriate, its branches, subsidiaries and the local offices of subsidiaries abroad (NewGlobe Schools Inc. in the US and Bridge in Kenya, Nigeria and Uganda) would have to be required to ensure MES, to be set by the home state, are complied with.

---

93 Similarly, see Olivier De Schutter et al, 'Commentary to the Maastricht Principles on Extraterritorial Obligations of States in the Area of Economic, Social and Cultural Rights' (2012) 34 Human Rights Quarterly 1084, 1142.

94 See e.g. ComRC, General Comment No 16: On State Obligations Regarding the Impact of Business on Children's Rights, UN Doc CRC/C/GC/16 (7 February 2013), para 42.

95 UN Human Rights Council, Open-Ended Intergovernmental Working Group, Second Revised Draft 6 August 2020, Legally Binding Instrument to Regulate, in International Human Rights Law, the Activities of Transnational Corporations and Other Business Enterprises (Draft UN Treaty), Art 6(1), (2), (3). See also John Ruggie, 'Report of the Special Representative of the Secretary-General: Guiding Principles on Business and Human Rights: Implementing the United Nations "Protect, Respect and Remedy" Framework', UN Doc A/HRC/17/31 (21 March 2011) (UNGPs), Guiding Principles 2–6. HRDD customarily covers the adoption of a human rights policy, assessing the human rights impacts of an enterprise's activities, integrating findings into corporate culture, management, and operation, and monitoring and reporting on compliance. See ibid Guiding Principles 15–22.

96 UN Human Rights Council, Open-Ended Intergovernmental Working Group, Second Revised Draft 6 August 2020, Legally Binding Instrument to Regulate, in International Human Rights Law, the Activities of Transnational Corporations and Other Business Enterprises (Draft UN Treaty), Art 1(4) ('business activities of a transnational character').

5.4. ADJUDICATIVE JURISDICTION

In recent years, there have been increased attempts to litigate human rights through private, notably tort, law in foreign jurisdictions – particularly those with a well-developed court system and law – with which a dispute may be connected. These cases have been termed 'foreign direct liability cases',[97] or there has been talk of 'transnational human rights litigation'[98] or 'transnational public law litigation'.[99] The defendants will often be private actors. The last term in particular, however, also covers governments.

As for the specific context of the transnational business activities of multinational corporations, Joseph mentions certain arguments against transnational human rights litigation. It might be seen as a form of 'judicial imperialism', retard the development of the legal systems of host countries, and threaten direct investment in developing countries. However, she considers its positive aspects to outweigh the negative ones. She refers to the 'moral' obligation of home countries for the good behaviour of 'their' multinationals abroad and the fact that remedies may be unavailable in host countries.[100] Moreover, transnational human rights litigation might lead to substantial damage awards, encourage out-of-court settlements, prompt thorough investigation, affect a wrongdoer company's reputation and its shares, raise the public profile of human rights NGOs, lead to legal responsibility, deter future human rights violations, and achieve vindication.[101] Enneking similarly opines that 'foreign direct liability' entails that an effective remedy becomes available for human rights violations. She considers tort law eminently suited to vindicate human rights in this manner. The malleable concept of 'a duty of care' facilitates this. However, she points out, success narrowly depends on which law is chosen.[102] Transnational human rights litigation would not only be important symbolically, raising awareness in the developed world for the human rights infringements committed by companies of the Global North in the Global South, but would also secure access to the sophisticated court system and law of a developed country and render possible enforcement measures that are very effective

---

97 See Liesbeth Enneking, *Foreign Direct Liability and Beyond: Exploring the Role of Tort Law in Promoting International Corporate Social Responsibility and Accountability* (Eleven International Publishing 2012).

98 See Craig Scott (ed), *Torture as Tort: Comparative Perspectives on the Development of Transnational Human Rights Litigation* (Hart Publishing 2001); Sarah Joseph, *Corporations and Transnational Human Rights Litigation* (Hart Publishing 2004).

99 See Harold H Koh, 'Transnational Public Law Litigation' (1991) 100 Yale Law Journal 2347.

100 Sarah Joseph, *Corporations and Transnational Human Rights Litigation* (Hart Publishing 2004) 148–151.

101 ibid 14–15.

102 Liesbeth Enneking, *Foreign Direct Liability and Beyond: Exploring the Role of Tort Law in Promoting International Corporate Social Responsibility and Accountability* (Eleven International Publishing 2012) 669–673.

'globally' (e.g. sanctions against, or the dissolution of, a controlling company). It might potentially lead to the formulation by the home state of (additional) 'duty of care' or HRDD obligations binding on home companies and entities acting abroad in developing countries.

Jurisdiction in relation to the extraterritorial duty to protect includes adjudicatory measures. This encompasses judicial remedies against the state under public law, but also judicial (and other) remedies against private providers or business enterprises. The ComRC holds that states should provide access to effective judicial (and other) mechanisms 'to provide remedy for children and their families whose rights have been violated by business enterprises *extra-territorially*'.[103] The main responsibility for remedies lies with the host state. As the CESCR points out, remedies must be made available '*especially* in cases where the remedies available to victims before the domestic courts of the State where the harm occurs are unavailable or ineffective'.[104] The UNGPs and the Abidjan Principles refer expressly to effective 'judicial mechanisms' and 'judicial means', respectively – their respective scope of application also covering the extraterritorial context.[105] Judicial remedies against private actors include administrative, criminal and civil law remedies. Private law actions vindicating human rights could be based on contract, delict or human rights directly. An effective remedy is one that is capable of leading to a thorough investigation, cessation of a violation that is ongoing, and adequate reparation, including compensation, satisfaction or guarantees of non-repetition.[106]

In the context of the transnational business activities of multinational edu- or other corporations, apart from the possibility of bringing private law actions against relevant actors in the host state – taking a cue from the Maastricht Principles – private law remedies should be made available by the home state of a multinational company against the home company where harm is suffered in another state, the host state, where that multinational company conducts business directly or through a branch, subsidiary or local office of a subsidiary.[107]

103 ComRC, General Comment No 16: On State Obligations Regarding the Impact of Business on Children's Rights, UN Doc CRC/C/GC/16 (7 February 2013), para 44 (own emphasis).

104 CESCR, General Comment No 24: State Obligations under the International Covenant on Economic, Social and Cultural Rights in the Context of Business Activities, UN Doc E/C.12/GC/24 (10 August 2017), para 30 (own emphasis).

105 John Ruggie, 'Report of the Special Representative of the Secretary-General: Guiding Principles on Business and Human Rights: Implementing the United Nations "Protect, Respect and Remedy" Framework', UN Doc A/HRC/17/31 (21 March 2011), Guiding Principles 25, 26; Guiding Principles on the Human Rights Obligations of States to Provide Public Education and to Regulate Private Involvement in Education, 13 February 2019, Abidjan, Côte d'Ivoire (Abidjan Principles), Guiding Principles 80(a), 89.

106 See e.g. Maastricht Principles on Extraterritorial Obligations of States in the Area of Economic, Social and Cultural Rights (2011), Principle 38.

107 See ibid Principle 37 ('judicial remedies'; as between host state and home state, 'any state concerned must provide remedies'), as read with Olivier De Schutter et al, 'Commentary to the Maastricht Principles on Extraterritorial Obligations of States in the Area of Economic, Social and Cultural Rights' (2012) 34 Human Rights Quarterly 1084, 1163–1164.

Where the remedy is founded on the contractual, delictual or human rights failings of the home company in respect of its worldwide operations and branches, subsidiaries and the local offices of subsidiaries, the jurisdictional link lies in the nationality (domicile) of the home company. Where the remedy is founded on the contractual, delictual or human rights failings of the actor acting abroad which may be ascribed or imputed to the home company or to which the latter contributed, the jurisdictional link may lie in:

- the 'home state' nationality (domicile) of a branch abroad; or
- the nationality (domicile) of the controlling company where the corporate veil of a subsidiary is lifted to prevent accountability being evaded; or
- acts of preparation or planning of business, or capital provision, by the home company (domiciled) in the home state, ultimately, through the actor acting abroad, leading to harm in the host state.

The August 2020 draft of the UN Treaty on Business and Human Rights provides that, in the case of 'human rights abuses', adjudicative jurisdiction vests in the courts of the state where

> a. the human rights abuse occurred;
> b. an act or omission contributing to the human rights abuse occurred; or
> c. the legal or natural persons alleged to have committed an act or omission causing or contributing to such human rights abuse in the context of business activities, including those of a transnational character, are domiciled.[108]

The exact extent to which these provisions allow for actions to be brought in the home state of a multinational company against the home company in the types of situations referred to in the previous paragraph is not really clear. It may commendably be noted that, under the draft treaty, none of the above courts in which jurisdiction vests – thus also not those of the home state of a multinational company – may argue that they are *forum non conveniens* and that the courts of another state, such as those of the host state, are better suited to hear a case.[109] It is also commendable that, in the case of a claim against a controlling company in the courts of the home state (court of domicile), victims can also pursue a claim against an overseas subsidiary in those courts, if the two claims are 'closely connected'.[110]

---

108 UN Human Rights Council, Open-Ended Intergovernmental Working Group, Second Revised Draft 6 August 2020, Legally Binding Instrument to Regulate, in International Human Rights Law, the Activities of Transnational Corporations and Other Business Enterprises (Draft UN Treaty), Art 9(1).

109 ibid Art 9(3).

110 ibid Art 9(4). The courts then are a form of *forum connexitatis* (controlling company as 'anchor' defendant).

Let us apply these insights to the case of Bridge International Academies, relying on the facts as borne out by the 2016 study on Kenya prepared by Education International. These clearly show that Bridge violates the right to education in Kenya. Should it be possible for a private law action to be brought before a court in the US, where NewGlobe Schools Inc., the controlling company, is incorporated (domiciled), for instance by a Kenyan NGO advancing children's rights?

First of all, is there an extraterritorial duty on the US to protect the right to education of Kenyan students? The US has not ratified any international human rights treaty that protects the right to education, including neither the ICESCR nor the CRC. Nevertheless, compulsory and free quality primary education for all forms part of customary international law,[111] which also binds the US. Bridge offers mainly primary education. The controlling company must accordingly be made to bear obligations of oversight with regard to its Kenyan subsidiary. The controlling company could perhaps be said to contribute to violations by providing the capital which makes Bridge operations possible at all. Perhaps there also exist reasons to lift the corporate veil of Bridge in Kenya. Overall, it seems possible to sue both the controlling company and its subsidiary in the US, the home state of the corporation.

The infringements of rights at issue here could be described as human rights violations, acts of delict or breaches of contract. From the delictual perspective, infringements of educational rights in the context of business activities would usually take the form of poor-quality education or lost educational opportunity, students, as it were, forfeiting the ability to fully develop their 'human personality'. This is an attack on their *dignitas*, an infringement of personality rights. However, there could also be patrimonial damage due to excessive school fees paid or in the form of lost future earnings. From the contractual perspective, quality education could be considered an implied contractual warranty.

Relief might be claimed in the form of an injunction that deficiencies be corrected, compensation for patrimonial damage, or satisfaction for infringement of personality rights. The court might even order the controlling company to close the Kenyan schools, able to enforce compliance with the order indirectly through a possible dissolution of the controlling company.

5.5. CHOICE OF LAW

Whatever law is applied to resolve a case, this must live up to the adjudicating state's domestic and extraterritorial duty to protect the right to education or any

111 Klaus D Beiter, *The Protection of the Right to Education by International Law: Including a Systematic Analysis of Article 13 of the International Covenant on Economic, Social and Cultural Rights* (Martinus Nijhoff Publishers 2006) 44–46.

other human right. The August 2020 draft of the UN Treaty on Business and Human Rights allows victims to request that a dispute be governed by either the law of the state where

> a. the acts or omissions that result in violations of human rights ... have occurred; or
> b. the natural or legal person alleged to have committed the acts or omissions that result in violations of human rights ... is domiciled.[112]

In other words, they may choose whichever of these two legal frameworks is more favourable to their claims. In the context of the transnational business activities of multinational edu- or other corporations, this would refer to the law of the home state of the multinational corporation or the law of the host state where an overseas actor acts. Again, there is no reason to construe a foreign *lex causae* as not covering another state's public law, including MES binding on private providers of education.

To ensure that the applicable foreign law affords adequate protection, it has been suggested that private international law might have to move towards the idea of an 'international public policy',[113] or a 'global regulatory public policy',[114] which, instead of, or additional to, a national *ordre public*, serves to ensure that 'rights established under international law' are respected,[115] or that 'a global minimum standard' to protect 'global goods' is observed.[116] Others hold that, in transnational human rights cases, there should be an application of 'transnational law' as substantive law, this being 'a hybrid between international and national law, where the interpretation and application of international human rights law is influenced by the national laws and the cultural context of all the states involved'.[117] Similarly, it has been stated that the law to be applied is 'cosmopolitan private law', which is built on domestic law interpreted in the light of foreign and international law, especially insofar as these address human rights.[118]

---

112 UN Human Rights Council, Open-Ended Intergovernmental Working Group, Second Revised Draft 6 August 2020, Legally Binding Instrument to Regulate, in International Human Rights Law, the Activities of Transnational Corporations and Other Business Enterprises (Draft UN Treaty), Art 11(2).

113 Alex Mills, *The Confluence of Public and Private International Law: Justice, Pluralism and Subsidiarity in the International Constitutional Ordering of Private Law* (CUP 2009) 275.

114 Matthias Lehmann, 'Regulation, Global Governance and Private International Law: Squaring the Triangle' (2020) 16 Journal of Private International Law 1, 27.

115 Alex Mills, *The Confluence of Public and Private International Law: Justice, Pluralism and Subsidiarity in the International Constitutional Ordering of Private Law* (CUP 2009) 276.

116 Matthias Lehmann, 'Regulation, Global Governance and Private International Law: Squaring the Triangle' (2020) 16 Journal of Private International Law 1, 28.

117 Sandra Raponi, 'Grounding a Cause of Action for Torture in Transnational Law' in Craig Scott (ed), *Torture as Tort: Comparative Perspectives on the Development of Transnational Human Rights Litigation* (Hart Publishing 2001) 375.

118 Mayo Moran, 'An Uncivil Action: The Tort of Torture and Cosmopolitan Private Law' in Craig Scott (ed), *Torture as Tort: Comparative Perspectives on the Development of Transnational Human Rights Litigation* (Hart Publishing 2001) 676–677, 682–683.

Any such 'enhanced' policy or law would thus also be heavily infused with right to education values.

Returning to the case of Bridge, the governing law applied by a US court would probably be either US or Kenyan law. The likely outcome of the hypothetical case cannot be predicted in any detail, of course. However, the US bears obligations under IHRL, domestic and extraterritorial, to guarantee free public primary education of a high quality and to strictly regulate private education providers, to ensure there is compliance with MES, which it must set. In the light of this, any resolution of the case – under whichever law and whether based on human rights, delict or contract – cannot ignore the fact that the very business model of Bridge, the reckless implementation thereof in practice, and the way the company treats learners, parents and teachers in developing countries violates rights to, and in, education, undermines the pursuit of education that fully develops human personality, and infringes universally agreed rights of teachers. Perceiving the poor in these countries as merely an unconquered market, to be provided with an education that lacks the attributes to be considered human rights-compliant, constitutes an attack on human dignity. Bridge's corporate philosophy is culturally imperialistic, neo-colonial and lacks the essential characteristics to be called morally decent.

6. RESULTS: A BLUEPRINT FOR THE DEVELOPMENT OF PRIVATE INTERNATIONAL LAW IN THE EDUCATION CONTEXT

The SDGs, including SDG 4, should be considered closely linked to IHRL, this also protecting the right to education. The SDGs should be seen as an agenda that may help achieve a realignment of private international law in terms of which the latter overcomes its 'tunnel-vision' and 'reappropriate[s] its political function'.[119] What currently comes as a technical approach in private international law may in reality hide the entrenchment of inequality. Also in the sphere of education, where private law and private international law are gaining relevance, private international law rules should be developed to provide greater protection to 'weaker' stakeholders in education, located notably in the Global South. At present, private international law rules often favour the global education industry with its base in the Global North.

The following 10 statements flow from the analysis in this chapter and may be seen to constitute a blueprint for the development of private international law norms applicable in the transnational education context.

---

119 Horatia Muir Watt, 'Private International Law: Beyond the Schism' (2011) 2 Transnational Legal Theory 347, 426.

1. IHRL protects the freedom of individuals and bodies to establish and direct educational institutions. Flowing from 'the duty to protect' the right to education, IHRL grants the freedom to establish private educational institutions subject to the proviso that MES, which states are obliged to lay down, must be complied with. The purpose of such MES is to protect the rights of students, parents or teachers to, and in, education.
2. There is, in the wake of neoliberalism, a trend of privatisation in education, covering phenomena such as the proliferation of for-profit private schools offering so-called 'low-cost' education, public educational institutions adopting business methods and practices, or PPPs becoming a notable feature of education systems. The privatisation of education is closely related to its liberalisation, globalisation and digitisation. In consequence, private law and private international law assume an increased role in education.
3. Private actors may play a *supplementary* role in the provision and funding of education. Beyond this point, privatisation undermines education as a public good and human right. Where private actors do operate legitimately, they must be strictly regulated – hence the importance of MES. This also has implications for private international law.
4. Choice-of-jurisdiction clauses in contracts between students or teachers and a private educational institution, referring a matter to the courts of the home state of a foreign private actor in education, are highly suspicious. Students or teachers cannot ordinarily be expected to bring a claim in the courts of any state other than that of their domicile. Choice-of-jurisdiction clauses in contracts between a state and a private actor in education (e.g. in a PPP agreement), referring a matter to the courts of the home state of a foreign private actor, may not result in the protective effect of MES of the host state being avoided.
5. In *'typical' private law actions* against the branch or subsidiary of a foreign private actor in education, or the foreign actor itself, based on contract or delict, in the courts of the *host state*, MES could be central to, but must at least constitute relevant background norms to, resolving a dispute. Should a foreign law apply, the protective effect of MES of the host state may not be avoided. To this end, host states must develop the concepts of overriding mandatory norms and *ordre public* as part of their private international law, and clearly link these to human rights, including the right to education, to safeguard MES. In *cases of violations of human rights* by any of the above private actors, host states must make available private law remedies directed at vindicating education as a human right and safeguarding the highest protective MES.
6. 'The duty to protect' the right to education has an extraterritorial dimension in terms of which the home state of an edu-business undertaking operations abroad must ensure that both the home company and, as appropriate, its branches, subsidiaries and the local offices of subsidiaries abroad comply with MES, which the home state is obliged to lay down.

7. Following from point 6, private law remedies against the home company, in the company's home state, to vindicate education as a human right, must be made available by home states: (a) Where the remedy is founded on the contractual, delictual or human rights failings of the home company in respect of its worldwide operations and branches, subsidiaries, and the local offices of subsidiaries, the jurisdictional link lies in the nationality (domicile) of the home company; (b) Where the remedy is founded on the contractual, delictual or human rights failings of the actor acting abroad which may be ascribed or imputed to the home company or to which the latter contributed, the jurisdictional link may lie in (i) the 'home state' nationality (domicile) of a branch abroad, (ii) the nationality (domicile) of the controlling company where the corporate veil of a subsidiary is lifted to prevent accountability being evaded, or (iii) acts of preparation or planning of business, or capital provision, by the home company (domiciled) in the home state, ultimately, through the actor acting abroad, leading to harm in the host state. Jurisdiction thus established must not be subject to the principle of *forum non conveniens.*
8. Private law remedies to vindicate education as a human right may also have to be made available by home states directly against the actors acting abroad. At any rate, if jurisdiction in accordance with the previous point exists, it must be possible to sue both the home company and the actor acting abroad in the home state, where the former is domiciled, if the two claims are 'closely connected'.
9. Whatever law is chosen to govern a *'typical' private law case*, or alternatively a *transnational human rights case*, by the courts of the *home state* of an edu-business, it is important that the adjudicating state, or its courts, comply with the right to education under IHRL. Regarding compliance by private actors in education with MES, the highest protective standards, if needs be those of the host state, should be secured. Choice-of-law rules should be developed to allow for the application of foreign regulatory rules (MES) even though they are norms of public law, form part of another state's public policy or constitute foreign overriding mandatory norms. Alternatively, private international law might have to move towards the idea of an 'international public policy', a 'global regulatory public policy', 'transnational law' or 'cosmopolitan private law' to ensure compliance with the substantive norms of IHRL, including those pertaining to the right to education.
10. Human rights NGOs should rely on 'transnational human rights litigation', grounded in contract, delict, human rights, etc., to vindicate the right to education in the courts of home states of multinational edu-businesses. Such litigation may secure access to a sophisticated system of courts and law, achieve 'tangible' and symbolic justice, and facilitate effective enforcement. It may thus form part of a strategy to put an end to violations of the right to education committed by multinational edu-businesses in developed countries operating 'low-cost' private schools in developing countries.

SDG 5: GENDER EQUALITY

Gülüm Bayraktaroğlu-Özçelik*

Goal 5: Achieve gender equality and empower all women and girls

5.1 End all forms of discrimination against all women and girls everywhere

5.2 Eliminate all forms of violence against all women and girls in the public and private spheres, including trafficking and sexual and other types of exploitation

5.3 Eliminate all harmful practices, such as child, early and forced marriage and female genital mutilation

5.4 Recognize and value unpaid care and domestic work through the provision of public services, infrastructure and social protection policies and the promotion of shared responsibility within the household and the family as nationally appropriate

5.5 Ensure women's full and effective participation and equal opportunities for leadership at all levels of decision-making in political, economic and public life

5.6 Ensure universal access to sexual and reproductive health and reproductive rights as agreed in accordance with the Programme of Action of the International Conference on Population and Development and the Beijing Platform for Action and the outcome documents of their review conferences

5.a Undertake reforms to give women equal rights to economic resources, as well as access to ownership and control over land and other forms of property, financial services, inheritance and natural resources, in accordance with national laws

5.b Enhance the use of enabling technology, in particular information and communications technology, to promote the empowerment of women

5.c Adopt and strengthen sound policies and enforceable legislation for the promotion of gender equality and the empowerment of all women and girls at all levels

* Email: gulum@bilkent.edu.tr.

1. INTRODUCTION

The Charter of the United Nations[1] (1945) and the Universal Declaration of Human Rights[2] (1948) were the first international instruments providing for equality between men and women. Since then, gender equality has been addressed both as a fundamental principle of human rights and as a key component of sustainable development.

However, despite all the efforts to increase awareness of the critical role played by gender equality and empowerment of women and the progress achieved in certain areas, significant disparities still exist as regards the status, rights and opportunities of women and girls as compared to men and boys in both the Global South and Global North. Such disparities, arising from either lack of legal protection or social, traditional or cultural realities, are found in relation to the

1 The Charter, in its preamble, sets out the goal to 'reaffirm faith in fundamental human rights, in the dignity and worth of the human person, in the equal rights of men and women and of nations large and small': Charter of the United Nations (signed 26 June 1945, entered into force 24 October 1945) 1 UNTS XVI.

2 Under Art 2 of the Universal Declaration of Human Rights '[e]veryone is entitled to all the rights and freedoms set forth in this Declaration, without distinction of any kind, such as race, colour, sex, language, religion, political or other opinion, national or social origin, property, birth or other status': Universal Declaration of Human Rights, UNGA Res 217 A(III) (adopted 10 December 1948).

status of women and girls within the household or in the workplace or their involvement in public and private spheres, as well as in terms of their access to some basic services such as health and education.[3] As of 2020, for example women do three times (4.1 hours/day) as much unpaid care and domestic work as men (1.7 hours/day), are paid 16 per cent less than men at the workplace, and 31 per cent of young women (aged between 15 and 24) are not in education, employment or training, which is the double rate (14 per cent) of young men.[4] Today, 39 per cent of women are employed in agriculture, fisheries and forestry, but only 14 per cent of agricultural landholders are women.[5] Women hold 25 per cent of seats in in national parliaments and make up 36 per cent of local government.[6] Violence against women and girls (including intimate partner violence, sexual violence and harassment, human trafficking, female genital mutilation and child marriage) still remains one of the most persistent human rights violations.

The goal of achieving gender equality and empowering all women and girls requires detailed assessments from both public and private law perspectives. This chapter discusses the contribution of private international law, through its methodologies and techniques, to achieving Sustainable Development Goal 5 (SDG 5). Due to the very wide scope of the goal, it focuses in particular on Target 5.1, on 'ending all forms of discrimination against all women and girls everywhere'. With this target in mind, the chapter starts with an overview of the main international and regional instruments providing for gender equality as a fundamental principle of human rights and as a crucial element of sustainable development. It should be underlined at the outset that although such instruments are undoubtedly relevant in cross-border matters, none of them specifically addresses this principle as regards issues of private international law. Thus, questions arise as to how classical techniques of private international law can be used to guarantee gender equality and eliminate gender-based discrimination. The chapter deals with issues of private international law, i.e. applicable law, jurisdiction, and recognition and enforcement of foreign judgments, as well as with the question of recognition of foreign marriages. The last part of the chapter is confined to the results and recommendations on the possible future regulatory framework to ensure gender equality and elimination of discrimination in the area of private international law.

3 For facts and figures see <https://www.unwomen.org/-/media/headquarters/attachments/sections/library/ publications/2020/gender-equality-womens-rights-in-review-key-facts-and-figures-en.pdf?la=en&vs=935> accessed 15 May 2020.

4 ibid.

5 ibid.

6 United Nations, 'The Sustainable Development Goals Report 2020' 10 <https://unstats.un.org/sdgs/report/2020/ The-Sustainable-Development-Goals-Report-2020.pdf> accessed 15 May 2020.

2. AN OVERVIEW: GENDER EQUALITY UNDER INTERNATIONAL AND REGIONAL INSTRUMENTS

Since the adoption of the Charter of the UN and the Universal Declaration of Human Rights, gender equality and the prohibition of gender-based discrimination have been subject to different international conventions and declarations recognising gender equality as a principle of human rights. These include the International Covenant on Civil and Political Rights (ICCPR)[7] (Art 3), the International Covenant on Economic, Social and Cultural Rights[8] (Arts 2(2), 3), the Declaration on the Elimination of Violence Against Women[9] (Art 4(f)), the Declaration on the Rights of Indigenous Peoples[10] (Art 22(2)), and the Convention on the Elimination of All Forms of Discrimination Against Women[11] (CEDAW), the latter being the most comprehensive one providing for gender equality and the rights and status of women.

At the regional level, the principle of gender equality is provided for by the European Convention for the Protection of Human Rights and Fundamental Freedoms[12] (ECHR) (Art 14) and in Protocols Nos 12[13] and 7[14] (Art 5) to the ECHR. In European Union law, equal treatment and non-discrimination is accepted as a general principle by the Court of Justice[15] and gender equality is made subject to provisions of the Treaty on European Union (TEU) (Arts 2, 3), the Treaty on the Functioning of the EU (TFEU) (Arts 8, 10, 19, 157) and the

---

7 International Covenant on Civil and Political Rights (adopted 16 December 1966, entered into force 23 March 1976) 999 UNTS 171.

8 International Covenant on Economic, Social and Cultural Rights (adopted 16 December 1966, entered into force 3 January 1976) 993 UNTS 3.

9 Declaration on the Elimination of Violence against Women, General Assembly Resolution 48/104 (20 December 1993) <https://www.ohchr.org/Documents/ProfessionalInterest/elimination vaw.pdf> accessed 12 May 2020.

10 United Nations Declaration on the Rights of Indigenous Peoples, General Assembly Resolution, UN Doc A/RES/61/295 (2 October 2007) <https://documents-dds-ny.un.org/doc/UNDOC/GEN/N06/512/07/PDF/N0651207.pdf?OpenElement> accessed 12 May 2020.

11 Convention on the Elimination of All Forms of Discrimination Against Women (adopted 18 December 1979, entered into force 3 September 1981) 1249 UNTS 13.

12 Convention for the Protection of Human Rights and Fundamental Freedoms, as amended by Protocols Nos 11 and 14 (opened for signature 4 November 1950, entered into force 3 September 1953) ETS No 5, <https://www.echr.coe.int/ Documents/Convention_ENG.pdf> accessed 12 May 2020.

13 Protocol No 12 to the Convention for the Protection of Human Rights and Fundamental Freedoms (opened for signature 4 November 2000, entered into force 1 April 2005) ETS No 177, <https://www.coe.int/en/web/conventions/full-list/-/conventions/treaty/177> accessed 12 May 2020.

14 Protocol No 7 to the Convention for the Protection of Human Rights and Fundamental Freedoms (opened for signature 22 November 1984, entered into force 1 November 1988) ETS No 117, <https://www.coe.int/en/web/conventions/full-list/-/conventions/treaty/117> accessed 12 May 2020.

15 Joined Cases 117/76 and 16/77 *Albert Ruckdeschel & Co and Hansa-Lagerhaus Ströh & Co v Hauptzollamt Hamburg-St. Annen; Diamalt AG v Hauptzollamt Itzehoe* [1977] ECR 1753, para 7.

Charter of Fundamental Rights of the EU[16] (Arts 21, 23). Secondary instruments are also in force that regulate the principle of equal treatment between men and women in different spheres and the improvement of certain rights of women.[17]

The African Charter on Human and Peoples' Rights of 1981[18] (Arts 2, 18(3)) and its Maputo Protocol[19] (Arts 2(1), (1)(b), (2)), the African Charter on the Rights and Welfare of the Child of 1990[20] (Arts 1(1), 3), the American Declaration on the Rights and Duties of Man of 1948[21] (Art 2), the American Convention on Human Rights of 1969[22] (Arts 1(1), 2) and its Protocol of San Salvador[23] (Arts 1, 3, 6.2, 8(i), 9) are other regional instruments that establish the principle of gender equality.

Gender equality (with its prerequisite 'empowerment of women and girls') has also been addressed on global platforms as a crucial component of sustainable development since the 1980s. These include the Fourth World Conference in Beijing (1995) and the Beijing Declaration and Platform for Action,[24] as well as the Global Action for Women towards Sustainable and Equitable Development of Agenda 21 (Chapter 24)[25] and the Rio Declaration (Principle 20), which were two of the outcomes of the UN Conference on Environment and Development (UNCED) of 1992.[26]

In the Millennium Development Goals (MDGs), adopted as a result of the UN Millennium Summit of 2000, promoting 'gender equality and empowerment

16 Consolidated versions of the Treaty on European Union and the Treaty on the Functioning of the European Union [2016] OJ C 202/1.

17 Regarding the principle of equal treatment and non-discrimination in EU law see Paul Craig and Gráinne de Búrca, *EU Law: Text, Cases, and Materials* (6th ed, OUP 2015) 892.

18 African Charter on Human and Peoples' Rights (adopted 27 June 1981, entered into force 21 October 1986) 1520 UNTS 217.

19 Protocol to the African Charter on Human and Peoples' Rights on the Rights of Women in Africa (adopted 1 July 2003, entered into force 25 November 2005) <https://au.int/en/treaties/protocol-african-charter-human-and-peoples-rights-rights-women-africa> accessed 12 May 2020.

20 African Charter on the Rights and Welfare of the Child (adopted 1 July 1990, entered into force 29 November 1999) <https://www.un.org/en/africa/osaa /pdf/au/afr_charter_ rights_ welfare_child_africa_1990.pdf > accessed 12 May 2020.

21 American Declaration of the Rights and Duties of Man (adopted 2 May 1948) <https://www.cidh.oas.org/basicos/english/basic2.american%20declaration.htm> accessed 12 May 2020.

22 American Convention on Human Rights (adopted 22 November 1969, entered into force 18 July 1978) 1144 UNTS 144.

23 Additional Protocol to the American Convention on Human Rights in the Area of Economic, Social and Cultural Rights (Protocol of San Salvador) (adopted 17 November 1988, entered into force 16 November 1999) <https://www.oas.org/juridico/english/treaties/a-52.html> accessed 12 May 2020.

24 Fourth World Conference on Women, Beijing Declaration <https://www.un.org/womenwatch /daw/beijing/platform/declar.htm> accessed 8 November 2020.

25 United Nations Conference on Environment & Development, Agenda 21, Rio de Janerio, Brazil, 3–14 June 1992, para 24.1 et seq <https://sustainabledevelopment.un.org/content/documents/Agenda21.pdf> accessed 15 September 2020.

26 UN General Assembly, Report of United Nations Conference on Environment and Development (Annex I- Rio Declaration on Environment and Development, UN Doc A/CONF.151/26 (Vol I)) (12 August 1992) 3, 7.

of women' was addressed as MDG 3, albeit in a modest manner, including the sole target of eliminating gender disparity in primary and secondary education by 2005 and at all levels of education by 2015 (Target 3.A), and addressing the issue as part of two other goals (Goal 1 (income poverty), Goal 2 (education)).

The outcome document of UN Conference on Sustainable Development (Rio+20) of 2012, which led to the development of the Sustainable Development Goals (SDGs) 2030, recognises gender equality both as a fundamental principle of human rights and as part of inclusive and people-centred sustainable development.[27] Compared to their predecessor, the SDGs address the goal of 'achieving gender equality and empowering all women and girls' (SDG 5) in a more comprehensive manner in terms of both the number and the scope of the targets and indicators that relate to the social, economic and political rights of women and girls.[28]

What should also be welcomed under the SDGs is the integration of gender equality and empowerment of women into other SGDs through some targets and indicators, rather than recognising it as an isolated task.[29] In fact, the multiplier effects of gender equality and empowerment of women are evident in all areas, and are thus critical to achieving any development in the whole agenda; for example, eliminating discrimination as regards women's access to decent work and regular income, will not only contribute to SDG 5 (Targets 5.1, 5.a) but also to reducing poverty (SDG 1) and supporting better education, health and nutritional outcomes for women and girls (SDGs 2, 3, 4).[30] Similarly, eliminating early and forced marriages (Target 5.3) will also contribute to ensuring access to education and lifelong opportunities for all (SDG 4). Reducing the amount of unpaid work performed by women (Target 5.4) is crucial for reducing poverty (SDG 1) as well as for the advancement of inclusive and sustainable economic growth (SDG 8),[31] while eliminating all forms of violence against women and

---

27 UN General Assembly, Resolution adopted by the General Assembly on 27 July 2012: The future we want, UN Doc A/RES/66/288 (11 September 2012) para 31.

28 For a comprehensive assessment on gender in SDGs see Karen Morrow, 'Gender and Sustainable Development Goals' in Duncan French and Louis J Kotzé (eds), *Sustainable Development Goals: Law, Theory and Implementation* (Edward Elgar Publishing 2018).

29 As such, gender equality and empowerment of women are specifically addressed as targets in SDGs 1, 2, 4, 6, 8, 11, 13. Also see Lynda M Collins, 'Sustainable Development Goals and human rights: challenges and opportunities' in Duncan French and Louis J Kotzé (eds), *Sustainable Development Goals: Law, Theory and Implementation* (Edward Elgar Publishing 2018) 84.

30 UN Women, 'Why Gender Equality Matters Across All SDGs – An Excerpt of Turning Promises into Action: Gender Equality in the 2030 Agenda For Sustainable Development' (2018) 5 <https://www.unwomen.org/-/media/headquarters/attachments/sections/library/publications/2018/sdg-report-chapter-3-why-gender-equality-matters-across-all-sdgs-2018 en.pdf? la=en&vs=5447> accessed 15 May 2020.

31 United Nations Development Programme, 'UNDP Support to the Integration of Gender Equality Across the SGDs including Goal 5' (February 2016) 4 <https://www.undp.org/content/dam/undp/library /SDGs/5_Gender_Equality_digital.pdf> accessed 15 May 2020.

girls (Target 5.2) is essential to ensuring healthy lives and well-being for people of all ages (SDG 3).[32]

3. PRIVATE INTERNATIONAL LAW DOCTRINES AND TECHNIQUES

In achieving the goal of gender equality, private international law also has a role to play. First and foremost, gender equality, being one of the fundamental principles of international human rights law, is to be taken into consideration in dealing with cross-border private law matters. Thus, although the above-mentioned international conventions do not particularly address issues of private international law, they have to be equally considered when dealing with matters that involve foreign element(s).

The principle of gender equality and the interests of women should be considered in a wide spectrum of cross-border issues, including family relations (such as women's rights and status in marriage and in its dissolution), property, inheritance and employment rights. There are also important questions as regards international surrogacy arrangements. Certain other issues have also arisen regarding the status and rights of migrant women as a result of the increase in the number of migrants in many countries.

Although academic work on gender and private international law is just emerging, the new approaches are promising, including feminist analysis of private international law,[33] or using the techniques of private international law (particularly of choice of law) to contribute to debates on feminism and multiculturalism[34] or analysing the involvement of women in the development of private international law.[35]

This section deals with the question of how classical techniques of private international law can be used to guarantee gender equality and eliminate gender-based discrimination. As such, the analysis covers the main issues of private international law, i.e. applicable law, international civil jurisdiction,

---

32 UN Women, 'Why Gender Equality Matters Across All SDGs – An Excerpt of Turning Promises into Action: Gender Equality in the 2030 Agenda For Sustainable Development' (2018) 5 <https://www.unwomen.org/-/media/headquarters/attachments/sections/library/publications/2018/sdg-report-chapter-3-why-gender-equality-matters-across-all-sdgs-2018 en.pdf? la=en&vs=5447> accessed 15 May 2020.

33 Roxana Banu, 'A Relational Feminist Approach to Conflict of Laws' (2017) 24(1) Michigan Journal of Gender and Law 1.

34 Karen Knop, Ralf Michaels and Annelise Riles, 'From Multiculturalism to Technique: Feminism, Culture, and the Conflict of Laws Style' (2012) 64 Stanford Law Review 589.

35 Mary Keyes, 'Women in Private International Law' in Susan Harris Rimmer and Kate Ogg (eds), *Research Handbook on Feminist Engagement with International Law* (Edward Elgar Publishing 2019) 103.

and recognition and enforcement of foreign judgments. Recognition of foreign marriages, which involves current debates in Europe in relation to polygamous and child marriages, is dealt with under a subsequent heading.

3.1. APPLICABLE LAW

In the area of applicable law, the principle of gender equality and prohibition of gender-based discrimination have to be taken into consideration, especially in the determination of connecting factors, and in the application of the public policy exception and of the overriding mandatory rules. The legal issues that concern gender equality in this area of private international law mostly relate to the law of persons, family law and succession law.

3.1.1. Ensuring Gender Equality through Conflict-of-Laws Rules

In private relationships involving foreign element(s), it is the conflict-of-laws rules of the forum that designate the law applicable to a given issue through connecting factors. Depending on the subject matter of the legal issue, different connecting factors may be preferred, such as 'nationality', 'domicile', 'habitual residence', 'the place where the property is located' or 'the place of performance of the contract'. Thus, the conflict-of-laws rules function in order to determine the law to be applied, rather than solving the issue itself.

Based on their purpose, it can be questioned whether such rules may themselves be in conflict with the principle of gender equality. However, in family matters where there is common life between the parties (such as the consequences of marriage, divorce, legal separation, matrimonial property, custody and parentage), connecting to the law of one of the spouses (e.g. national law or law of residence or domicile of the husband/father) and not the other (wife/mother) represents discrimination in itself, regardless of whether the substance of the designated law may in fact comply with the principle of equality.[36]

As a matter of fact, the gradual increase in the awareness of protection of women's rights in domestic laws and acceptance of the link between the conflict-of-laws rules and human rights have had a positive impact on the principle of gender equality being taken into consideration in the formulation of conflict-of-laws rules in European states. One of the early examples is the German Federal Constitutional Court's judgment of 1971 in *Spanier-Beschluss* that the

---

36 Pietro Franzina, 'The Law Applicable to Divorce and Legal Separation Under Regulation (EU) No. 1259/2010 of 20 December 2010' (2011) 3 Cuadernos de Derecho Transnacional 85, 99.

conflict-of-laws rules had to be in compliance with the German Constitution.[37] Following *Spanier-Beschluss*, the German conflict-of-laws rule requiring the application of the national law of the husband (where the nationalities of the spouses are different) in divorce cases (Art 17/I *Einführungsgesetz zum Bürgerlichen Gesetzbuche* (EGBGB)) was found unconstitutional by the decisions of 1982 and 1985 of the German Federal Court of Justice (*Bundesgerichtshof* (BGH))[38] and the Federal Constitutional Court (*Bundesverfassungsgericht* (BVerfG))[39] respectively. In 1983 the Federal Constitutional Court expressed the same view as regards the conflict-of-laws rules (Art 15/I, II EGBGB) requiring the application of the national law of the husband in matters of matrimonial property.[40] Such jurisprudence led to an amendment of German conflict-of-laws rules.

Similarly, the (then) Italian conflict-of-laws rules requiring the application of the national law of the husband (as regards marriage) and the national law of the father (as regards the relationship between the child and the spouses) were found to be in conflict with the Italian Constitution by the Italian Constitutional Court, which led to the adoption of the Italian Act on Private International Law of 1995. As such, the adoption of the new Act aimed to ensure compatibility of the conflict-of-laws rules with human rights, and in particular with the principle of gender equality as guaranteed by the Italian Constitution of 1948.[41]

Such rules, which were the reflection of the male dominance of their times over private international law,[42] are at odds with the principle of gender equality because they put an extra burden on the woman, making her subject to requirements of a law not known to her, and thus put her in a disadvantaged position in relation to her husband.[43] In cases where the conflict-of-laws rule

37 For an analysis of *Spanier-Beschluss* and subsequent case law on the compatibility of German conflict-of-laws rules with the German Constitution see Rainer Hofmann, 'Human Rights and the Ordre Public Clause of German Private International Law' (1994) 12 Tel Aviv University Studies in Law 145, 146 et seq.

38 BGH 8 December 1982, NJW 1983, 1260.

39 BVerfG 8 January 1985, 68 BVerfGE 384 (F.R.G.): Rainer Hofmann, 'Human Rights and the Ordre Public Clause of German Private International Law' (1994) 12 Tel Aviv University Studies in Law 145, 149, n 14.

40 BVerfG 22 February 1983, 63 BVerfGE 181 (F.R.G.): Rainer Hofmann, 'Human Rights and the Ordre Public Clause of German Private International Law' (1994) 12 Tel Aviv University Studies in Law 145, 149, n 15.

41 Tito Ballarino and Andrea Bonomi, 'The Italian Statute on Private International Law of 1995' (2000) 2 Yearbook of Private International Law 99, 101.

42 Council of Europe Parliamentary Assembly Committee on Equal Opportunities for Women and Men, 'Respect for the principle of equality in civil law' (Revised expert paper prepared by Stéphanie Billaud, 24 February 2006) 9.

43 ibid. As regards the common law rule on the dependency of the women's domicile on their husbands' see Mary Keyes, 'Women in Private International Law' in Susan Harris Rimmer and Kate Ogg (eds), *Research Handbook on Feminist Engagement with International Law* (Edward Elgar Publishing 2019) 107.

requires the national law of the husband to apply, it also gives him the opportunity – at least in theory – to change his nationality and obtain consequences favourable to him accordingly.[44]

One of the limited number of decisions of the European Court of Human Rights (ECtHR) on the impact of gender equality on the conflict-of-laws rules was *Losonci Rose and Rose v Switzerland*[45] where gender equality was discussed from the standpoint of the husband.[46] Under Swiss law, which requires the choice of a family name, the surname of the husband is accepted as the family name (except in exceptional situations where the spouses choose the surname of the wife). Under the Swiss PIL Act, the name of a person domiciled in Switzerland is governed by Swiss law (Art 37/I); however, a person may apply to have his or her name governed by his or her national law (Art 37/II). Mr Laszlo Losonci (Rose), a Hungarian national domiciled in Switzerland, and Ms Iris Rose, his wife, who held both Swiss and French nationalities, chose 'Rose' as their family name before marriage. Mr Losonci Rose subsequently requested that his surname be governed by his national law under Article 37/II of the Swiss PIL Act and that his name be replaced by 'Losonci'. This was then rejected by the Swiss authorities on the ground that a choice as to their family name had already been made by the spouses and that Mr Losonci Rose could no longer request the application of his national law to his surname. In the case before the ECtHR, the applicants claimed that Swiss law was in conflict with the prohibition of discrimination under Article 14 of the ECHR since the result would have been different if the wife had been a Hungarian national and the husband a Swiss national, where their family name would have been Rose automatically under Swiss law and the wife would have been able to choose the national law to apply to her surname. Accepting the arguments of the applicants and based on the ground that the difference in treatment was not justified, the ECtHR held that there was a breach of Article 14 read in conjunction with Article 8 (right to family life) of the Convention.

In modern private international law legislation, connecting factors which require application of the law of one of the spouses have mostly been replaced with others that ensure predictability and legal certainty for both spouses. These include the adoption of objective connecting factors common to both spouses (such as common habitual residence, last common habitual residence or common nationality) or providing for the possibility for the spouses to choose the applicable law.[47] However, even where party autonomy is the technique, there might be

---

44 Wilhelm Wengler, 'The Significance of the Principle of Equality in the Conflict of Laws' (1963) Law and Contemporary Problems 822, 831.

45 *Losonci Rose and Rose v Switzerland* App no 664/06 (9 November 2010).

46 Regarding *Losonci Rose and Rose v Switzerland* also see Louwrens Rienk Kiestra, *The Impact of the European Convention on Human Rights on Private International Law* (Springer 2014) 182.

47 See e.g. Arts 5 and 8 of Regulation (EU) No 1259/2010 of 20 December 2010 implementing enhanced cooperation in the area of the Law Applicable to Divorce and Legal Separation (Rome III Regulation); Arts 22 and 26/I of the Council Regulation (EU) No 2016/1103 of

situations which require the limitation of application of the chosen law in order to protect the interests of women. Such protection may be secured by specific provisions to this end.[48] One such example that considers the interests of the parties and provides for protective rules in cases of choice of law is to be found in Article 8(5) of the Hague Protocol of 2007 on the Law Applicable to Maintenance Obligations,[49] which – unless at the time of the designation the parties were fully informed and aware of the consequences of their designation – disregards the application of the law designated by the parties if the application of that law would lead to manifestly unfair or unreasonable consequences for any of the parties.

3.1.2. *The Public Policy Exception as a Technique to Eliminate Gender-Based Discrimination*

The public policy exception has been widely adopted as a technique of private international law to prevent the application of the otherwise applicable foreign law. Although there is no common definition of public policy,[50] principles protecting fundamental rights and freedoms, constitutional principles, and customary and ethical values of a society may be referred to as the values of public policy. In this regard it is mostly accepted that the general framework of public policy includes not only the values of a society and principles of national law but also the fundamental rights and freedoms as guaranteed under international norms, the latter also referred to as 'truly international public policy'.[51]

---

24 June 2016 implementing enhanced cooperation in the area of jurisdiction, applicable law and the recognition and enforcement of decisions in matters of matrimonial property regimes (EU Regulation on Matrimonial Property Regimes). Also see Arts 29 (personal relations between the spouses), 30/I and II (property relations between the spouses), 38/I (adoption) of the Reform of the Italian System of Private International Law (Law of 31 May 1995, No 218) (Italian PIL Act); Arts 48/I (personal effects of marriage), 52–54 (marital property relations) of the Swiss Federal Act of Private International Law of 18 December 1987 as amended until 1 January 2017 (Swiss PIL Act); Arts 13/III (personal effects of marriage), 14 (divorce and legal separation, maintenance claims between the spouses in case of divorce, custody), 15/I (matrimonial property) of the Turkish Act on Private International Law and International Civil Procedure, numbered 5718, dated 27 November 2007 (Turkish PIL Act).

48 As regards the role of gender on party autonomy in international family law see Cristina Gonzáles Beilfuss, 'Party Autonomy in International Family Law' (2020) 408 Recueil des cours 89, 201.

49 Hague Protocol of 2007 on the Law Applicable to Maintenance Obligations (concluded 23 November 2007, entered into force on 1 August 2013).

50 For a comprehensive assessment of the public policy exception in private international law see Paul Lagarde, 'Public Policy' in *International Encyclopedia of Comparative Law* (1994) vol 3, 3; Alex Mills, 'The Dimensions of Public Policy in Private International Law' (2008) 4(2) Journal of Private International Law 201; Ionna Thoma, 'Public policy (*ordre public*)' in *Encyclopedia of Private International Law* (2017) vol 2, 1453; Cecilia Fresnedo de Aguirre, *Public Policy: Common Principles in the American States,* Recueil des cours 379 (2016).

51 Louwrens Rienk Kiestra, *The Impact of the European Convention on Human Rights on Private International Law* (Springer 2014) 22.

When applying this exception, a 'manifest' conflict with the public policy of the forum is required due to its exceptional character.[52] Under certain legislation, 'proximity', i.e. a link between the legal issue with the forum state (e.g. where the parties are the nationals of the forum state or have their habitual residence in that state), may also be taken into consideration to trigger the public policy exception.[53]

The public policy exception can be regarded as the most effective tool to ensure gender equality and eliminate gender-based discrimination.[54] Thus, where the foreign law designated according to the conflict-of-law rules of the forum state is found to be manifestly in conflict with the principle of gender equality as adopted by the latter (e.g. as a constitutional principle and/or under an international convention to which the forum state is a party), the judge may decide to disregard its application on public policy grounds. Nevertheless, the public policy exception requires a case-by-case analysis; therefore the judge has to determine whether the application of a provision of foreign law would have discriminatory effects in the particular case and should thus be disregarded. For example, a foreign law which provides for the provision of maintenance only to sons may be regarded as discriminatory in the abstract, but may not discriminate in the particular case if the spouses only have sons.[55] In the latter case, it is clear that application of that foreign law provision cannot be disregarded under the public policy exception.

On the other hand, even though proximity with the forum state is generally required under certain states' legislation for the public policy exception, where gender equality is at issue, it should not further be discussed,[56] since gender equality is a fundamental element of international human rights law.

---

52 See e.g. Introductory Act to the German Civil Code, Art 6; Dutch Civil Code (*Burgerlijk Wetboek*), Book 10 on the Conflict of Laws (of 1 January 2012), Art 6; Turkish PIL Act, Art 5; Rome III Regulation, Art 12.

53 Regarding proximity in public policy see Louwrens Rienk Kiestra, *The Impact of the European Convention on Human Rights on Private International Law* (Springer 2014) 22; Susanne Lilian Gössl, 'The Public Policy Exception in the European Civil Justice System' (2016) 4 The European Legal Forum 85, 90.

54 For this finding as regards the Member States of the Council of Europe see Council of Europe Parliamentary Assembly Committee on Equal Opportunities for Women and Men, 'Respect for the principle of equality in civil law' (Revised expert paper prepared by Stéphanie Billaud, 24 February 2006) 14.

55 Aydanur Gürzumar, 'Türk Devletler Özel Hukuku Açısından Boşanma Davalarında Kamu Düzeninin Etkileri' [Effects of the Public Policy in Divorce Cases in Turkish Private International Law] (1994) 14(1) Milletlerarası Hukuk ve Milletlerarası Özel Hukuk Bülteni [Public and Private International Law Bulletin] 21, 37.

56 Where there is an infringement of fundamental rights proximity is not required: Cemal Şanlı, Emre Esen and Inci Ataman-Figanmeşe, *Milletlerarası Özel Hukuk [Private International Law]* (7th ed, Beta 2019) 81 (regarding Turkish law); Louwrens Rienk Kiestra, *The Impact of the European Convention on Human Rights on Private International Law* (Springer 2014) 179 (regarding the opinions of Swiss and Dutch doctrine); Susanne Lilian Gössl, 'The Public Policy Exception in the European Civil Justice System' (2016) 4 The European Legal Forum 85, 90 (regarding French and Spanish law). Also see Ionna Thoma, 'Public policy (*ordre public*)' in *Encyclopedia of Private International Law* (2017) vol 2, 1453, 1458.

Although the nature of the public policy exception precludes the possibility of listing discriminatory provisions, it may be inferred from the practice and doctrinal writings that the application of foreign law providing for a very low marriageable age for girls or different marriageable age for men and women, permitting celebration of polygynous marriages,[57] obliging the woman to use her husband's family name, without securing her right to keep her maiden name alone,[58] or providing for different rules on the transmission of the spouses' surnames to their children[59] may be considered discriminatory. On the same lines, application of foreign law that restricts the contractual capacity of married women and requires the consent of her husband for conclusion of contracts, that restricts her right to choose her place of residence or her profession or the disposition of matrimonial property,[60] or that requires the husband's consent for refusing succession may be accepted as contrary to the public policy of the forum.

In divorce cases, foreign law that provides for differences as to grounds and procedures for divorce between spouses and makes the women subject to more strict conditions,[61] or creates inequalities as regards the financial consequences of divorce may also be faced with public policy intervention. In particular in states which accept judicial divorces and the principle of equal access to divorce, the application of foreign law providing for *talaq* (repudiation) that is based solely on the discretion of one of the spouses (the husband)[62] may also lead to

57 Gülören Tekinalp and Ayfer Uyanık, *Milletlerarası Özel Hukuk-Bağlama Kuralları [Private International Law- Conflict-of-Laws Rules]* (12th ed, Vedat 2016) 142; Cemal Şanlı, Emre Esen and Inci Ataman-Figanmeşe, *Milletlerarası Özel Hukuk [Private International Law]* (7th ed, Beta 2019) 80.

58 See e.g. *Ünal Tekeli v Turkey* App no 29865/96 (16 November 2004) para 55; *Tuncer Güneş v Turkey* App no 26268/08 (3 September 2013) para 19.

59 See e.g. *Bijleveld v The Netherlands* App no 42973/98 (27 April 2000) 7.

60 For the decision of UN Human Rights Committee where the Peruvian Civil Code entitling only the husband to represent the matrimonial property before the courts was found in breach of Arts 3, 14(1) and 26 of the ICCPR: United Nations Office of the High Commissioner for Human Rights in Cooperation with the International Bar Association, *Human Rights in the Administration of Justice: A Manual for Judges, Prosecutors and Lawyers* (Professional Training Series No 9, 2003) 218 <https://www.ohchr.org/Documents/Publications/training9Titleen.pdf> accessed 15 May 2020.

61 According to the CEDAW Committee, the differences between standards of proof for wives and husbands as regards fault-based divorce regimes should be eliminated by the contracting states: Committee on the Elimination of Discrimination Against Women, General Recommendation on Art 16 of the Convention on the Elimination of All Forms of Discrimination against Women, UN Doc CEDAW/C/GC/29 (26 February 2013) para 39 <https://www.icj.org/wp-content/uploads/2013/05/General-Recommendation-CEDAW-29-economic-consequences-of-marriage-2013-eng.pdf> accessed 15 May 2020.

62 However, there are important differences in countries accepting *talaq* in terms of whether the will of the husband suffices or the involvement of an official authority of that country is required. For example, in Yemen, Saudi Arabia and Syria no such involvement is required, whereas in Tunisia and Algeria a decision of the court is required. For differing *talaq* procedures in Islamic countries see Susan Rutten, 'Recognition of Divorce by Repudiation

the public policy exception being invoked, especially if the foreign law does not provide for any other means of divorce (judicial or extrajudicial) for women.[63] Foreign law that only provides for the right to divorce for women subject to the consent of their husband should also be qualified as discriminatory.

In the EU, Article 10 of the Rome III Regulation obliges Member State courts to set aside the applicable law determined according to Articles 5 or 8 of the Regulation if it (makes no provision for divorce or) does not grant one of the spouses equal access to divorce or legal separation on grounds of sex and requires the forum to apply its own law. Article 10 is distinct from the public policy exception provided under Article 12 of the Regulation.[64] As indicated by Advocate General Saugmandsgaard Øe in his opinion in *Soha Sahyouni v Raja Mamisch*,[65] gender equality as enshrined in the founding treaties as well as in the EU Charter of Fundamental Rights is 'so fundamental as not to be open to restriction'; thus, unlike Article 12, Article 10 provides for 'an absolute rejection of the entirety of the law which would otherwise have had to be applied, with no scope for exceptions on a case-by-case basis'.[66] Thus, if the applicable law determined according to the Regulation provides for divorce by *talaq* by the husband, its application may be rejected on the basis of Article 10 of the Regulation. However, when applying the said provision, it should also be considered whether the applicable law grants the wife any access to divorce. If the applicable law provides for the right to divorce for the wife in any other way, it should continue to apply.[67]

In custody cases, provisions of foreign law which do not take the interests of the child into consideration or which give the custody of sons to the father and of daughters to the mother or of the children automatically to the father,[68]

(*talaq*) in France, Germany and the Netherlands' (2004) 11(3) Maastricht Journal of European and Comparative Law 263, 264; Muhammad Munir, 'Reforms in Triple *Talaq* in the Personal Laws of Muslim States and the Pakistani Legal System: Continuity versus Change' (2013) 1 International Review of Law 2.

63 See Pauline Kruiniger, *Islamic Divorces in Europe – Bridging the Gap between European and Islamic Legal Orders* (Eleven International Publishing 2015) 312 (as regards Dutch, English and French law); Gülören Tekinalp and Ayfer Uyanık, *Milletlerarası Özel Hukuk-Bağlama Kuralları [Private International Law- Conflict-of-Laws Rules]* (12th ed, Vedat 2016) 172 (as regards Turkish law); Zoé Papassiopi-Passia, 'The Applicable Law on Divorce and the "Ordre Public" Reservation in Greek Conflict of Laws' (2000) 60 Louisiana Law Review 1227, 1228 (as regards Greek law). On French and Dutch law also see Susan Rutten, 'Recognition of Divorce by Repudiation (*talaq*) in France, Germany and the Netherlands' (2004) 11(3) Maastricht Journal of European and Comparative Law 263, 271, 280.

64 Case C-372/16 *Soha Sahyouni v Raja Mamisch* [2017] ECLI:EU:C:2017:686, Opinion of AG *Saugmandsgaard Øe*, para 82.

65 ibid.

66 ibid para 70 et seq.

67 Thalia Kruger, 'Rome III and Parties' Choice' (2014) Familie & Recht <http://www.familyandlaw.eu/tijdschrift /fenr/2014/01/FENR-D-13-00010.pdf> accessed 16 May 2020.

68 As regards Turkish law see Cemile Demir-Gökyayla, *Yabancı Mahkeme Kararlarının Tanınması ve Tenfizinde Kamu Düzeni [Public Policy in the Recognition and Enforcement of Foreign Judgments]* (Seçkin 2001) 185.

and in the law of succession, foreign law which does not recognise women as heirs[69] or which differentiates shares of an inheritance based on the gender of the deceased[70] or differentiates between the shares of sons and daughters[71] may be disregarded based on the public policy exception. In the area of employment law, foreign law which provides for differentiation as to wages of the female and male employees may also be disregarded on the same ground.

3.1.3. Application of Overriding Mandatory Rules

Overriding mandatory rules (internationally mandatory rules/imperative norms/*lois de police/loi d'application immédiate/international zwingende Normen/Eingriffsnormen*) are substantive law provisions which are adopted to safeguard public interests of a state, such as the protection of its social, economic and political order.[72] They may exist in the law of the forum (*lex fori*) or in foreign law (*lex causae*) or in the law of a third country.

Overriding mandatory rules of the *lex fori* are applied to any situation that falls within their scope, irrespective of whether the issue involves a foreign element or not. In cross-border matters, application of such rules sets aside a foreign law that would otherwise be determined to be the applicable law by the conflict-of-laws rules of the forum state.[73] Determination of the overriding mandatory rules of the *lex fori* is a matter of interpretation that takes into consideration their nature and purpose. In this regard, a provision of *lex fori* safeguarding gender equality may be qualified as an overriding mandatory rule and may thus be applied, rejecting the otherwise applicable foreign law. Examples include: from the French Civil Code, Articles 220–222 on the rights and responsibilities of the spouses,[74]

69 Neşe Baran Çelik, *Milletlerarası Unsurlu Ölüme Bağlı Tasarruflara Uygulanacak Hukukun Tayini [Determination of the Applicable Law on Testamentary Dispositions with International Elements]* (Yetkin 2010) 210.

70 Directorate-General for Internal Policies of the Union (European Parliament), 'The state of implementation of the EU Succession Regulation's provisions on public policy's exception, universal application and renvoi, the European Certificate of Succession and access to registers' (20 November 2011) 2 <https://www.europarl.europa.eu/thinktank/lv/document.html?reference=IPOL_BRI(2017)596821> accessed 16 May 2020.

71 ibid.

72 For a comprehensive analysis of overriding mandatory rules see Andrea Bonomi, 'Mandatory Rules in Private International Law: The Quest for Uniformity of Decisions in a Global Environment' (1999) 1 Yearbook of Private International Law 215; Michael Wilderspin, 'Overriding Mandatory Provisions' in *Encyclopedia of Private International Law* (2017) vol 2, 1330.

73 See e.g. Inter-American Convention on the Law Applicable to Contracts, Art 11; Hague Convention of 1985 on the Law Applicable to Trusts and Their Recognition, Art 17; Hague Convention of 1989 on the Law Applicable to Succession to the Estates of the Deceased Persons, Art 6; Hague Convention of 2000 on International Protection of Adults, Art 20; Rome I Regulation, Art 9; Rome II Regulation, Art 16; EU Regulation on Matrimonial Property Regimes, Art 30(1); Swiss PIL Act, Art 18(1); Turkish PIL Act, Art 6; Italian PIL Act, Art 17.

74 Sarah Nietner, *Internationaler Entscheidungseinklang im europaeischen Kollisionsrecht* (Mohr Siebeck 2016) 289.

Article 215 on the matrimonial home[75] and Article 831 regarding preferential attribution in succession;[76] provisions of German employment law on conferral of maternity entitlements;[77] and provisions of the Turkish Labour Act on equal treatment (specifically Art 5) and on the protection of pregnant women and children.[78]

Nevertheless, depending on the forum state, there is always the possibility that an overriding mandatory rule of the *lex fori* may itself be discriminatory and may still be applied by the forum. In such a scenario, a judgment given that is in conflict with the principle of gender equality will be questionable from the point of international human rights law, and thus should not be recognised or enforced in other states.[79]

On the other hand, overriding mandatory rules may also exist in foreign law, i.e. in the *lex causae* – the applicable law determined by the conflict-of-laws rules of the forum or in the law of a third country. In conflict of laws, as a principle, the *lex causae* governs the legal issue in question as a whole. In this regard, if the provision of the *lex causae* to be applied has the character of an overriding mandatory rule that protects gender equality, it shall be applied as part of the *lex causae*. Where overriding mandatory rules exist in the law of a third country (i.e. in any law other than the *lex fori* and *lex causae*), depending on the provisions of the law of the forum on third-country mandatory rules, the judge should decide whether or not to apply/give effect to the rule that protects gender equality, or may refrain from applying/giving effect to it if he or she concludes that the rule conflicts with that principle.

3.2. INTERNATIONAL CIVIL JURISDICTION

The right of access to justice is one of the fundamental principles of the rule of law and one of the guarantees of the exercise of human rights.[80] Included in SDG 16,

---

75 Marie Cresp, Jean Hauser, Marion Ho-Dac and Sandrine Sana-Chaillé de Néré, *Droit de la famille: Droits français, européen, international et comparé* (Bruylant 2018) para 273.

76 Jan Peter Schmidt, 'Art. 30' in Anatol Dutta and Johannes Weber (eds), *Internationales Erbrecht* (C.H. Beck 2016) 269, para 23.

77 Michael Wilderspin, 'Overriding Mandatory Provisions' in *Encyclopedia of Private International Law* (2017) vol 2, 1332.

78 Doğa Elçin, *Milletlerarası Unsurlu Bireysel ve Toplu İş Sözleşmelerine Uygulanacak Hukuk [The Law Applicable to Personal Labour Contracts and Collective Labour Agreements with International Elements]* (Adalet 2012) 168; Belkıs Vural Çelenk, 'Yabancı Unsurlu İş Sözleşmelerinde For Devletinin Doğrudan Uygulanan Kurallarının Tespiti ve Uygulanması' [Determination and Application of the Overriding Mandatory Rules of the Forum State in Labour Contracts including Foreign Element] (2017) 3 Yıldırım Beyazıt Hukuk Dergisi [Yıldırım Beyazıt Law Review] 277, 291.

79 See *infra* section 3.3 (public policy in the recognition and enforcement of foreign judgments).

80 DCAF, OSCE/ODIHR and UN Women, 'Justice and Gender' in *Gender and Security Toolkit* (2019) 1.

access to justice is accepted as one of the main components of sustainable development.[81] International and regional conventions – including the ICCPR (Art 2(3)), the ECHR (Art 13), the African Charter on Human and Peoples' Rights (Art 7(a)) and the American Convention on Human Rights (Art 25) – oblige the contracting states to guarantee the right of effective remedy before national authorities to persons whose rights and freedoms are violated. The CEDAW also requires the contracting states to establish legal protection of the rights of women on an equal basis with men and to ensure through competent national tribunals and other public institutions the effective protection of women against any act of discrimination (Art 2(c)). It further requires equality between men and women at all stages of procedure in courts and tribunals (Art 15).

It is beyond doubt that the right of access to justice for women and girls is equally applicable in cross-border matters. It should be ensured both during the proceedings before a national court/authority with jurisdiction to adjudicate the matter and in the recognition and enforcement of foreign judgments.

As such, one of the main issues of access to justice is the determination of the national courts or authorities to adjudicate the case at hand.[82] Based on national sovereignty, every state has the power to determine the jurisdiction of its courts/the competence of its national authorities – where international conventions do not apply. In the formulation of the rules of (international) jurisdiction, states use certain criteria, including for example the habitual residence of the defendant, the place where the property is located or where the wrongful act or the result occurred. In this regard, the mechanism to ensure gender equality is the adoption of a jurisdiction criterion promoting that principle.

As regards the contracting states of the ECHR, this can also be accepted as a requirement arising from Article 6(1) of the Convention, which guarantees the right to a fair trial. In fact, as has been rightly pointed out, the obligations of the contracting states arising from the ECHR start from the moment when the claimant brings an action before their courts.[83] As such, the decision on

---

81 ibid.

82 Another central issue, but not specific to cross-border matters is the provision of legal aid to women. Provision of legal aid for women in need, covering the expenses of proceedings and ensuring assistance of a lawyer, plays a pivotal role for the exercise of their right of access to justice. However, today in most countries there are structural, cultural and gender-based barriers (such as lack of specialised legal aid services for women, consideration of overall household income rather than women's income specifically in the eligibility for legal aid, difficulties of confiding in a male legal aid provider and sharing intimate information related to a case). There is also a lack of awareness on the part of the women that legal aid services are available at little or no cost or on where to find legal assistance: United Nations Development Programme (UNDP) and United Nations Office on Drugs and Crime (UNODC), 'Global Study on Legal Aid – Global Report' (2016) 79 <https://www.unodc.org/documents/justice-and-prison-reform/LegalAid/Global_Study_on_Legal_Aid_-_FINAL.pdf> accessed 12 May 2020.

83 Louwrens Rienk Kiestra, *The Impact of the European Convention on Human Rights on Private International Law* (Springer 2014) 94. See also *Markovic and Others v Italy* where the ECtHR ruled that '[e]ven though the extraterritorial nature of the events alleged to have been at the

jurisdiction (whether to accept or to reject jurisdiction) should also comply with the Convention so as to guarantee the right to a fair trial.[84] In this regard, a jurisdiction rule based, for example, on a criterion which favours one of the spouses (the husband) would at least be controversial as regards prohibition of discrimination under Article 14 and as regards the right of access to a court, which is one of the elements of the right to a fair trial as provided under Article 6(1) of the Convention,[85] especially where the wife does not have the option to bring the action before the courts of that state under a different rule.

3.3. PUBLIC POLICY IN THE RECOGNITION AND ENFORCEMENT OF FOREIGN JUDGMENTS

Public policy may also prevent recognition and enforcement of foreign judgments if the foreign judgment would be manifestly incompatible with the public policy of the state in which recognition or enforcement is sought.[86] However, unlike the public policy exception in the conflict of laws, public policy in the recognition and enforcement of foreign judgments includes substantive as well as procedural matters (i.e. matters related to the procedure leading to the foreign judgment).

In the recognition and enforcement of foreign judgments, the prohibition of *révision au fond* prevents the requested court from revising the foreign judgment as to its substance. In this regard, the conflict-of-laws rules or the substantive provisions applied by the court of the requesting state in the main proceedings may not be reviewed by the requested court. Thus, application of conflict-of-laws rules or substantive provisions by the court of the requesting state which are different from, or even contrary to, the mandatory rules of the requested state or their misapplication may not trigger the public policy exception in the recognition or enforcement of a foreign judgment.

As regards promotion of gender equality, the public policy exception is a technique which is frequently used to reject the recognition or enforcement of a foreign judgment where, for example, the foreign judgment differentiates

origin of an action may have an effect on the applicability of Art. 6 and the final outcome of the proceedings, it cannot under any circumstances affect the jurisdiction *ratione loci* and *ratione personae* of the State concerned. If civil proceedings are brought in the domestic courts, the State is required by Art. 1 of the Convention to secure in those proceedings respect for the rights protected by Art. 6. The Court considers that once a person brings a civil action in the courts or tribunals of a State, there indisputably exists, without prejudice to the outcome of the proceedings, a "jurisdictional link" for the purposes of Art. 1': *Markovic and Others v Italy* App no 1398/03 (14 December 2006) para 54.

84 Louwrens Rienk Kiestra, *The Impact of the European Convention on Human Rights on Private International Law* (Springer 2014) 94.

85 *Golder v The United Kingdom* App no 4451/70 (21 February 1975) para 36.

86 See e.g. Hague Convention of 1970 on Recognition of Divorces and Legal Separations, Art 10; Regulation (EU) No 1215/2012 of the European Parliament and of the Council of

between succession shares of children or between the shares of spouses in matrimonial property based on their gender, or gives custody of the child automatically to the father without considering the best interest of the child and failing to establish personal relations with the mother.[87]

One of the most discussed issues in Europe in this regard has been the recognition of foreign divorces based on *talaq*. However, both the approach to recognition of foreign *talaq* and the weight given to public policy as a ground to refuse its recognition vary from country to country.[88] One important question that plays a role in the frequency of invoking the public policy exception is whether recognition of foreign *talaq* is made subject to special provisions in a particular country.[89] In countries such as the Netherlands and the UK where recognition of foreign *talaq* is subject to special provisions, derived from the Hague Convention of 1970 on Recognition of Divorces and Legal Separations (Art 1(1)),[90] it can be said that recognition is usually permissible once the

---

12 December 2012 on jurisdiction and the recognition and enforcement of judgments in civil and commercial matters (recast), Arts 45(1)(a), 46; Council Regulation (EC) No 2201/2003 of 27 November 2003 concerning jurisdiction and the recognition and enforcement of judgments in matrimonial matters and the matters of parental responsibility, repealing Regulation (EC) No 1347/2000 (Brussels II *bis*), Arts 22(2)(a), 23(2)(a), 31(2); Swiss PIL Act, Art 27(1); Italian PIL Act, Art 64; Turkish PIL Act, Art 54(1)(c).

87 Regarding this finding on Turkish law see Cemile Demir-Gökyayla, *Yabancı Mahkeme Kararlarının Tanınması ve Tenfizinde Kamu Düzeni [Public Policy in the Recognition and Enforcement of Foreign Judgments]* (Seçkin 2001) 185.

88 Although there is no special provision on *talaq* divorces in the Hague Convention of 1970 on the Recognition of Divorces and Legal Separations, a *talaq* divorce can still be recognised under the Convention if it involves the intervention of the public or religious authorities and can be regarded as proceedings: Hague Conference on Private International Law, Convention on the Recognition of Divorces and Legal Separations – Draft Adopted by the Eleventh Session and Explanatory Report by Messrs. P. Bellet and B. Goldman (English translation) (Permanent Bureau of the Hague Conference 1971) para 13. Also see Case C-372/16 *Soha Sahyouni v Raja Mamisch* in which the Court of Justice found that the Rome III and Brussels II *bis* Regulations do not apply to a divorce resulting from a unilateral declaration made by one of the spouses before a religious court: Case C-372/16 *Soha Sahyouni v Raja Mamisch* [2017] ECLI:EU:C:2017:988, para 35 et seq.

89 Recognition of foreign *talaq* is here dealt with as regards the public policy exception. Another important factor in the recognition of foreign *talaq* – which is not examined here but is still decisive – is whether it includes the involvement of a religious or administrative authority of that foreign country. In certain states (such as Germany, the Netherlands, England), recognition of foreign *talaq* is subject to different rules depending on whether there is an involvement of a public authority and whether some form of procedure is followed. In Turkish law *talaq* has to be approved by the courts of the foreign country to be recognised under the Turkish PIL Act. As regards different provisions applied to foreign *talaq* in German law see Susan Rutten, 'Recognition of Divorce by Repudiation (*talaq*) in France, Germany and the Netherlands' (2004) 11(3) Maastricht Journal of European and Comparative Law 263, 277. As regards Turkish law see Nuray Ekşi, *Yabancı Mahkeme Kararlarının Tanınması ve Tenfizi [Recognition and Enforcement of Foreign Judgments]* (Beta 2013) 537.

90 See e.g. Dutch Civil Code, Arts 10:57 (repudiations established under supervision or with the cooperation of the judge or another authority and following some form of procedure),

requirements provided are satisfied. Thus, in those states, even though public policy may also be accepted as a condition for recognition,[91] it is not frequently used since public interest is already taken into consideration in the formulation of the legal requirements.[92]

On the other hand, in countries where recognition of foreign *talaq* is not made subject to special provisions (such as Germany and Turkey) it can be said that public policy has a more prominent role. For example, in Germany and Turkey, the position of the woman (as well as proximity[93]) is of utmost importance in both substantive and procedural aspects of public policy in the recognition of foreign *talaq*. In this regard, where the wife has given her consent subsequently, public policy may not bar recognition since *talaq* in this case can be qualified as an uncontested divorce.[94] The same conclusion should be reached in situations where prior notice is given to the woman regarding *talaq* and she is given the opportunity to be heard.[95]

In France, which falls into the second group of countries, jurisprudence of *Cour de cassation* has shaped the discussions and the principle of gender equality has been given differing roles over the years: in certain decisions gender equality was given an important role in the recognition of foreign *talaq*, whereas in others it was taken into consideration as only one of the factors.[96] Nevertheless, via the decisions of *Cour de cassation* of 2004[97] it has now been accepted that a foreign

---

10:58 (repudiations where there is no such procedure followed), and 10:59 (public policy); English Family Law Act 1986, ss 46(1) (where some form of procedure is followed) and 46(2) (where no form of procedure is followed). Regarding implementation of the said provisions of English law see *Quazi v Quazi* [1979] 3 WLR 833 (HL); *Chaudhary v Chaudhary* [1985] Fam 19, [1984] 3 All ER 1017 (CA). Regarding recognition of foreign *talaq* in the Netherlands and in England see Pauline Kruiniger, *Islamic Divorces in Europe – Bridging the Gap between European and Islamic Legal Orders* (Eleven International Publishing 2015) 223, 267.

91 See Dutch Civil Code, Art 10:59; English Family Law Act, s 51(3)(c); and see Art 10 of the the 1970 Hague Divorce Convention.

92 Pauline Kruiniger, *Islamic Divorces in Europe – Bridging the Gap between European and Islamic Legal Orders* (Eleven International Publishing 2015) 325.

93 On such a finding regarding German and French law see Susan Rutten, 'Recognition of Divorce by Repudiation (*talaq*) in France, Germany and the Netherlands' (2004) 11(3) Maastricht Journal of European and Comparative Law 263, 278, 281.

94 See e.g. the decision of the (Istanbul) Kadıkoy Civil Court of First Instance where the court accepted that *talaq* before the Saudi Arabian *qadi* which was subsequently accepted by his spouse before the Jeddah Religious Court could be recognised in Turkey, as the divorce could be qualified as an uncontested divorce: Kadıkoy Civil Court of First Instance [*Kadıkoy Asliye Hukuk Mahkemesi*] (Second Chamber) 7 February 1991 (Registration No 1990/853, Decision No 1991/94): Nuray Ekşi, *Yabancı Mahkeme Kararlarının Tanınması ve Tenfizi [Recognition and Enforcement of Foreign Judgments]* (Beta 2013) 539.

95 Susan Rutten, 'Recognition of Divorce by Repudiation (*talaq*) in France, Germany and the Netherlands' (2004) 11(3) Maastricht Journal of European and Comparative Law 263, 278.

96 Regarding recognition of *talaq* in French case law see ibid 266.

97 Pauline Kruiniger, *Islamic Divorces in Europe – Bridging the Gap between European and Islamic Legal Orders* (Eleven International Publishing 2015) 312.

talaq judgment which is given as a result of fair proceedings may nevertheless be rejected on public policy grounds based on Article 5 of Protocol No 7 to the ECHR[98] on equality between the spouses.[99]

In the opinion of the present author, in states where public policy is used as a ground to reject recognition of foreign *talaq*, it would be appropriate to make an assessment according to the circumstances of the case rather than rejecting the foreign *talaq* categorically based on a strict application of the principle of gender equality, since there might be situations in which recognition would be more favourable to women. One such situation would be where recognition of *talaq* is requested by the wife,[100] since rejection of recognition may not be justified by the fact that *talaq* is merely based on the will of the husband. Rejection of *talaq* as such would place an extra burden on women to bring a new divorce action before the courts of the requested state. By contrast, if recognition is made possible, then the women would have the chance to make ancillary claims, such as for maintenance. This approach would also serve to avoid the undesirable situation of 'limping' marriages, i.e. marriages which are valid in some countries but not recognised in others.

As noted previously, the public policy exception in the recognition and enforcement of foreign judgments also includes procedural rights. As such, infringement of the parties' right to a fair trial in the foreign proceedings may be a reason for rejecting the recognition and enforcement of the judgment on public policy grounds. The principle of equality requires that the party against whom the request for recognition or enforcement is made has to be notified in due course, provided with the documents regarding the case and given the right to defend him- or herself before the foreign court.[101]

---

98 Under Art 5, '[s]pouses shall enjoy equality of rights and responsibilities of a private law character between them, and in their relations with their children, as to marriage, during marriage and in the event of its dissolution. This article shall not prevent States from taking such measures as are necessary in the interests of the children'.

99 For a critical assessment of the two-stage test of public policy in the recognition of *talaq* in France as applied by the *Cour de cassation* in its decisions of 2004 see Marie-Elodie Ancel, 'The New Policy of the Cour de Cassation Regarding Islamic Repudiations: A Comment on Five Decisions Dated 17 Feb. 2004' (2005) 7 Yearbook of Private International Law 261, 262.

100 For a decision of the Thessaloniki Court of First Instance of 17 July 2019 (No 8458/2019) recognising the judgment of Abdeen Court (Egypt) on *talaq* without invoking public policy if the applicant is the wife: Apostolos Anthimos, '*Talaq* Reloaded: Repudiation recognised if application filed by the wife' (9 September 2019) <https://conflictoflaws.net/2019/talaq-reloaded-repudiation-recognized-if-application-filed-by-the-wife/?print=pdf> accessed 1 May 2020.

101 See *Pellegrini v Italy* App no 30882/96 (20 July 2001) paras 44 et seq.

4. QUESTIONING PUBLIC POLICY IN THE RECOGNITION OF CONSEQUENCES OF MARRIAGES ACQUIRED VALIDLY ABROAD

As explained above, in the area of applicable law the public policy exception is an effective technique for disregarding the otherwise designated foreign law if the application of that law is considered manifestly contrary to the principle of gender equality and prohibition of gender-based discrimination as adopted by the forum state. As such, in countries where monogamy forms part of state policy, a polygynous marriage cannot be celebrated even where both spouses have foreign nationalities. In a similar vein, where the designated foreign law permits the celebration of marriages of women below the marriageable age specified by the forum state, the public policy exception shall bar the celebration of that marriage in the latter.

However, recognition of a marriage validly celebrated abroad in accordance with the foreign law designated by the conflict-of-laws rules of the forum should be treated as a separate question.[102] In such a case, certain consequences of that marriage may be recognised in the forum state to protect the interests of the women involved in the relationship. The importance of the question of recognition of marriages celebrated validly abroad has increased in recent years, due to the increase in the mobility of persons. In particular, the influx of Middle Eastern, African and South Asian immigrants into European countries has highlighted the discussions as regards recognition of certain consequences of polygynous and child marriages.

4.1. RECOGNITION OF POLYGYNOUS MARRIAGES

Polygyny refers to a marriage of a man with more than one wife at a time. Today it is accepted in Islamic law, as well as in certain West African countries by law and/or by practice. In certain countries, such as Nigeria, Ghana and Benin, polygynous marriages are prohibited by civil law but widespread in practice, whereas in others they are recognised by civil law (such as in Mali, Chad, Togo and Senegal) or by customary law and/or religious practices (including Niger and Liberia).[103]

---

102 The Hague Convention of 14 March 1978 on Celebration and Recognition of the Validity of Marriages requires the contracting states to recognise the validity of a marriage which is valid according to the law of the state of celebration, subject to certain limitations (Art 9). Under Art 11 of the Convention, the contracting states may refuse to recognise the validity of a marriage only if, at the time of the marriage, under the law of that state, inter alia one of the spouses was already married (Art 11(1)) or one of the spouses had not attained the minimum age required for marriage (Art 11(3)).

103 'Polygamy remains common and mostly legal in West Africa' (2019) 77 Maps & Facts <http://www.oecd.org/swac/maps/77-polygamy-remains%20common-West-Africa.pdf> accessed 20 May 2020.

In Iran, Saudi Arabia, Qatar, the United Arab Emirates, Pakistan and Morocco, polygyny is permissible, but subject to different conditions.

Although in monogamous countries celebration of a second (or third/fourth) marriage of a married man would be rejected on public policy grounds, if that marriage is already lawfully celebrated under the law of a foreign country, recognition of the consequences of such a marriage may be treated separately, with the aim of securing certain interests of second (or third/fourth) wife and the children born out of that relationship.[104]

In this regard, in certain European states, an approach based on the attenuated effect of public policy is adopted[105] where proximity with the forum state may be a decisive factor. As such, where the marriage has no significant connection with the forum state, spouses who are validly married in a country that accepts polygynous marriages would be considered to be legally married for the purposes of providing maintenance and succession rights, pension rights, and certain social security benefits and allowances, as well as of recognising the legitimacy of the children.[106] Thus, this approach disregards the intervention of the public policy exception and reflects that the status acquired under foreign law must be respected. Nevertheless, depending on the circumstances of each case – for example where one of the spouses is the citizen of the forum state – the connection with the latter would act as a bar to the cross-border recognition of the marriage.[107]

In *Wagner and J.M.W.L. v Luxembourg*,[108] which involved a dispute over non-recognition of a Peruvian 'judgment' on adoption in Luxembourg, the ECtHR held that, depending on the circumstances of the case, legal status acquired according to foreign law in good faith may be recognised if the persons

104 Regarding recognition of polygynous marriages see Karl Kreuzer, 'Clash of Civilizations and Conflict of Laws' (2009) 62 Revue Hellénique de Droit International 629, 644.

105 Council of Europe Parliamentary Assembly Committee on Equal Opportunities for Women and Men, 'Respect for the principle of equality in civil law' (Revised expert paper prepared by Stéphanie Billaud, 24 February 2006) 11.

106 E.g. in Germany, France, Italy and Belgium rights of maintenance, succession, pension rights and certain social security benefits are recognised: Sabine Corneloup, Bettina Heiderhoff, Costanza Honorati, Fabienne Jault-Seseke, Thalia Kruger, Caroline Rupp, Hans van Loon and Jinske Verhellen, 'Private International Law in a Context of Increasing International Mobility: Challenges and Potential' (European Parliament Policy Department for Citizens' Rights and Constitutional Affairs 2017) 23. In English common law, polygamous marriages concluded abroad are recognised since *The Sinha Peerage Claim* of 1939. As regards the recognition of consequences of polygamous marriages in England see David McClean and Verónica Ruiz Abou-Nigm, *Morris: The Conflict of Laws* (9th ed, Sweet & Maxwell 2016); Joost Bloom, 'Public Policy in Private International Law and Its Evolution in Time' (2003) Netherlands International Law Review 374, 383. As regards South African law see Jan L Neels, 'The Positive Role of Public Policy in Private International Law and the Recognition of Foreign Muslim Marriages' (2012) 28 South African Journal on Human Rights 219.

107 Karl Kreuzer, 'Clash of Civilizations and Conflict of Laws' (2009) 62 Revue Hellénique de Droit International 629, 646.

108 *Wagner and J.M.W.L. v Luxembourg* App no 76240/01 (28 June 2007).

concerned have legitimate expectations of the recognition of their family life.[109] Nevertheless, in *Mary Green and Ajad Farhat v Malta*,[110] where the rejection of registration of a second marriage by Maltese authorities on the grounds of public policy in the absence of proof of the dissolution of Mrs Green's first marriage was under consideration, the ECtHR took a different approach. It found that taking into account the interests of the Maltese community to ensure monogamous marriages, as well as the interests of Mrs Green's first husband, the domestic courts had not failed to strike a fair balance between the conflicting interests, and accordingly dismissed the complaint.[111]

However, even in countries where the effects of polygynous marriages are recognised, it seems that family reunification constitutes an important exception.[112] National legislation allowing family reunification only for one of the spouses and the children born out of that relationship was subject to decisions of the European Commission of Human Rights as early as the 1990s, where the Commission did not find any infringement of Article 8 of the Convention on the right to respect for private and family life. An example of such a decision is *E.A. and A.A. v The Netherlands*,[113] which concerned the rejection of E.A.'s application for a residence permit for his son A.A. in the Netherlands. A Moroccan national, E.A., who was already married in Morocco, entered into a second marriage in the Netherlands with another Moroccan national. He subsequently made an application for a residence permit in the Netherlands for his son, A.A., from his first marriage. This was rejected by the Dutch authorities based on, inter alia, the ground of the Dutch policy which authorised family reunification only for one spouse and the children born out of that relationship, since polygamy was contrary to Dutch public order. Although the Commission found that the ties between the applicants were covered by the concept of family life within the meaning of Article 8, and thus the refusal to grant a residence permit constituted an interference with their right to respect for family life, it

---

109 For a comprehensive assessment of *Wagner and J.M.W.L. v Luxembourg* see Hans van Loon and David Sindres, 'Cultural identities: Wagner v. Luxembourg' in Horatia Muir Watt, Lucia Biziková, Agatha Brandão de Oliveira and Diego P. Fernandez Arroyo (eds), *Global Private International Law* (Edward Elgar Publishing 2019) 530.

110 *Mary Green and Ajad Farhat v Malta* App no 38797/07 (6 July 2010).

111 Patrick Kinsch, 'Private International Law Topics Before the European Court of Human Rights – Selected Judgments and Decisions (2010–2011)' (2011) 13 Yearbook of Private International Law 37, 42.

112 Sabine Corneloup, Bettina Heiderhoff, Costanza Honorati, Fabienne Jault-Seseke, Thalia Kruger, Caroline Rupp, Hans van Loon and Jinske Verhellen, 'Private International Law in a Context of Increasing International Mobility: Challenges and Potential' (European Parliament Policy Department for Citizens' Rights and Constitutional Affairs 2017) 23. For a detailed assessment of family reunification in polygamous marriages see Nicole Stybnarova, 'Teleology Behind the Prohibition of Recognition of Polygamous Marriages Under the EU Family Reunification Directive: A Critique of Rule of Effectiveness' (2020) 40(1) Journal of Muslim Minority Affairs 104.

113 *E.A. and A.A. v The Netherlands* App no 14501/89 (6 January 1992).

nevertheless concluded that this interference was justified under Article 8(2), on the ground that it was in accordance with the law (Dutch Aliens Act) and was based on a legitimate measure of immigration control which was necessary in a democratic society for the economic well-being of the country. The Commission also rejected the complaints that the second applicant was discriminated against based on birth. According to the Commission, although the Dutch policy created a difference of treatment between children born out of subsequent marriages, it had an objective and reasonable justification for doing so because of the legal status of the second applicant, in that his mother continued to live in Morocco and was not entitled to live in the Netherlands.[114]

Today the EU Directive on the Right to Family Reunification[115] adopts a similar approach. It provides that where the sponsor already has a spouse living with him in the territory of a Member State, the Member State concerned shall not authorise the family reunification of a further spouse (Art 4(4)). On the other hand, the Directive leaves it to the Member States to decide whether they wish to authorise family reunification for minor children of a further spouse and the sponsor (Preamble, para 10; Art 4(4)). Although the approach provided in the Directive aims to respect the rights of women in polygynous marriages,[116] it is rather the rights of the wife who is resident in the Member States that are given priority, which results in exclusion of the other wife/wives and (depending on the discretion of the Member States) her/their minor children from the protection of EU law. The Directive gives the sole authority to the husband to choose unilaterally the wife who shall enjoy the right of residence in the EU Member State without any possible intervention in this choice by the other wife/wives or the children and without any assessment of this choice by the authorities of the Member State concerned.[117] This certainly leaves the 'other' wife/wives who is/are 'left' in the country of origin unprotected and in a situation where she/they can enjoy neither the benefits of an effective marriage nor the legal consequences of a divorce.[118]

Thus, the prevailing approach of recognising certain consequences of the validity of polygynous marriages abroad seems not to be applicable in the area of family reunification, the latter having been considered one of the main reasons

---

114 See also *M. and O.M. v The Netherlands* where the European Commission of Human Rights ruled as regards the Dutch family reunification policy in relation to polygamous marriages that discrimination based on birth may only be discussed for the minor children, thus rejecting the arguments based on that ground since the child in the case was 26 years old: *M. and O.M. v The Netherlands* App no 12139/86 (5 October 1987).

115 Council Directive 2003/86/EC of 22 September 2003 on the right to family reunification [2003] OJ L 251/12.

116 ibid Preamble, para 11.

117 Nicole Stybnarova, 'Teleology Behind the Prohibition of Recognition of Polygamous Marriages Under the EU Family Reunification Directive: A Critique of Rule of Effectiveness' (2020) 40(1) Journal of Muslim Minority Affairs 104, 112.

118 ibid.

for immigration into the EU.[119] A change in this attitude does not seem very probable either – at least in the near future – due to the migration pressure that has been felt in most of the EU Member States.

4.2. RECOGNITION OF CHILD MARRIAGES

'Child marriage' (or 'early marriage') is defined as 'any marriage where at least one of the parties is under 18 years of age'.[120] It prevents education of girls, who are the victims of child marriages in most cases, risks their health and subjects them to the risk of abuse and poverty.[121] It is also considered to be a type of forced marriage, since it undermines the full, free and informed consent of the child.[122]

Child marriages are prohibited by the Convention on Consent to Marriage, Minimum Age for Marriage and Registration of Marriages[123] (Art 2) and by the CEDAW (Art 16(2)).[124] Without specifying a marriageable age themselves, both instruments require the contracting states to specify a minimum age for marriage and provide that a marriage under this age shall have no legal effect.[125] The CEDAW further obliges the contracting states to make the registration of marriages in an official registry compulsory (Art 16(2)). Elimination of all harmful practices, such as child, early and forced marriage and female genital mutilation, is also provided as Target 5.3 of SDG 5.

119 European Commission, 'Family reunification' <https://ec.europa.eu/home-affairs/what-we-do/policies/legal-migration/family-reunification_en> accessed 16 April 2020.

120 Committee on the Elimination of Discrimination Against Women and Committee on the Rights of the Child, Joint General Recommendation No 31 of the Committee on the Elimination of Discrimination Against Women/General Comment No 18 of the Committee on the Rights of the Child on Harmful Practices, UN Doc CEDAW/C/GC/31-CRC/C/GC/18 (14 November 2014) para 20 <https://documents-dds-ny.un.org/doc/UNDOC/GEN/N14/627/78/PDF/ N1462778.pdf?OpenElement> accessed 20 May 2020.

121 For causes and consequences of child marriages see Anne Wijffelman, 'Child Marriage and Family Reunification: An Analysis under the European Convention on Human Rights of the Dutch Forced Marriage Prevention Act' (2017) 35(2) Netherlands Quarterly of Human Rights 104, 106.

122 Council of Europe Parliamentary Assembly, Forced Marriage in Europe, Resolution 2233 (2018) para 3 <http://assembly.coe.int/nw/xml/XRef/Xref-XML2HTML-en.asp?fileid=25016&lang=en> accessed 20 May 2020.

123 Convention on Consent to Marriage, Minimum Age for Marriage and Registration of Marriages (adopted 10 December 1962, entry into force 9 December 1964) 521 UNTS 231.

124 Other instruments such as the ICCPR (Art 23(2)) and the ECHR (Art 12) provide for the right to marry and to found a family for men and women 'of marriageable age'.

125 Under Art 2 of the Convention on Consent to Marriage, Minimum Age for Marriage and Registration of Marriages, marriage under the specified age can only be possible where a competent authority has granted a dispensation as to age, for serious reasons, in the interest of the intending spouses.

In recent years, due to amendments of national legislation increasing the marriageable age to 18, prohibiting child marriages and requiring the registration of all marriages, the number of child marriages has decreased worldwide.[126] Nevertheless, child marriage is still a reality in certain countries as a result of economic, cultural, religious and social factors. According to data provided by UNICEF, 37 per cent of young women in sub-Saharan Africa are married before they reach the age of 18 (76 per cent in Niger, 68 per cent in the Central African Republic, 67 per cent in Chad). Although 25 million child marriages were prevented in the last decade, more than 120 million girls are expected to get married before the age of 18 by 2030.[127]

The question which concerns us here is whether certain consequences of a child marriage which is validly entered into under the law of a foreign country should be recognised in another country which prohibits such marriages.

In recent years, the increase in the number of child marriages due to the increase in the number of migrants has triggered the national legislators of certain countries to provide express rules on not recognising such marriages. As such, the public policy exception as a classical technique of private international law in restricting the recognition of a status acquired abroad through a case-by-case analysis is replaced by mandatory prohibitions.[128] Examples of recent legislation prohibiting the recognition of child marriages include the German Law to Combat Child Marriages of 2017,[129] the Dutch Forced Marriage Prevention

---

126 Office of the UN High Commissioner for Human Rights, 'Preventing and Eliminating Child, Early and Forced Marriage', UN Doc A/HRC/26/22 (2 April 2014) para 25 et seq <https://documents-dds-ny.un.org/doc/UNDOC/GEN /G14/128 /76/PDF/G1412876.pdf?OpenElement> accessed 16 May 2020.

127 UNICEF, 'Child Marriage Around the World (infographic)' <https://www.unicef.org/stories/child-marriage-around-world> accessed 25 May 2020.

128 Regarding the role of public policy in the recognition of child marriages in Germany before the enactment of the Law to Combat Child Marriages see Andrea Büchler, *Islamic Law in Europe? Legal Pluralism and its Limits in European Family Laws* (Routledge 2011) 43; Nina Dethloff, 'Child Brides on the Move: Legal Responses to Culture Clashes' (2018) 32(3) International Journal of Law Policy and the Family 302, 310. Regarding Dutch law see Anne Wijffelman, 'Child Marriage and Family Reunification: An Analysis under the European Convention on Human Rights of the Dutch Forced Marriage Prevention Act' (2017) 35(2) Netherlands Quarterly of Human Rights 104, 105. Regarding Swedish law see Michael Bogdan, 'Some Critical Comments on the New Swedish Rules on Non-Recognition of Foreign Child Marriages' (2019) 15(2) Journal of Private International Law 247, 248. On the other hand, in English case law there are examples of both where public policy was used as a tool not to recognise a child marriage concluded abroad (e.g. *SB v RB (Residence: Forced Marriage; Child's Best Interests)* [2008] EWHC 938 (Fam)) and where such marriages were recognised without recourse to the public policy exception (e.g. *Mohammad v Knott* [1969] 1 QB 1; *Re K: A Local Authority v N and Others* [2005] EWHC 2956 (Fam)). As regards recognition of child marriages in England see James J Fawcett, Maire Ni Shuilleabhain and Sangeeta Shah, *Human Rights and Private International Law* (Oxford 2016) 647, para 11.157.

129 The German Law to Combat Child Marriage provides that a marriage concluded in Germany or abroad where one of the spouses is below 16 years of age shall be null and void in Germany from the date of its conclusion. If the spouses are between 16 and 18 years of age, the

Act of 2015[130] and the amendments of 2018 of the Swedish Act on Certain International Marriage and Guardianship Relations.[131]

Although the aforementioned national legislation aims to prevent child marriages, it is subject to criticism from the perspective of private international law. As a general point, it can firstly be mentioned that such prohibition will increase the phenomenon of 'limping' marriages and disregards the principle of protection of rights acquired legally abroad as well as the right to respect for family life. This approach may also leave the woman, as one of the parties to such a marriage, unprotected in her claims for divorce, maintenance, succession and matrimonial property, as well as regarding the paternity of any child born out of a child marriage. Similar questions may arise as regards family reunification and residence permits.[132]

This approach does not also take into account the reality for migrant women, who may agree to marry before they reach the marriageable age to protect themselves from sexual violence during their journey to the country of destination or in detention camps.[133] Rejection of recognition of certain consequences of child marriages is also open to criticism since this approach

---

marriage may be annulled by German courts. German Federal Court of Justice in its decision of 14 November 2018 found the Law contrary to the German Constitution since it declares the marriage invalid without taking the circumstances of the case into consideration and because of the fact that unlike marriages celebrated in Germany, the law also declares such foreign marriages which were celebrated even before the enactment of the new law to be invalid: BGH 14 November 2018 <http://juris.bundesgerichtshof.de/cgibin/rechtsprechung/document.py?Gericht=bgh&Art=en&sid=8f3f536fe9771956119dd3bf73cae3db&nr=90440&pos=0&anz=1> accessed 10 May 2020. The action taken before the German Federal Constitutional Court on the review of the Act was still pending at the time of writing this chapter. For a comprehensive analysis of child marriages in comparative law, including the recognition of foreign child marriages, prepared for the German Federal Constitutional Court see Max-Planck-Institut für ausländisches und internationales Privatrecht, 'Die Frühehe im Rechtsvergleich: Praxis, Sachrecht, Kollisionsrecht' (2020) 84(4) Rabels Zeitschrift für ausländisches und internationales Privatrecht 705.

130 The Dutch Forced Marriage Prevention Act permits the recognition of marriage contracted abroad by children under the age of 18 (child marriage) only once the spouses have reached the age of 18: Anne Wijffelman, 'Child Marriage and Family Reunification: An Analysis under the European Convention on Human Rights of the Dutch Forced Marriage Prevention Act' (2017) 35(2) Netherlands Quarterly of Human Rights 104, 105.

131 Under the new legislation, regardless of whether the spouses have any connection with Sweden at the time of the marriage, a marriage celebrated abroad after 1 January 2019 shall not be recognised in principle if one of the spouses is below 18 years of age at the time of the marriage: see Michael Bogdan, 'Some Critical Comments on the New Swedish Rules on Non-Recognition of Foreign Child Marriages' (2019) 15(2) Journal of Private International Law 247, 250 et seq; Maarit Jänterä-Jareborg, 'Non-recognition of Child Marriages: Sacrificing the Global for the Local in the Aftermath of the 2015 "Refugee Crisis"' in Gillian Douglas, Mervyn Murch and Victoria Stephens (eds), *International and National Perspectives on Child and Family Law: Essays in Honour of Nigel Lowe* (Intersentia 2018) 267, 275.

132 Under the EU Directive on the Right to Family Reunification the Member States may require the sponsor and his or her spouse to be of a minimum age, and at maximum 21 years old, before the spouse is able to join him or her in order to ensure better integration and to prevent forced marriages (Art 4(5)).

133 Sabine Corneloup, Bettina Heiderhoff, Costanza Honorati, Fabienne Jault-Seseke, Thalia Kruger, Caroline Rupp, Hans van Loon and Jinske Verhellen, 'Private International Law

equally empowers the husband by giving him the opportunity to remarry, mostly with a citizen of the country of destination, and thus become eligible to claim nationality or residence rights.[134]

In this regard, rather than categorically rejecting the recognition of all consequences of a child marriage celebrated abroad, an approach which gives the national authorities the option to take into account the circumstances of each case should be adopted. Accordingly, there might be situations where recognition of certain consequences of a child marriage would be in the best interests of the child as guaranteed by the Convention on the Rights of the Child (Art 3).[135] In its Resolution of 28 June 2018, the Parliamentary Assembly of the Council of Europe provided that the Member States should refrain from recognising forced marriages contracted abroad; it nevertheless advised recognising the effects of the marriage if this would enable the victim to secure rights which they could not otherwise claim (para 7.9).[136]

5. RESULTS AND RECOMMENDATIONS TO FURTHER THE ROLE OF PRIVATE INTERNATIONAL LAW IN ACHIEVING GENDER EQUALITY

As the preceding paragraphs demonstrate, gender equality has an impact on different issues of private international law with differing underlying principles. This precludes the adoption of a single global approach that is relevant for all such issues in order to secure gender equality and the elimination of discrimination; thus, each subject has to be considered and assessed independently.

Accordingly, recommendations on furthering the role of private international law to ensure gender equality differ as to the area concerned. Some would be strictly related to private international law techniques (such as in the selection of connecting factors or jurisdiction criteria favouring both spouses equally) or their mode of

in a Context of Increasing International Mobility: Challenges and Potential' (European Parliament Policy Department for Citizens' Rights and Constitutional Affairs 2017) 21. For a detailed assessment of Arts 3 and 8 of the ECHR as regards rejection of family reunification of the child brides see Anne Wijffelman, 'Child Marriage and Family Reunification: An Analysis under the European Convention on Human Rights of the Dutch Forced Marriage Prevention Act' (2017) 35(2) Netherlands Quarterly of Human Rights 104, 112.

134 Michael Bogdan, 'Some Critical Comments on the New Swedish Rules on Non-Recognition of Foreign Child Marriages' (2019) 15(2) Journal of Private International Law 247, 252.

135 Sabine Corneloup, Bettina Heiderhoff, Costanza Honorati, Fabienne Jault-Seseke, Thalia Kruger, Caroline Rupp, Hans van Loon and Jinske Verhellen, 'Private International Law in a Context of Increasing International Mobility: Challenges and Potential' (European Parliament Policy Department for Citizens' Rights and Constitutional Affairs 2017) 22; Nina Dethloff, 'Child Brides on the Move: Legal Responses to Culture Clashes' (2018) 32(3) International Journal of Law Policy and the Family 302, 314.

136 Council of Europe Parliamentary Assembly, Forced Marriage in Europe, Resolution 2233 (2018) <http://assembly.coe.int/nw/xml/XRef/Xref-XML2HTML-en.asp?fileid=25016&lang=en> accessed 20 May 2020.

application (such as the public policy exception in the conflict of laws and in the recognition and enforcement of foreign judgments, as well as in the recognition of polygynous marriages), whereas others would concern the substantive law of the relevant countries (such as the overriding mandatory rules of the *lex fori*) or may require amendments or new approaches therein (such as recognition of child marriages).

As such, it seems neither appropriate nor possible to recommend adoption of a single, binding private international law instrument to ensure gender equality and elimination of gender-based discrimination.[137] Nevertheless, it should still be possible to recommend soft law instruments, such as guiding principles on the realisation of gender equality in cross-border matters, covering all issues mentioned above. One such example, although not on gender equality in particular, is the Draft Resolution of the Fourth Commission of the Institute of International Law on 'Human Rights and Private International Law',[138] which deals with private international law issues through the lens of human rights.

In the opinion of the present author, similar work could be undertaken by the Hague Conference on Private International Law, considering the fact that the organisation's Strategic Plan for 2019–2022[139] provides for the development of legally non-binding instruments (model laws or principles) comprising private international law rules under Strategic Priority 1, and refers to the UN SDGs (albeit in the context of Strategic Priority 2 (non-normative work)). Despite not being binding such principles may identify how and where gender equality and prohibition of discrimination can be taken into account in different areas of private international law and can serve to establish *de lege ferenda* invaluable guidance for national legislators, administrative officials and judges.

---

[137] In 2007 the Committee on Equal Opportunities for Women and Men of the Council of Europe recommended that the Committee of Ministers draw up a new Protocol to the ECHR to ensure gender equality and eliminate gender-based discrimination in both domestic law and in private international law: Council of Europe Parliamentary Assembly Committee on Equal Opportunities for Women and Men, 'Respect for the principle of equality in civil law' (Rapporteur Svetlana Smirnova), Doc 11177 (6 February 2007) <https://assembly.coe.int/Documents/WorkingDocs/2007/EDOC11177.pdf> accessed 15 January 2021. Nevertheless, considering the existing legal instruments (Art 14 ECHR, Protocol No 12 and Art 5 of Protocol 7 to the ECHR, as well as Recommendations Rec(85)2 on legal protection against sex discrimination, Rec(2002)5 on the protection of women against violence, and Rec(2007)17 on gender equality standards and mechanisms) the Committee of Ministers did not see at that stage the need to draft a new protocol: Council of Europe Parliamentary Assembly, 'Respect for the principle of equality in civil law' (Reply to Recommendation: Recommendation 1798 (2007)) (Doc 11648 (20 June 2008) <https://pace.coe.int/pdf/23d1f928a398cb865fcac8910560313331cc5c093326667a8259ffe25682ae848428feba12/doc.%2011648.pdf> accessed 15 January 2021.

[138] Institute of International Law, Commission No 4, Draft Resolution: Human Rights and Private International Law (Rapporteur: Jürgen Basedow) (January 2017) <https://www.idi-iil.org/app/uploads/2017/08/Translation-draft-resolution-fourth-commission-human-rights-and-pril.pdf> accessed 15 May 2020.

[139] Hague Conference on Private International Law, Strategic Plan 2019–2022 <https://assets.hcch.net/docs/bb7129a9-abee-46c9-ab65-7da398e51856.pdf> accessed 15 November 2020.

SDG 6: CLEAN WATER AND SANITATION

Richard Frimpong OPPONG

Goal 6: Ensure availability and sustainable management of water and sanitation for all

6.1 By 2030, achieve universal and equitable access to safe and affordable drinking water for all
6.2 By 2030, achieve access to adequate and equitable sanitation and hygiene for all and end open defecation, paying special attention to the needs of women and girls and those in vulnerable situations
6.3 By 2030, improve water quality by reducing pollution, eliminating dumping and minimizing release of hazardous chemicals and materials, halving the proportion of untreated wastewater and substantially increasing recycling and safe reuse globally
6.4 By 2030, substantially increase water-use efficiency across all sectors and ensure sustainable withdrawals and supply of freshwater to address water scarcity and substantially reduce the number of people suffering from water scarcity
6.5 By 2030, implement integrated water resources management at all levels, including through transboundary cooperation as appropriate
6.6 By 2020, protect and restore water-related ecosystems, including mountains, forests, wetlands, rivers, aquifers and lakes
6.a By 2030, expand international cooperation and capacity-building support to developing countries in water- and sanitation-related activities and programmes, including water harvesting, desalination, water efficiency, wastewater treatment, recycling and reuse technologies
6.b Support and strengthen the participation of local communities in improving water and sanitation management

1. INTRODUCTION

In September 2015, the UN General Assembly adopted the 2030 Agenda for Sustainable Development (Agenda 2030).[1] It sets out an ambitious programme of goals, including Sustainable Development Goal 6 (SDG 6), which aims to 'ensure availability and sustainable management of water and sanitation for all' by the year 2030. Investments by transnational companies can play a significant role in achieving or undermining the Sustainable Development Goals,[2] including SDG 6. Indeed, attracting investment from multinational or transnational corporations has been a central tenet of the development efforts of most developing countries. This is reflected not only in national legislation and bilateral agreements, but also in various non-legislative initiatives. Multinational corporations have invested in many sectors in developing countries, ranging from agriculture – the heaviest user of water resources – to mining. Key sectors in which governments have sought foreign investment include water distribution, waste treatment, mining and agriculture.

Such investments can be instruments of sustainable development, but at the same time activities resulting from such investments can adversely affect the availability and sustainable management of water resources and sanitation. Mining-related water usage and investment in farmlands can have a significant impact on the quality, quantity and availability of water in countries around the world. Farmland investments, and the large-scale commercial farming they entail, can exacerbate the strain on water resources because of the vast amounts of water they require for their operations.[3] The amount of water extracted for farmland investments, and the quantity and nature of chemicals discharged by the use of pesticides and fertilisers, directly impact the water resources available for other users, including local communities, other investors or neighbouring states.[4] Similarly, mining and its by-products can damage or pollute water bodies, reducing communities' access to and utilisation of such water resources.

1 UN General Assembly, 'Transforming Our World: The 2030 Agenda for Sustainable Development', UN Doc A/RES/70/1 (21 October 2015).

2 ibid, para 67.

3 Makane Moïse Mbengue and Susanna Waltman, 'Farmland Investments and Water Rights in Africa: The Legal Regimes Converging over Land and Water', Investment Treaty News 6, no 3 (August 2015) 1.

4 ibid.

In several instances, investments by transnational corporations in these areas have gone bad, resulting in disputes and potentially undermining governments' efforts to ensure availability and sustainable development of water and sanitation for all. Accordingly, various attempts – both domestic and international – have been made by individuals and communities to hold multinational corporations judicially accountable for wrongful activities in developing countries that directly or indirectly affect water and sanitation. At the same time, multinational corporations have sought to hold governments accountable for actions and policies that adversely affect their investments before international arbitral tribunals.

This chapter seeks to examine whether private international law has a facilitative role in the attainment of SDG 6 at both the transactional and dispute settlement levels. It examines the extent to which the rules of private international law can be engaged in efforts to ensure the sustainable management of water resources in both the domestic and transboundary contexts. The chapter examines the appropriateness of resolving disputes affecting clean water and sanitation in foreign courts and international arbitral fora. It assesses the consequences of allowing such claims against or by multinational corporations to be resolved abroad on the development of host states' legal systems and the potential for judgments resulting from such claims to effect policy and legislative changes in developing countries.

The chapter is divided into four main sections. The first section is a general examination of the right to water and how it is related to SDG 6. The second section examines the current state of private international instruments, doctrines and methodologies to see the extent to which, at both the transactional and dispute settlement levels, they are suitable to advancing the goal of ensuring the availability and sustainable management of water and sanitation for all. The third section examines investment contracts that governments enter into with multinational corporations in the water and sanitation sectors. It examines how governments deal with private international law issues, such as the law that must govern such contracts and which dispute settlement mechanism to adopt in the event of a dispute. The final section of the chapter examines how national courts and international arbitration tribunals have dealt with claims brought by individuals against multinational corporations for harm to their water resources, as well as claims brought by multinational corporations against governments for governmental decisions that impact on their investments in the water and sanitation sectors.

2. AN OVERVIEW OF SDG 6

Water and sanitation are essential to life. Happily, the world is endowed with a vast number of rivers, lakes, aquifers and other vital water resources. These water resources, some of which are neglected or polluted due to human and industrial activities, are central to the realisation of SDG 6.

SDG 6 can be traced back to the Millennium Development Goals 2010, specifically Goal 7, Target 3, which called for the proportion of the world's population without sustainable access to safe drinking water and basic sanitation to be reduced by half by 2015. In 2015, the UN reported that globally, 147 countries had met the drinking water target, 95 countries had met the sanitation target, and 77 countries had met both.[5] Overall, the world was successful in achieving the target. Thus, SDG 6 aims, at least in part, to finish unfinished business arising from these achievements of the Millennium Development Goals.

The importance of SDG 6 lies in the fact that, regrettably, despite the progress made, an estimated 1.2 billion people lack access to safely managed drinking water services, 2.4 billion people do not have access to safely managed sanitation facilities, 4 billion people experience severe water scarcity during at least one month every year, and 0.5 billion people experience severe scarcity all year round.[6]

SDG 6 includes eight global targets. The targets are universally applicable and aspirational. Each government decides how to incorporate them into their national planning processes, policies and strategies, taking into account their national circumstances. The eight targets cover the entire water cycle, including the provision of drinking water (Target 6.1) and sanitation and hygiene services (Target 6.2), treatment and reuse of wastewater and ambient water quality (Target 6.3), water-use efficiency and scarcity (Target 6.4), transboundary cooperation in water resource management (Target 6.5), protecting and restoring water-related ecosystems (Target 6.6), international cooperation and capacity-building (Target 6.a) and participation in water and sanitation management (Target 6.b).[7] The full details of SDG 6 are presented in the introduction to this chapter.

SGD 6 is connected to and its realisation would support other SDGs, some of which make specific reference to water. As UN Secretary-General António Guterres observes, 'if we remain off track to deliver on SDG 6 then we jeopardize the entire 2030 Agenda for Sustainable Development'.[8] SDG 6 connects with SDG 3 (health and well-being), SDG 4 (quality education), SDG 11 (sustainable cities), SDG 12 (sustainable consumption and production) and SDG 15 (life on land). In essence, SDG 6 is a key multiplier-effect goal.[9]

In addition to its clear connections with environmental law, SDG 6 links closely with the human right to water and sanitation – a right that is widely

---

5 United Nations, *The Millennium Development Goals Report 2015* (2015) 7.

6 Jeffrey D Sachs et al, *Six Transformations to Achieve the Sustainable Development Goals (SDGs) Report* (Sustainable Development Solutions Network 2019) 25.

7 United Nations, *Sustainable Development Goal 6 Synthesis Report 2018 on Water and Sanitation* (2018) 11.

8 ibid, Foreword.

9 Godwell Nhamoa et al, 'Is 2030 too Soon for Africa to Achieve the Water and Sanitation Sustainable Development Goal?' (2019) 669 Science of the Total Environment 129, 131.

recognised by many countries[10] and by the United Nations.[11] The human right to water has progressively emerged from the interpretation of international human rights instruments regarding the human right to an adequate standard of living. The SDGs do not include any direct reference to a human right to water.[12] However, Target 6.1 focuses on universal and equitable access to safe and affordable drinking water for all. This is informed by international developments regarding the human right to water. The emergence of the human right to water has prominently focused on access to safe and clean drinking water and sanitation, but some have called for a broader interpretation of the right.[13]

Like most rights, the human right to water has procedural dimensions that are crucial to achieving its substantive dimensions. The procedural dimensions include access to information, public participation in decision-making, and international cooperation concerning water issues. Justiciability and the availability of judicial remedies when the right is violated are equally important to the realisation of the substantive dimensions of the human right to water. Private international law principles have a role to play in this regard. For example, as discussed below, the right to water can be relevant to investor–state arbitrations initiated under international investment treaties in connection with concessions for water-related services and large-scale land investments that often allocate water rights to foreign investors. Similarly, communities aggrieved by damage to their water resources by the activities of multinational corporations may seek remedy before domestic and foreign courts and engage private international law issues in the process.

3. PRIVATE INTERNATIONAL LAW INSTRUMENTS, DOCTRINES AND METHODOLOGIES AND SDG 6

A complex array of domestic and international laws and hard and soft laws could be engaged in efforts to ensure the availability and sustainable management of water and sanitation for all.[14] The relevant domestic laws vary from country to

---

10 A number of states guarantee the right to water in their constitutions or include it in their constitution as a directive principle of state policy. See e.g. Constitution of the Republic of South Africa 1996, s 27(1); Constitution of the Federal Democratic Republic of Ethiopia 1994, Art 90(1); Constitution of the Republic of Gambia 1997, Art 216(4); Constitution of Zambia 1996, Art 112(d).

11 UN General Assembly Resolution, The Human Right to Water and Sanitation, UN Doc A/RES/64/292 (28 July 2010) para 1.

12 However, in paragraph 7 of Agenda 2030 states reaffirmed their commitments regarding the 'human right to safe drinking water and sanitation'.

13 See recently Elisa Morgera et al, *The Right to Water for Food and Agriculture* (UN Food and Agriculture Organization 2020) 7–23 <http://www.fao.org/3/ca8248en/ca8248en.pdf> accessed 12 July 2021.

14 See generally Dante A Caponera, *Principles of Water Law and Administration – National and International* (3rd ed, Routledge 2019).

country. At the international level, especially in a transboundary context, issues affecting the availability and sustainable management of water and sanitation are subject to a plethora of public international laws[15] and regimes for international cooperation.[16] Although water has not yet been explicitly recognised as a self-standing human right in international treaties, as discussed above, such an independent right clearly is emerging. International law imposes specific obligations on states regarding access to safe drinking water.[17]

Indeed, in Agenda 2030, states expressly reaffirmed their commitment to international law and emphasised that the goals are to be 'implemented in a manner that is consistent with the rights and obligations of States under international law'.[18] In other words, international law is expressly recognised as the normative background for implementing the goals set out in Agenda 2030. Added to this, as Jolly and Trivedi have noted, 'international courts and tribunals have increasingly given due regard to the concept of sustainable development and sought to utilize it both as an aid to the interpretation and as a means of integration to contextualize their decisions within the broader normative framework'.[19]

Straddled between the domestic and international is private international law, a body of law traditionally defined as comprising rules for resolving claims involving foreign elements. There does not appear to be a significant number of international instruments that address the potential private international law issues that could be generated in the management of water resources. No Hague Conference on Private International Law convention directly addresses this issue.

Outside the Hague Conference, a few international instruments deal expressly with private international law issues affecting water and sanitation. The Protocol on Civil Liability and Compensation for Damage Caused by the Transboundary

---

15 E.g. Convention on the Law of the Non-Navigational Uses of International Watercourses, New York, 21 May 1997; Convention on the Protection and Use of Transboundary Watercourses and International Lakes, 1992.

16 Examples are the Alliance for Water Stewardship, and the UN Global Compact's CEO Water Mandate. See discussion in Mara Tignino, 'Private Investments and the Human Right to Water' in Yannick Radi (ed), *Research Handbook on Human Rights and Investment* (Edward Elgar Publishing 2018) 482–489. For a discussion on the regimes for transboundary management of water resources in the African context see Makane Moïse Mbengue and Susanna Waltman, 'Farmland Investments and Water Rights in Africa: The Legal Regimes Converging over Land and Water', Investment Treaty News 6, no 3 (August 2015) 37–45.

17 Sara De Vido, 'The Right to Water: From an Inchoate Right to an Emerging International Norm' (2012) 45 Belgian Review of International Law 517.

18 UN General Assembly, 'Transforming Our World: The 2030 Agenda for Sustainable Development', UN Doc A/RES/70/1 (21 October 2015), para 18. For other instances in which Agenda 2030 expressly underscores the role of international law see paras 10, 19, 23, 30, 35.

19 Stellina Jolly and Abhishek Trivedi, 'Implementing the SDG-13 Through the Adoption of Hybrid Law: Addressing Climate-Induced Displacement' (2019) Brill Open Law 69, 95 and the cases cited in n 119.

Effects of Industrial Accidents on Transboundary Waters of 2003,[20] which is not yet in force, provides a comprehensive regime for civil liability and adequate and prompt compensation for damage caused by the transboundary effects of industrial accidents on transboundary waters.[21] The Protocol has specific rules on the jurisdiction of courts,[22] arbitration,[23] *lis pendens* and related actions,[24] the applicable law,[25] and the recognition and enforcement of judgments and arbitral awards.[26] Similarly, the earlier, much broader, but equally not yet in force Convention on Civil Liability for Damage Resulting from Activities Dangerous to the Environment of 1993,[27] which aims at ensuring adequate compensation for damage resulting from activities dangerous to the environment,[28] also has specific rules on jurisdiction,[29] *lis pendens* and related actions,[30] and recognition and enforcement of judgments.[31]

The Protocol on Liability and Compensation for Damage Resulting from Transboundary Movements of Hazardous Wastes and their Disposal[32] provides a comprehensive regime for liability and adequate and prompt compensation for damage resulting from the transboundary movement of hazardous wastes and other wastes and their disposal, including illegal traffic in those wastes. The Protocol addresses the issues of jurisdiction,[33] related actions,[34] applicable law,[35] and the recognition and enforcement of judgments. The Bamako Convention on the Ban of the Import into Africa and the Control of Transboundary Movement and Management of Hazardous Wastes within Africa[36] envisaged the adoption

---

20 Protocol on Civil Liability and Compensation for Damage Caused by the Transboundary Effects of Industrial Accidents on Transboundary Waters, 2003 <https://www.unece.org/fileadmin/DAM/env/civil-liability/documents/protocol_e.pdf> accessed 12 July 2021 (Protocol on Civil Liability). For a discussion see Phani Dascalopoulou-Livada and Alexandros Kolliopoulos, 'The Kiev Civil Liability Protocol and the Interaction between Civil and Administrative Liability Regimes' (2017) 19 International Community Law Review 518.

21 Protocol on Civil Liability and Compensation for Damage Caused by the Transboundary Effects of Industrial Accidents on Transboundary Waters, 2003, Art 1 <https://www.unece.org/fileadmin/DAM/env/civil-liability/documents/protocol_e.pdf> accessed 12 July 2021.

22 ibid Art 13.

23 ibid Art 14.

24 ibid Art 15.

25 ibid Art 16.

26 ibid Art 18.

27 ETS 150 – Environment, 21.VI.1993 (Convention on Civil Liability for Damage).

28 ibid Art 1.

29 ibid Art 19.

30 ibid Arts 21–22.

31 ibid Art 23.

32 This Protocol was concluded under the Basel Convention on the Control of Transboundary Movements of Hazardous Wastes and their Disposal.

33 ibid Art 17.

34 ibid Art 18.

35 ibid Art 19.

36 <https://au.int/sites/default/files/treaties/7774-treaty-0015_-_bamako_convention_on_hazardous_wastes_e.pdf> accessed 12 July 2021.

of a protocol to deal with liabilities and compensation for damage resulting from the transboundary movement of hazardous waste. However, it appears no protocol has been adopted.

An important work in progress that may directly impact dispute settlement with transnational corporations, including, potentially, disputes related to activities affecting water resources and sanitation is the Draft Legally Binding Instrument to Regulate, in International Human Rights Law, the Activities of Transnational Corporations and other Business Enterprises of 2019.[37] It addresses the issues of jurisdiction,[38] the applicable law[39] and mutual legal assistance, including the recognition and enforcement of foreign judgments.[40]

The traditional doctrines, methodology and techniques of private international law are not designed for addressing the substantive objective of ensuring availability and sustainable management of water and sanitation for all. To a large extent, this is unremarkable. Indeed, the fact that existing doctrines, methodologies and techniques of other areas of law may be ill-suited to addressing sustainable development goals has been recognised. For example, it has been argued that public international law's restrictive traditional theoretical framework is ill-equipped to addressing the pluralistic concerns inherent in sustainable development. Rather, it has been suggested that a transnational law approach embracing more flexibly different elements which influence regulation, and which escape existing legal categories should be adopted.[41]

The traditional private international framework is limited and arguably ill-equipped to fully accommodate the challenges of implementing SDG 6. This is because, first, sustainable development issues such as ensuring the availability and sustainable management of water and sanitation for all often involve a complex network of elements, interests, actors and legal regimes, all animated by substantive objectives. However, it is arguable that the substance-neutrality of traditional choice-of-law methodology is particularly unsuitable for resolving water-related conflicts within this complex network. Traditional choice-of-law methodology's blindness to substance or its apparent goal of substantive neutrality suggests it does not have the necessary tools to accommodate or focus attention on the substantive interests of the parties.

Second, the focus of traditional choice-of-law analysis on state law as the main recognisable source of applicable law potentially excludes the relevance of

---

37 <https://www.ohchr.org/Documents/HRBodies/HRCouncil/WGTransCorp/OEIGWG_RevisedDraft_LBI.pdf> accessed 12 July 2021.

38 ibid Art 7.

39 ibid Art 9.

40 ibid Art 10.

41 Laure-Elise Mayard, 'Can A Transnational Law Approach Offer a Better Understanding of International Law's Contribution to Sustainable Hydropower Projects? A Test Case from the Mekong River Basin' (2019) 2 Brill Open Law 40.

soft law instruments or even international laws that states have not incorporated into their national laws, but which may be relevant in resolving water-related conflicts. Multinational corporations and various private actors have adopted soft law regulations and guidelines that could potentially inform their obligations regarding the management of water resources. However, traditional choice-of-law analysis makes it impossible, or challenging at best, to utilise these soft instruments in adjudication as part of the applicable law. As Mayard has noted, this 'reduces the depth or multi-dimension of private actors' functioning to an investment-centred role and also gives less normative power to "soft law" instruments, like codes of conduct'.[42]

Third, most developing countries have domestic laws and policies on water resources. But it is not uncommon that customary water rights, i.e. rights to water based on customary law, are not formally recognised. In most African countries, local communities typically hold their water rights in customary law.[43] This makes them legally vulnerable compared to foreign investors who often hold formal statutory, contractual and treaty-based rights from host states.[44] Adding to this disadvantage is the fact that, from a private international law perspective, such customary rights may not be considered a part of the applicable law, and even where so considered may be difficult to prove to the satisfaction of a foreign court. Indeed, as discussed below, to the extent that title to the water resource is at issue in a claim, a foreign court in a common law jurisdiction may consider the claim not justiciable because of the *Moçambique* rule.[45] In essence, the traditional private international law framework constrains the ability to litigate water conflicts in foreign courts.

The above does not mean that, in its current form, private international law is irrelevant to SDG 6. Like most natural resources, water is exploited and used by individuals, companies and states. Contracts for the exploitation of and conflicts between different users of water are not uncommon. Tortious conduct can also affect communities' access to water. When such contracts or conduct has a foreign element, as discussed below, the rules of private international law are necessarily part of the gamut of laws needed to structure and regulate the transaction, or to resolve conflicts, be they contractual or tortious.

---

42 ibid 67.

43 Makane Moïse Mbengue and Susanna Waltman, 'Farmland Investments and Water Rights in Africa: The Legal Regimes Converging over Land and Water', Investment Treaty News 6, no 3 (August 2015) 18–19.

44 ibid 2. See also See also Stefano Burchi, 'The Interface Between Customary and Statutory Water Rights – A Statutory Perspective' (FAO Legal Papers Online 45 Rome, FAO 2005) <http://www.fao.org/3/a-bb078e.pdf> Hitchin.

45 See e.g. *Dagi v Broken Hill Proprietary Co Ltd (No 2)* [1997] 1 VR 428, 433–441.

4. WATER AND SANITATION CONTRACTS AND PRIVATE INTERNATIONAL LAW

Water is a most valuable natural resource, indispensable to the sustenance of life on this planet. It is however coming under increased strain due to factors such as population growth, urbanisation and climate change. Indeed, billions of people around the world suffer from poor access to water, sanitation and hygiene.[46]

Notwithstanding its importance to life and human welfare, private investments in or affecting water resources are generally not governed by a distinct legal framework, but by the general legal framework of contract and investment treaties. Several legal regimes potentially govern investment in water resources and affect the rights of stakeholders. Truswell notes that 'despite the unique qualities of water, the legal obligations of a host government to protect the foreign investor are not moderated by that government's responsibility to provide safe water to its citizens'.[47] In such a setting, the contracts that underline investments in water resources become important fora for moderating the rights and obligations of stakeholders, which could impact on the goal of ensuring the availability and sustainable management of the water resource.

Investment contracts between private parties, as well as between governments and foreign investors, can impact water resources and sanitation, depending on the nature of the investment. Investments in farmlands for commercial agriculture and mining indirectly impact water resources. Other investments, such as for the production of hydroelectricity or the privatisation of the water and sewage sector, have water resources as their principal focus. In addition, governments may enter into contracts with foreign investors for waste treatment or disposal facilities and related services. Regardless of the nature of the contract or concession, water use resulting from such investments and how waste treatment facilities are operated directly affect communities.

In addition to addressing substantive issues such as price, quality and duration of the contracts, the parties to water and sewage contracts or concessions can also include provisions on the applicable law, as well as dispute resolution. Regarding dispute resolution, the three main options that parties may have resort to are: the courts of the host state; arbitration in the host state under domestic law; and international arbitration. Mbengue and Waltman have noted the significance of dispute resolution clauses in such investment contracts. They observe that:

> Procedural obligations are particularly important as they provide for the enforcement of legal rights. The dispute settlement mechanism available has a direct impact on the

[46] United Nations Children's Fund (UNICEF) and World Health Organization, *Progress on Household Drinking Water, Sanitation and Hygiene 2000–2017 – Special Focus on Inequalities* (2019).

[47] Emma Truswell, 'Thirst for Profit: Water Privatisation, Investment Law and a Human Right to Water' in Chester Brown and Kate Miles (eds), *Evolution in Investment Treaty Law and Arbitration* (CUP 2011) 570.

> practical situation. Local communities with their customary rights only have redress in domestic law, which may be bound to uphold the above terms of the contract. The investor, however, has the direct means to enforce its obligations against the state through arbitration. This is why investment treaties are particularly important, and why the dispute settlement clauses of contracts are also important.[48]

Like any international contracts, parties to water and sewage contracts or concessions can include a term dealing with the governing law of the contract. While the contractual aspects of the transaction would be governed by the law chosen by the parties, the proprietary consequence of the transaction will be governed by the *lex situs* – i.e. the law of the place where the water resource is located. Because water is a natural resource of immense value to life, it is arguable that governments entering into transactions for water-related investments should avoid agreeing to foreign law as the applicable law of the transaction. Having the host state's law as the applicable law enhances the government's regulatory capacity in respect of the investment, assuming the government has not contractually fettered its autonomy with other contractual provisions, such as a stabilisation clause.[49]

In some countries, there is a push toward governments assuming greater control of their natural resources, including by avoiding foreign law as the applicable law in resource transactions. This push can directly affect water resources. Tanzania recently enacted several laws aimed at protecting natural resources. This was done partly in reaction to several investment disputes Tanzania has been involved in, including, as discussed below, one that involved investment in the provision of water and sewer infrastructure and services.[50] These laws include the Natural Wealth and Resources Contracts (Review and Re-negotiation of Unconscionable Terms) Act of 2017 and the Natural Wealth and Resources (Permanent Sovereignty) Act of 2017. The latter provides that disputes arising from extraction, exploitation or acquisition and use of natural wealth and resources shall be adjudicated by judicial bodies or other organs established in Tanzania and accordance with Tanzanian laws.[51] Similarly, under the Public Private Partnership (Amendment) Act of 2018, all public–private

48 Makane Moïse Mbengue and Susanna Waltman, 'Farmland Investments and Water Rights in Africa: The Legal Regimes Converging over Land and Water', Investment Treaty News 6, no 3 (August 2015) 27. See also Carin Smaller, 'Investment Contracts for Farmland and Water: Ten Steps' (Institute for Sustainable Development 2013).

49 This is a clause often included in contracts with governments and international investment agreements to addresses how changes in law following the execution of the contract or investment agreement are to be treated, including the extent to which such changes modify the rights and obligations of the foreign investors under the contract or investment agreement. Foreign investors use stabilisation clauses to mitigate or manage the political risks associated with their projects.

50 *Biwater Gauff (Tanzania) Ltd v United Republic of Tanzania*, ICSID Case No ARB/05/22, Award, 24 July 2008.

51 Natural Wealth and Resources (Permanent Sovereignty) Act 2017, s 11.

partnerships agreements are subject to local arbitration under the arbitration laws of Tanzania and/or conclusively dealt with by Tanzanian courts.[52] More recently, under section 62(1) of Ghana's Public Private Partnership Act of 2020 (Act 1039), the 'governing law of a partnership agreement is the law of Ghana'. Therefore, a public–private partnership arrangement between the government or a state-owned entity and a private person (e.g. for the provision of water and sanitation services) under the Act cannot be governed by foreign law.

Given the importance of water as a natural resource, such attempts to localise transactions related thereto should be encouraged. This would ensure greater governmental regulatory capacity and control to advance the interests of the domestic population who rely on it. Significant domestic policy issues are often engaged when a government seeks to enhance access to water and provide better sanitation for its peoples through contracting with investors. Such issues are best addressed through the national legal framework. Hence, such contracts should not be externalised with foreign choice-of-law and jurisdiction agreements.

Another means of localising such transactions would be to award them to domestic investors. This would, potentially, mitigate the risk of assuming the consequences of the protections afforded foreign investors in bilateral investment treaties and international law. As Kynast observes, 'whenever foreign private investors are involved in providing essential services such as water and sanitation, investment protection rules and investor-state dispute settlement (ISDS) mechanisms can potentially come into play'.[53] This is avoided with localisation through domestic investors. The localisation of transactions related to water resources should be complemented by improvements in and reform of domestic laws related to water resources.

In a transboundary context, as noted above, water resources may be subject to a host of international laws. Contracts related to transboundary water resources call for careful consideration of how conflicts between national law and international should be resolved. It has been recommended that such 'contracts should also include a provision which provides that in the event of a conflict between the contract and obligations binding the host state in international law, the obligations under international law will prevail over the terms of the contract'.[54] While this recommendation may be appropriate in inter-state dealings, it may be inappropriate in transactions between governments and private parties. Such contracts should be governed by the law of the host state. Having said that, the recommendation reveals the potential utility of private

---

52 Public Private Partnership (Amendment) Act 2018, s 14, which amends s 22 of the parent Act.

53 Britta Kynast, 'Legal Barriers to Remunicipalisation? Trade Agreements and Investor-State Investment Protection in Water Services' (2019) 12 Water Alternatives 334.

54 Makane Moïse Mbengue and Susanna Waltman, 'Farmland Investments and Water Rights in Africa: The Legal Regimes Converging over Land and Water', Investment Treaty News 6, no 3 (August 2015) 60.

international law techniques even in inter-state dealings with transboundary water resources.

5. SDG 6-RELATED CLAIMS BEFORE ARBITRAL TRIBUNALS AND NATIONAL COURTS

Disputes before national courts and arbitral tribunals present the quintessential context for deploying private international law rules. The activities of states and private companies may affect water resources and sanitation, resulting in claims that engage the rules of private international law. Persons, including foreign investors, may seek to enforce or vindicate their rights in domestic and international fora. Individuals may bring claims against a foreign investor or multinational corporation for damage to community watercourses. Similarly, investors may bring claims against states for alleged breaches of investment contracts or bilateral investment treaties. The prospect or threat of claims by investors can affect the ability of governments to effectively regulate and manage their water resources. A government's decision to reallocate water resources to meet the needs of local communities, to take measures to prevent pollution of water bodies, to reduce water allocation to water-intensive projects such as dams, or to decrease water tariffs can all affect investments and result in claims.

Accordingly, national courts and international arbitral tribunals are important institutions in any discussion related to ensuring the availability and sustainable management of water and sanitation for all.[55] This section focuses on both institutions and how they have dealt with claims with foreign elements affecting water resources that have come before them.

5.1. ARBITRAL TRIBUNALS

The significant role international arbitral tribunals can play in ensuring rights to water has been recognised. Meshel has observed that 'arbitration tribunals are uniquely placed to strengthen and promote important human rights norms, such as the human right to water, that may be negatively impacted by investment protection measures. To this end, however, they must be more sensitive not only to the interests of foreign investors but also to those of local populations and focus on how these interests overlap rather than conflict'.[56]

55 See Rio+12: 'The Future We Want', Report of the United Nations Conference on Sustainable Development, Rio de Janeiro (Brazil) UN Doc A/CONF.216/16 (24 July 2012) para 43 where it is noted that 'judicial and administrative proceedings are essential to the promotion of sustainable development'.

56 Tamar Meshel, 'Human Rights in Investor-State Arbitration: The Human Right to Water and Beyond' (2015) 6 Journal of International Dispute Settlement 277, 278.

Issues concerning access to safe drinking water and damage to water resources have been raised before international arbitral tribunals. According to the UN Conference on Trade and Development (UNCTAD) Investment Dispute Settlement Navigator,[57] 'water collection, treatment and supply have been an issue in 19 international arbitration cases'. Most water resources-related investment disputes have resulted from the privatisation of the water and sewage sector and the decisions taken by governments or investors post-privatisation. As Farrugia summarises:

> Over the course of the last 15 years, a number of BIT [Bilateral Investment Treaties] arbitrations have emerged in relation to the water provision and sanitation industries. Indeed, with the active involvement of private actors in water supply, it is not surprising that many, if not most, of the disputes are startlingly similar: to modernize water supply/sanitation systems a state outsources the operation of the local water distribution system or wastewater treatment plant to a foreign investor (or consortium). The project seems to work well until, for various reasons, it is derailed by claims of tariff increases, water quality concerns, public health issues, and discrimination of access and provision – all of which could potentially represent a violation of human rights. Naturally, those claims then form the basis of the relevant governments' decision to close down the foreign investment activity and defend itself against claims of treaty breach.[58]

International arbitral tribunals have been called upon to resolve disputes arising from disagreements between investors and governments concerning tariff regimes and their effect on the affordability of water, failures to establish contractually agreed number of water connections, and threats of pollution of ground and drinking water resources.[59] From publicly available awards, conduct on the part of investors or governments that has precipitated some of these claims includes: failure to conduct contractually agreed repairs, leading to algae bloom and water contamination; community protest resulting from increases in water fees and impact of investors' operations on community wells; freezing of consumer water prices; failure to undertake the necessary expansion of service; and endangering access to water for citizens.[60] Another set of water-related claims before

57 <https://investmentpolicy.unctad.org/investment-dispute-settlement> accessed 12 July 2021.

58 Bree Farrugia, 'The Human Right to Water: Defences to Investment Treaty Violations' (2015) 31 Arbitration International 261, 268.

59 Ursula Kriebaum, 'The Right to Water Before Investment Tribunals' (2018) 1 Brill Open Law 16, 17.

60 *Aguas del Tunari, SA v Republic of Bolivia*, ICSID Case No ARB/02/3, Decision on Respondent's Objections to Jurisdiction, 21 October 2005; *Azurix Corp v The Argentine Republic*, ICSID Case No ARB/01/12, Award, 14 July 2006; *Suez, Sociedad General de Aguas de Barcelona SA and InterAguas Servicios Integrales del Agua SA v The Argentine Republic*, ICSID Case No ARB/03/17, Decision on Liability, 30 July 2010; *AWG Group Ltd v The Argentine Republic*, UNCITRAL, Decision on Liability, 30 July 2010; *Suez, Sociedad General*

international arbitral tribunals arises from the activities of mining companies. The harmful effects mining can have on water resources cannot be gainsaid.

Most of the disputes for which awards are publicly available are founded on BITs. The BITs' provisions on the applicable law provide the law for adjudicating the merits of the parties' claims. Thus, in *Azurix Corp v The Argentine Republic*,[61] the tribunal noted the agreement of the parties that the BIT was the point of reference for judging the merits of Azurix's claim.[62] Argentine law remained relevant, but, as the tribunal noted, 'only [as] an element of the inquiry because of the treaty nature of the claims under consideration'.[63]

To a large extent, it appears arbitral tribunals have avoided grounding their decisions on the right to water or SDG 6, even in cases where it has been directly argued by governments or in *amicus curiae* briefs. A case in point is *Biwater Gauff (Tanzania) Ltd v United Republic of Tanzania*, in which the *amici* submitted that:

> human rights and sustainable development issues are factors that condition the nature and extent of the investor's responsibilities, and the balance of rights and obligations as between the investor and the host State. ... [F]oreign corporations engaged in projects intimately related to human rights and the capacity to achieve sustainable development ... have the highest level of responsibility to meet their duties and obligations as foreign investors, before seeking the protection of international law. This is precisely because such investments necessarily carry with them very serious risks to the population at large.[64]

The tribunal found the *amici*'s submission 'useful' and suggested that the submission informed its analysis of the claims.[65] The tribunal, however, failed to address directly how sustainable development considerations may be useful in balancing the rights and obligations of investors and states.

---

de Aguas de Barcelona, SA and Vivendi Universal, SA v Argentine Republic, ICSID Case No ARB/03/19, Decision on Liability, 30 July 2010; *Impregilo SpA. v Argentine Republic*, ICSID Case No ARB/07/17, Award, 21 June 2011; *SAUR International SA v Republic of Argentina*, ICSID Case No ARB/04/4, Decision on Jurisdiction and Liability, 6 June 2012; *Urbaser SA and Consorcio de Aguas Bilbao Bizkaia, Bilbao Biskaia Ur Partzuergoa v The Argentine Republic*, ICSID Case No ARB/07/26, Award, 8 December 2016; *Biwater Gauff (Tanzania) Ltd v United Republic of Tanzania*, ICSID Case No ARB/05/22, Award, 24 July 2008. A full discussion of the substance of these cases is beyond the scope of this chapter. For a discuss see Ursula Kriebaum, 'The Right to Water Before Investment Tribunals' (2018) 1 Brill Open Law 16, 19–31; Tamar Meshel, 'Human Rights in Investor-State Arbitration: The Human Right to Water and Beyond' (2015) 6 Journal of International Dispute Settlement 277, 288–294; Yulia Levashova, 'The Right of Access to Water in the Context of Investment Disputes in Argentina: Urbaser and Beyond' (2020) 16 Utrecht Law Review 110.

61 ICSID Case No ARB/01/12, Award, 14 July 2006.

62 ibid para 65.

63 ibid para 67.

64 *Biwater Gauff (Tanzania) Ltd v United Republic of Tanzania*, ICSID Case No ARB/05/22, Award, 24 July 2008, para 380.

65 ibid para 392.

Following a detailed examination of three investment disputes between foreign investors and Argentina in which the human rights to water was argued, namely *AWG v Argentina*, *Impregilo v Argentina* and *Azurix v Argentina*,[66] Levashova observes that:

> In deciding whether the state's measures violated the obligations of investors under the IIAs, the arbitral tribunals considered arguments relating to the human right to water only to a limited extend, focusing primarily on the rights of investors and the impact on the investments. Tribunals in these cases have chosen not to examine the arguments related to the right of access to water. A view held by these and many other tribunals is that it is not their task to establish a hierarchy between human rights obligations and obligations towards foreign investors. Their task is to interpret the provisions of an applicable IIA, which is the legal basis of a dispute.[67]

Levashova contrasts the tribunals' approach in the three disputes with the tribunal's award in *Urbaser v Argentina* and notes that:

> The *Urbaser* tribunal demonstrated that counterclaims filed by host states against investors based on human rights violations may fall within the jurisdiction of investment tribunals. It clearly emphasised that companies cannot escape liability on the basis of the argument that they are not subjects of international law. … [T]he *Urbaser* tribunal considered these human rights arguments in detail. By examining the alleged violations of an investor under human rights treaties, the *Urbaser* tribunal not only stressed the investor's responsibilities but also emphasised that a state's right to regulate in providing adequate access to water may take precedence over the rights of investors under IIAs.[68]

In general, it has been suggested that:

> Investment tribunals have all found that investment law and human rights law obligations could be met at the same time. They did not accept a hierarchy between the right to water and investor rights. Furthermore, they did not frame the potential tensions between the right to water and investor rights as a normative conflict. Rather, tribunals have opted for a systemic integration of human rights obligations into investment law and found that both obligations apply in parallel and can be met at the same time.[69]

---

66 *AWG Group Ltd v The Argentine Republic*, UNCITRAL, Decision on Liability, 30 July 2010; *Impregilo SpA. v Argentine Republic*, ICSID Case No ARB/07/17, Award, 21 June 2011; *Azurix Corp v The Argentine Republic*, ICSID Case No ARB/01/12, Award, 14 July 2006.

67 Yulia Levashova, 'The Right of Access to Water in the Context of Investment Disputes in Argentina: Urbaser and Beyond' (2020) 16 Utrecht Law Review 110, 117–118.

68 ibid 120.

69 Ursula Kriebaum, 'The Right to Water Before Investment Tribunals' (2018) 1 Brill Open Law 16, 36.

The reluctance of arbitral tribunals to base their decisions on sustainable development considerations, including SDG 6, or human rights reflects the fact that an international arbitral tribunal has no specific mandate to examine issues of sustainable development; it is limited to deciding disputes under the rules of law agreed by the parties.

Although international arbitral tribunals can play a role in ensuring rights to water, an arbitral tribunal cannot order a state or an investor to take policy measures in its final award. Accordingly, the ability of tribunals to influence future conduct of the parties is limited in this regard.

5.2. NATIONAL COURTS

While investors have resorted to arbitral fora to vindicate their rights allegedly violated by governmental actions sometimes ostensibly aimed to ensure the availability of water to its residents, individuals have sued in foreign courts alleging torts and other causes of action arising from investors' dealings with water resources. In particular, individuals from affected communities have sought to hold accountable, especially in foreign courts, parent companies for torts committed by their subsidiaries in the host communities.

Individuals' efforts to hold multinational corporations accountable for wrongs committed within their communities have sometimes occurred without governmental support. This is because governments often have stakes in the subsidiaries of such transnational corporations operating – especially in the field of mining – within their jurisdiction. Governments may also calculate that the overall contribution of such corporations to national development far outweighs the harmful impacts on the affected communities and individuals. Indeed, governments have sometimes actively worked with multinational corporations to thwart efforts by individuals and communities to hold the former accountable in foreign courts.[70] Governments' disinterest in pursuing claims and sometimes outright hostility to such claims suggest the importance of the judicial process to ensuring that individuals and communities whose water resources and sanitary conditions are adversely affected by the activities of domestic and foreign companies are held accountable.

Because these are claims involving foreign elements, the first question courts have had to address within the traditional framework of private international

[70] See e.g. *Broken Hill Proprietary Co Ltd v Dagi* [1996] 2 VR 117 in which Broken Hill Proprietary Company Ltd was held to be in contempt of court because of its efforts to procure and draft an agreement with the government of Papua New Guinea in order to secure legislation aim at preventing the plaintiffs from continuing their claims against Broken Hill Proprietary Co Ltd in Australia. In *Vedanta Resources plc and Konkola Copper Mines plc v Lungowe* [2019] UKSC 20 the written intervention of the Attorney General of Zambia supported the defendant's position that the English court should decline jurisdiction in favour of Zambia.

law analysis is jurisdiction to hear the claim.[71] The rules on jurisdiction in international matters vary from country to country, except within the European Union where there are uniform rules in each of the member states.[72] This lack of uniformity poses a challenge to individuals and communities that seek to vindicate their rights abroad. They have to navigate the diverse sets of national rules to find the forum most suitable to their cause.

A very early case involving alleged damage to a watercourse is the Australian case of *Dagi v Broken Hill Proprietary Co Ltd (No 2)*.[73] In *Dagi*, the plaintiffs, who were residents of Papua New Guinea and members of various clans, brought claims in inter alia negligence, trespass and nuisance against the defendants. They alleged that they had in different ways been injuriously affected in their use of the water of the Ok Tedi River in Papua New Guinea and the lands adjacent to it because of the discharge of certain by-products of a copper mine operated by the defendants. One of the issues the court had to decide was jurisdiction in respect of the trespass and nuisance claims. The court held that, at common law, a court has no jurisdiction to entertain a claim which essentially concerns rights, whether possessory or proprietary, to or over foreign land. Such rights arise under the law of the place where the land is situated and can be litigated only in the courts of the place.[74] Thus, the claims in trespass and nuisance were held not to be justiciable in the State of Victoria, Australia.[75] It was however held that the court had jurisdiction with respect to the negligence claim.

Recherches Internationales Québec v Cambior Inc.[76] was a class action that arose from the spill of toxic effluents into Guyana's main waterway, the Essequibo, when the effluent treatment plant of a gold mine burst. The court noted that this waterway was the victims' principal source of potable drinking water and

---

71 I have focused in this section on cases from Australia, Canada and the United Kingdom. There have been significant judgments from the Netherlands not covered in this chapter. In January 2021, the Court of Appeal at The Hague held that the Nigerian subsidiary of Royal Dutch Shell was liable for the damage resulting from the leakage of certain pipelines it operates in Nigeria, which leaked in the towns of Oruma and Goi in the Niger Delta. The leaks contaminated the land and waterways of the communities. Another case involving an alleged oil well leak in Ikot Ada Udo is pending. The actions are governed by Nigerian law. For a short English summary of the judgments see: <https://www.rechtspraak.nl/Organisatie-en-contact/Organisatie/Gerechtshoven/Gerechtshof-Den-Haag/Nieuws/Paginas/Shell-Nigeria-liable-for-oil-spills-in-Nigeria.aspx> accessed 12 July 2021. For a general overview of the international legal claims brought against Shell for its operations in Nigeria see Amnesty International, *On Trial: Shell in Nigeria Legal Actions Against the Oil Multinational* (Amnesty International 2020).

72 An interesting case involving the application for European Union's uniform jurisdictional rules in a case that involved water pollution in a transboundary setting is Case 21/1976 *Bier v Mines de Potasse d'Alsace* [1976] ECR 1735.

73 [1997] 1 VR 428.

74 ibid 441.

75 ibid 441–442.

76 1998 CanLII 9780 (QC CS).

their source of water for bathing, washing clothes and dishes.[77] The gold mine was owned and operated by Omai Gold Mines Limited of Guyana. Cambior Inc., a Quebec corporation, was the majority shareholder of Omai. Some 23,000 victims of the spill brought an action in Quebec against Cambior. They were assisted by Recherches Internationales Quebec (RIQ), a Quebec company. Cambior contested the court's jurisdiction and denied responsibility for any acts of negligence of the Guyana company. RIQ argued that Cambior financed the project and made all the strategic decisions relating to the operations in Guyana.

Although the court found that Quebec and Guyana had jurisdiction to try the issues, it declined jurisdiction in favour of Guyana. In so deciding, the court took into account the fact that the mine was located in Guyana. Guyana was also the place where the victims resided, where the spill occurred, and where the victims suffered damage. Further, the law to determine the rights and obligations of the victims was the law of Guyana. All the evidence to establish liability or the lack thereof were also located primarily in Guyana.[78] The court did not accept RIQ's submission that the victims would be denied justice in Guyana should it decline to exercise its jurisdiction. If the case were to be heard in Guyana, the victims would lose the benefit of the class action vehicle available to them in Quebec. However, the court emphasised that it could not be said that the victims would be left without an adequate recourse in Guyana. They had available to them what was known as a representative action. Although this remedy did not appear to provide the victims with the same procedural and evidentiary advantages as a class action, it did permit them to sue Cambior collectively. They could also proceed by way of individual actions, should they so choose.[79] The court was of the opinion that Guyana's judicial system would provide the victims with a fair and impartial hearing.[80]

Vedanta Resources plc and Konkola Copper Mines plc v Lungowe[81] involved a claim brought by 1,826 Zambian nationals against Zambia-based Konkola Copper Mines plc (KCM) and its London-based parent company, Vedanta Resources plc. Vedanta was domiciled in England, but KCM was domiciled in Zambia. The claimants alleged that the Nchanga Copper Mine in the Republic of Zambia repeatedly discharged toxic chemicals into their local watercourses, polluting the only source of water for drinking and crop irrigation.[82] The claimants' claims were founded in negligence and breach of statutory duty under Zambian law.

77 ibid para 45.
78 ibid para 9.
79 ibid para 11.
80 ibid paras 72–88.
81 [2019] UKSC 20.
82 ibid [1].

The appeal before the UK Supreme Court concerned the English court's jurisdiction to hear the claim. For the purpose of this chapter, two of the issues are particularly important, namely whether England was the proper forum or proper place for the claim to be heard (*forum non conveniens*), and whether there was a real risk that substantial justice would not be obtained in Zambia. The court held that, on the facts, the claimants had failed to demonstrate that England was the proper place in which to bring their claims against the defendants, having regard to the interests of the parties and the ends of justice. In the words of Lord Briggs, 'Zambia was overwhelmingly the proper place for the claim to be tried'.[83] This was partly because Vedanta had offered to submit to the jurisdiction of the Zambia courts (which also had jurisdiction over KCM). The court, however, allowed the claim to proceed in England because it reasoned that there was a real risk that the claimants would not be able to obtain substantial justice in Zambia for two main reasons. First, it would be practically impossible for them to fund their claims given that they were in extreme poverty and there was neither legal aid nor the possibility of conditional fee agreements in Zambia.[84] Second, there were no suitably experienced legal teams in Zambia to pursue such specialised and complex environmental litigation.[85]

A case manifesting a most egregious threat to sanitation and its impact on human life involved Trafigura, a Dutch international petroleum trader.[86] In 2006, the ship Probo Koala, chartered by the London office of Trafigura, unloaded a highly toxic waste shipment at eight open-air sites in Abidjan, Ivory Coast. Remarkably, the Probo Koala had earlier attempted to discharge this waste at the port of Amsterdam. However, in Amsterdam, the port service would not accept the waste without an additional handling charge because of the waste's alleged toxicity, and the ship left Amsterdam without discharging its waste. Several unsuccessful attempts were made to dispose of the waste in Nigeria before the Probo Koala made its way to Abidjan.[87]

---

83 ibid [85].

84 ibid [89].

85 ibid [89].

86 See generally Sara Dezalay and Simon Archer, 'By-passing Sovereignty: Trafigura Lawsuits (re Ivory Coast)' in Horatia Muir Watt (ed), *Global Private International Law – Adjudication without Frontiers* (Edward Elgar Publishing 2019) 92; Amnesty International/Greenpeace Netherlands, *The Toxic Truth about a Company called Trafigura, a Ship Called Probo Koala and the Dumping of Toxic Waste in Cote D'Ivoire* (Amnesty International Publications 2012).

87 In 1988, Nigeria was a victim of an egregious dumping of toxic waste in Koko, a remote part of southern Nigeria. Through diplomatic channels, the Nigerian government succeeded in getting the Italian government and the Italian individual (then resident in Nigeria and working through a Nigerian company) that dumped the waste to lift the waste out of Nigeria, and take it back to Italy where it came from. This was followed by domestic legal and institutional reforms to avoid the recurrence of such an incident. The reforms included the enactment of the Harmful Waste (Special Criminal Provision Etc) Act 1988 and the establishment of the Federal Environmental Protection Agency. It appears no civil claim arose from this incident and it is reported no compensation was paid to the community.

After the waste from the ship was discharged in Abidjan, people living near the discharge sites began to suffer from a range of illnesses, including nausea, diarrhoea, vomiting, breathlessness, headaches, skin damage and swollen stomachs. Some people died, allegedly from exposure to this waste, and thousands more sought medical attention. The government of Ivory Coast reached a settlement of about $198 million with Trafigura, but that did not stop a group action filed in the United Kingdom against Trafigura in 2006.[88] The approximately 30,000 claimants alleged that that waste contained high levels of caustic soda, as well as a sulphur compound and hydrogen sulphide, making it hazardous waste as defined by the Basel Convention on the Control of Transboundary Movements of Hazardous Wastes. Although Trafigura denied responsibility, the case was ultimately settled in 2009.[89] Trafigura agreed to pay the claimants £30 million; the law firm that represented those claimants claimed £105 million, but ultimately walked away with a success fee of £40 million! Regrettably, many of the victims did not receive their compensation and had to subsequently bring an action against the law firm that represented them to recover what was due them.[90]

All the above cases reflect attempts by claimants from the Global South to seek justice in the Global North for wrongs allegedly committed against them. The cases reflect an expatriation of claims justiciable in the Global South to the Global North. This expatriation has been made even more possible by advances in technology which allow foreign courts to sit in outside their jurisdictions or hear evidence from witnesses based in the Global South via video link. In *Kalma v African Minerals Ltd*,[91] Turner J sat in Freetown, Sierra Leone for seven of the 14-day evidence hearing. In *Kimathi v Foreign and Commonwealth Office*,[92] witnesses gave evidence via a video link. And in *Vedanta*, Lord Briggs noted that modern facilities would reduce the inconvenience of having volumes of documents located in Zambia.[93]

The expatriation of claim has often been justified on the grounds of the ineffective judicial systems and non-viable remedies in the Global South. However, as Archer queries:

> how have domestic legal proceedings been characterised as ineffective, unavailable or otherwise failed? In whose view, and interest? Are those views and interests just

---

See generally Julius O Ihonvbere, 'The State and Environmental Degradation in Nigeria: A Study of the 1988 Toxic Waste Dump in Koko' (1994–1995) Journal of Environmental Systems 207.

88 In addition, there were lawsuits in Ivory Coast and the Netherlands. Criminal charges were also laid in the Netherlands. Also, in July 2010 a Dutch court fined Trafigura €1 million for illegally exporting toxic waste to Ivory Coast.

89 *Yao Esaie Motto v Trafigura Ltd & Trafigura Beheer BV*, Case Nos HQ06XO3370, HQ06XO3342, UK High Court (Macduff J), settlement approved 23 September 2009.

90 *Sylvie Aya Agouman v Leigh Day (a firm)* [2016] EWHC 1324 (QB).

91 [2020] EWCA Civ 144 [44].

92 [2018] EWHC 3144 (QB).

93 [2019] UKSC 20 [86].

> another form of 'environmental colonialism' or 'legal disaster capitalism', or more politely, a failure to fairly and properly evaluate the capacities of a state and its legal system in its own evolution?[94]

There is no gainsaying that allowing claims against multinational corporations to be litigated in the Global North is helpful towards increasing access to justice for the individuals and communities in the Global South that usually have weak governance systems, or where governments may be outright hostile to the claims against such multinationals. At the same time, it is arguable that litigating these claims outside the states where the harm occurred is at the expense of empowering the states in which the harm occurred, including those states' judicial and legal systems to develop the necessary expertise to handle those claims. Further, such externalisation of claims potential weakens the prospect of domestic mobilisation against the forces of corruption, bureaucratic inefficiencies, weak state institutional structures, and subtle neo-colonialist structures that make these legal wrongs possible in developing countries. For example, there are obvious reasons outside the strength of their respective legal systems that enabled the Probo Koala to dump its toxic waste in Abidjan, but not Amsterdam.

I argue that alternative arrangements should be explored to ensure that affected communities and individuals can vindicate their rights in their domestic legal systems, while at the same time bolstering the capacity of their national legal system to handle such complex claims.[95] For example, to the extent that the expertise of foreign counsel is needed,[96] the national laws of some countries allow, for example, foreign counsel to conduct litigation, usually with the approval of Chief Justice.[97] Thus, the merits of such claims could be litigated in the host states where the harm is done, with support of foreign counsel. Any eventual judgment could be enforced abroad, assuming there are not enough assets in the host state commensurate with the value of the judgment to satisfy it.

The host state's court is also in a better position to impose and supervise compliance with non-monetary obligations appropriate to address long-term

---

94 Simon Archer, 'The Trafigura Actions as Problems of Transnational Law' in Horatia Muir Watt (ed), *Global Private International Law – Adjudication without Frontiers* (Edward Elgar Publishing 2019) 106.

95 Sarah Joseph, *Corporations and Transnational Human Rights Litigation* (Hart Publishing 2004) 148–150.

96 In this regard, it is worth noting that almost all the recent English cases in which individuals have sought to bring proceedings in tort in England against English parent companies and their foreign subsidiaries in respect of events occurring in African countries where the subsidiaries carry on their operations have all been led by one and the same claimant law firm, Leigh Day Solicitors. See *Vedanta Resources* [2019] UKSC 20; *Okpabi v Royal Dutch Shell plc* [2018] EWCA Civ 191; *AAA v Unilever plc* [2018] EWCA Civ 1532; *Kalma v African Minerals Ltd* [2020] EWCA Civ 144.

97 See e.g. Nigeria: Legal Practitioners Act 1975, s 2(2).

damage to water resources and insanitary conditions, such as cleaning up of oil spills, remediation undertakings and proper waste disposal. A judge of the host state where the damage occurred is also more likely to be in a better position to assess the true social and economic consequences of the damage on the livelihood of the affected communities.[98]

Admittedly, there are significant challenges regarding standing, delay, corruption, judicial bias towards multinational corporations, and underdeveloped substantive laws that could affect litigating such claims in the Global South.[99] However, the expatriation of claims justiciable in the Global South to the Global North would not necessarily overcome these challenges, which tend to be endemic to legal systems in many developing countries; at best, it sidesteps the problems, and at worst contributes to the perpetuation of such problems. In general, a shift from domestic to transnational litigation may not necessarily be in the interest of the victims who experience harm from multinational corporations or the legal systems of the states where the harm is done. Given the asymmetrical relations between countries in the Global South and North, it remains important that multinational corporations in the North are held accountable in their home countries for legal wrongs committed in the South. However, this path to legal accountability should be complementary to, and not supersede or displace, accountability at the locus of the wrong in the Global South.

The recent jurisprudence of the English courts in *Vedanta* and *Okpabi*[100] has mitigated the scale of jurisdictional hurdles claimants from the Global South face in their efforts to hold multinational corporations accountable in the United Kingdom. Whether the claimants would succeed at the merits phase to establish liability remains to be seen. But, possibly, the jurisdictional success may force defendants into settlements to avoid further proceedings.[101]

---

98 See *Recherches Internationales Québec* 1998 CanLII 9780 (QC CS), para 52, where the court noted this point.

99 Eloamaka Carol Okonkwo, 'Assessing the Role of the Courts in Enhancing Access to Environmental Justice in Oil Pollution Matters in Nigeria' (2020) 28 African Journal of International & Comparative Law 195.

100 *Okpabi v Royal Dutch Shell plc* [2021] UKSC 3.

101 In 2015, Shell Petroleum Development Company of Nigeria (SDCCN) settled a claim that had been brought in the English courts by members of the Niger Delta Bodo community. SDCCN agreed to pay €70 million ($85 million) to the claimants. Under the settlement, SDCCN undertook to clean up Bodo's waterways, which had been devastated by giant oil spills. However, due to a lack of progress in this effort, and the ongoing harm suffered by the community, further legal action has been threatened against SDCCN in the UK courts. In this case, SDCCN and the claimants agreed that the English court should have jurisdiction to resolve the disputes which have arisen between them so jurisdictional battles were avoided. See *Bodo Community v Shell Petroleum Development Co of Nigeria Ltd* [2014] EWHC 1973 (TCC); *Bodo Community v Shell Petroleum Development Co of Nigeria Ltd* [2014] EWHC 2170 (TCC); *Bodo Community v CW Law Solicitors* [2014] EWHC 3675 (TCC); *King Berebon v Shell Petroleum Development Co of Nigeria Ltd* [2017] EWHC 1579 (TCC); *King Berebon v Shell Petroleum Development Co of Nigeria Ltd* [2018] EWHC 1377 (TCC).

If these jurisdictional decisions give a boost to responsible business conduct in developing countries, it would be positive. However, it could also result in a corporate backlash in the form of careful restructuring of parent company–subsidiary relations and decision-making. This would be done to avoid the potential for the liability of parent companies in relation to the activities of their subsidiaries in the Global South. The prospect for such backlash reinforces the importance of strengthening accountability channels at the locus of the wrongs in the Global South.

A recent case demonstrating what courts in the Global South can positively contribute is the Kenyan case of *KM v Attorney General*.[102] In this case, the petitioners are residents of Owino-Uhuru village in Mombasa County, Kenya. The respondents are various government agencies and two private companies, namely Metal Refinery (EPZ) Limited and Penguin Paper and Book Company. The two companies, however, did not participate in the proceedings. The petitioners alleged that a lead-acid battery recycling factory set up near their community produced toxic waste and that the waste seeped into the village, causing the petitioners and area residents various illnesses and ailments, and death. Among others, it was alleged that Metal Refinery (EPZ) Limited failed to construct proper drainage for its effluent, consequently releasing wastewater into the village, and that the lead seeped into the water from the shallow well used in the village. The petitioners sought declaratory relief regarding their constitutionally guaranteed rights to life, a clean and healthy environment, health, clean and safe water, and information. In addition, they sought compensation for damage to their health, environment and loss of life, and an order of mandamus to compel the government agencies to remediate the contaminated environment of Owino-Uhuru village.

In a very elaborate judgment, Justice Anne Omollo awarded the Owino-Uhuru community 1.3 billion Kenyan shillings (US $12,101,876.80) in damages. She also ordered the government and Metal Refinery (EPZ) Limited to clean up the soil and water and to remove any waste deposited in Owino-Uhuru within four months. In default, the sum of 700 million Kenyan shillings was awarded to the Center for Justice Governance and Environmental Action (an NGO suing on their behalf and on behalf of all the residents of Owino-Uhuru) to coordinate the clean-up exercise.

It is unlikely that a foreign court would have been able to hold the government and the private companies accountable using the type of relief granted by the Kenyan court. A foreign court is unlikely to issue public law remedies such as a mandamus to compel a foreign government and its agencies to act – indeed, such an order may entail judicial supervision, which the foreign court may be unable to exercise.

---

102 *KM v Attorney General*, Petition No 1 of 2016 (Environment and Land Court, Mombasa, 2020) [2020] eKLR.

Overcoming a jurisdictional challenge is only the first hurdle that individuals and communities must surmount in their efforts to hold multinational corporations accountable for damage done to their water resources and sanitary conditions. Whether the multinational corporation is liable in law would depend on the applicable law as determined by the choice-of-law rules of the forum. Claims against multinational corporations for damage to watercourses and the creation of insanitary conditions have usually been founded in tort and breach of statutory duty. The individuals and communities often do not have contracts with the corporations.[103]

In England and other major common law legal systems where such claims are litigated, the courts apply the law of the place where the tort was committed, which in most instances will be the law of the developing country where the harm was done. This has been the case with the very few cases that have passed the jurisdictional phase.[104] The claimants cannot choose to have applied to their claim, for example, the substantive law of the home state of the defendant multinational corporation. Although not directly an issue in the *Vedanta* case, it is implicit[105] from the judgment that the merits of the claim would have to be adjudicated using Zambia law as the applicable law, it being the law of the place where the tort and alleged breaches of statutory duty occurred. Obviously, because of the underdeveloped nature of Zambian tort law, existing gaps would have to be filled with persuasive foreign authority, which would most likely be English law.[106] More recently, in *Okpabi v Royal Dutch Shell plc*,[107] in which it was alleged that Royal Dutch Shell owed the appellants a common law duty of care, it was 'agreed that the issue of governing law should be approached on the basis that the laws of England and Wales and the law of Nigeria are materially the same'.[108] Accordingly, in these claims, the defendants would not be judged using the high tortious and safety standards that prevail in United Kingdom substantive law.

Regardless of whether the courts are dealing with jurisdiction or choice of law, it is evident from all the above cases that all the discussions and analyses were conducted through a traditional private international law methodological

103 This may change with the signing of community development agreements, especially with mining companies.

104 See e.g. *Kalma v African Minerals Ltd* [2020] EWCA Civ 144. The case did not involve damage to a water resource. *Bodo Community v Shell Petroleum Development Co of Nigeria Ltd* [2014] EWHC 1973 (TCC).

105 See e.g. *Vedanta Resources* [2019] UKSC 20 [85(iii)] where it is noted that 'it is common ground that all the applicable law is Zambian, even if that country may prove to follow the common law of England and Wales in material respects'.

106 *Vedanta Resources* [2019] UKSC 20 [56] where the court accepted that it was arguable that the Zambian courts would identify the relevant principles of Zambian common law in accordance with those established in England.

107 *Okpabi v Royal Dutch Shell plc* [2021] UKSC 3.

108 ibid [7].

lens. The fact that the courts were dealing with alleged damage to a water resource – something so vital for life – or the creation of insanitary conditions abroad for commercial gain hardly features in the courts' reasoning. One can easily substitute another resource or thing, and the decision would likely remain the same. For example, in assessing the appropriateness of the forum, neither the fact that the courts were dealing with foreign watercourses nor the importance of those watercourses were noted as relevant connecting factors.[109]

Even where the courts have recognised the gravity of harm done to water bodies and its impact on life, they have emphasised the need for the issues to be resolved using the existing traditional legal framework. In *Okpabi v Royal Dutch Shell plc*,[110] the Nigerian claimants sought damages for losses arising as a result of serious, and ongoing, pollution and environmental damage caused by leaks of oil from pipelines and associated infrastructure in and around the Niger Delta. The claimants contended that the first defendant, Royal Dutch Shell plc (RDS), and the second defendant, Shell Petroleum Development Company of Nigeria Ltd (SPDC), were responsible for the damage. The oil leaks had contaminated the land, swamps, groundwater and waterways of the communities of the claimants, and they claimed that there had been no adequate cleaning or remediation, with the consequence that the natural water sources could not be used for drinking, agricultural, washing or recreational purposes. The jurisdiction of the court to try the claims turned upon whether RDS owed a duty of care to the claimants. The majority of the English Court of Appeal held that the claimants had been unable demonstrate a properly arguable case that RDS owed them a duty of care to them on the basis either of assumed responsibility for devising a material policy the adequacy of which was the subject of the claim, or on the basis that it controlled or shared control of the operations which were the subject of the claim.[111] In his judgment, Sir Geoffrey Vos noted that:

> the fact that none of the judgments in this case dwells upon the underlying facts of the claims should not be taken as any depreciation of their gravity. The severe pollution caused by the repeated large oil spills in respect of which these claims are made has impacted the lives, health and local environment of some 50,000 people forming part of the communities in the Niger Delta represented by the appellants. Despite the gravity of the public health situation and the fact that clean-up operations are still incomplete, *it is necessary for this court to focus on the legal foundation of the claims against the anchor first defendant*, RDS. If those claims cannot be shown to have a real prospect of success, jurisdiction cannot be established in England and Wales and none of the claims can proceed.[112]

---

109 *Vedanta Resources* [2019] UKSC 20 [85]–[87]; *Recherches Internationales Québec* 1998 CanLII 9780 (QC CS) paras 34–63.

110 *Okpabi v Royal Dutch Shell plc* [2018] EWCA Civ 191.

111 ibid [132] and [206].

112 ibid [175] (emphasis added).

Similarly, Simon LJ noted the importance of distinguishing a duty of care owed to the claimants 'from the more abstract (although no less important) concepts of moral responsibility: for example, to reduce global warming and to protect the environment'.[113] In essence, the Court of Appeal grounded its decision on the technical nuances of positive law, uninfluenced by extralegal or policy considerations. The UK Supreme Court overturned the Court of Appeal's decision because there were errors of law in the approach the court adopted, and it was wrong for the court to hold that there was no real issue to be tried regarding whether RDS owed the claimants a common law duty of care.[114] However, like the Court of Appeal, the Supreme Court's decision was grounded in positive law.

An important issue is the potential for claims before international arbitral tribunals and foreign courts to effect governmental policy and legislative changes in the Global South so as to advance the goal of ensuring the availability and sustainable management of water and sanitation for all. In the cases and awards reviewed for this chapter, the relief sought has been mainly for monetary compensation for damage done. The prospect for such relief to effect governmental policy or legislative changes is minimal. Furthermore, compared to the courts of a host country, a foreign court or an international arbitral tribunal is in a very weak position to compel policy or legislative changes in another country. Claims before international arbitral tribunals and foreign courts may vindicate the rights of communities, individuals and investors. However, they leave largely unaddressed the legal and policy deficiencies, including weak institutional frameworks and capacities,[115] that constrain the effective management of water resources and create the environment for such claims to arise.

6. CONCLUSION

The need for substantial investments in water supply and sanitation facilities and infrastructure, including sewage treatment, should be at the top of the list of all governments, especially governments in developing countries, where the need is often most pressing. Governmental action has to be expedited in this regard if the SGD 6 targets are to be achieved. At present, the world is not on track to achieve

113 ibid [88].

114 *Okpabi v Royal Dutch Shell plc* [2021] UKSC 3.

115 Southern African Development Community, *Regional Water Policy* (2005) 8, where a weak legal and regulatory framework, inadequate institutional capacities of national water authorities and of regional or river basin organisations, and a weak policy framework for sustainable development of national water resources are identified by the Southern African Development Community as key issues for or constraints on effective development of the water sector in the region.

the global SDG 6 targets by 2030.[116] Writing on Africa, Nhamoa, Nhemachenab and Nhamoc have called on African governments to 'leapfrog to avoid being left behind when it comes to attaining universal water and sanitation access by 2030'.[117] They observed disturbing trends in countries such as the Comoros and Zimbabwe, where basic drinking water services have been in decline. They also observed similar trends for basic sanitation services in Chad, the Democratic Republic of the Congo, Equatorial Guinea, the Gambia, Kenya, Nigeria, Somalia and Zimbabwe.[118]

While substantial investments in water supply and sanitation facilities and infrastructure are essential, ultimately good water governance is a critical pillar for implementing and achieving SDG 6.[119] This chapter has recounted, through judicial and arbitral decisions, the potentially deleterious consequences that such investments can visit on communities without good water governance and sanitation management. Confronted with perceived weaknesses in the capacities of their legal systems to hold foreign investors accountable for the deleterious effects of the foreign investors' operations in the Global South, various communities have sought remedy in courts in the Global North, often aided by cause lawyers and non-governmental organisations. Their claims have met varying degrees of success, although there appears to be a perceptible trend towards greater accountability.

Private international law has a facilitative role to play in the governance of water and sanitation resources and related services. This is so especially in developing appropriate legal frameworks, structuring of transactions, including the use of conflict-avoidance techniques, and in dispute resolution. This facilitative role of private international law could be enhanced by embracing soft law as part of the applicable law, encouraging the localisation of international contracts through using choice-of-law and jurisdiction agreements, and developing local legal expertise, including the capacity of courts in the Global South to handle transnational claims involving damage to water resources and sanitation.

Having said that, ultimately the issues involved in achieving SDG 6 are too complex and multifaceted to be resolved through traditional private international law methodologies, and adversarial litigation or international arbitration – the quintessential fora where the rules of private international law hold sway. Accordingly, while one should not diminish the role of private international law, its potential contribution should also not be exaggerated.

116 United Nations, *Sustainable Development Goal 6 Synthesis Report 2018 on Water and Sanitation* (2018) 21.

117 Godwell Nhamoa et al, 'Is 2030 too Soon for Africa to Achieve the Water and Sanitation Sustainable Development Goal?' (2019) 669 Science of the Total Environment 129, 138.

118 ibid 138.

119 United Nations, *Sustainable Development Goal 6 Synthesis Report 2018 on Water and Sanitation* (2018) 15.

SDG 7: AFFORDABLE AND CLEAN ENERGY

Nikitas E. HATZIMIHAIL

Goal 7: Ensure access to affordable, reliable, sustainable and modern energy for all

7.1 By 2030, ensure universal access to affordable, reliable and modern energy services
7.2 By 2030, increase substantially the share of renewable energy in the global energy mix
7.3 By 2030, double the global rate of improvement in energy efficiency
7.a By 2030, enhance international cooperation to facilitate access to clean energy research and technology, including renewable energy, energy efficiency and advanced and cleaner fossil-fuel technology, and promote investment in energy infrastructure and clean energy technology
7.b By 2030, expand infrastructure and upgrade technology for supplying modern and sustainable energy services for all in developing countries, in particular least developed countries, small island developing States, and land-locked developing countries, in accordance with their respective programmes of support

1. INTRODUCTION

It takes only a cursory look at world history to realise that energy has been the bedrock, indeed a precondition, of development. Ever since the invention of fire, energy has been increasingly vital in the cooking and maintenance of food.[1] Its use has led to marked improvements in all aspects of the quality of human life – including education, communication and transportation. Its availability has also led to the temporal and spatial expansion of human life. Distances have been shrunk, leading inevitably to our planetary civilisation and a global circulation of humans, commodities and ideas. Humans have been empowered to live productive – and fulfilling – lives in the night as well as under the daylight, and even in the most extreme weather conditions. Energy has empowered but also defined human societies: the prehistoric hearth may have been initially used for cooking, warmth and security, but it eventually acquired social and even spiritual significance. Human civilisations have been shaped – and reshaped – depending on the availability of energy.

At the same time, there has been a dark side of the human use of energy. This is epitomised by fire, the earliest non-organic type and, probably to this day, the archetype of energy. Fire has both empowered humans and cost human lives – whether through malicious intent or by accident. It has also taken millennia for humans to understand its environmental consequences – from air poisoning at the micro level to the devastation of soil and living organisms at the macro level. The same has been exponentially true of other energy forms. Coal enabled long-distance travel and significantly added to global pollution levels. Nuclear energy is largely emissions-free but nuclear accidents can have devastating ecological circumstances – and the weaponisation of nuclear power could lead to the extinction of human life. Even more benevolent sources of energy have taken a serious toll on local ecology, cultural heritage and traditional ways of life: directly, in the case of the big hydroelectric construction projects, and indirectly, in the scramble for the natural resources needed as raw materials, such as the balsa wood used in wind turbines.[2] It could be said that the more complex an energy source, the higher the ecological and public-health stakes are likely to be. Moreover, the more costly – or dependent on primary resources not readily available – an energy source, the bigger the possible inequality between those who have access to that type of energy and those who either cannot or would have to expand a significant part of their own resources to obtain such access. Ethics and morality aside, such energy inequality can lead to the unravelling of social cohesion, and even war.

---

1 Yuval Noah Harari, *Sapiens: A Brief History of Humankind* (HarperCollins 2015) 12–13.

2 See e.g. 'Is that wind turbine made from illegally harvested Balsa wood?' (27 November 2020) <https://timbercheck.blog/2020/11/27/is-that-wind-turbine-made-from-illegally-harvested-balsa-wood/> accessed 19 July 2021.

It is thus imperative to work towards covering the basic energy needs of all humanity and universal access to energy is essential in this regard. It is also vital to ensure *affordable* energy, as energy infrastructures are built across the world, and to ensure no one falls off the grid, in the developing and developed world alike. Ensuring universal access to clean and affordable energy would constitute one of the goals, indeed conditions, for sustainable development. But there are also inherent contradictions in the pursuit of a sustainable universal energy policy. Increased energy consumption – and demand – has been the catalyst for environmental and geopolitical transformation, all the way to today's climate change. As humans were provided with more – and less costly – energy, their energy needs tended to grow: time and again, cost-efficient provision of energy has even led to resource-inefficient use of energy.

This is the background that informs Sustainable Development Goal 7 (SDG 7), one of the new goals that were added to the original Millennium Development Goals in 2015. The balance sought between development and sustainability is expressed in the short form 'clean and affordable energy', which is often used to describe SDG 7 and reflects the growing awareness both of energy poverty and of the environmental repercussions of energy proliferation. The fulfilment of SDG 7 requires balancing exercises between industry and nature, private and public law, global and local action, fostering innovation and regulating human activity. Whereas a change in attitudes is certainly needed, we must also work on solutions that take into account the past and present mindsets and historical trends. Environmental sustainability is a global problem that requires addressing local conditions. Access to energy is a set of local problems with global implications, and solutions.

Law is a critical arm of sustainable energy policy and this certainly holds true, more specifically, as to private international law, the legal discipline tasked with regulating – and even conceptualising – cross-border private activity and its consequences. From a practical point of view, private international law operates as a toolkit available to policymakers, practitioners, entrepreneurs and civil society: it provides them with a framework for the conduct and planning of their activities, as well as with concrete solutions. From a governance point of view, private international law epitomises the notion of decentralised governance, drawing distinctions as well as connections between private individuals and public authorities, fusing global and local sensibilities into a coherent outlook. When it comes to clean and affordable energy, this contribution is twofold: on the one hand, the legal treatment of technological innovation and the organisation of investment towards clean, efficient and affordable energy solutions; on the other hand, dealing with the cross-border implications and effectiveness of regulatory policies, as they are enforced by a variety of means.

The private international law aspects of promoting technological cooperation and innovation constitute the main focus of this chapter. This is better explained as we first consider, in section 2, the concrete targets and indicators set in SDG 7, and then attempt, in section 3, a comprehensive picture of the interaction of private international law with the goal of 'ensuring access to affordable, reliable, sustainable and modern energy for all'. Section 4 then focuses on the management of transactional risk, as technology is shared, rights infringed and claims enforced across borders.

2. SDG 7: ACCESS TO AFFORDABLE, RELIABLE, SUSTAINABLE AND MODERN ENERGY

The idea of universal ('ensure … for all') and effective ('affordable, reliable') access to energy is accordingly enshrined in the first target of SDG 7. The next two targets, on renewable energy and energy efficiency, embrace the concept of 'sustainable' energy but their achievement should make a lasting positive contribution to universal access. SDG 7 seeks to overcome the long-term challenges noted above by embracing the notion of 'modern' energy, which is central to all targets and especially the means of implementation, which emphasise the role of international cooperation in improving infrastructure and technology. New technologies and technical improvements can lead us to cleaner energy sources, ecologically friendly new materials and more energy-efficient devices that meet humanity's increased energy needs. Innovative thinking would then be needed in making cleaner and efficient energy products affordable and more widely accessible.

SDG 7 includes two indicators of progress towards achieving 'universal access to affordable, reliable and modern energy services'.

The first indicator concerns the proportion of the population with access to electricity.[3] The latest report notes an acceleration in electrification, which may however not be enough to fully meet the target by 2030. In absolute numbers, we have gone from 1.22 billion people without access to electricity in 2010 to 759 million in 2019.[4] In that same period, the share of the global population with access to electricity went up from 83 per cent to 90 per cent;[5] moreover, the acceleration rate increased over time, from an average of 0.77 per cent in 2010–2016 to 0.82 per cent in 2016–2018.[6] But for Indicator 7.1.1 to be met, that rate would need to be increased to an annual average of 0.87 per cent for the period 2018–2030.[7] It is also imperative to address the problem in sub-Saharan

3 Indicator 7.1.1.

4 'Progress towards the Sustainable Development Goals', Report of the Secretary General to the Economic and Social Council, UN Doc E/2021/58, para 85.

5 ibid.

6 'Accelerating SDG7 Achievement in the Time of COVID-19' Policy Brief in Support of the High-Level Political Forum 2020 (UN 2020), 27.

7 <https://unstats.un.org/sdgs/report/2020/goal-07/> accessed 19 July 2021. According to the UN Secretary General, 'there may still be as many as 660 million people without access worldwide in 2030': 'Progress towards the Sustainable Development Goals', Report of the Secretary General to the Economic and Social Council, UN Doc E/2021/58, para 85.

Africa, where the 'world's deficit is increasingly concentrated'.[8] Whereas other regions of the developing world exceeded 98 per cent rates of access to electricity, in sub-Saharan Africa over 548 million people – representing just over half the population (53 per cent) – continued to lack access.[9]

The COVID-19 pandemic has brought attention to a specific dimension of the goal: the need for reliable and affordable energy in health centres. According to a survey of selected developing countries, one-quarter of health facilities were not electrified, while 'another quarter had unscheduled outages, affecting their capacity to deliver essential health services'.[10]

The second indicator concerns the proportion of population with primary reliance on clean fuels and technology.[11] As of 2018, a staggering 2.8 billion do not have such access. Moreover, even though the share of the global population with access to clean fuel and technologies for cooking increased, between 2010 and 2018, from 56 per cent to 63 per cent,[12] the absolute number has remained largely unchanged since 2010 – in fact, over the past two decades, in sub-Saharan Africa population growth has outpaced the acceleration of access to clean cooking technologies.[13] It is estimated that 4 million people die annually from 'illnesses attributable to household air pollution from inefficient cooking practices using polluting stoves paired with solid fuels and kerosine'.[14]

The most polluting form of energy is coal, which still accounts today for 27 per cent of the raw energy used to power everything from barbecue grills and cars to electric grids: its consumption is actually growing in Asia, which now accounts for 77 per cent of all coal use and most new coal plants being built.[15] It is estimated that, since 2009, coal consumption fell by 34 per cent in America and Europe and grew by a quarter in Asia, especially China and India.

The first critical observation that can be made about access to energy around the world concerns the marked, and persisting, regional disparity in terms of actual access, energy infrastructure and reliability of the energy networks. In addition to the global policies about promoting technological innovation, sub-Saharan Africa in particular will require massive investment in infrastructure, with technology and capital flows, in order to cover the electrification deficit.[16]

---

8 'Progress towards the Sustainable Development Goals', Report of the Secretary General to the Economic and Social Council, UN Doc E/2020/57, para 68.

9 ibid.

10 <https://unstats.un.org/sdgs/report/2020/goal-07/> accessed 19 July 2021.

11 Indicator 7.1.2.

12 <https://unstats.un.org/sdgs/report/2020/goal-07/> accessed 19 July 2021.

13 'Progress towards the Sustainable Development Goals', Report of the Secretary General to the Economic and Social Council, UN Doc E/2020/57, para 69.

14 <https://www.who.int/news-room/fact-sheets/detail/household-air-pollution-and-health> accessed 19 July 2021.

15 'Make coal history', *The Economist* (3 December 2020).

16 Sándor Szabó et al., 'Mapping of affordability levels for photovoltaic-based electricity generation in the solar belt of sub-Saharan Africa, East Asia and South Asia' (2021) 11 Scientific Reports 3226.

Custom solutions that take into account the facts and capabilities on the ground are also needed. A notable example concerns the so-called microgrids,[17] i.e. small, freestanding energy networks (grids), which can be established and maintained more easily, integrating a variety of energy sources, or even the promotion of off-grid power systems, especially drawing on solar energy. The second critical observation concerns the means to achieve universal access efficiently and cleanly. The recent growth of coal in Asia may drive home the point that the carbon prices and scheduled caps can only take care of the problem in part, and not soon enough. A more potent tool is to provide competitive alternatives. Thus, coal consumption in the US continued to fall during the Trump presidency, despite the Trump Administration's political and cultural support for coal, including attempts to de-regulate its use, due to the availability of cheaper natural gas and – increasingly – sources of renewable energy.[18] This underlines the potential of technological innovation, and diffusion, in helping humanity meet SDG 7.

Renewable energy represents an obvious alternative to fossil fuels, but also, increasingly, to nuclear energy: at present, nuclear plants are certainly cleaner than fossil-fuel power plants,[19] but also decisively more expensive. As the costs of renewable energy decrease,[20] achieving Target 7.2, which is to 'increase substantially the share of renewable energy in the global energy mix' by 2030, becomes more feasible. The target's single indicator concerns the renewable energy share in the total final energy consumption.[21] In 2018, the renewable energy share was at 17.1 per cent, up from 16.4 per cent in 2010, but the share of modern renewable sources in total final energy consumption remained below 11 per cent, rising by only 2.5 per cent in a decade.[22]

Technological and logistical innovation should also help achieve Target 7.3, which is to 'double the global rate of improvement in energy efficiency' by 2030. The target's indicator concerns energy intensity measured in terms of primary energy and GDP.[23] In 2018, global primary energy intensity was measured

---

17 Adam Hirsch, Yael Parag and Josep Guerrero 'Microgrids: A review of technologies, key drivers, and outstanding issues' (2018) 90 Renewable and Sustainable Energy Reviews 402–411.

18 'Make coal history', *The Economist* (3 December 2020).

19 For each kWh, nuclear plants emit 4–110 grams of equivalent CO2, compared to 400 grams for gas and 800 grams for coal.

20 In 2012, the cost per MWh was $70 for gas, $100 for nuclear, $80 for onshore wind and $220 for rooftop solar photovoltaics, but it was estimated that the cost of the last two would be reduced to $60 and $50 by 2018.

21 Indicator 7.2.1.

22 'Progress towards the Sustainable Development Goals', Report of the Secretary General to the Economic and Social Council, UN Doc E/2021/58, para 87. The 2020 Report gives 17 per cent for 2015 and 17.3 per cent for 2017.

23 Indicator 7.3.1.

at 4.8 MJ/$, down from 5.6 in 2010.[24] This represents an annual rate of up to 2.2 per cent, which is still below the target of 2.7 per cent.[25]

The three targets of SDG 7 are complemented by the two targets pertaining to means of implementation, Targets 7.a and 7.b. The indicator for meeting Target 7.a concerns '[i]nternational financial flows to developing countries in support of clean energy research and development and renewable energy production, including in hybrid systems.'[26] The indicator for meeting Target 7.b looks at 'investments in energy efficiency as a percentage of GDP and the amount of foreign direct investment in financial transfer for infrastructure and technology to sustainable development services.'[27]

In 2017, international financial flows to developing countries in support of clean and renewable energy reached $21.4 billion: this is 13 per cent higher than in 2016 and a 'twofold increase from flows committed in 2010'.[28] Only 12 per cent of these flows went to least developed countries. Moreover, almost half of these flows (46 per cent) went into hydropower projects, followed by – less ecologically intense – solar (19 per cent), wind (7 per cent) and geothermal (6 per cent) projects. In 2018, international financial flows decreased considerably to $14 billion, but there was an improved mix, with 27 per cent going to hydropower projects, 26 per cent to solar, 5 per cent to wind 8 per cent to geothermal and 34 per cent to 'multiple or other renewable energies'.[29]

These goals can only be met by massive flows of private capital. In order to achieve this, we must encourage investment in energy projects, enhance the role of the Global South in global supply chains for high-end technological products, and nurture a culture of innovation and entrepreneurship, in the spirit of environmental sustainability.

3. THE PRIVATE INTERNATIONAL LAW OF SDG 7

The contribution of law, and private international law, in helping meet the goals of clean and affordable energy rests on two pillars. It goes without saying that energy policy is shaped and enforced by regulatory institutions: originally

---

24 'Progress towards the Sustainable Development Goals', Report of the Secretary General to the Economic and Social Council, UN Doc E/2021/58, para 88. At the time of the Report, it was estimated that the improvement rate for 2019 would be at 2 per cent and for 2020 at only 0.8 per cent, due to the pandemic.

25 3 per cent would be needed to meet Target 7.3 by 2030: ibid.

26 Indicator 7.a.1.

27 Indicator 7.b.1.

28 'Progress towards the Sustainable Development Goals', Report of the Secretary General to the Economic and Social Council, UN Doc E/2020/57, para 72.

29 'Progress towards the Sustainable Development Goals', Report of the Secretary General to the Economic and Social Council, UN Doc E/2021/58, para 89.

viewed as creatures of 'domestic', 'public' law, regulators have been increasingly faced with the cross-border dimension and experimenting with a variety of means to achieve enforcement. There is thus an increasing role for private enforcement of such regulatory policies, as discussed in section 3.5 below. At the same time, energy policy is also served by traditional functions of private law. In our case, fostering a legal culture of entrepreneurship, which rewards success but also manages failure, should facilitate the twin goals of fostering technological innovation and enhancing its global dissemination, by incentivising technology transfers and technology-sharing. The two main dimensions involved are intellectual property and the protection of private investment, discussed in sections 3.1 and 3.2 below. Sections 3.3 and 3.4 consider two additional dimensions, rights over raw materials and legal treatment of supply chains.

3.1. TECHNOLOGICAL INNOVATION

Technological innovation must play a vital part with regard to the production and circulation of energy, but also in facilitating communication and information flows. Another important aspect concerns financial technology and innovative thinking about facilitating payment systems that minimise transaction costs and enable poorer people, especially in poorer areas, to afford access to needed energy resources.[30]

Protection of intellectual property appears paramount if we are to foster innovation. This should involve primarily the legal treatment of technological inventions, namely patents, and to a lesser extent distinctive marks, such as trademarks. A role for copyright and neighbouring rights may also be conceivable in the case of educational material, literary or audio-visual works promoting the goal of clean and affordable energy.

The protection of intellectual property rights has long involved policy discussions as to the level of protection, especially with regard to the duration of exploitation rights. Another point of contention, especially with regard to patents, involves the ability of third parties to compel the rights-holder to allow (to license) the use of the protected technology. This matter relates to broader debates about technology transfer between North and South. More generally, global intellectual property law has involved debates about the territorial scope of intellectual property rights (e.g. generic drugs).

Today, more than ever, patents are everywhere, and patent applications have proliferated. A lot of patents serve legitimate interests in safeguarding technological investment, but patents are also used as a weapon aiming at

---

30 Whitney Lisa Pailman, Wikus Kruger and Gisela Prasad, 'Mobile Payment Innovation for Sustainable Energy Access', *2015 International Conference on the Domestic Use of Energy (DUE)* (2015) 39–44.

preventing competitors from entering a field or at least delaying them in imitating the patent-holder's success. On the face of it, it is the former and not the latter group of patents that really serve technological innovation and thus SDG 7, but we must consider the patent landscape as a whole.

At the same time as patents are weaponised, many businesses opt not to protect their most important inventions via patents. The main reason for this is the publicity required in a patent application, raising the possibility of valuable information or know-how becoming available to third parties or competitors; in the medium to long -term, patented inventions enter the public domain. A contractual alternative is used instead: confidentiality or non-disclosure agreements (NDAs).

Cases concerning intellectual property rights fall into three, but essentially two, types. The first type are contractual cases involving especially licensing agreements. To them we may add employment agreements or work contracts, which determine who owns the right itself, and of course non-disclosure agreements. The second type of cases are tort cases involving infringement of the intellectual property right by a third party (or a licensee, if for some reason a tort claim is chosen). To the second group we may add other tort claims. The so-called 'complementary torts' include breach of confidence, breach of competition rules, unfair competition and passing off.[31] Tort bases such as civil conspiracy can be especially useful in establishing jurisdiction in a different state or joining together multiple defendants.

The third group of cases concerns the validity of the right itself: these cases should be distinguished conceptually from the other two groups, as they involve property rights and not an obligation. They are often subjected to different private international law norms, namely strict territoriality. But in legal practice, validity questions are usually connected to disputes about the exploitation of an intellectual property right, even if filed as a separate case.

These issues arise in the context of a relatively diverse legal environment – in fact, more diverse than as regards more ordinary civil and commercial cases.

Providing a uniform treatment of applicable law matters and facilitating the mutual recognition and enforcement of judgments by means of a global treaty has been a foundational idea at least since the mid-19th-century formation of the discipline of private international law.[32] Over time, it became commonly

31 James Fawcett and Paul Torremans, *Intellectual Property and Private International Law* (2nd ed, OUP 2011).

32 TMC Asser, 'De l'effet ou de l'exécution des jugements rendus à l'étranger en matière civile et commerciale' (1869) 1 Revue de droit international et de législation comparée 82–99; P-S Mancini, 'De l'utilité de rendre obligatoires pour tous les États, sous la forme d'un ou de plusieurs traités internationaux, un certain nombre des règles générales du Droit international privé pour assurer la décision uniforme des conflits entre les différentes législations civiles et criminelles' (1874) 1 Journal du droit international privé 221–239, 285–304.

accepted that the diversity of jurisdictional doctrines was the major obstacle to such an instrument. A century and a half later, the main effort of global ambition has been the Jurisdiction and Judgments Project, hosted by the Hague Conference on Private International Law.[33] The first result of the project was the 2005 Hague Choice-of-Court Convention.[34] 2019 saw the conclusion of a Hague Convention on the Recognition and Enforcement of Foreign Judgments in Civil or Commercial Matters (Hague Judgments Convention), not yet in force.[35] Discussions on further instruments pertaining to jurisdiction continue. Moreover, 'intellectual property' matters have been left out of the material scope of the 2019 Hague Judgments Convention.[36] The 2005 Hague Choice-of-Court Convention only covers cases involving the contractual exploitation of intellectual property rights.[37]

As a result, the most important legal sources remain those at the regional level, with the European Union having been the most successful actor in its regard. The Brussels I *bis* Regulation extends over the bulk of civil and commercial matters, including all aspects of intellectual property litigation.[38] The Lugano Convention extends the territorial scope of the Brussels I regime over a few more European countries. An Inter-American Convention dealing with the recognition and enforcement of judgments is also in force,[39] but it assumes a common jurisdictional framework between its contracting states.

In the absence of such instruments, residual national law applies. In the European Union, this has led to a binary system. For cases falling under the territorial scope of the EU instruments, jurisdiction will be exercised in accordance with the EU regime. For the rest, Member State courts will exercise their jurisdiction in accordance with their – more expansive and more diverse – national jurisdictional regimes ('residual jurisdiction'). Judgments made under that jurisdiction will also enjoy the benefits of the EU when it comes to their recognition and enforcement in other Member States. This has provided a strong incentive for claimants to seek to litigate cases in the courts of EU Member States. In the United States, most state laws have extended their courts' civil jurisdiction

33 For the legislative history of the project see the Hague Conference's website at <https://www.hcch.net/en/projects/legislative-projects/jurisdiction-project> accessed 17 July 2021.

34 Convention of 30 June 2005 on Choice of Court Agreements. <https://www.hcch.net/en/instruments/conventions/specialised-sections/choice-of-court> accessed 19 July 2021.

35 Convention of 2 July 2019 on the Recognition and Enforcement of Foreign Judgments in Civil or Commercial Matters <https://www.hcch.net/en/instruments/conventions/specialised-sections/judgments> accessed 19 July 2021.

36 Hague Judgments Convention, Art 2(1)(m).

37 Hague Choice-of-Court Convention, Art 2(2)(n): the Convention does not apply to 'the validity of intellectual property rights other than copyright and related rights'.

38 Regulation (EU) No 1215/2012 of the European Parliament and of the Council on jurisdiction and the recognition and enforcement of judgments in civil and commercial matters (recast) (Brussels I *bis* Regulation) [2012] OJ L 35/1.

39 Inter-American Convention on Extraterritorial Validity of Foreign Judgments and Arbitral Awards <https://www.oas.org/juridico/english/treaties/b-41.html> accessed 19 July 2021.

as far as the due process clause of the federal constitution would allow (the so-called long-arm jurisdiction doctrine).

It is precisely the regions most challenged in terms of meeting the SDGs, that is Asia and Africa, which are left out of this picture. Most developing countries having been under Western colonial rule, their private international law tends to reflect a version of the respective colonial power's legal tradition, which is not necessarily up to date. For example, the former British colonies follow the common law tradition in the conflict of laws, which should at the very least constitute a common reference framework and make it easier to incorporate new legal doctrines by judicial means. Yet the systematic survey of the conflict of laws in Commonwealth Africa by Richard Frimpong Oppong has revealed considerable diversity on the ground.[40]

Things are similar when it comes to applicable law. The few Hague Conventions on specific aspects of commercial relations have had relatively limited scope, especially when it comes to North–South relations, or have been superseded by developments in international uniform law (notably regarding the sale of goods). Regional activity has been more successful – and predominantly concentrated in the Western world. The European Union has issued two influential Regulations, on contractual (Rome I) and extra-contractual (Rome II) obligations respectively: both these Regulations have fully replaced the national choice-of-law norms in matters falling within their scope.[41] In the Western hemisphere, the 1994 Inter-American Convention on International Contracts has only been ratified by the two states needed for it to come into force: Mexico and Venezuela.[42]

In fact, the most important intergovernmental global instrument in this regard is a 'soft law' one: the 2015 Hague Principles on Choice of Law in International Commercial Contracts.[43]

Other, non-governmental soft law texts have also been influential in producing a common frame of reference. Specifically in matters concerning the conflict of laws in intellectual property we have the American Law Institute's Principles Governing Jurisdiction, Choice of Law, and Judgments in Transnational Disputes[44] and the CLIP Principles on Conflict of Laws in Intellectual Property.[45]

---

40 Richard Frimpong Oppong, *Private International Law in Commonwealth Africa* (CUP 2013).

41 Regulation (EC) No 593/2008 of the European Parliament and the Council on the law applicable to contractual obligations (Rome I Regulation) OJ L 177/7; Regulation (EC) No 864/2007 of the European Parliament and the Council on the law applicable to non-contractual obligations (Rome II Regulation) OJ L 199/40.

42 Inter-American Convention on the Law Applicable to International Contracts <http://www.oas.org/juridico/english/treaties/b-56.html> accessed 19 July 2021.

43 <https://www.hcch.net/en/instruments/conventions/specialised-sections/choice-of-law-principles> accessed 19 July 2021.

44 American Law Institute, *Intellectual Property: Principles Governing Jurisdiction, Choice of Law, and Judgments in Transnational Disputes* (2008).

45 European Max Planck Group on Conflict of Laws in Intellectual Property (CLIP), *Principles on Conflict of Laws in Intellectual Property* (2011).

International arbitration enjoys a more universal legal framework. With 166 contracting parties, the 1958 New York Convention on the Recognition and Enforcement of Foreign Arbitral Awards is one of the most successful international instruments of any kind, setting the main standard for the enforcement of both arbitration agreements and arbitral awards. The UNCITRAL Model Law on International Commercial Arbitration, which provides a comprehensive framework for international commercial arbitration processes, has also been adopted in 84 states (and a total of 117 jurisdictions), including most Asian and many African developing countries. Most commercial arbitrations take place under the auspices (and Rules) of one of a constellation of arbitral institutions. This includes the WIPO Arbitration and Mediation Center, which for the past quarter-century has provided an established venue for intellectual property disputes. So far, most of its cases have centred geographically on Europe and Asia.

3.2. PROTECTION OF PRIVATE INVESTORS

Much of the 'international financial flows' envisaged under Targets 7.a and 7.b should come from private parties, including 'angel' investors, venture capitalists, investment funds or even groups of small-scale investors. Even some of the money provided by the public funds of more developed countries will often use the mechanisms of private investment.[46]

Direct investment by foreign entities is often protected under international investment law, such as bilateral investment treaties, which often provide a right to investor–state dispute settlement, notably arbitration. Such cases fall outside the scope of this chapter. On the contrary, some attention must be paid to foreign investment in existing, possibly local, entities. Such investment will take the form of shareholder participation or a financing agreement.

Financing agreements may take the form of a simple loan or include a stock option. In either case, this brings us into contract law properly speaking. These agreements tend to have jurisdiction and choice-of-law clauses, commonly referring to English or New York law (or the investor's own law).

Shareholder (equity) participation involves investors taking a minority stock position in a company. In that case, issues may arise, first, as to the investors' actual legal rights (ability to participate in company decisions, monitor company finances) and, second, as to their effective exercise of such rights. In some cases, minority shareholders could even have the right to bring *derivative actions* on behalf of the company. Here as well, the starting point is a contractual undertaking; the agreement may be detailed enough to deal with most possible issues and it

---

[46] See the chapter on SDG 9 on this volume, with its emphasis on state investors.

may even designate the forum and the law applicable to any disputes, in which case the real question would be whether such arrangements are enforceable. But these issues are by default classified under company rather than contract law. In many cases, contractual arrangements may even be pre-empted by public policy considerations regarding corporate governance and capital markets. A company has to be set up under the rules of the law of its 'nationality' and basic matters pertaining to its operation will be litigated in that *forum societatis*.[47] But there is a well-known global divergence between legal systems that look, for both jurisdiction and applicable law, to the place of registration or incorporation and those that give preference to the place of central management (the 'real seat'). The former approach is followed by common law jurisdictions and corporate hubs. The latter approach still holds in continental jurisdictions. The approach espoused by the EU is characteristic: a company may be regarded as having its 'domicile' in either the statutory seat, or the place of central administration, or its principal place of business.[48]

Equity investment usually takes place in stock companies, but it is also possible for the more ancient business form of partnership to be selected instead: this option has the benefit of the general partner or partners (the entrepreneur or his or her company) being personally liable for the business, in exchange for having full control over its management. A partnership can also have a prescribed duration. In many jurisdictions, partnerships provide a more affordable business arrangement than incorporation. But partnership arrangements raise different kinds of problems.[49] General partners remain liable in full for the partnership's debts, but many legal systems do not acknowledge that partnerships possess a distinct legal personality. This matter has to be determined by looking to the law of the place where the partnership was organised. The same holds true for business associations whose legal status as a company is either pending or not recognised: such de facto companies may be treated as a partnership if the applicable law so allows.

This is an area where international uniform law has been gaining increasing importance. The United Nations Commission on International Trade Law (UNCITRAL), originally set up in order to help provide a common legal framework for international commerce, inclusive of the concerns of the Global South, has been especially active. Its initiatives of note include the 2019 Legislative Guide on Key Principles of a Business Registry[50] and the Model Laws

---

47 See e.g. Brussels I *bis* Regulation, Art 24(2).

48 Brussels I *bis* Regulation, Art 63(1).

49 In the words of Adrian Briggs, *Private International Law in English Courts* (OUP 2015), 831: 'Though its history is long, the private international law of partnerships is still less than fully formed'.

50 <https://uncitral.un.org/en/texts/msmes/legislativeguides/business_registry> accessed 19 July 2021.

on Cross-Border Insolvency (1997) and on the Recognition and Enforcement of Insolvency-Related Judgments (2018).[51]

On the regional level, some attention must be paid to the work of the Organization for the Harmonization of Business Law in Africa (OHADA). This international organisation comprises 17 Western African countries, almost all of them former French or Belgian colonies.[52] OHADA has produced several uniform laws on matters of business organisation, dispute resolution, and the simplification of recovery procedures and execution measures between its members.[53] For example, the OHADA Uniform Act on Company Law pays particular attention to the legal treatment of de facto companies.[54]

3.3. EXPLOITATION OF NATURAL RESOURCES

A number of issues arise from the demand for raw materials for the production of the equipment needed for new energy forms. Most of the supply must be met by the exploitation of resource-rich areas in the developing world. The principal instance involves the 17 rare-earth minerals necessary for many high-end technological products, the best known of which may be the lithium required for electric-car batteries.[55] But organic materials have also been in high demand, such as the balsa wood needed for wind turbines.[56]

Such cases involve questions of property rights over the raw materials themselves and the land, forests and sub-terrain where they are harvested. These matters involve land rights and are thus normally governed by the law of the place where the land is situated (*lex rei sitae*).[57] This same law – i.e. *lex situs* at the decisive moment – will determine whether a claim will be classified as a property claim or an obligation, or whether the thing in question is regarded as movable or immovable.[58] This is a settled principle everywhere.[59] Complications do arise

51 <https://uncitral.un.org/en/texts/insolvency/modellaw/cross-border_insolvency> and <https://uncitral.un.org/en/texts/insolvency/modellaw/mlij> both accessed19 July 2021.

52 Guinea-Bissau is a former Portuguese colony. Cameroon is regarded as a bilingual, mixed jurisdiction, with its northwestern part having been under British colonial rule and English common law maintained in that province. OHADA instruments have broken the hold of English commercial law in that territory as well.

53 See <www.ohada.org> accessed 19 July 2021.

54 Medret Lekunga Ndangoh, 'The OHADA Company Law and de facto companies' (2020) 15 Uniform Law Review 300.

55 See e.g. 'An increasingly precious metal', *The Economist* (16 January 2016).

56 See e.g. 'A worrying windfall', *The Economist* (30 January 2021) 37–39.

57 See e.g. Caroline Rupp, 'The *lex rei sitae* and its Neighbours – Debates, Developments and Delineating Boundaries Between PIL Rules' (2018) 7 European Property Law Journal 267.

58 See e.g. *Re Hoyles* [1911] 1 Ch 179 (CA).

59 In the words of Richard Frimpong Oppong, *Private International Law in Commonwealth Africa* (CUP 2013) 263: 'the lex situs rule … serves a practical end. It can ensure that immovable properties are not dealt with in a manner detrimental to national laws or interests.'

in countries, including notably some in sub-Saharan Africa, where there can be an 'internal' conflict of laws between state law and the custom of indigenous communities with claims to the land.

Another set of problems involves attempts by governments to regulate the movement of raw materials across borders and indirectly the ownership of natural resources in question. As to the former, import or export controls have been the main tool.[60] As to the latter, we have been observing a proliferation of investor screening regimes.[61]

On a different note, exploding demand for such raw materials has led to environmental devastation and brought challenges for the sustainability of indigenous communities and the traditional way of life.[62] This should give rise to civil claims best covered in the treatment of other Goals.[63]

3.4. SUPPLY CHAINS

The equipment used in the production and distribution of energy is the result of complex international supply chains of materials and components. Global supply chains, which rely on comparative advantage and economies of scale, promote efficiencies, dissemination of know-how and interdependence, but they also often trigger legal issues regarding the sale and carriage of goods. It is in these two areas that we find the most prominent types of international contracts, which have led to specific, global legal regimes.

When it comes to the international sale of goods, the two 1958 Hague Conventions (on critical conflict-of-laws aspects)[64] have been largely superseded by the 1980 UN ('Vienna') Convention on Contracts for the International Sale of Goods. 94 contracting parties, including many African countries, have joined the Vienna Convention, but its biggest success may well be the impressive corpus of doctrine and case law it has given rise to.

Carriage of goods may be by road, rail, air, sea or a combination of the above ('multimodal'). Different international instruments govern each of them. The dominant one is still carriage of goods by sea, where we observe a certain diversity in national legislations regarding the degree of carriers' protection from liability.

60 See e.g. 'China tightens rare-earth regulations, policing entire supply chain' *NikkeiAsia* (16 January 2021).

61 See e.g. Mikko Rajavuori and Kaisa Huhta, 'Investment screening: implications for the energy sector and energy security' (2020) 144 Energy Policy 111646.

62 See the chapter on SDG 11 in this volume. See also Jiunn-Cheng Lin et al 'Risk Analysis of Regions with Suspicious Illegal Logging and Their Trade Flows' (2021) 13 Sustainability 3549.

63 See the chapter on SDG 6 in this volume.

64 Conventions of 15 April 1958 on the jurisdiction of the selected forum in the case of international sales of goods and on the law governing transfer of title in international sales of goods.

The more carrier-friendly International Convention for the Unification of Certain Rules of Law relating to Bills of Lading (better known as the Hague-Visby Rules) still provides the international regime most commonly incorporated into carriage contracts.[65] The 1978 Hamburg Rules, proposed by the United Nations Commission on Trade and Development (UNCTAD), never obtained much traction in shipping practice. In an attempt to breach the gap, while taking into account modern technological developments such as electronic bills of lading and the realities of multimodal transportation, UNCITRAL fostered the 2009 Rotterdam Rules (the UN Convention on Contracts for the International Carriage of Goods Wholly or Partly by Sea). However, even though the US and most EU Member States are among its signatories, the Convention appears unlikely to come into force in the near future.

3.5. REGULATORY ENFORCEMENT

Achieving SDG 7 will require a diverse regulatory framework, using multiple tools to achieve several objectives. The starting point concerns the regulation of energy-related emissions. Some types of energy production are being phased out or prohibited; caps on emissions or on consumption are being placed on other types of energy; while yet other types must be subjected to strict rules of operation and severe scrutiny. Apart from the duties imposed on energy actors, regulatory law also tries to incentivise them to fulfil regulatory objectives: positive incentives may include tax credit or other benefits; negative incentives include the transaction costs of, for example, being subjected to lengthy, expensive proceedings. The actual operation of energy business also involves other regulatory domains, in addition to energy regulators. Competition law is an important tool for ensuring technological innovation and consumer choice, but even securities regulation has a part to play in safeguarding investors' interests. Data protection is also acquiring increasing importance in a data-driven global economy.

Private international law can play an important part in the achievement of regulatory objectives.[66] International agreements can only go so far in bridging the regulatory gap between North and South. In any case, in the short term some countries will be moving forward with higher standards and some will not. Private international law can provide tools that prevent a regulatory race to the bottom and may in fact help create a regulatory race to the top: a business

65 The Hague-Visby Rules are the original 1924 Convention ('Hague Rules') as amended by the 1968 Protocol. Countries may accede to the Convention or incorporate the Rules into domestic law.

66 See e.g. Hannah Buxbaum, 'Public Regulation and Private Enforcement in a Global Economy: Strategies for Managing Conflict' (2019) 399 Recueil des Cours 265–442.

operating in a country with lower standards that has to take into account, in these operations, the higher standards of another jurisdiction may even be incentivised to adopt uniformly a higher standard.

Public law has provided the principal means of enforcement of regulatory policies, in the form of prohibitions and penalties. The question is phrased in terms of determining the scope of a regulatory authority's jurisdiction over a case. If the authority has jurisdiction, it will apply its own substantive law. In the absence of an international agreement, jurisdiction is here asserted unilaterally, on the basis of the actual or potential effects of the regulated activity in the regulator's territory.

Modern regulatory law has also been increasingly embracing the concept of private enforcement of regulatory objectives, where private parties may sue the party in violation of regulatory norms. The pioneering field has been competition law: private enforcement of anti-trust claims has been a mainstay of US law for quite some time and has been gaining ground in the EU. Regulatory law provides the standard for judging whether a breach of statutory duty may be alleged against a business. In the case of a company violating a sectoral agreement, other businesses could bring an action in tort for the damage it has caused them. A major problem posed for the effectiveness of private enforcement has often been the relatively low monetary stakes of individual injured parties. A way out of this has been to promote collective redress mechanisms: class actions can level the playing field and help tackle the problems of litigation costs, under-compensation and under-regulation.[67]

Collective redress is not without its problems. Claims may be governed by different laws, when injury has occurred in more than one country, as for example in a transnational product liability case involving multiple states, and this adversely affects the above-mentioned interests.[68] A solution might be to devise a specific choice-of-law rule that determines the law applicable to the claim. A more modest proposal would be to have a single law apply as to regulatory purposes, while allowing compensation to be determined by several laws.[69]

The regulatory environment also includes efforts to achieve regulatory objectives by more consensual means.[70] For example, agreements may be reached between the regulator and an industry sector (*co-regulation*),[71] or

67 Ralf Michaels, 'European Class Actions and Applicable Law' in Arnaud Nuyts and Nikitas Hatzimihail (eds), *Cross-Border Class Actions: The European Way?* (Sellier 2013) 117–118.

68 ibid 118–120.

69 ibid 123–124, noting that 'such a splitting up of what is a single action would not go well at least with a European understanding of law. Although considerations of regulation and of compensation may lead us in somewhat different directions, they must in the end be treated together.'

70 See Marie-Anne Frison-Roche (ed), *Régulation, supervision, compliance* (LGDJ 2017).

71 Jean-Philippe Coulson and Pascale Idoux, *Droit public économique* (9th ed, LGDJ 2018).

specific enterprises: this would a more efficient way of achieving objectives, on the part of the regulator, and avoiding sanctions or proceedings, on the part of the businesses. Incentives also constitute a form of *consensual enforcement*. A state may provide clean energy certification to a business meeting its standards, even for operations taking place abroad. Commodities produced under certain energy standards may be exempt from tariffs or other regulatory barriers. On the whole, the regulatory environment aims to motivate the industry towards compliance.

Regulatory policy may also be enforced by more conventional conflict-of-laws means: Regulatory norms may be characterised as constituting mandatory rules (*lois de police*) from which there can be no derogation by the application of a foreign law. Even when a foreign norm is applicable, the court may still take into account the impact its application in the individual case might have on the forum's policy regarding the promotion of clean and affordable energy and invoke the *ordre public* exception. The result in either case would be to hold a contracting party (the promisee) to a higher standard of performance than it may have expected at the time the contract was concluded, or, conversely, to excuse its non-performance in order to comply with energy standards.

4. DEALING WITH THE RISK

The assessment, allocation and management of risk, including legal risk, is an essential part of business activity. Such risk is increased – and even takes new dimensions – when it comes to cross-border economic activity and especially the medium- to long-term relations that technological innovation and cooperation call for. In fact, the assessment and management of cross-border legal risk has been presented as the defining idea of modern international commercial litigation.[72]

4.1. CONTRACTUAL MANAGEMENT OF LITIGATION RISK

Contract litigation may arise in relation to licensing agreements, agency and distribution agreements, the sale of goods (independently or as part of supply chains) and employment contracts (especially with regard to works made for hire and non-disclosure agreements). In all these cases, the primary distinction is between contracts involving a forum selection or an applicable law clause, and those without one.

Jurisdiction agreements are today common in international contracts. International instruments and national legislation tend to acknowledge their

72 Richard Fentiman, *International Commercial Litigation* (2nd ed, OUP 2015) 3 et seq.

validity. The formal requirements for them have been simplified. A noticeable development in modern law is that agreements are presumed to stipulate the exclusive jurisdiction of the chosen forum. Especially in advanced commercial jurisdictions, drafting practice has become more sophisticated and even the judicial interpretation of such clauses has been increasingly emphasising the commercial expediency.

This however still leaves a few problem areas. First, in countries not party to international instruments – and these countries are overwhelmingly in the developing world – the law still embodies a certain degree of scepticism towards agreements divesting their courts of default jurisdiction. Especially in Commonwealth jurisdictions, absent a legislative provision to the contrary, courts have discretion to stay proceedings in favour of the foreign court designated in the agreement; a jurisdiction agreement is an important factor to consider but not the only one.[73] Moreover, courts may be reluctant to affirm the validity or existence of such an agreement.

Second, modern practice has seen more complex agreements, including a proliferation of asymmetrical and hybrid jurisdiction agreements.[74] In asymmetrical agreements, one party to the agreement is bound to the exclusive jurisdiction of the selected forum (*forum prorogatum*), whereas the other party has additional options. In hybrid agreements, one party is bound to the exclusive jurisdiction of the *forum prorogatum*, whereas the other one has the option of arbitration. The legal treatment of these agreements is at present debated. English law, for example, finds no fault with them. On the other hand, the French Court of Cassation has found asymmetrical jurisdiction clauses to be invalid. The consensus seems to be that such agreements are not covered by the Hague Choice-of-Court Convention.

Third, certain types of contracts where one kind of party habitually has limited bargaining power, invite special treatment. This is notably the case of employment contracts, which are left out of the Hague Choice-of-Court Convention.[75] The Brussels I *bis* Regulation provides a special regime for these contracts, under which a choice-of-court agreement may only add to the jurisdictional bases available to the employee (who can only be sued in his or her domicile but may sue even an employer domiciled in a third country at the place where work was carried out or where the 'business which engaged the employee is or was situated').[76] By carving out these exceptions, it should be easier for legal systems to take a more liberal position as to the jurisdictional clauses

73 There are, however, benefits in allowing judges a certain degree of discretion. See Richard Fentiman, *International Commercial Litigation* (2nd ed, OUP 2015), 102 et seq.

74 See also Mary Keyes (ed), *Optional Choice of Court Agreements in Private International Law* (Springer 2020).

75 Art 2(1(b) Hague Choice-of-Court Convention.

76 Arts 21–23 Brussels I *bis* Regulation.

in commercial agreements. At the same time, this may create issues of legal characterisation as to who constitutes an 'employee' rather than an independent contractor (or even a 'consumer' rather than a business).

Arbitration agreements should provide fewer challenges. The New York Convention provides an effective global legislative framework for the enforcement of arbitration agreements. Procedural formalities such as official translation and document certification requirements must be taken into account in estimating the costs of doing business in some jurisdictions, but this is an area where global standards have developed, and information is generally available. A more challenging subject, treated in various ways under national laws, regards the arbitrability of certain disputes.

Party autonomy constitutes the principal rule when it comes to the law applicable to contracts.[77] It is today common practice to include an applicable law provision in the contract.

Party autonomy is noticeably limited with regard to consumers and employees. In some African countries, domestic employment law applies to all employment relations in the territory.[78]

4.2. CONTRACT LITIGATION IN THE ABSENCE OF A PARTY AGREEMENT

Absent an enforceable agreement between the parties as to jurisdiction, the place of the defendant's domicile (the *general* or *personal* jurisdiction) constitutes a commonly accepted jurisdictional basis.[79]

Parallel to the *forum rei*, legal systems tend to acknowledge some form of *forum contractus*, i.e. that the courts of a place connected to the transaction itself should be able to hear the case. There is however some variety in how wide such a basis may be. A common law forum would have jurisdiction if the contract was 'made within the jurisdiction' or 'by an agent trading or residing within the jurisdiction', or if breach of contract was 'committed within the jurisdiction', or if 'the contract is by its terms, or by implication, governed by English law'.[80] On the contrary, EU private international law has viewed the 'special jurisdiction' of the *forum contractus* as an exception from the general jurisdiction rule, attempting to localise it to the 'place of performance of the obligation in question', and even defining statutorily this latter in cases of contracts for the sale of goods or services as the place where, under the contract, goods and services were or

77 Alex Mills, *Party Autonomy in Private International Law* (CUP 2018), 313 et seq.

78 See e.g. Employment Act 2006, s 4(a), of Uganda, as discussed by Richard Frimpong Oppong, *Private International Law in Commonwealth Africa* (CUP 2013) 139–140.

79 In the EU, see Art 4 Brussels I *bis* Regulation.

80 RSC Ord 11, r 1(1).

should have been delivered – thus eliminating, among others, the possibility of grounding jurisdiction on payment being due or effected in the forum.[81]

With regard to applicable law, in the absence of an agreement by the parties there exists a noticeable diversity of approaches. The ancient rule that the law where the contract was made shall apply has lost ground in much of the world but persists in some countries.[82] Parties being far more likely than in the past to expressly state their intention, the old practice of courts reading into the contract a tacit agreement by the parties to have the law of the forum apply to their case has waned or morphed into the concept of the *proper law of the contract*, under which the judge determines by considering the totality of the facts of the case, in order to ascertain the legal system with which the contract has the closest and most real connection.[83] The proper law approach was carried over from England to all Commonwealth countries[84] but has also been adopted across the globe. At the same time, the approach has been subject to criticism for the potentially large number of indicators the judge may have to consider. It has also led to issues concerning performance abroad being carved out from the proper law.[85] This explains the approach recently adopted in EU private international law: the 1980 Rome Convention embraced the concept of 'characteristic performance' and the Rome I Regulation that replaced it developed concrete, almost mechanical rules for the major types of transactions. Proper law survives as an escape device in these cases, as well as for those contracts where it is not possible to determine characteristic performance.

When it comes to the scope of the *lex contractus*, we observe that the historic diversity as to the characterisation of prescription, burden of proof or even remedies as matters of substantive or procedural law still persists, with continental jurisdictions (and EU instruments) following the former approach and common law jurisdictions the latter.[86]

4.3. INFRINGEMENT LITIGATION

More questions are raised with regard to tort litigation. The absence of a contractual relation between the parties reduces the possibilities of risk management. At the same time, tort litigation in commercial matters often involves tactical considerations: it is not uncommon for a party to a transactional relation to make tort rather than contract claims, in order to avoid precisely choice-of-forum and choice-of-law agreements or litispendence. When it comes

81 See Art 7(1) Brussels I *bis* Regulation.

82 For example, Algeria and Argentina.

83 See e.g. *Coast Lines Ltd v Hudig & Veder Chartering LV* [1972] 2 QB 34 (CA).

84 Richard Frimpong Oppong, *Private International Law in Commonwealth Africa* (CUP 2013) 131.

85 See e.g. ibid 146–148.

86 ibid 7–11.

to intellectual property litigation, things are further complicated because of the stronger territoriality element: for both copyright and industrial property, the main rule is that the applicable law in an infringement claim would be the law of the territory in which protection is sought (*lex loci protectionis*).[87] Industrial property rights granted by an administrative agency are moreover territorially limited. Given that contesting the validity of an intellectual property claim is a frequent defence to an infringement suit, this often leads to parallel proceedings or even the suspension of the infringement action, as an action contesting the validity of a patent may only be brought in the jurisdiction which granted that patent in the first instance. The EU, which brought to light the notion of such a 'torpedo' has attempted to deal with the problem via the creation of a Community Patent Court, but this not a realistic global solution.[88]

General jurisdiction is again the starting point in infringement litigation. However, compared to contract litigation, problems involving general jurisdiction multiply in tort litigation: on the one hand, plaintiffs have an incentive to 'discover' a defendant who allows them to establish jurisdiction in a convenient forum; on the other hand, potential defendants have at least as strong an incentive to insulate themselves from legal actions, by spinning off subsidiary and related companies, or by subcontracting.

Identifying the place of infringement is also an increasingly complex exercise. In EU private international law, 'the place where the harmful event occurred or may occur'[89] has been taken to encompass both the place of the event giving rise to the damage and the place where the damage occurred.[90] The possibility of granting the claimant too many options was mitigated by the adoption of the so-called mosaic principle: claimants have the option either to sue the defendant, under the general jurisdiction ground, for all their damages in the defendant's place of domicile, or to sue the defendant in one or more *loci delicti commissi*, presumably including their own domicile.[91] This equilibrium has been challenged by the advent of the internet and the ubiquity of online content. The CJEU has created more claimant-friendly exceptions in cases involving online violations of personality rights,[92] but it has been reluctant to abandon the territoriality element attached to intellectual property rights.[93]

---

87 See James Fawcett and Paul Torremans, *Intellectual Property and Private International Law* (2nd ed, OUP 2011), 799 et seq.

88 Alberto Miglio 'The Jurisdiction of the Unified Patent Court: A Model for the Application of the Brussels I Regulation to non-EU Disputes?' in Alexander Trunk and Nikitas Hatzimihail (eds), *EU Civil Litigation and Third Countries: Which Way Forward?* (Nomos/Hart 2021).

89 Art 7(2) Brussels I *bis* Regulation.

90 Case 21/76, *Bier v Mines de Potasse*, ECLI:EU:C:1976:166.

91 Case C-68/93, *Shevil v Presse Alliance*, ECLI:EU:C:1995:61.

92 Case C-509/09, *eDate* and C-161/10, *Martinez*, ECLI:EU:C:2011:685; Case C-194/16, *Bolagsupplysningen*, ECLI:EU:C:2017:766.

93 Case C-523/10, *Wintersteiger*, ECLI:EU:C:2012:220; Case C-170/12, *Pinckney*, ECLI:EU:C:2013:635; Case C-441/13, *Hejduk*, ECLI:EU:C:2015:28.

In matters of applicable law, just like jurisdiction, infringement of intellectual property rights is treated as a tort. A possible hurdle to claims concerns the common law rule of double actionability, which has been abandoned in an increasing number of jurisdictions but still holds in some Commonwealth countries. The rule can indeed operate as 'a test of jurisdiction rather what it truly is – a choice of law rule'.[94]

4.4. ENFORCEMENT

In most of the world, enforcement of judgments is grounded on national statutory provisions or on international instruments. Given that international instruments, both bilateral and multilateral, have a defined territorial and subject-matter scope, national legislation provides the default regime. But these regimes are not always comprehensive. For example, Russian law makes enforcement conditional upon the existence of a treaty arrangement between the Russian Federation and the state of the judgment court.[95] Absent that, the foreign judgment should be recognised in accordance with 'federal law',[96] but at present such a provision, requiring reciprocity, exists only for bankruptcy judgments.[97] In other continental jurisdictions, the reciprocity requirement persists, with a distinction being made between 'diplomatic' reciprocity (when an agreement is in place between the judgment country and the enforcement country) and the 'legislative' or 'judicial' reciprocity of requiring that the enforcement country's judgments be enforced in the judgment country.[98] In many continental jurisdictions, the foreign judgment must undergo the process of being declared enforceable (*exequatur*) in order to produce any legal effects.[99]

In the member countries of the British Commonwealth, there is no default statutory provision for third-country judgments and the residual regime for treating foreign judgments is via the common law means of an action on the judgment.[100] As a result, forum jurisdiction would have to be established, on the basis of the defendant residing or having assets therein. There is limited

---

94 Richard Frimpong Oppong, *Private International Law in Commonwealth Africa* (CUP 2013) 152.

95 Art 221 of the Arbitrazh Procedure Code; Art 409 of the Code of Civil Procedure, as discussed in Vladimir Yarkov, 'Recognition and Enforcement of Judgments Between the European Union and Russia: Possible Prospects' in Alexander Trunk and Nikitas Hatzimihail (eds), *EU Civil Litigation and Third Countries: Which Way Forward?* (Nomos/Hart 2021).

96 Art 241 of the Russian Arbritazh Procedure Code.

97 Art 1 of the Russian Federal Bankruptcy Law.

98 See e.g. Michael Stöber, 'Recognition and Enforcement of Foreign Court Decisions in Colombia' in Alexander Trunk and Nikitas Hatzimihail (eds), *EU Civil Litigation and Third Countries: Which Way Forward?* (Nomos/Hart 2021), 215–217.

99 See e.g. Art 607 of the Colombian General Code of Procedure.

100 See e.g. Richard Fentiman, *International Commercial Litigation* (2nd ed, OUP 2015), 620 et seq.

discussion, and some diversity of opinion, as to the theoretical foundation of thus enforcing foreign judgments.[101] That discussion may have practical consequences, if it leads to a hard or soft reciprocity requirement. Moreover, by converting the foreign judgment into a debt, the scope of enforcement may be limited to money judgments, and a stricter time limitation may apply.[102]

In the EU, the *exequatur* was abolished with the recast Brussels I *bis* Regulation. Whereas the same grounds for refusing the recognition or enforcement of a judgment have remained under the new regime, there is a noticeable effort to compel the judgment debtor to litigate in good faith in the judgment country, with certain defences not being available before the enforcement court if they had not been raised before the judgment country's courts.[103] The EU regime sets the minimum grounds for non-enforcement: a judgment 'manifestly' contrary to public policy (*ordre public*); a judgment in default when the defendant was not duly served (with the additional condition that the defendant must have challenged the judgment in the judgment country's courts if at all possible); a judgment irreconcilable with a judgment given between the same parties in the enforcement country, or an earlier judgment in another Member State or third country 'involving the same cause of action and between the same parties' provided that judgment meets the conditions for recognition/enforcement; and a judgment violating the exclusive jurisdiction grounds of the Regulation.[104] This regime is more liberal than national regimes. For example, Colombia would not recognise judgments pertaining to rights *in rem* over goods situated in its territory when the proceedings were commenced or when a lawsuit involving the same cause of action is pending before Colombian courts.[105]

The Hague Judgments Convention offers a more comprehensive, modern approach. The Convention distinguishes between those types of cases where enforcement may be refused, possibly precluding another attempt, and those cases where recognition/enforcement 'may be postponed or refused' without preventing a subsequent application to the same effect. As to the former, four of the six grounds correspond to Article 45(1) of Brussels I *bis*, with the Convention elaborating more on the due service requirement[106] and on the definition of

[101] Richard Frimpong Oppong, *Private International Law in Commonwealth Africa* (CUP 2013) 316 enumerates comity, the doctrine of obligation, 'reciprocity and the advantage to be gained therefrom', and facilitating international trade and commerce.

[102] ibid 318.

[103] Arnaud Nuyts, 'Exequatur going global: The doctrine of exhaustion of remedies in the Member State of origin of the judgment' in Charalambos Pamboukis (ed) *Symposium on the Future of Global Law* (Nomiki Bibliothiki 2021).

[104] Art 45 Brussels I *bis* Regulation.

[105] Michael Stöber, 'Recognition and Enforcement of Foreign Court Decisions in Colombia' in Alexander Trunk and Nikitas Hatzimihail (eds), *EU Civil Litigation and Third Countries: Which Way Forward?* (Nomos/Hart 2021).

[106] Art 7(1)(a): 'the document which instituted the proceedings or an equivalent document, including a statement of the essential elements of the claim (i) was not notified to the

ordre public.[107] Given that the Convention does not provide a jurisdictional regime, the relevant ground concerns judgments obtained in violation of a jurisdiction agreement.[108] An additional ground addresses judgments obtained by fraud.[109] The latter group concerns proceedings pending 'between the same parties on the same subject matter' in the courts of the requested state, provided that there is a 'close connection' between the dispute and the requested state and that 'the court of the requested state had been seised before the court of origin'.[110]

5. APPRAISAL AND REFORM PROPOSALS

Ensuring access to affordable, reliable, sustainable and modern energy for all requires an approach which is both systemic and decentralised. We must be aware of the connections between SDG 7 and the other SDGs. We must also appreciate the balance that needs to be struck, in the fulfilment of these goals, between them and other fundamental values. At the same time, successfully balancing the twin goals of clean and affordable energy serves as a compelling narrative for sustainable development. In operational terms, achieving SDG 7 also requires a decentralised approach, which takes into consideration local circumstances and encourages local solutions. It must also be a mixed solution, bringing together public regulation and planning with private initiative and self-interest.

Private international law can make a vital contribution in all these regards. First, in terms of dealing with the more traditional subjects of private law, i.e. contracts and rights over tangible and intangible property, private international law can help expedite the international flows of information, financial, technological and material resources needed in order to make energy access both truly universal and truly sustainable. Private international law is about the legal risks involved in international transactions: identifying them and proposing to lawmakers, on the one hand, and entrepreneurs and other stakeholders,

---

defendant in sufficient time and in such a way as to enable them to arrange for their defense, unless the defendant entered an appearance and presented their case without contesting notification in the court of origin, provided that the law of the State of origin permitted notification to be contested; or (ii) was notified to the defendant in the requested State in a manner that is incompatible with fundamental principles of the requested State concerning service of documents'

107 Art 7(1)(c): 'recognition or enforcement would be manifestly incompatible with the public policy of the requested State, including situations where the specific proceedings leading to the judgment were incompatible with fundamental principles of procedural fairness of that State and situations involving infringements of security or sovereignty of that State'.

108 Art 7(1)(d): 'the proceedings in the court of origin were contrary to an agreement, or a designation in a trust instrument, under which the dispute in question was to be determined in a court of a State other than the State of origin'.

109 Art 7(1)(b).

110 Art 7(2).

on the other hand, how to manage and most efficiently allocate them. Private international law is moreover a tool for decentralised governance, in the sense that it aims to manage legal diversity, rather than eliminating it. Such an approach may in fact be not only more pragmatic, but also more effective in terms of fostering creativity and customised solutions.

Second, the idea of decentralised governance also pertains to the regulatory function of private international law. To national regulators, it can bring mindfulness of the cross-border implications of their actions, but also the territorial limits of their individual ambition. On the global scale, by the promotion and careful management of private enforcement, it could also contribute to a certain degree of harmonisation of regulatory standards, and even achieving regulatory objectives in an efficient manner.

Third, private international law is capable of promoting a comprehensive outlook in the governance of human affairs. At the same time, global thinking and interdisciplinarity has a transformative potential for private international law and international commercial law.

With this in mind, our survey has shown a marked divergence between Global North and Global South. In much of the former, regional and international instruments have achieved a remarkable degree of convergence and homogenisation of rules on jurisdiction and the enforcement of judgments. But the same phenomenon is not observed in the legal systems of most developing countries. In particular, African private international law still relies on the conflict-of-laws doctrine inherited from colonial times.

On the other hand, even the fact that we can speak of 'African private international law' is propitious. In the past two decades, a new generation of scholars has been making a strong contribution to the doctrinal discussion and systematic examinations of the private international law of developing countries. This has also coincided with and been nurtured by increased participation of developing countries in international organisations, such as UNCITRAL and the Hague Conference, as well as by regional initiatives.

Such increased participation augurs well. It should allow for the interests, and practical limitations, of developing countries to be considered more seriously both when drawing up international instruments and when discussing how to monitor and facilitate their application. Since the early days of the discipline of private international law, the story of international legislative projects has centred around the interests and doctrinal debates in the most advanced legal systems, to the point that we may forget the value of instruments that are less ambitious in their subject matter but more far-reaching in their geographic scope, setting certain minimum standards. Both the Hague Conference and UNCITRAL have devoted a significant amount of their work to developing guides and guidelines, both as means of facilitating the application of certain of their most successful instruments and even as 'soft law' instruments.

The value of soft law must also not be underestimated. The various Principles may provide a common frame of reference and discussion between lawyers from different legal traditions (and legal systems at different levels of development). This is also a function shared by international legislative projects that may not have come into force but often represent the state of the art in the field and point to directions to follow.

A booming transnational legal practice has led to extremely sophisticated contracts and complex dispute management strategies. A lot of international contracts are so detailed as to minimise the role of the legal system providing the applicable law. Certain jurisdiction agreements extend over several pages, setting out custom processes for the resolution of potential disputes. Such customisation is quite costly; it often runs in parallel with the proliferation of standard-form agreements and use of boilerplate language.

To a great extent, these practices have helped resolve and even pre-empt legal problems. Legal certainty is especially important in commercial transactions, with uncertainty often deterring investment. But customised legal advice can also entail significant costs, which may even be prohibitive for new entrants, especially from developing countries. Transnational legal practice may thus provide advantages to established players from developed, powerful countries (and markets), to the point of undermining the objectives of promoting entrepreneurship, local solutions, etc. A solution would be to promote the drafting of more standard form contracts from neutral actors (intergovernmental organisations, industry, academic or non-profit initiatives).

Providing for the energy needs of humanity in a sustainable manner is a matter of long-term survival. It calls for us to bundle together a variety of doctrinal tools, while remaining mindful of the diverse interests that need to be balanced, the nuances in the application of principles and even the antinomies inherent in the life of the law. Private international law can help with the development and execution of a truly global strategy – in spatial but especially in analytical and policy terms. Hopefully, it can also contribute to the cautious, pragmatic and persistent optimism that has been a beacon of our discipline since the first doctrinal musings on the subject.

SDG 8: DECENT WORK AND ECONOMIC GROWTH

Ulla LIUKKUNEN

Goal 8: Promote sustained, inclusive and sustainable economic growth, full and productive employment and decent work for all

8.1 Sustain per capita economic growth in accordance with national circumstances and, in particular, at least 7 per cent gross domestic product growth per annum in the least developed countries
8.2 Achieve higher levels of economic productivity through diversification, technological upgrading and innovation, including through a focus on high-value added and labour-intensive sectors
8.3 Promote development-oriented policies that support productive activities, decent job creation, entrepreneurship, creativity and innovation, and encourage the formalization and growth of micro-, small- and medium-sized enterprises, including through access to financial services
8.4 Improve progressively, through 2030, global resource efficiency in consumption and production and endeavour to decouple economic growth from environmental degradation, in accordance with the 10-year framework of programmes on sustainable consumption and production, with developed countries taking the lead
8.5 By 2030, achieve full and productive employment and decent work for all women and men, including for young people and persons with disabilities, and equal pay for work of equal value
8.6 By 2020, substantially reduce the proportion of youth not in employment, education or training
8.7 Take immediate and effective measures to eradicate forced labour, end modern slavery and human trafficking and secure the prohibition and elimination of the worst forms of child labour, including recruitment and use of child soldiers, and by 2025 end child labour in all its forms
8.8 Protect labour rights and promote safe and secure working environments for all workers, including migrant workers, in particular women migrants, and those in precarious employment
8.9 By 2030, devise and implement policies to promote sustainable tourism that creates jobs and promotes local culture and products

8.10	Strengthen the capacity of domestic financial institutions to encourage and expand access to banking, insurance and financial services for all
8.a	Increase Aid for Trade support for developing countries, in particular least developed countries, including through the Enhanced Integrated Framework for Trade-Related Technical Assistance to Least Developed Countries
8.b	By 2020, develop and operationalize a global strategy for youth employment and implement the Global Jobs Pact of the International Labour Organization

1. INTRODUCTION

Sustainable Development Goal 8 (SDG 8) brings a strong social dimension to Agenda 2030, reflecting the aspirations behind the Decent Work Agenda of the International Labour Organization (ILO), which in recent years has become central to the organisation's renewed strategy.[1] Decent work is an ambitious objective linked to the pressing need to achieve sustainable social progress in order to combat problems of exclusion and inequality in the global labour

[1] See also ILO Centenary Declaration for the Future of Work, adopted by the International Labour Conference, 108th Session, Geneva, 21 June 2019; and *Decent Work: Report of the Director-General* (International Labour Conference, 87th Session, Geneva, International Labour Organization 1999).

market. The ILO Decent Work Agenda rests on four pillars, namely employment creation, rights at work, social protection, and social dialogue, that together are integral to SDG 8. In Agenda 2030, decent work has been set side by side with economic growth and concretised with 12 particular targets.[2] However, it can – and should – simultaneously be read in the context of the strategy of the ILO, where it has gained significance in strengthening the role of fundamental labour rights and a labour rights-based approach to working life regulation more generally. Thus, the regulatory context for decent work offered by the ILO draws the objective of decent work to the core of the system of international labour standards.[3] Decent work as a goal captures long-term efforts in the tripartite work of the ILO.[4] Decent work as an objective of labour standards has also been gradually integrated with development of the ILO international labour standards system.[5]

Decent work as an ILO objective can originally be traced back to Director-General Juan Somavia's initiative.[6] It has assumed an increasingly strong role in managing the social dimension of globalisation,[7] emphasising the need for adequate protection of all who work, and simultaneously challenging old Western categorisations of labour law. Although these have played a major role in shaping regulatory frameworks for labour protection, coverage of decent work is much broader, aligning with the ILO Constitution,[8] which states that conditions of labour must be improved. This requirement is not dependent on the form of

---

2 See Resolution adopted by the UN General Assembly on 25 September 2015: 'Transforming Our World: The 2030 Agenda for Sustainable Development', UN Doc A/RES/70/1 (21 October 2015).

3 See Ulla Liukkunen, 'The ILO and Transformation of Labour Law' in Tarja Halonen and Ulla Liukkunen (eds), *International Labour Organization and Global Social Governance* (Springer 2021).

4 Tripartism is a defining characteristic of the norm-creation pattern of the ILO as an organisation. Social dialogue is central to the organisation itself and, in terms of achieving both social and economic progress, to the ILO Decent Work Agenda. See *Social Dialogue and Tripartism: A Recurrent Discussion on the Strategic Objective of Social Dialogue and Tripartism, under the Follow-up to the ILO Declaration on Social Justice for a Fair Globalization, 2008* (Report VI, International Labour Conference, 107th Session, Geneva, International Labour Organization 2018) 3.

5 See for example, Protocol of 2014 to the Forced Labour Convention, 1930, adopted by the International Labour Conference, 103rd Session, Geneva, 11 June 2014, whose Preamble recognises that the prohibition of forced or compulsory labour forms part of the body of fundamental rights, and asserts that forced or compulsory labour violates the human rights and dignity of millions of women and men, girls and boys, contributes to the perpetuation of poverty and stands in the way of achieving decent work for all.

6 See *Decent Work: Report of the Director-General* (International Labour Conference, 87th Session, Geneva, International Labour Organization 1999).

7 This was advanced by the ILO World Commission on the Social Dimension of Globalization. See World Commission on the Social Dimension of Globalization, *A Fair Globalization: Creating Opportunities for All* (International Labour Organization 2004).

8 Constitution of the ILO, adopted by the Peace Conference in April 1919, became Part XIII of the Treaty of Peace of Versailles (28 June 1919). The Constitution has been amended in 1922, 1945, 1953, 1962, 1972, 1986 and 1997.

labour, be it work in an employment relationship or some other way of working. This frame brings about a remarkable challenge in terms of finding appropriate tools to achieve progress towards SDG 8. In particular, it is not enough to maintain contract-based work at the level of an employment relationship because a large number of workers are unprotected by labour legislation.[9] Many developments combine to challenge old patterns of regulation of labour and major unresolved issues, such as work in the informal economy and human trafficking.[10] These issues need to be properly addressed when seeking development towards decent work. Another important perspective on decent work highlights its universal nature as an objective. This means that decent work is an objective to be set both in developed and developing countries as well as each region and continent. Importantly, this also implies that diverse means at international, regional and national levels are needed to achieve progress towards decent work.

Literally, SDG 8 connects decent work and economic growth. Although this chapter focuses on decent work, fostering the objective of decent work requires an approach that does not set aside the interrelation between the 'social' and the 'economic'. As SDG 8 links decent work and sustainable economic growth, the combination calls for a perspective which enables integrating labour protection and economic growth.[11] Thus, the objective of sustained growth involves a commitment to growth which is inclusive. This approach calls for critically rethinking regulatory frames that prioritise 'economic' at the cost of 'social' and in addition the attribute 'sufficient', which is often the label used to treat labour-protective elements of law as secondary in global economic processes.

The objective of decent work reflects a pressing need to safeguard social protection globally and to ensure that the social dimension of globalisation is answered fairly and sustainably.[12] On the one hand, it should be noted that basically the idea of decency is not dependent on economic growth as it should govern all work, whatever the economic circumstances. On the other hand,

9 As the most recent World Employment and Social Outlook report of the ILO emphasises, '[t]he ILO's Decent Work Agenda does not only deal with access to employment opportunities; it also requires that an employment relationship should provide an adequate minimum wage and guarantee rights at work and access to social protection. Yet such conditions are not being fulfilled for a large proportion of workers worldwide'. See *World Employment and Social Outlook: Trends 2020* (International Labour Organization 2020).

10 See *Decent Work in Global Supply Chains* (Report IV, International Labour Conference, 105th Session, Geneva, International Labour Organization 2016); *Global Estimates of Child Labour: Results and Trends, 2012–2016* (International Labour Organization 2017); *Women and Men in the Informal Economy: A Statistical Picture* (3rd ed, International Labour Organization 2018); and *Ending Forced Labour by 2030: A Review of Policies and Programmes* (International Labour Organization 2018).

11 Critically from the human rights perspective, see Diane F Frey, 'Economic Growth, Full Employment and Decent Work: The Means and Ends in SDG 8' (2017) 21 International Journal of Human Rights 1164.

12 The World Commission on the Social Dimension of Globalization elaborated the idea of decent work and fair globalisation, see World Commission on the Social Dimension of

sustainable economic development is important to the well-being of workers who suffer harsh economic times in ways that often bear consequences for the realisation of labour rights and social protection. In order to pursue the goal of decent work it should also be emphasised that SDG 8 is strongly interconnected with other SDGs and that the theme of decent work and economic growth is related to many other goals set by Agenda 2030. In essence, the SDGs should be viewed as an entity. Many aspects of decent work remain unachievable if goals expressed in other SDGs are also not achieved. Therefore, the analysis offered by this chapter should be read with that in mind. To illustrate, combating poverty and lack of sufficient social protection as well as advocating gender equality go hand in hand with decent working conditions and labour protection.[13] As the COVID-19 pandemic has had significant economic and labour market impacts, new and wide-ranging challenges in terms of SDG 8 have emerged. These challenges have shaken existing regulatory frameworks and again emphasise a holistic perspective of Agenda 2030. Simultaneously, recent adverse economic and social developments have brought the goal of decent work to the fore even more than previously. As pointed out by Joseph E Stiglitz, a post-pandemic world will need more global cooperation with better social governance.[14]

This chapter focuses on SDG 8 and the goal of decent work from a private international law perspective. First of all, it delimits the view on certain central aspects of decency that bear relevance from a cross-border perspective. Secondly, it addresses the question of decent work from the perspective of regulatory developments of a private international law nature. Cross-border work takes shape in highly diverse forms. Some of these forms are more susceptible to lack of labour protection than others. Private international law approaches of regulatory actors have an effect on the extent to which cross-border protection of workers is possible. However, they need to be seen in a wider context to evaluate their effectiveness. Therefore, connections between labour law and private international law need to be fully acknowledged and viewed from the perspective of key aspects of decent work. Observations offered on regulatory frameworks are used first and foremost to point out major opportunities and challenges for private international law in terms of promotion of decent work. Transnational labour law developments offer a third perspective on decent

---

Globalization, *A Fair Globalization: Creating Opportunities for All* (International Labour Organization 2004).

13 See *Social Protection Floor for a Fair and Inclusive Globalization. Report of the Advisory Group Chaired by Michelle Bachelet Convened by the ILO with the Collaboration of the WHO* (International Labour Organization 2011); *Universal Social Protection for Human Dignity, Social Justice and Sustainable Development* (Report III, Part B, International Labour Conference, 108th Session, Geneva, International Labour Organization 2019); and *Gender Equality at the Heart of Decent Work* (Report VI, International Labour Conference, 98th Session, Geneva, International Labour Organization 2009).

14 Joseph E Stiglitz, 'Postscript' in Tarja Halonen and Ulla Liukkunen (eds), *International Labour Organization and Global Social Governance* (Springer 2021) 145.

work, discussed in this chapter through an analysis of relevant regulatory frameworks beyond national states. These frameworks point to development trends that demonstrate regulatory efforts within private rule-making involving transnational normativities.[15] At the same time, they illustrate continuing challenges in terms of private labour governance.

2. FUNDAMENTAL LABOUR RIGHTS AND DECENT WORK

The ILO's 1998 Declaration on Fundamental Principles and Rights at Work emphasises the universal nature of fundamental labour rights, namely freedom of association and effective recognition of the right to collective bargaining, elimination of forced or compulsory labour, abolition of child labour, and elimination of discrimination in respect of employment and occupation.[16] These core labour standards are included in a total of eight ILO conventions, also referred to as the ILO core or key or fundamental conventions.[17] Based on the number of ratifications of conventions on which the core labour standards are founded and the ILO's follow-up data on the 1998 Declaration, it has become evident that despite some success – for example with the global ratification of the Worst Forms of Child Labour Convention No 182[18] – significant progress is

[15] See also Jürgen Basedow, *The Law of Open Societies – Private Ordering and Public Regulation of International Relations* (Hague Academy of International Law 2013) 50–51.

[16] See ILO Declaration on Fundamental Principles and Rights at Work and its Follow-up, adopted by the International Labour Conference, 86th Session, Geneva, 18 June 1998 (Annex revised 15 June 2010).

[17] These conventions are the Convention concerning Freedom of Association and Protection of the Right to Organise (No 87), adopted by the International Labour Conference, 31st Session, Geneva, 9 July 1948; the Convention concerning the Application of the Principles of the Right to Organise and to Bargain Collectively (No 98), adopted by the International Labour Conference, 32nd Session, Geneva, 1 July 1949; the Convention concerning Forced or Compulsory Labour (No 29), adopted by the International Labour Conference, 14th Session, Geneva, 28 June 1930 (and its Protocol of 2014 to the Forced Labour Convention, adopted by the International Labour Conference, 103rd Session, Geneva, 11 June 2014); the Convention concerning the Abolition of Forced Labour (No 105), adopted by the International Labour Conference, 40th Session, Geneva, 25 June 1957; the Convention concerning Minimum Age for Admission to Employment (No 138), adopted by the International Labour Conference, 58th Session, Geneva, 26 June 1973; the Convention concerning the Prohibition and Immediate Action for the Elimination of the Worst Forms of Child Labour (No 182), adopted by the International Labour Conference, 87th Session, Geneva, 17 June 1999; the Convention concerning Equal Remuneration for Men and Women Workers for Work of Equal Value (No 100), adopted by the International Labour Conference, 34th Session, Geneva, 29 June 1951; and the Convention concerning Discrimination in Respect of Employment and Occupation (No 111), adopted by the International Labour Conference, 42nd Session, Geneva, 25 June 1958.

[18] See 'ILO Child Labour Convention achieves Universal Ratification' (4 August 2020) <https://www.ilo.org/ankara/news/WCMS_749858/lang--en/index.htm> accessed 11 March 2021.

lacking in realising core labour standards, particularly in the poorest countries. If we measure the coverage of ratifications against the global number of workers, we find that a remarkable number of workers are not protected by all ILO fundamental conventions.[19] Fundamental labour rights also remain out of reach in work that drops out of the scope of any formal regulatory frameworks; indeed, work in the informal economy largely remains 'below the radar' in terms of promoting decent work.[20]

If we want to achieve better protection of fundamental labour rights it is not enough to focus solely on a ratification-centred approach. Rather, a view is needed which acknowledges the relevance of various institutions, actors and approaches that enhance labour rights protection and broaden the spectrum of regulatory mechanisms that play a role in institutional and legal environments where labour rights are dealt with.[21] To illustrate, major institutional features of the ILO often eclipse well-established technical work of the organisation, which includes assistance for individual countries to improve and promote implementation of international labour standards and which in the long term supports countries in building stronger implementation structures and institutions at local level.[22]

The purpose of defining core labour standards has been to further the management of the social dimension of globalisation. The 1998 ILO Declaration on Fundamental Labour Rights has come to concretise conditions for decent work. The decent work objective should also be viewed in relation to the regulatory framework of the ILO international labour standards system, where decent work as an aim is supported by several ILO conventions and related mechanisms of implementation. Despite problems related to their observance,

---

19 See 'Ratifications of Fundamental Conventions by Country' <https://www.ilo.org/dyn/normlex/en/f?p=1000:10011:::NO:10011:P10011_DISPLAY_BY,P10011_CONVENTION_TYPE_CODE:1,F> accessed 11 March 2021. The numbers of ratifications of each fundamental convention were: Freedom of Association and Protection of the Right to Organise Convention No 87: 157; Right to Organise and Collective Bargaining Convention No 98: 168; Forced Labour Convention No 29: 179; Abolition of Forced Labour Convention No 105: 176 (denounced: 2); Minimum Age Convention No 138: 173; Worst Forms of Child Labour Convention No 182: 187; Equal Remuneration Convention No 100: 173; and Discrimination (Employment and Occupation) Convention No 111: 175.

20 See *Women and Men in the Informal Economy: A Statistical Picture* (3rd ed, International Labour Organization 2018); and Organisation for Economic Co-operation and Development and International Labour Organization, *Tackling Vulnerability in the Informal Economy* (OECD Publishing 2019). See also Tiziano Treu, 'The ILO and the Future of Work' in Adalberto Perulli and Tiziano Treu (eds), *The Future of Work: Labour Law and Labour Market Regulation in the Digital Era* (Wolters Kluwer 2020) 15–16.

21 See also Ulla Liukkunen and Yifeng Chen, 'Developing Fundamental Labour Rights in China: A New Approach to Implementation' in Ulla Liukkunen and Yifeng Chen (eds), *Fundamental Labour Rights in China – Legal Implementation and Cultural Logic* (Springer 2016).

22 See *The Committee on the Application of Standards of the International Labour Conference: A Dynamic and Impact Built on Decades of Dialogue and Persuasion* (International Labour Organization 2011).

core labour standards are widely approved internationally and are recognised in several significant international and regional human rights documents.[23] In addition, they are included in most of the central public guidelines laid out for multinational enterprises, such as the OECD Guidelines for Multinational Enterprises[24] and the Tripartite Declaration of Principles concerning Multinational Enterprises and Social Policy of the ILO.[25] Crucially, these guidelines emphasise the need to respect fundamental labour rights regardless of the existing regulation of the host state where multinationals operate.[26]

Fundamental labour rights, being strongly interrelated, are core goals in terms of promoting decent work and equality.[27] Globally, realising these goals also depends on multinational enterprises as regulatory actors and corporate social responsibility (CSR) strategists, and the weight they give to sustainable production. Realising these rights may require resolving regime collisions that necessitate a broader perspective on private international law and its ability to resolve such collisions than any perspective that can be derived from state-centric regulatory settings.

3. DECENT WORK AND PRIVATE INTERNATIONAL LAW: POINTS OF DEPARTURE

Labour law is characterised by a multi-layered normative framework – a framework shaped by different kinds of normative actors and their interplay. The mix of private ordering and public regulation is of a particular nature in labour law and causes

23 See for example, the International Convention on the Elimination of All Forms of Racial Discrimination, adopted by the UN General Assembly on 21 December 1965; the International Covenant on Civil and Political Rights, adopted by the UN General Assembly on 16 December 1966; and the International Covenant on Economic, Social and Cultural Rights, adopted by the UN General Assembly on 16 December 1966.

24 See Organisation for Economic Co-operation and Development, *OECD Guidelines for Multinational Enterprises* (OECD Publishing 2011). The Guidelines are a part of the OECD Declaration on International Investment and Multinational Enterprises adopted by the governments of OECD member countries on 21 June 1976. They have been revised in 1979, 1982, 1984, 1991, 2000 and 2011.

25 See Tripartite Declaration of Principles concerning Multinational Enterprises and Social Policy of the ILO, adopted by the Governing Body, 204th Session, Geneva, November 1977, and amended at its 279th, 295th and 329th Sessions in November 2000, March 2006 and March 2017.

26 See Organisation for Economic Co-operation and Development, *OECD Guidelines for Multinational Enterprises* (OECD Publishing 2011) Part I Concepts and Principles, para 2; and Tripartite Declaration of Principles concerning Multinational Enterprises and Social Policy of the ILO, adopted by the Governing Body, 204th Session, Geneva, November 1977, and amended at its 279th, 295th and 329th Sessions in November 2000, March 2006 and March 2017, para 8.

27 See *Decent Work: Report of the Director-General* (International Labour Conference, 87th Session, Geneva, International Labour Organization 1999).

tensions when labour rights are addressed in the contexts of self-regulation and related transnational contractual arrangements. The complex interaction between private and public in labour law also complicates the legal environment where cross-border work is regulated.[28] The fact of public law elements being present in diverse ways in the regulatory modes of domestic labour laws triggers a need to use caution in approaching perspectives that highlight contractual relations and their private law frame as the sole point of departure for the private international law of employment contracts and labour relations. In general, the objectives behind labour law and embedded public law-related elements have been channelled into regulatory private international law in ways that have rejected or restricted party autonomy and shaped the connecting factors used, as well as increased the role of mandatory rules in choice of law.

The tendency to use the law of the habitual place of work as the point of departure in choice of law concerning individual employment contracts is explained by the nature and rationale of labour law.[29] However, work across borders in its various forms challenges the idea of solely focusing on the law of the habitual workplace as the one producing socially just outcomes. Work carried out in a cross-border setting takes diverse forms and needs to be seen from a more nuanced perspective.[30] This in turn requires broadening the view to different ways of promoting the objective of decent work via means of private international law.

Recent labour market developments have given birth to new types of work which challenge traditional categorisations used in private international law as the basis for protection. Different forms of self-employment and atypical work are characterised by the temporary nature of work as well as heightened unpredictability, which also complicates determination of the applicable private international law rules. In addition to the growth of forms of atypical employment-type work, working without an employment contract or an employment relationship takes different forms that require more precise attention in terms of the protection that can be offered by rules of private international law.[31] With new kinds of multi-party contractual arrangements, platformisation has given rise to a need to rethink existing regulatory approaches to labour protection in

---

28 See Ulla Liukkunen, 'Introduction' in Ulla Liukkunen (ed), *Employment and Private International Law* (Edward Elgar Publishing 2020).

29 See also Martin Franzen, 'Conflicts of Laws in Employment Contracts and Industrial Relations' in Roger Blanpain (ed), *Comparative Labour Law and Industrial Relations in Industrialized Market Economies* (9th ed, Wolters Kluwer 2008) 224–225; and Franz Gamillscheg, *Rules of Public Order in Private International Labour Law* (Hague Academy of International Law 1983).

30 See also Otto Kahn-Freund, 'Notes on the Conflict of Laws in Relation to Employment in English and Scottish Law' in *Selected Writings* (Stevens 1978).

31 See Guy Davidov, 'The Three Axes of Employment Relationships: A Characterization of Workers in Need of Protection' (2002) 52 University of Toronto Law Journal 357.

a private international law setting.[32] It is not possible to limit evaluation of the sufficiency of existing safeguards to workers with employee status, as there is a need for broader assessment of forms of work that are dependent on platforms and in various ways based on multi-party contractual constellations.[33]

Sustainability concerns should be seen as part of the dilemma inherent in the decent work deficit, which is caused by a certain mismatch between existing private international law rules and workers' need for protection. The lack of sufficient protection for cross-border work necessitates a critical evaluation of existing regulatory approaches and in addition a re-orientation towards global developments in the labour market. This is needed in order to create sustainable regulatory responses to changes caused by the transformation of work that have produced entirely novel phenomena in the labour arena. Regulatory approaches that are designated to protect weaker parties in a cross-border setting need to be more inclusive to encompass new forms of work and be equipped to deal with related inequalities. The question arises as to whether more uniform private international law rules between states could bring about the improvements that would be needed to remove existing problems of lack of protection and social dumping in its diverse forms.[34]

There is a need to search for new ways to enhance cross-border protective frameworks on a more informed basis. With private rule-making related to transnational labour law developments, new actors have entered the arena of international labour regulation, while new categories of cross-border contractual relationships have emerged. Transnational forms of governance require new ways of viewing values and rights manifested in the decent work objective in regulatory contexts where they become apparent, transforming how collisions that emerge are to be dealt with. Constructing responses to private normativities of a cross-border nature presupposes rejecting the rigid separation between private international law and labour law, on the one hand, and between public international law and labour law, on the other hand. This understanding also underpins the idea of viewing private international law and public international law as interrelated in framing articulation of labour rights in a transnational era where economic success may be accompanied by cheap labour or where labour moves without a regulatory realm affording protection.[35]

---

32 See also *World Employment and Social Outlook 2021: The Role of Digital Labour Platforms in Transforming the World of Work* (International Labour Organization 2021).

33 See Janine Berg, Marianne Furrer, Ellie Harmon, Uma Rani and M Six Silberman, *Digital Labour Platforms and the Future of Work: Towards Decent Work in the Online World* (International Labour Organization 2018).

34 See Lisa Berntsen and Nathan Lillie, 'Breaking the Law? Varieties of Social Dumping in a Pan-European Labour Market' in Magdalena Bernaciak (ed), *Market Expansion and Social Dumping in Europe* (Routledge 2015).

35 See Ulla Liukkunen, 'Introduction' in Ulla Liukkunen (ed), *Employment and Private International Law* (Edward Elgar Publishing 2020). See also Horatia Muir Watt, 'Private International Law Beyond the Schism' (2011) 2 Transnational Legal Theory 347.

4. DECENT WORK AND PRIVATE INTERNATIONAL LAW: A LABOUR RIGHTS-BASED APPROACH

Different dimensions of protection that private international law rules offer to weaker parties bring to the fore the mandatory nature of central labour legislation. From the regulatory perspective, decent work as an objective should be viewed in the context of the system of international labour standards with a focus on fundamental labour rights as defined by the ILO in its 1998 Declaration. Adoption of the Declaration marked a turning point in terms of defining fundamental labour rights in an internationally uniform way. From the perspective of the entity formed by these rights, collective labour rights can be viewed as necessary to the development of other labour rights. This means that cross-border protection of collective labour rights should be kept in mind and in focus, along with individual rights, when regulatory private international law frameworks are rethought. However, there are also other ILO conventions than the fundamental ones, such as those that regulate safety and health at work and other conditions of labour protection that are essential to decent work. From the viewpoint of governance, the ILO has also designated four of its conventions as governance instruments because of their importance for the functioning of the international labour standards system.[36]

Adopting a labour rights-based approach to decent work in private international law would broaden the perspective on existing regulatory approaches in private international law so that laws and legal practices could be evaluated from the viewpoint of protection of labour rights and their existence. Consequently, tools for promoting decent work can be sought from labour rights schemes in a cross-border setting so that private international law means of ensuring application of mandatory substantive rules would be utilised more broadly. Labour rights-oriented regulatory approaches can be linked to private international law developments that in diverse ways highlight the role of mandatory rules in choice of law. While internationally recognised labour standards form a frame for labour rights to evolve, private international law is needed to ensure that these rights can be assured in a cross-border setting. However, the realisation of fundamental labour rights is also dependent on overall respect for human rights and the rule of law, which draws attention to SDG 16 promoting peaceful and inclusive societies for sustainable development, providing access to justice

---

36 The four governance conventions are the Convention concerning Labour Inspection in Industry and Commerce (No 81), adopted by the International Labour Conference, 30th Session, Geneva, 11 July 1947; the Convention concerning Employment Policy (No 122), adopted by the International Labour Conference, 48th Session, Geneva, 9 July 1964; the Convention concerning Labour Inspection in Agriculture (No 129), adopted by the International Labour Conference, 53rd Session, Geneva, 25 June 1969; and the Convention concerning Tripartite Consultations to Promote the Implementation of International Labour Standards (No 144), adopted by the International Labour Conference, 61st Session, Geneva, 21 June 1976.

for all, and building effective, accountable and inclusive institutions at all levels. It is not possible to evaluate the status of labour rights without paying heed to the broader societal framework of these rights and their evolution. The perspective of a changing labour market and the transformation of work should be integrated with the labour rights approach so that new needs for protection can be taken into account. Moreover, the rights-based approach requires tackling the structural causes of lack of labour protection.

Cross-border collective bargaining brings out a particular perspective on global labour governance. In several labour law regimes, collective agreements play an essential role in regulating minimum terms of employment and they can also govern work performed abroad.[37] In recent decades, the international dimension of collective bargaining has changed profoundly and cross-border dimensions of collective agreements have become more manifold. This means that the regulatory framework for collective bargaining across borders should be viewed from a private international law perspective which is nuanced enough to govern diverse developments. Cross-border social dialogue has much potential in terms of promoting labour rights and decent work. The ILO has called for the strengthening of cross-border social dialogue, including by economic sector or region, to generate a virtuous circle of dialogue at the national level for tackling the impact of the COVID-19 pandemic, and to devise appropriate recovery strategies.[38] Efficiency of collective bargaining requires recognition of the relevance of private international law rules to cross-border collective agreements. Importantly, the approach towards fundamental labour rights in private international law affects the way choice-of-law questions related to cross border collective agreements are dealt with.

Although internationally uniform regulation is absent from employment-related private international law, some particular regulatory contexts should be noted. First of all, the regulatory framework for public procurement is important to social protection of workers in a cross-border setting. Social considerations in public procurement regulation are also relevant to regulatory private international law. ILO Convention No 94 on public contracts[39] is applicable in a cross-border context so that it affects choice of law.[40] The Convention and

37 See Ulla Liukkunen, 'The Role of Collective Bargaining in Labour Law Regimes: A Global Approach' in Ulla Liukkunen (ed), *Collective Bargaining in Labour Law Regimes: A Global Perspective* (Ius Comparatum – Global Studies in Comparative Law, vol 32, Springer 2019).

38 See 'Peak-level Social Dialogue as a Governance Tool during the COVID-19 Pandemic: Global and Regional Trends and Policy Issues' (26 October 2020) <https://www.ilo.org/wcmsp5/groups/public/---ed_dialogue/---dialogue/documents/briefingnote/wcms_759072.pdf> accessed 11 March 2021, 28.

39 Labour Clauses (Public Contracts) Convention (No 94), adopted by the International Labour Conference, 32nd Session, Geneva, 29 June 1949.

40 The Convention has been ratified by 63 states. See 'Ratifications of C094 – Labour Clauses (Public Contracts) Convention, 1949 (No 94)' <https://www.ilo.org/dyn/normlex/en/f?p=1000:11300:0::NO:11300:P11300_INSTRUMENT_ID:312239> accessed 11 March 2021.

related Recommendation No 84[41] focus on procurement contracts that involve employment of workers. These contracts are required to guarantee an acceptable level of social protection.[42] The Convention, which also applies under certain conditions to posted workers, aims at guaranteeing that minimum terms of employment are protected from the downside of competition caused by tenders.[43] The Convention requires that public contracts include labour clauses concerning wages, working hours and other conditions of work. The Convention also covers temporary work performed in a contracting state on the basis of a supply contract; here, some difficult questions of its compatibility with EU law on posted workers have arisen. Secondly, international trade and investment agreements that include labour clauses with dispute settlement mechanisms may have important connections to private international law.[44] Although often loosely formulated, labour clauses that involve international labour standards should also be considered in terms of how related dispute settlement mechanisms can promote objectives of labour protection in a cross-border setting.

It is noteworthy that result-oriented considerations in choice of law that emphasise weaker party protection have shaped regulatory private international law rules concerning employment contracts. The impact of mandatory rules on choice of law has risen with the increasing result-selectivism and materialisation of private international law where material justice considerations guide the pursuit of 'conflicts justice'.[45] The decent work objective can also be considered in the light of particular developments in the EU that demonstrate the materialisation of private international law in the use of private international law rules outside their traditional function. These developments deserve more attention in terms of enhancing labour rights protection beyond regional legal integration. Private international law has been used by the EU in a manner that differs from its traditional use, especially when employee participation rights have been developed to govern the cross-border dimension. Although participation rights are not included in ILO fundamental labour rights, and the ILO has not set labour standards on informing and consulting employees, it is important to note the

41 Labour Clauses (Public Contracts) Recommendation, 1949 (No 84), adopted by the International Labour Conference, 32nd Session, Geneva, 29 June 1949.

42 See also *Labour Clauses (Public Contracts) Convention, 1949 (No 94) and Recommendation (No 84): A Practical Guide* (International Labour Organization 2008).

43 See Maria Anna Corvaglia, *Public Procurement and Labour Rights: Towards Coherence in International Instruments of Procurement Regulation* (Hart Publishing 2017).

44 On labour clauses in international trade agreements from a comparative perspective, see Ronald C Brown, 'Asian and US Perspectives on Labor Rights under International Trade Agreements Compared' in Axel Marx, Jan Wouters, Glenn Rayp and Laura Beke (eds), *Global Governance of Labour Rights: Assessing the Effectiveness of Transnational Public and Private Policy Initiatives* (Edward Elgar Publishing 2015). See also *Assessment of Labour Provisions in Free Trade and Investment Agreements* (International Labour Organization 2016).

45 See also Symeon C Symeonides, 'Result-Selectivism in Conflicts Law' (2009) 46 Willamette Law Review 1.

unity between social dialogue, industrial relations and employee participation as a frame which is central to promoting labour rights and enabling the collective voice of workers also in a cross-border setting. This frame has been added a new layer with the European Works Council Directive,[46] in that European Works Councils have assumed tasks that do not derive from their regulatory frame but rather from the transnational operational environment in which they communicate with the management of multinational enterprises where they function as cross-border institutions for employee information and consultation. EU legislation, which sets out the framework for European Works Councils, has focused on establishing rules on cross-border information and consultation and builds on a particular use of private international rules to enable an institution backed up by diverse domestic models of employee participation.[47] However, with transnational company agreements between multinational enterprises and employee representatives on labour issues, European Works Councils have expanded their role beyond this. They have contributed to the evolution of cross-border social dialogue within multinationals and have become significant actors in terms of private governance in transnational labour law.

5. REGULATORY PRIVATE INTERNATIONAL LAW AND INDIVIDUAL EMPLOYMENT CONTRACTS

The lack of globally unified private international rules on employment contracts and labour relations more generally emphasises the role of regional and state-level regulatory solutions. The concept of the individual employment contract is central to regulatory private international law. Employment status determines the protection that choice-of-law rules can afford. From the classic private international law perspective, decent work as a goal draws attention to the protection afforded by the law with the closest connection to the employment contract in choice of law and the means available to ensure this protection. In some legal systems, mandatory rules play a heightened role in choice of law. Importantly, for example, the experience of the US shows that concepts deriving from the system of international labour standards can be turned to in labour cases.[48]

---

46 See Directive 2009/38/EC of the European Parliament and of the Council of 6 May 2009 on the Establishment of a European Works Council or a Procedure in Community-scale Undertakings and Community-scale Groups of Undertakings for the Purposes of Informing and Consulting Employees (Recast) [2009] OJ L 122/28.

47 See also Manfred Weiss, 'The Development of Employee Involvement in the EU: Lessons to Be Learned' in Valeria Pulignano and Frank Hendrickx (eds), *Employment Relations in the 21st Century: Challenges for Theory and Research in a Changing World of Work* (Wolters Kluwer 2019) 184–185.

48 See William B Gold IV, 'Labor Law Beyond U.S. Borders: Does What Happens Outside of America Stay Outside of America?' (2010) 21 Stanford Law and Policy Review 401.

Some countries do not allow party autonomy in employment contracts, whereas others permit it but limit its effects.[49] Despite allowing party autonomy in employment contracts, a point of departure in choice of law can be to ensure application of the mandatory employee-protective rules of the law closest to the contract. The heightened role of mandatory rules can also come into play in the opportunity to apply overriding mandatory rules (*lois de police*) of a law other than the *lex causae*. Accordingly, in cases where the law of closest connection does not afford sufficient protection, it may be possible to apply overriding mandatory rules of the *lex fori* or, to certain extent, even third countries.[50] As regards the substance of these rules, guidance could be sought more directly from internationally recognised labour standards, fundamental labour rights being at the core of them. With the human rights nature of core labour standards, it would be possible to rely on them when defining the content of rules that have to be respected in choice of law regardless of the *lex causae*. In the end, the public policy (*ordre public*) principle, which enables courts to refuse to apply foreign laws or to recognise or enforce foreign judgments that are contrary to the public policy of the *lex fori*, can become applicable.[51] Fundamental labour rights at work connect the idea of decency to workers' human rights. For example, the link between forced labour and lack of decent work is clear; here, the public policy principle which embodies human rights concerns may offer a last resort in protecting people in forced labour.[52]

While particular rules have been created to protect weaker parties to employment contracts, at the same time weaker parties without formal employee status in the labour market have been excluded from similar protection. Arguably, traditional labour legislation, with its protective elements and particular monitoring mechanisms, has been unable to keep up with changes in ways of working. As a result, a large number of workers who remain outside the scope of application of labour law rules are unprotected.[53] For private international

49 See also Symeon C Symeonides, 'The Scope and Limits of Party Autonomy in International Contracts: A Comparative Analysis' in Franco Ferrari and Diego P Fernández Arroyo (eds), *Private International Law: Contemporary Challenges and Continuing Relevance* (Edward Elgar Publishing 2019).

50 For example, Bogdan states that '[m]ost overriding mandatory rules of private-law nature are provisions favouring the party considered worthy of special protection, such as children, women, employees or consumers, but more general protective rules are also conceivable'. See Michael Bogdan, *Private International Law as Component of the Law of the Forum* (Hague Academy of International Law 2012) 183. See also Andrea Bonomi, 'Mandatory Rules in Private International Law: The Quest for Uniformity of Decisions in a Global Environment' in *Yearbook of Private International Law* (vol 1, Otto Schmidt/De Gruyter European Law Publishers 1999) 215.

51 See for example, Alex Mills, 'The Dimensions of Public Policy in Private International Law' (2008) 4 Journal of Private International Law 201.

52 On different aspects of forced labour, see *Ending Forced Labour by 2030: A Review of Policies and Programmes* (International Labour Organization 2018).

53 See Ulla Liukkunen, 'Introduction' in Ulla Liukkunen (ed), *Employment and Private International Law* (Edward Elgar Publishing 2020).

law, this means that non-employment contract-based forms of work also need to be given attention so that protective devices can be applicable and developed further in order to guarantee appropriate and inclusive protection of those who work in a cross-border setting.

Overriding mandatory rules have the potential to assume a growing role in the protection of the weaker party in choice of law so that diverse forms of work can be more broadly governed. However, although the significance of mandatory rules in choice of law has grown, overriding mandatory rules are known to be difficult to identify. In Article 3(1) of the Posted Workers Directive,[54] the EU legislature has set out a list of applicable terms and conditions of employment of host state law as having overriding mandatory status. It has also confirmed the overriding mandatory nature of essential collective agreement provisions.[55] In essence, the specific use of mandatory provisions, which limits the scope of party autonomy, reflects the effect of substantive labour law on choice of law. Notably, not only statutory provisions, but also provisions of collective agreements can be employed in order to protect the weaker party in the framework of international transactions that involve the performance of work in another country. The trend of enabling application of substantive labour law rules of a law other than the *lex causae* is a significant part of the materialisation of private international law.

Protecting the individual and collective interests of workers in cross-border work through private international law means has become more complex in a still globalising world. This means a regulatory challenge that cannot be overcome without searching for new ways of developing an international protective framework with means that private international law can afford. A broader recognition of labour protection issues embedded in cross-border settings is needed to develop measures that can contribute to promoting decent work. The ILO Decent Work Agenda could also be reviewed with the cross-border setting of regulatory needs and transnational labour governance in mind.[56] The ILO has not focused in its regulatory activities on legal questions of a cross-border nature. Nor is there any other global actor which would have taken on such activity.[57] Therefore, the content of private international rules that relate

---

54 See Directive 96/71/EC of the European Parliament and of the Council of 16 December 1996 concerning the Posting of Workers in the Framework of the Provision of Services [1997] OJ L 18/1; and Directive 2018/957/EU of the European Parliament and of the Council of 28 June 2018 amending Directive 96/71/EC concerning the Posting of Workers in the Framework of the Provision of Services [2018] OJ L 173/16.

55 See Ulla Liukkunen, *Cross-Border Services and Choice of Law: A Comparative Study of the European Approach* (Peter Lang 2007).

56 See Ulla Liukkunen, 'The ILO and Transformation of Labour Law' in Tarja Halonen and Ulla Liukkunen (eds), *International Labour Organization and Global Social Governance* (Springer 2021) 45.

57 For example, the Hague Principles on Choice of Law in International Commercial Contracts, approved on 19 March 2015, do not apply to employment contracts. Similarly, the Hague

to employment contracts and labour relations is decided by states themselves or regional actors such as the EU. As a result, outcomes are diverse. Moreover, no forum is yet available for discussion of these issues with a view to attempting to find a global perspective. The Hague Conference on Private International Law, whose purpose is to work for progressive unification of the rules of private international law, has not addressed these issues either.[58]

In regulatory approaches of private international law, protective mechanisms are used to emphasise different points of departure. In the EU, the Brussels I Regulation (recast)[59] includes specific rules on jurisdiction that protect employees as weaker parties to employment contracts. According to Article 21 of Brussels I, an employer domiciled in an EU Member State may be sued in the courts of its domicile or at the place where or from where employees habitually carry out their work or the last place where they did so. If there is no habitual place of work, the employer can be sued in the place where the business which engaged the employee is or was situated. In addition, the Posted Workers Directive contains a particular jurisdictional rule on postings occurring in the framework of provision of services.[60] As regards choice of law, the special rules on individual employment contracts in Article 8 of the Rome I Regulation[61] lean on similar points of departure to Brussels I, namely the habitual place of work and the place where the business which engaged the employee is situated. Party autonomy in choice of law is permitted. However, a special minimum protection rule is included in Rome I. A choice-of-law clause in an employment contract cannot have the result of depriving employees of the protection afforded by mandatory rules of the law applicable in the absence of choice. When determining the content of employee-protective rules, the question of whether the rules serve to protect the employee should be understood broadly.[62] Article 9 of Rome I contains provisions on the application of overriding mandatory rules.

Further, in countries where regulatory private international law is relatively young, there are specific protective rules of private international law on

---

Convention of 30 June 2005 on Choice of Court Agreements does not apply to employment contracts.

58 See Art 1 of the Statute of the Hague Conference on Private International Law, adopted by the Hague Conference on Private International Law, 7th Session, the Hague, 31 October 1951, entered into force on 15 July 1955.

59 Regulation (EU) No 1215/2012 of the European Parliament and of the Council of 12 December 2012 on Jurisdiction and the Recognition and Enforcement of Judgments in Civil and Commercial Matters [2012] OJ L 351/1.

60 See Art 6 of Directive 96/71/EC of the European Parliament and of the Council of 16 December 1996 concerning the Posting of Workers in the Framework of the Provision of Services [1997] OJ L 18/1.

61 Regulation (EC) No 593/2008 of the European Parliament and of the Council of 17 June 2008 on the Law Applicable to Contractual Obligations (Rome I) [2008] OJ L 177/6.

62 See for example, Mario Giuliano and Paul Lagarde, Report on the Convention on the Law Applicable to Contractual Obligations [1980] OJ C 282/1.

employment contracts. For example, Article 469(1) of the Civil Procedure Code of Vietnam sets out jurisdictional rules for employment contracts in a way which highlights the jurisdiction of the Vietnamese courts. Accordingly, the Vietnamese courts have jurisdiction over disputes arising out of an employment relationship with foreign elements if the defendant is a natural person who resides, works or has lived for a long time in Vietnam; if the defendant has properties in Vietnam; if the relationship was established, changed or terminated in Vietnam, or its objects are acts performed in Vietnam; or if the basis for the establishment, change, implementation or termination of such relationship arises in a foreign country but involves the rights and obligations of Vietnamese agencies, organisations and natural persons, or agencies, organisations and natural persons that are headquartered or reside in Vietnam.[63] As regards choice of law, the protection afforded by the *lex fori* is emphasised. Article 683 of the Civil Code of Vietnam, which includes choice-of-law rules on contractual relationships, states that if the applicable law selected by the parties for their employment contract adversely affects the minimum interests of the employee as prescribed in Vietnamese law, the law of Vietnam will be applied instead of the chosen law.[64] This article aims at safeguarding the minimum protection of employees afforded by Vietnamese labour legislation. Vietnamese regulatory private international law has its origins in legislative development during the 1980s and 1990s and has to be seen in the context of the particular societal system. The experience of applying employee-protective rules has remained limited.

In China,[65] too, regulatory development – which has entailed resolving legal problems relating to the applicable law from the viewpoint of employment relationships, and which entails enactment of the choice-of-law rules applicable to employment contracts – has occurred in a notably short timeframe.[66] Although Chinese legislation on choice of law is by and large based on similar principles that EU regulatory private international law manifests, there are differences in the ways in which it protects employees. Additionally, the particular nature of the legal system, with its interconnections with the political system, influences the role of the rules. According to Article 43 of the Law on Choice of Law for Foreign-related Civil Relationships, the law at the working locality of employees

63 See Art 469(1) of the Civil Procedure Code, National Assembly of the Socialist Republic of Vietnam, issued 25 November 2015, effective 1 July 2016 <https://thuvienphapluat.vn/van-ban/Thu-tuc-To-tung/Bo-luat-to-tung-dan-su-2015-296861.aspx#tab2> accessed 11 March 2021.

64 See Art 683(5) of the Civil Code, National Assembly of the Socialist Republic of Vietnam, issued 24 November 2015, effective 1 January 2017 <https://thuvienphapluat.vn/van-ban/Quyen-dan-su/Bo-luat-dan-su-2015-296215.aspx> accessed 11 March 2021.

65 China and the People's Republic of China (PRC) are used in this chapter interchangeably.

66 See also Ulla Liukkunen, 'Chinese Context and Complexities – Comparative Law and Private International Law facing New Normativities in International Commercial Arbitration' (2020) 1 Ius Comparatum 254, 275–276.

applies to employment contracts with foreign-related elements.[67] If it is difficult to determine the working locality of an employee, the law at the employer's main business place will apply. It is also noteworthy that, according to Article 4 of the same law, it is possible to apply overriding mandatory rules of the PRC.[68] According to Interpretation I of the Supreme People's Court, these rules include, for example, rules relating to protection of the rights and interests of the employee.[69]

6. POSTING OF WORKERS

The phenomenon of posted workers is known globally to create problems of inequality and social dumping that persist in cross-border work which is temporarily carried out in another country.[70] In postings, it is necessary to pay attention not only to the protective rules in the host state's regulation but also to posted workers' rights, which often remain limited. For example, long and complicated subcontracting chains, diverse forms of temporary agency work and other kinds of multi-party work – these, as well as sectoral characteristics of working conditions that shape the legal environment, pose constant challenges. These challenges cause difficulties for the efficient regulation of the phenomenon highlighted by the temporary nature of work in one host state or several host states in succession.

A striking feature of the global phenomenon of posted workers temporarily carrying out their work in another country is that their legal position has remained particularly weak. The dilemma of transnational social dumping relates to the

---

67 See Art 43 of the Law of the People's Republic of China on Choice of Law for Foreign-related Civil Relationships, Standing Committee of the National People's Congress, issued 28 October 2010, effective 1 April 2011 <https://www.pkulaw.com/en_law/7674d9626365d7e3bdfb.html?keyword=Choice%20of%20Law%20for%20Foreign> accessed 11 March 2021.

68 See Art 4 of the Law of the People's Republic of China on Choice of Law for Foreign-related Civil Relationships, Standing Committee of the National People's Congress, issued 28 October 2010, effective 1 April 2011 <https://www.pkulaw.com/en_law/7674d9626365d7e3bdfb.html?keyword=Choice%20of%20Law%20for%20Foreign> accessed 11 March 2021.

69 See Art 10 of the Interpretations of the Supreme People's Court on Several Issues Concerning Application of the Law of the People's Republic of China on Choice of Law for Foreign-related Civil Relationships (I), Supreme People's Court, issued 28 December 2012, effective 7 January 2013 <https://www.pkulaw.com/en_law/98b84ea968652f04bdfb.html?keyword=Choice%20of%20Law%20for%20Foreign> accessed 11 March 2021.

70 See for example, Nathan Lillie and Ian Greer, 'Industrial Relations, Migration, and Neoliberal Politics: The Case of the European Construction Sector' (2007) 35 Politics & Society 551; Lisa Berntsen and Nathan Lillie, 'Breaking the Law? Varieties of Social Dumping in a Pan-European Labour Market' in Magdalena Bernaciak (ed), *Market Expansion and Social Dumping in Europe* (Routledge 2015); and Ines Wagner and Karen Shire, 'Labour Subcontracting in Cross-Border Labour Markets: A Comparison of Rule Evasion in Germany and Japan' in Jens Arnholtz and Nathan Lillie (eds), *Posted Work in the European Union: The Political Economy of Free Movement* (Routledge 2019).

highlighted inefficiency of regulation and different kinds of regulatory lacunae, as well as structural problems of regulatory frameworks. Vulnerability related to the legal status of cross-border workers hampers the realisation of labour rights.[71] Often, clarity is lacking in terms of the jurisdictional and choice-of-law rules to be applied and no attempt might be made at even settling the content of these rules as the period spent in a foreign country remains limited and mobile workers are seldom capable of claiming their rights on foreign soil. In addition, questions of enforcement of judgments and cross-border cooperation between authorities are of particular importance for enhancing access to labour rights.

The posting of workers dilemma has a global dimension – a dimension that is growing in relevance. This is demonstrated, for example, by developments related to the Belt and Road Initiative (BRI), launched by the Chinese government in 2013,[72] which has led to a growing number of cross-border contracts that encompass posting of workers to countries with less developed private international law regimes. These host countries may often also have low labour standards. China has sought to develop regulatory efforts at different regulatory levels to deal with the posting phenomenon, with the aim of improving protection of workers in Chinese overseas enterprises, as well as Chinese workers posted abroad.[73] The BRI involves different kinds of linkages to the decent work objective.[74] The ILO has noticed opportunities embedded in this initiative and elaborated cooperation with China in the form of Memorandums of Understanding concluded

---

71 See Yifeng Chen and Ulla Liukkunen, 'Enclave Governance and Transnational Labor Law – A Case Study of Chinese Workers on Strike in Africa' (2019) 88 Nordic Journal of International Law 558 in more detail.

72 See Ministry of Foreign Affairs of the People's Republic of China, 'President Xi Jinping Delivers Important Speech and Proposes to Build a Silk Road Economic Belt with Central Asian Countries' (7 September 2013) <https://www.fmprc.gov.cn/mfa_eng/topics_665678/xjpfwzysiesgjtfhshzzfh_665686/t1076334.shtml> accessed 11 March 2021. There are currently 143 countries involved in the Belt and Road Initiative. For details, see Office of the Leading Group for the Belt and Road Initiative, 'International Cooperation – Profiles' <https://eng.yidaiyilu.gov.cn/info/iList.jsp?cat_id=10076> accessed 11 March 2021.

73 See for example, Ministry of Commerce, the Ministry of Foreign Affairs, the State-owned Assets Supervision and Administration Commission and All-China Federation of Industry and Commerce of the People's Republic of China, Guidelines for the Management of Employees of Overseas Chinese-funded Enterprises (Institutions), issued and effective 14 March 2011 <https://www.pkulaw.com/en_law/36f09548b40ff0e4bdfb.html?keyword=%E5%A2%83%E5%A4%96%E4%B8%AD%E8%B5%84%E4%BC%81%E4%B8%9A%28%E6%9C%BA%E6%9E%84%29%E5%91%98%E5%B7%A5%E7%AE%A1%E7%90%86%E6%8C%87%E5%BC%95> accessed 11 March 2021; and State Council of the People's Republic of China, Regulation on the Administration of Foreign Labor Cooperation, issued 4 June 2012, effective 1 August 2012 <https://www.pkulaw.com/en_law/6179b62e12581de2bdfb.html?keyword=%E5%AF%B9%E5%A4%96%E5%8A%B3%E5%8A%A1%E5%90%88%E4%BD%9C%E7%AE%A1%E7%90%86%E6%9D%A1%E4%BE%8B> accessed 11 March 2021.

74 See also Donald J Lewis, Xiaohua Yang, Diana Moise and Stephen John Roddy, 'Dynamic Synergies between China's Belt and Road Initiative and the UN's Sustainable Development Goals' (2021) 4 Journal of International Business Policy 58.

with Chinese partners that aim to improve labour and social protection in the context of the BRI.[75]

With the BRI and related efforts to facilitate regional economic cooperation by China, the Chinese regulatory approach to cross-border work has increased in relevance both in Asia and elsewhere.[76] However, simultaneously, BRI-related cross-border projects illustrate the fragile nature of the legal protection of posted workers afforded by regulatory private international law and highlight the adverse consequences of the pluralism of private international law approaches to individual employment contracts. The lack of protection visible in cross-border work related to various BRI investments has heightened the need and demand for regulatory solutions that are more inclusive and effective in terms of mobile labour protection.[77] In addition, BRI-related cross-border work has drawn attention to the regulatory challenges that characterise work carried out by posted workers with very loose connections to the host state's regulatory and societal framework.[78] This development has revealed difficulties in achieving cross-border labour protection when regulatory models of different countries are based on highly diverse points of departure, but it also points to widely known problems related to the posting phenomenon. Characteristically, posted workers are seldom capable of demanding their rights; moreover, structures that would be supportive in terms of meeting their needs are largely lacking.

From the labour rights perspective, regulatory solutions to posting have not provided sufficient protection if we compare the legal status of posted workers to other categories of workers. Posted workers are not adequately entitled to a full set of legal rights in the host country where they work only on a temporary basis.[79] The EU regulatory formula on posted workers is illustrative. In the EU Member States, the most important sources for choice-of-law rules concerning

---

75 See 'ILO Broadens Cooperation with its Chinese Partners under the Belt and Road Initiative' (29 April 2019) <https://www.ilo.org/beijing/information-resources/public-information/press-releases/WCMS_695356/lang--en/index.htm> accessed 11 March 2021.

76 See also Mimi Zou, 'Labour Standards Along "One Belt One Road"' in Lutz-Christian Wolff and Chao Xi (eds), *Legal Dimensions of China's Belt and Road Initiative* (Wolters Kluwer 2016).

77 See Aaron Halegua and Xiaohui Ban, 'Labour Protections for Overseas Chinese Workers: Legal Framework and Judicial Practice' (2020) 8 Chinese Journal of Comparative Law 304; Aaron Halegua, 'Where is the Belt and Road Initiative Taking International Labour Rights? An Examination of Worker Abuse by Chinese Firms in Saipan' in Maria Adele Carrai, Jean-Christophe Defraigne and Jan Wouters (eds), *The Belt and One Road Initiative and Global Governance* (Edward Elgar Publishing 2020); and Ivan Franceschini, 'As Far apart as Earth and Sky: A Survey of Chinese and Cambodian Construction Workers in Sihanoukville' (2020) 54 Critical Asian Studies 512.

78 See also Yifeng Chen and Ulla Liukkunen, 'Enclave Governance and Transnational Labor Law – A Case Study of Chinese Workers on Strike in Africa' (2019) 88 Nordic Journal of International Law 558.

79 ibid 572.

employment contracts of posted workers are the Rome I Regulation and the Posted Workers Directive. Rome I sets out the general conflict rules on contractual obligations and the scope of application of the Regulation is considerably more extensive than that of the Directive.[80] When determining the law applicable to an international employment contract of a posted worker, Rome I and the Directive may both have to be considered. However, the interplay between these two has proven complex.

Basically, the Posted Workers Directive reflects the aim of establishing a balance between two principles: promotion of free movement of services in the EU and the need for minimum protection of posted workers.[81] The Directive aims at clarifying the legal status of both posted workers and undertakings that post workers by determining the sphere of the host state's labour law provisions applicable to posted workers, but without prohibiting the application of more favourable provisions of the *lex causae*. Taking into account the nature of the provisions referred to in the 'hard core' list of the Posted Workers Directive, it is clear that the objective of the Directive is to make those rules of the host country that are considered most important applicable to posted workers. The aim is not to govern all employee-protective provisions of the host country.[82] The regulatory approach of the Directive, which, along with setting certain minimum standards, allows a variety of differences in transposition, has turned out to be complicated.[83] The EU legislature has reformed the posted workers legislation with the aim of ensuring that posted workers are better protected under the host state's law and that enforcement of EU legislation on posting is more efficient, noting the particular problems of cross-border work that make it more difficult for workers to demand their rights.

However, a differentiation remains between workers temporarily carrying out their work in the host state and workers who work there on some other legal basis. The basic dilemma derives from the regulatory approach that differentiates

---

80 See also recital 10 of the Directive 96/71/EC of the European Parliament and of the Council of 16 December 1996 concerning the Posting of Workers in the Framework of the Provision of Services [1997] OJ L 18/1.

81 According to the Explanatory Memorandum, the objectives of the proposal were to remove obstacles and uncertainties likely to hamper free movement of services. This was to be achieved, in particular, by clear identification of the applicable rules of the host state. See Commission of the European Communities, Proposal for a Council Directive concerning the Posting of Workers in the Framework of the Provision of Services COM (91) 230 final – SYN 346 [1991] OJ C 225/6, 2–4 and 13.

82 See ibid 15.

83 See Ulla Liukkunen, 'Collision Between the Economic and the Social – What Has Private International Law Got to Do with It?' in Pia Letto-Vanamo and Jan Smits (eds), *Coherence and Fragmentation in European Private Law* (Sellier European Law Publishers 2012); and Jonas Malmberg and Tore Sigeman, 'Industrial Actions and EU Economic Freedoms: The Autonomous Collective Bargaining Model Curtailed by the European Court of Justice' (2008) 45 Common Market Law Review 1115.

between how posted workers and workers in these other groups are protected by host state law. The Enforcement Directive,[84] which seeks to improve enforcement of the rules on posted workers, as well as the recent revision of the Posted Workers Directive, have opened up prospects for improved protection for posted workers in the EU. However, they do not remove vulnerabilities that are typically present in the posting phenomenon. The regulatory environment lacks foreseeability, as posting typically involves cases where circumstances change and workers are engaged very temporarily, that is, with short postings in different countries. This causes difficulty in determining under which law posted workers are or should be protected. Typically, short postings may follow each other and the law of one host state is thus not applicable to all postings. Moreover, as posting is a global phenomenon, building protection on regional or individual state-level regulatory instruments remains piecemeal, while improving the legal status of posted workers would require global efforts.

The adverse working conditions of posted workers easily open paths to work in the informal economy. Transnational social dumping practices undermine existing regulatory frameworks and make formal work informal.[85] Although work in the informal economy per se encompasses a wide variety of forms of work and circumstances, the relevance of posting as a regulatory challenge in terms of combating informal work cannot be ignored. It is important to note that combating social dumping in its various cross-border forms can contribute to the transition of informal workers to formal work. Promotion of fundamental labour rights is an essential means to deal with work in the informal economy and it also provides a useful point of departure for developing the regulatory frameworks provided by private international law rules and regulatory mechanisms embedded in transnational labour governance. Access to formal economy jobs is enabled by a legal framework which recognises the relevance of fundamental labour rights in a cross-border setting and provides safeguards that ensure respect for and access to these rights in various forms of temporary work abroad.

As ILO Recommendation No 204 points out, the informal economy is a major challenge for the rights of workers, including fundamental labour rights, and for social protection, decent working conditions, inclusive development and the rule of law. The informal economy also has a negative effect on the development of sustainable enterprises, public revenues and governments' scope

84 Directive 2014/67/EU of the European Parliament and of the Council of 15 May 2014 on the Enforcement of Directive 96/71/EC concerning the Posting of Workers in the Framework of the Provision of Services and Amending Regulation (EU) No 1024/2012 on Administrative Cooperation through the Internal Market Information System (the IMI Regulation) [2014] OJ L 159/11.

85 See *Decent Work in Global Supply Chains* (Report IV, International Labour Conference, 105th Session, Geneva, International Labour Organization 2016).

of action.[86] The Recommendation advocates an integrated policy framework which encompasses various kinds of measures. However, this framework should also include measures related to cross-border settings deriving from private international law and transnational labour governance. Among the reasons behind work in the informal economy are adverse structural factors that are not revealed and addressed if the analysis and measures adopted do not govern cross-border regulatory efforts.

7. THE RIGHT TO STRIKE AFTER THE *LAVAL* AND *VIKING* JUDGMENTS

In the EU, fundamental labour rights protections concerning the right to take collective action for the protection of workers have confronted challenges that derive from the strengthened position of fundamental economic freedoms in the Union. In the *Laval*[87] and *Viking*[88] judgments, the Court of Justice of the European Union (CJEU) assigned more weight to the market freedom aspects of EU law than to the labour rights aspects. These rulings reveal a certain mismatch in regional private international law in terms of labour protection as they illustrate a balancing of the 'economic' and the 'social' on the axis between fundamental economic freedoms and fundamental labour rights. As EU internal market law highlights a favourable framework for economic transactions, protection of labour rights confronts obstacles that derive from legal considerations promoting economic integration.[89]

With *Viking* and *Laval*, the CJEU has taken a stance which makes the right to industrial action subordinate to the doctrine of the conditions under which fundamental economic freedoms can be restricted. It is difficult to undertake a prior assessment of the conformity of industrial action involving fundamental economic freedoms with the conditions set by the CJEU concerning permitted restrictions on free movement of services and freedom of establishment. This means a serious de facto restriction of the right to strike. The practice of the ILO supervisory organs has developed a clear stance on the nature of restrictions which can be placed on the right to strike. Limitations on the right to take collective action adopted by the CJEU would not be recognised by ILO

86 See Transition from the Informal to the Formal Economy Recommendation, 2015 (No 204), adopted by the International Labour Conference, 104th Session, Geneva, 12 June 2015.

87 Case C-341/05 *Laval un Partneri Ltd v Svenska Byggnadsarbetareförbundet, Svenska Byggnadsarbetareförbundets avdelning 1, Byggettan and Svenska Elektrikerförbundet* [2007] ECR I-11767.

88 Case C-438/05 *International Transport Workers' Federation and Finnish Seamen's Union v Viking Line ABP and OÜ Viking Line Eesti* [2008] OJ C 51/11.

89 See Simon Deakin, 'Regulatory Competition after Laval' (2008) 10 Cambridge Yearbook of European Legal Studies 581.

case law.[90] Limiting the right to take collective action to grounds based on an assessment of justified restrictions of fundamental economic freedoms of the EU may affect the balance of the labour market parties in a way which in the worst case forces individual employees to compete against each other with the price of their work.[91]

The linkage of internal market law developments to EU legislation on determining jurisdiction and the applicable law concerning cross-border strike disputes is noteworthy. According to Brussels I, the court of the country where industrial action has been taken does not have jurisdiction in disputes involving that action, even though the law of that country would be applicable to the case. The regulatory approach of the Rome II Regulation[92] on non-contractual obligations is based on the general principle of application of the law of the place where industrial action is or has been taken. As party autonomy in determining the applicable law enabled by Article 14 of Rome II may only be used after industrial action has taken place, it can be presumed to play a narrow role in industrial action disputes. On the whole, the regulatory framework is complicated, as the rules on jurisdiction to be found in Brussels I and the rules on determining the applicable law to be found in Rome II as well as Rome I do not form a coherent entity.[93] Because of globalisation, there is an increasing need to evaluate the development of regulatory approaches to cross-border industrial action even more broadly so that the global context of labour rights is acknowledged. Different kinds of cross-border collective action play a role in the cross-border labour settings, with international and domestic trade unions taking action in order to safeguard the labour rights of employees on the move whose working conditions are susceptible to social dumping.

8. TRANSNATIONAL LABOUR LAW DEVELOPMENTS: DECENT WORK IN A NON-STATE CONTEXT

Globalisation has raised several challenges for the system of international labour standards. It also poses a test for regionally and nationally adopted labour

90 See ILO Committee of Experts, *General Report and Observations concerning Particular Countries* (Report III, Part 1A, International Labour Conference, 99th Session, Geneva, International Labour Organization 2009) 209.

91 See also Brian Bercusson, 'The Trade Union Movement and the European Union: Judgment Day' (2007) 13 European Law Journal 279.

92 Regulation (EC) No 864/2007 of the European Parliament and of the Council of 11 July 2007 on the Law Applicable to Non-contractual Obligations (Rome II) [2007] OJ L 199/40.

93 See also Ulla Liukkunen, 'The Right to Strike in the International and European Context – Viking, Laval and Beyond' in Jürgen Basedow, Su Chen, Matteo Fornasier and Ulla Liukkunen (eds), *Employee Participation and Collective Bargaining in Europe and China* (Mohr Siebeck 2016).

law rules when multinational enterprises are operating on a transnational basis in various regions and countries. The regulatory framework governing multinational enterprises is manifold, consisting of multiple overlapping regimes, broader than the law of national states. By means of public guidelines related to international labour standards, states and international organisations seek to advocate a consistent rationale for those normative regimes governing multinationals. Public guidelines often refer to fundamental labour rights. Additionally, decent work has been incorporated into several guidelines targeted at multinationals.[94]

There is a pressing need to strengthen transnational labour governance. This, in turn, draws attention to labour relations and their regulatory framework at the level of multinational enterprises. Beyond the traditional sphere of collective autonomy in labour relations, transnational labour law regimes have enabled the gradual development of what might be called multinational enterprise-level industrial relations. Evolving transnational negotiations between multinationals and employee representatives have brought about transnational company agreements with their own characteristics that do not fit into traditional conceptions of cross-border collective bargaining. Indeed, these have raised complex legal questions. Yet transnational agreements open a horizon on development where labour rights and their collective settings are not tied to territories but they stem from a transnational frame where the regime of multinational companies provides a regulatory point of departure.[95]

Private international law has been blamed for not being well-suited to tackling legal challenges posed by transnationality. However, private international law has acquired new roles in labour governance enabled by developments in transnational labour law, and private international law methodology is needed to shape responses to transnational regime collisions.[96] Transnational

---

94 See for example, The Ten Principles of the UN Global Compact. Principle One: Human Rights <https://www.unglobalcompact.org/what-is-gc/mission/principles/principle-1> accessed 11 March 2021. The UN Global Compact is a voluntary initiative designed to promote innovation in relation to corporate sustainability. It is a principle-based framework for businesses, stating ten principles in the areas of human rights, labour, the environment and anti-corruption. The Ten Principles of the UN Global Compact are derived from the Universal Declaration of Human Rights, the 1998 ILO Declaration on Fundamental Principles and Rights at Work, the Rio Declaration on Environment and Development (adopted by the UN Conference on Environment and Development, Rio de Janeiro, 14 June 1992), and the UN Convention Against Corruption (adopted by the UN General Assembly on 31 October 2003). See also Tripartite Declaration of Principles concerning Multinational Enterprises and Social Policy of the ILO, adopted by the Governing Body, 204th Session, Geneva, November 1977, and amended at its 279th, 295th and 329th Sessions in November 2000, March 2006 and March 2017, para 2.

95 See also Rüdiger Krause, 'The Promotion of Labour Standards through International Framework Agreements' in Henner Gött (ed), *Labour Standards in International Economic Law* (Springer 2018).

96 See also Robert Wai, 'Transnational Liftoff and Juridical Touchdown: The Regulatory Function of Private International Law in an Era of Globalization' (2002) 40 Columbia Journal of Transnational Law 209.

labour law embraces and produces normativities independent from the state-centred context, where private international law of labour relations has traditionally operated. For private international law, this means a call to obtain adaptive capacity in response to collisions caused by transnationality and the normativities involved. In a transnational setting, material justice sought by identifying fundamental labour rights and decent work as an objective cannot be achieved merely through material regulation. Nor does it suffice to maintain the public international law scheme.

Managing changes in working life caused by globalisation poses a central challenge for labour law. Typically, development in the labour market has increased decentralisation and diversification of labour standard-setting – the growth of private regulators being an indication of this. For example, from the employee viewpoint, increasing reorganisation of cross-border business operations occurs in a complex legal framework built on several sources of norms at different levels. In the creation of labour standards, the impact of globalisation is illustrated by the growth and increasing complexity of the interplay between international, regional, national and corporate-level sources of norms.[97]

A scenario of another kind arises from developments of private governance in transnational labour law. Collective contractual arrangements in the form of transnational company agreements between multinational enterprises and employee representatives also involve Global or European Works Councils. Thus, a new breed of actors has been thrust into the sphere of what was previously the domain of traditional regulatory actors in labour law. Despite varied experiences, transnational agreements add new regulatory frameworks and mechanisms to collective labour law.[98] They demonstrate transnational normativities that develop collective rule-making capacities which overcome jurisdictional boundaries.

Transnational company agreements encompass a variety of forms of agreement concluded between multinational enterprises on the one side, and on the other side international or national trade union federations or some other party representing employees, typically a Global or European Works Council. These agreements consist of European-level transnational agreements and international framework agreements with global reach, each having their particular characteristics in terms of objectives and content. European-level agreements typically deal with the social effects of restructuring. International framework agreements are agreements that mostly seek to promote compliance with fundamental labour rights and the CSR strategy of the company in question.

97 See Katherine Van Wezel Stone, 'Labour and the Global Economy: Four Approaches to Transnational Labour Regulation' (1995) 16 Michigan Journal of International Law 987.

98 See Ulla Liukkunen, 'The Role of Collective Bargaining in Labour Law Regimes: A Global Approach' in Ulla Liukkunen (ed), *Collective Bargaining in Labour Law Regimes: A Global Perspective* (Ius Comparatum – Global Studies in Comparative Law, vol 32, Springer 2019).

The objective is often to commit to fundamental labour rights, both across the company, and increasingly also so that supply chains are governed. These agreements may create obligations which a multinational enterprise owes to its subcontractors or other actors within the global supply chain.[99] The labour protection sought by these kinds of contractual arrangements often poses complex legal questions.[100] Several legal challenges are involved in the question of the legally binding nature of transnational company agreements and their effects; to resolve them, private international law rules are needed.

Transnational labour governance would require more precise attention to be paid to the objective of decent work. Notably, fundamental labour rights have become a widely debated issue in the context of corporate codes of conduct. Although promoting labour rights should not be equated with protecting them, the interaction between CSR strategies and the transnational contractual commitments of multinationals is relevant. The impact of private international law should also be viewed from the perspective of this interplay and the regulatory context offered by transnational settings. Adopting a labour rights-based approach to decent work in private international law provides a useful point of departure for evaluating the transnational contractual arrangements of multinationals.

9. AN EXCURSION: MULTINATIONAL ENTERPRISES AND FUNDAMENTAL LABOUR RIGHTS

9.1. INTRODUCTION

As transnational company agreements have continued to evolve and spread their linkages to CSR, strategies of multinational enterprises have prompted questions that relate to the interaction between contractual arrangements and commitments by multinationals to labour rights in general.[101] It is not a matter for indifference how and to what extent multinationals commit to these rights, as, in addition to the economic power they exercise, their operations govern countries and regions at very different stages of development in terms of labour protection.

---

99 See also International Labour Organization, Organisation for Economic Co-operation and Development, International Organization for Migration and United Nations Children's Emergency Fund, *Ending Child Labour, Forced Labour and Human Trafficking in Global Supply Chains* (2019).

100 See also Lance Compa, 'Corporate Social Responsibility and Workers' Rights' (2008) 30 Comparative Labor Law & Policy Journal 1.

101 See Ulla Liukkunen, 'Transnational Labour Law and Fundamental Labour Rights: Making Chinese Workers Matter?' in Ulla Liukkunen and Yifeng Chen (eds), *China and ILO Fundamental Principles and Rights at Work* (Bulletin of Comparative Labour Relations No 86, Kluwer Law International 2014).

Some observations regarding the developments in terms of promoting decent work can be made by looking at publicly available CSR documentation and existing transnational company agreements of the 30 biggest multinational enterprises globally.[102] With these observations, a more concrete, albeit limited, look can be taken at the commitment to fundamental labour rights and decent work. The extent to which CSR documentation and transnational company agreements govern fundamental labour rights and address decent work as an objective varies. From the viewpoint of private international law, the transnational context where CSR strategies and contractual commitments interact affects the way cross-border collisions are dealt with. The content of transnational company agreements of multinationals is of particular interest as cross-border contractual arrangements can promote decent work through contractual obligations. The majority of the 30 biggest multinationals under scrutiny are located in the US (15) and the PRC (seven). The rest are located in France, Germany, Hong Kong,[103] Japan, the Netherlands, Saudi Arabia and South Korea.

The regulatory framework of fundamental labour rights within the regulatory sphere of multinational enterprises highlights the complexity of promoting decent work in global production systems.[104] CSR has been defined in multiple ways. For example, the ILO considers it to be how enterprises view the impact of their operations on society and affirm their principles and values in their own internal methods and processes as well as in interaction with other actors. It is a voluntary, enterprise-driven initiative and refers to activities considered to exceed compliance with the law.[105] On the one hand, it is important to note that the conceptualisation of CSR and transnational company agreements is rooted in a Western framework where it has also been defined in a vast number of different ways.[106] On the other hand, CSR is to be understood as having diverse

---

102 The biggest companies under survey are the top 30 according to Forbes Global 2000 (2020). Information on multinational corporations was gathered from Andrea Murphy, Hank Tucker, Marley Coyne and Halah Touryalai, 'GLOBAL 2000 – The World's Largest Public Companies' <https://www.forbes.com/global2000/#5367cee6335d> accessed 11 March 2021. Information about CSR documentation and transnational agreements were gathered from the official websites of the corporations as available there. The present author is grateful to Le Bao Ngoc Pham for her assistance with gathering the information.

103 The Hong Kong Special Administrative Region of the People's Republic of China.

104 See also Stephanie Barrientos, *Global Production Systems and Decent Work,* Working Paper No 77 (International Labour Organization 2007).

105 *InFocus Initiative on Corporate Social Responsibility (CSR): (A) Strategic Orientations* (Governing Body, 295th Session, Geneva, International Labour Organization 2006) para 1.

106 See for example, Ruben Zandvliet and Paul van der Heijden, 'The Rapprochement of ILO Standards and CSR Mechanisms: Towards a Positive Understanding of the "Privatization" of International Labour Standards' in Axel Marx, Jan Wouters, Glenn Rayp and Laura Beke (eds), *Global Governance of Labour Rights. Assessing the Effectiveness of Transnational Public and Private Policy Initiatives* (Edward Elgar Publishing 2015).

meanings in the context of different jurisdictions. For example, in the PRC, the concept has its own characteristics but is not clear and is still evolving.[107]

9.2. PERSPECTIVES ON CSR DOCUMENTATION AND TRANSNATIONAL COMPANY AGREEMENTS

All 30 of the biggest multinationals have adopted CSR-related documentation which deals with labour rights in diverse forms. As regards fundamental labour rights, most of the multinationals have in some way included non-discrimination in respect of employment and occupation, prohibition of child labour and prohibition of forced labour in their CSR documents. Nearly half of them also referred to freedom of association, although the right to collective bargaining was less governed. While some of the references to fundamental labour rights were loosely formulated, others were based on explicit references to the 1998 ILO Declaration on Fundamental Labour Rights, as well as ILO fundamental conventions and other international human rights documents. Some CSR documents referred to public codes of conduct, such as the principles of the UN Global Compact and the OECD Guidelines for Multinational Enterprises. However, there was notable ambiguity in some CSR documents on the commitment to promote collective labour rights that did not make full or clear reference to freedom of association and the right to collective bargaining. The majority of multinationals under scrutiny have adopted supplier codes of conduct, which lay down commitments to promote some core labour standards.

On the basis of the information available on the official websites of multinationals, only three of the 30 biggest multinationals have concluded transnational company agreements. Parties to these agreements from the workers' side include Global and European Works Councils, European Trade Union Organisations, and Global Union Federations.

Allianz SE has three transnational agreements covering the European region. One of these, the Agreement concerning the Participation of Employees in Allianz SE, states that the Allianz Group stands by the goal of observing and implementing the principles of the UN Global Compact and the OECD Guidelines for Multinational Enterprises, as well as ILO fundamental rights and principles at work. The agreement also covers the information, consultation

107 See Ulla Liukkunen, 'Transnational Labour Law and Fundamental Labour Rights: Making Chinese Workers Matter?' in Ulla Liukkunen and Yifeng Chen (eds), *China and ILO Fundamental Principles and Rights at Work* (Bulletin of Comparative Labour Relations No 86, Kluwer Law International 2014); and Guangjian Tu and Si Chen, 'China' in Catherine Kessedjian and Humberto Cantú Rivera (eds), *Private International Law Aspects of Corporate Social Responsibility* (Ius Comparatum – Global Studies in Comparative Law, vol 42, Springer 2020).

and co-determination rights of Allianz SE employees, as well as a basis for cooperation between the committees of employees and their unions and the managements of the Allianz Group that are of importance in the European context. It also deals with other labour issues, namely lifelong learning and work and health protection.[108]

The Corporate Social Responsibility – Total Global Agreement governs all entities of Total in more than 130 countries. As stated in this international framework agreement, Total is committed to applying the principles enshrined in the eight ILO fundamental conventions. The agreement also emphasises promotion of human rights in the workplace and diversity, with specific commitments concerning gender equality, involvement of employees and their representatives in conducting and developing social dialogue, and workplace health and safety. According to the agreement, these are priorities for everyone in the extended corporate community, and in selecting service providers and suppliers. The agreement also governs insurance coverage as well as measures to anticipate and support changes within the Group's organisation and CSR, as Total commits to develop its operations in harmony with surrounding communities.[109]

The third company which has concluded transnational agreements is Volkswagen. One of its global agreements, the Declaration by the Volkswagen Group on Social Rights, Industrial Relations and Business and Human Rights, is an international framework agreement with global reach to all parts of the company. Through the agreement, Volkswagen reaffirms its support for the eight ILO fundamental conventions and the Tripartite Declaration of Principles concerning Multinational Enterprises and Social Policy of the ILO, as well as other international human rights documents and public codes of conduct. The agreement deals with freedom of association and collective bargaining, prohibition of discrimination and harassment, and prohibition of child labour and forced labour. In addition, it governs compensation and benefits, working hours, occupational health and fire safety at the workplace. Other issues, such as protection of personal data and confidential information, freedom of conscience, expression and religion, and bodily integrity, are also covered.[110]

---

108 Other European-level transnational agreements are the Agreement on Guidelines concerning Lifelong Learning and the Agreement on Guidelines concerning Work Related Stress.

109 Total has three other transnational agreements maintained at European level, namely the Social Platform Total Group – European Agreement; the European Agreement on Equal Opportunity – Total Group; and the European Agreement – Assistance in Creation, Purchase or Development of Small and Medium Sized Businesses.

110 Volkswagen has three other global agreements, namely the Charter on Temporary Work for the Volkswagen Group; the Charter on Labour Relations within the Volkswagen Group; and the Charter on Vocational Education and Training within the Volkswagen Group.

9.3. PERSPECTIVES ON TRANSNATIONAL CONTRACTUAL COMMITMENTS

Fundamental labour rights play an important role in counterbalancing efforts that relate to asymmetries in transnational industrial relations.[111] This emphasises their role in transnational labour governance. However, critical attention needs to be paid to how fundamental labour rights are defined in CSR documents of multinationals and how de facto commitments to respect them are made. Diverse ways of presenting labour rights and commitment thereto are typical of multinationals' CSR documents as well as of their transnational company agreements. However, transnational agreements can concretise the commitment to fundamental labour rights beyond what has been expressed in unilateral CSR documents and develop social dialogue.

On the other hand, in general, European agreements refer to labour issues that are relevant in a European context and their contents can be considered as essential in achieving decent work from a regional perspective. Importantly, a perspective on decent work offered by transnational company agreements broadens the view of these contractual arrangements in navigating global and regional labour governance. While decent work for all as an objective requires a perspective which crosses borders, it simultaneously requires region-specific and country-specific, as well as sector-specific, approaches in order to combat particular obstacles to decency of work. For regulatory private international law, this means that the question of the inclusivity of the protection afforded needs to be seen from a broad enough perspective. A nuanced perspective on decency is also required from the labour rights-based approach to private international law advocated in this chapter.

Where transnational company agreements exist, there are also differences in terms of their impact and efficiency depending, for example, on whether the state in question, in which a multinational has personnel, is in the role of the company's host state or home state. It should also be noted that different kinds of legal, structural or institutional constraints can occur at the level of domestic collective bargaining regimes. These constraints can hinder or complicate entering into transnational contractual arrangements.[112] This question should be given more attention in order to unlock the potential of transnational agreements in advancing decent work. As regards implementing and enforcing

---

111 See Marie-Ange Moreau, 'The Reconceptualization of the Employment Relationship and Labour Rights through Transnationality' (2013) 34 Comparative Labor Law & Policy Journal 697.

112 To illustrate, see Takashi Araki, 'Japan' in Ulla Liukkunen (ed), *Collective Bargaining in Labour Law Regimes: A Global Perspective* (Ius Comparatum – Global Studies in Comparative Law, vol 32, Springer 2019); and Campos Medina Maia, 'Brazil' in Ulla Liukkunen (ed), *Collective Bargaining in Labour Law Regimes: A Global Perspective* (Ius Comparatum – Global Studies in Comparative Law, vol 32, Springer 2019).

transnational company agreements, even where a commitment to core labour standards has been clearly formulated, problems of efficiency are well known.[113] Some transnational agreements provide specific procedures at the company level to ensure efficient implementation so that the employee side is a party to these procedures.[114]

In terms of the efficiency of transnational company agreements, it would be of great importance for the applicable private international law rules to be foreseeable and the regulatory approach to be consistent with these agreements' particular nature. When a labour rights-based approach to decent work in private international law is advocated, transnational company agreements and their personal sphere should be paid particular heed. The interaction between multinationals' CSR strategies of and transnational company agreements may either weaken or strengthen these agreements. The context where private international law operates in a transnational setting should thus be viewed from the perspective of multiple mutually interacting regulatory regimes and mechanisms, noting that collisions between these influence transnational labour governance.

10. CONCLUSIONS

Significant challenges from a cross-border perspective complicate progress in the social dimension of Agenda 2030 and the goal of decent work set out in SDG 8. From a private international law point of view, the existing legal framework for cross-border work based on diverse regulatory approaches can be considered incapable of providing adequate labour protection on a global scale. Developing more uniform and inclusive regulatory approaches would require efforts at the international level. There is a need to search for more inclusive regulatory models to develop protection so that it encompasses different forms and categorisations of cross-border work and labour relations. International level solutions that could broaden the applicability of protective labour standards in a cross-border setting could be advanced by the ILO.[115] When developing a stronger role for those standards, fundamental labour rights provide a point of departure highlighted by the decent work objective.

---

[113] See also Ulla Liukkunen, 'Transnational Labour Law and Fundamental Labour Rights: Making Chinese Workers Matter?' in Ulla Liukkunen and Yifeng Chen (eds), *China and ILO Fundamental Principles and Rights at Work* (Bulletin of Comparative Labour Relations No 86, Kluwer Law International 2014).

[114] For example, the international framework agreement of the Volkswagen Group sets out a reporting obligation of the company management to the Global Works Council and its Steering Committee.

[115] See also *Work for a Brighter Future: Report of the Global Commission on the Future of Work* (International Labour Conference, 108th Session, Geneva, International Labour Organization 2019).

Transnational company agreements concluded by multinationals and trade unions, as well as Global or European Works Councils, demonstrate developments that can advance fundamental labour rights and decent work.[116] However, greater effort is needed to enhance more efficient labour rights protection. The complex context of globalisation, with constant changes in global production systems and corporate strategies, requires heed to be paid to transnational industrial relations, company behaviour and labour rights realisation as a whole.[117] Regulatory regimes of multinationals have taken shape in a way which enables development of cross-border company-level industrial relations, at the same time creating new opportunities in terms of pursuit of fundamental labour rights through contractual arrangements in a transnational setting.

While some transnational company agreements raise prospects for a global horizon of more inclusive modes of private governance related to decent work, nevertheless, there is a need for further efforts to incorporate core labour standards in private governance. This would involve strengthening the role and coverage of those standards in transnational company agreements. Private international law perspectives should be strongly integrated in this effort. Transnational agreements would benefit from foreseeability of applicable private international law rules and from a regulatory approach that is consistent with the nature of these agreements in advancing labour rights and social protection. Importantly, evidence shows that transnational labour governance involves mechanisms that are capable of promoting more inclusive labour protection and higher labour standards, although concretisation of the rights-based approach needs further affirmation.[118] The labour rights-based approach to private international law proposed in this chapter should be developed so that particular characteristics of transnational company agreements are heeded.

There is also a need to view transnational regulatory developments from a broader perspective so that the decent work objective and the related need to strengthen fundamental labour rights are taken as a point of departure. The ILO Decent Work Agenda lacks a transnational dimension, which it should have.[119]

---

116 See also Lance Compa, 'Corporate Social Responsibility and Workers' Rights' (2019) 5 Law Journal of Social and Labor Relations 52.

117 See Ulla Liukkunen, 'Transnational Labour Law and Fundamental Labour Rights: Making Chinese Workers Matter?' in Ulla Liukkunen and Yifeng Chen (eds), *China and ILO Fundamental Principles and Rights at Work* (Bulletin of Comparative Labour Relations No 86, Kluwer Law International 2014).

118 See Ulla Liukkunen, 'The Role of Collective Bargaining in Labour Law Regimes: A Global Approach' in Ulla Liukkunen (ed), *Collective Bargaining in Labour Law Regimes: A Global Perspective* (Ius Comparatum – Global Studies in Comparative Law, vol 32, Springer 2019). See also Konstantinos Papadakis, 'Introduction and Overview' in Konstantinos Papadakis (ed), *Shaping Global Industrial Relations. The Impact of International Framework Agreements* (International Labour Organization and Palgrave Macmillan 2011).

119 See Ulla Liukkunen, 'The ILO and Transformation of Labour Law' in Tarja Halonen and Ulla Liukkunen (eds), *International Labour Organization and Global Social Governance* (Springer 2021) 44–45.

Although the organisation has paid growing attention to various forms of transnational rule-making and legal policies that in diverse ways guide private actors that attend to transnational regulatory efforts, the ILO has not comprehensively addressed the transnational dimension of decent work and social justice and related regulatory challenges. Dealing strategically with transnational labour governance would strengthen the perspective offered by the ILO on core labour standards in a cross-border setting.

This chapter has advocated a labour rights-based approach to decent work in developing regulatory private international law in order to advance adequate protection for workers and decent work for all. Attention has been paid to the inability of existing regulatory approaches to provide sufficient protection and combat different forms of transnational social dumping. The weak legal position of posted workers has become a persistent problem of private international law and it has also opened a gateway to the informal economy. It has proved troublesome to eliminate abusive practices in cross-border work where the regulatory framework remains fragmented, biased and underdeveloped. Although states' private international law rules govern individual employment contracts, the protection offered by those rules varies and it does not reach posted workers in such a way as would meet the needs of protection. Nor does the protection afforded by private international law rules adequately extend to forms of cross-border work that are not based on employment contracts. The line between the employee and the self-employed is growing more ambiguous. Rather than only pointing out individual obstacles, it is important to address the structural causes of the lack of protection and the problems hindering the objective of decent work.

Transnational social dumping involves complex legal problems of implementation and enforceability that point to the need to further develop enforcement mechanisms. In addition to jurisdiction and choice of law, questions of enforcement of judgments and cross-border cooperation between authorities are of particular importance for enhancing access to labour rights in mobile work, where workers are known to have particular difficulties in demanding their rights through the courts. While in the EU some improvement has been achieved with recent reforms to the posted workers legislation, more needs to be done. A global perspective on posting as a regulatory dilemma is needed.

Regulatory frameworks, and the pluralism of their approaches, need critical evaluation, which should reach the level of problems recognised in legal practice. Several challenges for the inclusivity of protection derive from the divergence of countries' private international law models when it comes to the protection of workers. The level of development of countries' labour law models and their larger societal framework also affect how their private international law rules can protect workers. A more comprehensive approach would be needed to labour rights, both individual and collective, as well as to situations where workers' cross-border protection should be guaranteed. The idea of protection of the weaker party should be expanded so that protective frames of regulatory private international law govern different categories of workers. This also means taking into account the opportunities that the heightened role of mandatory rules of substantive law in choice of law entails.

In search of more inclusive labour protection in a cross-border setting, perspectives on the social dimension of Agenda 2030 and the objective of decent work amalgamate public and private governance. Illustrative of this is the impact of fundamental labour rights on choice of law enabled by overriding mandatory rules. This encapsulates materialisation of regulatory private international law as an increasingly important development in terms of improving weaker party protection. The growing relevance of mandatory rules in choice of law is characteristic of regulatory private international law. Overriding mandatory rules have the potential to assume a larger role in weaker party protection so that diverse forms of work can be governed. However, further concretisation is needed of the substantive law rules that can be considered overriding mandatory by nature.[120]

A serious problem in relation to ensuring respect for fundamental labour rights in choice of law is the influence of some countries' non-ratification of ILO fundamental conventions. However, a ratification-centred perspective is not alone enough for the promotion of these rights.[121] In order to govern diverse cross-border settings, means of private international law are needed to foster respect for fundamental labour rights that highlight the human rights dimension of the decent work objective. Moreover, developments in transnational labour governance and private ordering at the level of multinationals should be fully taken into account. This requires a broader perspective on private international law in regulating collective labour relations. Fundamental labour rights concerns in the context of cross-border collective bargaining also need attention.

More uniform regulatory private international law would better protect labour rights in a globalised world.[122] A labour rights-based approach to decent

---

120 See also Yifeng Chen and Ulla Liukkunen, 'Enclave Governance and Transnational Labor Law – A Case Study of Chinese Workers on Strike in Africa' (2019) 88 Nordic Journal of International Law 558.

121 See Ulla Liukkunen and Yifeng Chen, 'Developing Fundamental Labour Rights in China: A New Approach to Implementation' in Ulla Liukkunen and Yifeng Chen (eds), *Fundamental Labour Rights in China – Legal Implementation and Cultural Logic* (Springer 2016). See also Bernd Waas, 'How to Improve Monitoring and Enforcement of International Labour Standards?' in Tarja Halonen and Ulla Liukkunen (eds), *International Labour Organization and Global Social Governance* (Springer 2021).

122 In 1981, the Japanese government proposed to the Hague Conference on Private International Law that it should study the feasibility and theoretical questions of the law applicable to employment contracts. See *Actes et Documents* (Hague Conference, XIVth Session, 1980) I-156. See also Hans van Loon, *The Global Horizon of Private International Law, Inaugural Lecture, Private International Law Session, 2015* (Hague Academy of International Law 2016) para 58, where the question of drafting specific rules for party autonomy on weaker party contracts, consumer transactions and employment contracts is taken up.

work in private international law has been highlighted in this chapter as a route to improving promotion of the decent work objective set out by SDG 8. The labour rights perspective connects regulatory private international law and transnational labour governance. Enabling application of overriding mandatory rules in choice of law could promote fundamental labour rights protection in concrete cases so that, in identifying such mandatory rules, guidance is sought from internationally recognised labour standards, with fundamental labour rights at their core. Additionally, the classic public policy principle may come to play a role in private international law decision-making. At the same time, basic elements of private international law decision-making have to be seen in the context of particular vulnerabilities often related to cross-border work. This, in turn, highlights the need to pay heed to implementing and enforcing rules so that the classic problems of applying private international law rules, which are disruptive of the goal of cross-border labour protection, would be better tackled.

On the basis of the above analysis, it can be proposed that the Hague Conference on Private International Law could take the initiative to draft uniform private international law rules on employment contracts and labour relations. With the suggested labour rights-based approach to decent work in private international law as a point of departure, attention would need to be paid to fundamental labour rights and the system of international labour standards as a whole. Therefore, it can be proposed that the ILO, as the principal international institution which formulates and develops international labour standards, could be invited to cooperate with the Hague Conference in the regulatory effort. This would also open up an opportunity to develop a transnational dimension for the ILO Decent Work Agenda.

SDG 9: INDUSTRY, INNOVATION AND INFRASTRUCTURE

Vivienne BATH

Goal 9: Build resilient infrastructure, promote inclusive and sustainable industrialization and foster innovation

9.1 Develop quality, reliable, sustainable and resilient infrastructure, including regional and transborder infrastructure, to support economic development and human well-being, with a focus on affordable and equitable access for all

9.2 Promote inclusive and sustainable industrialization and, by 2030, significantly raise industry's share of employment and gross domestic product, in line with national circumstances, and double its share in least developed countries

9.3 Increase the access of small-scale industrial and other enterprises, in particular in developing countries, to financial services, including affordable credit, and their integration into value chains and markets

9.4 By 2030, upgrade infrastructure and retrofit industries to make them sustainable, with increased resource-use efficiency and greater adoption of clean and environmentally sound technologies and industrial processes, with all countries taking action in accordance with their respective capabilities

9.5 Enhance scientific research, upgrade the technological capabilities of industrial sectors in all countries, in particular developing countries, including, by 2030, encouraging innovation and substantially increasing the number of research and development workers per 1 million people and public and private research and development spending

9.a Facilitate sustainable and resilient infrastructure development in developing countries through enhanced financial, technological and technical support to African countries, least developed countries, landlocked developing countries and small island developing States

9.b Support domestic technology development, research and innovation in developing countries, including by ensuring a conducive policy environment for, inter alia, industrial diversification and value addition to commodities

9.c Significantly increase access to information and communications technology and strive to provide universal and affordable access to the Internet in least developed countries by 2020

1. INTRODUCTION

Sustainable Development Goal 9 (SDG 9) is far-reaching and, like all the SDGs, ambitious. It covers a broad range of important areas for sustainable development, with a focus on developing and less-developed countries, including infrastructure, inclusive and sustainable industrialisation, assistance to smaller enterprises and improvements in scientific research, technical capacity, research and innovation, particularly in developing countries. This chapter looks especially at infrastructure, an important focus of SDG 9, which provides for the development of infrastructure (Target 9.1), the upgrading of infrastructure and refitting of industries to make them sustainable (Target 9.4), and the facilitation of sustainable and resilient infrastructure in developing countries through enhanced financial, technological and technical support (Target 9.a).

SDG 9 is firmly located within the 2030 Agenda for Sustainable Development. Achieving the objective of providing necessary infrastructure, increased industrialisation and innovation is closely related to – and indeed a prerequisite to the accomplishment of – other SDG goals, such as the provision of water and electricity (SDGs 6 and 7) and the reduction of poverty (SDG 2).[1] The construction and implementation of infrastructure projects, the focus of

[1] Xubei Luo and Xuejiao Xu, 'Infrastructure, Value Chains, and Economic Upgrades' (2018) 2(2) Journal of Infrastructure, Policy and Development <https://systems.enpress-publisher.com/index.php/jipd/article/viewFile/691/448> accessed 7 May 2021.

this chapter, that advance these broader goals also implicates other SDGs, such as the need to ensure that infrastructure takes into account equality dimensions in planning and execution (SDG 5), the promotion of access to justice for all and accountable and inclusive institutions (SDG 16) and avoiding degradation of the environment (SDGs 6 and 13). The emphasis on growth and expansion implicit in SDG 9 thus clearly presents the potential tension between rapid and extensive construction and industrialisation and sustainable development.

The basic criteria for infrastructure and its role in sustainable development are laid out in Target 9.1: 'Develop quality, reliable, sustainable and resilient infrastructure, including regional and transborder infrastructure, to support economic development and human well-being, with a focus on affordable and equitable access for all.' The scope of infrastructure is thus very broad, and includes not just infrastructure necessary for transport, telecommunications, energy, water waste management and electricity, but also social infrastructure.[2] The construction and retrofitting of infrastructure – for example, 'hard' infrastructure, such as roads, railways, energy and telecommunications – has a major long-term economic and social impact. SDG 9 requires that infrastructure be both high quality and reliable, that is, fit for purpose now and in the future. It must similarly be sustainable and resilient and support economic development as well as human well-being and accessibility. This is supported by the indicators for Target 9.1, which look at both accessibility and usage in the form of passenger and freight volumes.[3]

Implementation of SDG 9 involves the financing, construction and operation of infrastructure projects and extends to consideration of the interests of numerous stakeholders. These include the host state and local governments; project financiers, lenders, investors and parties involved in construction; and occupiers of land, workers (local and foreign), displaced persons, businesses and individuals benefiting from – and disrupted by – additional connectivity and other factors such as the environmental and social impact of the project. A related factor is the financial impact on the host state and its citizens of infrastructure construction and implementation, and its potential impact on the ability of the government to provide other services to its population. Major infrastructure projects may also present significant sustainability concerns in terms of potential degradation of the environment, the need to preserve critical habitats and natural resources, relocation of residents and impacts on local

2 Scott Thacker, Daniel Adshead, Marianne Fay et al, 'Infrastructure for sustainable development' (2019) 2 Nature Sustainability 324.

3 Global indicator framework for the Sustainable Development Goals and targets of the 2030 Agenda for Sustainable Development, Resolution adopted by the General Assembly on Work of the Statistical Commission pertaining to the 2030 Agenda for Sustainable Development, UN Doc A/RES/71/313, Annex A, 21.

stakeholders, including social, health and safety impacts, as well as employment. Thus, in considering sustainability and resilience in relation to infrastructure and SDG 9, it is necessary to consider both the sustainability of the entire infrastructure project and its contribution to sustainable infrastructure and thus the development of the host state. This includes consideration of the project's short- and long-term impact on the local stakeholders it is intended to benefit, a close examination of the basic contracts and legal frameworks which make infrastructure possible, and an assessment of the potential impact of disputes on the project and the host state.[4]

Both the construction and the updating and retrofitting of major infrastructure are expensive, and international financing and investment are often required. The intellectual property and technology[5] and the skills, labour, materials and equipment required for the efficient and prompt construction and operation of most forms of infrastructure are often beyond the capability or means of developing countries and must be imported. Private international law plays an important role in infrastructure due to the international nature of many infrastructure transactions, which bring with them the involvement of multiple legal systems, cross-border dispute resolution and international enforcement. For an infrastructure project to be sustainable, principles of sustainability and sustainable development should also be incorporated and implemented and private international law potentially has a role to play in this regard as well.

This chapter considers the structuring of infrastructure projects; the role that private international law plays in the implementation of infrastructure and infrastructure projects as a conduit of practices and values; its role in dispute resolution, both contractual and as a result of treaty obligations; and state liability and enforcement. It concludes by examining the ways in which regulatory private international law rules could play a positive role in the implementation of sustainable infrastructure.

2. MAJOR INFRASTRUCTURE PROJECTS

There are a number of different parties and systems of law potentially involved in a major infrastructure project. The variety of parties and their differing

---

4 ibid. Martin Dietrich Brauch, 'Contracts for Sustainable Infrastructure: Ensuring the economic, social and environmental co-benefits of infrastructure investment projects', IISD Report (December 2017) <https://www.iisd.org/sites/default/files/publications/contracts-sustainable-infrastructure.pdf> accessed 15 April 2021; Shawn Shieh, Lowell Chow, Zhong Huang and Jinfei Yue, 'Understanding and mitigating social risks to sustainable development in China's BRI', ODI Report (April 2021) <https://cdn.odi.org/media/documents/ODI_social_risks_BRI_Nepal_and_Zambia_final0104.pdf> accessed 7 May 2021.

5 Janice Denoncourt, 'Companies and UN 2030 Sustainable Development Goal 9 Industry, Innovation and Infrastructure' (2020) 20(1) Journal of Corporate Law Studies 199.

financial, political, legal and regulatory, and project-related interests and risks[6] all contribute to the complexity of the transactions and the related private international law issues.

The host state plays an important role in an infrastructure transaction, whether or not it is an actual party to the financing and construction contracts. First, it creates and maintains the legislative and regulatory environment which will govern the construction and operation of the infrastructure. Host state law should therefore include principles and rules designed to promote and ensure the sustainability of both the construction and the implementation and ongoing operation of infrastructure projects through, for example, environmental legislation and rules relating to land and water use. The host state, directly or indirectly, will be involved in the requisition of land and the provision of specific concessions and benefits to the project. It may, directly or through an agency, provide support for the financing for a project, as a borrower from an international agency, a lender, a guarantor, an issuer of state-backed bonds, an equity investor or one or more of these.[7] It may also offer support to investors in the project through its network of bilateral (and plurilateral) investment agreements and free trade agreements (IIAs), which are designed to promote investment in return for the promise of legal protection for investors.[8] The host state is also responsible for the protection of the interests of domestic stakeholders who may be affected by, or benefit from, the project, through, for example, legislation to protect employees and small business and provisions for proper payment on requisition of land.

Secondly, the project must be constructed – often by an international specialist construction company, which will be supported by multiple sub-contractors, both foreign and domestic. Equipment must be purchased, specialist services provided, construction workers employed, land requisitioned, operating permits obtained, and environmental rules complied with. Thirdly, the project must be commissioned and implemented on an ongoing basis. A project company will often be established to operate, or possibly own, the infrastructure in accordance with the regulatory regime of the host state.[9] This involves multiple connected

---

6 See e.g. Dentons.com, 'A Guide to Project Finance' (2013) 53, Fig 14 <https://www.dentons.com/~/media/6a199894417f4877adea73a76caac1a5.ashx> accessed 15 April 2021.

7 For a discussion of the disparate sources of infrastructure financing, see OECD, 'Increasing complexity in the financing for sustainable development system – instruments, income and interlinkages' in *Global Outlook on Financing for Sustainable Development 2019: Time to Face the Challenge* (OECD Publishing 2019).

8 UNCTAD, Investment Policy Hub, International Investment Agreements Navigator <https://investmentpolicy.unctad.org/international-investment-agreements> accessed 7 May 2021, states that there are 3,269 IIAs and treaties with investment provisions, of which 2,622 are in force, and a total of 1,104 reported investment dispute settlement cases: <https://investmentpolicy.unctad.org/investment-dispute-settlement> accessed 7 May 2021.

9 There are many different options in relation to a project company. See, for example, UNCITRAL, Legislative Guide on Public–Private Partnerships, United Nations, Vienna, 2020, 'I. General legal and institutional framework', 25 (UNCITRAL PPP Guide).

contracts, many of them transnational, thus raising obvious private international law issues.

Finally, due to the high cost of infrastructure, finance plays a major role in shaping an infrastructure transaction and the related contractual arrangements.[10] Finance may be provided in a range of different ways, including loans and guarantees from international organisations, multilateral investment banks, state-sponsored credit agencies and private lenders, or guarantees, direct funding and bond issues raised by the host government. It can take the form of direct foreign investment (equity investment) by private parties into a project company, joint venture or other entity, with the infrastructure being funded through limited or non-recourse project finance. It can also take the form of investment through a public–private partnership (PPP), in which both private investors and governments participate, a form of finance to which considerable attention has been given by international agencies.[11] Project and political risk insurance will also need to be obtained.

The overall transaction for the construction of infrastructure requires the participation of all the principal parties set out above and hence a complex structure of contracts and agreements between the numerous parties involved in arranging and effecting the transaction. Domestic stakeholders are affected in their roles as employees, landholders, small businesses, suppliers, consumers and beneficiaries of the project. The structure and content of the financing, construction and operational transactions potentially have major direct and indirect effects on these stakeholders, even though they are not parties to the funding and construction documents, and this should be considered in assessing the overall sustainability of the project.[12]

---

10 Marianne Fay et al, 'Hitting the Trillion Mark: A Look at How Much Countries Are Spending on Infrastructure', World Bank Policy Research Working Paper 8730 (World Bank 2019) 46 <http://documents1.worldbank.org/curated/en/970571549037261080/pdf/WPS8730.pdf> accessed 22 April 2021; Judith Tyson, 'Private infrastructure finance for developing countries: Five challenges, five solutions', ODI Working Paper 536 (August 2018) <https://odi.org/en/publications/private-infrastructure-finance-in-developing-countries-five-challenges-five-solutions/> accessed 15 April 2021.

11 The World Bank, 'Public–Private Partnerships' https://www.worldbank.org/en/topic/publicprivatepartnerships accessed 23 April 2021; World Bank Public-Private Partnership Legal Resource Center (PPPLRC), 'Government Guarantees for Mobilizing Private Investment in Infrastructure' (24 December 2019) <https://ppp.worldbank.org/public-private-partnership/library/government-guarantees-mobilizing-private-investment-infrastructure> accessed 15 April 2021; Timothy E Nielander, *Public–Private Partnerships in Global Development: Supporting Sustainable Development Goals* (Edward Elgar Publishing 2020); Maria Jose Romero, 'History RePPPeated – How public–private partnerships are failing', European Network on Debt and Development (in conjunction with Heinrich Böll Stiftung) (2018) <https://www.eurodad.org/historyrepppeated> accessed 15 April 2021.

12 Benedict Kingsbury, 'Infrastructure and InfraReg: on rousing the international law "Wizards of Is"' (2019) Cambridge International Law Journal 171.

3. PRIVATE INTERNATIONAL LAW AND INFRASTRUCTURE

Private international law plays an important role in infrastructure projects. On the one hand, it supports the internationalisation of law and dispute resolution through the principle of party autonomy. Parties can thereby mitigate anticipated legal and financial risks and achieve the feasibility of major projects through the choice of non-host state law as a governing law for major contracts and offshore dispute resolution, and offshore enforcement of judgments and awards. On the other hand, this use of private international law rules may also result in the fragmentation of disputes relating to infrastructure projects, and encourage the de-linking of the host state, domestic stakeholders and host state law (including provisions relevant to sustainability) from dispute settlement. Further private international law issues may be presented by investor–state dispute settlement (ISDS) of disputes arising in relation to a project under IIAs or investment contracts and the international enforcement of liabilities against the assets of the host state.

3.1. CASE STUDY

An illustration of the complex contractual and private international law issues in a major transaction can be found in the structure of – and litigation surrounding – the construction of a large and economically important resort complex in The Bahamas.[13] Loan finance was provided by China Export-Import Bank pursuant to a facility agreement governed by English law, with an agreement that English courts would be the most appropriate and convenient to resolve any disputes. The principal construction contract was entered into between the American developer of the project and China State Construction Engineering Corp. Ltd (CSCEC), a Chinese company, and subsequently assigned to an indirect Bahamas subsidiary of CSCEC. A shareholders' agreement between the developer and CSCEC and its subsidiaries, all of whom invested equity into the project through a project company, was governed by New York law and courts. Both the construction contract and the assignment and assumption agreement were also governed by New York law, with disputes subject to the jurisdiction of the New York courts. Other agreements related to the facility agreement were governed by the laws of England, British Columbia, Texas and New York.[14]

---

13 *BML Properties Ltd v China Construction America Inc., et al.*, 101 N.Y.S. 3d 597 (N.Y. App. Div. 2019); *BML Props. Ltd v China Constr Am. Inc.*, 2020 N.Y. Slip. Op. 30816 (U).

14 Summary from *In re Northshore Mainland Services, Inc.*, 537 B.R. 192 (2015) Sept. 15, 2015 United States Bankruptcy Court for the District of Delaware Case No. 15-11402 (KJC), Kevin J. Carey.

Only the agreements relating to the grant of security to China Export-Import Bank over assets in The Bahamas were governed by Bahamian law.

The government of The Bahamas was not a party to any of these documents. It was, however, actively involved in negotiations around the project and the investment and granted a number of important concessions and contributions to make the project viable.[15] The government was also involved in the liquidation proceedings in The Bahamas.[16]

Overlapping proceedings in relation to this project involved an action in the English High Court against CSCEC (relating to a performance guarantee),[17] litigation in New York in relation to the construction contract, and competing winding-up proceedings in the United States federal court in Delaware and The Bahamas. Ultimately, however, the Attorney-General of The Bahamas led a delegation to Beijing to negotiate with China Export-Import Bank and CSCEC to seek a resolution, which resulted in the winding up and sale of the project to a Hong Kong corporation.[18] Litigation by the developer against the construction company and its parents continues in the New York courts.[19]

This case illustrates a number of issues which this type of cross-border structuring presents, not only for the financiers and investors, but also for the ultimate stakeholders – the government and people of The Bahamas, where the majority of the debtors were incorporated, and the project, the assets, employees and other stakeholders were located.

3.2. CHOICE OF LAW AND CHOICE OF FORUM

Private international law plays an important role in major projects in mitigating perceived risks arising from the inadequacies of host state law and the host state's legal system. Thus, the parties to the financing or commercial contracts may agree that a particular (non-host state) system of law will govern the contract,

15 Larry Smith, 'Tough Call: Deadlock At Baha Mar', *The Tribune* (17 June 2015) <http://www.tribune242.com/news/2015/jun/17/tough-call-deadlock-baha-mar/> accessed 15 April 2021.

16 Summary from *In re Northshore Mainland Services, Inc.*, 537 B.R. 192 (2015) Sept. 15, 2015 United States Bankruptcy Court for the District of Delaware Case No. 15-11402 (KJC), Kevin J. Carey.

17 Baha Mar Ltd, press release, 'Baha Mar Files Claim Form With English High Court Against China State Construction Engineering Corporation', *PR Newswire* (30 June 2015) <https://www.prnewswire.com/news-releases/baha-mar-files-claim-form-with-english-high-court-against-china-state-construction-engineering-corporation-300106704.html> accessed 15 April 2021.

18 Khrisna Virgil, 'Chinese "Agree" To Complete Baha Mar', *The Tribune* (25 May 2016) <http://www.tribune242.com/news/2016/may/26/chinese-agree-complete-baha-mar/> accessed 15 April 2021.

19 Natario McKenzie, 'Sarkis wins: US Supreme Court dismisses CCA counterclaim', *Eyewitness News* (20 March 2020) <https://ewnews.com/sarkis-wins> accessed 7 May 2021.

and may also submit to the jurisdiction of a non-host state court or international arbitration.[20] The basis for the effectiveness and enforceability of this choice is twofold: first, the principle of party autonomy of choice of law in commercial contracts, and, secondly, the concept of the parties' freedom to choose both the method of dispute resolution (arbitration or litigation) and the forum. These are both well-established private international law rules in a wide range of jurisdictions.[21] The doctrine of autonomy is supported by international initiatives such as the Hague Principles on Choice of Law in International Commercial Contracts,[22] the aim of which is to encourage 'the spread of this [autonomy] concept to States that have not yet adopted it, or have done so with significant restrictions' (Preamble, I.4). The right of the parties to a commercial contract to choose an appropriate forum for the resolution of disputes is supported by the recognition (and in the case of the common law courts, enforcement, through judicial doctrine, backed up by anti-suit injunctions)[23] of exclusive jurisdiction and arbitration clauses, as well as, for example, the Convention on Choice of Court Agreements.[24]

There are some limits to the enforcement of exclusive jurisdiction clauses imposed by domestic systems and courts.[25] The Choice of Court Agreements Convention allows Member States to reserve the right for their courts to refuse to take cases where there is no connection with the court or to refuse enforcement if all connections with the case are with the state of the requested court.[26] Some domestic laws, Chinese law for example, go further and require an actual connection between a dispute, the parties or the location of the dispute and will

20 Daniel Reichert-Facilides, 'Dispute Resolution and Conflict of Laws Risks' in David F Amus (ed), *The Project Finance Law Review* (2nd ed, The Law Reviews 2020) <https://thelawreviews.co.uk/edition/1001490/the-project-finance-law-review-edition-2> accessed 15 April 2021.

21 Maria Hook, *The Choice of Law in Contract* (Bloomsbury Publishing 2016) 54–55.

22 HCCH, 40: Principles on Choice of Law in International Commercial Contracts (approved 19 March 2015) <https://www.hcch.net/en/instruments/conventions/full-text/?cid=135> accessed 7 January 2021 (incorporated or otherwise in used in a way compatible with the principles in eight domestic arbitration centres and implemented by legislation in Paraguay and Uruguay: <https://www.hcch.net/en/publications-and-studies/details4/?pid=6300&dtid=41> accessed 7 January 2021).

23 Andrew Dickinson, 'National Report, United Kingdom' in Jürgen Basedow, Giesela Rühl, Franco Ferrari and Pedro de Miguel Asensio, *Encyclopedia of Private International Law* (Edward Elgar Publishing 2017); Stacie I Strong, 'Anti-Suit Injunctions in Judicial and Arbitral Procedures in the United States' (2018) 66 American Journal of International Law 153.

24 HCCH, 37: Convention on Choice of Court Agreements (concluded 30 June 2005, in force 1 October 2015) <https://assets.hcch.net/docs/510bc238-7318-47ed-9ed5-e0972510d98b.pdf> accessed 15 April 2021.

25 See, for example, *The Hollandia* [1983] AC 565; Carriage of Goods by Sea Act 1991 (Cth), s 11(2)(c) (overriding a foreign choice of court or arbitration clause). See also Peter Hay, 'Forum Selection Clauses – Procedural Tools or Contractual Obligations? Conceptualization and Remedies in American and German Law' (2021) 35 Emory International Law Review 1.

26 HCCH, 37: Convention on Choice of Court Agreements (concluded 30 June 2005, in force 1 October 2015) <https://assets.hcch.net/docs/510bc238-7318-47ed-9ed5-e0972510d98b.pdf> accessed 15 April 2021, Arts 19 and 20.

not recognise the choice of a third-party neutral forum if there is no connection between the forum and any of the parties or the subject matter of the dispute.[27] The general principle in relation to commercial contracts, however, is that the parties should be held to their bargain.

A range of factors may lead to the choice of certain systems of law and particular fora in an infrastructure project: a preference by the lenders for a sophisticated system of law with substantial experience in international financing;[28] the location and experience of large law firms who handle project financing work; the experience and reputation of the dispute resolution venue (combined with considerations of ease of enforcement); distrust of, or inadequacy of, the law, judicial system or governance of the host state; convenience of a particular party; and other factors.[29] English and New York law appear to be the current preferred systems of financial law[30] (although China is aiming to expand the use of Chinese law in cross-border transactions, in conjunction with the Belt and Road Initiative).[31]

The applicable law is not necessarily the same as the law of the chosen forum, but there is a strong correlation between the choice of law and choice of forum (even though there is strong competition between competing fora offering international dispute resolution services).[32] In major cross-border transactions, these factors may well lead away from the host state and its domestic law.

3.3. PRIVATE INTERNATIONAL LAW AND THE ROLE OF THE HOST STATE

Commentators on the sustainable development of infrastructure emphasise the need for project parties to work with local regulation – and similarly emphasise the desirability of local dispute resolution – as a means of building up the capability of the host state's legal system and providing effective remedies to

27 Law of Civil Procedure of the PRC, National People's Congress, as revised 1 July 2017; Vivienne Bath, 'Overlapping Jurisdiction and the Resolution of Disputes before Chinese and Foreign Courts' (2015–2016) 17 Yearbook of International Private Law 111.

28 Philip R Wood, 'Ten Points for Choosing the Governing Law of an International Business Contract', Business Law International (2020) <https://www.ibanet.org/> accessed 15 April 2021.

29 Daniel Reichert-Facilides, 'Dispute Resolution and Conflict of Laws Risks' in David F Amus (ed), *The Project Finance Law Review* (2nd ed, The Law Reviews 2020) <https://thelawreviews.co.uk/edition/1001490/the-project-finance-law-review-edition-2> accessed 15 April 2021.

30 ibid.

31 Supreme People's Court of the PRC, Opinions on Further Supply of Judicial Services and Safeguards by the People's Courts for the 'Belt and Road' Construction, Fa [2019] No 29 (9 December 2019), Art 3(20).

32 Note, for example, the role of international commercial arbitration and the new International Commercial Courts; Andrew Godwin, Ian Ramsay and Miranda Webster, 'International Commercial Courts: The Singapore Experience' (2017) 18(2) Melbourne Journal of International Law 18.

local stakeholders.[33] However, they also acknowledge the commercial realities of risk allocation reflected in the parties' choice of law and designation of a method and forum for dispute resolution. The 2017 version of the World Bank Guidelines for PPPs[34] was in fact criticised for failing to consider the perspective of the host state's contracting authority as opposed to the private parties involved, including by focusing on the disadvantages of utilising host state domestic law as the law governing the PPP contract notwithstanding the importance of host state law in relation to domestic public policy issues and the issue of licences for the implementation of the project.[35] This is especially important in relation to the sustainability of the project, which will be an important goal for the host state but not necessarily for the contract parties. The 2019 edition is considerably more neutral on the question of governing law. However, it draws heavily on the concept of 'bankability' (that is, the ability to obtain finance for the project) in its discussion on choice of law (due to the risk that there may be a change to substantive law[36] and the need to obtain political risk insurance)[37] and choice of dispute resolution forum. Realistically, the message is the same: the financiers and sponsors of the transaction will require foreign law and dispute resolution if they consider it too risky to submit to the law and legal system of the host state.[38]

The preference for a law other than the law of the host state is also quite common in loan transactions involving sovereign debt. Multilateral development banks (MDBs) may prefer not to use host state law in non-sovereign backed funding. The AIIB Operational Policy on Financing,[39] for example, provides that the governing law generally applicable to non-sovereign-backed financing in cross-border loans will be a 'suitable law' which will be a law 'usually other than

33 Martin Dietrich Brauch, 'Contracts for Sustainable Infrastructure: Ensuring the economic, social and environmental co-benefits of infrastructure investment projects', IISD Report (December 2017) <https://www.iisd.org/sites/default/files/publications/contracts-sustainable-infrastructure.pdf> accessed 15 April 2021.

34 World Bank Group, *Guidance on PPP Contractual Provisions* (15 September 2017) <https://ppp.worldbank.org/public-private-partnership/library/guidance-ppp-contractual-provisions-2017-edition> accessed 18 May 2021.

35 Foley Hoag, 'Summary Comments on the World Bank Group's 2017 Guidance on PPP Contractual Provisions' (15 September 2017) <https://us.boell.org/en/2017/09/15/summary-comments-world-bank-groups-2017-guidance-ppp-contractual-provisions> accessed 15 April 2021.

36 World Bank Group, *Guidance on PPP Contractual Provisions* (International Bank for Reconstruction and Development 2019) s 3.2.1.2 Bankability, 68.

37 ibid.

38 See also UNCITRAL, Legislative Guide on Public–Private Partnerships, United Nations, Vienna, 2020, 'I. General legal and institutional framework', 25 (UNCITRAL PPP Guide) 175 (sub-contractors), 248 (loan agreements).

39 AIIB, Operational Policy on Financing (Annex 2, Special Provisions Applicable to Non-Sovereign-Backed Financing) s 5.2, <https://www.aiib.org/en/policies-strategies/_download/operation-policy/Operational-policy-on-financing-March-20-2020.pdf> accessed 15 April 2021; John W Head, 'Evolution of the Governing Law for Loan Agreements of the World Bank and Other Multilateral Development Banks' (1996) 90(2) American Journal of International Law 214.

the law of the jurisdiction in which the Loan Beneficiary is established', and local law where the governing law is 'of necessity' local law.[40] Similarly, state-owned or commercial banks often have a policy of requiring the use of their own domestic law and dispute resolution fora.[41]

In relation to dispute resolution, the availability of international arbitration in a foreign venue is often offered as an incentive to investment by host states, even where host state law applies to a particular contract. Thus, PPP or joint venture laws may allow for international arbitration between the investor and the host state despite requiring that the PPP project company be domestically established and subject to local law.[42] International programmes encourage smaller states to accede to the New York Convention[43] on the basis that providing a mechanism for the enforcement of international arbitral awards will assist them to attract foreign investment.[44]

This has two important consequences. First, in a multi-party infrastructure transaction, the different interests and preferences of parties involved in contracts, combined with the utilisation of the principle of party autonomy, may well result in a variety of governing laws, fora and methods of dispute resolution in the same project. This can and does result in a multiplicity of litigation and arbitrations in different international and host state fora as disputes arise. In the case study above, the main transaction documents were under the laws of England, New York, The Bahamas, Texas and British Columbia, with different dispute resolution methods and fora in each contract and winding-up and liquidation proceedings initiated in both Delaware and The Bahamas. Host state laws emphasising sustainability may not be applied at all in these disputes nor will it be necessary for the viability or sustainability of the underlying project to be considered, depending on the disputed contract. Depending on the

40 Art 3.1.5 (c) also allows the AIIB to require that the member in whose territory the project is to be carried out guarantee a non-sovereign-based loan if the recipient of the AIIB loan or guarantee is not the member itself.

41 See Anna Gelpern, Sebastian Horn, Scott Morris, Brad Parks and Christoph Trebesch, 'How China Lends: A Rare Look into 100 Debt Contracts with Foreign Governments', Peterson Institute for International Economics, Kiel Institute for the World Economy, Center for Global Development, and AidData at William & Mary (March 2021) Tables A5 to A8 <https://docs.aiddata.org/ad4/pdfs/How_China_Lends__A_Rare_Look_into_100_Debt_Contracts_with_Foreign_Governments.pdf> accessed 15 April 2021.

42 See, for example, Kingdom of Cambodia, Law on Concessions, Art 24 <https://ppp.worldbank.org/public-private-partnership/library/cambodia-law-concessions> accessed 15 April 2021. The concessionaire is, however, free to choose the governing law for any ancillary contract.

43 Convention on the Recognition and Enforcement of Foreign Arbitral Awards (adopted 10 June 1958, entered into force 7 June 1959) 330 UNTS I-4739 (New York Convention).

44 For example, Marketscreener, 'ADB Asian Development Bank: Papua New Guinea Accedes to New York Convention on Arbitration' (24 July 2019) <https://www.marketscreener.com/news/latest/ADB-Asian-Development-Bank-nbsp-Papua-New-Guinea-Accedes-to-New-York-Convention-on-Arbitration--28948636/> accessed 15 April 2021.

transaction structure and the parties to particular contracts, it is quite possible that neither the host state nor its stakeholders will have a right to participate in the contractual disputes. The government of The Bahamas in the case study was not a party to the transaction documents, and the resolution of the contractual disputes in such a way as to ensure the continuation of the project was thus dealt with by a combination of political intervention and winding-up proceedings, with the original developer and investor left to pursue remedies for an alleged fraud in the courts of New York.

There can also be distinct disadvantages for the host state in insisting on the use of domestic law. An agreement by commercial or other parties to use host country law may come with the requirement that the host state provide direct assurances of support and protection by entering into an investment agreement or giving a specific binding commitment in the form of a stabilisation agreement, that is, that it agree not to apply law changes after the date of the agreement against the foreign investor or concessionaire (freezing clauses), or that it promise indemnification for the consequences of such changes (economic equilibrium clauses).[45] The host state's commitments in its IIAs for the benefit of investors may also have an impact on its freedom to regulate.[46]

In summary, private international law rules potentially facilitate the separation of the legal system of the host state, as well as the host state and domestic stakeholders, from implementation, adjudication and dispute resolution of major projects. Sustainability principles relevant to the construction and operation of the project that are incorporated in host state law are thereby potentially excluded, and an offshore forum is generally not obliged to apply those principles and laws. As Wai comments, the consequence of the de-linking of host state law is that 'greater social concerns embodied in national laws that arguably have more to do with the transaction' may be excluded from consideration.[47] Similarly, the scope of application of protective domestic law and access for local stakeholders to rapid resolution of local disputes – and associated opportunities to upgrade or improve local skills, legal and judicial capacity, and the legal system itself – may be reduced. This structure can also be highly costly in real financial terms if, due to the fragmented process of dispute resolution, major disputes (and the enforcement of awards or claims) must be argued by foreign legal experts in foreign fora. The 'offshoring' of negotiations, contract drafting, deal structuring and dispute resolution also

45 See Jola Gjuzi, *Stabilization Clauses in International Investment Law – A Sustainable Development Approach* (Springer 2018).

46 Lise Johnson, Lisa Sachs and Nathan Lobel, 'Aligning International Investment Agreements with the Sustainable Development Goals' (2019) 58 Columbia Journal of Transnational Law 58.

47 Robert Wai, 'Private v Private: Transnational Private Law and Contestation in Global Economic Governance' in Horatia Muir Watt and Diego P Ferández Arroyo (eds), *Private International Law and Global Governance* (OUP 2015) 256.

represents a potential lost opportunity for the acquisition of experience and expertise by the state's administrators, lawyers and regulatory and judicial systems in dealing with major cross-border projects.

3.4. PRIVATE INTERNATIONAL LAW AND THE DOMESTIC STAKEHOLDERS

The domestic stakeholders have a strong interest in the sustainability of infrastructure. They are potentially affected as employees seeking fairly paid employment and training with the project, small businesses that may lose existing opportunities or seek new ones, landholders whose interests in land or just compensation are affected by the project, contractors and others, all of whom have interests which need to be protected, ideally in an efficient, convenient and coherent manner. As a matter of principle, there is much to be said for the view that the law of the jurisdiction where the infrastructure will be located, the work will take place and domestic workers are employed, the ultimate stakeholders are located and the benefits (or disadvantages) of the project will accrue should apply. Domestic dispute resolution (including by arbitration) presents opportunities not just for the consistent and consolidated resolution of disputes involving local stakeholders but for the improvement and development of the legal system and dispute resolution mechanisms (SDG 16, and, in particular, newly added Indicator 16.3.3, which provides for monitoring access to civil justice).[48] The International Institute for Sustainable Development recommends that preference in dispute settlement in local disputes be given to domestic courts over arbitration, with an opportunity for non-party stakeholders to participate.[49]

In terms of private international law rules, however, a foreign contractor is generally not bound to enter into contracts governed by domestic law and may prefer not to. This raises the question whether and what matters should be exclusively subject to local law or local jurisdiction, how to ensure that other matters in which the state has an interest are subject to local law and resolution,[50]

---

48 Kristin Bergtora Sandvik, 'The SDGs, access to civil justice, and legal technology', *Devpolicy Blog* (18 May 2020) <https://devpolicy.org/access-to-civil-justice-20200518-1/> accessed 22 April 2021. Oslo Governance Centre, 'UNDP support to reporting on the global SDG 16 indicators under targets 16.3, 16.6 and 16.7' <https://www.undp.org/content/oslo-governance-centre/en/home/our-focus/sdg-16/undp-support-to-reporting-on-the-global-sdg-16-indicators.html> accessed 4 January 2021.

49 Martin Dietrich Brauch, 'Contracts for Sustainable Infrastructure: Ensuring the economic, social and environmental co-benefits of infrastructure investment projects', IISD Report (December 2017) 13 <https://www.iisd.org/sites/default/files/publications/contracts-sustainable-infrastructure.pdf> accessed 15 April 2021.

50 Martin Wilderspin, 'Overriding mandatory provisions', Ch O.3 in Jürgen Basedow, Giesela Rühl, Franco Ferrari and Pedro de Miguel Asensio, *Encyclopedia of Private International Law* (Edward Elgar Publishing 2017).

and, if they are not, whether private international law rules can assist to ensure the application of domestic protective rules outside the host state.[51]

There is some agreement internationally in relation to the applicable law and, to a lesser extent, exclusive jurisdiction, in relation to certain areas such as immovables, including land, and related security interests, which are generally agreed to be subject to the *lex situs*.[52] This is particularly relevant to infrastructure, which necessarily involves the acquisition and use of land and other resources. In the Bahamian project above, for example, security interests over land and local companies were granted under local law. The AIIB Operational Policy on Financing[53] similarly provides that local law will apply, in the case of instruments such as mortgage agreements, equity subscription agreements and security interests and equipment, where the governing law is 'of necessity' local law.[54]

There is, however, a wider category of matters in which the domestic jurisdiction arguably has the primary interest and a duty to protect the interests of local stakeholders in order to support the sustainable and consistent implementation of the project. Many of these matters implicate other SDGs, such as employment (SDG 8). An issue which should be considered in relation to infrastructure projects, however, is the importance of a consolidated and consistent approach to protection of stakeholders such as persons employed to construct or operate the project or small business owners, suppliers and independent contractors dealing with foreign contractors, or a foreign-controlled PPP company.[55] The issue presented here is how and whether private international law can contribute to the coherent and consolidated resolution of issues relating to the sustainability of the project as a whole and the enforceability of host state protective regulation outside the host state.[56]

---

51 UNCITRAL, Legislative Guide on Public–Private Partnerships, United Nations, Vienna, 2020, 'I. General legal and institutional framework', 25 (UNCITRAL PPP Guide) 176, for example, notes that domestic law does not generally prescribe the governing law of contracts entered into by the private partner, which can therefore be subject to foreign law. However, they should still be subject to the host state's mandatory laws, such as environment, labour, safety or security laws and regulations.

52 Eva-Maria Kieninger, 'Immovable Property', Ch I.2 in Jürgen Basedow, Giesela Rühl, Franco Ferrari and Pedro de Miguel Asensio, *Encyclopedia of Private International Law* (Edward Elgar Publishing 2017).

53 AIIB, Operational Policy on Financing (Annex 2, Special Provisions Applicable to Non-Sovereign-Backed Financing) s 5.2, <https://www.aiib.org/en/policies-strategies/_download/operation-policy/Operational-policy-on-financing-March-20-2020.pdf> accessed 15 April 2021.

54 ibid, Art 5.2.

55 See *Proactive Building Solutions v Mackenzie Keck* [2013] NSWSC 1500, in which the NSW court disregarded the choice of English law and courts as it would result in the builder losing the protection of the Building and Construction Industry Security of Payment Act 1999 (NSW).

56 Ralf Michaels, 'Towards a Private International Law for Regulatory Conflicts' (2016) 59 Japanese Yearbook of International Law 175; Matthias Lehmann, 'Regulation, global governance and private international law: squaring the triangle' (2020) 16(1) Journal of Private International Law 1.

3.5. INVESTMENT AND PRIVATE INTERNATIONAL LAW

An important source of private financing for infrastructure projects is foreign direct investment (FDI). Foreign investment is essentially a creature of domestic – that is, host state – law and international organisations have put considerable effort into assisting developing countries to develop investment legislation which both promotes and regulates foreign investment and, more recently, forwards sustainable development goals.[57] Promotion of FDI is also supported by IIAs and investment agreements between host states and investors, pursuant to which host states offer guarantees of protection to foreign investors. Many IIAs contain expansive definitions of 'investment' and thus PPPs, joint venture projects, and construction, operating and licence arrangements relating to infrastructure, including project finance transactions, government issued bonds,[58] intellectual property licences and other arrangements, may well come within the definition. These IIAs (and investment agreements) provide an avenue for both investors and contractors to seek remedies directly from the host state through ISDS instead of – or in addition to – contractual claims under the project contracts.[59] The UNCITRAL PPP Guide in fact includes in its discussion on dispute resolution in PPPs the possibility of resolving disputes between the host state and the PPP investor under the Washington Convention[60] or a bilateral investment treaty.

Statistics issued by the International Center for the Settlement of Investment Disputes (ICSID) show that a substantial number of disputes before the ICSID are related to infrastructure or infrastructure-related projects, including

57 For example, see UNCITRAL, Investment Policy Hub, Investment Policy Framework <https://investmentpolicy.unctad.org/> accessed 15 April 2021.

58 Freshfields Bruckhaus Deringer, 'Project finance lenders may seek protection under international investment treaties against state measures adversely affecting the project' (28 August 2020) <http://knowledge.freshfields.com/en/Global/r/4302/project_finance_lenders_may_seek__protection_under> accessed 15 April 2021; Stratos Pahis, 'BITs and Bonds: The International Law and Economics of Sovereign Debt' (29 July 2020) <https://ssrn.com/abstract=3663299> accessed 22 April 2021.

59 See, for example, 2013 China–Tanzania Investment Agreement (signed 24 March 2013, effective 17 April 2014) Art 1, definition of 'investment' paras (f) and (g). In contrast, the 2015 Model Indian BIT focuses on long-term investment in assets and long-term contracts and does not refer to construction at all (Art 1.4).

60 UNCITRAL, Legislative Guide on Public–Private Partnerships, United Nations, Vienna, 2020, 'I. General legal and institutional framework', 237 et seq; Convention on the Settlement of Investment Disputes between States and nationals of other States (signed Washington 1996, effective 14 October 1996) 575 UNTS 159. There are currently 155 parties to the Convention: <https://icsid.worldbank.org/resources/rules-and-regulations/convention/overview> accessed 15 April 2021.

electric power and energy, transportation, construction, information and communications, and water, sanitation and flood protection.[61] Cases brought under IIAs or otherwise directly against a state weigh heavily on developing countries.[62] Of the 39 heavily indebted poor countries (HIPCs) in the IMF debt-relief programme, for example, 18 are, or have been, respondents to investor–state arbitrations, led by Bolivia (17 cases), Tanzania (eight cases), and Burundi, Madagascar, Senegal and the Democratic Republic of Congo (DRC) (four each).[63]

ISDS raises some particularly problematic private international law issues due to its public international law origins and the fact that investment takes place – and must operate – under domestic law. There are therefore a number of possibilities in relation to applicable law, the main ones of which are public international law (particularly in the case of disputes arising under a treaty rather than an investment contract), the law nominated by the parties (if any) and the law of the host state where the investment takes place.[64] Article 42(1) of the Washington Convention[65] provides that the applicable rules of law to be applied may be agreed by the parties (either separately or as part of the relevant treaty). However, in the absence of agreement, 'the Tribunal shall apply the law of the Contracting State (including its rules on the conflict of laws) and such rules of international law as may be applicable.'[66] Spiermann comments that the

---

61 ICSID, The ICISD Caseload – Statistics (Issue 2021-1) <https://icsid.worldbank.org/sites/default/files/publications/The%20ICSID%20Caseload%20Statistics%20%282021-1%20Edition%29%20ENG.pdf> accessed 15 April 2021.

62 Tim R Samples, 'Winning and Losing in Investor-State Dispute Settlement' (2019) 65(1) American Business Law Journal 115. According to the ICSID, of the 123 cases brought under an investment contract under the Washington Convention or the ICSID Additional Facility, all but one were brought against developing states: <https://icsid.worldbank.org/cases/case-database> accessed 15 April 2021.

63 International Monetary Fund, 'Debt Relief Under the Heavily Indebted Poor Countries (HIPC) Initiative and Multilateral Debt Relief Initiative (MDRI)' <https://www.imf.org/en/About/Factsheets/Sheets/2016/08/01/16/11/Debt-Relief-Under-the-Heavily-Indebted-Poor-Countries-Initiative> accessed 12 July 2021. UNCTAD Investment Policy Hub, Investment Dispute Settlement Navigator <https://investmentpolicy.unctad.org/investment-dispute-settlement> accessed 12 July 2021.

64 See Christophe Schreuer et al, *The ICSID Convention: A commentary* (2nd ed, CUP 2009) Art 42, 550 et seq; Ole Spiermann, 'Investment Arbitration: Applicable Law', Ch 11.IV in Marc Bungenberg, John Griebel, Stephan Hove and August Reinish (eds), *International Investment Law* (Beck/Hart/Nomos 2015) 1373; Benedetta Cappiello, 'Applicable Law in Investment Arbitration' in Julian Chaisse, Leïla Choukroune and Sufian Jusoh (eds), *Handbook of International Investment Law and Policy* (Springer 2020).

65 Schreuer, ibid.

66 See also the ICSID Additional Facility Rules (Art 54(1)), which also grant the tribunal considerable flexibility: <https://icsid.worldbank.org/sites/default/files/AFR_2006%20English-final.pdf> (2006 version) accessed 15 April 2021.

principle of party autonomy of choice of law in contract in the commercial sphere has flowed over into the sphere of investor–state contracts and agreements. Nevertheless, the application by arbitral tribunals of the concept of *pacta sunt servanda* and the so-called internationalisation of investment contracts tends to result in the application of international law rather than host state law.[67]

In all cases, the international tribunal has considerable flexibility both in determining which law should apply to a particular dispute and whether to apply the host state's domestic law or to determine that international law and standards operate to impose liability on the state regardless of its own laws. While the rationale behind this is clear (holding the state to its bargain to protect foreign investment and preventing it from changing the law for its own convenience), the reference of a dispute to ISDS means that decision-making in this area, including on the choice of law to be applied and, indeed, the content, validity, application and amendment of domestic law and policies (including laws designed to promote sustainable investment), is in the hands of international arbitrators. It is not a surprise then that the content of IIAs, the way in which to ensure the importance of sustainability is recognised in IIAs[68] and ISDS, and the implications of IIAs and ISDS for the host state and its regulatory system are hotly debated.[69]

3.6. HOST STATE LIABILITY, ENFORCEMENT AND SOVEREIGN IMMUNITY

In the case of a developing country, where much of the infrastructure financing is public or supported, directly by guarantees, investment agreements, concessions and other government commitments, or indirectly through IIAs, there is a very real prospect of host state liability – and related international enforcement actions – arising in connection with infrastructure projects. For poorer developing countries and emerging states, this may also be related to the issue of high levels of sovereign debt.[70]

---

67 Ole Spiermann, 'Investment Arbitration: Applicable Law', Ch 11.IV in Marc Bungenberg, John Griebel, Stephan Hove and August Reinish (eds), *International Investment Law* (Beck/Hart/Nomos 2015) 1377, citing Böckstiegel.

68 Lise Johnson, Lisa Sachs and Nathan Lobel, 'Aligning International Investment Agreements with the Sustainable Development Goals' (2019) 58 Columbia Journal of Transnational Law 58.

69 Yannick Raid, 'Balancing the Public and the Private in International Investment Law' in Horatia Muir Watt and Diego P Ferández Arroyo (eds), *Private International Law and Global Governance* (OUP 2015). See also UNCITRAL, Working Group III: Investor-State Dispute Settlement Reform <https://uncitral.un.org/en/working_groups/3/investor-state> accessed 15 April 2021.

70 This has been aggravated by the COVID-19 pandemic. Colby Smith, 'IMF calls for urgent action to prevent debt crisis in emerging economies' *Financial Times* (1 October 2020) <https://www.ft.com/content/b61c8dea-58bc-476d-ae9f-c2de104808de> accessed 22 April 2021.

The question of the liability of a sovereign state to suit is subject to a range of different rules and considerations.[71] At an international level, there continue to be differences in approach in relation to the enforcement of judgments against a foreign state and the question whether the state is entitled to immunity from suit or execution in a domestic court, the extent of that immunity and whether it should be restricted to non-commercial matters (and how these are defined), and what effect this has on attempts by a claimant to recover under a judgment or award.[72] As a result, for the purpose of recognition and enforcement of foreign judgments or arbitral awards, enforcement actions in domestic courts must be argued under local law, and determined either by statute or by custom, or both.[73]

Although some states (notably China) adhere to an absolute standard in relation to sovereign immunity,[74] many (particularly developed states) apply the 'commercial' exception to immunity[75] and the concept that the state may waive its immunity by specific agreement or, for example, by entering into an arbitration agreement. A distinction is, however, drawn between adjudication and the waiver of immunity in the adjudicatory stage, and execution against the assets of a state in the enforcement stage, which tends to be more difficult.[76] Thus, under the Washington Convention, the state consents to arbitration under Article 53 and recognition and enforcement of such an award is required by Article 54, but domestic rules on immunity from execution apply pursuant to Article 55.[77]

---

71 Stefan Kröll, 'Enforcement of Awards', Ch 11.VII, in Marc Bungenberg, John Griebel, Stephan Hove and August Reinish (eds), *International Investment Law* (Beck/Hart/Nomos 2015) 1499 et seq; Jasper Finke, 'Sovereign Immunity: Rule, Comity or Something Else' (2011) 21(4) European Journal of International Law 853 on the nature of sovereign immunity under international law and the public–private distinction; Hayk Kupelyants, *Sovereign Defaults Before Domestic Courts* (OUP 2018) ch 8, 'Enforcement of Sovereign Debt', 277.

72 Finke, ibid; UN General Assembly, Convention on Jurisdictional Immunities of States and Their Property (adopted 2 December 2004) UN Doc A/59/508, UN Doc A/RES/59/38 (not in force), particularly Arts 10 and 19.

73 Adrian Lai, 'State Immunity in the Context of Enforcement of Investment Arbitration Awards' in Julian Chaisse, Leïla Choukroune and Sufian Jusoh (eds), *Handbook of International Investment Law and Policy* (Springer 2020).

74 Affirmed in *Democratic Republic of the Congo and others v FG Hemisphere Associates LLC* [2011] HKCFA 41; (2011) 14 HKCFAR 95; [2011] 4 HKC 151. China is a signatory (but not a party) to the UN General Assembly, Convention on Jurisdictional Immunities of States and Their Property (adopted 2 December 2004) UN Doc A/59/508, UN Doc A/RES/59/38 (not in force).

75 See, for example, Convention on Jurisdictional Immunities, ibid, Art 10, Commercial transactions.

76 Stefan Kröll, 'Enforcement of Awards', Ch 11.VII, in Marc Bungenberg, John Griebel, Stephan Hove and August Reinish (eds), *International Investment Law* (Beck/Hart/Nomos 2015) 1485; Adrian Lai, 'State Immunity in the Context of Enforcement of Investment Arbitration Awards' in Julian Chaisse, Leïla Choukroune and Sufian Jusoh (eds), *Handbook of International Investment Law and Policy* (Springer 2020).

77 Convention on the Settlement of Investment Disputes between States and nationals of other States (signed Washington 1996, effective 14 October 1996) 575 UNTS 159. For a recent case on the interaction of these Articles, see *Kingdom of Spain v Infrastructure Services Luxembourg Sarl* [2021] FCAFC 3.

Arbitration awards against a state can also potentially be enforced (where a distinction is drawn between enforcement and execution against assets) under the New York Convention or national law.[78] As a method of risk mitigation for the private commercial parties therefore, both private lawyers and the World Bank Group Public-Private Partnership Legal Resource Center (PPPLRC)[79] recommend that in project financing and PPP transactions the host state be required to waive sovereign immunity in respect of both adjudication of disputes and enforcement, including execution.

Although the logic for this is clear, this potentially weighs heavily on developing states, and has a potential impact on the sustainability of major projects, for several reasons. First, as noted above, much of the finance for infrastructure in the developing world requires state support. In PPP arrangements, for example, which have been strongly supported by the World Bank and other international institutions as a means of obtaining private finance for infrastructure (and equally strongly criticised as unfair, costly and inefficient),[80] the state or its agencies are required to provide support to the project, opening up the state to a wide range of claims and potential liabilities, in addition to its other commitments. This in turn may have an impact on its overall debt position and direct or indirect impacts on other projects or state responsibilities to its citizens.[81] This potentially open-ended state liability is highly relevant to the overall question of sustainability.

Secondly, the terms of a specific waiver of immunity can be very broad and extend to a wide range of state assets. For example, the waiver recommended by the PPPLRC covers sovereign immunity and acts of state, all property and assets of the host state, whenever acquired, the institution and all aspects of legal proceedings, and enforcement and execution. It further includes an irrevocable and unconditional acknowledgement that the agreement is private and commercial

---

78 Stefan Kröll, 'Enforcement of Awards', Ch 11.VII, in Marc Bungenberg, John Griebel, Stephan Hove and August Reinish (eds), *International Investment Law* (Beck/Hart/Nomos 2015) 1488 et seq.

79 PPPLRC, 'Checklist on Sovereign Immunity' <https://ppp.worldbank.org/public-private-partnership/ppp-overview/practical-tools/checklists-and-risk-matrices/checklist-sovereign-immunity> accessed 3 January 2021.

80 Philip Alston, 'Report of the Special Rapporteur on Extreme Poverty and Human Rights: The Parlous State of Poverty Eradication', UN Doc A/HRC/44/40 (2 July 2020) para 49 and sources cited therein; Maria Jose Romero, 'History RePPPeated – How public–private partnerships are failing', European Network on Debt and Development (in conjunction with Heinrich Böll Stiftung) (2018).

81 Romero, ibid. See, in relation to a US$10 billion award against Nigeria arising from a failed infrastructure project see Victor Akazue Nwakasi and Ugochukwu Eze, 'Arbitral Awards as Sovereign Debt Risks: Impact of P&ID and Eurafic Cases', Legal Business Day (last updated 10 October 2020) <https://legal.businessday.ng/2020/10/02/arbitral-awards-as-sovereign-debt-risks-impact-of-pid-and-eurafic-cases/> accessed 3 January 2021; Jonathan Bonnitcha, 'Corruption and confidentiality in contract-based ISDS: The case of P&ID v Nigeria', Investment Treaty News (23 March 2021).

and not a public act of the signing authority.[82] The authors further suggest that there be a careful definition of those assets available for seizure in view of rules in various jurisdictions on execution and sovereign immunity and that the waiver include a waiver of execution against 'any property or assets whatsoever (irrespective of its use or intended use)'.

Where execution against state assets is permitted under domestic law, states generally maintain a distinction between activities and assets of a state which are considered to be 'commercial' and therefore do not enjoy immunity, and 'non-commercial', which do. Thus, execution of a judgment or award against a state clearly presents the issues that arise from the need to distinguish between state assets (often held offshore) which should be made available to meet commercial debts and state assets which should be protected from execution because they are held for use – or otherwise required – for social and other state purposes. In the case of a small state (as discussed in the Australian High Court case of *Firebird Global Master Fund II Ltd v Republic of Nauru*),[83] there may be very little difference between the two.[84]

An example of these issues is provided by the multi-jurisdictional enforcement actions taken by FG Hemisphere, a vulture fund, against the DRC and its assets, which started with commercial arbitrations in respect of a dispute over the financing of the construction of a hydroelectric facility and electric transmission lines,[85] and subsequently involved enforcement actions in Belgium, Bermuda and South Africa, Hong Kong,[86] Canada, the United States,[87] Australia,[88] South Africa and Jersey[89] (and possibly others). Overall, this was an expensive and

82 See PPPLRC, 'Checklist on Sovereign Immunity' <https://ppp.worldbank.org/public-private-partnership/ppp-overview/practical-tools/checklists-and-risk-matrices/checklist-sovereign-immunity> accessed 3 January 2021.

83 [2015] HCA 43.

84 See, however, Lee Jones and Shahar Hameiri, 'Debunking the Myth of "Debt-trap Diplomacy"', Chatham House Research Paper, Asia-Pacific Programme (2020) <https://www.chathamhouse.org/sites/default/files/2020-08-25-debunking-myth-debt-trap-diplomacy-jones-hameiri.pdf> accessed 15 April 2021, commenting on the domestic mismanagement and corruption preceding Chinese funding of projects in Sri Lanka and Malaysia.

85 Shen Wei, 'FG Hemisphere Associates v. Democratic Republic of the Congo' (2014) 108(4) American Journal of International Law 776.

86 Unsuccessful due to the absolute view on sovereign immunity taken by the Chinese government: *Democratic Republic of the Congo and others v FG Hemisphere Associates LLC* [2011] HKCFA 41; (2011) 14 HKCFAR 95; [2011] 4 HKC 151, per Chan PF, Ribeiro PG and Mason NPJ, [384]–[393].

87 Hemisphere obtained – inter alia – a contempt order against the DRC for its failure to cooperate in providing lists of its assets. Aff. US Court of Appeals, District of Columbia Circuit in *FG Hemisphere Associates, LLC, Appellee v Democratic Republic of Congo*, Appellant Nos 10-7040, 10-7046 (15 March 2011).

88 *FG Hemisphere Associates LLC v Democratic Republic of Congo* [2010] NSWSC 1394. Award for approximately US$30 million plus expenses and interest. Costs were awarded against the DRC on an indemnity basis.

89 Action against a state-owned entity failed in the Supreme Court. *La Générale des Carrières et des Mines v FG Hemisphere Associates LLC* [2012] UKPC 27.

time-consuming exercise for both the claimant and the DRC, which finally launched proceedings in France in 2018 to have the underlying award annulled and recognition and enforcement of the Swiss award overturned.[90]

4. REGULATORY PRIVATE INTERNATIONAL LAW AND SDG 9: SUGGESTIONS FOR REFORM

The discussion above highlights a number of practical issues which private international law rules can present in relation to the inclusion of the concept of sustainable development objectives in the implementation of a major project. On the one hand, there is international support from the United Nations and other international organisations, states and private bodies both for the principle of sustainability and the sustainable development of developing and less-developed countries, and for the incorporation into domestic law of principles and regulations designed to promote sustainability. This is reflected in the SDGs themselves, as well as in other international initiatives such as the UN Guiding Principles on Business and Human Rights.[91] UNCTAD's Investment Policy Framework for Sustainable Development,[92] for example, makes detailed recommendations for the inclusion of sustainability considerations in host state investment law and for improving the drafting of IIAs to include considerations of sustainable development, by clarifying the right of the host state to regulate and by imposing compliance obligations on investors. The EU's recent proposal for amendments to the Energy Charter Treaty (ECT)[93] includes draft provisions specifically recognising the right of contracting parties to determine their own sustainable development policies and priorities and to regulate accordingly. Draft Part III on Regulatory Measures, for example, refers to the right of the host

90 See Stefaan Smis, Dan N Kashironge and Jean-Paul Mushagalusa, 'The FG Hemisphere Case: Congo's Resistance to Investor-State Arbitration or Just a Malaise with Vulture Funds?' (August 2020) Transnational Dispute Management (Provisional). See also Human Rights Council Advisory Committee, 'Draft final report on the activities of vulture funds and the impact on human rights', prepared by Jean Ziegler, Rapporteur, UN Doc A/HRC/AC/22/CRP.1 (8 February 2019); Aren Goldsmith and Guillaume de Rancourt, 'Trading in International Arbitral Awards: Developments in French Case Law Could Have a Chilling Effect' (2019) 262(10) New York Law Journal S8.

91 UN Human Rights Office of the High Commissioner website <https://www.ohchr.org/Documents/Publications/GuidingPrinciplesBusinessHR_EN.pdf> accessed 22 April 2021.

92 UNCTAD, Investment Policy Framework for Sustainable Development (2015) ch IV, 'Framework for International Investment Agreements', 73–124 <https://unctad.org/system/files/official-document/diaepcb2015d5_en.pdf> accessed 22 April 2021.

93 European Union, EU text proposal for the modernisation of the Energy Charter Treaty (ECT) (2020) <https://trade.ec.europa.eu/doclib/docs/2020/may/tradoc_158754.pdf> accessed 22 April 2021, Draft Articles on Sustainable Development, 10–12. The Energy Charter Treaty (17 December 1994, entered into force 16 April 1998) 2080 UNTS 95.

state to regulate to achieve legitimate policy objectives and specifically states that a contracting party does not commit *not* to change the legal and regulatory framework in a way which may negatively affect an investor.[94]

On the other hand, private international law rules relating to choice of law, jurisdiction and enforcement have played an important role in resolving some of the difficulties in structuring and financing infrastructure transactions. In particular, they materially assist to mitigate perceived legal and adjudication risks by supporting the choice by the parties of internationally favoured systems of law and the nomination of offshore litigation and arbitration. They have, however, been less successful in assuring sustainability.

The question therefore is whether (and how) regulatory private international law rules could, and should, play a role in supporting the aim of sustainability in relation to infrastructure and other major development projects.[95]

4.1. SUSTAINABILITY, APPLICABLE LAW AND DISPUTE RESOLUTION

The first issue relates to the role of international dispute resolution and the potential de-linking of host state law and dispute resolution from infrastructure project contracts. This raises the question of the extent to which – when the applicable law is not the law of the host state and the forum for dispute resolution is similarly located outside the host state – private international law rules could allow for, or require, consideration of sustainability generally or of host state laws and regulations designed to support sustainability. Can, or should, the court or tribunal take into account the sustainability of the infrastructure project as a whole as a relevant factor? Can, or should, it consider the laws, or the policies and regulatory interests, of the host state in sustainable development as relevant to the performance of the particular contract or decisions under that contract relating to termination, suspension, remedies or other issues? This could be material, for example, in relation to excuses for non-performance or delay due

94 ibid 4–5.

95 See more generally Robert Wai, 'Private v Private: Transnational Private Law and Contestation in Global Economic Governance' in Horatia Muir Watt and Diego P Ferández Arroyo (eds), *Private International Law and Global Governance* (OUP 2015) 256; Ralf Michaels, 'Towards a Private International Law for Regulatory Conflicts' (2016) 59 Japanese Yearbook of International Law 175; Matthias Lehmann, 'Regulation, global governance and private international law: squaring the triangle' (2020) 16(1) Journal of Private International Law 1; Bram van der Eem, 'Financial Stability as a Global Public Good and Private International Law as an Instrument for its Transnational Governance – Some Basic Thoughts' in Horatia Muir Watt and Diego P Ferández Arroyo (eds), *Private International Law and Global Governance* (OUP 2015) 293; Mauro Megliani, 'For the Orphan, the Widow, the Poor: How to Curb Enforcing by Vulture Funds against the Highly Indebted Poor Countries' (2018) 31 Leiden Journal of International Law 363.

to host state laws or policies relating to sustainability (such as environmental legislation); contract changes or unanticipated increases in costs resulting from the implementation of sustainability policies (in relation, for example, to environmental assessment requirements or regulations relating to the acquisition or preservation of arable land) and overall issues of interpretation of contracts.

Generally speaking, where parties choose a particular law to govern a contract, they also exclude the operation of other systems of law. Exceptions to the principle of party autonomy are limited, and dominated by the private international law rules of the forum. Thus Article 11 of the Hague Principles on Choice of Law in International Commercial Contracts[96] provides that a court is not prevented from applying overriding mandatory laws of the forum *which apply irrespective of the law chosen by the parties* (Art 11(1), author's emphasis); the law of the forum determines when overriding mandatory provisions of another law must be applied or taken into account (Art 11(2)); a provision of chosen law may be excluded 'only if and to the extent that the result of such application would be manifestly incompatible with fundamental notions of public policy … *of the forum*' (Art 11(3), author's emphasis); and the law of the forum determines if a court may or must apply or take into account the public policy 'of a State the law of which would apply if there were no choice of law' (Art 11(4)) (which might, but would not necessarily, lead to the law of the host state).[97] In principle, where dispute resolution takes place in a non-host state forum, host state laws, including laws designed to promote sustainability, will not be applied unless a formulation can be found that requires the forum to recognise the importance of sustainability and the host state's interest in promoting it.

The Commentary on Article 11[98] focuses on the difficult concept of illegality in the state of performance (often, in common law systems, based on the decision in *Ralli Bros v Cia Naviera Sota y Aznar*)[99] or attempts to undermine the laws of foreign states, both of which may give rise to public policy considerations *in the forum*.[100] In practice, the application of these principles is essentially defensive and far from routine. The public policy exception is applied with great reticence

96 HCCH, 40: Principles on Choice of Law in International Commercial Contracts (approved 19 March 2015) <https://www.hcch.net/en/instruments/conventions/full-text/?cid=135> accessed 7 January 2021, Art 11.

97 In relation to Art 11(5), the Principles leave the consideration of mandatory law other than applicable law or public policy up to the arbitral tribunal, 'if the arbitral tribunal is required or entitled to do so.'

98 HCCH, 40: Principles on Choice of Law in International Commercial Contracts, Text and Commentary <https://www.hcch.net/en/instruments/conventions/full-text/?cid=135#text> accessed 10 May 2021.

99 [1920] 2 KB 287; discussed in *Ryder Industries v Woo* [2015] HKCFA 32. See also Martin Davies, Andrew Bell, Paul Le Gay Brereton and Michael Douglas, *Nygh's Conflict of Laws in Australia* (10th ed, LexisNexis Butterworths 2020) 503–505.

100 See the much-criticised decision in *Kaufman v Gerson* [1904] 1 KB 591; *Royal Boskalis Westminster NV v Mountain* [1999] QB 674.

by domestic courts, and cases involving public policy mainly involve requests that the court not enforce particular contracts or judgments rather than that they give effect to foreign laws. If the forum is not located in the host state, the scope for application of mandatory laws of the host state which relate to sustainability, such as environmental laws, is thus potentially limited.

In this regard, Lehmann looks at reform of private international law for the purpose of causing private international rules and lawyers to engage more with foreign (in this case, host state) regulation in a less defensive fashion.[101] This would include revising the rule whereby the forum court generally considers only the public policy of the forum (which would generally exclude the enforcement of foreign governmental interests) and requiring the forum to give more emphasis to relevant foreign public policy rules. Van Loon raises the possibility of expanding the scope of public policy considerations generally by referring to 'internationally recognised human rights norms that may inform … public policy.' This could be expanded to include an internationally accepted concept of sustainable development.[102] This would also allow the forum to give effect to overriding mandatory rules of 'another legislator who has a legitimate interest in the application of its regulation.'[103] Michaels suggests the development of a new private international law which would allow and facilitate the extraterritorial application of foreign (in this case, host state) regulation on the basis, among other things, of a doctrine of 'positive comity'.[104]

This concept should also potentially be extended to the application in foreign courts of regulatory rules of the host state implemented to support sustainable development (such as environmental regulation), as well as protective host state laws and regulations designed to provide protection for vulnerable domestic stakeholders in an infrastructure project (for example, employees and consumers, and potentially small businesses and contractors). Although the principle of party autonomy generally allows parties to nominate the use of foreign law in smaller cross-border transactions in the private international law context, instruments such as the Choice of Court Agreements Convention (Art 2(1)) specifically exclude consumer and employment contracts from the scope of civil and commercial agreements, thus implicitly acknowledging the interest of the host state in those relationships. It can also be argued that the host state has a role and interest in regulating to ensure the prompt, consistent and effective protection of

---

101 Matthias Lehmann, 'Regulation, global governance and private international law: squaring the triangle' (2020) 16(1) Journal of Private International Law 1 16, 21.

102 Hans van Loon, 'The Global Horizon of Private International Law', Inaugural Lecture, Private International Law Session, 2015 (vol 380) [59].

103 ibid 22.

104 Ralf Michaels, 'Towards a Private International Law for Regulatory Conflicts' (2016) 59 Japanese Yearbook of International Law 175, 194. See for fuller discussion, 192–197.

domestic stakeholders in an infrastructure project, and the host state could certainly put in place a mandatory domestic dispute resolution process to achieve this result. It may, however, be difficult to find strong public policy grounds supporting the enforcement of these requirements in foreign courts unless the size and nature of the disputes and the nature of the beneficiaries is tightly drawn and the need for protective legislation is very clear.

Widening the current very narrow view of public policy should, as suggested above, take the form of allowing the forum to incorporate into its own public policy the public policy concerns of the state where the infrastructure project is located. Private international law rules of the forum should also incorporate recognition of international support for sustainable development into domestic public policy and thus give the forum the scope to take sustainability into account in interpreting a contract and deciding appropriate remedies. This would allow, or require, the forum to take into account potentially relevant requirements of host state laws specifically implementing the SDGs in relation to the project, even if host state law is not the governing law. As noted above, support for a wider application of sustainability principles can be obtained from international initiatives and agreements, including the SDGs themselves, the EU's suggested amendment to the ECT, and bilateral and plurilateral agreements such as the Trans-Pacific Partnership[105] (now in force, with some amendments, as the Comprehensive and Progressive Agreement for Trans-Pacific Partnership).[106] The Trans-Pacific Partnership, for example, while recognising the 'sovereign right' of each party to establish its own laws and policies (Art 20.3), requires the effective enforcement of, for example, environmental law (Art 20.4) by states and sets out detailed requirements in relation to a range of environmental issues.

In conjunction with this, a more general purposive approach to the interpretation of treaties and contracts could be adopted which incorporates the concept of sustainable development and recognises the significance of a disputed contract which is part of an infrastructure project in implementing a sustainable infrastructure project.[107]

---

105 Trans-Pacific Partnership Agreement between the Government of Australia and the Governments of: Brunei Darussalam, Canada, Chile, Japan, Malaysia, Mexico, New Zealand, Peru, Singapore, United States of America and Vietnam [2016] ATNIF 2 (TPP).

106 Comprehensive and Progressive Agreement for Trans-Pacific Partnership (Santiago, 8 March 2018) [2018] ATS 23 (CPTPP), incorporating most of the terms of the Agreement for Trans-Pacific Partnership (TPP).

107 See also UNCITRAL, Working Group 3, 'Interpretation of investment treaties by treaty Parties, Note by the Secretariat', UN Doc A/CN.9/WG.III/WP.191 (17 January 2020) 7, noting the inclusion of policy objectives such as sustainable development in the Preamble to order to provide 'context' and an 'object and purpose' for the purposes of interpretation.

4.2. SUSTAINABILITY OF THE INFRASTRUCTURE PROJECT

The discussion above considers the role of the forum in relation to a single contract dispute. However, another very important issue in relation to multi-party infrastructure projects is the practical question of what private international law could do to maintain the sustainability of an infrastructure project taken as a whole – from inception through the various stages of implementation and dispute resolution in event of a dispute – and to reduce the impact on the project of the splintering of disputes and inconsistent methods and results of dispute resolution and enforcement across different parts of the same infrastructure project. The Bahamas case study discussed above[108] is a good example of how this can happen (and how it is facilitated by existing private international law rules) and the difficulties this can cause the host state and the stakeholders, as well as the contract parties.

Here it is suggested that private international law rules should support an internationally purposive approach to jurisdiction which builds on existing case law on the importance of consolidation of disputes and gives priority to the importance of supporting sustainability objectives through a 'whole project approach' to dispute resolution and enforcement even where the contract parties have failed to negotiate a consolidated approach to dispute resolution. This would require modification of the current rigorous approach towards strict enforcement of exclusive jurisdiction clauses in individual contracts expressed, for example, in the Choice of Court Agreements Convention, EU law[109] and statutory law, and require a return to a form of judicial discretion to override an exclusive jurisdiction clause in favour of consolidating related proceedings. It would in some cases require courts (or tribunals) to extend their jurisdiction so that they could hear all disputes related to the project. It would also oblige other courts or adjudicative bodies to surrender jurisdiction over disputes related to the project (despite the presence of an exclusive jurisdiction clause or arbitration agreement) and to enforce the resulting judgment (or award).[110] It would also require a review of the current strict requirements relating to compliance with, and enforcement of, international arbitration agreements – a major step in view

108 See section 3.1.

109 See, for example, Regulation (EU) No 1215/2012 of the European Parliament and of the Council of 12 December 2012 [2012] OJ l 351/1 (Brussels I Recast) Art 31(2).

110 See generally Lise Johnson, Lisa Sachs and Nathan Lobel, 'Aligning International Investment Agreements with the Sustainable Development Goals' (2019) 58 Columbia Journal of Transnational Law 58. See also the interesting discussion in Cedric Ryngaert, *Selfless Intervention: The Exercise of Jurisdiction in the Common Interest* (OUP 2020) 16, presenting a theory supporting 'selfless' cosmopolitan extraterritoriality by means of the exercise of jurisdiction, and using as one 'manifestation' of this port state jurisdiction over illegal, unreported and unsustainable fishing and marine pollution.

of the growth in international arbitration and the respectful consideration given to agreements to arbitrate worldwide.[111]

The importance of consolidating multiple disputes relating to the same issue is already recognised in both litigation and arbitration.[112] A significant reason used by common law courts in exercising their discretion to override an exclusive jurisdiction clause is the risk of fragmentation of proceedings leading to parallel proceedings and an adverse impact on third parties.[113] Resolving disputes relating to a large-scale and important infrastructure project in a cohesive and manner and with a view to preserving the sustainability of the project taken as a whole should be an appropriate public policy consideration which is relevant to the court's decision to consolidate proceedings.[114] Taking steps to ensure the efficient and unified resolution of all disputes relating to the project would further support sustainability by supporting the efficient administration of justice. Interested parties and stakeholders could also be granted a broader right to participate in – or to make submissions in – the litigation or arbitration to reflect the substantial interests of the host state and the domestic stakeholders in the infrastructure project.

The issue here is that the exercise of discretion by one court enabling it to hear all related disputes could, instead of consolidating proceedings, contribute to an increase in parallel and overlapping proceedings and competition between courts to hear cases. The circumstances under which one court could adjudicate the entire project would therefore have to be strictly defined. If the parties are unable to achieve agreement on one venue in the contract documents, the most effective way to implement such a rule may well be by drafting an international instrument or revising such instruments as the Choice of Court Agreements Convention, first, to set out objective criteria for determining the appropriate court or tribunal to hear such consolidated litigation (for example, closest

111 See generally discussion in Robert Wai, 'Private v Private: Transnational Private Law and Contestation in Global Economic Governance' in Horatia Muir Watt and Diego P Ferández Arroyo (eds), *Private International Law and Global Governance* (OUP 2015).

112 The 2021 version of the International Chamber of Commerce International Arbitration Rules (Rules 7–10) provides for joinder of additional parties, multiple party arbitrations, claims under more than one contract and consolidation of claims. The Rules are, however, limited by the scope of, and the parties to, the arbitration agreement. <https://iccwbo.org/dispute-resolution-services/arbitration/rules-of-arbitration/> accessed 23 April 2021.

113 See, for example, *Donohue v Armco Inc* [2002] 1 Lloyd's Rep 425, 433, per Lord Bingham; *CSR Ltd v Cigna Insurance Australia Ltd* (1997) 189 CLR 345. Practice among common law courts varies, however. See e.g. discussion in Anthony Kennedy, 'Approaches to Jurisdiction Clauses in Anglophone African Common Law Countries: Principle and Policy' (2019) 27 African Journal of International and Comparative Law 378.

114 See *Incitec Ltd v Alkimos Shipping Corp* [2004]138 FCR 496, 506 per Allsop J: 'What really are of importance in weighing against the operation of the exclusive jurisdiction clause are … (c) any other appropriate public policy consideration than can be discerned in all the circumstances.'

connection with the project (which would often be the host state), location of the project, jurisdiction nominated for disputes in the principal project agreement (for example, construction or financing) or a majority of the project agreements, court already engaged in hearing proceedings in relation to the project); secondly, to require other courts (or tribunals) to refuse or surrender jurisdiction; thirdly (and ideally), for investors and contractors to waive rights under IIAs or include IIA claims in the consolidated proceeding; and finally, to require courts both to enforce the resulting judgments and awards and to refuse enforcement of competing judgments and awards.

All of the proposals above would of course represent major modifications to the well-entrenched principle of party autonomy and divergence from the policy of holding the parties to a commercial contract to their bargain.[115] They are particularly difficult in the context of international arbitration, given its highly independent and de-linked operation as a mechanism of global governance. However, as Wai suggests,[116] it is probably time to look again at party autonomy and the deference given to international commercial arbitration. This reconsideration should be done generally, not just in relation to consolidation of proceedings but also in projects which are important to sustainable development, to ensure that the interests of the host state and domestic stakeholders in the sustainable completion of infrastructure projects are adequately considered.

4.3. IIAs AND ISDS

A number of studies have highlighted the lack of provisions in IIAs which emphasise or give effect to the importance of sustainable development, particularly in IIAs to which less-developed and developing countries are parties.[117] In particular, the question arises as to how the state can ensure that,

---

115 See HCCH, 37: Convention on Choice of Court Agreements (concluded 30 June 2005, in force 1 October 2015) <https://assets.hcch.net/docs/510bc238-7318-47ed-9ed5-e0972510d98b.pdf> accessed 15 April 2021, Art 5, limiting the ability of the court to refuse to take jurisdiction; Robert Wai, 'Private v Private: Transnational Private Law and Contestation in Global Economic Governance' in Horatia Muir Watt and Diego P Ferández Arroyo (eds), *Private International Law and Global Governance* (OUP 2015) 245 et seq, on 'anti-comity',

116 Robert Wai, 'Private v Private: Transnational Private Law and Contestation in Global Economic Governance' in Horatia Muir Watt and Diego P Ferández Arroyo (eds), *Private International Law and Global Governance* (OUP 2015) 50–52.

117 See, for example, UNESCAP, 'Policy Brief: Sustainable Development Provisions in Investment Treaties' (22 October 2018) <https://www.unescap.org/resources/sustainable-development-provisions-investment-treaties> accessed 15 April 2021, commenting that BITs of Asia-Pacific LDCs and LLDCs contain smaller numbers of sustainable development provisions; Gudrun Monika Zagel, 'India's International Investment Agreements (IIAs) and Sustainable Development: Friends or Foes?' (2020) XII Indian Journal of International Economic Law 1 (analysing India's reform of its IIAs from the perspective of incorporating sustainability considerations into IIAs).

in an ISDS proceeding, the principles of sustainability, the specific provisions of host state law directed at sustainable development and the ability of the host state to change its law in order to support its aspirations of sustainable development are considered and given appropriate weight.[118] Many suggestions have been made on how to improve the drafting of IIAs, by, for example, including provisions relating to sustainability as a principle of interpretation of the IIA, allowing the state contracting parties to issue interpretations of articles of the treaty,[119] and clarifying the host state's ongoing right to regulate in the public interest.[120]

These initiatives support a greater emphasis being placed on host state regulation and regulatory power to support sustainability, together with improvements to host state regulation on matters such as the environment to comply with international treaties and standards. In ISDS, therefore, it is important that sustainability objectives of the host state are not considered to be purely a matter of host state law which can be sidelined or ignored by the use of private international law principles to apply international law to claims under IIAs. Similarly, sustainability should not be taken into consideration in disputes only if specific references to sustainable development or particular sustainable issues such as the environment are specifically incorporated in the treaty. In addition, therefore, to the suggestions of UNCITRAL and other commentators on the incorporation of considerations of sustainability into IIAs, choice-of-law rules applied by tribunals resolving investor–state disputes should provide a greater role to host state law, in particular by giving due regard to the importance of the sustainable objectives and aspirations of the host state. Consideration of both the host state's international commitments in relation to sustainability (for example, the environment) and international moves toward sustainability, through such initiatives as the UN Guiding Principles on Business and Human Rights[121] and the SDGs, should also be taken into account in the interpretation of the treaty and the application of international law principles to the implementation of the IIA.

---

118 See discussion in Lise Johnson, Lisa Sachs and Nathan Lobel, 'Aligning International Investment Agreements with the Sustainable Development Goals' (2019) 58 Columbia Journal of Transnational Law 58.

119 See Comprehensive and Progressive Agreement for Trans-Pacific Partnership (Santiago, 8 March 2018) [2018] ATS 23 (CPTPP), incorporating most of the terms of the Agreement for Trans-Pacific Partnership (TPP), Art 9.26.

120 Lise Johnson, Lisa Sachs and Nathan Lobel, 'Aligning International Investment Agreements with the Sustainable Development Goals' (2019) 58 Columbia Journal of Transnational Law 58, 116 et seq. See also European Union, 'EU text proposal for the modernisation of the Energy Charter Treaty (ECT)' (2020), <https://trade.ec.europa.eu/doclib/docs/2020/may/tradoc_158754.pdf> accessed 22 April 2021, draft Articles on Sustainable Development, 10–12.

121 See UN Human Rights Office of the High Commissioner website <https://www.ohchr.org/Documents/Publications/GuidingPrinciplesBusinessHR_EN.pdf> accessed 22 April 2021.

4.4. ENFORCEMENT AND HOST STATE LIABILITY

UNCTAD, in developing its Investment Policy Framework for Sustainable Development, sets out as one of its objectives for the reform of IIAs '[s]hielding host countries from unjustified liabilities and high procedural costs'.[122] As discussed above, public financing and support often plays an important role in infrastructure projects and the host state may therefore incur liabilities for infrastructure, not just through IIAs, but also for loan commitments, bond issues, guarantees, concessions, government undertakings and supports, stabilisation clauses and breaches of contract. The full extent of these potential liabilities may not be readily quantifiable either at the inception of the project or thereafter. A sovereign state, even if poorly managed, has ongoing obligations to its citizens in terms of economic and social responsibilities, the preservation and protection of public assets for the benefit of its citizens and the sustainability – both short term and long term – of all of its activities. Host state liability, sovereign debt, and the enforcement of judgments and awards against the state and its assets under the differing sovereign immunity rules in force across the world can therefore raise important questions of sustainability for less-developed and emerging states. This is particularly relevant in relation to infrastructure projects, which are both long term and likely to be expensive.

One option is to address the liability of the host state to its creditors as a systemic issue. Thus, just as commercial parties limit their liability through non-recourse financing agreements, holding companies, special purpose vehicles, planned insolvencies and contractual limits on liability, a state could – by contract or legislation or both – impose a limit on its liability in relation to a specified investment, investment contract or project agreement (as well as in relation to guarantees and miscellaneous project supports). The challenge for private international law would be ensuring that this limit – which represents an important public interest of the host state – is recognised in enforcement and other proceedings outside the host state.[123] The challenge for the host state would be in negotiating such a limit, or in attempting retrospectively to impose it in respect of liabilities including under its IIAs.

---

122 See UNCTAD, Investment Policy Framework for Sustainable Development, 8 <https://unctad.org/en/PublicationsLibrary/diaepcb2015d5_en.pdf> accessed 12 July 2021, which addresses the issue of preserving space to regulate and shielding host countries from 'unjustified liabilities and excessive costs,' and the challenge of striking an appropriate balance between regulation and an open economy (17 et seq).

123 Note, for example, that the 2019 HCCH Convention on the Recognition and Enforcement of Foreign Judgments in Civil or Commercial Matters (adopted 2 July 2019, not in force) <https://www.hcch.net/en/instruments/conventions/full-text/?cid=137> accessed 23 April 2021, specifically excludes from enforcement 'sovereign debt restructuring through unilateral State measures' (Art 2.1(q)), although it does not exclude enforcement against states or attempt to deal with the issue of immunities of states (Arts 2.4 and 2.5).

The second option is to use principles of sustainability to exercise a degree of control over international enforcement actions. As discussed above, domestic rules on state immunity are often based on the UN Convention on the Jurisdictional Immunity of States, which separates commercial and non-commercial activities and transactions of states in determining whether immunity applies at the adjudication or enforcement and execution stage.[124] The rules of the forum of enforcement may therefore require a distinction to be drawn between the commercial and non-commercial use of assets, impose different rules on the burden of proof, and raise the question how much credence should be given to certificates issued by the debtor state.[125] This can, however, be a problematic distinction, particularly in the case of smaller states with limited assets, since execution of judgments against bank accounts and other assets of the state – even if deemed to be used for 'commercial purposes' – may well have an adverse effect on the state's ability overall to satisfy its own social and economic obligations. Execution on a court-by-court, country-by-country, asset-by-asset basis – whether contested by the state or pursuant to a waiver of sovereign immunity – does not currently require or allow the courts to consider the impact on the overall social stability of the state or the question of sustainability.

Megliani,[126] drawing, inter alia, on the UNCTAD Principles on Promoting Responsible Sovereign Lending and Borrowing,[127] proposes several ways in which private international law could be utilised to assist heavily indebted states. One of these is drawing on the concept of 'international public policy' to incorporate acknowledgement of the duty of the state to provide essential services to its citizens as a basis for the suspension of the recognition and enforcement of a foreign judgment against a heavily indebted state.[128] The second proposes the recognition in a foreign forum of the duty of the state to provide services as an overriding mandatory rule of the host state[129] as a basis on which the host state could resist – or suspend – a claim that could threaten the performance of this obligation. Sustainability, and the duty of the state towards its citizens in respect of sustainable development, could also be relevant here.

---

124 Adrian Lai, 'State Immunity in the Context of Enforcement of Investment Arbitration Awards' in Julian Chaisse, Leïla Choukroune and Sufian Jusoh (eds), *Handbook of International Investment Law and Policy* (Springer 2020) 27.

125 ibid.

126 Mauro Megliani, 'For the Orphan, the Widow, the Poor: How to Curb Enforcing by Vulture Funds against the Highly Indebted Poor Countries' (2018) 31 Leiden Journal of International Law 363, 372.

127 Amended and restated as of 10 January 2012. See <https://unctad.org/system/files/official-document/gdsddf2012misc1_en.pdf> accessed 7 May 2021.

128 Mauro Megliani, 'For the Orphan, the Widow, the Poor: How to Curb Enforcing by Vulture Funds against the Highly Indebted Poor Countries' (2018) 31 Leiden Journal of International Law 363, 379.

129 ibid 380.

At a minimum, rules relating to the execution of a judgment against specific sovereign assets should move away from the commercial and non-commercial distinction. Particularly in the case of developing countries, courts asked to enforce host state debts should be required to consider whether the state legitimately requires the assets for social or economic purposes, including vital sustainable development projects, rather than determining whether particular assets are used or set aside for a particular commercial or non-commercial purpose. The decision of the High Court of Australia in *Firebird v Nauru*[130] that it is necessary to look behind what appears to be a commercial activity to determine whether it is in fact the provision of essential services and noting that the circumstances of one foreign state may differ from another[131] may be of assistance in supporting an argument that domestic rules on sovereign immunity should also take into account considerations of sustainability in looking at execution over state assets. This should be no more difficult than the current detailed analysis of the use or purpose of each asset.

5. CONCLUSION

SDG 9 on 'industry, innovation and infrastructure' has a broad scope, and is particularly important for less-developed and emerging countries. This chapter focuses on Target 9.1 and sustainable infrastructure – that is, the construction and operation of high-quality, reliable and resilient infrastructure that is fit for purpose now and in the future. Sustainable infrastructure must not just support economic development – it must also support human well-being, accessibility and connectivity. Infrastructure projects, which will often be large and expensive, take large amounts of time to build and have a wide-reaching impact on the host state, investors, financiers, contractors and domestic stakeholders, must also be sustainable.

Private international law has a significant role to play in infrastructure projects. It is relevant to the contractual elements of financing, constructing and operating an infrastructure project and its related contracts, as well as to the resolution of disputes, international enforcement (including, potentially, against the host state) and host state liability under international investment agreements. Utilisation of the doctrine of party autonomy in choice of law and dispute resolution, for example, serves as a means of risk mitigation for the financiers, contractors and other parties by allowing for the internationalisation of major contracts and related disputes. However, it may also separate the host state, its legal system (including its interests in sustainability and the sustainability of

130 *Firebird v Nauru* [2015] HCA 43, [112] et seq, per French CJ and Kiefel J.

131 ibid [125].

the project) and the domestic stakeholders in a major project from the dispute resolution process and enforcement. The application of private international law rules relating to choice of law and forum, as well as rules on jurisdiction and enforcement, may affect the overall sustainability of the project by allowing for the fragmentation of disputes and disparate decisions on liability. In the case of investor–state disputes, private international law may facilitate the use of international or foreign law in place of host state investment regulation which incorporates sustainable development principles. Developing and emerging states may also be adversely affected by international enforcement of state debt liabilities incurred as a result of state support for major projects.

The discussion shows that regulatory private international law has a potential role to play in supporting the overall sustainability of infrastructure development projects and sustainable infrastructure, primarily through requiring the recognition of the importance of sustainability of the project and sustainable development. This should apply at a number of levels. Private international law could, and should, provide – in the case of a dispute conducted under a law other than host state law, and in an international forum – for the recognition as a matter of public policy both of the relevance and importance of the concept of sustainability and of host state regulations designed to support sustainability. Private international law should move away from the priority given to party autonomy and the unchallenged right of parties to select dispute resolution fora by adopting an approach to jurisdiction which allows a court or tribunal to consolidate disputes relating to an infrastructure project in order to support the interests of the host state and its stakeholders in the completion and sustainable implementation of the project. It should also move towards an approach to applicable law in ISDS which gives priority to the importance of sustainability and sustainable development regulation in the implementation of investment policy and, finally, it should support consideration of the importance of sustainability in relation to enforcement of liabilities against states, particularly less-developed and emerging states, arising from disputes over infrastructure.

In short, while there are considerable practical difficulties in moving away from the current approach, it is suggested that private international law rules should and can be less focused on enforcement of the commercially based doctrines of autonomy in choice of law and the importance of holding contractual parties to their choice of forum, and more focused on requiring the application of a more purposive approach in relation to sustainability, sustainable infrastructure and the SDGs. This would recognise both international support for the principle and importance of sustainability and the relevance and importance of host state law directed at implementing the SDGs.

SDG 10: REDUCED INEQUALITIES

Thalia Kruger

Goal 10: Reduce inequality within and among countries

10.1 By 2030, progressively achieve and sustain income growth of the bottom 40 per cent of the population at a rate higher than the national average

10.2 By 2030, empower and promote the social, economic and political inclusion of all, irrespective of age, sex, disability, race, ethnicity, origin, religion or economic or other status

10.3 Ensure equal opportunity and reduce inequalities of outcome, including by eliminating discriminatory laws, policies and practices and promoting appropriate legislation, policies and action in this regard

10.4 Adopt policies, especially fiscal, wage and social protection policies, and progressively achieve greater equality

10.5 Improve the regulation and monitoring of global financial markets and institutions and strengthen the implementation of such regulations

10.6 Ensure enhanced representation and voice for developing countries in decision-making in global international economic and financial institutions in order to deliver more effective, credible, accountable and legitimate institutions

10.7 Facilitate orderly, safe, regular and responsible migration and mobility of people, including through the implementation of planned and well-managed migration policies

10.a Implement the principle of special and differential treatment for developing countries, in particular least developed countries, in accordance with World Trade Organization agreements

10.b Encourage official development assistance and financial flows, including foreign direct investment, to States where the need is greatest, in particular least developed countries, African countries, small island developing States and landlocked developing countries, in accordance with their national plans and programmes

10.c By 2030, reduce to less than 3 per cent the transaction costs of migrant remittances and eliminate remittance corridors with costs higher than 5 percent

1. INTRODUCTION

Sustainable Development Goal 10 (SDG 10) is to reduce inequality within and among countries. Inequality exists on many levels and between many groups of people. The current COVID-19 pandemic has exposed and enhanced existing inequalities[1] and seems even to be increasing inequality.[2]

The purpose of this chapter is to critically look at current private international law rules of jurisdiction and connecting factors to appoint applicable law in the light of the goal to reduce inequality. The focus will be on economic and financial inequality. More specifically, Targets 10.1, 10.2, 10.4, 10.5 and 10.c will be under consideration. Gender equality will not be dealt with in this chapter, as it is analysed in the discussion of SDG 5.

After setting the context (section 2 below), the next section (section 3) will discuss existing private international law instruments and doctrines in various fields that affect SDG 10. Section 4 will narrow the focus to the European Parliament's Resolution about value chain due diligence. It will analyse whether current proposals succeed in attaining Target 10.2, namely including all potential victims of human rights abuses, irrespective of their ethnicity, origin and race. Thereafter section 5 will consider reform proposals, i.e. where current private international law can be improved to better ensure income growth (Target 10.1), economic, social and political inclusion of all persons (Target 10.2), and reduce unequal outcomes (Target 10.4). The concluding section (section 6) will collect the results of sections 3–5.

2. SDG 10: CONTEXT

In the period 2012–2017, the bottom 40 per cent of the world's population received less than 25 per cent of the overall income or consumption, while the top 10 per cent received at least 20 per cent of the income.[3] Some countries fare a lot worse than others. The Gini index, calculated by the World Bank, shows which the most unequal countries are.[4] Private international law, with its focus on cross-border relations and disputes, could play a role in the reduction of inequality among countries. This could happen through a fairer distribution

---

1 See United Nations, 'Progress towards the Sustainable Development Goals', Report of the UN Secretary-General, UN Docs E/2020/57 (28 April 2020) <https://undocs.org/en/E/2020/57> accessed 4 December 2020.

2 See for instance 'Companies have raised more capital in 2020 than ever before', *The Economist* (9 December 2020) <https://www.economist.com/business/2020/12/09/companies-have-raised-more-capital-in-2020-than-ever-before> accessed 10 December 2020.

3 Of all countries for which data exist. See United Nations, 'Progress towards the Sustainable Development Goals', Report of the UN Secretary-General, UN Docs E/2020/57 (28 April 2020) <https://undocs.org/en/E/2020/57> accessed 4 December 2020.

4 <https://databank.worldbank.org/reports.aspx?source=2&series=SI.POV.GINI&country=> accessed 13 December 2020.

of transaction costs, a reduction of remittance costs and a fairer allocation of goods and property. Although indirectly, private international law could also help to reduce inequalities within countries. This would be through targeted use of supply-chain legislation, in order to ensure that foreign undertakings (or multinationals) respect human rights in the places where they are active.

The problem of inequality has drawn the attention of economists,[5] lawyers,[6] activists[7] and authors generally.[8] The Club of Rome, an international and interdisciplinary group of experts set up at the end of the 1960s,[9] identified 'poverty in the midst of plenty' as one of the 'complex of problems troubling men of all nations'.[10] They saw the challenge of 'relationships between producer and consumer nations as the remaining resources become concentrated in more limited geographical areas'.[11] This realisation brings private international law to the centre stage: it is private international law that will determine the law applicable to transactions between big and small traders, between exporters and importers, between sellers and consumers, whenever they are cross-border transactions.

The way in which so-called connecting factors (connecting a fact, dispute or transaction to a particular legal system) operate will determine who gets protection when. Connecting factors for property law, contract law, tort law, corporate law, insolvency law and succession law may all be relevant in the fight against inequality.

---

5 Donella H Meadows, Dennis L Meadows, Jørgen Randers and William W Behrens III, *The Limits to Growth* (Universe Books 1972); full text also available at <http://www.donellameadows.org/wp-content/userfiles/Limits-to-Growth-digital-scan-version.pdf> accessed 14 May 2021; Thomas Piketty, *Capital in the Twenty-First Century* (English ed, Belknap Press 2017); Kate Raworth, *Doughnut Economics* (Penguin Random House 2017); Sander Heijne and Hendrik Noten, *Fantoomgroei* [Phantom Growth] (Business Contact 2020); Institute of New Economic Thinking, mentioning as one of its key principles that '*inequality and distribution* matter as much to the economy as growth and productivity': <https://www.ineteconomics.org/about/our-purpose> accessed 14 May 2021.

6 Katharina Pistor, *The Code of Capital: How the Law Creates Wealth and Inequality* (Princeton University Press 2019).

7 E.g. those involved in the French Revolution; Karl Marx and Frederick Engels, *Communist Manifesto* <https://www.marxists.org/archive/marx/works/1848/communist-manifesto/> accessed 14 May 2021.

8 Thomas More, *Utopia*, first published in Latin in Leuven in 1516; despite the author's instruction that the text should only be read in Latin, it has been translated into several languages; George Orwell, *Animal Farm* (first published in England in 1945); Jo Walton, *The Just City* (Corsair 2014).

9 The group was established after a first gathering called by Aurelio Peccei in Rome in 1968.

10 Donella H Meadows, Dennis L Meadows, Jørgen Randers and William W Behrens III, *The Limits to Growth* (Universe Books 1972); full text also available at <http://www.donellameadows.org/wp-content/userfiles/Limits-to-Growth-digital-scan-version.pdf> accessed 14 May 2021, 10.

11 ibid 67.

While the milestones are measured by the comparison of incomes, inequalities must be understood in terms of both income and capital.[12] Dealing with inequality can therefore not be restricted to employment, but must take into account the shifting of money and under which conditions such shifting takes place, i.e. transactions (contracts) between undertakings or individuals.

At first sight, private international law is not relevant for Target 10.1, as calculations to measure the attainment of this target are national and do not gauge inequality between persons in different countries. However, the wages paid by businesses that mainly export goods to richer countries can have an influence on income growth. The businesses that import the goods have some leverage to improve these wages. This can be addressed through value chain due diligence, as will be discussed in section 4 below.

Regarding Target 10.2, private international law can be instrumental to the implementation of policies that aim at social, economic and political inclusion and that have effects across borders. This can be done by making stringent laws with high thresholds of due diligence accessible to persons living and working in countries where the legal thresholds are not as high. Such accessibility depends on rules of civil jurisdiction and on connecting factors in contract law, tort law and corporate law. This will be further discussed in section 4 below.

Current private international law rules often lead to unequal outcomes, contrary to what Target 10.3 envisages. These rules for instance provide a forum for some persons (consumers or employees) who have suffered from torts (including human rights infringements) but not for others. They apply different legal standards to the same tort depending on where the damage arose.

Private international law determines which law governs wage and social protection, referred to in Target 10.4: see the discussion in this volume of SDG 8 by Ulla Liukkunen. Private international law moreover determines which businesses will be subjected to the regulation and monitoring of global financial markets and institutions under Target 10.5. Targets 10.6, 10.a and 10.b operate more on the public international level and this chapter will not focus on them.[13] Private international law also plays an important role in the attainment

---

12 This is a central argument made by Thomas Piketty, *Capital in the Twenty-First Century* (English ed, Belknap Press 2017) 32–36. He shows that inequality grows as long as return on capital is higher than the growth of the economy. He also compares the level of wealth to how long it takes to gather the same amount through income.

13 Concerning international trade, see Bernd G Janzen and Emily S Fuller, 'Assessing the UN Sustainable Development Goals through the Lens of International Trade Law' (2015) 44(1) International Law News 23, referring at 25 to the Transatlantic Trade and Investment Partnership and the possible contribution to the attainment of SDG 10 by its anticorruption provisions. Foreign direct investment is also relevant here and that field is on the cusp of public and private international law, but this falls beyond the scope of the current chapter. See however Clair Gammage, 'Investment Facilitation for Development: A Rights Perspective of Multilateral Governance' (2019) 10 Indian Journal of International Economic Law 31.

of Target 10.7 on orderly, safe, regular and responsible migration and mobility of people. Sabine Corneloup and Jinske Verhellen discuss the issue in this volume in relation to SDG 16. Finally, introducing international administrative cooperation, a well-known tool of private international law, could assist in reducing remittance costs in accordance with Target 10.c.

3. EXISTING PRIVATE INTERNATIONAL LAW RULES

3.1. PROPERTY

In property law, the connecting factor is generally quite straightforward: the law of the place where the property is situated is applicable. This law determines who the owner of the property is. It also determines whether other real rights can be affixed to the property, such as securities, hypothecs and retention of title.[14] This connecting factor has different effects for movables and for immovables, and for corporeal and incorporeal property.

3.1.1. Movable Property, Especially Cultural Property

For movables, questions arise when a thing does not stay in the same place and might at some point be found at a place where it was not supposed to be. This is the problem of *conflit mobile*: the place where the thing was located at what point in time? The way in which this *conflit* is solved has an important influence on the social inclusion of all persons (Target 10.2), especially equal access to cultural heritage. Many objects of cultural value were removed from their places of origin by former colonial powers. Similarly, in the Second World War, various objects of art were displaced. In order to ensure a resolution of the issue in a way that treats all involved in an equal manner, the connecting factor should point to the law of the place where the property was located at the moment it was stolen or illicitly removed. If the (cultural) property was removed from a place where private ownership was not acknowledged, but rather the property was deemed to belong to a community, that view of ownership should apply. Taking the property away from the community should be considered illicit according to the law of that place.

Attempting to solve the *conflit mobile* may require a complex investigation of a series of property transfers over a number of years: each transfer of the property would have to be investigated according to the law of the place where it was at the time of the transfer. This is difficult, but it can be, and has been, done.

---

14 See for instance Regulation (EU) No 2015/848 of 20 May 2015 on insolvency proceedings, Art 10 on retention of title.

The Museum of Fine Arts in Ghent houses a painting entitled 'Portrait of Ludwig Adler' by Oskar Kokoschka. In 2009 the descendants of the heirs of a Jewish art collector claimed restitution of the painting on the basis that the collector was forced by the Nazi regime to sell it. The city of Ghent appointed a commission to investigate the claim. The commission traced back the various transfers and considered the law to be applied to each one of these.[15] The investigation did not have a positive result for the claimants in this instance, mainly[16] because the transfer by the art collector was found to be pursuant to a valid and voluntary sale, before the persecution of his family started. However, the meticulous way in which the connecting factors were considered is an example of what can be done.

The EU,[17] UNESCO[18] and UNIDROIT[19] rules on cultural property have the aim of ensuring the restitution of such property if it is stolen or illicitly exported. However, obligations of restitution apply to objects that were removed after the instruments came into force.[20] This means that the current owners of property illicitly removed a long time ago (e.g. during the colonialist period or during the Second World War) are not subject to these duties. This has led to various communities not being able to get their cultural property back, even from countries that ratified the instruments by the time they claimed restitution. Adjudicators less diligent than Ghent city's commission could get away with only considering the current location of the goods rather than their previous location. Under the law of the current location of the property, the possessor could acquire ownership after only a few years. This was the case with 'Master Zhang Gong', a Song-Dynasty Buddha statue, which Chinese villagers unsuccessfully claimed back in a Dutch court.[21] A group of Hopi Native Americans faced the same kind of rejection when they claimed restitution of Katsina masks, which were considered inalienable property under their law, but not under French law, where the masks were at the time of the proceedings.[22] A better approach in

15 Johan Erauw, 'The City of Ghent on 16 June 2011 declined the request for restitution of a Kokoschka-painting presently in the Ghent Museum of Fine Arts and sold late 1937-early 1938 by a German Jewish family from Dresden' (2011) 2 Tijdschrift@ipr.be 140.

16 The Commission also considered the prescription of the claim.

17 Directive 2014/60/EU of 15 May 2014 on the return of cultural objects unlawfully removed from the territory of a Member State, available at <https://eur-lex.europa.eu/legal-content/EN/TXT/?uri=CELEX%3A02014L0060-20140528> accessed 12 July 2021.

18 UNESCO Convention on the Means of Prohibiting and Preventing the Illicit Import, Export and Transfer of Ownership of Cultural Property, concluded in Paris on 14 November 1970.

19 UNIDROIT Convention on Stolen or Illegally Exported Cultural Objects, concluded in Rome on 24 June 1995.

20 UNIDROIT Convention on Stolen or Illegally Exported Cultural Objects, Art 10; Directive 2014/60/EU, Art 14.

21 Evelien Campfens, 'Whose Cultural Property? Introducing Heritage Title for Cross-Border Cultural Claims' (2020) 67 Netherlands Review of International Law 257, 258.

22 ibid 259. The author points out that stolen artefacts often surface only decades later (at 261).

private international law would be to always consider the historical location of (cultural) property. If a country or community considers something to be part of their cultural heritage, that thing could be deemed to be situated in that place. If a question about ownership arises years later, those deciding on the matter would have to look at the law where the thing is deemed to be situated rather than where it is located when the question arises.

When disputes arise, the bases of jurisdiction determine which courts can hear these disputes. In the EU, a claim for the recovery of cultural property can be brought in the EU country where the property is found.[23] This forum for the revindication claim may be useful to those who want to ensure the attainment of Target 10. 2, i.e. the inclusion of all to have access to their cultural heritage. However, having access to a court will not be sufficient if the difficulty of the *conflit mobile* is not resolved.

3.1.2. Immovable Property

For immovables, the connecting factor of the place of location allows states to adopt certain policies with respect to ownership, real rights and lease. They will see those policies applied to all immovable property within their territory. If the state seeks to introduce rules of redistribution to address past injustices or effects of war, these will without question apply to all the immovable property in the state. If the state wants to regulate sales prices, it can do so throughout the country. It is not relevant whether the owners, intending buyers or lessors live in the state or have its nationality. This is an inclusive rule, thus complying with Target 10.2. By the same token, where states decide to limit purchase of property by foreign nationals or foreign businesses, their policies will also apply to all the immovable property in their territory. The same is true for policies of expropriation and nationalisation. In this sense, the connecting factor permits states to reduce inequalities in their state.

However, authorities do not always apply this clear connecting factor in a precise manner. This can lead to increased inequality. Two examples are worth noting in this regard. The first concerns a recent incident in Flanders, Belgium.[24] A number of families were evicted from subsidised rented houses because an investigation found that they owned immovable property in other states.[25]

---

23 Regulation (EU) No 1215/2012 of the European Parliament and of the Council of 12 December 2012 on jurisdiction and the recognition and enforcement of judgments in civil and commercial matters (Brussels I), Art 7(4). This provision did not exist in the previous versions, but was inserted in the 2012 version of the Regulation for the first time.

24 The matter at hand falls under the competence of the Regions and not of the Federal State.

25 Stef Meerbergen, '25 gezinnen moeten sociale woning in Lier verlaten, omdat ze ook vermogen hebben in het buitenland', *vrt NWS* (21 March 2021) <https://www.vrt.be/vrtnws/nl/2021/03/21/25-gezinnen-moeten-sociale-woning-in-lier-verlaten-omdat-ze-ook/> accessed 24 April 2021.

The families concerned mostly had roots in other countries, such as Turkey. They owned or co-owned houses, apartments or land in these countries. Let us assume that Belgian and Flemish law apply to the rental contracts.[26] Inequalities can emerge when considering the value of these properties and the access that the families have to the property and what they can do with it. Under the current rules, these aspects do not play a role. The tenants are considered to be relatively poor by the standards of Belgian society, otherwise they would not be granted the subsidies. Through private international law, authorities should take into account the concepts of property (and co-property) and the value of the property in the country where the property is situated. This could help to reduce the (possibly unintentional) unequal treatment of persons.

The second example concerns Chinese investment in Namibia and Zimbabwe. The laws of Namibia and Zimbabwe apply to rights on immovable property, such as mining concessions. These laws are however not always applied strictly for a number of reasons, including a need for help by China, a 'colonial legal hangover', poor laws or poor enforcement mechanisms, and possibly also corruption.[27] Mapaure gives the example of the Zimbabwean Indigenization and Empowerment Act of 2008, which concerns the ceding of 51 per cent of shareholdership to black Zimbabweans. A Chinese company active in Zimbabwe was exempted from this requirement (thus it did not have to cede 51 per cent of shareholdership). The Zimbabwean government viewed it as inappropriate to apply the requirement in the same way to a Chinese company as to Western corporations such as Standard Chartered and Barclays. The argument was that the Chinese company helped in the government's farm mechanisation programme, while the Western corporations did nothing to support the land reform programme and even tried to sabotage it.[28] Even though this example does not involve the ownership of land, it does illustrate the point of inconsistent application of laws. Here the correct use of private international law would indeed assist in reducing inequalities: those between various investors and between foreign investors and local companies and communities. Disregarding equal application of the laws might achieve a short-term goal (such as mechanisation of farms), but can exacerbate inequality in the

---

26 If no choice of law is made in an agreement for the lease of immovable property, the agreement is governed by the law of the place where the property is situated: Regulation (EC) No 593/2008 of the European Parliament and of the Council of 17 June 2008 on the law applicable to contractual obligations (Rome I), Art 4(1)(c).

27 See the informative and nuanced report by Clever Mapaure, 'Chinese Investments in Zimbabwe and Namibia: A Comparative Legal Analysis' (2014) esp 14 and 21 <https://www.researchgate.net/profile/Clever-Mapaure/publication/311875115_Chinese_Investments_in_Zimbabwe_and_Namibia_A_Comparative_Legal_Analysis/links/5b2799b5aca2723fbeef7dbb/Chinese-Investments-in-Zimbabwe-and-Namibia-A-Comparative-Legal-Analysis.pdf> accessed 24 April 2021.

28 ibid 25.

long run, with local communities still not having their country's wealth (fertile soil and a rich deposit of various minerals) in their own hands.

Disputes regarding immovable property will most often have to be brought to court at the place where the property is located.[29] This rule of jurisdiction enables states to have disputes heard in their domestic courts, which will apply their own law. Thus, the rules on jurisdiction echo the connecting factors and can help to attain the same goals of the reduction of inequality. Private international law offers appropriate tools here, but as set out in the previous paragraphs, the local legal structure and enforcement mechanisms also have to be adequate in order to ensure that inequality can effectively be reduced.

3.2. CONTRACT

Contract law facilitates the transfer of property and capital. The connecting factor linking a contract to the law of a particular country can help to increase income growth (Target 10.1) and in reducing inequalities of outcome (Target 10.4), or can have the opposite effect.

3.2.1. The Law Chosen by the Parties

Contract law is in the first place an area of party autonomy. This is also true for private international law: contracting parties can choose the law that they wish to have their contract governed by. This approach is broadly accepted worldwide, for example in the Hague Principles of 2015,[30] in the Inter-American Convention,[31] in the Rome I Regulation,[32] in the OHADAC Draft Model Law on Private International Law[33] and a suggested set of principles for Africa,[34] as well as in many domestic legal systems.[35]

The general freedom in contract law is limited in some areas, where legislators have thought it appropriate to protect vulnerable parties such as consumers

---

29 Brussels I, Art 24(1).

30 Hague Principles on Choice of Law in International Commercial Contracts (2015), Art 2.

31 Inter-American Convention on the Law Applicable to International Contracts (Mexico, 1994), Art 7.

32 Rome I, Art 3.

33 OHADAC Draft Model Law of Private International Law (2014), Art 45.

34 See also Jan L Neels, 'The African Principles on the Law Applicable to International Commercial Contracts – a first drafting experiment' (2021) Uniform Law Review, 1, 5–6.

35 See for instance Richard Frimpong Oppong, *Private International Law in Commonwealth Africa* (CUP 2013) 135; Chikwuma Samuel Adesina Okoli and Richard Frimpong Oppong, *Private International Law in Nigeria* (Hart Publishing 2020) 187; Christopher F Forsyth, *Private International Law* (5th ed, Juta 2012) 317; Swiss Code of Private International Law, Art 116.

and employees.[36] Where party autonomy is accepted, it allows resourceful (and wealthy) individuals and corporations to navigate between legal systems in a way that maintains, consolidates or increases capital where it is.[37] A broad recognition of private international law of party autonomy as a connecting factor therefore could increase or at least preserve inequality, rather than reducing it.

This issue is exacerbated in today's global trade where contracts are single links in a much larger value chain, including several sales, (multiple stages of) transport and insurance contracts.[38] These chains can increase inequalities as businesses source their goods in countries where labourers are paid less in order to reduce the price of the goods and increase their profit margin. Such a global system increases inequality: the businesses make more profit and consumers in rich countries can buy more goods with the same money, but at the same time workers in poor countries do not see their income increasing. We see this happening in the textile industry, in manufacturing technologies and in agriculture.[39] Rather than reducing wage gaps, they stay the same or increase.

Legislators (at the regional level, for example in the EU, but also at the national level) have been seeking to regulate value chains to some extent and to introduce value chain due diligence. The EU adopted rules on supply chain due diligence with respect to certain minerals and metals in 2017.[40] The rules apply to 'Union importers' of the minerals and metals concerned.[41]

---

36 For example, for consumers, Rome I designates the law of the place of their habitual residence (Art 6) while in normal sales contracts the connecting factor is the habitual residence of the seller (Art 4(1)(a)). A choice of law cannot detract the protection the consumer would have had under the otherwise applicable law according to the latter conflict-of-law rule.

37 Katharina Pistor, *The Code of Capital: How the Law Creates Wealth and Inequality* (Princeton University Press 2019).

38 Tomaso Ferrando, 'About capitalism and private international law' in Horatia Muir Watt, Lucia Bíziková, Agatha Brandão de Oliveira and Diego P Fernández Arroyo, *Global Private International Law* (Edward Elgar Publishing 2019) 237–243. Regarding transport, including multimodal transport and the role that contract law can play in sustainability, see Ellen Eftestøl-Wilhelmsson, 'European Sustainable Freight – The Role of Contract Law', Helsinki, Legal Studies Research Paper No 8 <https://papers.ssrn.com/sol3/papers.cfm?abstract_id=1865791> accessed 10 December 2020.

39 For a discussion of the latter, see Samuel Fulli-Lemaire, 'Grappling with (global supply) chains: transnational human rights litigation in the agribusiness sector' in Horatia Muir Watt, Lucia Bíziková, Agatha Brandão de Oliveira and Diego P Fernández Arroyo, *Global Private International Law* (Edward Elgar Publishing 2019) 244–253.

40 Regulation (EU) No 2017/821 of 17 May 2017 laying down supply chain due diligence obligations for Union importers of tin, tantalum and tungsten, their ores, and gold originating from conflict-affected and high-risk areas, consolidated version, available at <https://eur-lex.europa.eu/legal-content/EN/TXT/?uri=CELEX%3A02017R0821-20201119> accessed 12 July 2021. The Regulation applies from 1 January 2021. EU legislation follows on from the introduction of US rules requiring listed companies to disclose the use of conflict minerals under the US Dodd-Frank Act. See also Victoria Stork, 'Conflict Minerals, Ineffective Regulations: Comparing International Guidelines to Remedy Dodd-Frank's Inefficiencies' (2016-2017) 61 New York Law School Law Review 429.

41 Regulation 2017/821, Arts 1(2) and 2(l).

The sphere of application is further defined neither by the places of residence or business of the importers nor by the law applicable to the transactions, but by the specified metals.[42] This is not a traditional connecting factor in private international law.

If we were to apply standard private international law connecting factors, the contracting parties would be able to choose the law applicable to each separate contract and thus turn a blind eye to atrocities that happen higher up in the chain.[43] On the other hand, businesses could use their bargaining power to require their contracting partners to comply with due diligence. In this way they can oblige their contracting partners to implement their own due diligence standards in their contracts, as well as in the next link up the chain.[44] This way of securing due diligence and human rights compliance is determined by businesses' own codes of conduct or reporting duties, where they exist. According to some, more than nudging is needed to implement such chains of diligence (see section 4 below for a discussion of initiatives taken in this regard).

3.2.2. *In the Absence of Choice: The Closest Connection*

In the absence of choice by the parties, a contract is governed by the law with which it is most closely connected. How this close connection is determined depends on the details of the private international rules of each system.

Some have a broad and flexible rule. The Second Restatement in the US, for example, contains rather weak presumptions, in other words leaving a large discretion to the judges. The Inter-American Convention on the Law Applicable to International Contracts again takes a flexible approach, referring to the law of the state with which the contract has the closest ties. To determine this, courts will take into account 'all objective and subjective elements of the contract' and also 'the general principles of international commercial law recognized by international organizations.'[45] Common law countries in Africa also generally follow a flexible approach, with courts looking at objective factors.[46] South Africa uses the imputed chosen law, in other words the law that the parties *ought* to have chosen. This is a rather open-ended approach to get to the law that

42 Regulation 2017/821, Art 1 and Annex I.

43 See Tomaso Ferrando, 'About capitalism and private international law' in Horatia Muir Watt, Lucia Bíziková, Agatha Brandão de Oliveira and Diego P Fernández Arroyo, *Global Private International Law* (Edward Elgar Publishing 2019) 237–238.

44 See Samuel Fulli-Lemaire, 'Grappling with (global supply) chains: transnational human rights litigation in the agribusiness sector' in Horatia Muir Watt, Lucia Bíziková, Agatha Brandão de Oliveira and Diego P Fernández Arroyo, *Global Private International Law* (Edward Elgar Publishing 2019).

45 Inter-American Convention on the Law Applicable to International Contracts, Art 9.

46 Richard Frimpong Oppong, *Private International Law in Commonwealth Africa* (CUP 2013) 131–138.

is most closely connected to the contract. Of the factors South African law takes into account, particular importance is attached to the place of performance.[47]

Other legal systems have stronger presumptions. The Rome I Regulation in the EU belongs to this category, referring to the habitual residence of the party effecting the characteristic performance and for the most common contracts defining who that party is (e.g. the seller, the service provider and so forth).[48] If all the circumstances show that the contract is manifestly more closely connected to a legal system other than the one designated by the connecting factor (the habitual residence of the party effecting the characteristic performance),[49] the contract shall be governed by the former legal system.[50] In considering this closer connection, whether the contract has a very close connection to another contract shall be taken into account. This is only mentioned in a recital, not in the provisions themselves, and it is only one of the relevant elements (as indicated by the words 'inter alia').[51]

The drawback of the flexible approach is that it is not always certain and predictable to contracting parties. The drawback of the approach with strong presumptions is that it might too easily tilt the balance in favour of the stronger party: the seller, the service provider, etc. This will not assist in reducing inequality. In particular, the fact that Rome I does not take account of the place where the contract was performed, but of the habitual residence of the party effecting that performance, could have this effect.

The Hague Convention on the Law Applicable to the International Sale of Goods[52] has struck a different balance: the starting point (in the absence of choice) is that the law of the seller's place of business applies. However, if the contract provides expressly that the seller had to deliver the goods in the state of the buyer's place of business, the law of the latter applies.[53] In this way, the Convention does not necessarily give preference to the law of the stronger party and could lead to a better and more equal inclusion of all parties (Target 10.2) and to equality of outcomes (Target 10.4). Von Mehren

47 Christopher F Forsyth, *Private International Law* (5th ed, Juta 2012) 329–335.

48 Rome I, Art 4. The OHADAC Draft Model Law of Private International Law, Art 46 and the Swiss Code on Private International Law, Art 118 are very similar.

49 Rome I, Art 3(1) pointing at the party effecting the characteristic performance for the most common contracts (e.g. the seller for sales contracts) and Art 3(2) containing the general rule for all other contracts.

50 Under Rome I: Art 4(3).

51 Rome I, Recital 20.

52 Convention on the Law Applicable to the International Sale of Goods of 22 December 1986 (not yet in force).

53 Hague Convention on the Law Applicable to the International Sale of Goods, Art 8(2). This exception also applies if negotiations were conducted and the contract concluded by and in the presence of the parties, in the state of the buyer's pace of business or if the contract was concluded on terms determined mainly by the buyer and in response to a call for tenders by the buyer.

in the Explanatory Report to the Convention points out that this provision, in its original version, was introduced upon a proposal by the delegation of Algeria, which had argued that it was the 'sole achievement of the developing countries which were often buyers and wished to see the buyer's law applied, at least in certain cases.'[54] Unfortunately, the Convention was not successful in gaining contracting states. The potential of private international law is thus not fully used.

3.3. TORT

The applicable tort law will determine whether the claimants will be able to get compensation for the wrongs committed against them and also what the level of such compensation would be. Linked to the issue of value chains introduced in the previous subsection is the situation in which victims of human rights abuses (often in poor countries) seek compensation from businesses lower down the value chain (those that ordered the goods and sell them at a large profit). Can the inequality that has been expressed above be reduced by applying a tort law that will ensure proper accountability?[55] And which is the most appropriate law to get proper compensation? How can the connecting factor ensure that there are no undue money flows that increase instead of reduce inequality?

In tort law, the rule that the law of the place of the tort (*lex loci delicti*) applies is broadly followed.[56] Some countries follow the double actionability rule, which means that the claimant has to show that the alleged tort is wrongful both in the state of the forum and in the state where it was committed.[57] Some have a more flexible approach: seeking the law that is most closely connected to the tort by considering various relevant factors.[58]

---

54 Arthur Taylor von Mehren, 'Convention on the Law Applicable to the International Sale of Goods: Explanatory Report' (1987) para 70 <https://assets.hcch.net/docs/b9e13840-b2af-4456-bd48-31b3bbd8eecf.pdf> accessed 26 August 2021, quoting verbatim from the proceedings of the Special Commission.

55 Reporting and codes of conduct can assist victims in establishing liability in tort: Rachel Chambers and Anil Yilmaz-Vastardis, 'The New EU Rules on Non-Financial reporting. Potential Impacts on Access to Remedy?' (2016) 10 Human Rights and International Legal Discourse 18, 32; Lara Blecher, 'Codes of Conduct: The Trojan Horse of International Human Rights Law' (2017) 38 Comparative Labour Law and Policy Journal 437, 439 and 456–467.

56 Christopher F Forsyth, *Private International Law* (5th ed, Juta 2012) 354.

57 Richard Frimpong Oppong, *Private International Law in Commonwealth Africa* (CUP 2013) 149–153. See also Chikwuma Samuel Adesina Okoli and Richard Frimpong Oppong, *Private International Law in Nigeria* (Hart Publishing 2020) 204–207, explaining that the double actionability rule is applied as a jurisdiction rule in Nigeria, while the country applies the *lex loci delicti* as connecting factor for applicable law.

58 Second Restatement of Conflict of Laws in the US.

The general rule under the EU's Rome II Regulation[59] is that the applicable law is that of the place where the damage occurs, 'irrespective of the country in which the event giving rise to the damage occurred' (Art 4). This is a specific application of the *lex loci delicti* rule. The provision contains an exception: if the tort is manifestly more closely connected to the law of another country, that law will apply. This is an escape clause, and shall not be applied too lightly.[60] For environmental damage, the connecting factor is broader, allowing the claimant to choose whether to base their claim on the law of the country of the damage or the law of the country where the event giving rise to the damage occurred (Art 7). This choice is not available to the claimant in relation to tortious claims for human rights abuses. Giving victims this choice could assist in the pursuit for equality and inclusion for all (Target 10.2). It would give them the option of relying on the strictest law, for example that imposing a high standard of environmental protection and high compensation for victims. Thus, this is an area where private international law techniques could be further developed to pursue equality and inclusion for all.

3.4. CORPORATIONS

In corporate law, the two conflicting approaches to finding the home of a corporation are well known.[61] Some legal systems adhere to the real seat theory, i.e. considering a corporation to be at home at the place where it has its main activities, principal place of business and/or central administration. Others prefer the statutory seat theory, considering a corporation to be at home at the place where it is registered/incorporated.

The statutory seat theory promotes legal certainty (SDG 16) and autonomy for corporations and the people behind them, while the real seat theory allows states to regulate the activities on their territory in a more targeted fashion. States could for instance regulate reporting duties on corporate social responsibility and due diligence for all companies that are managed from their territory.[62] This would allow them to cast the net more broadly rather than

---

59 Regulation (EC) No 864/2007 of 11 July 2007 on the law applicable to non-contractual obligations.

60 Recital 18, Rome II.

61 See for instance the studies by Justin Borg-Barthet, *The Governing Law of Companies in EU Law* (Hart Publishing 2012); Miroslawa Myszke-Nowakowska, *The Role of Choice of Law Rules in Shaping Free Movement of Companies* (Intersentia 2014).

62 Obligations to report on human rights due diligence or to disclose risks will fit into the annual reporting duties the law imposes on companies. See Rachel Chambers and Anil Yilmaz-Vastardis, 'The New EU Rules on Non-Financial reporting. Potential Impacts on Access to Remedy?' (2016) 10 Human Rights and International Legal Discourse 18, 25.

restricting the policies to those companies that have chosen the state as their place of incorporation. It would allow a pursuit of equality in the regulation and monitoring of financial markets (Target 10.5). Reporting on corporate social responsibility and due diligence, as explained in section 3.2.1 above, can assist in reducing the inequalities that can arise in the value chain when businesses buy cheap commodities or rely on cheap labour further up the chain.[63]

In the EU, for example, targeting of policies through the use of the real seat doctrine has been made more difficult by the freedom of establishment: Member States are not permitted to impose undue restrictions on companies' freedom of establishment under the EU Treaty.[64] The CJEU's case law increasingly put pressure on the use by Member States of the real seat theory because of the restrictions it places on free movement in the EU. This pressure has led several Member States to amend their legislation and cross over to the statutory seat approach.[65]

This prevalence of the statutory seat theory reduces legislators' room for imposing certain policies, for example of corporate social or environmental responsibility, often imposed by way of reporting duties (Target 10.5).

In its pure form, the statutory seat theory in combination with the focus on single legal entities instead of economic conglomerates, allows businesses to shirk any due diligence requirements by moving to a place with no or fewer such requirements.

---

63 There is some debate about the effectiveness of reporting in order to ensure remedies for victims. See Adam S Chilton and Galit A Sarfaty, 'The Limitations of Supply Chain Disclosure Regimes' (2017) 53 Stanford Journal of International Law 1; Rachel Chambers and Anil Yilmaz-Vastardis, 'The New EU Rules on Non-Financial reporting. Potential Impacts on Access to Remedy?' (2016) 10 Human Rights and International Legal Discourse 18; Lise Smit, Claire Bright, Irene Pietropaoli, Juliane Hughes-Jennett and Peter Hood, 'Business Views on Mandatory Human Rights Due Diligence: A Comparative Analysis of Two Recent Studies' (2020) 5 Business and Human Rights Journal 261. On the difficulty to measure impact, see Liliana Lizarazo-Rodríguez, 'The UN "Guiding Principles on Business and Human Rights": Methodological Challenges to Assessing the Third Pillar: Access to Effective Remedy' (2018) 36 Nordic Journal of Human Rights 353.

64 CJEU C-212/97 *Centros v Erhvervs- ogSelskabsstyrelsen* (9 March 1999) ECLI:EU:C:1999:126; CJEU C-208/00 *Überseering BV v Nordic Construction Company Baumanagement* (5 November 2002) ECLI:EU:C:2002:632; CJEU 167/01 *Kamer van Koophandel en Fabrieken voor Amsterdam v Inspire Art* (30 September 2003) ECLI:EU:C:2003:512; CJEU C-210/06 *Cartesio* (16 December 2008) ECLI:EU:C:2008:723; CJEU C-106/16 *Polbud- Wykonawstwo* (25 October 2017) ECLI:EU:C:2017:804. See also Justin Borg-Barthet, *The Governing Law of Companies in EU Law* (Hart Publishing 2012) and Miroslawa Myszke-Nowakowska, *The Role of Choice of Law Rules in Shaping Free Movement of Companies* (Intersentia 2014).

65 For a discussion of the recent reform of Belgian company law, among others to change from the real seat to the statutory seat theory, see Robby Houben and Johan Meeusen, 'The competition for corporate charters: Belgium wants a (bigger) piece of the pie' (2020) Zeitschrift für Europäisches Privatrecht 11.

3.5. ADMINISTRATIVE COOPERATION

In contemporary private international law, increasing attention is being paid to cross-border cooperation on administrative and judicial levels.[66] Such cooperation, especially of the administrative nature,[67] can play diverse roles with respect to the transferring of funds. Two specific scenarios are briefly discussed below.

One role of administrative cooperation is to facilitate transfers of funds and to reduce costs. Target 10.c is that transaction costs of migrant remittances must be reduced to less than 3 per cent by 2030. Remittances are important for communities where an extended group of people (not only direct family members) depend on money sent back by one person working abroad. For these community members and for the individual working abroad, it is important to get as much money as possible back to the community and to lose as little as possible to administrative costs. Remittances are an important source of income for some countries and formal remittances to developing countries reach huge amounts, to the extent that they are one of the most significant international flows of funds.[68] Finding solutions that allow remittances at reasonable costs, while stamping out risks such as money laundering and terrorist financing, requires public–private partnerships between regulators and banks.[69] Such partnerships could be enhanced if regulators in different countries worked together and created cross-border systems for the transfer of funds. The Permanent Bureau of the Hague Conference on Private International Law raised the idea of working on this topic as early as 2006[70] and on

66 See for instance Andrea Schulz, 'The Cooperation between Central Authorities under the Brussels IIa Regulation' in Ilaria Viarengo and Francesca Villata, *Planning the Future of Cross Border Families* (Hart Publishing 2020) 399–425, showing the important role of central authorities in matters of parental responsibility. The increasing importance can also be seen in the mounting number of provisions in conventions and EU Regulations on cooperation: Hague Conventions rely on this form of international cooperation; the recently adopted Regulation (EU) No 2019/1111 of 25 June 2019 on jurisdiction and the recognition and enforcement of judgments in matrimonial matters and the matters of parental responsibility, and on international child abduction (Brussels II *ter*) contains numerous and detailed provisions.

67 Judicial cooperation is no less important, but there is not a close link to the topics under discussion in this chapter. Issues such as cooperation to gather evidence or gain knowledge of foreign law are not discussed here.

68 According to Louis De Koker, Supriya Singh and Jonathan Capal, 'Closure of Bank Accounts of Remittance Service Providers: Global Challenges and Community Perspectives in Australia' (2017) 36 University of Queensland Law Journal 119, 120, formal remittances to developing countries reached US$442 billion in 2016.

69 ibid.

70 See Permanent Bureau of the Hague Conference on Private International Law, 'Some Reflections on the Utility of Applying Certain Techniques for International Co-operation Developed by the Hague Conference on Private International Law to Issues of International Migration', Preliminary Document No 8 of March 2006 for the attention of the Special Commission of April 2006 on General Affairs and Policy of the Conference, 7–8 <https://www.hcch.net/en/governance/council-on-general-affairs/archive> accessed 26 August 2021.

various subsequent occasions.[71] The project has to date not evolved to the stage of a working group.[72]

A second role of administrative cooperation is to ensure fairness and correctness in the transfers of funds, and to avoid corruption and bribes. This is a role that is present in the cross-border enforcement of maintenance claims. In international adoption, central authorities have the task of being a filter between intending parents (often in rich countries) and orphanages or organisations caring for children (often in poorer countries).[73] By funnelling adoptions through these central and other appointed or approved authorities, which cooperate with each other internationally, illicit or inappropriate payments for adoption can be avoided.[74]

3.6. OVERRIDING MANDATORY LAW AND PUBLIC POLICY

Some principles are so crucial for the political, economic or social order of a state that their application cannot be set aside by connecting factors pointing to another legal system.[75] This is a higher threshold than for domestically mandatory rules. The latter refers to principles that cannot be derogated from by contract when the contract is attached to that legal system.[76]

Private international law instruments allow for the application of overriding mandatory law.[77] These rules can be useful in ensuring that policies aimed at businesses can be applied in a coherent way, working towards equality of outcome for all involved and not only victims in that particular country (Target 10.2).

71 See the Preliminary Documents prepared for the General Affairs and Policy meetings of the following years (until 2010): <https://www.hcch.net/en/governance/council-on-general-affairs/archive> accessed 26 August 2021.

72 The Tourists and Visitors Project (<https://www.hcch.net/en/projects/legislative-projects/protection-of-tourists> accessed 26 August 2021) addresses entirely different matters.

73 Hague Convention of 29 May 1993 on Protection of Children and Co-operation in Respect of Intercountry Adoption.

74 Hague Adoption Convention, Arts 7 and 8.

75 Definition by the CJEU in Joined Cases C-369/96 *Arblade* and C-376/96 *Leloup* (23 November 1999) ECLI:EU:C:1999:575, para 30; subsequently taken over in Rome I, Art 9(1). The same wording is also used by the OHADAC Draft Model Law on Private International Law, Art 69(1).

76 Rome I, Art 3(3) and (4).

77 Hague Principles on Choice of Law in International Commercial Contracts, Art 11(1) and (2); Hague Convention of 22 December 1986 on the Law Applicable to Contracts for the International Sale of Goods (not yet in force), Art 17; Rome I, Art 9(2) and (3); Rome II, Art 16; Inter-American Convention on the Law Applicable to International Contracts, Art 11; OHADAC Draft Model Law on Private International Law, Art 69. See also Swiss Code of Private International Law, Art 18. See also the contribution by Ulla Liukkunen in this volume, explaining the potential of overriding mandatory rules.

For instance, seeing rules on due diligence as overriding mandatory provisions could lead to their application regardless of the choice made by the parties in their contracts. Such overriding mandatory provisions set their own scope. They do not necessarily follow the logic of the connecting factors as discussed above. A legislator[78] can for instance impose due diligence duties on businesses operating within its market or importing goods into its market. The effect will be that businesses will be held to those rules no matter which corporate law applies to them (for instance due to their place of incorporation, their statutory seat) and no matter which law they elect to govern their contracts and no matter which law applies to contracts further up the supply chain.

In a similar way as for overriding mandatory law, private international law makes provision for public policy. If the connecting factors lead to foreign rules that are repugnant to the legal system of the forum, their application can be refused via the public policy exception. This provision is even more prevalent in multilateral private international law instruments.[79] It is however, more of a post facto equaliser than a tool for legislators to ensure equality of outcome upfront.

4. SPECIFIC APPLICATION

The European Parliament on 10 March 2021 approved a Resolution on corporate due diligence and corporate accountability.[80] The Resolution is addressed to the European Commission and requests the latter to initiate legislation on this topic.[81]

---

78 This can be a national, regional or international legislator. EU law, for instance, can also qualify as overriding mandatory principles: CJEU C-381/98 *Ingmar v Eaton Leonard Technologies* (9 November 2000) ECLI:EU:C:2000:605. See also Xandra E Kramer, 'The interaction between Rome I and mandatory EU private rules – EPIL and EPL: communicating vessels?' in Peter Stone and Youseph Farah (eds), *Research Handbook on EU Private International Law* (Edward Elgar Publishing 2017) 248–284.

79 Hague Principles on Choice of Law in International Commercial Contracts, Art 11(3) and (4); Hague Convention of 2 October 1973 on the Law Applicable to Products Liability, Art 10; Hague Convention of 22 December 1986 on the Law Applicable to Contracts for the International Sale of Goods, Art 18; Rome I, Art 21; Rome II, Art 26; Inter-American Convention on the Law Applicable to International Contracts, Art 18; Inter-American Convention on General Rules of Private International Law (Montevideo, 1979), Art 5; OHADAC Draft Model Law on Private International Law, Art 68.

80 European Parliament Resolution of 10 March 2021 with recommendations to the Commission on corporate due diligence and corporate accountability, 2020/2129(INL) <https://www.europarl.europa.eu/doceo/document/TA-9-2021-0073_EN.html#title1> accessed 26 August 2021.

81 Under EU law, legislation must be initiated by the European Commission, but the European Parliament can request it to do so (Art 225 Treaty on the Functioning of the European Union). If the Commission receives such a request, but refrains from initiating legislation, it must inform the European Parliament of its reasons.

Some states also have legislation on value chain due diligence, but this chapter will not be able to discuss this.[82]

4.1. INTRODUCING THE EUROPEAN PARLIAMENT'S RESOLUTION

The Resolution is aimed at holding corporations that operate in the European Union accountable for human rights abuses higher up the value chain. It refers in its preamble to the Sustainable Development Goals. It does not single out any of them, but its aims are in line with Target 10.2 (among others). It refers to levelling the playing field and mitigating unfair competitive advantages due to lower standards of protection.[83] By seeking to oblige businesses to conduct due diligence over their entire supply chains, the Resolution aims to reduce inequalities in who is protected by policies and legislation on due diligence and human rights protection. People anywhere in the world, irrespective of their origin or race, should benefit from the enhanced due diligence: victims should be able to hold undertakings liable for damage caused by undertakings under their control in cases of human rights violations or environmental harm.[84]

The Resolution considers that '[s]ound due diligence requires that all stakeholders be consulted effectively and meaningfully'.[85] 'Stakeholders' is defined broadly:

> individuals, and groups of individuals whose rights or interests may be affected by the potential or actual adverse impacts on human rights, the environment and good governance posed by an undertaking or its business relationships, as well as organisations whose statutory purpose is the defence of human rights, including social and labour rights, the environment and good governance. These can include workers and their representatives, local communities, children, indigenous peoples, citizens' associations, trade unions, civil society organisations and the undertakings' shareholders.[86]

The European Parliament thus seeks to ensure that the due diligence obligations on undertakings benefit not only citizens living in the EU, where the legislation

82 For an overview see British Institute of International and Comparative Law, Civic Consulting, Directorate-General for Justice and Consumers (European Commission) and LSE, 'Due Diligence requirements through the supply chain', Study commissioned by the European Commission (January 2020) 170–175 <https://op.europa.eu/en/publication-detail/-/publication/8ba0a8fd-4c83-11ea-b8b7-01aa75ed71a1/language-en> accessed 26 August 2021.

83 Resolution, para 1.

84 Resolution, para 26.

85 Consideration 38 of the proposed Directive, annexed to the Resolution.

86 Proposed Directive, Art 3(1).

is made, but also in the countries where undertakings carry out their mining or production operations. In this way, it is aiming at social and economic inclusion of all.

4.2. CONTEXT OF UN ACTION

The European Parliament's Resolution subscribes to the United Nations Guiding Principles on Business and Human Rights (UNGPs)[87] and their three-pronged approach of protect, respect and remedy. 'Protect' refers to the state's duty to protect against human rights abuses.[88] 'Respect' means that corporations have the responsibility to respect human rights. 'Remedy' focuses on the right of access to remedies for victims of human rights abuses.

The UN Draft Treaty on Business and Human Rights, dating from 2018 (the 'Zero Draft')[89] and revised in 2019[90] and in 2020,[91] should also be mentioned. This Treaty would oblige states parties to require their business enterprises to exercise human rights due diligence (Art 6 2020 Draft). States would also have to ensure access to remedies and legal liability for human rights violations (Arts 7 and 8), but the Treaty does not foresee harmonisation of this aspect. This liability should also cover activities of a transnational character and failures to prevent harmful activities by other legal or natural persons with whom the business enterprise has contractual relationships (Art 8(7)). Thus, the protection seeks to be inclusive of all potential victims and reduce inequalities between them due to differences between legal systems.

Introducing standards of due diligence is a way for states to *prevent* human rights abuses. How far they can prevent abuses taking place on or outside their territory by corporations domiciled in or active in their territory is a matter for

87 Endorsed by the Human Rights Council of the UN in its Resolution 17/4 of 16 June 2011. The principles are available at <https://www.ohchr.org/documents/publications/guidingprinciplesbusinesshr_en.pdf> accessed 26 August 2021. See also Humberto Cantu Rivera, 'Negotiating a Treaty on Business and Human Rights: The Early Stages' (2017) 40 University of New South Wales Law Journal 1200 and Julia Bialek, 'Evaluating the Zero Draft of a UN Treaty on Business and Human Rights: What Does it Regulate and How Likely is its Adoption by States?' (2019) 9 Goettingen Journal of International Law 501.

88 See also Marco Fasciglione, 'The Enforcement of Corporate Human Rights Due Diligence. From the UN Guiding Principles on Business and Human Rights to the Legal Systems of EU Countries' (2016) 10 Human Rights and International Legal Discourse, 94.

89 Draft of 16 July 2018 <https://www.ohchr.org/Documents/HRBodies/HRCouncil/WGTransCorp/Session3/DraftLBI.pdf> accessed 26 August 2021.

90 Draft of 16 July 2019 <https://www.ohchr.org/Documents/HRBodies/HRCouncil/WGTransCorp/OEIGWG_RevisedDraft_LBI.pdf> accessed 26 August 2021.

91 Draft of 6 August 2020 <https://www.ohchr.org/Documents/HRBodies/HRCouncil/WGTransCorp/Session6/OEIGWG_Chair-Rapporteur_second_revised_draft_LBI_on_TNCs_and_OBEs_with_respect_to_Human_Rights.pdf> accessed 26 August 2021.

private international law.[92] One of the examples given in the Commentary to the UNGPs is the duty placed on parent companies to report on the global operations of the entire enterprise. Reporting duties would fall under the corporate law applicable to the parent company.[93] In some states, this would be the place of their statutory seat; in others, the place of their central administration or main activities.

Moreover, private international law is indispensable for ensuring *respect* by all corporations, in an inclusive way, regardless of where they are registered and where they conduct their activities. The UNGPs emphasise the need to respect all human rights. They acknowledge that some industries or contexts may bring higher risks of abuses and that specific groups may require particular attention, and aim to be inclusive (Target 10.2).[94] Principle 13 of the UNGPs requires businesses to 'prevent or mitigate adverse human rights impacts that are directly linked to their operations, products or services by their business relationships, even if they have not contributed to those impacts.' Principle 17 echoes this approach by explaining that an undertaking's due diligence should encompass impacts that it may 'cause or contribute to through its own activities, or which may be directly linked to its operations, products or services by its business relationships.'

Where undertakings contract across borders and where abuses occur somewhere in their value chain, ensuring that all in that value chain are equally included in the envisaged protection is a matter for private international law. This branch of the law defines whether the said undertakings can be held liable under tort law for actions that occurred elsewhere. Moreover, the said undertakings can also insert clauses guaranteeing human rights standards into their contracts with direct suppliers. They could impose duties on their direct suppliers to include these clauses into contracts further up the value chain. In the absence of such liability in the applicable tort or contact law, a last resort of private law is to consider value chain due diligence as overriding mandatory law or invoke it through public policy.

Establishing *remedies* that can work across borders, not only for those who live in the same country as the undertaking, is another challenge for private international law. States should avoid a situation where victims face a denial of justice in the host state and have no access to a court in the home state.[95] The Principles thus seek to ensure that remedies are available for all, irrespective of origin.

---

92 See for instance Principle 2 of the UNGPs: '*States should set out clearly the expectation that all business enterprises domiciled in their territory and/or jurisdiction respect human rights throughout their operations.*'

93 Principle 3(b) of the UNGPs refers to corporate law. The commentary also refers to non-discrimination, labour, environmental, property, privacy and anti-bribery laws.

94 Commentary to Principles 12 and 20 of the UNGPs.

95 Commentary to Principle 26 of the UNGPs.

4.3. PRIVATE INTERNATIONAL LAW AND THE EUROPEAN PARLIAMENT'S RESOLUTION

The Resolution does not propose to harmonise civil liability for cases of human rights infringement, and for this aspect, national law will continue to apply,[96] which is the entry point for private international law. The Resolution addresses private international law both directly and indirectly. It contains a provision specifying that the 'relevant provisions of this Directive are considered overriding mandatory provisions' under the Rome II Regulation (direct).[97] This is a watered-down version of the Motion for Resolution by the Committee on Legal Affairs,[98] which contained proposals for the amendment of the Rome II and Brussels I Regulations. Regarding minimum requirements for reporting and due diligence duties, the proposed Directive's scope extends beyond businesses that fall under EU law according to traditional connecting factors for corporations (indirect role for private international law).

4.3.1. *Law Applicable to Torts*

For applicable law, the UN Draft Treaty distinguishes between matters regarding substance of procedure of claims not specifically regulated in the instrument on the one hand, and human rights law relevant to the claims on the other hand (Art 11). The law applicable to the former category is that of the forum, including its conflict-of-law rules (Art 11(1)). This provision in essence means that the Draft Treaty, at least in its current form, does not address the matter of applicable law, but leaves this up to the national law of the forum state.[99] Relevant human rights matters may, upon request of the victim, be governed by the law of another state where the acts or omissions occurred or where the

96 See also Jan von Hein, 'Back to the Future – (Re-)Introducing the Principle of Ubiquity for Business-related Human Rights Claims', *Conflict of Laws* (October 2020) <https://conflictoflaws.net/2020/back-to-the-future-re-introducing-the-principle-of-ubiquity-for-business-related-human-rights-claims/> accessed 26 August 2021. He notes that this choice by the legislator is in line with existing approaches in EU legislation and with the principle of subsidiarity.

97 Resolution, Art 20.

98 See Report by the Committee of Legal Affairs and Motion for a European Parliament Resolution with recommendations to the Commission on corporate due diligence and corporate accountability, 2020/2129(INL) <https://www.europarl.europa.eu/doceo/document/A-9-2021-0018_EN.html> accessed 26 August 2021.

99 See also Claire Bright, 'Comment on Article 9 (Applicable Law) of the Revised Draft of the Proposed Business and Human Rights Treaty', Submission to the intergovernmental working group on transnational corporations and other business enterprises with respect to human rights (OEIGWG, July 2020) <https://www.biicl.org/publications/submission-on-the-issue-of-the-applicable-law-in-the-revised-draft-of-the-business-and-human-rights?cookiesset=1&ts=1614612697> accessed 26 August 2021, calling for the application of forum law to the exclusion of its conflict-of-law rules.

alleged infringer is domiciled (Art 11(2)). Let us take the example of victims whose health was harmed by operations of a local mining company that is the subsidiary of a large business established in a rich country. On the tort aspects of their claim, the victims should rely on the connecting factors of the forum, for example the place of the tort. Only on the abuse of human rights can they revert to the law of the place where the infringer is domiciled. If they manage to show that the infringer is the mother undertaking (which is not easy), they would have to separate the human rights and tort aspects of their claim. This might be artificial and difficult to do in practice: which aspects of harm to health are tort and which are human rights infringements? The draft rule in fact amounts to little more than an acknowledgement that courts are permitted to use human rights law as overriding mandatory law.

The European Parliament's Resolution does not contain a specific rule on the law applicable to tort. The Motion for Resolution, however, did contain a provision specifically for the law applicable to human rights abuses by undertakings operating in the EU. It sought to open up the options to the claimant in the same way as the current provision on environmental damage in Rome II, but went even further. Besides the law of the countries of the damage and of the event giving rise to the damage, claimants could also rely on the law of the parent company's domicile or the place where it operates (proposed Art 6a):

> In the context of business-related civil claims for human rights violations within the value chain of an undertaking domiciled in a Member State of the Union or operating in the Union within the scope of Directive xxx/xxxx on Corporate Due Diligence and Corporate Accountability, the law applicable to a non-contractual obligation arising out of the damage sustained shall be the law determined pursuant to Article 4(1), unless the person seeking compensation for damage chooses to base his or her claim on the law of the country in which the event giving rise to the damage occurred or on the law of the country in which the parent company has its domicile or, where it does not have a domicile in a Member State, the law of the country where it operates.

The four options are alternatives in a non-hierarchical way. The claimant could thus choose any of them. There are potentially more than four options, as 'domicile' could refer to the place of incorporation (statutory seat), central administration or principal place of business.[100]

100 According to Art 63 Brussels I. See also Geert van Calster, 'First analysis of the European Parliament's draft proposal to amend Brussels Ia and Rome II with a view to corporate human rights due diligence', *GAVC law – Geert van Calster* (October 2020) <https://gavclaw.com/2020/10/02/first-analysis-of-the-european-parliaments-draft-proposal-to-amend-brussels-ia-and-rome-ii-with-a-view-to-corporate-human-rights-due-diligence/> accessed 26 August 2021.

The drafters seemed to presume that their own legislation would grant better protection than other legal systems. They wanted to ensure that victims, wherever they may be situated, could benefit from the value chain due diligence. In this approach they seek to promote social and economic inclusion for all, irrespective of people's origin.

Commentators' responses to the suggestions varied. Álvarez-Armas was in favour of the approach, as it empowered victims, giving them the choice on applicable law and not only the option to request that a particular law be applied.[101] Von Hein and Thomale, on the other hand, considered the four alternative connecting factors to be excessive, impractical and detrimental to foreseeability.[102] Rühl was of the view that allowing victims to unilaterally choose the applicable law *ex post* would cause legal uncertainty for companies.[103] Álvarez-Armas, responding to this criticism, explained that for businesses it means complying with the most stringent legal systems among those potentially applicable, something an undertaking can assess *ex ante*.

4.3.2. Overriding Mandatory Law

The European Parliament's Resolution did not follow the ambitions of the Legal Affairs Committee concerning their private international law proposals. The Resolution's Recommendation for a Directive contains a brief reference to the Rome II Regulation. It stipulates that:

> Member States shall ensure that relevant provisions of this Directive are considered overriding mandatory provisions in line with Article 16 of Regulation (EC) No 864/2007 [Rome II].

This provision has two weaknesses. First, the provision leaves the determination of what is mandatory up to the Member States rather than stipulating itself what is mandatory. As explained above, that would have been perfectly possible, as

---

101 Eduardo Álvarez-Armas, 'Potential human-rights-related amendments to the Rome II Regulation (II): The proposed Art. 6a; Art. 7 is dead, long live Article 7?', blog entry, January 2021, <https://conflictoflaws.net/2021/alvarez-armas-on-potential-human-rights-related-amendments-to-the-rome-ii-regulation-ii-the-proposed-art-6a-art-7-is-dead-long-live-article-7/> accessed 26 August 2021.

102 Jan von Hein, 'Back to the Future – (Re-)Introducing the Principle of Ubiquity for Business-related Human Rights Claims', *Conflict of Laws* (October 2020) <https://conflictoflaws.net/2020/back-to-the-future-re-introducing-the-principle-of-ubiquity-for-business-related-human-rights-claims/> accessed 26 August 2021, and Chris Thomale, 'The EP Draft Report on Corporate Due Diligence', *Conflict of Laws* (October 2020) <https://conflictoflaws.net/2020/chris-thomale-on-the-ep-draft-report-on-corporate-due-diligence/> accessed 26 August 2021.

103 Giesela Rühl, 'Human rights in global supply chains: Do we need to amend the Rome II-Regulation?', *Conflict of Laws* (October 2020) <https://conflictoflaws.net/2020/human-rights-in-global-supply-chains-do-we-need-to-amend-the-rome-ii-regulation/> accessed 26 August 2021.

EU law can be of a mandatory nature. Second, having to rely on overriding mandatory law can be more difficult and uncertain than relying on a connecting factor which makes the entire legal system of a particular country applicable (and not only certain provisions). This is the same problem that the current version of the UN Draft Treaty contains. As explained above, in the case of harm done to a community in a poor country, it might be unclear for which aspects they can rely on which law. Perhaps only some rules qualify as mandatory (e.g. prohibition of torture), while for other aspects of the dispute (e.g. polluted air) the standard connecting factors have to be applied.

4.3.3. *Corporations Law*

The scope of the Directive proposed by the Resolution encompasses not only undertakings that fall under the law of an EU Member State or that are incorporated in a Member State. It also covers large undertakings, publicly listed small and medium-sized undertakings and small and medium-sized undertakings operating in high-risk sectors when these undertakings operate in the EU's internal market by way of selling products or providing services there.[104] In this way the Resolution introduces a scope rule that defies traditional notions in corporate private international law. It determines its scope not by a connecting factor that attaches to some quality of the undertaking itself, but by a place where the undertaking conducts an activity. That activity (selling goods onto the EU's market) does not have to be the undertaking's main activity for it to be covered by the Directive.

4.3.4. *Jurisdiction*

The rules on the protection and respect of human rights, in the form of due diligence duties, would be incomplete if victims were not provided with an effective remedy in case of violations (the 'remedy' approach of the UNGP).

The UN 2020 Draft Treaty's provision on jurisdiction would make a wide range of fora available: that of the place where the human rights abuse occurred, that of the place where an act or omission contributing to the human rights abuse occurred, and that of the domicile of the alleged infringers who committed an act or omission causing or contributing to such human rights abuse in the context of business activities, including those of a transnational character (Art 9(1) 2020 Draft). Domicile has a broad meaning: the place of incorporation, statutory seat, central administration, or principal place of business (Art 9(2) 2020 Draft). The 2019 Draft contained an even broader interpretation, referring in the fourth option to 'substantial business interests' (Art 7(2) 2019 Draft).

104 Proposed Directive (annex to the Resolution), Art 2.

While the European Parliament's Resolution does not address jurisdiction, the Motion for Resolution included recommendations for the amendment of Brussels I. The proposals were aimed at ensuring social, economic and political inclusion of vulnerable groups. It would reduce the inequality of remedies between victims harmed by undertakings managed from their own country and victims harmed by foreign undertakings (or by undertakings that were local in name but were in fact managed from abroad).

The Legal Affairs Committee proposed inserting two new bases of jurisdiction: a new special basis of jurisdiction and a *forum necessitatis*.

The new special basis of jurisdiction was to be inserted in the provision on multiple defendants, actions in warranty and counter-claims (Art 8):[105]

> (5) In matters relating to business civil claims for human rights violations within the value chain within the scope of Directive xxx/xxxx on Corporate Due Diligence and Corporate Accountability, an undertaking domiciled in a Member State may also be sued in the Member State where it has its domicile or in which it operates when the damage caused in a third country can be imputed to a subsidiary or another undertaking with which the parent company has a business relationship within the meaning of Article 3 of Directive xxx/xxxx on Corporate Due Diligence and Corporate Accountability.

From a private international law perspective, this is a rather unusual approach: the provision started by saying that an undertaking could be sued in the Member State where it was domiciled and then went on to set a condition, even though the possibility of suing an undertaking at its home place is widely accepted.[106]

Unlike the first, the second proposed insertion in Brussels I would be a true change, i.e. the inclusion of *forum necessitatis* (proposed Art 26a):

> Regarding business-related civil claims on human rights violations within the value chain of a company domiciled in the Union or operating in the Union within the scope of Directive xxx/xxxx on Corporate Due Diligence and Corporate Accountability, where no court of a Member State has jurisdiction under this Regulation, the courts of a Member State may, on an exceptional basis, hear the case if the right to a fair trial or the right to access to justice so requires, in particular:
>
> (a) if proceedings cannot reasonably be brought or conducted or would be impossible in a third State with which the dispute is closely related; or

105 The proposal was to add a fifth subsection to this Article, referring to the Directive that the European Parliament wants the Commission to initiate (hence the reference to 'xxx/xxxx').

106 Brussels I, Art 4. This argument is also raised by Chris Thomale, 'The EP Draft Report on Corporate Due Diligence', *Conflict of Laws* (October 2020) <https://conflictoflaws.net/2020/chris-thomale-on-the-ep-draft-report-on-corporate-due-diligence/> accessed 26 August 2021.

(b) if a judgment given on the claim in a third State would not be entitled to recognition and enforcement in the Member State of the court seised under the law of that State and such recognition and enforcement is necessary to ensure that the rights of the claimant are satisfied; and the dispute has a sufficient connection with the Member State of the court seised.

The current Brussels I Regulation does not contain a *forum necessitatis* clause.[107] Brussels I would not apply in these situations, as it only applies if the defendant is domiciled in the EU, if the parties agreed to a forum in the EU, if the dispute concerns an exclusive basis of jurisdiction under the Regulation (such as rights in rem in immovable property, tenancy, validity of legal persons or decisions by their organs, validity of intellectual property rights, validity of entries in public registries), or if the claimant is a consumer or an employee in the EU. If none of these criteria apply, the national law of the forum determines jurisdiction (Art 6 Brussels I). National law could contain such *forum necessitatis*,[108] but whether it does or not is beyond the scope of EU law as it currently stands. To bring this matter under EU law would ensure a further harmonised approach in the EU: all Member States would have this additional basis of jurisdiction.

The question, however, is whether an amendment to jurisdiction rules is necessary. If the aim is to hold businesses domiciled in the EU accountable for human rights infringements elsewhere in which they had a part through their value chain, then jurisdiction is simply established by the general rule. Any business can be sued at its domicile. This includes its statutory seat, central administration or principal place of business.[109]

The real issue is thus whether the EU branch of the business is the one that can be held liable. This issue came out clearly in the *Shell*[110] and *Vedanta*[111] cases in the Netherlands and the UK.[112] The difficulty that the victims of the

---

107 The European Commission, in its original proposal to recast Brussels I, did foresee such a change: it attempted to broaden the scope of Brussels I so that it would cover all civil and commercial claims that fall within its material scope of application. This means that no room would be left for national bases of jurisdiction. This proposal however did not survive the negotiation process.

108 E.g. Belgian Code of Private International Law, Art 11; Dutch Code of Civil Procedure, Art 9c.

109 Brussels I, Art 63.

110 Gerechtshof Den Haag 29 January 2021, ECLI:NL:GHDHA:2021:132, ECLI:NL:GHDHA:2021:133 and ECLI:NL:GHDHA:2021:134; *Okpabi v Royal Dutch Shell* [2021] UKSC 3.

111 *Vedanta Resources plc and Another v Lungowe and Others* [2019] UKSC 20.

112 See for instance the debate in *Okpabi v Royal Dutch Shell* [2021] UKSC 3. See also Marilyn Croser, Martyn Day, Mariëtte van Huijstee and Channa Samkalden, 'Vedanta v Lungowe and Kiobel v Shell: The Implications for Parent Company Accountability' (2020) 5 Business and Human Rights Journal 130; Marios Koutsias, 'Corporate domicile and residence' in Peter Stone and Youseph Farah (eds), *Research Handbook on EU Private International Law* (Edward Elgar Publishing 2017) 344–378, esp at 350.

alleged abuses in Nigeria and Zambia (respectively) faced was getting to the European mother companies, namely showing that they were involved. If the EU Directive that the Resolution proposes makes clear that there is such liability, the jurisdiction issue in such cases would be solved.

More difficult are perhaps the cases where neither the alleged infringing company nor their parent is domiciled in the EU. If the products do not enter the EU market, there is no one to be held responsible in the EU and possibly no EU court is available. If the Directive becomes law, however, these would be situations where there is really hardly any link with the EU. We can think for instance of South American companies exploiting local communities. Their goods might be sold down the value chain to several countries in the world, but not any EU countries. Does such a case belong in an EU court, one might wonder.

Whether the company can be sued at the place where the tort occurs depends on the bases of jurisdiction in the law of that place. Some legal systems have a basis of jurisdiction at the place where the tort occurred or where the cause of action arose.[113] This basis of jurisdiction is not universally accepted, as it might be unfair towards a defendant who could not have foreseen being sued at a distant place where unforeseen damage occurred.[114] The availability of a forum at the place of the tort or the place of the damage is not something that the EU can regulate beyond its borders. Within its borders, it already has a broad basis of jurisdiction for tort.

Forum necessitatis would provide a forum in the situation of foreign torts by foreign companies and where hardly any link with the EU exists. One could perhaps think of the situation where a business in the EU has provided consulting services to one of the undertakings. But it should be used restrictively. Where proper rules on liability exist and the defendant is thus brought within reach by liability rules, the *forum necessitatis* becomes less necessary. The European Court of Human Rights in the *Naït-Liman* case found that states are not obliged to have universal bases of jurisdiction and are not obliged to make their *forum necessitatis* available without requiring a certain connection to their state (they have a large margin of appreciation).[115]

---

113 E.g. in the EU Art 7(2) Brussels I. South African law provides for jurisdiction at the place of the cause of action (Superior Courts Act 10 of 2013, s 21) combined with either submission or attachment of property.

114 This is indeed the case in the US, where jurisdiction is tested against the due process requirement of the fourteenth amendment of the Constitution: see *Daimler AG v Bauman, et al*, 571 U.S. 117 (2014).

115 ECHR *Naït-Liman v Switzerland* App no 51357/07 (15 March 2018). See also the Report of the European Group for Private International Law's meeting in Antwerp (2018) <https://www.gedip-egpil.eu/reunionstravail/Anvers%202018/PV-TRAV-v4-7.02.19.pdf> accessed 26 August 2021.

5. REFORM PROPOSALS

5.1. PROPERTY

The general connecting factor should remain that the law of the place where it is situated governs property. However, this should be nuanced in cases of movable cultural property that has long since left its original place (i.e. was illegally exported a long time ago): the law of the place of its original situation should be applied.[116] As defined in a resolution by the International Law Institute, this should be the 'country with which the property concerned is most closely linked from the cultural point of view'.[117] For immovable property, no change is needed, only coherent application of the connecting factor.

5.2. CONTRACT

Party autonomy as a general rule is in line with freedom in contract law in general, but it should be handled with care in order not to reinforce existing inequalities. The rule should be tempered for vulnerable contracting parties. Moreover, when the choice is not truly free for one of the parties, the choice should not be enforceable and the default connecting factors should come into play.

Value chain due diligence should encourage contracting parties to impose due diligence obligations on parties higher up in the value chain through contractual clauses. For businesses that cannot escape due diligence duties because they are obliged to report, it makes sense to choose the law that also imposes the obligation in its contracts. In this way, reporting and liability can have a spill-over effect on contracts.

Where the parties have not made a choice of law, equality of outcomes (Target 10.4) should play a role alongside, and not subject to, legal certainty. In other words, connecting factors should not too rigidly refer to the law of the habitual residence of the party effecting the characteristic performance, but should also take into account other factors that point to another legal system, such as the place of performance and the position of the other party. Guidance can be derived from the Hague Convention on the Law Applicable to Contracts for the International Sale of Goods. Moreover, when considering the 'closest

116 For support of this approach, see Evelien Campfens, 'Whose Cultural Property? Introducing Heritage Title for Cross-Border Cultural Claims' (2020) 67 Netherlands Review of International Law 257, 274.

117 Institute of International Law, 'The International Sale of Works of Art from the Angle of the Protection of the Cultural Heritage' (Basel, 1991) Art 1(b) <https://www.idi-iil.org/app/uploads/2017/06/1991_bal_04_en.pdf> accessed 26 August 2021.

connection' of a contract and factors to determine such connection, courts should be able to take account of related contracts in the value chain.

Suppose that business R contracts to take minerals from developing country X to developing country Y where technological products are manufactured, then brings them to rich country R from where they are sold to various buyers across the world, among others to developing countries D and E and to rich country H. Business R has its habitual residence in country R. In the absence of choice of law, the applicable law should not automatically be that of country R. Let us now assume that country H has legislation on value chain due diligence, but country R does not. In order to provide more effective protection, the law applicable to R's contract with party H in country H should not automatically be the law of country R; rather, the contract's link to the other contracts should be taken into account. In addition, the contract chain's connections to countries X and Y should be considered when ascertaining the applicable law.

5.3. TORT

In tort law, victims should have the choice of basing their claim on the law of the place of the damage or the place of the wrongful act. This choice already exists under Rome II for environmental torts. By expanding the range of possibly applicable legal systems, the responsibility of businesses is also expanded. Such approach would assist in reducing inequalities (Target 10.2): businesses would not be able to rely only on the law of the place of the damage, which might contain less stringent laws. They would also have to comply with the laws of the place where they act. In the *Shell* case in the Netherlands, the claimants argued that the wrongful act consisted of the decisions made in the Netherlands.[118] This argument was abandoned in the appeal case, but nevertheless provides an interesting path to explore.

Permitting this choice still complies with the broadly accepted *lex loci delicti* rule. It does not amount to legal uncertainty: surely businesses know where they act.

5.4. CORPORATIONS

Private international law should take account of economic realities and not only separate legal entities. This will allow legislators to impose reporting duties more broadly than only on the legal entities with statutory or real seats on its territory.

[118] Gerechtshof Den Haag, 29 January 2021, ECLI:NL:GHDHA:2021:132, ECLI:NL:GHDHA:2021:133 and ECLI:NL:GHDHA:2021:134.

Adhering to the statutory seat theory makes it easy for companies to join the race to the bottom, as well as to escape reporting duties and related diligence requirements. This makes it difficult for legislators to ensure the 'inclusion [in its policies] of all' possible victims (Target 10.2) and to monitor financial markets (Target 10.5). It is advisable to, if not entirely reject the statutory seat theory, at least mitigate it. A solution could be to use the compromise that has long since been reached in the field of insolvency law as inspiration: let us assume that a corporation is at home where it has the centre of its main interests (COMI). Let us call it 'Statutory Seat+': a corporation is at home at its statutory seat unless that place is not where it really conducts its activities. For the purposes of insolvency law, the presumption that the COMI is at the statutory seat can be set aside by taking into account what is foreseeable for third parties (most importantly creditors). For corporate due diligence, the focus should not be on third parties or creditors but on the influence on the market.

There are already signs of the acknowledgment that sticking to the application of the law of the statutory seat is insufficient. The EU's Directive on the annual financial statements, consolidated financial statements and related reports of certain types of undertakings[119] provides one. Its sixth recital sets out this approach:

> The scope of this Directive should be principles-based and should ensure that it is not possible for an undertaking to exclude itself from that scope by creating a group structure containing multiple layers of undertakings established inside or outside the Union.

The provisions of the Directive follow this approach by sometimes allowing and sometimes requiring reporting on group level. Furthering this broad view of companies and their actions, the European Commission in its Guidelines on non-financial reporting (methodology for reporting non-financial information)[120] gives examples of key performance indicators that relate not only to the activities of the reporting company, but also to consequences for its supply chain.

The connecting factor should take into account the real activities of corporations. Operating in a certain market should be enough to draw a corporation under due diligence rules.[121]

---

119 Directive 2013/34/EU of 26 June 2013 of the European Parliament and of the Council of 26 June 2013 on the annual financial statements, consolidated financial statements and related reports of certain types of undertakings, amending Directive 2006/43/EC of the European Parliament and of the Council and repealing Council Directives 78/660/EEC and 83/349/EEC [2013], consolidated version available at <http://data.europa.eu/eli/dir/2013/34/2014-12-11> accessed 13 December 2020.

120 [2017] OJ C 215/1.

121 See for instance Committee on Legal Affairs of the European Parliament Draft Report with recommendations to the Commission on corporate due diligence and corporate accountability, 2020/2129(INL) (11 September 2020) <https://www.europarl.europa.eu/doceo/document/JURI-PR-657191_EN.pdf> accessed 26 August 2021, Art 1, referring to 'undertakings operating in the internal market'.

5.5. OVERRIDING MANDATORY LAW

Overriding mandatory law can be a powerful tool to ensure the application of legislation beyond what would normally be appointed by standard connecting factors. Such broad application might be necessary to ensure that policies can be implemented in a way that reduces inequality, for example that human rights standards apply not only to a part of the population but to all, including potential victims in distant countries.

5.6. JURISDICTION

The jurisdiction of the place of the domicile of the defendant goes a long way if this defendant is subject to due diligence duties under the applicable law. A *forum necessitatis* is only necessary if the defendant is not liable and cannot be tried according to the due diligence liabilities.

6. RESULTS AND CONCLUSION

By way of conclusion, private international law contains tools to reduce inequalities and work towards the attainment of SDG 10. In some fields the tools can be sharpened, while in other fields they have to be rediscovered and dusted off.

6.1. PROPERTY

Applying the law of the place of the situation of property is logical, clear and easy. However, in the case of long-lost cultural property, it might not lead to the most equitable results. For these cases, the rule should be flexible enough to take account not of the current situation of the property but of the place where it should have been.

6.2. CONTRACT

Party autonomy conforms to the field of contract law where freedom is the rule. However, the connecting factors of private international law should admit situations in which the choice is not truly free and allow it to be set aside. Similarly, weaker parties should be protected against a 'choice' that was imposed on them. Such choices of law should be admitted only to the extent that they do not undermine or detract from the protection that these parties would have had by the law appointed in the absence of choice.

In the absence of choice, the closest connection between the parties and the contract should be determined by taking into account not only the habitual residence of the party effecting the characteristic performance, but also other factors linked to the contract, including other contracts in the value chain.

6.3. TORT

Tort law is important to ensure remedies for victims of human rights and other abuses by large undertakings. It is tort law that can ensure a remedy, as required by the UNGP. In ensuring such a remedy, it would be a mistake to oblige victims to make hard and unnatural distinctions between civil law torts and human rights infringements. These two aspects can be caused by the same event. Victims' access to remedies should not be unnecessarily complicated.

The connecting factor should give the claimant a choice between the law of the place where the wrongful act was committed and the law of the place of the damage. Both of these aspects are part of the tort, and allowing victims to choose between them offers them broad protection. At the same time, allowing these options to the victims should not cause too much uncertainty to businesses: they know where they take decisions, where they implement these decisions, where they operate and where their operations have effects. The same is true for the effects of their subsidiaries' operations.

The European Parliament's Resolution on value chain due diligence would make businesses liable for rights infringements up their value chain. When such infringements take place and civil liability arises, a connecting factor based on choice, as referred to above, should accompany the new legal provisions in order to ensure equal protection for all and equal access to compensation for all.

6.4. CORPORATIONS

In corporate law, the push in the EU towards the statutory seat theory can have the effect of enhancing inequality. The real seat theory allows for a better grip on businesses, making it more difficult to hide from strict reporting duties on human rights and due diligence. The statutory seat theory should thus be rejected, if not in general, then at least for reporting duties. If it is followed, this should be mitigated by a COMI-type connecting factor to alleviate harsh effects.

Moreover, private international law should take into account economic reality and not only single legal entities. This is even more important if the statutory seat approach survives.

Reporting duties on undertakings should be imposed on a broader basis than the current statutory or real seat theories. The European Parliament's Resolution on value chain due diligence takes this broader approach: it defines its scope as encompassing all undertakings that are active on the EU's market. This scope rule has an equalising effect: it ensures that all goods on the specific market come into the market on the same conditions. The reporting duties apply with respect to all undertakings that bring goods into the market. This should reduce the potential to make a profit at the expense of persons living and working in poor conditions. No matter where the goods originate, are manufactured or finished, or pass through – no matter whose hands they pass through – human rights standards have to be respected for all.

6.5. OVERRIDING MANDATORY LAW

For the remaining situations in which inequality is still generated by the use of the connecting factors, states can qualify certain rules as being mandatory. Such overriding mandatory law can be used as a last resort to work towards reducing inequality. Rules of a regional nature (such as the European Parliament's Resolution and proposed Directive) or an international nature (such as the UNGP and possibly the UN Draft Treaty) can also qualify as overriding mandatory law.

6.6. JURISDICTION

If a clear system of liability is in place for undertakings, victims should be able to sue businesses at the home of the victims. In this sense, the domicile of the defendant is a sufficient basis for jurisdiction. However, where such rules of liability are not in place, a *forum necessitatis* rule can give victims access to court.

SDG 11: SUSTAINABLE CITIES AND COMMUNITIES

Klaas Hendrik ELLER

Goal 11: Make cities and human settlements inclusive, safe, resilient and sustainable

11.1 By 2030, ensure access for all to adequate, safe and affordable housing and basic services and upgrade slums
11.2 By 2030, provide access to safe, affordable, accessible and sustainable transport systems for all, improving road safety, notably by expanding public transport, with special attention to the needs of those in vulnerable situations, women, children, persons with disabilities and older persons
11.3 By 2030, enhance inclusive and sustainable urbanization and capacity for participatory, integrated and sustainable human settlement planning and management in all countries
11.4 Strengthen efforts to protect and safeguard the world's cultural and natural heritage
11.5 By 2030, significantly reduce the number of deaths and the number of people affected and substantially decrease the direct economic losses relative to global gross domestic product caused by disasters, including water-related disasters, with a focus on protecting the poor and people in vulnerable situations
11.6 By 2030, reduce the adverse per capita environmental impact of cities, including by paying special attention to air quality and municipal and other waste management
11.7 By 2030, provide universal access to safe, inclusive and accessible, green and public spaces, in particular for women and children, older persons and persons with disabilities
11.a Support positive economic, social and environmental links between urban, peri-urban and rural areas by strengthening national and regional development planning
11.b By 2020, substantially increase the number of cities and human settlements adopting and implementing integrated policies and plans towards inclusion, resource efficiency, mitigation and adaptation to climate change, resilience to

disasters, and develop and implement, in line with the Sendai Framework for Disaster Risk Reduction 2015–2030, holistic disaster risk management at all levels
11.c Support least developed countries, including through financial and technical assistance, in building sustainable and resilient buildings utilizing local materials

1. INTRODUCTION: THE 'GLOCALISATION' OF URBAN DEVELOPMENT

The Sustainable Development Goals (SDGs) of 2015 recognise that cities around the world are playing an increasingly central role in sustainable development by going beyond the previous Millennium Development Goals (MDGs)[1] and dedicating SDG 11 explicitly to urban development. Together with other international documents, notably the United Nations' New Urban Agenda adopted at Habitat III, and the Pact of Amsterdam[2] within the EU, both from 2016, SDG 11 posits cities as crucial arenas and actors for sustainability. SDG 11 contains the pledge to 'make cities and human settlements inclusive, safe, resilient and sustainable'. It stands out vis-à-vis other SDGs in that it seems to formulate a geographically limited ambition, whereas other SDGs are formulated without geographic specifications. On the other hand, multiple overlaps with other SDGs intuitively underline that the urban space is not an isolated island requiring exclusively city-specific responses, but that cities stand at the intersection of complementary and conflicting SDGs. This can be said above all of health and

---

1 Noora Arajärvi, 'Including Cities in the 2030 Agenda – A Review of the Post-2015 Process' in Helmut Aust and Anél du Plessis (eds), *The Globalisation of Urban Governance. Legal Perspectives on Sustainable Development Goal 11* (Routledge 2019) 17, 18 et seqq.

2 <https://ec.europa.eu/regional_policy/sources/policy/themes/urban-development/agenda/pact-of-amsterdam.pdf>. All websites last accessed 8 August 2021.

well-being (SDG 3), clean water and sanitation (SDG 6), resilient infrastructure (SDG 9), the eradication of inequalities (SDG 10), sustainable consumption and waste management (SDG 12), climate change (SDG 13) and democratic institution-building (SDG 16).

The growing role of cities for sustainable development manifests itself in many ways today. Both the urbanisation rate and the number of 'megacities' are constantly on the rise, not only in the Global North, but specifically in the Global South.[3] The OECD declared a 'Metropolitan Century',[4] in which cities would serve even more firmly as engines of concentrated economic growth and innovation. In a setting in which social, economic and political life worldwide is increasingly organised in and around cities, the ambivalence of cities in the quest for sustainability is easy to grasp. Cities' vibrancy and avant-gardist role has stirred both magnetic attraction and repulsion throughout history.[5] Today again, cities seem to be part of both the problem and the solution since they combine unparalleled challenges for sustainability with a unique potential to address them in novel ways. This moves cities into the spotlight as condensed socio-spatial labs for applying and learning about many of the most pressing issues on the sustainability agenda. To be sure, the priorities on this agenda differ across cities and stages of development, but generally include fair and accessible housing, mobility, pollution and waste management, infrastructure, and economic development, to name only a few. Urban struggles are moreover perceived as proxies for society-wide struggles, as in the cases of the of Occupy and Extinction Rebellion protest movements, which portrayed their struggle for financial and environmental justice as 'urban' movements.[6] A growing number of points on the sustainability agenda have concrete local ramifications and it is at the urban level where the course is set for addressing them. By consequence, many cities have become involved in global networks of para-diplomatic activities[7] and frequently partner with international

---

3 Gavin Shatkin, 'Global cities of the South: Emerging perspectives on growth and inequality' (2007) 24 Cities 1.

4 Cf OECD, *The Metropolitan Century: Understanding Urbanisation and its Consequences* (OECD Publishing 2015). See also Parag Khanna, 'Beyond City Limits', Foreign Policy of 6 August <https://foreignpolicy.com/2010/08/06/beyond-city-limits/> ('The 21st century will not be dominated by America or China, Brazil or India, but by the city.').

5 See e.g. Georg Simmel, 'The Metropolis and Mental Life' (1903) in Malcom Miles, Tim Hall and Iain Borden (eds), *The City Cultures Reader* (2nd ed, Routledge 2000) 12 et seqq; on similar tensions in Walter Benjamin's work cf Greame Gilloch, *Myth & Metropolis. Walter Benjamin and the City* (Polity Press 1996).

6 Cf Justus Ultermark and Walter Nicholls, 'How Local Networks Shape a Global Movement: Comparing Occupy in Amsterdam and Los Angeles' (2012) 11 Social Movement Studies 295; Guillaume Marche and Jean-Baptiste Velut, 'All Contentious Politics is Local: Studying the Occupy Movement from Below, in Oakland and Atlanta' (2016) 148 Revue Française d'Etudes Américaines 98; generally Bettina Köhler and Markus Wissen, 'Glocalizing Protest: Urban Conflicts and Global Social Movements' (2003) 27 International Journal of Urban and Regional Research 942.

7 Examples include the C40 network (www.c40.org), ICLEI – Local Governments for Sustainability (https://iclei.org) and the Global Covenant of Mayors for Climate and Energy

organisations such as UN Habitat or private foundations to increase their capacities and share best practices. The implementation of the Paris Agreement[8] and the emergence of 'sanctuary cities'[9] for immigrants and refugees are powerful illustrations of the global dimension of municipal activities. Cities employ their global reach and membership in international alliances and adhere to international rules to strengthen their local powers.[10] In some cases, cities may for a number of structural reasons be better positioned to develop and implement progressive environmental policies than the national (federal) level and are increasingly taking centre stage in the international development apparatus.[11] In short, cities are, as former UN Deputy Secretary General Jan Eliasson phrased it, 'where the battle for sustainable development will be won – or lost if we fail.'[12] Urban development is currently at a crossroads and calls for particular attention to the various factors that will shape its future.

Against this backdrop, SDG 11 is driven by the idea that cities are not merely the *site* where sustainability risks materialise and where they can and should be addressed. Rather, *urban dynamics* – political, legal, economic and cultural – are *themselves a productive force* in shaping sustainable futures. These urban dynamics are best described as 'glocal' since they manifest themselves in a local setting but are nonetheless shaped by the integration of big cities into the global economy and more broadly globalisation at large. In the words of Boaventura Santos,[13] cities could be regarded both as 'globalized localism' (describing the global replication and dissemination of a specific economic, cultural phenomenon) and as 'localized globalism' (denoting the local repercussions of transnational practices and imperatives). Against this background, this chapter advances a twofold argument. First, identifying, understanding and potentially altering such 'glocal' urban dynamics is central for the agenda of sustainable development. Second, not only does law play a constitutive role in shaping such dynamics, but it also does so through new legal tools and fields which gain significance in the urban context. Tensions between the national level and local government law have long dominated our thinking about urban ramifications of law. National legislation sees its

---

(<www.globalcovenantofmayors.org>), three global coalitions committed to reducing greenhouse gas emissions.

8 See e.g. David Gordon, *Cities on the World Stage. The Politics of Urban Climate Governance* (CUP 2020); Danielle Spiegel-Feld and Katrina Wyman, 'Cities as Global Environmental Actors: The Case of Marine Plastics' (2020) 62 Arizona Law Review 487.

9 See e.g. City of Sanctuary UK (<https://cityofsanctuary.org>).

10 Gerald Frug and David Barron, 'International Local Government Law' (2006) 38 The Urban Lawyer 1, 13.

11 Benjamin Barber, *If Mayors Rules the World. Dysfunctional Nations, Rising Cities* (Yale University Press 2013); Sergio Montero, 'Leveraging Bogotá: Sustainable development, global philanthropy and the rise of urban solutionism' (2020) 57 Urban Studies 2263.

12 UN Deputy Secretary General, Press Release, DSG/SM/874-HAB/229 of 9 June 2015.

13 Boaventura de Sousa Santos, 'Globalizations' (2006) 23 Theory, Culture & Society 393.

regulatory reach contested and finds itself squeezed between pioneering municipal regulation on the one hand and a rise in transnational regulation on the other. If urban governance today is 'glocal', the global embeddedness of cities and actors of urban governance in regulatory, economic and technological networks urges us to look beyond local rules and capture what might be called, 'connectivity norms':[14] the normative mechanisms that shape the framework and very possibility of urban development by governing the transfer of capital, products, ideas or knowledge in and across cities. Public (international) law is increasingly taking this step, entirely reversing the classical domestic view of cities as mere 'political subdivisions' and 'agencies' of the state,[15] and investigating cities' autonomy in setting and implementing international norms.[16]

This chapter puts forward the idea that private law and private international law, in turn, even if seldom discussed in this context, play an unquestionably important role in the legal array shaping urban development.[17] Rather than focusing on municipalities as agents of global interurban relations or processes of urban democracy, private law forms a more contextual legal infrastructure of economic and technological dynamics that leave a structural imprint on today's cities. This is the case for several fields of private and economic law, including data protection and IP law. This chapter will specifically cover private international law and explore inroads for private international law doctrines and thinking for urban development under SDG 11. How can the vast experience of private international law in detecting, delineating and processing 'conflicts' contribute to the creation of an adequate 'forum' for questions of spatial justice in a global city?[18] This new formative role of private law and private international law has largely gone unnoticed because of shared deficits of both disciplines in retracing and curtailing the fluid dynamics of private power in the global economy in general and in their manifestation in specific sites in particular. Private law for the most part grapples with tying its doctrines to the institutions that arise from the aggregate use of freedom of contract or the

14 Poul F Kjær, 'Constitutionalizing Connectivity: The Constitutional Grid of World Society' (2018) 45 Journal of Law and Society 114.

15 *Ballard v Hunter*, 204 U.S. 241 (1907).

16 See Gerald Frug and David Barron, 'International Local Government Law' (2006) 38 The Urban Lawyer 1; Yishai Blank, 'The City and the World' (2006) 44 Columbia Journal of Transnational Law 868; Yishai Blank, 'Localism in the New Global Legal Order' (2006) 47 Harvard International Law Journal 263; Helmut Aust, *Das Recht der globalen Stadt. Grenzüberschreitende Dimensionen kommunaler Zusammenarbeit* (Mohr Siebeck 2017).

17 In fact, the very origins of European private international law in the writings of Bartolus are tied to inter-city law in Northern Italy, see Magnus Ryan, 'Bartolus of Sassoferrato and Free Cities. The Alexander Prize Lecture' (2000) 10 Transactions of the Royal Historical Society 65.

18 On the current lack of such a legal-institutional forum Olatunde Johnson, 'Unjust Cities? Gentrification, Integration, and the Fair Housing Act' (2019) 53 University of Richmond Law Review 835.

corporate form.[19] Within private international law, in turn, concepts of territory and space have a long pedigree,[20] but are often employed too rigidly to map the multiple and permeating actors, norms and processes at play in global cities.[21]

The chapter proceeds as follows. The next section (section 2) will seek to elucidate further the hitherto absent private law conceptualisation of global cities as a performative site of globalisation. Reading the city as a social institution that provides the context and playing field in and on which private law operates allows private law and its theory to take a more active stance in realising the ambition of SDG 11. Drawing on this framework, the chapter then turns more specifically to private international law's intersections with SDG 11 (section 3). We will see how an urban perspective on private international law emblematises a move beyond the abstractions of the liberal and Westphalian paradigm with private autonomy and sovereignty as the stable cornerstones of what were perceived as distinct 'private' and 'public' spheres.[22] Two main illustrations will be provided, namely the financialisation of real estate and infrastructure (section 3.1) and the various initiatives linked to the cross-cutting trend towards 'smart cities' (section 3.2). Some paths for future inquiries and practical reforms conclude the chapter (section 4).

2. SDG 11 AND THE ROLE OF LAW IN URBAN DEVELOPMENT

The increasing role of private and also private international law for the trajectories of global cities appears to be backed by the vision of urban development that underlies SDG 11 and the SDGs more generally.

---

19 One recent example is the conceptualisation of global value chains under contract law, see Klaas Hendrik Eller, 'Is "Global Value Chain" a Legal Concept? Situating Contract Law in Discourses Around Global Production' (2020) 16 European Review of Contract Law 3.

20 See Ralf Michaels, 'Territorial Jurisdiction after Territoriality' in Piet Jan Slot and Mielle Bulterman (eds), *Globalization and Jurisdiction* (Kluwer Law International 2004) 105.

21 This resonates with the discipline's ongoing self-ascertainment to global governance, see Horatia Muir Watt, 'Private International Law Beyond the Schism' (2011) 2 Transnational Legal Theory 347; Robert Wai, 'Private v Private – Transnational Private Law and Contestation in Global Economic Governance' in Horatia Muir Watt and Diego Fernández Arroyo (eds), *Private International Law and Global Governance* (OUP 2014) 34; Ralf Michaels, 'The Re-State-ment of Non-State Law. The State, Choice of Law, and the Challenge from Global Legal Pluralism' (2005) 51 Wayne Law Review 1209; Hans van Loon, 'The Global Horizon of Private International Law' (2016) 380 Collected Courses of the Hague Academy of International Law 1. On the *trias* of 'actors, norms and processes (ANT)' as vectors of transnational law cf Peer Zumbansen, 'Defining the Space of Transnational Law: Legal Theory, Global Governance and Legal Pluralism' in Gunther Handl, Joachim Zekoll and Peer Zumbansen (eds), *Beyond Territoriality. Transnational Legal Authority in an Age of Globalization* (Brill/Nijhoff 2012) 53.

22 *Locus classicus* Duncan Kennedy, 'The Stages of the Decline of the Public/Private Distinction' (1982) 130 University of Pennsylvania Law Review 1349.

2.1. SDG 11: A POLYCENTRIC UNDERSTANDING OF URBAN DEVELOPMENT

The attention paid to cities under the SDGs seems in line with the broader conceptual shift that occurred between the MDGs of 2000 and the SDGs of 2015. Contrasting the regulatory paradigms underlying both codices allows a clearer picture of the peculiar potential contained in SDG 11. The MDGs remained much more state-centred in their regulatory approach, entailing a primary responsibility of governments and the development community to bring about targeted reforms on specific issues and geographies. In this, the MDGs formed an inter-state consensus along the lines of (public) international soft law and envisioned a linear regulatory process. The SDGs, in turn, take the interconnectedness of business, society and the environment as their starting point and advocate for an integrated, holistic and collaborative approach.[23] In this, the SDGs follow a reflexive regulatory paradigm[24] that directly responds to the complexity of modern society and is geared towards the transformation of systemic enabling conditions. These are understood to include not only social but also planetary boundaries, which stress the sustainability goals of natural resource preservation, waste disposal and energy consumption.[25]

This broad perspective on sustainability is clearly reflected in SDG 11, which covers vast ground within the urban agenda until 2030. It comprises seven substantive targets alongside three targets that further spell out the means of implementation. The goals address, inter alia, housing (Target 11.1), transport systems, especially for people in need of public transportation (Target 11.2), disaster resilience (Target 11.5), air quality and waste management (Target 11.6), and participatory governance of urbanisation (Target 11.3). As cross-cutting ambitions, the targets of SDG 11 stress a concern for health-related risks, such as through disasters and climate change, and highlight the need for positive relations between urban, peri-urban and rural areas, as well as on the national and regional level. The general phrasing of these goals does not deny the diverse cultural, economic and regulatory contexts of cities around the world and the fact that an agenda of combating spatialised injustice may have different

---

23 See United Nations Department of Economic and Social Affairs (UN DESA), *The SDG Partnership Guidebook*, (v. 1.01, 2020); also SDG 17 ('global partnership for sustainable development').

24 See Gunther Teubner, 'Substantive and Reflexive Elements in Modern Law' (1983) 17 Law and Society Review 239 and Colin Scott, 'Reflexive Governance, Regulation and Meta-Regulation: Control or Learning' in Olivier de Schutter and Jacques Lenoble (eds), *Reflexive Governance: Redefining the Public Interest in a Pluralistic World* (Hart Publishing 2010) 43.

25 See Kate Raworth, *Doughnut Economics: Seven Ways to Think Like a 21st-Century Economist* (Random House 2017); for an initial application of the economic model at the city level see 'The Amsterdam City Doughnut. A Tool for Transformative Action' (2020) <https://www.kateraworth.com/wp/wp-content/uploads/2020/04/20200416-AMS-portrait-EN-Spread-web-420x210mm.pdf>.

priorities and leverage points between the Global North and the Global South. Yet, despite these differences, the growth of global cities in the second half of the 20th century marked the beginning of a global model of urbanity that gradually fostered a more universal topography and structural similarities among such cities. Overall, cities merit being placed at the forefront of a future-oriented discourse of sustainability, partly since they are – as explained – the locus where much of the sustainability agenda needs to gain traction, and partly because of the untapped potential of an urban angle to contrast the dominance of national policies.

2.2. THE LEGAL ARCHITECTURE OF GLOBAL CITIES: MOVING BEYOND 'HOME RULE'

Understanding urban development as an interplay of various actors and both local and global factors also requires adjustments to the established legal perspective on urban governance. Conventionally, urban matters are thought to be addressed by a specific set of rules of municipal law (and by-laws), including planning, zoning and land use law. Cities, to be sure, are the cradle of public governance[26] and feature prominently in progressive debates on reforming democracy.[27] Historically, establishing the principal architectural, logistical and cultural character of a city was the domain of municipal law, notably zoning law. For monumental projects such as Haussmann's reforms of Parisian streets, private property rights were clearly subordinated to public planning. To this day, detailed public planning faces many fewer objections at the municipal level than at the national level.[28] Naturally, local government and zoning law differ substantially between countries (and cities) and depend, for example, on the size, constitutional status and institutional organisation of the respective city. However, the shared feature is a reliance on public ordering in both urban governance and planning of matters such as housing, pollution and transportation. Underlying this is the central concept of local government law, namely subsidiarity, or 'home rule'.[29] 'Home rule' moves away from the

26 Jürgen Osterhammel, *The Transformation of the World. A Global History of the Nineteenth Century* (Princeton University Press 2014) 241 et seqq; Roscoe Pound, 'Law and the State: Jurisprudence and Politics' (1944) 57 Harvard Law Review 1193, 1194–1201.

27 See e.g. Mark Purcell, 'The right to the city: The struggle for democracy in the urban public realm' (2013) 43 Policy & Politics 311.

28 See already *Village of Euclid v Ambler Realty*, 272 U.S. 365 (1926).

29 For an overview Gerald E Frug and David J Barron, 'City Bound: How States Stifle Urban Innovation' (Cornell University Press 2008) 60–74; Richard Briffault, 'Our Localism: Part I – The Structure of Local Government Law' (1990) 90 Columbia Law Review 1; on the alternative conception of local power as state creature (which predated home rule in the US) cf Hendrik Hartog, *Public Property and Private Power: The Corporation of the City of New York in American Law, 1730–1870* (Cornell University Press 1983).

understanding of cities as mere creatures of the state and grants localities the power to regulate matters of 'local' concern out of their own right. The exact scope and understanding of this concept are contested and allude to different images of government as either 'localist' or 'centralist'.

However, the democratic promise of 'home rule' has been hollowed out by the transformation that has dragged cities into the whirlwinds of globalisation and digitalisation. The controversy around 'home rule' has played the sceptics of both local and central government against each other and has ultimately promoted market-based solutions as a perceived third way.[30] In the US context, scholars have found that the powers conferred under 'home rule' left cities largely powerless with regard to private and economic law matters[31] and that this petrified a self-image of cities as mere passive facilitators of markets. This conceptual absorption of cities' authority to regulate markets into the debate around 'home rule', leaving cities with formal regulatory authority yet few practical means, has become even more fraught with consequences today.

The exacerbating factor stems from the embeddedness of cities in global markets for products, labour and finance. With fewer and fewer matters being of merely 'local nature', a strict adherence to 'home rule' leaves municipal decision-makers with a fairly shallow array of competences. This mechanism is familiar from EU law debates, where the increasing transboundary setup of markets puts pressure on the principle of subsidiarity and increasingly justifies moving regulatory competencies upwards to the EU level. Even if often understood as a formal cornerstone of multi-level democracy that is protective of national competence by default, the principle of subsidiarity has become a vehicle for substantive transformation of economic policy in the EU. Faced with transboundary markets, subsidiarity flips its normative orientation and puts increasing pressure on Member States to justify regulation at the national level.[32]

It seems likely that, in an era of global cities,[33] 'home rule' will over time produce similar effects for municipal regulation. Matters that were long treated as the paradigm cases for local government, such as housing, transportation and local commerce, have spill-over effects on the broader metropolitan regions, on national economies and on other major cities around the world. In an interconnected world, the idea of matters that are local by their *nature* needs to be revisited just as much as the assumption that the 'local' is a dependent

---

30 See for the US context David J Barron, 'Reclaiming Home Rule' (2003) 116 Harvard Law Review 2255, 2265.

31 Paul Diller, 'The City and the Private Right of Action' (2012) 64 Stanford Law Review 1109; Gerald Frug, 'The City as a Legal Concept' (1980) 93 Harvard Law Review 1057.

32 See Jacob Öberg, 'Subsidiarity as a Limit to the Exercise of EU Competences' (2017) 36 Yearbook of European Law 391.

33 Saskia Sassen, *Global Networks Linked Cities* (Routledge 2002); Saskia Sassen, *The Global City: New York, London, Tokyo* (Princeton University Press 1991); Peter Hall, *The World Cities* (Weidenfeld & Nicolson 1984).

subdivision of the 'national'. Cities are a *condensed locus of globalisation and modern capitalism* inasmuch as urban development reflects stages in the evolution of capitalism.[34] Even in (semi-)planned economies, the urban level is where economic planning conflicts and coalesces most explicitly with neoliberal models of urban development.[35] Global cities reject the traditional idea of being the lower echelon of administration by stepping out of the state-centred frame that prevails in economic and legal models. New York and Karachi, São Paulo and Manila, Berlin and Guangzhou may in several respects share more with each other than these cities do with other domestic municipalities. Major cities have become principal economic zones, making urban economic performance a better indicator of economic development than national figures such as the GDP.[36] Taken together, SDG 11 rightly recognises cities as sites in their own right and projects sustainability as a powerful yardstick that can guide the current urban transformations. The rationale of SDG 11 sees this transformation as systemic, involving multiple actors and levels of governance, and hence calls for reforms beyond the confines of local government.[37] This speaks to the fact that cities are connected more tightly than ever before to global trends. It would be insufficient to merely shift regulatory power vertically from the national to the urban level to increase the leverage of local decision-making. Rather, urban governance under globalisation requires an *expansion of the regulatory and conceptual toolkit to address global urban dynamics*.

This entails taking a closer look at the changing legal venues for questions of 'urban equity' and 'spatial justice' today. In addition to the public and administrative law arsenal mentioned above, regimes of private and economic law, most notably contract and property law, alongside private international law and arbitration, as well as IP and data protection, shape urban trajectories. Increasingly since the 1980s, cities' involvement in a global competition for capital investment[38] and a prominent position in global supply chains has triggered structural changes within them and has marked their integration into the world economy.[39] As a consequence, many of the contemporary

---

34 David Harvey, 'From managerialism to entrepreneurialism: The transformation in urban governance in late capitalism' (1989) 71 Human Geography 3.

35 Yi-Ling Chen and Hyun Bang Shin (eds), *Neoliberal Urbanism, Contested Cities and Housing in Asia* (Palgrave Macmillan 2019).

36 Jane Jacobs, *Cities and the Wealth of Nations: Principles of Economic Life* (Vintage Books 1984).

37 Particular emphasis on the public dimension by Helmut Philipp Aust and Anél du Plessis, 'Introduction: The Globalization of Urban Governance – Legal Perspectives on Sustainable Development Goal 11' in Helmut Philipp Aust and Anél du Plessis (eds), *The Globalisation of Urban Governance. Legal Perspectives on Sustainable Development Goal 11* (Routledge 2019) 3, 4.

38 Richard C Schragger, 'Mobile Capital, Local Economic Regulation, and the Democratic City' (2009) 123 Harvard Law Review 482.

39 John Friedmann, 'The world city hypothesis' (1986) 17 Development & Change 69; RB Cohen, 'The new international division of labor, multinational corporations and urban hierarchy' in Michael Dear and Allen Scott (eds), *Urbanization and Urban Planning in Capitalist Society* (Methuen 1981) 287.

developments in fields like urban labour or the financialisation of housing and infrastructure follow a geographic dispersion of economic power. The legal institutions of property, contract and tax play a facilitative role that allows real estate investments to be turned into tradeable financial assets.[40] The circulation of labour, capital, materials and information is not only constitutive of a localised urban economy but attracts and directs international investment flows that operate independently of their spatial effects on urban development. By consequence, globalisation has partly broken apart the traditional links between cities and their local industry, agriculture and service sector.[41]

Alongside economic globalisation, the digitalisation and data-driven governance of the economy are also increasingly leaving a mark on urban development. 'Smart city'[42] has become an alluring signifier for the digital enhancement of public services and infrastructure. Such digitally mediated infrastructure and the digital platforms that draw on it (like Airbnb and Yelp) are redefining individual and collective opportunities in the urban sphere, value creation and power allocation.[43] Consider Amazon's city competition to host its second headquarters ('HQ2'), in response to which 238 US cities submitted their bids in anticipation of a boost to their local areas. Besides commitments to large public funds, often bypassing regular planning rules, the bids contained comprehensive data on city infrastructure, allowing Amazon to assess how an entire city, including its transportation, workforce and cultural system, could be mobilised for its purposes.[44]

The above requires zooming in on the legal construction of competition between global cities. Overall, the change of perspective suggested in this chapter places the trajectories of urban sustainability within legal realms that have not conventionally been analysed from an urban perspective.

40 Rachel Weber, 'Selling City Futures: The Financialization of Urban Redevelopment Policy' (2010) 86 Economic Geography 251; Katharina Pistor, *How the Law Creates Wealth and Inequality* (Princeton University Press 2019) 23.

41 Richard Florida, *The New Urban Crisis* (Basic Books 2017) 173 et seqq.

42 On this multifaceted notion see Germaine R Halegoua, *Smart Cities* (MIT Press 2019); Robert G Hollands, 'Will the Real Smart City Please Stand Up? Intelligent, Progressive or Entrepreneurial?' (2008) 12 City 303.

43 See Petter Törnberg and Justus Uitermark, 'Complex Control and the Governmentality of Digital Platforms' (2020) 2 Frontiers in Sustainable Cities, DOI: 10.3389/frsc.2020.00006.

44 See Priya S Gupta, 'The fleeting, unhappy affair of Amazon HQ 2 and New York City' (2019) 10 Transnational Legal Theory 97; similar bids occur for the Olympics and other major sports competitions, cf Stefan Kipler and Roger Keil, 'Toronto Inc? Planning the Competitive City in the New Toronto' (2002) 34 Antipode 227 and – on the FIFA Worldcup's Memorandum of Understanding with host states and cities – Tomaso Ferrando, 'Private Legal Transplant: Multinational Enterprises as Proxies of Legal Homogenisation' (2014) 5 Transnational Legal Theory 20. For the neoclassical model of competition between municipalities around the optimal level of provision of public goods cf Charles Tiebout, 'The Pure Theory of Local Expenditure' (1956) 64 Journal of Political Economy 416 and David Schleicher, 'The City as a Law and Economic Subject' (2010) University of Illinois Law Review 1507.

'Seeing like a city'[45] provides an angle from which to recast the legal array of 'enabling conditions' of unsustainable urban practices and spatial injustice, rather than merely concentrating on discourses around remedies and redress that leave the enabling set of norms and practices intact. This resonates with recent scholarship on legal institutionalism[46] that has put the often indirectly and incrementally facilitative role of private law for the global economy to the fore. Such a focus is reflective of the transformative agenda of the SDGs. At the same time, it makes the quest for urban sustainability more fragmented, eclectic and hence demanding. It stresses how the centralised implementation of SDG 11 through planning and design remains limited to the more conventional tools of ('public' or 'municipal') urban governance. It also, however, invites sustainability in as a broad and much-needed normative yardstick[47] that identifies cities in their global interconnections beyond their territorial anchoring and that can reshape the economic, environmental and social viability of urban communities.

2.3. A TRANSNATIONAL LEGAL PERSPECTIVE ON URBAN DEVELOPMENT

Giving adequate room to the global entanglements of cities and both their public and private legal infrastructure requires a legal conception of cities as social institutions that cannot be described in spatial terms alone. The types and layers of norms that animate the concurrent plurality of urban dynamics do not form a comprehensive regulatory framework.[48] Capturing them proves to be particularly challenging, given that the most vivid discussions of global cities have so far been in international and administrative law, with a certain blind spot for informal, bottom-up legal practice. Moreover, private law's methodological individualism as reflected in several of its basic notions leaves it ill-prepared to apprehend the complex and overlapping normative order of social institutions.[49] Similarly, private international law in its perception of

45 Marina Valverde, 'Seeing Like a City: The Dialectic of Modern and Premodern Ways of Seeing in Urban Governance' (2011) 45 Law and Society Review 277.

46 Simon Deakin et al, 'Legal Institutionalism: Capitalism and the constitutive role of law' (2017) 45 Journal of Comparative Economics 188; Katharina Pistor, *How the Law Creates Wealth and Inequality* (Princeton University Press 2019) 23.

47 On the role of such 'imaginaries' in law cf Marija Bartl, 'Socio-Economic Imaginaries and European Private Law' in Poul F Kjaer (ed), *The Law of Political Economy: Transformation in the Function of Law* (CUP 2020) 228.

48 Cf generally, albeit with a focus on the national political constitution, Gunther Teubner, *Constitutional Fragments. Societal Constitutionalism and Globalization* (OUP 2012) 17 et seqq.

49 Cf Dan Wielsch, 'The Function of Fundamental Rights in EU Private Law – Perspectives for the Common European Sales Law' (2014) 10 European Review of Contract Law 365, 371; for a similar starting point with regards to fundamental rights cf Thomas Vesting, Stefan Korioth and Ino Augsberg (eds), *Grundrechte als Phänomene kollektiver Ordnung* (Mohr Siebeck 2014).

affected interests oscillates between 'governmental versus individual' interests, thereby leaving little room to capture policies and interests of intermediaries, groups and sub- or supra-national political entities in a more granular manner.[50] Methodological individualism renders it difficult to address the meso level of complex systems like the urban economy and its global connecting points, which are in constant evolution, animated by countless individual and collective decisions.[51] Despite recent interest in the 'scales' of private law, this scholarship focuses on translations between micro and macro and only adds to the impression of the meso as a void in private law analysis.[52] This chapter puts forward a transnational law perspective,[53] with private international law at its core,[54] to grasp the socio-legal arrangements that embed global cities in a web of economic, political and cultural relations. In addition to the micro-level analysis of private law relationships and the macro level of political economy, socio-legal analysis is attuned to the meso level of urban institutions and assemblages.

Despite the rising prominence of cities in legal discourse, the role of private authority as an animating force of city trajectories has so far remained underexplored. While law was initially hesitant to follow other social sciences' renewed enthusiasm for cities linked to the 'spatial turn',[55] in part because of the legally scattered nature of related questions, the rise of global cities was first traced by scholars interested in international administrative networks and the status of cities under international law.[56] At a time when private

---

50 See for an early account Christian Joerges, *Zum Funktionswandel des Kollisionsrechts – Die "Governmental Interest Analysis" und die "Krise des Internationalen Privatrechts"* (de Gruyter 1971) 151 et seqq.

51 For such a systemic understanding of cities cf Michael Batty, *Cities and complexity. Understanding Cities with cellular automata, agent-based models, and fractals* (MIT Press 2005); see generally Kenneth J Arrow, 'Methodological Individualism and Social Knowledge' (1994) 84 American Economic Review 1.

52 Andrew Gold and Henry Smith, 'Sizing up private law' (2020) 70 University of Toronto Law Journal 489.

53 See most recently Peer Zumbansen, 'Transnational Law: Theories and Applications', forthcoming in Peer Zumbansen (ed), *The Oxford Handbook of Transnational Law* (OUP 2021).

54 See Ralf Michaels, 'Globalisation and Law: Law Beyond the State' in Reza Banakar and Max Travers (eds), *Law and Social Theory* (Hart Publishing 2013) 289.

55 John Agnew and Stuart Corbridge, *Mastering Space. Hegemony, Territory, and International Political Economy* (Routledge 1995).

56 See pioneering Gerald Frug and David Barron, 'International Local Government Law' (2006) 38 The Urban Lawyer 1; Yishai Blank, 'The City and the World' (2006) 44 Columbia Journal of Transnational Law 868; Yishai Blank, 'Localism in the New Global Legal Order' (2006) 47 Harvard International Law Journal 263; Fernanda G Nicola and Sheila Foster, 'Comparative Urban Governance for Lawyers' (2014) 42 Fordham Urban Law Journal 1; Andreas Philippopoulos-Mihalopoulos (ed), *Law and the City* (Routledge 2007); most recently Chrystie Swiney, 'The Urbanization of International Law and International Relations: The Rising Soft Power of Cities in Global Governance' (2020) 41 Michigan Journal of International Law 227.

international law scholars were wary of foreign regulatory influence on private relationships,[57] (international) administrative lawyers demonstrated how cities' external political relations grant them a de facto status as important actors in an emerging global legal order.

Accordingly, the fact that cities remain for the most part excluded from the group of signatories of treaties, for example on climate change, waste management or sustainable transportation, has inspired calls to 'pierce the veil of sovereign nation states'[58] with the aim of recognising cities as basic political units. This lacuna of international law is echoed by the domestic law of many states, which explicitly prohibit local governments from engaging in foreign affairs.[59] Cities, as public international and administrative lawyers have recognised, adopt a state-like role as generators and enforcers of global norms.[60] The concept of 'urban citizenship' captures the particular proximity between public power and individual autonomy at the urban level and expresses the fact that cities are increasingly replacing states in the construction of social and cultural identities.[61] (Global) cities are becoming the central nodes of many functional systems, including the economy and politics, as well as media and culture, and provide a degree of global interconnection and multiplicity of individual experiences, which McLuhan referred to as the 'global village'.[62]

At the same time, this illustrates how an understanding of cities primarily as local government[63] and the faith placed on democratic governability of global cities may fall short of grasping the flows of global data, finance, commodities and labour migration that permeate city walls. A (private) legal perspective on global cities faces the constant challenge of attending to local effects of such law on the one hand and not reducing global cities to spatial bounds on the other.

---

57 Matthias Lehmann, 'Regulation, global governance and private international law: Squaring the triangle' (2020) 16 Journal of Private International Law 1.

58 Yishai Blank, 'Localism in the New Global Legal Order' (2006) 47 Harvard International Law Journal 263, 267.

59 Gerald Frug and David Barron, 'International Local Government Law' (2006) 38 The Urban Lawyer 1; on the suggestion of a 'city supplement' to international treaties cf Danielle Spiegel-Feld and Katrina Wyman, 'Cities as Global Environmental Actors: The Case of Marine Plastics' (2020) 62 Arizona Law Review 487.

60 Barbara Oomen and Moritz Baumgärtel, 'Frontier Cities: The Rise of Local Authorities as an Opportunity for International Human Rights Law' (2018) 29 European Journal of International Law 607.

61 Peter Taylor, 'World Cities and Territorial States: The Rise and Fall of their Mutuality' in Paul Know and Peter Taylor (eds), *World Cities in a World System* (CUP 1995) 48, 58.

62 Marshall McLuhan, *The Gutenberg Galasy: The Making of Typographic Man* (first published 1962, University of Toronto Press 2011) 3; for a legal perspective on his work cf Thomas Vesting, *Computernetzwerke. Die Medien des Rechts* (vol 4, Velbrück Wissenschaft 2015) 110–125.

63 See explicitly Chrystie Swiney, 'The Urbanization of International Law and International Relations: The Rising Soft Power of Cities in Global Governance' (2020) 41 Michigan Journal of International Law 227, 228, n 4.

While scholars in law-and-geography have recognised law as a productive force shaping material, social and mental spaces,[64] spatial thinking can also prove limiting in discerning the city as a social institution.[65] Rather, studying the transnational legal dynamics that englobe cities requires 'following the policy' across the many sites and processes that make and unmake such policies.[66] Despite its local 'touchdown' point,[67] contemporary urban governance requires a multi-sited – *transnational* – analysis.

'Seeing like a city' through the lens of private law seems apt to do just this, namely to unpack cities as globally embedded sites of overlapping normativities and spatially concentrated social interactions resulting from diverse forms of life.[68] Complementing scholarship in international and administrative law that portrays cities as actors at the international level, a private law perspective turns to the internal dynamics within and between cities. It can draw on extensive work in urban philosophy and sociology that engages with the relation between individuals and urban communities, to the extent that cities may invite exploring legal concepts of organising social life beyond individualism. In fact, most trajectories of urban development are 'spontaneous' and 'natural' only at first glimpse; for the most part, they are constructed by an array of legal, economic and political contextualising elements. Gentrification – i.e. the transformation of neighbourhoods caused by an influx of more wealthy incomers and businesses, resulting in displacement of residents from a lower socio-economic background[69] – is not merely a cultural process but is deeply anchored in a capitalist urban development that invites a private law conceptualisation.[70] While not underestimating the important role and potential of municipal

---

64 Yishai Blank and Issi Rosen-Zvi, 'The spatial turn in legal theory' (2010) 10 Hagar: Studies in Culture, Polity and Identity 39; Irus Braverman et al, 'Introduction: Expanding the Spaces of Law' in Irus Braverman et al (eds), *Expanding the Spaces of Law: A Timely Legal Geography* (Stanford University Press 2014) 1; from within private international law Richard Ford, 'Law's Territory (A History of Jurisdiction)' (1999) 97 Michigan Law Review 843 and Ralf Michaels, 'Territorial Jurisdiction after Territoriality' in Piet Jan Slot and Mielle Bulterman (eds), *Globalization and Jurisdiction* (Kluwer Law International 2004).

65 For a critique of the understanding of space as easily malleable through law see Yishai Blank and Issi Rosen-Zvi, 'The spatial turn in legal theory' (2010) 10 Hagar: Studies in Culture, Polity and Identity 39; for scepticism vis-à-vis the concept of 'space' in theories of society see Rudolf Stichweh, 'Raum, Region und Stadt in der Systemtheorie' in *Die Weltgesellschaft. Soziologische Analysen* (Suhrkamp 2000) 184.

66 Jamie Peck and Nik Theodore, 'Follow the policy: A distended case approach' (2012) 44 Environment and Planning A 21.

67 On a (national) 'touchdown' of transnational normative regimes cf Robert Wai, 'Transnational Liftoff and Juridical Touchdown: The Regulatory Function of Private International Law in an Era of Globalization' (2002) 40 Columbia Journal of Transnational Law 209.

68 Karl-Heinz Ladeur, 'Netzwerkrecht als neues Ordnungsmodell des Rechts' in Martin Eifert and Tobias Gostomzyk (eds), *Netzwerkrecht* (Nomos 2018) 169, 175.

69 Neil Smith, 'New Globalism, New Urbanism: Gentrification as Global Urban Strategy' (2002) 34 Antipode 427.

70 ibid.

regulation, such an approach investigates how local regulatory power is conditioned through transnational legal mechanisms.

In brief, a transnational legal perspective on the analysis of urban governance can (1) allow the effects of national policies (e.g. of austerity) and economic globalisation to be more effectively counterbalanced at the urban level by focusing not only on the formal level of rules applicable in and enacted by cities, but also on the legal construction and translation of general policies and market dynamics at the urban level, and (2) address conflicts – interpersonal, group-based and institutional ones – across cultural, social and other barriers that mark urban life in global cities.

3. INTERSECTIONS BETWEEN SDG 11 AND PRIVATE INTERNATIONAL LAW

The above understanding of and perspective on urban development also sheds light on the role of private international law in particular. A multiplicity of normative systems and the absence of a central regulator mark the usual terrain of private international law. The rules and doctrines of this discipline seem ubiquitous in a global city, populated by people from diverse backgrounds and home to numerous firms with foreign parent companies and cross-border transactions. At the same time, the exact role of private international law remains enigmatic and difficult to pinpoint. Providing us with a technique for determining the jurisdiction, applicable law and place of enforcement for a given conflict, private international law certainly does not have a single decisive lever to pull in order to enhance sustainability in the urban sphere. No rules of private international law carry an explicit 'urban imprint' – none are designed to take effect specifically in an urban environment and none incorporate a comprehensive idea of urban development, let alone urban justice. The doctrines of private international law seem, at first sight at least, to be insensitive towards the societal stakes identified for sustainability in the urban sphere. While the intersections between private international law and SDG 11 are manifold and example cases around investment, commercial sales, consumer contracts or data protection in a transboundary setting come to mind easily, the regulatory effects of private international law on the urban fabric are much more difficult to detect. Here, the abstract nature of private international law's toolkit shines through, along with the fact that even if a certain implicit orientation in terms of political economy may be ingrained, it is not tailored to the urban context.

The perspective on global urban governance outlined above brings several of private international law's foundational concepts to the table, including sovereignty, territoriality, nationality, identity and sense of belonging (as in the personal connecting factors of domicile and habitual residence). In particular, this invites perspectives that bring out the governance dimension of this body of law and identify private international law as a constitutive factor in the global political economy,[71] as well as perspectives which mobilise the toolkit of private international law to address questions of identity and difference in pluralistic societies.[72] Not least because the driving force of urbanisation, especially in the Global South, has often been displacement through coercion, both physical and economic, engaging with the genealogy of urban structures may also shed light on lines of continuity with colonial and other pasts.

Overall, recent years have witnessed considerable attention paid to the unmasking of the allegedly technical nature and multilateralism of private international law doctrines.[73] One strand explores the substantive goals behind much of private international law's mechanisms[74] – goals that have become most apparent in the functionalism of the EU internal market (e.g. consumer rights and access to courts), but can be found beyond. A second strand investigates the role of private international law in regulatory conflicts and asks how it ought to react to the strategic circumvention of regulatory standards and to the exploitation of regulatory gaps through corporate structures and contractual arrangements.[75] To be sure, many standards that apply in the urban sphere are local by nature and allow rather little arbitrage (e.g. logistical and safety standards, construction law). The standards in question pertain mostly to economic conduct, such as in antitrust, securities or tax law, and touch upon the financial side of corporate activities in global cities. As the above discussion of the features of urban development

71 Horatia Muir Watt and Diego Fernández Arroyo (eds), *Private International Law and Global Governance* (OUP 2015); Horatia Muir Watt et al (eds), *Global Private International Law. Adjudication without Frontiers* (OUP 2019); Christopher A Whytock, 'Conflict of Laws, Global Governance, and Transnational Legal Order' (2016) 1 UC Irvine Journal of International and Transnational & Comparative Law 117; on economic models Ralf Michaels, 'Two Economists, Three Opinions? Economic Models for Private International Law – Cross-Border Torts as Example' in Jürgen Basedow, Toshiyuki Kono and Giesela Rühl (eds), *An Economic Analysis of Private International Law* (Mohr Siebeck 2006) 143.

72 See e.g. Annelise Riles, 'Cultural Conflicts' (2008) 71 Law and Contemporary Problems 273; Annelise Riles, 'A New Agenda for the Cultural Study of Law: Taking on the Technicalities' (2005) 53 Buffalo Law Review 1018; Ralf Michaels, 'Banning Burkas – The perspective of Postsecular Comparative Law' (2018) 28 Duke Journal of Comparative and International Law 213.

73 Ralf Michaels, 'Towards a Private International Law for Regulatory Conflicts?' (2016) 59 Japanese Yearbook of International Law 175.

74 Symeon Symeonides, *The 'Private' in Private International Law* (Eleven Publishing 2019); Yves Lequette, 'Les mutations du droit international privé: Vers un changement de paradigme?' (2017) 387 Cours général de droit international privé 9.

75 Ralf Michaels, 'Towards a Private International Law for Regulatory Conflicts?' (2016) 59 Japanese Yearbook of International Law 175; Laura Carballa Piñeiro and Xandra Kramer, 'The Role of Private International Law in Contemporary Society: Global Governance as a Challenge' (2014) Erasmus Law Review 109.

has shown, the national level is no longer undisputed as the most significant norm-setter. This poses considerable challenges for a private international law which, even in its regulatory theorisations, has a traditional focus on national law and treats the determination of sub-national law as a domestic matter.[76] *Ordre public*, for instance, is commonly understood as referring to a *national* public policy[77] and cannot easily encompass particularly progressive municipal policies, for example in matters of equality and non-discrimination,[78] or reflect urban customary law[79] or municipal commitments to sustainability, for example 'Fair Trade Town'[80] partnerships. It is no coincidence that many of the newly rising financial marketplaces around the world are in city-states, islands and enclave economies, such as Singapore, Hong Kong, The Bahamas, Luxembourg or Bahrain.[81] Their peculiar setting allows national rules to be primarily geared towards integration into global markets,[82] not mediating domestically between different urban areas, regions and hinterlands, as in bigger nation states.

For private international law, SDG 11 raises the question of how the urban level can be addressed without distortions created by the intermediary of the national level and without losing sight of the global interconnections across urban spaces, actors, norms and processes. Moreover, it brings the rather underexplored question to the table of whether existing private international law rules have an implicit 'city bias' behind allegedly 'national' policies, i.e. by being particularly conducive to interests grouped in big cities. One example would be broad rules on jurisdiction over non-residents ('long-arm statutes')[83] that favour the dispute resolution business typically located in big cities. In addition, party autonomy does allow for a choice of jurisdiction or seat of arbitration in cities.[84]

---

76 See e.g. Vincent Schröder, *Die Verweisung auf Mehrrechtsstaaten im deutschen Internationalen Privatrecht* (Mohr Siebeck 2007).

77 See for European private international law e.g. Art 21 Rome I Regulation (Regulation (EC) No 593/2008).

78 See e.g. Jason Pierceson, 'Theoretical Perspectives on Subnational Public Policy and LGBT Law' in *Oxford Research Encyclopedia: Politics* (23 May 2019).

79 For local customary law cf BGH, Judgment of 21 November 2008 – V ZR 35/08 (holding that in a fen area of East Frisia on the North German coast, a local customary law has been recognised since the 19th century, according to which a marginal strip must be kept free along the Iwieken canal as access for the users of the properties behind it.

80 Cf <http://www.fairtradetowns.org>.

81 Ronen Palan, 'International Financial Centers: The British-Empire, City-States and Commercially Oriented Politics' (2010) 11 Theoretical Inquiries in Law 149.

82 Parag Khanna, 'Beyond City Limits', Foreign Policy of 6 August <https://foreignpolicy.com/2010/08/06/beyond-city-limits/> speaks of 'Venices of the 21st century'.

83 E.g. the Alien Tort Statute in 28 U.S.C. §1350.

84 In 2018, the most popular seats of arbitration were London, Paris, Singapore, Hong Kong and Geneva, cf White & Case, '2018 International Arbitration Survey: The Evolution of International Arbitration' <http://www.arbitration.qmul.ac.uk/media/arbitration/docs/2018-International-Arbitration-Survey---The-Evolution-of-International-Arbitration-(2).pdf>.

Choice of law, in turn, continues to be restricted to national laws, at least before domestic courts.[85] A principal reason for this, of course, is the lack of substantive private law orders at the urban level, with the exception of city-states. A certain historical precursor for sub-national law can be found in the early, medieval *lex mercatoria* that arose out of the prevalence of local communities over distant central legislators. This law of merchants was a set of rules emanating from localised marketplaces, such as Venice and other European principalities, and served as a specialised and functional normative regime between experienced traders.[86] Certainly, links to specifically urban development were not spelled out – yet the *lex mercatoria* was credited with having positive effects on economic growth. Arguably, the 'new *lex mercatoria*', an evolving contemporary set of rules and laws for transnational and cross-cultural legal transactions,[87] also originated and finds its main application in the principal trading places of the world, which for the most part are big cities. However, rather than to a specific city, such rules and norms are attributed to the business organisations, expert bodies or communities of legal practitioners that develop them.

At a conceptual level, the rise of cities might mean for private international law that local or community-based connecting factors will gradually gain prominence.[88] One might also say *regain* prominence, since the initial environment of the *lex mercatoria*, and private international law more generally, was, as we have seen, one of inter-local and intercity conflicts,[89] long before nation states became the primary point of reference for the discipline. Overall, a supportive role for private international law as regards the goals of SDG 11 could best be achieved by mobilising the discipline's unparalleled experience in and technique of situating and contextualising conflicts, in other words translating a novel type of social *problématique* into a legal question and providing an adequate

---

85 See Markus Petsche, 'The Application of Transnational Law (Lex Mercatoria) by Domestic Courts' (2013) 10 Journal of Private International Law 489; for arbitration Ulla Liukkunen, 'Lex Mercatoria in International Arbitration' in Jan Klabbers and Touko Piiparinen (eds), *Normative Pluralism in International Law: Exploring Global Governance* (CUP 2013) 201.

86 Ron Harris, *Going the Distance: Eurasian Trade and the Rise of the Business Corporation, 1400–1700* (Princeton University Press 2020); on the contemporary rediscovery of this concept Alec Stone Sweet, 'The new Lex Mercatoria and transnational governance' (2006) 13 Journal of European Public Policy 627.

87 See for an overview Jeremy J Kingsley, 'Introduction: *Reimagining* Lex Mercatoria' (2020) 40 Comparative Studies of South Asia, Africa and the Middle East 257, and the Special Issue it introduces.

88 See for a perspective of inter-systemic conflict resolution (without specific attention to cities) e.g. Gunther Teubner, *Constitutional Fragments. Societal Constitutionalism and Globalization* (OUP 2012) 154 et seqq.

89 See Magnus Ryan, 'Bartolus of Sassoferrato and Free Cities. The Alexander Prize Lecture' (2000) 10 Transactions of the Royal Historical Society 65; Bertrand Ancel, *Eléments d'histoire du droit international privé* (Panthéon-Assas 2017).

forum for its resolution.[90] Conflicts around urban development presently lack such adequate legal-institutional fora, for they are either – as we will see in the next sections – conceived of as merely local or, on the contrary, decided with disregard for their local urban implications. Private international law is apt to render visible the urban development implications of a finance-mediated globalisation of rental markets and the digitalisation of urban services, both because of its own contribution to such phenomena of value creation[91] and its conceptual affinity with a multi-level analysis of conflicts. Private international law would, ideally, mirror a macro-level study of the global economy onto the meso and micro level of its urban ramifications. What is, for instance, the role of finance in big infrastructure consortia, which account for much of contemporary urban design and architecture, including their often-robust exclusionary effects, which put onerous and unequal constraints on the use of public space?[92] This parallel orientation towards micro, meso and macro moreover prevents the rise of the urban being seen as a return to territorialism and treats space as an important, yet decentred category in a deterritorialised world.

3.1. FINANCIALISATION OF REAL ESTATE AND PRIVATISATION OF PUBLIC SPACE

SDG 11 sets out the goal of adequate, safe and affordable housing and basic services, as well upgrading slums (Target 11.1). The quality and location of housing is a bottleneck for participation in society and central to questions of health, economic well-being and social interactions. The vocabulary used in SDG 11 certainly translates differently between municipalities at different stages of development. The recent rise in rent control legislation in several countries and localities[93] reflects the centrality of housing in the Global North, too, which is also threatened by evictions, energy poverty, rising homelessness and a backlash against social housing, possibly propelled by the Covid-19 pandemic. Housing policy and regulation in global cities has to respond to shortages, rising housing

---

90 Andreas Maurer and Moritz Renner, 'Kollisionsrechtliches Denken in der Rechtstheorie' (2010) 125 Archiv für Rechts- und Sozialphilosophie 207; Gunther Teubner, 'Alienating Justice: On the surplus value of the twelfth camel' in David Nelken and Jirí Prabán (eds), *Consequences of Legal Autopoiesis* (Aldershot 2001) 21.

91 See e.g. Horatia Muir Watt, 'Private International Law's Shadow Contribution to the Question of Informal Transnational Authority' (2018) 25 Indiana Journal of Global Legal Studies 37.

92 See on the regulatory character of 'urban design tactics' around street layouts, sidewalks, elevators and other facilities Sarah Schindler, 'Architectural Exclusion: Discrimination and Segregation Through Physical Design of the Built Environment' (2015) 124 The Yale Law Journal 1934; Leslie Kern, *Feminist City* (Verso 2020).

93 Christoph Schmid (ed), *Tenancy Law and Housing Policy in Europe* (vol 1, Edward Elgar Publishing 2018); Duncan Kennedy, 'In Defense of Rent Control and Rent Caps', LPEblog (3 February 2020) <https://lpeblog.org/author/dkennedylpe/>.

costs, restrictions of public budgets and a related growing privatisation.[94] Arguably, the most significant transformation of the housing market and urban infrastructure stems from its financialisation.[95] When land becomes a financial commodity, this delocalises the value generated through real estate and decouples price levels from their local context and the often-convoluted settings of local actors.[96] Urban geographers like David Harvey have long highlighted the link between capitalism and its geographical expansionary logic ('spatial fix') that seeks surplus through investments in local housing markets across the world.[97] While commodification of land first found attention with regard to agricultural and rural land,[98] the role of private developers and investors was foregrounded during Leilani Farha's tenure as UN Special Rapporteur on adequate housing (2014–2020).[99] Today, large-scale infrastructure and real estate projects have become inconceivable without significant involvement of private investment funds.[100] Blackstone Group, for instance, has become the world's biggest landlord, with a real estate portfolio in major cities around the globe.[101] Moreover, financial service providers and law and accounting firms are clustered in global cities and add to urban hierarchy. They make use of the 'transnational lift-off'

94 See Rashmi Dyal-Chand, *Collaborative Capitalism in American Cities. Reforming Urban Market Regulations* (CUP 2019).

95 For an early account of the influence of financial hotspots on architecture cf Carol Willis, *Form Follows Finance* (Princeton Architectural Press 1995). See, moreover, Samuel Stein, *Capital City. Gentrification and the Real Estate State* (Verso 2019); David Bassens and Michiel Van Meeteren, 'World cities under conditions of financialized globalization: Towards an augmented world city hypothesis' (2015) 39 Progress in Human Geography 752; Manuel Aalbers, *The Financialization of Housing: A Political Economy Approach* (Routledge 2016); Gertjan Wijburg, 'De de-financialization of housing: Towards a research Agenda' (2020) Housing Studies, DOI: 10.1080/02673037.2020.1762847.

96 Roger Sherman, *L.A. Under the Influence: The Hidden Logic of Urban Property* (University of Minnesota Press 2010).

97 David Harvey, 'Globalization and the "Spatial Fix"' (2001) Geographische Revue 23; pioneering Henri Lefebvre, *The Production of Space* (first published 1974, Blackwell 1991).

98 Cf recently Olivier de Schutter and Balakrishnan Rajagopal (eds), *Property Rights from Below. Commodification of Land and the Counter-Movement* (Routledge 2020).

99 See UN Human Rights Council, 'Guidelines for the Implementation of the Right to Adequate Housing' Report of the Special Rapporteur on adequate housing as a component of the right to an adequate standard of living, and on the right to non-discrimination in this context, 43rd Session (24 February–20 March 2020).

100 See for a typology of actors involved in financing urban infrastructure Phillip O'Neill, 'The financialization of urban infrastructure: A framework of analysis' (2019) 56 Urban Studies 1304, 1314; Fritz-Julius Grafe and Harald A Mieg, 'Connecting financialization and urbanization: The changing financial ecology of urban infrastructure in the UK' (2019) 6 Regional Studies, Regional Science 496.

101 See Letter by Surya Deva, UN Chair-Rapporteur of the Working Group on the issue of human rights and transnational corporations and other business enterprises, and Leilana Farha, Special Rapporteur on adequate housing as a component of the right to an adequate standard of living, and on the right to non-discrimination in this context, to Blackstone's CEO Steve Schwarzman of 22 March 2019, Ref. OL OTH 17/2019 <https://www.ohchr.org/Documents/Issues/Housing/Financialization/OL_OTH_17_2019.pdf>.

allowed for by choice of law and jurisdiction under private international law[102] to create largely self-contained regimes. For instance, the rise and volatility of secondary mortgage markets has led the US financial industry to develop a way of bypassing the recordation obligations imposed by states' real property law in the case of mortgage transfer. The Mortgage Electronic Registration System (MERS)[103] is a privately administered and owned registry which runs in parallel to the land recordation system. Funded by banks as its members, MERS serves as intermediary platform and nominal owner of mortgages, facilitating the circulation of mortgages among member banks.

The flow of capital, enabled and channelled through private law, including private international law,[104] transforms and reconstitutes cities with regard to conventional housing,[105] digital platform-based short-term rentals and large infrastructure projects. Even if party autonomy remains for the most part subject to (overriding) municipal regulation, such local rules are in praxis contested in different ways. In addition to office towers, malls and other premises in Central Business Districts (CBDs) which integrate cities into global value chains,[106] real estate portfolios comprise important infrastructure sites, ranging from ports and train stations to digitised warehouses for online retail. The increasing number of properties in global cities that are held by a small number of institutional investors poses problems of concentration and isomorphism across cities. Moreover, it is common to use 'share deals' in transferring rights to real estate in order to avoid transfer taxes and allow for a quicker market pace. Lastly, most funds are set up as temporary, imposing a timeline on their rentability that may collide with timelines of sustainable urban planning.

---

102 Horatia Muir Watt, 'Party Autonomy in Global Context: The Political Economy of a Self-Constituting Regime' (2015) 58 Japanese Yearbook of International Law 175.

103 See Sjef van Erp, 'Lex Rei Sitae: The Territorial Side of Classical Property Law' in Christine Godt (ed), *Regulatory Property Rights: The Transforming Notion of Property in Transnational Business Regulation* (Brill/Nijhoff 2016) 78; Julie Cohen, *Between Truth and Power. The Legal Constructions of Informational Capitalism* (OUP 2019) 34–37; Amnon Lehavi, *Property Law in a Globalizing World* (CUP 2019) 91–125.

104 Philip Wood, *Conflict of Laws and International Finance* (Sweet & Maxwell 2007); Caroline Bradley, 'Private International Law-making for the Financial Markets' (2005) 29 Fordham International Law Journal 127; Matthias Lehmann, 'Private international law and finance: nothing special?' (2018) Nederlands Internationaal Privaatrecht 3.

105 E.g. David Birchall, 'Human rights on the altar of the market: The Blackstone letters and the financialization of housing' (2019) 10 Transnational Legal Theory 446. The 'right to housing' as a fundamental right, to the contrary, conceptualises housing as bilateral relations and hence remains largely insensitive to the structural factors. See Irina Domurath and Chantal Mak, 'Private Law and Housing Justice in Europe' (2020) 83 The Modern Law Review 1188; generally on this structural weakness of human rights Samuel Moyn, *Not Enough: Human Rights in an Unequal World* (Harvard University Press 2018).

106 Saskia Sassen, 'Global Inter-city networks and commodity chains: Any intersections?' (2010) 10 Global Networks 150; Christof Parnreiter, 'Global cities and the geographical transfer of value' (2019) 56 Urban Studies 81; E Brown et al, 'World City Networks and Global Commodity Chains: Towards a world-systems' integration' (2010) 10 Global Networks 12.

The more public space becomes absorbed by private investors, the more questions of urban governance shift from zoning and local government law to the realm of contractual agreements with investors and developers. Those arrangements therefore merit extra scrutiny reflective of their public nature.[107] The urban level is generally where the rise of market-based regulation, privatisation and a disciplinary ethos as central tenets of neoliberal policies are felt most immediately, for example in the gradual withdrawal of the state from the funding of housing, schools, hospitals, transportation and in some countries even prisons.[108] Cuts in municipal budgets have not only led to patterns of municipal expenses that disadvantage lower socio-economic groups,[109] but have also exposed municipal budgets to the risk of bankruptcy. Detroit's 2013 bankruptcy under Chapter 9 of the US Bankruptcy Code is among the most prominent illustrations and has in turn fostered the privatisation of infrastructure and private investments in Detroit.[110]

Three specific examples may illustrate private (international) law's heightened role under such conditions.

A first example pertains to the privatisation of urban infrastructure through long-term public–private partnerships with advertising and media companies.[111] Much of today's small-scale infrastructure, like street furniture (bus shelters, benches, street signs, public toilets), billboards or self-service rental bikes, is provided by private actors in exchange for exclusive advertising rights in the public realm. For instance, the French limited company JCDecaux, a global market leader, operates in 75 countries and over 4,000 cities alone. The long-term nature of most such agreements and the relation-specific investments generate risks for both parties, which make clauses on cancellation and adjustment of contractual obligations and dispute mechanisms crucial. Municipal decisions to discontinue such relations have given rise to challenges under international investment law.[112]

107 Max Schanzenbach and Nadav Shoked, 'Reclaiming Fiduciary Law for the City' (2018) 70 Stanford Law Review 565.

108 Gilles Pinson and Christelle Morel Journel, 'The City – Theory, Evidence, Debates' (2016) 4 Territory, Politics, Governance 137; David Jaffee, 'Neoliberal urbanism as "Strategic Coupling" to global chains: Port infrastructure and the role of economic impact studies' (2019) 37 Environment and Planning C: Politics and Space 119; see from a legal perspective Honor Brabazon (ed), *Neoliberal Legality. Understanding the Role of Law in the Neoliberal Project* (Routledge 2016); David Singh Grewal and Jedediah Purdy, 'Introduction: Law and Neoliberalism' (2014) 77 Law and Contemporary Problems 1.

109 Destin Jenkins, *The Bonds of Inequality. Debt and the Making of the American City* (Chicago University Press 2021).

110 Michael J Deitch, 'Time for an Update: A New Framework for Evaluating Chapter 9 Bankruptcies' (2015) 83 Fordham Law Review 2705.

111 Kurt Iveson, 'Branded cities: Outdoor advertising, urban governance, and the outdoor media landscape' (2012) 44 Antipode 151.

112 See the ongoing ICSID Case No ARB/20/33, *JCDecaux SA v Czech Republic* pursuant to the Bilateral Investment Treaty between France and the Czech Republic of 1990.

A second and related example pertains to so-called privately owned public space (POPS). Cities increasingly make major construction permits – malls, office towers – conditional upon the provision of publicly accessible space surrounding these estates, often in exchange for exemptions from otherwise applicable restrictions, for example on building height.[113] What appears to be public domain – parks, squares, walkways, atriums – are in fact public spaces owned and designed by private developers. Often, no demarcations or other signs hint at the private nature of such spaces, and yet they are governed by exclusionary house rules, surveilled by private security companies and subject to other limitations to social heterogeneity that would be inconceivable in the public domain. From a private international law perspective, this raises the question of how foreign investors formulate such private access or house rules and how local regulatory standards can be guaranteed.

A third example comes from short-term rentals through digital platforms, notably the market leader, Airbnb. Airbnb's global rise has rapidly paced up and digitised the market for short-term rentals, previously dominated by hotels with stable business models and market structures. In addition, this transformation impacts on city economics, influencing tourism destinations, the composition of neighbourhoods and concepts of 'mobility' and 'home'. Airbnb engages in a 'servicification' of 'home' in a similar way as WeWork does for the workplace. From a legal perspective, this implies first of all that comprehensive property or usage rights are dissolved as a service, thereby often bypassing public regulations.[114] Moreover, platforms increase the spatial gap between value generation and value capture. Ultimately, alleged discrimination[115] and localised disputes between guests and hosts are absorbed by algorithmic governance and online dispute mechanisms.[116] The responses by municipalities have so far been mixed and based on a plurality of legal and policy approaches, some using digital platform regulation (e.g. Milan), others housing and land use (e.g. Paris), and again others using tourism regulation (e.g. Barcelona).[117] At the same time, Airbnb itself

---

113 Sarah Schindler, 'The "Publicization" of Private Space' (2018) 103 Iowa Law Review 1093.

114 See e.g. on the heavily regulated market for taxis in NYC Katrina Wyman, 'Problematic Private Property: The Case of New York Taxicab Medallions' (2013) 30 Yale Journal on Regulation 125.

115 *Selden v Airbnb, Inc*, Case No 16-cv-933 (CRC) (D.D.C. Dec. 19, 2016); David Restrepo Amariles and Gregory Lewkowicz, 'Global contract governance: Selden v. Airbnb' in Horatia Muir Watt et al (eds), *Global Private International Law. Adjudication without Frontiers* (OUP 2019) 416; Benjamin Edelman and Michael Luca, 'Digital Discrimination: The Case of Airbnb.com', Harvard Business School Working Paper No 14-054 (January 2014).

116 On Airbnb's dispute mechanism cf Nofar Sheffi, 'The Fast to the Furious' in Derek McKee, Finn Makela and Teresa Scassa (eds), *Law and the 'Sharing Economy'* (University of Ottawa Press 2018) 73.

117 Thomas Aguilera, Francesca Artioli and Claire Colom, 'Explaining the diversity of policy responses to platform-mediated short-term rentals in European cities: A comparison of Barcelona, Paris and Milan' (2019) 1 Economy and Space.

clearly lobbies – and litigates[118] – for global legal homogenisation in order to allow for easier scaling of its business model.[119] The case of Airbnb illustrates how digitally mediated relations are part and parcel of urban transformation,[120] relativising the concept of 'space' by moving towards the digital and affecting not only individuals – as is the common focus for example in the debate around employment status of Uber drivers[121] – but the urban community at large.

3.2. 'SMART CITIES' AS SUSTAINABLE UTOPIAS?

The embeddedness of urban justice in digital infrastructure becomes even more striking when considering the most avant-gardist scenarios that presently excite urban planners and designers. 'Smart city' is the *mot du jour* that spurs the collective imagination of urban futures,[122] praised as a sustainable utopia by some and portrayed as the ultimate dystopia by others. Several targets of SDG 11 may be addressed, among them specifically 'safe, affordable, accessible and sustainable transport systems' (Target 11.2) and air quality and waste management (Target 11.6). The 'smart' image presents urban life as knowable and governable through the use of aggregate data collected through sensors, cameras or GPS. Critics however argue that the quest for (optimised) digital 'solutions' to given 'problems' represents far too narrow a view of urban space as an actual habitat with lived experiences. Only in rare cases is an entire city planned as a 'smart' tabula rasa, as in China's Songdo;[123] the more frequent examples consist in specific data-driven services that are used to advance the city's real-time decision-making abilities on matters as diverse as traffic, energy, safety or general logistics.[124]

---

118 'Airbnb to America's Big Cities: See You in Court', Bloomberg (14 February 2020) <https://www.bloomberg.com/graphics/2020-airbnb-ipo-challenges/>.

119 Cf Airbnb Policy Tool Chest 2.0 <https://www.airbnbcitizen.com/home-sharing-policy-approaches-that-are-working-around-the-world/>.

120 For a synthesis cf Francesca Artioli, 'Digital platforms and cities', Cities are back in town Working Paper 01/2018, Sciences Po Urban School (May 2018).

121 *Uber BV v Aslam* [2021] UKSC 5; on the policy context cf Brishen Rogers, 'Employment Rights in the Platform Economy: Getting Back to Basics' (2016) 10 Harvard Law & Policy Review 479.

122 Thaddeus R Miller, 'Imaginaries of Sustainability: The Techno-Politics of Smart Cities' (2020) 29 Science as Culture 365.

123 Shannon Mattern, 'A City Is Not a Computer' (February 2017) Places Journal, DOI: 10.22269/170207; Martina Löw, 'Songdo: Raumkonstruktion in digitalisierten Lebensräumen' in Nicole Burzan (ed), *Komplexe Dynamiken globaler und lokaler Entwicklungen. Verhandlungen des 39. Kongresses der Deutschen Gesellschaft für Soziologie in Göttingen 2018* (Deutsche Gesellschaft für Soziologie 2019) <http://publikationen.soziologie.de/index.php/kongressband_2018>.

124 See e.g. LocalData (<http://localdata.com>) for an example of a non-profit that collects and visualises community-generated data, e.g. on street-level conditions such as property damage, delivery routes for goods and services, vacant resources and environmental damage. For further illustrations cf Souvanic Roy, 'The Smart City Paradigm in India: Issues and

Such technologies are being experimented with in global cities all over the world; some stress a 'smart' trajectory more than others. Despite the novelty of jargon, it is important to recall that information circulation has shaped cities since the early modern age, through, for example, the installation of an urban bureaucratic apparatus of edifices and clerks for deeds, taxes, passports and regulations mostly in city centres. Today, some 'smart' applications are careful reminders of the fact that the globalisation of cities is not restricted to city centres, with splendid boulevards and shopping malls, Central Business Districts and principal tourist spots. Importantly, the periphery of global cities has become a hub for IT infrastructure, warehouses and transportation services that are denoted as a 'logistical city'.[125] Located at the margins of the city, such sites operate largely unnoticed in the background and exemplify how capitalism works, with deliberate obfuscations so as not to disclose where goods and services truly stem from.[126]

Urban tech and digital urbanism are receiving more and more attention on the SDG agenda. The widespread use of sensors and cameras, operating jointly with individual devices like smartphones, to link urban services together is hailed as a way of scaling efficient resource use (e.g. of energy, waste or parking spaces) and foster social and technological connectivity. Given the long-standing role of centralised planning in the urban sphere, the idea of 'programming' urban life towards a rational order is endorsed by tech firms as well as planning officials – arguably overlooking the often rather evolutionary process of urban life. Some suggest that the collection of local data might help to localise global supply chains without the impetus of economic nationalism, because data, not physical commodities, will be the primary resource travelling along supply chains and enabling domestic and circular production. On the flipside of the positive connotations of the concept, smart cities can be said to euphemise surveillance tools and anchor them in everyday life, such as for predictive policing. What is more, data-driven solutions may deepen the social disconnect of the most marginalised groups of the urban population and may add the digital divide to a long list of factors sustaining urban segregation. While the spatialisation of inequality currently manifests itself in uneven access to the basic infrastructure of clean drinking water, sanitation, electricity or transportation, digital access will generate a new fault line.

A promising legal inroad is offered by thinking holistically about the role of infrastructure, understood as including material and informational devices

Challenges of Sustainability and Inclusiveness' (2016) 44 Social Scientist 29; Taylor Shelton, Matthew Zook and Alan Wiig, 'The "Actually Existing Smart City"' (2015) 8 Cambridge Journal of Regions, Economy and Society 13.

125 Steven Erie, *Globalizing L.A.: Trade, Infrastructure and Regional Development* (Stanford University Press 2004).

126 Cf Anna Tsing, *Friction: An Ethnography of Global Connection* (Princeton University Press 2004).

alongside legal institutions and governance regimes. For private international law, this may for instance entail an interest in transport routes and trade logistics such as in the Chinese Belt and Road Initiative or in the various techno-legal elements of global data governance.[127] Thinking infrastructurally, especially in the urban realm, means imagining infrastructure not as inert things that merely enable, but as active and performative agents.[128] From this perspective, law and material and technological infrastructure appear interconnected, not ontologically separate. This interweaving of the social, technological and organisational dimension of infrastructure indicates its centrality as a medium of power and contestation to which law contributes in numerous ways, for example through global data and IP law. Law at times blends into infrastructure and becomes itself infrastructural, thereby not losing its significance as a tool for social ordering but requiring more indirect and procedural concepts of regulation via infrastructure. The quest for sustainable urban development will constitute a central arena for this conceptual challenge. Again, the doctrines of private international law are contextual to this. As 'smart cities' are gradually taking shape and being experimented with, private international law will be called upon to decide on the applicable privacy standards in urban data-collecting services used by locals and travellers with various personal connecting factors.

4. RESULTS AND OUTLOOK

This chapter has sought to illustrate the role of private law and private international law in sustainable urban transformations. While global cities are increasingly being identified as pivotal sites for sustainable futures – a fact that led them to be addressed in a separate SDG – an engagement with the legal underpinnings of this transformation has thus far been sporadic. Although cities are a renewed field of interest for international lawyers, existing work mostly portrays cities as novel political and regulatory actors in a still largely state-dominated international order. Yet, beyond the novel role of global cities as generators and enforcers of norms as highlighted by public international lawyers, sustainable urban development hinges upon the fact that global cities

127 For current European and transnational initiatives on harmonising data regulation cf Sjef van Erp, 'Data Regulation: A Race to …?' (2020) 7 European Journal of Comparative Law and Governance 335.

128 Benedict Kingsbury, 'Infrastructure and InfraReg: On Rousing the international law "Wizards of Is"' (2019) 8 Cambridge International Law Journal 171; Boris Vormann, 'Toward an infrastructural critique of urban change' (2015) 19 City 356; Boris Vormann, 'Infrastrukturen der globalen Stadt. Widersprüche des urbanen Nachhaltigkeitsdiskurses am Beispiel Vancouvers' (2014) 34 Zeitschrift für Kanada-Studien 62; Ronen Shamir, *Current Flow: The Electrification of Palestine* (Stanford University Press 2013).

are loci of global markets and subject to digital transformations. This inner, social and performative side of current urban change, as described for instance in urban studies, political economy and media and communication studies, calls for private law to play a role in moderating social innovation. Examples from the financialisation of real estate and the trajectory of 'smart cities' show how private law paves the way for the delocalisation of urban social relations, exposing them to the dynamics of financialisation, digital platform dispute resolution or algorithmic governance. Paradoxically, strengthening private law's constitutive role for the urban space then implies reaching beyond the category of 'space' and retracing how legally mediated non-spatialised processes manifest themselves inside the city walls.

As regards private international law more specifically, the above analysis has shown that the discipline is yet to unpack its role in shaping urban sustainability and SDG 11.

This can best be explained by the lack of doctrines or treaties which bear an explicit urban imprint: even if questions of private international law seem ubiquitous in global cities with companies and individuals of different nationalities and residencies, the discipline does not have one single, targeted lever to move towards urban governance. Rather, private international law is contextual to many of the economic and digital trends that mark today's global cities. It seems likely that these trends will only exacerbate in the future and lead to further example cases of the role of private international law. Continuing this line of conceptual investigation may be among the biggest contributions private international law can make to SDG 11.

Overall, the rise of global cities poses a series of challenges to a private international law the primary objective of which is the *national* attribution of disputes. Sub-national attributions, such as the decision on governing law in multi-law states and on domestic jurisdiction, are treated as domestic matters. Here, private international law – in many ways similar to its public counterpart – shuts itself off from reflecting the state-like qualities of many global cities. At a time when global cities are increasingly becoming the economic, political and cultural proxies of their englobing territorial states and sharpening the centre/periphery divide at the national level, private international law continues to treat nation states as proxies for global cities. Normatively, the relegation of global cities to a mere sub-division of the national falls short of cities' role as sites of globalisation. Stichweh has argued that such cities 'always function … as a spatially bounded representation of world society'.[129] During the COVID-19 pandemic, the global nature of the health crisis was commonly illustrated by

[129] Rudolf Stichweh, 'The Eigenstructures of World Society and the Regional Cultures of the World' in Ino Rossi (ed), *Frontiers of Globalization Research. Theoretical and Methodological Approaches* (Springer 2007) 133, 145.

media reports from different global cities as places which people around the globe can easily relate to. This world-relevance of global cities may put them on the radar of private international law. On applicable law, one should note, however, that despite the activities of global cities in setting and implementing international rules and standards,[130] there is typically no private legal order specific to individual cities or even shared within city networks. Legislative powers for private law usually lie with the national or state level.[131] A welcoming approach within private international law towards private law rules for global cities might foster the development of such local initiatives, similar to the many existing urban rules on regulatory matters. If such rules are developed, private international law should use corresponding local connecting factors that express the idea of urban citizenship.

Moreover, urban policies should form a more prominent part of the *ordre public*, which is mostly understood as a reservation linked to shared *national* (or in the EU even supranational) norms and principles. Such an *ordre public local* would ensure that urban policies are not contracted around via, for example choice-of-law provisions by real estate or infrastructure investors.

Lastly, private international law can be mobilised to better express the public nature of large-scale urban infrastructure projects. Such projects, even if supported and legitimised by local government authorities, can give rise to disputes that raise vital issues for urban sustainability under SDG 11. The city should hence serve as seat of jurisdiction (or arbitration) in order to embed such disputes in urban debates and allow critical scrutiny by civil society. For real estate-related disputes, this will often already be governed by *forum rei sitae*. However, we saw examples of, for example, urban partnerships with advertising companies like JCDecaux where investors may press for foreign jurisdiction. A local jurisdiction clause could be anchored in the contractual practice of municipalities (or, of course, in private international laws and treaties). Potentially, existing networks of exchange between global cities could back this by developing and endorsing a model jurisdiction clause for projects on 'urban infrastructure and investments related to SDG 11'. Such a coordinated effort would increase the leverage of each of the municipalities through network effects and provides an illustration of how regulatory corporation between global cities can extend to private law and private international law.

---

130 See Yishai Blank, 'The City and the World' (2006) 44 Columbia Journal of Transnational Law 868.

131 This was at the heart of the German Constitutional Court's recent decision to invalidate rent cap legislation in Berlin (Gesetz zur Neuregelung gesetzlicher Vorschriften zur Mietenbegrenzung of 11 February 2020), see BVerfG, Order of 25 March 2021, 2 BvF 1/20 and others, ECLI:DE:BVerfG:2021:fs20210325a.2bvf000120.

SDG 12: SUSTAINABLE CONSUMPTION AND PRODUCTION

Geneviève SAUMIER*

Goal 12: Ensure sustainable consumption and production patterns

12.1 Implement the 10-year framework of programmes on sustainable consumption and production, all countries taking action, with developed countries taking the lead, taking into account the development and capabilities of developing countries

12.2 By 2030, achieve the sustainable management and efficient use of natural resources

12.3 By 2030, halve per capita global food waste at the retail and consumer levels and reduce food losses along production and supply chains, including post-harvest losses

12.4 By 2020, achieve the environmentally sound management of chemicals and all wastes throughout their life cycle, in accordance with agreed international frameworks, and significantly reduce their release to air, water and soil in order to minimize their adverse impacts on human health and the environment

12.5 By 2030, substantially reduce waste generation through prevention, reduction, recycling and reuse

12.6 Encourage companies, especially large and transnational companies, to adopt sustainable practices and to integrate sustainability information into their reporting cycle

12.7 Promote public procurement practices that are sustainable, in accordance with national policies and priorities

12.8 By 2030, ensure that people everywhere have the relevant information and awareness for sustainable development and lifestyles in harmony with nature

12.a Support developing countries to strengthen their scientific and technological capacity to move towards more sustainable patterns of consumption and production

* The author is grateful for research assistance provided for this chapter by Jeanne Mayrand-Thibert (BCL/JD McGill 2023) and funded by the Peter M. Laing Q.C. Chair.

12.b Develop and implement tools to monitor sustainable development impacts for sustainable tourism that creates jobs and promotes local culture and products

12.c Rationalize inefficient fossil-fuel subsidies that encourage wasteful consumption by removing market distortions, in accordance with national circumstances, including by restructuring taxation and phasing out those harmful subsidies, where they exist, to reflect their environmental impacts, taking fully into account the specific needs and conditions of developing countries and minimizing the possible adverse impacts on their development in a manner that protects the poor and the affected communities

Sustainable Development Goal 12 (SDG 12) aims to 'ensure sustainable consumption and production patterns'.[1] Although presented as an autonomous goal, it is directly or indirectly related to many other SDGs, to the point where its realisation would 'simultaneously contribute significantly to the achievement of almost all of the SDGs.'[2] Sustainable consumption and production (SCP) can thus be understood as both a fundamental and a transversal objective of the SDG programme. SCP is also recognised to be a 'wicked problem',[3] making it both rich and unwieldy. On the one hand, this increases its potential to interact with private international law in the abstract. On the other hand, it makes it challenging to present anything that interacts in a concrete manner.

---

1 It also provides for specific targets that include references to natural resources, waste, including food and chemical, public procurement, corporate practice, education and information, scientific and technological capacity in developing countries, tourism and fossil fuel subsidies.

2 UN High Level Political Forum (HLPF) 2018 – Review of SDGs Implementation: SDG12, 4 <sustainabledevlopment.un.org/hplf/2018>. See also Catherine Tinker, 'Ensuring sustainable consumption and production patterns through the United Nations' global goals: the international law and policy perspective' (2016) 107 Revista de Direito do Consumidor 385, 390 and Des Gasper et al, 'The Framing of Sustainable Consumption and Production in SDG 12' (2019) 10 Supplement 1 Global Policy 83, 87.

3 Oksana Mont, 'Introduction' in Oksana Mont (ed), *A research agenda for sustainable consumption governance* (Edward Elgar Publishing 2019) 1, 7.

This contribution will attempt both, seeking to answer the overall question whether private international law can play a role in supporting and furthering the achievement of SDG 12.

Section 1 of the chapter will outline what 'sustainable consumption and production' entails, highlighting the debates surrounding these two distinct yet intertwined concepts. Much of the literature is drawn from social sciences, as there is a scarcity of legal treatments of these concepts. Section 2 will first consider whether private international law has anything to offer in general and then look at selected targets of SDG 12 that could provide fertile ground to establish links between SCP and private international law: sustainable production practices (Target 12.6), public procurement (Target 12.7) and consumer information, including eco-labels (Target 12.8). This examination of the intersection between private international law and SDG 12 will identify some promising opportunities for a positive interaction.

1. UNDERSTANDING SUSTAINABLE CONSUMPTION AND PRODUCTION

The UN website on the SDGs currently defines sustainable consumption and production as follows:

> Sustainable consumption and production is about doing more and better with less. It is also about decoupling economic growth from environmental degradation, increasing resource efficiency and promoting sustainable lifestyles.[4]

The imperative of SCP was articulated in Agenda 21, an outcome of the 1992 Rio Summit, in unambiguous terms and the onus was put squarely on states to 'reduce and eliminate unsustainable patterns of production and consumption'.[5] By 1994, this was further refined at the Oslo Symposium to refer to 'the use of goods and services that respond to basic needs and bring a better quality of life, while minimising the use of natural resources, toxic materials and emissions of waste and pollutants over the life cycle, so as not to jeopardise the needs of future generations.'[6] At the Rio+20 Summit in 2012, a 10-year framework of programmes (10YFP) on SCP patterns was adopted, although it expressly stated that participation in the programmes was voluntary.[7] The first 'Global Meeting

4 <https://www.un.org/sustainabledevelopment/sustainable-consumption-production/>.

5 Principle 8, Rio Declaration on Environment and Development (1992), UN Doc A/CONF.151/26, vol I.

6 Oslo Roundtable on Sustainable Consumption and Production (see the timeline at <https://sustainabledevelopment.un.org/topics/sustainableconsumptionandproduction>).

7 Implementation of Agenda 21, the Programme for the Further Implementation of Agenda 21 and the outcomes of the World Summit on Sustainable Development and of the United Nations Conference on Sustainable Development, UN Doc A/70/472/Add.1, paras 224–226.

of the 10YFP' was held in 2015, a year after the adoption of Agenda 2030.[8] The UNEP website dedicated to SCP reports only two formal activities since then, the 2018 and 2021 High-Level Political Forum on Sustainable Development.[9] The purpose of that forum is to review progress on the implementation of some key SDGs, including SDG 12. The 2018 forum was preceded by an Expert Group Meeting on SDG 12 where it was concluded that while some progress had been made, 'significant gaps remain and implementation efforts have been seriously under-resourced'.[10] Further HLPF meetings were held in July 2020 and 2021, but their focus was mainly on the impact of the COVID-19 pandemic. Still, the overall conclusion on progress on Agenda 2030 is rather grim, with implementation said to be 'too slow and uneven and … either stalled or … reversed in some areas.'[11] Data and reports regarding SCP are particularly disquieting. Global domestic material consumption rose 7 per cent and the global material footprint[12] rose 17.4 per cent between 2010 and 2017.[13] North America and Europe consume at a rate 40 per cent above the world average. E-waste increased by 38 per cent from 2010 to 2019, while environmentally sound recycling of e-waste grew more slowly and still stands at less than 20 per cent of all e-waste.[14] While 79 countries and the EU reported at least one national policy instrument relating to SCP as of 2019, 40 per cent of those were limited to the production side in terms of reducing greenhouse gas emissions.[15]

What makes SCP such a challenging goal? Writing in 1997 in a widely cited article on SCP, Salzman suggested that it is the sustainable consumption dimension that is the most elusive objective, in part because its partner, sustainable production, has attracted the most attention.[16] Indeed, from the early days of sustainable development, the focus has been on pollution caused by industrial production, and its environmental impacts have been the subject of decades of scientific research, concrete state intervention and some voluntary industry responses, both domestically and internationally.[17]

---

8 Transforming our World: The 2030 Agenda for Sustainable Development <https://sdgs.un.org/2030agenda>.

9 <https://sustainabledevelopment.un.org/hlpf>.

10 2018 HLPF Review of SDGs implementation: SDG 12 – Ensure sustainable consumption and production patterns, available at <https://sustainabledevelopment.un.org/hlpf/2018>, in tab 'Inputs and Background Notes'.

11 Ministerial Declaration, E/2020/L.20–E/HLPF/2020/L.1.

12 This refers to the use of natural resources.

13 Progress towards the Sustainable Development Goals – Report of the Secretary-General, UN Doc E/2020/57 (28 April 2020) para 107.

14 *ibid* para 109.

15 United Nations, 'Sustainable Development Goals Report 2020', Goal 12 <https://unstats.un.org/sdgs/report/2020/goal-12/>.

16 James Salzman, 'Sustainable Consumption and the Law' (1997) 27 Environmental Law 1243, 1253.

17 ibid 1253–1254.

Recycling programmes are perhaps the notable early exception, targeting consumers directly in the sustainability project.[18] Since the turn of the century, the social aspects of sustainability on the production side have also become the subject of significant research, governmental policies,[19] soft law[20] and voluntary industry engagement or initiatives.[21] And while production patterns certainly do not currently meet the SDGs, a range of 'toolkits' have been developed to lead the way.[22] The path to sustainable *production* patterns has been defined and no one engaged in production of goods or services can claim to lack information about what to do.[23] The sustainable *consumption* part of SCP, on the other hand, remains much more diffuse and elusive, both as a concept and as an objective.

One of the causes of this elusiveness is what Oksana Mont refers to as the 'lack of consensus about what constitutes the field of sustainable consumption, even though the terminology … can be traced back to Agenda 21 from 1992'.[24] SDG 12 refers to 'consumption patterns', but does not specify whether sustainability requires changes to 'what' we consume as opposed to 'how much' we consume.[25] As Salzman put it in 1997: 'there is neither a common understanding of the problem nor of the solution. If our current practices represent overconsumption, then what level of consumption is sustainable?'[26] Over 20 years later, nothing much seems to have changed, given that 'various disciplines have a different understanding of what constitutes the problem of sustainable consumption, what its origins are and what the solutions to the problems look like'.[27]

18 Magnus Bengtsson et al, 'Transforming systems of consumption and production for achieving the sustainable development goals: moving beyond efficiency' (2018) 13 Sustainability Science 1533, 1534.

19 For example the recently created Canadian Ombudsperson for Responsible Enterprise <https://core-ombuds.canada.ca/core_ombuds-ocre_ombuds/index.aspx?lang=eng>.

20 For example the 2001 OECD Guidelines for Multinational Enterprises <http://mneguidelines.oecd.org/> and the 2011 UN Guiding Principles on Business and Human Rights <https://www.ohchr.org/Documents/Publications/GuidingPrinciplesBusinessHR_EN.pdf>.

21 For example through the UN sponsored Global Compact <https://www.unglobalcompact.org/> or the Voluntary Principles <https://www.voluntaryprinciples.org/>.

22 For example the OECD Sustainable Manufacturing Toolkit <www.oecd.org/innovation/green/toolkit/48704993.pdf> and numerous documents in the 'take action' section of the Global Compact website.

23 Of course financial and other resources remain an issue, particularly for developing countries, which explains the reference to both, including capacity-building with regards to technology, in the targets of SDG 12.

24 Oksana Mont, 'Introduction' in Oksana Mont (ed), *A research agenda for sustainable consumption governance* (Edward Elgar Publishing 2019) 1, 7.

25 James Salzman, 'Sustainable Consumption and the Law' (1997) 27 Environmental Law 1243 referred to the distinction between patterns of consumption and levels of consumption, giving as examples of each mandatory catalytic converters and limits on car purchases per household (at 1253).

26 ibid 1255.

27 Oksana Mont, 'Introduction' in Oksana Mont (ed), *A research agenda for sustainable consumption governance* (Edward Elgar Publishing 2019) 1, 7.

The literature does reflect an apparent divide between two ideological stances regarding sustainable consumption: weak versus strong sustainability.[28] According to the former, sustainable consumption is to be sought through technological innovation and more efficient production processes. Coupled with increased education and information directed at consumers, through media campaigns and eco-labelling for example, this is expected to lead to changes in patterns of consumption compatible with sustainability.[29] In other words, weak sustainability 'strives to achieve *relative* improvements of product performance, but does not refer to *absolute* ecological limits'.[30] The strong sustainability view rejects this option completely, considering that only a dramatic reduction in current consumption levels can have any measurable impact, particularly from an environmental perspective.[31] Critics of the weak view challenge the rationality paradigm of consumer behaviour, thereby denying that information-based approaches have any significant effect on sustainability.[32] In addition, they argue that the weak version reflects corporate interests and their resistance to any market intervention that would affect their bottom line.[33] But the strong sustainability view is also said to be politically unacceptable, given that it involves 'redesigning the economic system, associated infrastructures, dominant cultures and lifestyles'.[34]

This sharp dichotomy is rejected by the most recent scholarship, which sees more benefit in thinking in terms of complementarity or continuity between approaches.[35] For example, Oksana Mont suggests a middle ground between

---

28 For a description and critique of this view, see generally, Magnus Bengtsson et al, 'Transforming systems of consumption and production for achieving the sustainable development goals: moving beyond efficiency' (2018) 13 Sustainability Science 1533; for support of this view in a non-English language source, see Marine Friant-Perrot, 'La consommation durable et la protection des consommateurs: réflexions sur les nouveaux rapports entre le droit de la consommation et le concept de développement durable' in Geneviève Parent (ed), *Production et consommation durables: de la gouvernance au consommateur-citoyen* (Éditions Yvon Blais 2008) 569.

29 Candice Stevens, 'Linking sustainable consumption and production: The government role' (2010) 34(1) Natural Resources Forum 16, 17–20.

30 Magnus Bengtsson et al, 'Transforming systems of consumption and production for achieving the sustainable development goals: moving beyond efficiency' (2018) 13 Sustainability Science 1533, 1535.

31 ibid.

32 Oksana Mont, 'Introduction' in Oksana Mont (ed), *A research agenda for sustainable consumption governance* (Edward Elgar Publishing 2019) 1, 8–9; see also generally Christian Brodhag, 'A differentiated approach for sustainable consumption and production policies' (2010) 34(1) Natural Resources Forum 63.

33 Des Gasper et al, 'The Framing of Sustainable Consumption and Production in SDG 12' (2019) 10 Supplement 1 Global Policy 83, 84–87.

34 Magnus Bengtsson et al, 'Transforming systems of consumption and production for achieving the sustainable development goals: moving beyond efficiency' (2018) 13 Sustainability Science 1533, 1535.

35 See, for example, ibid, 1536.

systemic optimisation (weak sustainability) and *systemic reorientation* (strong sustainability), which she calls *systemic transformation* and which would involve ramping up current technological and efficiency approaches while transitioning to a 'planned reorientation of society towards slower economic growth or, when feasible, degrowth'.[36]

This diversity in academic views flows from the absence of any set definition of SCP in SDG 12. Still, most scholars argue that, with a few exceptions, and without downplaying the overall benefits of the Agenda 2030 initiative, 'SDG 12 mainly represents an *efficiency* approach to SCP and, as such, its overall efficacy can be doubted'.[37] Looking at the question from a policy perspective, Des Gasper concludes that the approach in SDG 12 'emphasizes voluntary, informed consumption and production decisions, rather than regulation' in a manner that undermines its transformative power.[38]

This cursory overview of sustainable consumption highlights the complexity of this part of SDG 12. This will necessarily transpose itself onto any examination of what role law, let alone private international law, can play on this terrain.

Before moving to that task, it is worth pausing to note that whereas sustainable development is a robust field of research in law,[39] in particular in relation to environmental issues, there is a relative dearth of legal research related to sustainable consumption.[40] While the general field of sustainable consumption is said to be relatively new,[41] although growing exponentially, with a 'six-fold increase [in peer-reviewed academic publications] from 1980–2018',[42]

---

36 Oksana Mont, 'Introduction' in Oksana Mont (ed), *A research agenda for sustainable consumption governance* (Edward Elgar Publishing 2019) 1, 9. Within this third way, Mont would include, among others, 'alternative consumption models such as peer-to-peer sharing and alternative business models (e.g. the circular economy)'.

37 ibid.

38 Des Gasper et al, 'The Framing of Sustainable Consumption and Production in SDG 12' (2019) 10 Supplement 1 Global Policy 83, 92.

39 For example, the McGill Journal of Sustainable Development Law has been published since 2005.

40 See Ipshita Chaturvedi, 'Sustainable Consumption: Scope and Applicability of Principles of International Law' (2018) 2 Chinese Journal of International Law 5, 14; but see James Salzman, 'Sustainable Consumption and the Law' (1997) 27 Environmental Law 1243 and some contributions to G Parent (ed), *Production et consommation durables: de la gouvernance au consommateur-citoyen* (Éditions Yvon Blais 2008).

41 Oksana Mont, 'Introduction' in Oksana Mont (ed), *A research agenda for sustainable consumption governance* (Edward Elgar Publishing 2019) 1, 4.; Alberto do Amaral Junior, Lucila de Almeida, Luciane Klein Vieira, 'An Introduction to Sustainable Consumption and the Law' in Alberto do Amaral Junior, Lucila de Almeida, Luciane Klein Vieira (eds), *Sustainable Consumption* (Springer 2020) 1.

42 Oksana Mont, 'Introduction' in Oksana Mont (ed), *A research agenda for sustainable consumption governance* (Edward Elgar Publishing 2019) 1, 4. Magnus Bengtsson et al, 'Transforming systems of consumption and production for achieving the sustainable development goals: moving beyond efficiency' (2018) 13 Sustainability Science 1533 notes that a search of SCP on Google Scholar results in 5,980 publications between 2008 and 2012 and over 12,600 between 2013 and 2017 (at 1534).

law does not appear within the six main disciplines within which sustainable consumption is a field of study.[43] In two monographs dealing with research in sustainable consumption (from 2015 and 2019), none of the contributors was a jurist.[44] This 'silence of legal scholars' is mentioned by the editors of a recent collection on sustainable consumption and law published in 2020.[45]

2. SCP AND PRIVATE INTERNATIONAL LAW

SCP envisages, at minimum if following the *efficiency* or *weak sustainability* view outlined previously, a change in the *objects* of consumption, be they goods or services. This change could occur as a result of changes in the offer of products or services, changing consumer choices, or a combination of the two. In developed economies, these changes are largely left to market forces, following classical assumptions concerning supply and demand, with governments intervening mainly to control for risks to human health and for fairness in transactions. But there is also increasing evidence of government intervention to restrict consumer and producer options for environmental purposes. Early examples include leaded gasoline and CFC bans; more recent initiatives include extended producer responsibility and bans on single-use plastic bags (both of which are mainly directed at reducing waste). These public policies are consistent with increasing references to the 'circular economy' or 'product lifecycle' approaches. Otherwise, when it comes to making sustainable *consumption* choices, individual liberty – or consumer sovereignty – continues to be the dominant paradigm, constrained only by personal values, financial resources (or access to credit) and access to products and services, which e-commerce has significantly amplified. While some consumers do choose 'green' options, this rarely amounts to more than 10 per cent of consumer purchases on average.[46] Government intervention is usually limited to financial (dis)incentives through taxation or subsidies, which are only effective at the margins.

---

43 These are environmental science, management, social sciences, economics, energy and engineering (ibid).

44 Oksana Mont, 'Introduction' in Oksana Mont (ed), *A research agenda for sustainable consumption governance* (Edward Elgar Publishing 2019); Lucia Reisch and John Thøgersen, *Handbook of Research on Sustainable Consumption* (Edward Elgar Publishing 2015).

45 Alberto do Amaral Junior, Lucila de Almeida, Luciane Klein Vieira, 'An Introduction to Sustainable Consumption and the Law' in Alberto do Amaral Junior, Lucila de Almeida, Luciane Klein Vieira (eds), *Sustainable Consumption* (Springer 2020) 1.

46 But see a recent US study that reports a significant increase in recent years for packaged goods marketed using some form of sustainability labelling. While those goods had only a 16.6 per cent market share, sales growth was 50 per cent of the entire market for the period 2013–2018, indicating growing consumer interest (see Randi Kronthal-Sacco et al, 'Sustainable Purchasing Patterns and Consumer Responsiveness to Sustainability Marketing Messages' (2020) 2(2) Journal of Sustainability Research (<https://doi.org/10.20900/jsr20200016>).

Short of some cataclysmic global event that would lead governments to impose limits on levels of consumption (think of rationing in wartime), it seems likely that national government and legislative focus will continue to be on the *production* side. Targeting production can have an effect on reducing consumption (think of compulsory health warnings on cigarettes) but is more likely to shift consumption (think of compulsory GMO labelling). And while the current COVID-19 pandemic has shown that governments are capable of dramatically curtailing consumption (just think of air travel), this is viewed as an extraordinary and temporary step the reversal of which is anxiously awaited despite the evident positive impacts it has had on some environmental indicators, such as air quality. The short-term limits on air travel may have a more lasting effect as people recognise the feasibility and flexibility of virtual meetings. However, the great increase in online shopping during full or partial lockdowns, made possible by the maintenance of international cargo flights, may mitigate any gains.

Within this conception of weak sustainability, the question here is what role private international law can play. Traditionally, private international law has focused on cross-border legal relations between private parties. From that starting point, there are obvious links between private international law and issues of production and consumption. These links may arise in relation to contracts for the sale of goods and services that cross borders. They may arise in relation to claims of liability for personal or property injury caused by activity or products, particularly when the causal agent is a foreign entity. These linkages flow from the fact that rules of private international law determine where a claim can be brought, what law will apply to the claim and whether any resulting judgment will be enforceable elsewhere. In many legal systems, there are even specific private international law rules to deal with consumer contracts, product liability and environmental damage. These potential intersections between private international and SCP justify further inquiry into whether, and how, these can be harnessed to *support and further* SCP patterns.

In many legal systems, private international law is often presented as being 'neutral', in the sense that in addressing cross-border legal relations, its rules refer to local or foreign law according to objective connections that are indifferent to the substantive content of the designated law. This idea of 'neutrality' is closely associated with 'choice of law' issues, that is, the subset of private international law that deals with identifying the law applicable to the substance of a dispute. However, even jurisdictional issues can be described as neutral whenever a court's jurisdiction, or the recognition of a foreign judgment, is determined according to objective connecting factors that treat foreign and local connections on an equal footing. This presumption of neutrality, if consistently valid, would diminish the potential role that private international law could play in support of sustainable development goals, given its predicate that substantive outcomes are not its concern. Such a view is, however, open to challenge. Indeed, the idea that private international law can pursue policy objectives, although classically rejected (or camouflaged through other doctrines, such as renvoi), is increasingly being recognised.[47] Whether in jurisdictional or choice-of-law terms, private international rules are often fashioned to support a particular end, whether it be access to local courts for consumers, access to a more protective law for victims of defective products or environmental damage, formal validity of juridical acts, or establishment of filiation, to name only a few.

Beyond the express formulation of policy-oriented rules in existing legislation or international instruments, it is worth exploring whether there is further scope for expanding the policy reach of private international law in pursuit of SDG 12. There is a growing literature on the 'regulatory' or 'governance' function of private international law that would see it bridge regulatory gaps exploited by transnational actors and establish higher-level standards.[48] Given the challenges presented by much of SDG 12, a reconceptualisation of private international law along those lines may well be necessary for it to play a supporting role in Agenda 2030. This is a controversial approach, however, and one that would need to attract greater consensus lest it be interpreted as illegitimate extraterritorial overreach.[49]

Even without venturing too far beyond orthodoxy, however, it is arguable that existing private international law rules and methodologies can be reimagined or redeployed with a view to supporting SDG 12. Looking first at the issue of international jurisdiction, there is no doubt that broad access to judicial redress can support many of the *production* targets of SDG 12. Whether with reference to contractual or extra-contractual claims against producers, enabling judicial recourse against producers allows for both public scrutiny of and accountability for their activity. Taken together, these outcomes support SDG 16, in particular Target 16.3 on promoting the rule of law and access to justice. Since most private

---

47 On this 'materialisation' of private international law, see, for example, Yves Lequette, 'Les mutations du droit international privé: vers un changement de paradigme? Cours général de droit international privé' (2017) 387 Recueil des Cours 9, 240–255; Symeon C Symeonides, 'Private International Law: Idealism, Pragmatism, Eclecticism' (2017) 384 Recueil des Cours 9, 195–255.

48 See, for example, Horatia Muir Watt et al (eds), *Global Private International Law: Adjudication Without Frontiers* (Edward Elgar Publishing 2019); Christopher A Whytock, 'Conflict of Laws, Global Governance, and Transnational Legal Order' (2016) 1 UC Irvine Journal of International, Transnational and Comparative Law 117; Horatia Muir Watt and Diego P Fernández Arroyo (eds), *Private International Law and Global Governance* (OUP 2014); Laura Carballo Pineiro and Xandra Kramer, 'The Role of Private International Law in Contemporary Society: Global Governance as a Challenge' (2014) 7(3) Erasmus Law Review 109; Robert Wai, 'Transnational Lift-off and Juridical Touchdown: The Regulatory Function of Private International Law in a Global Age' (2002) 40(2) Columbia Journal of Transnational Law 209.

49 For discussion, see Hannah L Buxbaum, 'Public Regulation and Private Enforcement in a Global Economy: Strategies for Managing Conflict' (2019) 399 Recueil des Cours 268.

international law systems provide for jurisdiction in the defendant's home state, claims related to foreign or cross-border activity of corporations should never suffer from an absence of available fora. In jurisdictions that provide for the aggregation of claims, such as class actions, this can quite readily stimulate such proceedings, overcoming the usually dramatic asymmetry of resources and bargaining power between consumers and multinationals. As class actions become more widespread,[50] the potential for multinationals to exploit the procedural differences between states via private international law rules on jurisdiction over legal persons will be reduced.

This positive aspect can be undermined in those jurisdictions that recognise court discretion to decline to exercise jurisdiction, generally referred to as *forum non conveniens*.[51] Typical of common law systems, this limitation on access to a defendant's home state jurisdiction is often decried as one of the failures of private international law's ability to regulate transnational activity.[52] This was stated forcefully, 30 years ago, by a US judge in the following terms:

> [T]he doctrine of *forum non conveniens* is obsolete in a world in which markets are global and in which ecologists have documented the delicate balance of all life on this planet. The parochial perspective embodied in the doctrine of *forum non conveniens* enables corporations to evade legal control merely because they are transnational.[53]

The ILA Committee on International Civil and Commercial Litigation has twice called for reconsideration of recourse to this discretion where jurisdiction is established in the corporate defendant's home state.[54] But these invitations

---

50 See, for example, the 30 June 2020 adoption of the Directive of the European Parliament and of the Council on representative actions for the protection of the collective interests of consumers <https://data.consilium.europa.eu/doc/document/ST-9223-2020-INIT/en/pdf>.

51 Another avenue for domestic defendants to seek to escape the jurisdiction of courts in common law jurisdictions is through the 'abuse of process' route, which English courts have recently admitted being available even where jurisdiction is established under the Brussels recast regime, which excludes recourse to *forum non conveniens*. This argument was recently successful at first instance in *Município de Mariana v BHP Group plc* (Rev 1) [2020] EWHC 2930 (TCC) concerning the collapse of the Fundão dam in Brazil in 2015.

52 See, for example, in the context of environmental claims, Hans van Loon, 'Principles and Building Blocks for a Global Legal Framework for Transnational Civil Litigation in Environmental Matters' (2018) 23(2) Uniform Law Review 298, 309.

53 *Dow Chemical Co v Alfaro*, 786 S.W. (2d) 674 at 689 (Tex. Sup. Ct. 1990), Doggett J, concurring, *certiorari* denied, 498 U.S. 1024, 111 S. Ct. 671.

54 'Third Interim Report – Declining and Referring Jurisdiction in International Litigation' (2000) 69 International Law Association Reports of Conferences 137, 161, adopted as 'Resolution No 1/2000: International Civil and Commercial Litigation' (2000) 69 International Law Association Reports of Conferences 13; 'Resolution No 2/2012: International Civil Litigation and the Interests of the Public' (2012) 75 International Law Association Reports of Conferences 19 (Sofia Guidelines on Best Practices for International Civil Litigation for Human Rights Violations (2012), Guideline 2.5(1)).

do not appear to have been taken up by any of the relevant jurisdictions.[55] It is noteworthy that the latest August 2020 draft of the proposed UN treaty on business and human rights also excludes *forum non conveniens*.[56]

On the other hand, most private international law systems in the civil law tradition do not recognise *forum non conveniens* and a corporate defendant's home forum will typically be available to claimants, whether in a contractual or extra-contractual context.[57] Moreover, special jurisdictional rules for consumer or employment contract claims and for claims by victims of product liability or environmental damage can facilitate access to those claimants' local courts, thus increasing their access to justice even against foreign defendants. The same may result from rules extending jurisdiction over foreign co-defendants (such as under Art 8(1) Brussels I)[58] or by recourse to the exceptional *forum necessitatis* ground, which is intended to prevent a denial of justice.[59] As will be discussed below, some of the SDG 12 targets may give rise to justiciable private law claims against producers. As such, generous private international law jurisdictional rules could be understood to further those targets.

Of course, access to courts does not necessarily entail success on the merits. From a private international law perspective, this will first depend on the law applicable to the dispute. Typically, claimants will select a forum, if there is an option, taking into account the substantive law that will eventually be applied by that forum's court. Working backwards, a claimant should consider which potentially applicable law is likely to lead to a successful outcome and then

55 See, for example, *Garcia v Tahoe Resources*, 2017 BCCA 39 (British Columbia Court of Appeal), leave to the Supreme Court of Canada denied, 2017 CanLII 35114. Although the Court of Appeal reversed the lower court's finding that it was *forum non conveniens*, it did so on the exceptional ground that sending the plaintiffs to Guatemala, where the damage occurred, would be tantamount to a denial of justice. The Court of Appeal did not even consider whether it should refrain from exercising its discretion to decline jurisdiction on the basis that the corporate defendant was domiciled in British Columbia.

56 See Legally Binding Instrument to Regulate, in International Human Rights Law, the Activities of Transnational Corporations and Other Business Enterprises, Art 7(5). The draft is accessible at <https://www.ohchr.org/EN/HRBodies/HRC/WGTransCorp/Pages/IGWGOnTNC.aspx>.

57 This had also been the case in the UK with respect to defendants domiciled there given the exclusion of *forum non conveniens* under the Brussels Regulation, as confirmed by the ECJ in Case C-281/02 *Owusu v Jackson* [2005] ECR I-1383. This should no longer be the case post-Brexit (see Andrew Dickinson, 'A View from the Edge', Oxford Legal Studies Research Paper No 25/2019, available at SSRN: <https://ssrn.com/abstract=3356549>).

58 A proposal to amend Art 8(1) to include jurisdiction over parent companies for harm caused abroad by their foreign subsidiaries or other undertakings, based in third (non-EU) states, in their supply chain has been proposed by the European Parliament this past October 2020, see <https://www.europarl.europa.eu/doceo/document/JURI-PR-657191_EN.pdf>.

59 This so-called 'forum of necessity' is expressly provided for in some Canadian provinces such as Quebec (see Art 3136 Civil Code) and British Columbia (see Court Jurisdiction and Proceedings Transfer Act, SBC 2003, c 28, s 6). A proposal to add this jurisdictional ground to the Brussels I regime is also being considered (see *supra*).

identify the forum where that law will be considered to govern the claim. In other words, even though substantive law is not, per se, the object of private international law, its content can have a significant impact on litigation strategy. Therefore, even if private international law rules on applicable law do not, in themselves, expressly favour a particular policy outcome, the result in a given case may well be equivalent. A few examples will illustrate how this works.

First, with respect to claims of environmental damage, a choice-of-law rule can be formulated to make the defendant subject to a higher standard, by giving the claimant the right to designate either the law of the place of the damage or the law of the place of the wrongful conduct, assuming one is more stringent than the other. This is, for example, the choice-of-law rule in the Rome II Regulation applicable in all EU Member States (Art 7).[60]

Second, even where the choice-of-law rule is framed in more neutral terms, such as the traditional *lex loci delicti* rule, courts could articulate or apply the rule in a manner that would make a corporate defendant subject to more stringent domestic law in the place of acting rather than laxer foreign law in the place of injury (or vice versa). A key passage from the Supreme Court of Canada's seminal case on choice of law in tort suggests as much:

> [A]s a general rule, the law to be applied in torts is the law of the place where the activity occurred, i.e., the *lex loci delicti*. There are situations, of course, notably where an act occurs in one place but the consequences are directly felt elsewhere, when the issue of where the tort takes place itself raises thorny issues. In such a case, it may well be that the consequences would be held to constitute the wrong. Difficulties may also arise where the wrong directly arises out of some transnational or interprovincial activity.[61]

Claimants in recent Canadian litigation related to the Rana Plaza disaster attempted to make this argument (essentially to avoid limitation periods under Bangladeshi law).[62] The Canadian corporate defendants, who were the main purchasers of garments produced by suppliers operating in the Rana Plaza, were alleged to have failed in their duty to ensure the safety of the workplace as required by their own supplier code of conduct. The claimants argued that this failure occurred in Ontario, where the defendants were located and where decisions were made, thereby situating the tort in Ontario and attracting the application of Ontario law as the *lex loci delicti*.[63] Unfortunately, this argument

---

60 The European Parliament proposal to amend Article 8(1) regarding jurisdiction also includes adding a new provision to Rome II allowing for greater choice of applicable law by the victim of human rights violations, including the law of the parent company's domicile.

61 *Tolofson v Jensen* [1994] 3 SCR 1022, 1049–1050.

62 *Das v George Weston Limited*, 2018 ONCA 1053 (Ontario Court of Appeal), leave to appeal to the Supreme Court of Canada denied (2019 CanLII 73201).

63 ibid para 85.

was rejected by the Ontario Court of Appeal,[64] arguably on a misreading of the above paragraph, and the Supreme Court denied leave to appeal. Despite this missed opportunity, the point remains that even an apparently neutral choice-of-law rule could be interpreted to further the goal of subjecting transnational corporate defendants to their home state law, where doing so would lead to outcomes more compatible with sustainability goals.

Finally, where the choice-of-law rule itself does not provide a helpful avenue, the forum seised of an action may have recourse to other mechanisms to hold domestic defendants to account for their foreign damaging activities. For example, the law of the forum may include a mandatory rule that is applicable notwithstanding the fact that a different law would be designated under the forum's choice-of-law rules. France's 2017 *Loi sur la vigilance* may provide an example.[65] Enacted with a view to regulating French multinationals regarding, among other things, the environmental impacts of their activities, whether directly through subsidiaries or throughout the entire value chain, the statute provides for private claims in damages. The statute does not expressly state that it applies regardless of whether the place of injury or of acting is elsewhere. However, the entire purpose of the statute would be defeated if French courts did not apply it to determine the liability of the multinationals targeted by the legislation.[66] Recourse to mandatory rules of the forum to displace the otherwise applicable law is permitted under the Rome II Regulation, thereby providing a direct route for such a result in French courts.[67]

Where a particular private international law system does not include such a mechanism, a similar result could be achieved by appealing to the almost universally accepted public policy exception, which allows for a refusal to apply an otherwise applicable foreign law when the outcome under that law is manifestly incompatible with fundamental values of the forum. It is certainly arguable that a state's public endorsement of SDG 12, particularly if accompanied by domestic implementation, could fit within the purview of the public policy exception.

---

64 ibid paras 85–91.

65 *Loi no 2017-399 relative au devoir de vigilance des sociétés mères et entreprises donneuses d'ordre*. Similar legislative interventions are being contemplated in Germany, Switzerland and the Netherlands. The first case launched based on the French statute involves French multinational Total and its oil field in Uganda. It has not proceeded beyond a first internal jurisdictional issue where the Tribunal de grande instance de Nanterre declared, on 30 January 2020, that it was not competent to hear the claim which should instead have been instituted before the Tribunal de commerce. The decision was appealed to the Cour d'appel de Versailles in March 2020 and was confirmed by that court on 10 December 2020. A further appeal to the Cour de Cassation was launched in April 2021. For the history of the proceedings, see <www.totalautribunal.org and https://survie.org/mot/ouganda>.

66 Which multinationals are targeted is actually not that clear – see Etienne Pataut, 'Le devoir de vigilance – Aspects de droit international privé' (2017) Droit Social 833.

67 This characterisation of the French statute is debatable (see Pataut, ibid), but a similar result could be achieved through application of other exceptions to the usual *lex loci delicti* of Art 4(1) Rome II, such as Arts 4(3), 17 and 26.

Even if a multinational could be held to account in court, and either ordered to pay damages for past harm caused or be enjoined to modify its practices for the future, such a judgment would only be effective in the state whose court issued it. Indeed, save in the presence of a treaty,[68] there is no international law obligation on states to recognise or give effect to foreign judgments. While many states' private international law provides for recognition and enforcement of foreign judgments, this is an additional hurdle that can mitigate the impact of a favourable judgment. This provides an additional reason for ensuring that jurisdiction is available in the home state of corporate defendants, since any judgment rendered by home courts will be enforceable under domestic law.

Having provided an overview of the general components of private international law and how they might currently support, or be generously interpreted to support, SDG 12, some of the specific targets of SDG 12 will be considered in the next section, to examine more concrete scenarios.

3. SDG 12 TARGETS AND PRIVATE INTERNATIONAL LAW

The definitions of 'sustainable consumption and production patterns' examined in section 1 invite further exploration of certain points of potential intersection with private international law, with particular focus on the targets of SDG 12. I will consider, in turn, sustainable production practices (Target 12.6), public procurement (Target 12.7) and consumer information, including eco-labels (Target 12.8).

3.1. TARGET 12.6: SUSTAINABLE PRODUCTION PRACTICES

Gasper argues, persuasively, that the vision of SCP in Agenda 2030, and in its various iterations since at least the turn of the millennium leading up to Agenda 2030, if not since the Rio Summit in 1992, has been strongly influenced by corporate and industrial interests,[69] and their preferences for self-regulation. Far from translating into a refusal to engage with sustainability, many business voices called for reconciling growth with environmental protection, for example endorsing the 'polluter pays' principle and calling for an end to subsidies for

---

[68] Such as the Lugano Convention and, within the EU, the Brussels Regulation. A new multilateral Convention on the recognition and enforcement of judgments in civil or commercial matters was adopted by the Hague Conference on Private International Law in July 2019, but it has not yet been ratified by any state (see <www.hcch.net>).

[69] Des Gasper et al, 'The Framing of Sustainable Consumption and Production in SDG 12' (2019) 10 Supplement 1 Global Policy 83, 84.

unsustainable production processes.[70] According to a 2017 review of 200 of the largest global companies, 94 per cent published sustainability reports and set specific sustainability goals.[71] Whether motivated by business or moral imperatives, transnational corporations appear to speak the language of sustainable development, suggesting that Target 12.6 is already met. The real question, of course, is whether these declarations of commitment to sustainable production are more than just non-binding promises. This formulation provides a potential entry point for private litigation and therefore for private international law.[72]

The 2019 UK Supreme Court decision in *Vedanta v Lungowe*[73] may be instructive on this point. The case concerns a claim brought by Zambian villagers against Vedanta Resources plc, an English-domiciled company, and KCM, its Zambian subsidiary, for injuries resulting from toxic emissions from a mine operated by KCM in Zambia. The claim against the parent company was based on 'material published by Vedanta in which it asserted its responsibility for the establishment of appropriate group-wide environmental control and sustainability standards, for their implementation throughout the group by training, and for their monitoring and enforcement.'[74] The defendant argued that 'a parent could never incur a duty of care in respect of the activities of a particular subsidiary merely by laying down group-wide policies and guidelines, and expecting the management of each subsidiary to comply with them'.[75] The court rejected this view, stating instead that:

> [Corporate] group guidelines about minimising the environmental impact of inherently dangerous activities, such as mining, may be shown to contain systemic errors which, when implemented as of course by a particular subsidiary, then cause harm to third parties[, giving rise to a duty of care].[76]
>
> Even where group-wide policies do not of themselves give rise to such a duty of care to third parties, they may do so if the parent does not merely proclaim them, but takes active steps, by training, supervision and enforcement, to see that they are implemented by relevant subsidiaries. *Similarly, it seems to me that the parent may incur the relevant responsibility to third parties if, in published materials, it holds itself out as exercising that degree of supervision and control of its subsidiaries, even if it*

---

70 ibid 85.

71 See <https://sustainablebrands.com/read/marketing-and-comms/the-rise-of-corporate-sustainability-goals-some-hard-data>.

72 For a detailed analysis of the private law dimension see Anna Beckers, *Enforcing Corporate Social Responsibility Codes: On Global Self-Regulation and National Private Law* (Hart Publishing 2015).

73 [2019] UKSC 20.

74 ibid para 55.

75 ibid para 52.

76 ibid.

does not in fact do so. In such circumstances its very omission may constitute the abdication of a responsibility which it has publicly undertaken.[77] (emphasis added)

While the judgment was strictly concerned with a threshold jurisdictional issue[78] (which it answered in favour of the English court seised by the claimants), and thus it did not actually decide whether Vedanta owed any duty to the Zambian villagers, the quoted passages reveal an opportunity to hold corporate groups accountable *in private law* for unfulfilled assertions of commitments to sustainability. Ironically, for Vedanta, such a possibility arises whether or not the applicable law is English law or Zambian law, since the latter is based on English common law.[79] This implies that tort liability for environmental damage allegedly arising as a result of an English parent company's failure to respect its sustainability commitments in a foreign country that follows English common law will be determined by the law of its home jurisdiction.[80] Albeit for reasons partially unconnected to private international law (i.e. the colonial legacy of English law), the net effect is akin to the French *Loi sur la vigilance*.

When it comes to Target 12.6, therefore, private international law may well play a supporting role if, (1) jurisdictional rules are developed, interpreted or applied in ways that allow transnational corporations to be sued at home for any activity of their corporate group, or even throughout their global value chain, that causes injury elsewhere, and (2) if choice-of-law rules or methodologies allow for the designation or application of a law that can hold them accountable for damage caused either by the violation of their sustainable production promises or their failure to implement them adequately. This could be accomplished by adopting choice-of-law rules with alternative connecting factors, pointing either to the law of the place of injury, of the wrongful act or

---

77 ibid para 53. It is interesting that the court insisted that this was not a 'novel' category, despite the fact that it did not point to any precedent (ibid para 54).

78 The court ultimately held that both defendants could be sued before the English courts. While fascinating, the reasons for that holding are not relevant for my purposes here.

79 The parties apparently agreed that Zambian law would apply and that it would likely be equivalent to English law (ibid paras 44, 56).

80 It is worth noting that in the Canadian case discussed previously (*Das v George Weston Limited*, 2018 ONCA 1053 (Ontario Court of Appeal), leave to appeal to the Supreme Court of Canada denied (2019 CanLII 73201)), the Court of Appeal held that it was 'plain and obvious' that no duty of care arose between the Canadian companies and the employees of their suppliers in Bangladesh on the basis of the companies' 'supplier code of conduct' (at paras 127–194). It did so on the basis that the law of Bangladesh applied to the issue and that a court in Bangladesh would look to English law if needed. The Court of Appeal did not have the advantage of the UK Supreme Court's decision in *Vedanta v Lungowe* (which was rendered subsequently) and relied upon the English Court of Appeal's decision in that case (which the UK Supreme Court upheld but on distinct reasoning regarding the duty of care issue), and in another case (*Okpabi v Shell plc* [2018] EWCA Civ 191) that was also reversed by the UK Supreme Court in February 2021 (2021 UKSC 3).

of the parent's domicile, at the choice of the claimant, following the *ubiquity* principle found in relation, for example, to environmental damage and proposed for human right violations.

3.2. TARGET 12.7: PUBLIC PROCUREMENT

Public procurement is a significant source of global economic activity. Recent data indicates that 12 per cent of GDP, and 29 per cent of government expenditures, is spent on procurement by OECD countries.[81] Efforts in relation to procurement practices have tended to focus on fair processes, transparency and fighting corruption,[82] but the turn to 'green' public procurement (GPP), although initially directed at environmental concerns, has more recently been broadened to 'sustainable public procurement',[83] more in line with SCP.[84] The European Commission has defined the two concepts as follows:

> Green Public Procurement (GPP) means that public authorities seek to purchase goods, services and works with a reduced environmental impact throughout their life-cycle compared to goods, services and works with the same primary function which would otherwise be procured.
>
> Sustainable Public Procurement (SPP) is a process by which public authorities seek to achieve the appropriate balance between the three pillars of sustainable development – economic, social and environmental – when procuring goods, services or works at all stages of the project.[85]

There are now innumerable national, regional and international instruments and initiatives on GPP/SPP.[86] While many tend to involve voluntary standards, the EU Commission announced, in March 2020, a proposal to introduce

---

[81] OECD, Highlights of Reforming Public Procurement: Progress in Implementing the 2015 OECD Recommendations (2019) 4 <https://www.oecd.org/gov/public-procurement/public-procurement-progress-report-highlights.pdf>.

[82] See for example the 2012 OECD Recommendation on Fighting Bid Rigging in Public Procurement, available at <https://www.oecd.org/competition/oecdrecommendationonfightingbidrigginginpublicprocurement.htm> and the 2011 UNCITRAL Model Law on Public Procurement (which replaced the earlier version from 1994).

[83] The term 'circular procurement' may soon replace 'green procurement' and 'sustainable procurement' given increased focus on the notion of circular economy. There is no need to provide granular distinctions for the purpose of this chapter.

[84] '69% of OECD countries are measuring results of GPP policies and strategies.' See <https://www.oecd.org/gov/public-procurement/green/>.

[85] <https://ec.europa.eu/environment/gpp/versus_en.htm>.

[86] See for example the 2017 Global Review of Sustainable Public Procurement, prepared and published as part of the 10YFP for SDG 12, through the One Planet network: <https://www.oneplanetnetwork.org/resource/2017-global-review-sustainable-public-procurement>.

'minimum mandatory green public procurement (GPP) criteria and targets in sectoral legislation' by 2021.[87] Because green or sustainable public procurement policy impacts both the demand (consumption) and supply (production) side, and given its scale and global reach, it carries significant promise for achieving SDG 12.[88]

Public procurement is a multi-step process, involving first a public administrative process of defining needs (which increasingly include sustainable production conditions),[89] soliciting bids and selecting the successful bidder, followed by a contractual relationship between the public body and the supplier providing the goods or services. Target 12.7 may find support through challenges to the bidding process or the selected bid, based on claims that sustainable elements were not respected. It is not obvious what role private international law may play even where the process allows for bids from foreign suppliers, which is often provided for in bilateral or multilateral trade agreements.[90]

In a recent document on public procurement, the European Commission noted that '[t]hird country bidders, goods and services are not always bound by the same, or equivalent, environmental, social or labour standards as those applicable to EU economic operators', giving rise to 'a need to apply the EU public procurement rules so as to ensure that the same, or equivalent, standards and requirements apply to EU and third country bidders'.[91] While this view may appear to be supportive of SDG 12, it does not account for the possibility that third-country bidders are subject to more stringent SCP requirements under their own law. Private international law methodology may offer a means to address this.

Thinking in terms of choice of law, a procurement process requiring that each supplier meet (or surpass) any sustainable production requirements applicable under its national law, and indicating how this impacts the quality and cost of its proposal, would highlight stronger sustainability standards. Assessment of

---

87 This is part of its Circular Economy Action Plan, intended to implement the 2019 European Green Deal: <https://ec.europa.eu/environment/circular-economy/pdf/new_circular_economy_action_plan.pdf> 8 and 26. This would appear to go beyond existing requirements under Directive 2014/24/EU on public procurement, which requires compliance with environmental, social and labour law.

88 On the imperative of addressing both consumption and production directly and jointly, see Candice Stevens, 'Linking sustainable consumption and production: The government role' (2010) 34(1) Natural Resources Forum 16.

89 For example, the EU GPP website specifies that 'GPP requires the inclusion of clear and verifiable environmental criteria for products and services in the public procurement process': <https://ec.europa.eu/environment/gpp/index_en.htm>.

90 This is typically determined by bilateral or multilateral trade agreements, such as the WTO Agreement on Government Procurement, last revised in 2014 <https://www.wto.org/english/tratop_e/gproc_e/gp_gpa_e.htm>.

91 European Commission, 'Guidance on the participation of third country bidders and goods in the EU procurement market', C(2019) 5494 final, 3.

bids would then take account of each supplier's contribution to sustainability.[92] In other words, where there are different sustainable production standards across states, Target 12.7 would be furthered if procurement processes were designed to reflect this diversity and support a race to the top rather than to the bottom. This would reconcile sustainable production with the non-discrimination conditions that typically define trade agreements dealing with public procurement.

Alternatively, the UN's Sustainable Procurement Indicators,[93] approved in 2019, could well be designated by national governments in their procurement processes, as incorporation by reference, which is often merely a weaker form of choice of law. As green/sustainable procurement standards become embedded in procurement processes with governments or international organisations, they may even rise to the level of a 'general principle of international commercial law', or less ambitiously, to the level of international practice, binding on all procurement processes and parties regardless of the applicable law.

3.3. TARGET 12.8: CONSUMER INFORMATION

This target is the only one in SDG 12 directed at sustainable *consumption*, or perhaps more accurately, directed at *consumers* as opposed to *producers*. As noted in the first section, the literature on SCP is clear: both must be pursued simultaneously if there is any hope of effectiveness. While strategies to influence consumer behaviour through education and information can give results, these are generally viewed as insufficient to make a meaningful impact.[94] The most pessimistic view argues that without a dramatic – and unlikely – systemic change in *values*, targeting consumption is a losing strategy.[95] And yet there is no doubt that bottom-up consumer-driven calls for sustainability have had an influence on the production side,[96] either directly through pressure on firms to act, or indirectly as a result of electing governments willing (or claiming to be willing) to take legislative action directed at the production side.

It is worth noting that, unlike with the production side discussed in the previous section, there is no indication that legislatures are moving toward imposing obligations directly on consumers to behave in ways that are

---

92 Admittedly this adds a layer of complexity to an already complex process.

93 <https://www.ungm.org/Shared/KnowledgeCenter/Pages/SustainableProcurementIndicatorProject>.

94 On this 'weak sustainability' approach, see the overview in Oksana Mont, 'Introduction' in Oksana Mont (ed), *A research agenda for sustainable consumption governance* (Edward Elgar Publishing 2019) 1, 7–8.

95 ibid 8–10 (discussing this 'strong sustainability' view).

96 See Wencke Gwozdz, Lucia Reisch and John Thøgersen, 'Behaviour Change for Sustainable Consumption' (2020) 43 Journal of Consumer Policy 249.

consistent with SDG 12. As Target 12.8 indicates, the objective is to provide consumers with the necessary *information* and *awareness* to be in a position to make choices that support SDG 12. Those choices may well be *influenced* by incentives, such as subsidies for electric vehicles or tax deductions for energy-saving home renovations, but these governmental programmes are marginal in relation to overall consumption and different in kind from policies that would actively discourage or even sanction unsustainable consumption. Moreover, and differently from the case of producers, such direct limitations on unsustainable consumption would likely unduly target vulnerable populations, given that less sustainable options are typically cheaper and therefore often the only choice for poorer consumers. In this context, the possibility that private international law may be deployed to make consumers subject to higher sustainability standards *in consumption* can only arise if such standards arise first within substantive law, which remains unrealised at this point.

The role for private international law in relation to Target 12.8 is thus currently limited to its potential to support *production*-related obligations; these typically engage the consumer/producer relationship through the lens of contract or delict. The consumer protection focus of much national law has recognised the vulnerability of the consumer in the market and intervened in various ways to seek to address it. Private international law has often followed, providing rules tailored to the consumer position in law and in practice. Hence consumers are often granted jurisdictional and legislative protections that are not afforded to other parties to cross-border legal relations. At its most basic, in the contract context, this involves some guarantee of access to local courts by denying the effect of forum selection or arbitration clauses.[97] Mandatory substantive law protections are preserved as a limit to party autonomy with regard to applicable contract law.[98] With respect to product liability, the victim of a defective product is commonly granted access to domestic courts and may even be entitled to choose the most beneficial applicable law.[99] In such an environment, it is possible, at least in theory, for transnational corporations to be held to higher standards even if they are headquartered or domiciled in jurisdictions with laxer standards. As national legislators adopt sustainable policies, private international law can operate to extend their reach beyond the purely domestic sphere.

Paradoxically, expanding the scope for consumer claims against foreign vendors of goods or services may be detrimental to SCP. If the only way to

97 As e.g. in Art 3149 of the Civil Code of Québec and Arts 17–19 of the Brussels I Regulation.

98 As e.g. in Art 3117 of the Civil Code of Québec and Art 6 of the Rome I Regulation.

99 See e.g. Arts 3148(3) and 3128 of the Civil Code of Québec; see also the Hague Convention of 2 October 1973 on the Law Applicable to Products Liability, which provides for alternative choice-of-law rules depending on the factual matrix but without giving the victim any choice as to the applicable law.

achieve sustainable consumption is by *reducing* consumption in absolute terms, maintaining legal obstacles to the international circulation of goods and services may be a preferable policy. Even without reducing consumption per se, local purchasing or minimising transportation costs related to consumption could be consistent with a weak sustainability approach. From a private international law perspective, this could be supported by excluding consumer access to domestic courts for claims against foreign vendors, particularly in the context of e-commerce,[100] on the assumption that court redress is a relevant factor in consumer decision-making, which is highly doubtful.[101] In any event, such an approach would entail a reversal of the dominant paradigm of supporting e-commerce by providing accessible dispute resolution. As with many other aspects of a strong sustainability thesis, such a view is so contrary to contemporary discourse about consumer sovereignty, choice and empowerment that it is likely a non-starter in political terms.[102]

Access to courts may support Target 12.6 in other ways. The growth in producers' sustainability claims regarding consumer goods and services opens up the option of court scrutiny pursuant to laws governing unfair business practices.[103] Because unfair business practices are typically remedied through injunctions, this approach arguably holds corporations to their unilateral sustainability statements or subjects them to the risk of severe reputational damage and loss of market share. The existing EU Injunctions Directive,[104] although underutilised, is an example of a type of instrument that could be developed regionally or globally to police producers' sustainability claims in the consumer market. This is one positive aspect of consumer sovereignty and empowerment that can translate into support for SDG 12.

---

100 While the COVID-19 pandemic has spelled disaster for many retailers, leading to expectations of reduced consumption, total US online sales in June 2020 were 75 per cent higher than in June 2019: <https://www.digitalcommerce360.com/article/coronavirus-impact-online-retail/>.

101 Consumers' knowledge about their rights and options for redress is notoriously poor. For a discussion see Hans-W Micklitz, 'General Report' in Hans-W Micklitz and Geneviève Saumier, *Enforcement and Effectiveness of Consumer Law* (Springer 2018) 3–45.

102 Oksana Mont, 'Introduction' in Oksana Mont (ed), *A research agenda for sustainable consumption governance* (Edward Elgar Publishing 2019) 1, 8. See also Ipshita Chaturvedi, 'Sustainable Consumption: Scope and Applicability of Principles of International Law' (2018) 2 Chinese Journal of International Law 514–15.

103 See Anna Beckers, *Enforcing Corporate Social Responsibility Codes: On Global Self-Regulation and National Private Law* (Hart Publishing 2015) and Borko Mihajlović, 'The Role of Consumers in the Achievement of Corporate Sustainability through the Reduction of Unfair Commercial Practices' (2020) 12(3) Sustainability 1.

104 Directive 2009/22/EC of the European Parliament and of the Council of 23 April 2009 on injunctions for the protection of consumers' interests (codified version) [2009] OJ L 110/30. This Directive is likely to be replaced in the near future as part of the 'New Deal for Consumers' initiative.

An obvious concrete example concerns labelling, in particular 'eco-labels'. These labels have become ubiquitous[105] and the sustainable consumption literature is replete with research on them.[106] Whether or not eco-labels have concrete sustainability impacts remains empirically uncertain,[107] but support for their use is widespread among governments, producers and even activists.[108] What is noteworthy about eco-labels is that they target both consumers and producers, thus potentially jointly contributing to furthering SCP. Indeed, if eco-labels can be conceived in a manner that positively influences consumer choice, this could have a knock-on effect, leading producers to invest in developing products that satisfy the certification requirements of the most effective eco-labels. The widespread use of eco-labels indicates that producers are already aware of their market value. The well-known examples of McDonald's endorsement of the Marine Stewardship Council eco-label for its fish fillet, or Lipton Tea sourcing its leaves from the Rainforest Alliance, demonstrate the acknowledged value of these labels.[109] But for eco-labels to further SCP, they must be meaningful and avoid the risk of so-called 'greenwashing'.[110] Even though the challenge of devising effective eco-labels cannot be understated, and their impact on consumer behaviour remains difficult to measure, the promise of eco-labels as part of an SCP policy is evident.

Unlike internal CSR codes, eco-labels are affixed on products or used in advertising and therefore fall within most consumer law governing unfair business practices. They may even intersect with competition law, particularly in the case of misrepresentation or greenwashing.[111] As noted by Mihajlovic, unfair business practices can provide a legal route for consumers (and consumer regulators) to push for sustainable production.[112] The same arguments made previously with respect to the role of private international law concerning access

---

105 Ecolabel Index, a global directory of ecolabels, lists 457 ecolabels in 199 countries, and 25 industry sectors: <www.ecolabelindex.com>.

106 See for example Magnus Boström and Mikael Klintman, *Eco-Standards, Product Labelling and Green Consumerism* (Palgrave Macmillan 2008); Jason J Czarnezki et al, 'Eco-labelling' in Emma Lees and Jorge E Viñuales (eds), *The Oxford Handbook of Comparative Environmental Law* (OUP 2019) 996; Caroline L Noblet and Mario F Teisl, 'Eco-labelling as sustainable consumption policy' in Lucia Reisch and John Thøgersen, *Handbook of Research on Sustainable Consumption* (Edward Elgar Publishing 2015) 300; Hamish van der Ven, *Beyond Greenwash? Explaining Credibility in Transnational Eco-Labeling* (OUP 2019).

107 Noblet and Teisl, ibid 301; Jason J Czarnezki, K Ingemar Jönsson and Katrina Kuh, 'Crafting Next Generation Eco-Label Policy' (2018) 48(3) Environmental Law 409, 422–423.

108 Hamish van der Ven, *Beyond Greenwash? Explaining Credibility in Transnational Eco-Labeling* (OUP 2019) 2–3.

109 Ibid 10.

110 This refers to the practice of using eco-labels to make false or meaningless claims about a product. See van der Ven, ibid.

111 See for example the US FTC Guides for the Use of Environmental Marketing Claims ('Green Guides'), last updated in 2012.

112 Borko Mihajlović, 'The Role of Consumers in the Achievement of Corporate Sustainability through the Reduction of Unfair Commercial Practices' (2020) 12(3) Sustainability 1.

to courts and applicable law are relevant here as well. Given that many consumer goods are produced by multinational corporations,[113] any increased opportunity to hold them to account regarding the use of eco-labels through courts should be seen as a way to contribute to SDG 12.

4. RESULTS

The previous sections reveal that private international law has a role to play in supporting the goal of 'ensuring sustainable consumption and production patterns', through existing rules and doctrines. It could expand its role by expressly adopting a sustainability-endorsing approach that seeks to bridge the regulatory gaps that can be exploited by multinational producers to defeat national attempts to reach sustainable development goals.

First, regarding the jurisdictional dimension of private international law rules, these should be interpreted to secure access to courts for claims against corporate defendants whose activities violate existing domestic regulation related to SDG 12 or engage in unfair business practices relating to sustainable production claims. Current proposals to modify the Brussels I regime to broaden jurisdiction over corporate groups go in this direction. Moreover, existing rules establishing jurisdiction in the defendant's home state should be strengthened by eliminating avoidance mechanisms such as *forum non conveniens*. There is multilateral consensus in soft-law instruments for such an approach in relation to human rights violations and this view should be extended to the environmental aspect of sustainability that is at the heart of SDG 12. Rules allowing for joinder of foreign co-defendants should be expanded to facilitate efficient resolution of claims in a single forum and eliminate strategic jurisdictional litigation that serves only to delay proceedings and increase the cost for claimants, both detrimental to access to justice. The exceptional jurisdictional basis of necessity should be more widely admitted as another tool against regulatory or accountability avoidance by multinational producers. To be fully effective, this broadening of jurisdictional rules needs to be recognised as legitimate at the judgment enforcement stage as well.

Second, in relation to choice-of-law rules, there is significant scope for both generous interpretation of existing rules and development of new targeted rules for issues relating to SDG 12. For example, with regard to tort liability of parent companies for injurious acts of their foreign subsidiaries, it is possible

[113] Data from 2016 compiled by the OECD shows that multinational enterprises and their foreign affiliates account for one-third of world output and GDP and two-thirds of international trade: Koen De Backer et al, 'Multinational enterprises in the global economy: Heavily discussed, hardly measured' (25 September 2019) <https://voxeu.org/article/multinational-enterprises-global-economy>.

to interpret the *lex loci delicti* as including the place where the parent's policy decision was taken, which in turn enabled the foreign subsidiary (or supplier) to act (or fail to act). Where this points to a law that imposes higher standards, either accountability and compensation for the injured party may result, or, *ex ante*, deterrence of harm-causing behaviour through respect for higher standards may be expected. More generally, choice-of-law rules that allow the claimant to choose between alternative applicable laws, such as exist in relation to environmental damage under the Rome II Regulation, also provide *ex ante* incentives for producers to follow higher standards of potentially applicable laws even if only as a liability avoidance strategy. This model should be more widely adopted.

SDG 12 may also be supported through the significant cross-border activity occasioned by public procurement. Choice-of-law methodology can be referenced to structure procurement processes that incorporate preferences for strong sustainable production standards.

5. CONCLUSION

Research for this contribution revealed a paradox. There is an apparently infinite number of sources on SCP, from academic papers in all fields of the humanities and sciences, to government reports and legislative agendas, international organisation soft-law instruments and practice guides, industry and civil society initiatives, social media posts, blogs, etc. And yet, as the UN Secretary-General reported in April 2020, there is little to celebrate in terms of progress in meeting the sustainable development goals of Agenda 2030.[114] Asking how private international law could support Agenda 2030 seems almost whimsical in such a context!

Nevertheless, this contribution sought to examine how SDG 12 on sustainable consumption and production patterns might intersect with private international law and how the discipline might contribute to the ongoing discourse on sustainability. My conclusion is that while private international law is currently a marginal player, reflecting on how it might further be deployed to support the objectives of SDG 12 and sustainable development generally reveals some promising insights. I have tried to show that access to courts, in particular in relation to claims against transnational corporations, is a key issue and one that rules on international jurisdiction can facilitate. This would go some ways to addressing the 'regulatory gap' that transnational corporations are otherwise able to exploit, to the detriment of individuals and the environment across

114 Progress towards the Sustainable Development Goals – Report of the Secretary-General, UN Doc E/2020/57 (28 April 2020) para 107.

the globe. But equally important is the availability of remedies that are responsive to the SDGs, which in turn depends on the content of substantive law and the choice-of-law rules that designate it in cross-border litigation. Policy-oriented choice-of-law rules, such as Article 7 of the Rome II Regulation in relation to environmental damage, are obvious options, but these are only as effective as the substantive law that they refer to. Recent developments regarding corporate group liability for environmental damage discussed in this chapter suggest there is progress on that front. To a lesser degree the same might be said of public procurement and eco-labelling.

I close with cautious optimism regarding the role that private international law may be able to play in supporting the sustainable development agenda. As long as unsustainable consumption and production result from human activities that largely escape the reach of law, whether domestic or international, it is incumbent on jurists, including private international law specialists, to engage with this pressing challenge to our common future.

SDG 13: CLIMATE ACTION

Eduardo Álvarez-Armas*

Goal 13: Take urgent action to combat climate change and its impacts*

13.1 Strengthen resilience and adaptive capacity to climate-related hazards and natural disasters in all countries
13.2 Integrate climate change measures into national policies, strategies and planning
13.3 Improve education, awareness-raising and human and institutional capacity on climate change mitigation, adaptation, impact reduction and early warning
13.a Implement the commitment undertaken by developed-country parties to the United Nations Framework Convention on Climate Change to a goal of mobilizing jointly $100 billion annually by 2020 from all sources to address the needs of developing countries in the context of meaningful mitigation actions and transparency on implementation and fully operationalize the Green Climate Fund through its capitalization as soon as possible
13.b Promote mechanisms for raising capacity for effective climate change-related planning and management in least developed countries and small island developing States, including focusing on women, youth and local and marginalized communities

* Acknowledging that the United Nations Framework Convention on Climate Change is the primary international, intergovernmental forum for negotiating the global response to climate change.

* This chapter contains arguments presented in the VIII Journal of Private International Law Biannual Conference, held in Munich on 12–14 September 2019, as well as arguments taken and/or adapted from Eduardo Álvarez-Armas, *Private International Environmental Litigation before EU Courts: Choice of Law as a Tool of Environmental Global Governance* (Université catholique de Louvain/Universidad de Granada 2017).

When exploring how private international law may help '[t]ake urgent action to combat climate change and its impacts' a first possibility that immediately comes to mind is private international climate change litigation (PICCL). I define PICCL as litigation (1) amongst private parties; (2) of a private law (generally tort law) nature; (3) conducted on the basis of private international law notions and rules; (4) over damage threatened or caused by climate-change-derived phenomena. Private law (mostly tort law) litigation is conceived by economic analysis of law as a means to force polluters (in this case, greenhouse gas emitters) to internalise environmental externalities (in this case, greenhouse gas emissions).[1] Thus, in a cross-border setting, such litigation-based internalisation may contribute to attaining 'development that

[1] On economic analysis of law and environmental damage: M Faure, *L'analyse économique du droit de l'environnement* (Bruylant 2007). On economic analysis of tort law in general, other than the usual citation of Calabresi, see, amongst others, A M Polinsky and S Shavell, 'Economic Analysis of Law' in L Blume and S Durlauf (eds), *The New Palgrave Dictionary of Economics* (SSRN version, 2005: <http://ssrn.com/abstract=859406> 8 et seq) including the work cited therein.

meets the needs of the present without compromising the ability of future generations to meet their own needs'.[2]

Clearly, for transnational climate change litigation to be undertaken by private parties, rules on international jurisdiction of courts and applicable law in civil and commercial matters are required. Without them, this kind of litigation would often not be possible. This first level of intervention/contribution simply reflects the paradigm of neutral – policy-blind – private international law. However, beyond this, PICCL conducted on the basis of so-called 'content-oriented' private international law rules may further foster the global enhancement of climate change mitigation and adaptation policies,[3] and contribute to the attainment of the United Nations' Sustainable Development Goal 13 (SDG 13) through the involvement of private parties.

Further interfaces between SDG 13 and private international law arise outside the realm of PICCL. However, these pages will largely focus on the latter (notwithstanding the importance of the former), if anything due to the political significance of climate litigation (both private and public). As a result of the limited success that diplomatic efforts have yielded in respect of tackling what has been labelled a 'climate crisis',[4] climate change litigation is gaining momentum. This momentum seems (so far) to be less related to its potential to provide redress for climate-change-related damage, or to facilitate climate change mitigation and adaptation, than to its potential to spark public debate on global warming.[5] But the tendency may be changing.[6]

---

2 World Commission on Environment and Development, 'Our Common Future' (1987) para 27 <https://sustainabledevelopment.un.org/content/documents/5987our-common-future.pdf> accessed 1 February 2021 (Brundtland Commission report).

3 'Mitigation' is a 'human intervention to reduce the sources or enhance the sinks of greenhouse gases (GHGs)'; 'adaptation' is '[t]he process of adjustment to actual or expected climate and its effects. In human systems, adaptation seeks to moderate or avoid harm or exploit beneficial opportunities. In some natural systems, human intervention may facilitate adjustment to expected climate and its effects'. K J Mach, S Planton and C von Stechow (eds), 'IPCC, 2014: Annex II: Glossary' in R K Pachauri and L A Meyer (eds), *Climate Change 2014: Synthesis Report. Contribution of Working Groups I, II and III to the Fifth Assessment Report of the Intergovernmental Panel on Climate Change* (IPCC 2014) 117, 118 and 125 respectively <https://www.ipcc.ch/site/assets/uploads/2018/02/AR5_SYR_FINAL_Annexes.pdf> accessed 1 February 2021.

4 This language is used by the United Nations Organization itself <http://un.org/en/un75/climate-crisis-race-we-can-win> accessed 1 February 2021.

5 M Lehmann and F Eichel, 'Globaler Klimawandel und Internationales Privatrecht – Zuständigkeit und anzuwendendes Recht für transnationale Klagen wegen klimawandelbedingter Individualschäden' (2019) 83(1) Rabels Zeitschrift für ausländisches und internationales Privatrecht 77, 82. They consider that civil courts have become a forum for public debate on issues of global environmental governance. Cf Shi-Ling Hsu, 'A realistic evaluation of climate change litigation through the lens of a hypothetical judgment lawsuit' (2008) 79 University of Colorado Law Review 701, 717: 'By targeting deep-pocketed private entities that actually emit greenhouse gases … a civil litigation strategy, if successful, skips over the potentially cumbersome, time-consuming, and politically perilous route of pursuing legislation and regulation.'

6 See, notably MilieuDefensie 2019 (described below, in section 2.3).

This chapter begins by unpacking SDG 13 (section 1) and presenting the notion of PICCL (section 2), before assessing its sustainability-enhancing potential (section 3), including the possibility that it may indirectly contribute to the development of international negotiations within the scheme arising from the United Nations Framework Convention on Climate Change (UNFCCC). This is followed by an exploration of the challenges PICCL faces as a tool to foster sustainability (section 4), some of which are shared by private international litigation in respect of other SDGs beyond SDG 13. Finally, after briefly introducing some illustrations of further interfaces between private international law and SDG 13 (section 5), some concluding remarks are provided (section 6), and results are summarised (section 7).

1. UNPACKING SDG 13

'Climate change is regarded by many as a defining challenge of our times and thus it is not surprising that one of the SDGs (13) concerns "urgent action to combat climate change and its impacts"'.[7] It is scientifically demonstrated and politically acknowledged that Planet Earth is undergoing a human-induced process of 'changes in [its] climate system'.[8] The anthropogenic emission of CO2 and other greenhouse gases (GHGs) and their accumulation in the atmosphere are causing a rise in global average temperatures. This, in turn, is resulting in the intensification and multiplication of 'extreme weather and climate events',[9] which are already having dramatic consequences for Earth's biodiversity and for human lives.[10] Beyond pure ecological outcomes (melting of glaciers, acidification of oceans, rise of sea levels, etc.), clear human-felt impacts are quickly crystallising around the planet: lengthier and more severe droughts, compromising freshwater supplies and food production;[11] changes in patterns of distribution of infectious diseases;[12] increases in natural-resources-related

7 B M Campbell et al, 'Urgent action to combat climate change and its impacts (SDG 13): transforming agriculture and food systems' (2018) 34 Current Opinion in Environmental Sustainability 13.

8 IPCC, 'IPCC, 2013: Summary for Policymakers' in T F Stocker et al (eds), *Climate Change 2013: The Physical Science Basis. Contribution of Working Group I to the Fifth Assessment Report of the Intergovernmental Panel on Climate Change* (CUP 2013) 15.

9 ibid 4.

10 Food and Agriculture Organization of the United Nations (FAO), 'Sustainable development goals – Take urgent action to combat climate change and its impacts' <http://www.fao.org/sustainable-development-goals/goals/goal-13/en/> accessed 1 February 2021.

11 ibid.

12 World Health Organization (WHO), Regional Office for Europe, 'SDG 13: Health and climate action' <https://www.euro.who.int/en/health-topics/health-policy/sustainable-development-goals/publications/2019/policy-briefs-on-health-and-the-sustainable-development-goals/sdg-13-health-and-climate-action> accessed 1 February 2021.

conflicts, political instability and migration;[13] and disruptions in national economies,[14] just to name a few examples.

The 'urgent action' mentioned in SDG 13 is required in order to succeed in adapting to and mitigating these as well as further and more profound impacts.[15] Specifically, other than developing 'prevention, protection and response measures',[16] GHG emissions need to be cut almost by 50 per cent by 2030 in order to cap further temperature increases at 1.5°C above pre-industrial levels, which would allow disastrous global-scale consequences to be averted.[17] This will require systemic shifts[18] and a significant 'scaling-up of technological, economic, institutional and behavioural changes',[19] including 'appropriate financial flows, a new technology framework and an enhanced capacity building framework'.[20]

Accordingly, SDG 13 breaks down into five targets, accompanied by eight indicators, which aim at tackling what has been depicted. It is contended, however, that SDG 13 just reinstates a series of pre-existing international legal obligations, for, ultimately, its content and objectives could be traced back to a series of multilateral legally-binding international treaties, amongst which the UNFCCC, the Kyoto Protocol and the Paris Agreement.[21] Other than these instruments, it is also contended that SDG 13, and specifically Target 13.2 (integration of climate change measures into national policies, strategies, and planning), can be traced back to more general overarching principles of public international law (as applied to climate change).[22] Amongst the latter would be

13 ibid.

14 United Nations, 'Goal 13: Take urgent action to combat climate change and its impacts' <https://www.un.org/sustainabledevelopment/climate-change/> accessed 1 February 2021.

15 K Lofts et al, 'Brief on Sustainable Development Goal 13 on Taking Action on Climate Change and Its Impacts: Contributions of International Law, Policy and Governance' (2017) 13(1) McGill Journal of Sustainable Development Law 183, 191.

16 World Health Organization (WHO), Regional Office for Europe, 'SDG 13: Health and climate action' <https://www.euro.who.int/en/health-topics/health-policy/sustainable-development-goals/publications/2019/policy-briefs-on-health-and-the-sustainable-development-goals/sdg-13-health-and-climate-action> accessed 1 February 2021.

17 ibid.

18 United Nations Department of Economic and Social Affairs, 'Take urgent action to combat climate change and its impacts' <https://sdgs.un.org/goals/goal13> accessed 1 February 2021.

19 World Health Organization (WHO), Regional Office for Europe, 'SDG 13: Health and climate action' <https://www.euro.who.int/en/health-topics/health-policy/sustainable-development-goals/publications/2019/policy-briefs-on-health-and-the-sustainable-development-goals/sdg-13-health-and-climate-action> accessed 1 February 2021.

20 United Nations, 'Goal 13: Take urgent action to combat climate change and its impacts' <https://www.un.org/sustainabledevelopment/climate-change/> accessed 1 February 2021.

21 K Lofts et al, 'Brief on Sustainable Development Goal 13 on Taking Action on Climate Change and Its Impacts: Contributions of International Law, Policy and Governance' (2017) 13(1) McGill Journal of Sustainable Development Law 183, 186.

22 ibid 189.

the *sic utere tuo ut alienum non laedas* principle, i.e. the 'general obligation of States to ensure that activities within their jurisdiction and control respect the environment of other States or of areas beyond national control'.[23]

2. PRESENTATION OF PICCL: DELIMITATION FROM OTHER CLIMATE CHANGE LITIGATION AND ILLUSTRATIONS

2.1. DEFINING AND DISTINGUISHING PICCL

While climate change litigation has existed (relatively discreetly) for possibly almost three decades,[24] it has attracted broader attention in recent times. Most notably so since the historic judgment rendered by the District Court of The Hague (the Netherlands) on 24 June 2015 in the so-called 'Urgenda climate case', where the Urgenda Foundation[25] successfully conducted litigation against the government of the Netherlands for its lack of efforts to combat climate change.[26] In its landmark ruling (whose essence was ultimately upheld on 20 December 2019 by the Dutch Supreme Court),[27] the District Court established that 'the State must take more action to reduce the greenhouse gas emissions in the Netherlands. The State also has to ensure that the Dutch emissions in the year 2020 will be at least 25% lower than those in 1990.'[28] The *Urgenda* case seems to have inspired, or at least to have provided further momentum to,

23 J Brunnée, 'Sic utere tuo ut alienum non laedas' in R Wolfrum (ed), *The Max Planck Encyclopedia of Public International Law* (OUP 2010, online edition).

24 For an overview of (broadly conceived) climate change litigation, its evolution over time, its key features and stakes: G Ganguly, J Setzer and V Heyvaert, 'If at First You Don't Succeed: Suing Corporations for Climate Change' (2018) 38(4) Oxford Journal of Legal Studies 841, 846 et seq. The authors place the beginning of the 'first wave' of what they call 'private' climate litigation (i.e. litigation against private parties, irrespective of whether initiated by public or private subjects) around 2005 in the United States.

25 Reportedly, Urgenda is 'a citizens' platform which develops plans and measures to prevent climate change [which] also represent[ed] 886 individuals in this case.' <http://deeplink.rechtspraak.nl/uitspraak?id=ECLI:NL:RBDHA:2015:7196> accessed 1 February 2021.

26 For a description and timeline: <https://www.urgenda.nl/en/themas/climate-case/climate-case-explained/> accessed 1 February 2021. For further commentary, see inter alia: R Suryapratim and E Woerdman, 'Situating Urgenda v the Netherlands within comparative climate change litigation' (2016) 34(2) Journal of Energy & Natural Resources Law 165 (on the initial decision); H van Loon, 'Strategic climate litigation in the Dutch courts: a source of inspiration for NGO's elsewhere?' (2020) 4 Acta Universitatis Carolinae – Iuridica 69 (on the three instances of the case).

27 Urgenda, 'The Urgenda climate case against the Dutch Government' <http://www.urgenda.nl/en/climate-case/> accessed 1 February 2021.

28 An English version of the District Court of The Hague's 2015 judgment can be found at <http://deeplink.rechtspraak.nl/uitspraak?id=ECLI:NL:RBDHA:2015:7196> accessed 1 February 2021 (quotation taken from the summary provided in the same webpage).

similar sets of proceedings around the world.[29] These include, other than actions by NGOs against public bodies for lack of action as regards climate change, actions by public bodies against private actors for climate-change-related effective or potential damage, for instance.[30]

It is common to refer to public versus private climate litigation, depending on whether the defendant is a public entity or a private person. However, it may be more appropriate to differentiate along two axes of coordinates: domestic versus international litigation, and public versus private litigation, further restricting the latter to situations where both claimant and defendant are private parties, and the relevant cause of action is of a private law nature. In this sense, *Urgenda* would be an example of 'domestic' (plaintiffs and defendant are contained within a single state) and public (the defendant is a public entity) litigation. Although it may be difficult to draw clear-cut distinctions (notably as climate change is, by definition, an 'international'/global phenomenon), differences in legal and non-legal stakes along both axes justify the classification effort. The presence of a public entity on either side of the legal relationship will frequently bring various complexities into the picture: potential international law immunities and doctrines such as the 'act of state' when litigation targets a public defendant; questions as to whether the lawsuit is grounded on public prerogatives/State authority when litigation is brought by a public plaintiff. This latter aspect is key. Moreover, (domestic) political and (international) diplomatic dynamics differ widely in function of the public or private nature of the parties involved.

Accordingly, PICCL features, other than a cross-border/transboundary dimension, one or several private party claimants (as opposed to public bodies) and one or several private party defendants (as opposed to public entities), the latter generally being one (or several) of the so-called 'Carbon Majors': a group of 90 corporations, which, according to the scientific evidence, produced '63% of cumulative worldwide emissions of industrial CO2 and methane between 1751 and 2010'.[31] Claims in PICCL generally rest on tortious or non-contractual liability, aiming at providing compensation for damage suffered and/or, where available, injunctive relief, and/or provisional measures, etc.

---

29 See, most recently, German Constitutional Court, 24 March 2021 (1 BvR 2656/18 et al); English press release available at <https://www.bundesverfassungsgericht.de/SharedDocs/Pressemitteilungen/EN/2021/bvg21-031.html> accessed 25 March 2021.

30 Two key databases offer an 'inventory' of cases and information on climate change litigation around the globe: the one held by the Grantham Research Institute on Climate Change and the Environment <https://climate-laws.org/cclow/litigation_cases> and the one held by the Sabin Center for Climate Change Law <http://climatecasechart.com/> both accessed 1 February 2021.

31 R Heede, 'Tracing anthropogenic carbon dioxide and methane emissions to fossil fuel and cement producers, 1854–2010' (2014) 122 Climatic Change 229. For updated data: <https://climateaccountability.org/carbonmajors.html> accessed 1 February 2021.

2.2. CLIMATE-RELEVANT ELEMENTS OF PRIVATE INTERNATIONAL LAW

Unsurprisingly, there are no specific private international law rules devoted to climate matters. On the one hand, as mentioned, general climate litigation's momentum and the general public's climate awareness are relatively recent. On the other hand, where general environmental policies and sensibilities have crystallised into special private international law rules on environmental matters, those rules possibly suffice to manage at least the core aspects of most climate-related cases. Additionally, the prospect of a potential inception of specific climate-relevant private international law rules at the international level seems far out of reach: the Hague Conference attempted during the 1990s to work towards drafting a convention on private international law aspects of (general) environmental liability to no avail (the item was ultimately eliminated from the Hague Conference's agenda).[32]

As PICCL is sustained by the broader framework of private international law – both its general rules and (where available) its specific experience with environmental matters – this subsection will only present climate-significant elements within that framework briefly. The following pages will deal with those elements in further detail as appropriate.[33] To a limited extent, mention will be made of climate-relevant conclusions that may be derived from environmental but non-climate-related elements. This will be so to avoid unnecessary repetitions. Elements of general private international 'environmental' litigation are discussed in the chapters of the volume on SDG 14 ('Conserve and sustainably use the oceans, seas and marine resources for sustainable development') and SDG 15 ('Protect, restore and promote sustainable use of terrestrial ecosystems, sustainably manage forests, combat desertification, and halt and reverse land degradation and halt biodiversity loss').

Overall, while PICCL is a novelty from the standpoint of climate litigation, from a private international law perspective it is no more than a specific application to a given context (climate matters) of general principles of private international environmental litigation. This 'mirrors' the fact that SDG 13 is, to a certain extent, a specific and explicit application of values underlying SDGs 14 and 15. In other words, SDG 13 could potentially have been 'diluted' into SDGs 14 and 15, notably as Targets 14.2, 14.3, 15.1, 15.2, 15.3, 15.4 and 15.5 (amongst others) are connected with climate-mitigation or climate-adaptation

---

32 H van Loon, 'Principles and building blocks for a global legal framework for transnational civil litigation in environmental matters' (2018) 23 Uniform Law Review 298, 314.

33 For a similar account to the one provided here, see E-M Kieninger, 'Conflicts of jurisdiction and the applicable law in domestic courts' proceedings' in W Kahl and M-P Weller (eds) *Climate Change Litigation – a handbook* (Beck 2021).

objectives. However, SG13 is a standalone SDG due to its political significance, and the very intense sense of urgency of the 'climate crisis'.

PICCL may be typically developed wherever any of the two following rules of international jurisdiction of courts in civil and commercial matters are available. First, *actor sequitur forum rei*, or the rule providing jurisdiction to the courts of the 'home' country of the defendant (provided that no relevant subject-matter or other restrictions interfere). The specific connecting factors used to identify whether the defendant has their 'home' within a given jurisdiction (domicile, habitual residence, registered office, etc.) and their definition will vary from one system of private international law to another. The second typical possibility for jurisdiction over PICCL is *forum loci deliciti commissi*, or the rule providing jurisdiction to the courts of the 'place of the tort'. Either one of the two understandings of the 'place of' transboundary torts may give rise to relevant jurisdiction: jurisdiction at the place of materialisation of the injury or jurisdiction at the place of the conduct. Here again, availability of only one possibility or both may vary from one system of private international law to another. These rules entail that, in principle, jurisdiction over PICCL may be asserted in the home country of the emitter, in the country/countries where they emit from, and/or in the country/countries where the victim(s) suffered/will suffer climate-change-related damage. As a consequence, where a plaintiff in the Global South alleges injuries caused by a polluter in the Global North, that plaintiff can, in principle, bring suit in their home courts, or in the defendant's home state in the Global North.

Beyond these two key rules, further possibilities may be available in certain countries, like, for instance, 'doing business' grounds of jurisdiction, which allow, under certain conditions, jurisdiction to be asserted over subjects that perform economic activities within the relevant territory. However, these three, and any other possibilities, may be restricted, in certain countries, by institutions like *forum non conveniens*, a discretionary prerogative allowing a given court, at a defendant's request, to stay or dismiss a case that it is entitled to hear, due to the fact that there is an allegedly more appropriate venue to hear the case elsewhere.[34]

Once jurisdiction is established, the applicable law is usually determined through specific choice-of-law rules for environmental torts, or through broad/comprehensive choice-of-law rules on (general) torts. Irrespective of the specific focus of the rule, what is actually relevant is: (1) what the relevant

[34] This definition has been elaborated drawing elements from G Betlem, 'Transnational Litigation Against Multinational Corporations Before Dutch Civil Courts' in M T Kamminga and S Zia-Zafiri (eds), *Liability of Multinational Corporations Under International Law* (Kluwer Law International 2000) 283–284; and R A Brand, 'Challenges to Forum non conveniens', (2013) 45 NYU Journal of International Law and Politics 1003, 1005 et seq.

connecting factor(s) is/are; (2) what their structural relationship is, if there are several of them; (3) whether the rule reflects the complexity of transboundary situations; and (4) whether the rule is policy-blind, or whether it embodies any sort of substantive policy (like, for instance, environmental protection). Typically, the relevant connecting factor will be one of several possible manifestations of the 'place of the tort', thus leading to the application of either the law of the place of materialisation of the injury, the law of the place of the conduct, or the law chosen between these two alternatives by either the victim or the court. This latter possibility (alternative structure with a choice prerogative) is one of several possibilities that reflect pro-environmental content-orientedness in choice of law, the main example thereof being Article 7 of the European Union's Rome II Regulation.[35] These ideas will be discussed in further detail below.[36]

Finally, the recognition and enforcement of foreign judicial decisions dealing with environmental torts may face difficulties deriving, for instance, from the distinct legal personality of the various units of a transnational corporation, or from lack of connection of the matter with the country where recognition and enforcement are sought. An infamous and recent example in this sense (notwithstanding the cases' other difficulties and controversies) are the negative results obtained by Ecuadorian plaintiffs in their attempts to obtain recognition and enforcement of the Ecuadorian Supreme Court's ruling against Chevron in the Lago Agrio saga in various jurisdictions.[37] Other aspects and difficulties relating to the recognition and enforcement of foreign judicial decisions and foreign public acts will be discussed below.[38]

2.3. ILLUSTRATIONS OF PICCL: *MILIEUDEFENSIE* 2019 AND *LLIUYA*

PICCL is a (relatively) new tendency within climate change litigation. Research in the Grantham Research Institute and Sabin Center climate cases databases shows two ongoing illustrations thereof, both taking place before EU courts.[39] As of 1 February 2021, only one more case could potentially respond to the features of PICCL as described above: *Friends of the Earth*

---

35 Regulation (EC) No 864/2007 of the European Parliament and of the Council of 11 July 2007 on the law applicable to non-contractual obligations (Rome II) [2007] OJ L 199/40.

36 See section 3.1.

37 See 'Canadian proceedings' and 'Proceedings in other countries' at <https://www.business-humanrights.org/en/latest-news/texacochevron-lawsuits-re-ecuador-1> accessed 16 May 2021.

38 See section 5.

39 <https://climate-laws.org/cclow/litigation_cases> and <http://climatecasechart.com/> both accessed 1 February 2021.

(Les amis de la terre) et al v Total.[40] However, its file specifies that the claimants are focusing on human rights and conventional pollution issues, and are only collaterally arguing 'that Total's vigilance plan does not properly account for the project's potential life cycle greenhouse gas emissions'. Beyond this, some further five or six cases, located in non-EU jurisdictions such as Argentina and Australia, could potentially be classified as PICCL, but their files do not contain enough information to ascertain whether that is indeed the case.

In *Milieudefensie v Shell* 2019,[41] seven Dutch NGOs and over 17,000 individuals have brought Royal Dutch Shell before the District Court of The Hague, on the basis of both EU and Dutch rules of private international law (Royal Dutch Shell has its registered office in the United Kingdom and its principal place of business in the Netherlands). The claimants seek to obtain the transposition of the legal reasoning of the *Urgenda* case to private subjects (corporations). Specifically, they seek to obtain, inter alia, an order that Shell limits 'the joint volume of all CO2 emissions associated with its business activities and fossil fuel products in such a way that the joint volume of those emissions is reduced by (net) 45% by 2030 compared to 2010 levels'.[42] They rest their claim on Dutch tort law, under which Shell would have 'a duty of care towards the claimants to contribute to preventing [climate-change-derived] danger and to act in line with … Paris climate target[s]'.[43] Their position is further sustained, amongst other grounds, on a claim to indirect horizontal effect of Articles 2 ('right to life') and 8 ('Right to respect for private and family life, home and correspondence') of the European Convention of Human Rights (ECHR).[44] On 26 May 2021, the trial level decision was issued. The District Court of The Hague

> orders [Shell], both directly and via the companies and legal entities it commonly includes in its consolidated annual accounts … to limit or cause to be limited the aggregate annual volume of all CO2 emissions into the atmosphere … due to the business operations and sold energy-carrying products of the Shell group to such an

---

40 <https://www.climate-laws.org/geographies/france/litigation_cases/friends-of-the-earth-et-al-v-total> accessed 1 February 2021.

41 <https://en.milieudefensie.nl/climate-case-shell/climate-case-against-shell> (not to be confused with the 2008 *Milieudefensie v Shell* 'common' environmental litigation <https://en.milieudefensie.nl/shell-in-nigeria>) both accessed 1 February 2021.

42 Page 205 of the unofficial translation of the court summons, which can be found under the 'summons' link at <http://climatecasechart.com/non-us-case/milieudefensie-et-al-v-royal-dutch-shell-plc/> accessed 1 February 2021.

43 ibid paras 38–39.

44 ibid paras 40, 50–55. For a broad overview of the interface between climate change and human rights, see T Gross, 'Climate change and duties to protect with regards to fundamental rights' in W Kahl and M-P Weller (eds) *Climate Change Litigation – a handbook* (Beck 2021), especially 85–90.

> extent that this volume will have reduced by at least net 45% at end 2030, relative to 2019 levels.[45]

This ruling has been welcomed as a 'turning point': '[f]or the first time in history',[46] a court has ruled in this sense against a corporation within climate change litigation.

Lliuya v RWE[47] is a case pending before German courts which is likely to become a milestone in climate change litigation due to the creativity of the plaintiff's counsel. The plaintiff, Saúl Lliuya, lives in Huaraz, a city in Peru situated in the Andes mountains, at the foot of a glacier that global warming is melting, increasing the volume of water in a lake (Palcacocha) that will eventually overflow and flood his property.[48] Mr Lliuya, backed up by German NGO Germanwatch, has sued, on the basis of EU rules of private international law, German electricity provider RWE in order to avoid damage to his property. He contends, on the basis of scientific data/evidence, that, as RWE has contributed to 0.47 per cent of all GHG emissions since the beginning of the industrial era,[49] it is liable to contribute to 0.47per cent of the costs of the 'appropriate safety precautions' (building/construction works) required to prevent his property from being flooded.[50]

Lliuya's approach is undoubtedly creative: by focusing on the claimant's aspiration to protect his own property from future damage, the case circumvents several difficulties typically encountered in environmental litigation (*locus standi* in respect of diffuse interests and 'visibility' of latent damages). Despite this focus on private rights and interests, the case, if successful, would indirectly produce climate-beneficial results. Nevertheless, *Lliuya* still faces significant challenges from the standpoint of tort law, notably as regards establishing the causal link between the (potential) damage and RWE's actions.[51] As explained by Lehmann

---

45 Point 5.3 of the Court-issued English translation of the District Court Judgment <http://climatecasechart.com/climate-change-litigation/wp-content/uploads/sites/16/non-us-case-documents/2021/20210526_8918_judgment-2.pdf > accessed 14 July 2021.

46 Statements of Milieudefensie representatives <https://en.milieudefensie.nl/news/historic-victory-judge-forces-shell-to-drastically-reduce-co2-emissions> accessed 14 July 2021.

47 For general information on the case: Germanwatch, 'Saúl versus RWE – The Huaraz Case' <https://www.germanwatch.org/en/huaraz> accessed 1 February 2021.

48 ibid.

49 *Lliuya v RWE*, Statement of claim, 18 pt 8.2 <https://www.germanwatch.org/sites/germanwatch.org/files/announcement/20822.pdf> accessed 1 February 2021.

50 ibid 2. Idea adapted from the *petitum*.

51 For an assessment of this case under German substantive private law, which concludes that Lliuya's chances of success are 'limited', see G Wagner and A Antz, 'Liability for climate damages under the German law of torts' in W Kahl and M-P Weller (eds) *Climate Change Litigation – a handbook* (Beck 2021), especially 422–27.

and Eichel,[52] while 'non-degradable, anthropogenic' surpluses of GHGs may certainly be considered to be polluting elements, their traceability to any specific emitter is complicated by at least two factors: 'the greenhouse effect also takes place without human intervention and is subject to natural fluctuations that vary in space and time', and anthropogenic GHG emissions 'are absorbed by natural *"CO2 sinks"* (such as land surfaces or water)'. Moreover, for Lehmann and Eichel, establishing a causal link/chain in respect of material or financial damage attributable to global warming is further complicated by the fact that the specific material or financial damage suffered by a person is preceded by impacts on two 'environmental goods': first, changes in the atmosphere (GHGs not 'absorbed' by water or soil intensify the natural greenhouse effect, leading to increases in the average temperature on Earth); and second, changes in the environment that result from the latter, for instance rising sea levels, severe droughts or the melting of glaciers. Therefore, in their view, overall, 'the damage suffered by the plaintiff is not directly and monocausally attributable to an act of the defendant, but is mediated through general global warming. This distinguishes it from actions for directly caused environmental disasters … At the level of national law, this leads to challenges in proving causality and in selecting the liable debtor'.[53]

At the time of writing, both cases are still 'ongoing'. Shell has announced an appeal to the District Court of The Hague's decision.[54] In *Lliuya*, the action did not succeed at trial level before the District Court in Essen, precisely due to issues of causality (despite scientific evidence offered to the court in the statement of claim). However, an appeal is currently pending before the Higher Regional Court in Hamm. It is unlikely that there will be developments in the case before late 2021, for the court hearing the appeal wants to take evidence *in situ* in Peru.[55] This is possible, to begin with, because the said court has, in principle, accepted the causal link.[56]

---

52 The entirety of the remainder of the paragraph is a translation/paraphrasis of M Lehmann and F Eichel, 'Globaler Klimawandel und Internationales Privatrecht – Zuständigkeit und anzuwendendes Recht für transnationale Klagen wegen klimawandelbedingter Individualschäden' (2019) 83(1) Rabels Zeitschrift für ausländisches und internationales Privatrecht 77, 79–80.

53 ibid 80.

54 <https://www.shell.nl/media/persberichten/media-releases-2021/reactie-shell-op-uitspraak-klimaatzaak.html#english> accessed 14 July 2021.

55 Germanwatch, 'Saúl versus RWE – The Huaraz Case' <https://www.germanwatch.org/en/huaraz> accessed 1 February 2021. See especially the entries after 30 November 2017.

56 <https://www.germanwatch.org/en/15999> accessed 1 February 2021 ('The decision by the Higher Regional Court Hamm to enter into the evidentiary stage is a historic breakthrough: it is the first time that a court has recognised that "a private company is in principal [sic] responsible for its share in causing climate damages in other countries"').

3. ASSESSING THE SUSTAINABILITY-ENHANCING POTENTIAL OF PICCL

There are at least four dynamic ways of conceptualising PICCL as linking private international law and SDG 13, and contributing towards sustainability, conceived as a 'long-term goal'.[57]

3.1. CONTENT-ORIENTEDNESS: FACILITATING THE IMPLEMENTATION OF GREEN POLICIES AT THE TRANSNATIONAL LEVEL

Multilateral choice-of-law rules may, instead of being policy-blind (as in the 'neutral' paradigm described in the introduction), follow a functionalist approach. 'Content-oriented' or 'result-selective' choice-of-law rules consider the content of the substantive law to be applied; they are inspired by substantive concerns and pursue specific substantive results, which are frequently expressly stated in their very wording.[58] Accordingly, as operationalised through PICCL, content-oriented choice-of-law rules may elevate into the transnational sphere the (substantive) climate change mitigation or adaptation policies of concerned fora. This may happen, for instance, by providing potential GHG emitters with tort-based economic incentives not to emit (i.e. via striving to achieve tort-based deterrence from emitting, beyond compensation and/or injunctive-relief potential). The most common means to try to do this is resorting to 'alternative' choice-of-law rules,[59] i.e. rules designating two or more legal systems as potentially applicable, and establishing that the one to be effectively applied is the one which allows the desired result to be obtained.[60] An illustration in this

57 As explained by the United Nations Educational, Scientific and Cultural Organization (UNESCO): 'Sustainability is often thought of as a long-term goal (i.e. a more sustainable world), while sustainable development refers to the many processes and pathways to achieve it (e.g. sustainable agriculture and forestry …)': <https://en.unesco.org/themes/education-sustainable-development/what-is-esd/sd> accessed 1 February 2021.

58 See, amongst others: B Audit, 'Le caractère fonctionnel de la règle de conflit (Sur la « crise » des conflits de lois)' (1984) 186 Recueil des Cours de l'Académie de Droit International 219, 363; P Lagarde, 'Le principe de proximité dans le droit international privé contemporain; cours général de droit international privé' (1986) 196 Recueil des Cours de l'Académie de Droit International 9, 56.

59 A Bucher ('La dimension sociale du droit international privé – Cours general' (2009) 341 Recueil des Cours de l'Académie de Droit International 28) identifies alternative structures with content-orientedness. However, content-orientedness may also be achieved through other technical means (like 'waterfall' structures); see P Lagarde, 'Le principe de proximité dans le droit international privé contemporain; cours général de droit international privé' (1986) 196 Recueil des Cours de l'Académie de Droit International 9, 57.

60 P Lagarde, 'Le principe de proximité dans le droit international privé contemporain; cours général de droit international privé' (1986) 196 Recueil des Cours de l'Académie de Droit International 9, 56–57.

sense, as mentioned, is Article 7 of the Rome II Regulation. This provision, which addresses environmental damage broadly, and has been used both in *Lliuya* and *Milieudefensie* 2019 for climate change purposes specifically, reads as follows:

> The law applicable to a non-contractual obligation arising out of environmental damage or damage sustained by persons or property as a result of such damage shall be the law determined pursuant to Article 4(1) [law of the country where the damage materialises], unless the person seeking compensation for damage chooses to base his or her claim on the law of the country in which the event giving rise to the damage occurred.

Article 7 Rome II finds its roots in certain principles of EU environmental law and policy, as enshrined in the Treaty on the Functioning of the European Union (TFEU). Specifically, as explicitly established by recital 25 Rome II:

> Article [191 TFEU], which provides that there should be a high level of protection based on the precautionary principle and the principle that preventive action should be taken, the principle of priority for corrective action at source and the principle that the polluter pays, fully justifies the use of the principle of discriminating in favour of the person sustaining the damage.

Through the choice between the two referred potentially applicable laws, victims are offered the option to maximise the reparation to be paid by the polluter by choosing the legal system that will lead to more substantial economic compensation. Allegedly,[61] this strategic privilege is meant to produce an enhanced deterrence effect upon potential polluters, thus amounting to an increase in the level of environmental protection in force in the international scene:[62] 'the point is not only to respect the victim's legitimate interests but also to establish a legislative policy that contributes to raising the general level of environmental protection'.[63]

However, irrespective of mitigation potential via (potential) emissions deterrence, provisions like Article 7 Rome II elevate into the transnational

[61] See section 4.1.

[62] See Art 7, recital 24 and recital 25 Rome II Regulation, and the Explanatory Memorandum to the Commission's Proposal for a Regulation of the European Parliament and the Council on the law applicable to non-contractual obligations (Rome II), COM(2003)427 final, 19–20. L Enneking ('The Common Denominator of the Trafigura Case, Foreign Direct Liability Cases and the Rome II Regulation – An Essay on the Consequences of Private International Law for the Feasibility of Regulating Multinational Corporations through Tort Law' [2008] European Review of Private Law 283, 289–291) explicitly addresses this point, which is not explicitly addressed in the aforementioned legislative document (only implicitly).

[63] Explanatory Memorandum to the Commission's Proposal for a Regulation of the European Parliament and the Council on the law applicable to non-contractual obligations (Rome II), COM(2003)427 final, 19.

sphere climate adaptation policies inasmuch as they contribute, for instance, to enhancing victims' chances of obtaining compensation for expenses incurred/to be incurred in preventing future climate-related damage.

While nothing prevents jurisdictions other than the EU from enacting similar rules, equivalent results may be obtained with less environmentally focused provisions. Examples in this sense may be found in Article 138 of the Swiss Law on Private International Law (which, in strict terms, does not deal with environmental damage but with '*immissions*')[64] and paragraph 1 of Article 52 of the recent Uruguayan General Act on Private International Law (which is a general provision on torts).[65] Both provisions bear an alternative structure and confer the prerogative of choosing the applicable law to the victim.

3.2. A SENSE OF GLOBAL CLIMATE JUSTICE: ACCESS TO JUSTICE AND THE PRIVATE MOBILISATION OF CLIMATE-RELEVANT CAPITAL

It is conventional wisdom in the realm of 'business and human rights' that opening the door to litigation in the Global North to claimants from the Global South (in respect of those activities of Global North corporations having an impact on the former) facilitates an access to justice that oftentimes would not happen otherwise, for various reasons.[66] In this respect, the openness and wide interpretation of rules of international jurisdiction in civil (private law) matters in the Global North are of cardinal importance.

Irrespective of the state of access to justice in Peru, in *Lliuya* the claimant decided to benefit from the openness of the EU's system of international jurisdiction in civil matters to start PICCL in the Global North. Per the unofficial English translation of his statement of claim,[67] Mr Lliuya pleaded the international jurisdiction of German courts on the basis of Article 4(1) – in relation to Article 63 – of the Brussels I *bis* Regulation,[68] the EU's general

---

64 *Loi fédérale du 18 décembre 1987 sur le droit international privé* (LDIP), RS 291.

65 *Ley General de Derecho Internacional Privado*, Ley 19.920, Diario Oficial 30568, 16 December 2020.

66 See, amongst a profuse literature: C Burke Robertson, 'Transnational Litigation and Institutional Choice' (2010) 51 Boston College Law Review 1081; C A Whytock and C Burke Robertson, 'Forum Conveniens and the enforcement of foreign judgments' (2011) 111 Columbia Law Review 1444; D E Childress III, 'Forum Conveniens: The Search for a Convenient Forum in Transnational Cases' (2012) 53(1) Virginia Journal of International Law 157; R A Brand, 'Challenges to Forum non conveniens', (2013) 45 NYU Journal of International Law and Politics 1003.

67 *Lliuya v RWE*, Statement of claim, 20–24 <https://www.germanwatch.org/sites/germanwatch.org/files/announcement/20822.pdf> accessed 1 February 2021.

68 Regulation (EU) No 1215/2012 of the European Parliament and of the Council of 12 December 2012 on jurisdiction and the recognition and enforcement of judgments in civil and commercial matters (recast) [2012] OJ L 351/1.

instrument on international jurisdiction and the recognition and enforcement of judgments in civil and commercial matters. Article 4(1) Brussels I *bis* confers general jurisdiction in respect of disputes on civil and commercial matters to the courts of the country of the domicile of the defendant.[69] The notion of domicile of a 'company or other legal person or association of natural or legal persons' is defined in Article 63 as being 'the place where it has its (a) statutory seat; (b) central administration; or (c) principal place of business'. The availability of resort to these provisions for non-EU claimants is firmly established by the CJEU's *Josi* case law.[70] Thus, EU GHG emitters whose emissions have contributed/will contribute to climate-change-related harm in third countries can be brought to justice before an EU court by using the general criterion of jurisdiction of the domicile of the defendant.

Unfortunately, not all systems of private international law around the Global North are equally receptive to foreign claimants. Significant difficulties may arise wherever restrictive approaches to access to courts exist,[71] amongst which *forum non conveniens*. Some countries generally use the latter to restrict access to their courts by foreigners,[72] especially in respect of 'common' environmental tort cases.[73] It is to be expected that a similar restrictive approach may be followed as regards PICCL.

Obviously, all of this is without prejudice to the possibility that where logistically and legally feasible (i.e. notably where rules of international jurisdiction on private law matters so allow, for instance on the basis of the *locus damni*),[74] PICCL before Global South courts would be a significant

---

69 Two remarks: first, this general rule does not operate whenever a given case involves the exclusive grounds of jurisdiction in the Regulation (Art 24); second, in *Lliuya*, the specific domestic jurisdiction of the District Court of Essen is sustained by German Procedural Law Rules.

70 Case C-412/98 *Group Josi Reinsurance Company SA* [2000] ECR I-5925, ECLI:EU:C:2000:399.

71 In respect, for instance, of the United States' restrictive reading of its Alien Tort Statue, see H van Loon, 'Principles and building blocks for a global legal framework for transnational civil litigation in environmental matters' (2018) 23 Uniform Law Review 298, 306 et seq.

72 C Burke Robertson, 'Transnational Litigation and Institutional Choice' (2010) 51 Boston College Law Review 1081; C A Whytock and C Burke Robertson, 'Forum Conveniens and the enforcement of foreign judgments' (2011) 111 Columbia Law Review 1444; D E Childress III, 'Forum Conveniens: The Search for a Convenient Forum in Transnational Cases' (2012) 53(1) Virginia Journal of International Law 157; R A Brand, 'Challenges to Forum non conveniens', (2013) 45 NYU Journal of International Law and Politics 1003.

73 See, for instance, the well-known *forum non conveniens* decisions in the *Bhopal* (*In re Union Carbide Corp Gas Plant Disaster at Bhopal India in December 1984*, 809 F.2s 195) and *Chevron-Lago Agrio* (*Aguinda v Texaco* INC 2000 10650) cases.

74 As reported by G Ganguly, J Setzer and V Heyvaert, 'If at First You Don't Succeed: Suing Corporations for Climate Change' (2018) 38(4) Oxford Journal of Legal Studies 841, 862. P E Seley and R Dudley mention that following the petition filed in 2015 before the Commission on Human Rights of the Philippines, (*Philippines Reconstruction Movement and Greenpeace v Carbon Majors*, Case No CHR-NI-2016-0001 (2015)) 'residents of several other

development: attracting Global North corporate emitters before Global South courts for trial over private-law-based climate liability would certainly have an impact on climate-related global politics, diplomacy and international relations.

In any case, where available, PICCL conducted on the basis of broadly open rules of international jurisdiction in civil (private law) matters directly connects with SDG 16 ('Promote peaceful and inclusive societies for sustainable development, provide access to justice for all and build effective, accountable and inclusive institutions at all levels') and specifically with Target 16.3 'Promote the rule of law at the national and international levels and ensure equal access to justice for all'.

However, beyond this first generic sense of global justice to which PICCL may contribute (just like other forms of business and human rights litigation or general transnational environmental litigation), there is a second, more climate-specific sense. PICCL may also respond to a constant issue over the course of almost 30 years of climate negotiations: common but differentiated climate responsibilities between states. By allowing private–private actions to be tried and adjudicated upon, private international law may take a step forward and go beyond the stalemate of diplomatic negotiations in respect of climate-mitigating and adapting finance. If Global North countries do not honour their pledge to 'mobiliz[e] jointly $100 billion annually by 2020 from all sources to address the needs of developing countries in the context of meaningful mitigation actions' (Target 13.a), PICCL may facilitate the mobilisation of capital from Global North private parties to Global South private parties. This would be so because successful PICCL would force private parties from the Global North to step in and provide redress in lieu of the expected public party financing. Thus, rules of international jurisdiction that facilitate private-law-based litigation build a specific policy of global justice: one which would correspond to the longstanding revindications to discern historical responsibilities and differentiated contributions in respect of climate change.[75] Additionally, this second sense of global justice could be conceived as further connecting with

southeastern countries – including Vanuatu, Kiribati, Tuvalu, Fiji and the Solomon Islands – declared their intent to file similar petitions'. It would not have been surprising to see PICCL spark in these jurisdictions, if feasible. However, a search on the Sabin and Graham databases on 14 July 2020 shows no results at all for the aforementioned jurisdictions.

75 On how this discourse and its crystallisation in a principle of differentiated responsibilities has allegedly hindered the incursion of public international law's *sic utere tuo ut alienum non laedas* principle in the realm of climate change, see B Mayer, 'The Relevance of the No-Harm Principle to Climate Change Law and Politics' (2016) 19 Asia-Pacific Journal of Environmental Law 79; B Mayer, 'Climate Change Reparations and the Law and Practice of State Responsibility' (2017) 7 Asian Journal of International Law 185 (cf the latter with the impact of the polluter-pays principle on private litigation, and full compensation in tort law, as briefly discussed in the penultimate paragraph of section 4.3).

SDG 17 ('Strengthen the means of implementation and revitalize the Global Partnership for Sustainable Development'), both indirectly with Target 17.2 ('Developed countries to implement fully their official development assistance commitments …'), and directly with Target 17.3 ('Mobilize additional financial resources for developing countries from multiple sources').

3.3. FACILITATING THE DEVELOPMENT OF ENVIRONMENTALLY RELEVANT SUBSTANTIVE RIGHTS

PICCL may become the basis and testing ground for the development of environmentally relevant and sustainability-enhancing legal arguments coming from other areas of law, where litigation structure and procedural laws (including provisions on *locus standi*, etc.) allow it. In other words, wherever procedurally possible, it may be worth exploring the 'bundling' of novel progressive legal arguments stemming from other fields of law to private law substrata, as a means to test their potential to make the global legal framework on climate change evolve towards a greater integration of sustainability. An example in this sense may be found in *Milieudefensie* 2019, where the claimants, beyond Dutch tort law, have pleaded for an indirect horizontal effect of the ECHR.[76] They seem to have been successful to a certain extent, as, at trial level, the court has ruled that 'Milieudefensie et al. cannot directly invoke these human rights with respect to [Shell]', but it has 'factor[ed] in the human rights and the values they embody' in its decision.[77] Overall, while it may be extremely difficult to have human rights enforced horizontally, developments in this sense are visible in certain jurisdictions, as for instance the Canadian Supreme Court's decision in the *Nevsun* case.[78]

Additionally, it may be conceivable to attempt similar bundling even in cases like *Lliuya*, where an individual private claimant starts private-law-based

[76] Unofficial translation of the *Milieudefensie* 2019 court summons, para 666 et seq. <http://climatecasechart.com/non-us-case/milieudefensie-et-al-v-royal-dutch-shell-plc/> accessed 1 February 2021.

[77] Points 4.4.9 and following of the Court-issued English translation of the District Court Judgment <http://climatecasechart.com/climate-change-litigation/wp-content/uploads/sites/16/non-us-case-documents/2021/20210526_8918_judgment-2.pdf> accessed 14 July 2021.

[78] *Nevsun Resources Ltd v Araya*, 2020 SCC 5. For commentary, see J Haynes, 'The confluence of national and international law in response to multinational corporations' commission of modern Slavery: Nevsun Resources Ltd. V. Araya' [2020] Journal of Human Trafficking, DOI: 10.1080/23322705.2020.1832785J; J Yap, 'Nevsun Resources Ltd. v. Araya: What the Canadian Supreme Court decision means in holding Canadian companies accountable for human rights abuses abroad' <https://www.business-humanrights.org/sites/default/files/documents/BHRRC%20Blog%20Submission%20James%20Yap-FINAL.pdf> accessed 1 February 2021.

litigation in respect of their own life, health or property (environmental damage *lato sensu*).[79] For instance, the individual could be joined in a voluntary intervention, where procedurally possible, by environmental and/or human rights NGOs, as parties representing an interest in (climate-related aspects of) the environment *stricto sensu*. Admittedly, this proposal may face structural difficulties. Just to name one, there may be diverging views as regards the acceptability of a voluntary intervention on the basis of non-identical legal interests – the environment *lato sensu* and *stricto sensu*. Nevertheless, this approach remains worth exploring in practice.

3.4. SPARKING NEGOTIATION AND LEGISLATIVE CHANGE

If PICCL worked, beyond facilitating the flow of private capital from the Global North to the Global South for climate mitigation and adaptation purposes, it would possibly provide strong incentives for the negotiations in the framework of the UNFCCC to move forward, and/or for legislative changes to be made.

As regards the first aspect, all lists of the SDGs are accompanied by a disclaimer in respect of SDG 13, which establishes that the intent to '[t]ake urgent action to combat climate change and its impacts' is put forward while '[a]cknowledging that the United Nations Framework Convention on Climate Change is the primary international, intergovernmental forum for negotiating the global response to climate change'.

As counterintuitive as it may seem prima facie, PICCL may actually contribute to sparking progress in those negotiations: while it may be thought that, in certain instances, private litigation can cause tension and disruption in diplomatic processes, it is contended that moderate diplomatic friction 'actually promotes long-run international cooperation by providing stronger incentives to negotiate'.[80] In this sense, if PICCL were conducted against foreign emitters, states other than the forum state may consider the outcomes to which PICCL leads to be unpalatable (especially if they involve the projection of values through content-oriented choice-of-law rules), and the ensuing diplomatic tension may in turn force negotiations to develop.

---

79 Traditionally, it is possible to distinguish between environmental damage *lato sensu* (damage to property or human health due to an environmental contamination, 'thus including both physical and economic damage') and environmental damage *stricto sensu* (damage to the environment itself, irrespective of any damage to property or health, thus 'damage to natural habitats and protected species'). See F Munari and L Schiano di Pepe, 'Liability for Environmental Torts in Europe: Choice of Forum, Choice of Law, and the Case for Pursuing Effective Legal Uniformity' in A Malatesta (ed), *The unification of choice of law rules on torts and other non-contractual obligations in Europe. The 'Rome II' proposal* (CEDAM 2006) 173, 204.

80 W S Dodge, 'Extraterritoriality and Conflict-of-Laws Theory: An Argument for Judicial Unilateralism' (1998) 39 *Harvard International Law Journal* 101, 106.

A rather graphic example of these diplomatic dynamics – not PICCL but climate change litigation in the broad sense, containing an implicit (public) choice-of-law element – can be found in the *Air Transport Association of America and Others* CJEU judgment and the events that have ensued.[81] In its decision, the CJEU ruled that the applicability of the European Union Emission Trading scheme (EU ETS)[82] to any air carrier – thus, also non-European-based ones – whose flights departed or landed in EU airports[83] did not breach international law. Moderate diplomatic tensions ensued, and the EU froze the applicability of the EU ETS to the air carriers concerned. However, what could have been seen as caving due to international pressure has actually contributed to a series of negotiations within the framework of the International Civil Aviation Organization (ICAO), which have led to a 'global market-based mechanism addressing international aviation emissions'.[84] The so-called CORSIA (Carbon Offsetting and Reduction Scheme for International Aviation) 'aims to stabilise CO2 emissions at 2020 levels by requiring airlines to offset the growth of their emissions after 2020',[85] notwithstanding the fact that the economic impact of travel restrictions related to the COVID-19 pandemic may interfere with its ambitions.

Beyond these ideas, PICCL may provide strong incentives for significant (but not necessarily positive) legislative changes to be made. Suits against Global North emitters in their home jurisdictions may trigger a 'protectionist' private (international) law movement: such suits may provide incentives for states to modify domestic private law and/or private international law rules to shield their industries. However, private domestic climate change litigation (where global economic and geopolitics are not as directly at stake) may actually spark a movement in the opposite direction: Ganguly, Setzer and Heyvaert, who address climate change litigation broadly, expect that the proliferation of this kind of dispute will lead to an easing of the requirements of evidence in private

81 Case C-366/10 *Air Transport Association of America and Others v Secretary of State for Energy and Climate Change* [2011] ECR I-13755, ECLI:EU:C:2011:864. For a contextualisation of this 'unilateral' climate change decision in the frame of the EU's climate change policy: K Kulovesi, 'Climate change in EU external relations: please follow my example, or I might force you to' in E Morgera (ed), *The External Environmental Policy of the European Union – EU and International Law Perspectives* (CUP 2012) 115, 139–146.

82 The scheme is built on the basis of multiple legal texts and amendments, but ultimately its core piece of legislation is Directive 2003/87/EC of the European Parliament and of the Council of 13 October 2003 establishing a scheme for greenhouse gas emission allowance trading within the Community and amending Council Directive 96/61/EC [2003] OJ L 275/32.

83 Per the amendment made by Directive 2008/101, para 2 of the introduction preceding the table set out in Annex I to Directive 2003/87 ('Categories of activities to which this Directive applies') had the following subparagraph added to it: 'From 1 January 2012 all flights which arrive at or depart from an aerodrome situated in the territory of a Member State to which the Treaty applies shall be included'. See also para 125 of the decision.

84 <https://ec.europa.eu/transport/modes/air/environment_nl> accessed 1 February 2021.

85 <https://ec.europa.eu/clima/policies/transport/aviation_en> accessed 1 February 2021.

law causation along the lines of the legislative changes sparked by the waves of tobacco and asbestos litigation.[86] This domestic trend might counteract the 'shielding' temptation: those governments which would feel pressured from the inside in such a sense would not engage in establishing private law or private international law restrictions.

Having described PICCL's four core sustainability-enhancing potentials, let us now address the limitations that private international law's involvement with SDG 13 may face.

4. SOME DIFFICULTIES FACED BY PICCL

PICCL, as a tool to foster SDG 13, may face three major difficulties. All three of them are transversal challenges that private international law is generally likely to face in its interactions with those SDGs that are more strongly connected with the environmental pillar of sustainable development.

4.1. THE RELATIVITY OF DETERRENCE IN RESPECT OF TRANSNATIONAL CORPORATE TORTS

The potential of private (international) tort actions for GHG-emission deterrence (and for deterrence in respect of transnational corporate torts in general) is not limitless.

Without delving too much into considerations on the functions of tort law,[87] for an abstract climate victim, tort law has *in abstracto* compensatory potential, even if it may be blunted *in casu*, depending on various factors. However, for an abstract GHG emitter, tort law does not necessarily have *in abstracto* deterrent value. The latter will only appear *in casu*, depending on several factors, for instance the potential intervention of other fields of law (for example, criminal liability). Where there is no (efficient) intervention by other fields of law, the potential deterrent value of tort law will always ultimately be dependent on an *in casu* cost–benefit analysis.

At the time of writing, PICCL is still too 'novel', in comparison with general private international environmental litigation, for most emitters to have

---

86 G Ganguly, J Setzer and V Heyvaert, 'If at First You Don't Succeed: Suing Corporations for Climate Change' (2018) 38(4) Oxford Journal of Legal Studies 841, 858.

87 As a token of a very extensive literature: A Tunc, 'Introduction' in A Tunc (ed), *International Encyclopedia of Comparative Law. Vol XI: Torts* (Brill 1977) ch 1, 87 et seq; R Stevens, *Tort and Rights* (OUP 2007) 323 et seq; J Gordley and A T Von Mehren, *An Introduction to the Comparative Study of Private Law – Readings, Cases, Materials* (CUP 2006) 236–240; B S Markesinis and S F Deakin, *Tort Law* (4th ed, OUP 1999) 36 et seq.

factored it into any proper conscious cost–benefit analysis of emitting GHGs. However, when the time comes, the potential economic impact of (cross-border) civil remedies and other potential economically significant 'market sanctions'[88] will be weighed against the economic benefit that GHG emitters may derive from causing harm. Notwithstanding the said market sanctions, for tort's compensation dimension to become a deterrent, the potential payment needs to be so economically damaging that the mere prospect of having to face it renders the risk associated with the relevant course of action unworthy. This, of course, will depend on the specific economic power of the tortfeasor, the (projected) status of their finances when the (possible) obligation to compensate materialises (if it does/in the event it did), and their overall economic planning and strategy. Thus, the same amount of compensation may be ridiculous for a given tortfeasor and totally burdensome for another. Economically healthy corporate tortfeasors may decide to simply absorb the impact themselves, or transfer it to the market through price increases. However, the market will only 'accept' the re-transferring of a certain amount of tort compensation through market prices. Beyond a given point, the tortfeasor will need to absorb it themselves, which may be economically 'harmful' and may ultimately exclude them from the market. Thus, in order for tort-based compensation (i.e. the internalisation of environmental externalities, like GHGs) to become a deterrent, it needs to pass a certain benchmark of significance for the tortfeasor concerned.

Parallel reasoning has been put forward in respect of the capacity of the EU ETS to incentivise the reduction of carbon emissions: the overabundance of available emissions allowances (which does not allow for their prices to rise sufficiently high to become a deterrent) entails that many enterprises simply prefer to buy emissions allowances over investing in new procedures and equipment to avoid emitting in the first place.[89]

In sum, as tort law's deterrence arises only where *ex ante* cost–benefit analyses result in economic stimuli in favour of not polluting, environmental and climate deterrence (which, allegedly, are key values/goals for the EU, embodied in Article 7 Rome II) will be difficult to achieve, due to the economic power of corporate polluters/emitters. This will especially be the case if not coupled with 'market sanctions', as suggested above. Although these ideas do not entail discarding tort-law-induced deterrence, they largely diminish the case for it in instances of international environmental and climate occurrences.

All of this being said, in the specific context of PICCL, it is to be expected that if Mr Lliuya ends up being successful in his German litigation against RWE, the 'litigation floodgates' will open. The potentially overwhelming number of

88 Notably, reputational damage and consumer 'retaliation', penalties/increases in insurance policies, etc.

89 C Cheneviere, *Le système d'échange de quotas d'émission de gaz à effet de serre – Protéger le climat, préserver le marché intérieur* (Bruylant 2018) 40.

cases that may be filed by countless claimants from around the world, against not only RWE but potentially any other carbon major, may produce deterrent effects vis-à-vis future carbon-emissions-related decisions. This would be the case because the potential costs may become so immense that cost–benefit calculations would clearly tip against emitting. In any case, beyond deterrence (or lack thereof), tort's compensation potential as such may fulfil, at the very least, climate adaptation goals (as expected in *Lliuya*), and, where available, tort's injunctive potential may force GHG emitters to turn to greener energy sources (as in the trial-level decision in *Milieudefensie* 2019).

4.2. DIFFICULTIES ARISING FROM THE PUBLIC NATURE OF LEGAL GOODS EMBODIED IN CERTAIN SDGs

Other than SDG 13, those SDGs which are more directly connected with the environmental branch of sustainable development, for instance SDG 15, face a general complication: a conceptual, idiosyncratic and structural mismatch between the content and structure of the legal good that is 'the environment' (*stricto sensu*) and the notions, structure, tools and mechanisms of private law.

It is generally considered that the environment *stricto sensu* – without taking into account possible damage to human health and human property – is the object of a so-called 'diffuse interest'; as a legal good it cannot be submitted to any sort of individualisation which would allow the introduction of individual claims concerning identifiable parts thereof. Whatever the relevant definition of the environment, it is a 'common' or 'collective' legal good.

This means that the involvement of private subjects in redressing environmental damage *stricto sensu* and in the legal protection of the environment *stricto sensu* is problematic: environmental protection is simply not structurally suited to being privately enforced in the first place. Any debate revolving around its private enforcement therefore needs to answer three questions. Firstly, who has the condition of rights-holder over such *stricto sensu* environment? Secondly, can that rights-holder start private law judicial proceedings in respect of environmental damage *stricto sensu* (and if not, who can do so on their behalf)? Thirdly, what kind of remedy can be obtained (and if the remedy is pecuniary in nature, who should benefit from it and on what conditions)?

All in all, claims in respect of this common good, unless channelled through the intervention of a public subject, require a 'converter' in order to function properly within the realm of private law claims. In other words, unless a given legal order specifically provides for a special legal tool, claims for environmental damage per se cannot easily come from private subjects, insofar as this kind of damage is inflicted on a collective legal good. The kind of adaptation referred to, which may allow private subjects to 'step forward', may be achieved, for instance, through the introduction of so-called collective redress or the official conferral of *locus standi* to NGOs. Roughly speaking, collective redress may be characterised as various forms of (mainly procedural) legal mechanisms which may allow various private subjects to overcome the complexities arising from the diffuse nature of a given interest in order to access justice in respect thereof.

In this sense, those jurisdictions where class or representative actions, or similar institutions, are available – and allow private parties in a sense to 'solidify' diffuse interests – have an advantage in respect of facilitating private international environmental litigation, broadly conceived, including PICCL. Among the Global North countries where these institutions may contribute to PICCL are, for instance, Canada and the United States, even if the latter, as mentioned, is not very 'open' to asserting jurisdiction over claims in which Global South claimants sue domestic corporations for transnational torts. As for the EU, notwithstanding the scarce, isolated and non-comprehensive developments at Member State level,[90] nowadays there is no general 'converter' which may help 'translate' the common legal good of the environment *stricto sensu* into private law 'terms',[91] in order to facilitate and allow its introduction, for redress purposes, in private law proceedings.

In fact, one of the senses in which *Lliuya* is creative and clever in its legal approach, is precisely the way in which the above-described difficulties, typically found in environmental litigation, have been circumvented: a single claimant has introduced a claim over his own environment *lato sensu* (his property), in the hope that such claim will lead to a deterrence-yielding outcome from which the global climate may benefit (i.e. the environment *lato sensu* acting as an indirect 'proxy' for the environment *stricto sensu*). However, wherever environmental collective redress is available, it may open further doors for PICCL, potentially allowing the introduction of direct claims over the environment *stricto sensu* (global climate and/or environment as impacted by climate-change-related phenomena).

Overall, in any case, it is important to remember that in order to seriously envisage the private enforcement of rights over the environment *stricto sensu*, an 'adaptation' becomes mandatorily required: within the framework of private

---

90 Following L Carballo Piñeiro ('La construcción del mercado interior y el recurso colectivo de consumidores' in F Esteban de la Rosa (ed), *La protección del consumidor en dos espacios de integración: Europa y América: Una perspectiva de Derecho internacional, europeo y comparado* (Tirant lo Blanch 2015) 1055, 1060–1062), as of 2015, around 12 EU Member States possessed some kind of 'compensatory' (as opposed to injunctive-only) collective redress mechanism, whether general (Portugal, Sweden, Denmark, the Netherlands), or sector-specific (Spain, Finland, Bulgaria, Greece, Italy and Germany – in many cases, consumer-specific).

91 In November 2020 Directive (EU) 2020/1828 of the European Parliament and of the Council of 25 November 2020 on representative actions for the protection of the collective interests of consumers and repealing Directive 2009/22/EC [2020] OJ L 409/1 was adopted. As its title indicates, it only deals with consumer issues.

enforcement logic, the collective/common dimension of the damaged legal good must be somehow 'translated' into private law and/or civil proceeding elements. In the absence of any such 'converter' or 'adaptation', rights over the environment *stricto sensu*, or similar 'public legal goods', cannot be privately enforced in practice.

4.3. *DATUMTHEORIE*

The so-called *Datumtheorie* is a threat to the goal of ensuring the deterrence of environmentally damaging activities (including the emission of GHGs) through private international environmental litigation (and specifically PICCL).

The 'local and moral data' theory was developed by Ehrenzweig under the acknowledged inspiration of Currie's notion of 'datum' and other influences coming from Europe.[92] In a nutshell, local data are 'questions which typically can or must be subjected to foreign rules without resort to a "choice of law"'.[93] In the realm of admiralty law, Ehrenzweig would contend that: 'such foreign rules as fixed speed limits or pilotage and manning requirements [apply], without recourse to choice of law, as local data under the local law of the defendant's conduct'.[94]

This theory (and any legal provision or case law development that operationalises it in a given legal system) runs against the economic reasoning that underpins content-oriented choice-of-law provisions which try to maximise compensation in order to cause tort-based deterrence. This is because it may allow the 'legality' of the tortfeasor's activities under the law of the country where those activities take place to be factored in: if the behavioural standards in force in the place where a damaging activity occurs are taken into consideration for liability-excluding or liability-reducing purposes, private international law's potential for deterrence will be undermined.

In the EU, for instance, Article 17 of the Rome II Regulation (entitled 'Rules of safety and conduct') embodies this theory.[95] This provision establishes that:

> In assessing the conduct of the person claimed to be liable, account shall be taken, as a matter of fact and in so far as is appropriate, of the rules of safety and conduct which were in force at the place and time of the event giving rise to the liability.

---

92 A A Ehrenzweig, 'Local and moral data in the conflict of laws: terra incognita' (1966–1967) 16 Buffalo Law Review 55. On the distinction between local data and moral data, see further A A Ehrenzweig, *Conflicts in a nutshell* (3rd ed, West Publishing 1974) 95.

93 A A Ehrenzweig, *Private international law: a comparative treatise on American international conflicts law, including the law of admiralty* (vol I, Sijthoff 1967) 83.

94 ibid 84.

95 This provision, however, is not a novelty in private international law. See Explanatory Memorandum to the Commission's Proposal for a Regulation of the European Parliament and the Council on the law applicable to non-contractual obligations (Rome II), COM(2003)427

On the basis of this provision, certain authors argue that the public (administrative) law provisions that regulate environmentally damaging activities (like emitting GHGs) in the state where the action takes place should nuance or discard liability altogether even when the applicable law chosen by the victim is the *lex loci damni*.[96] This conclusion, reportedly, should extend to situations where an administrative permit/authorisation allows the activity in the state where the action takes place, as could allegedly be the case of the European emission allowances under the EU ETS.[97] Thus, in *Lliuya*, if the claimant had decided to opt for Peruvian law, RWE could have tried to plead that Article 17 Rome II should limit or eliminate their liability altogether.

While the *Datumtheorie* is possibly convenient and adequate in other contexts (Article 17 is a general provision), it seems hard to reconcile with the specificities that characterise the phenomenon of environmental liability, especially within the EU legal order, for a number of reasons.[98] First, the polluter-pays principle – one of the explicit rationales behind Article 7 of Rome II – tends to impose full reparation.[99] Thus, if within the context of environmental damage the polluter-pays principle requires that reparation be made in full, there is no room for considering nuancing/softening the obligation to compensate. Furthermore, following de Sadeleer, the polluter-pays principle would establish a conception of liability based on strict liability.[100] This idea,

final, 25: 'This article is based on the corresponding articles of the Hague Conventions on traffic accidents (Article 7) and product liability (Article 9). There are equivalent principles in the conflict systems of virtually all the Member States, either in express statutory provisions or in the decided cases'.

96 See, amongst others, S C Symeonides, 'Rome II and Tort Conflicts: A Missed Opportunity' (2008) 56(1) The American Journal of Comparative Law 173, 212–215.

97 M Lehmann and F Eichel, 'Globaler Klimawandel und Internationales Privatrecht – Zuständigkeit und anzuwendendes Recht für transnationale Klagen wegen klimawandelbedingter Individualschäden' (2019) 83(1) Rabels Zeitschrift für ausländisches und internationales Privatrecht 77, 98.

98 For an equally critical assessment of Lehmann and Eichel's opinion on the role of Article 17 Rome II, see E-M Kieninger, 'Conflicts of jurisdiction and the applicable law in domestic courts' proceedings' in W Kahl and M-P Weller (eds) *Climate Change Litigation – a handbook* (Beck 2021) 141–44.

99 N de Sadeleer, *Les principes du pollueur-payeur, de prévention et de précaution – Essai sur la genèse et la portée juridique de quelques principes du Droit de l'Environnement* (Bruylant-AUF 1999) 65 and 69. Further support for this idea may be drawn from comparative tort law, where the principle of full reparation/compensation bears a strong relevance. See, for instance, J Spier (ed), *The limits of liability: keeping the floodgates shut* (Kluwer Law International 1996) 1 et seq; C Von Bar, *The common European law of torts. Vol 2: Damage and damages, liability for and without personal misconduct, causality, and defences* (OUP 2000) 106. Cf, however, E Rehbinder, 'Climate damages and the "Polluter Pays" Principle' in W Kahl and M-P Weller (eds) *Climate Change Litigation – a handbook* (Beck 2021), especially 59–60.

100 Notwithstanding the fact that the point is controversial, N de Sadeleer, *Les principes du pollueur-payeur, de prévention et de précaution – Essai sur la genèse et la portée juridique de quelques principes du Droit de l'Environnement* (Bruylant-AUF 1999) 91 considers that several elements 'suggest that the polluter pays principle requires the establishment of

coupled with the fact that the explanatory memorandum of the Rome II proposal establishes that 'recent … environmental protection policy', which inspires Article 7, 'tends to support strict liability', would further close the door to a pro-polluter use of Article 17.[101]

Having presented the obstacles that PICCL may face, let us map other potential forms of intervention that private international law may take in respect of climate action.

5. FURTHER POTENTIAL: INTERFACES WITH OTHER SDGs AND BRIEF MENTION OF RECOGNITION

Despite the significance of PICCL, further possibilities for private international law involvement arise, on the one hand from the connections that SDG 13 has with other SDGs, and on the other hand from a wider understanding of 'recognition'.

As regards the first possibility, as a result of the 'interlinkages and integrated nature of the Sustainable Development Goals',[102] important synergies can be established between them, to the point that private international law contributions and interventions in respect of other SDGs may have an indirect impact on SDG 13 (and vice versa). For example, private international law action taken in respect of SDG 7 ('Ensure access to affordable, reliable, sustainable and modern energy for all'), and specifically Target 7.2 (on clean energy mix), will have a clear impact on SDG 13. In particular, any private international law interaction with SDG 7 as regards IP and technology transfer may indirectly contribute to SDG 13. Similarly, action in respect of SDG 13 may contribute to SDG 14 ('Conserve and sustainably use the oceans, seas and marine resources for sustainable development'), specifically in respect of Target 14.3 (acidification and its impact on life below water).

As regards the second possibility, further potential for contribution and involvement between private international law and the SDGs arises from the notion of recognition, beyond the traditional understanding thereof

a strict liability regime'. Cf L Kramer, 'Le principe du pollueur-payeur ("Verursacher") en droit communautaire, interprétation de l'article 130 R du Traité CEE' [1991] Aménagement-Environnement 3, 3. For a nuanced position: E T Larson, 'Why environmental liability regimes in the United States, the European Community and Japan have grown synonymous with the polluter pays principle' (2005) 38-2 Vanderbilt Journal of Transnational Law 541, 541.

101 The French and Spanish linguistic versions confirm that it is the 'policy' what 'tends to support' strict liability.

102 UN General Assembly, 'Transforming Our World: The 2030 Agenda for Sustainable Development', UN Doc A/RES/70/1 2 (21 October 2015).

(recognition of foreign judgments and foreign public acts). An extended notion of 'recognition' as a technique would allow, for instance, 'recognising' the (purported) applicability of a given foreign legal instrument following the self-determination of its own scope of territorial application,[103] or else 'recognising' given legal institutions or entities in cross-border situations. An example in the latter sense, even if it leads back to litigation to some extent, could be 'recognising' the legal standing of foreign environmental associations and NGOs (as granted by their own law) in cross-border proceedings where their capacity to act may be called into question in fora with restrictive approaches to these issues.

Obviously, the above is no obstacle to also considering recognition in a 'classical' sense. In this respect, any instrument contributing to the recognition and enforcement of foreign judicial decisions may facilitate the development of private international environmental litigation generally, and PICCL specifically. This potentially includes, albeit to a very limited extent, the not-yet-in-force Hague Convention of 2 July 2019 on the Recognition and Enforcement of Foreign Judgments in Civil or Commercial Matters. Article 5 thereof, on the 'Bases for recognition and enforcement', establishes that: '1. A judgment is eligible for recognition and enforcement if … (j) the judgment ruled on a non-contractual obligation arising from death, physical injury, damage to or loss of tangible property, and the act or omission directly causing such harm occurred in the State of origin, irrespective of where that harm occurred'.[104] In the light of this, a Peruvian judgment in *Lliuya* would not have been recognisable under the 2019 Convention. This curtails (where available) an environmental/climate victim's potential freedom of choice of the relevant forum, unless the relevant judgment can be recognised and enforced 'under national law' (as permitted by Article 15 of the Convention). At the time of writing, only Uruguay and Ukraine have ratified the Convention.

6. CONCLUDING REMARKS

Previous pages have explored the potential of private international law to foster sustainable development in relation to climate change issues, placing a

---

103 H Muir Watt, 'Future Directions?' in H Muir Watt and D P Fernández Arroyo (eds), *Private International Law and Global Governance* (OUP 2014) 343, 367–369. For further insights into the wider notion of recognition, I Isailovic, 'Political Recognition and Transnational Law: Gender Equality and Cultural Diversification in French Courts' in H Muir Watt and D P Fernández Arroyo (eds), *Private International Law and Global Governance* (OUP 2014) 318.

104 For criticism of Art 5(1)(j), see H van Loon, 'Towards a Global Hague Convention on the Recognition and Enforcement of Foreign Judgments in Civil or Commercial Matters' (2020) 38 Nederlands Internationaal Privaatrecht 1, 13–14.

special focus on PICCL. By forcing the internalisation of GHG-derived externalities, PICCL may contribute to pushing emitters towards the goal of sustainability in several ways, amongst which the need to reduce costs to keep their business afloat, which may trigger innovation and steer them towards sustainable practices. This is just a reflection of the fact that private international environmental litigation, broadly conceived, may contribute to environmental protection, and to sustainable development, in various ways, notably by facilitating the internalisation of environmental externalities.

As a part of the assessment undertaken by this contribution, PICCL's potential, as well as the possible threats that may undermine it, have been explored. Amongst the former, for instance, PICCL's potential to activate private climate-relevant Global North–South financial flows, or its potential to foster Global North–South climate negotiations as a possible consequence of victims from the Global South litigating against corporations from the Global North (thus sparking the concerns of Global North states). Amongst the possible threats lies the fact that the *Datumtheorie* jeopardises the economic reasoning that (partially) justifies the involvement of private international law in climate change matters and, more broadly, environmental protection. For PICCL to fully reveal its potential, wherever any embodiment of the *Datumtheorie* is available, appropriate legal provisions or case law will need to be introduced to neutralise it in respect of climate-related damage.

Beyond the interventions depicted in the previous pages, it is possible to conceive of further potential private international law involvement in climate change matters, many of which could clearly be qualified as utopian. For instance, resort to uniform law conventions on 'private' climate liability (along the lines of the International Convention on Civil Liability for Oil Pollution Damage[105] and the Nuclear Liability Conventions)[106] is currently out of the question. On the one hand, climate-change-related international agreements of any sort are complicated to negotiate, as demonstrated by the evolution of negotiations in successive sessions of the Conference of the Parties. On the other hand, there is a clear reluctance on the part of Global North countries to conceive of any form of 'liability' in respect of climate change at the international substantive level, as demonstrated by the explicit exclusion thereof in one of the accompanying

[105] Adopted on 29 November 1969; entered into force on 19 June 1975; amended by a 1992 Protocol, which entered into force on 30 May 1996.

[106] Convention on Third Party Liability in the Field of Nuclear Energy (Paris Convention – established on 29 July 1960 under the auspices of the OECD Nuclear Energy Agency); Convention on Civil Liability for Nuclear Damage (Vienna Convention – established on 21 May 1963 under the auspices of the International Atomic Energy Agency); Joint Protocol Relating to the Application of the Vienna Convention and the Paris Convention of the 21st of September 1988; Convention Relating to Civil Liability in the Field of Maritime Carriage of Nuclear Material of 17 December 1971.

Decisions to the Paris Agreement (Decision 1/CP.21).[107] Along the same lines, any sort of PICCL development within the framework of the Hague Conference seems to be currently beyond reach, especially taking into account the failure in the 1990s of the attempts to put forward a Hague Convention on private international law aspects of environmental liability.[108]

However, overall, private international law's involvement with SDG 13 is promising, and, as explored, can directly contribute to, or provide suitable 'substitutes' for, Targets 13.1 and 13.a, as well as provide indirect incentives to progress in respect of other targets, like Targets 13.b or especially 13.2 ('Integrate climate change measures into national policies, strategies and planning'). At the very minimum, due to PICCL's media profile, and the power of the social movements and communication strategies created by NGOs around this kind of litigation, it can certainly contribute to Target 13.3 ('Improve education, awareness-raising and human and institutional capacity on climate change mitigation, adaptation, impact reduction and early warning').

7. RESULTS

The following eight points summarise the core findings of this chapter:

1. Private international law may contribute to sustainable development by means of so-called private international climate change litigation (PICCL). Beyond neutral/policy-blind facilitation of cross-border redress, PICCL conducted on the basis of content-oriented private international law rules may enhance climate change mitigation and adaptation policies.
2. One of the potential ways in which this may happen is by providing potential GHG emitters with tort-based economic incentives not to emit, i.e. PICCL could potentially achieve tort-based deterrence from emitting, beyond its compensation and/or injunctive relief potential. This can be achieved by targeting climate-change-related torts via appropriate (specific or general) content-oriented choice of law rules.
3. Additionally, irrespective of mitigation potential via (potential) emissions deterrence, those content-oriented choice-of-law rules elevate into the transnational sphere climate adaptation policies inasmuch as they can be used, for instance, to enhance victims' chances of obtaining compensation for expenses incurred/to be incurred in preventing future climate-related damage.

---

107 Para 51: 'Article 8 of the Agreement does not involve or provide a basis for any liability or compensation'.

108 See H van Loon, 'Principles and building blocks for a global legal framework for transnational civil litigation in environmental matters' (2018) 23 Uniform Law Review 298, 314.

4. Moreover, PICCL can foster a sense of global climate justice – firstly, by facilitating access to justice through open and broadly interpreted rules on international jurisdiction (thus, notably avoiding *forum non conveniens*); and secondly, by ultimately allowing the private mobilisation of climate-relevant capital from the Global North to the Global South, thus contributing to the principle of common but differentiated climate responsibilities between states.
5. Where litigation structure and procedural laws (including provisions on *locus standi*, etc.) allow it, PICCL may facilitate the evolution of the global legal framework on climate change towards greater integration of the environmental dimension of sustainability. It suffices to try to 'bundle' novel progressive legal arguments stemming from other fields of law with pure private law argumentative substrata.
6. PICCL may also contribute to sparking progress in climate-related diplomatic negotiations within the UNFCCC. If it is conducted against foreign emitters, states other than the forum state may consider the outcomes to which PICCL leads to be unpalatable (especially if these outcomes involve the projection of values through content-oriented choice-of-law rules), and the ensuing diplomatic tension may in turn force negotiations to develop.
7. However, PICCL may face difficulties stemming from: the relativity of tort law's deterrence potential in respect of corporate actors; the difficulties derived from the 'public' nature of the legal goods involved (thus, requiring the involvement of collective redress or a 'private attorney general'); or the so-called '*Datumtheorie*'.
8. Nevertheless, all in all, the potential of PICCL deserves to be further explored.

SDG 14: LIFE BELOW WATER

Tajudeen Sanni

Goal 14: Conserve and sustainably use the oceans, seas and marine resources for sustainable development

14.1 By 2025, prevent and significantly reduce marine pollution of all kinds, in particular from land-based activities, including marine debris and nutrient pollution

14.2 By 2020, sustainably manage and protect marine and coastal ecosystems to avoid significant adverse impacts, including by strengthening their resilience, and take action for their restoration in order to achieve healthy and productive oceans

14.3 Minimize and address the impacts of ocean acidification, including through enhanced scientific cooperation at all levels

14.4 By 2020, effectively regulate harvesting and end overfishing, illegal, unreported and unregulated fishing and destructive fishing practices and implement science-based management plans, in order to restore fish stocks in the shortest time feasible, at least to levels that can produce maximum sustainable yield as determined by their biological characteristics

14.5 By 2020, conserve at least 10 per cent of coastal and marine areas, consistent with national and international law and based on the best available scientific information

14.6 By 2020, prohibit certain forms of fisheries subsidies which contribute to overcapacity and overfishing, eliminate subsidies that contribute to illegal, unreported and unregulated fishing and refrain from introducing new such subsidies, recognizing that appropriate and effective special and differential treatment for developing and least developed countries should be an integral part of the World Trade Organization fisheries subsidies negotiation

14.7 By 2030, increase the economic benefits to Small Island developing States and least developed countries from the sustainable use of marine resources, including through sustainable management of fisheries, aquaculture and tourism

14.a	Increase scientific knowledge, develop research capacity and transfer marine technology, taking into account the Intergovernmental Oceanographic Commission Criteria and Guidelines on the Transfer of Marine Technology, in order to improve ocean health and to enhance the contribution of marine biodiversity to the development of developing countries, in particular small island developing States and least developed countries
14.b	Provide access for small-scale artisanal fishers to marine resources and markets
14.c	Enhance the conservation and sustainable use of oceans and their resources by implementing international law as reflected in UNCLOS, which provides the legal framework for the conservation and sustainable use of oceans and their resources, as recalled in paragraph 158 of The Future We Want

1. INTRODUCTION

If there is a resource which signifies the interconnectedness of humanity across borders and boundaries, the ocean it is. We are entirely reliant upon the ocean which covers more than 70 per cent of the planet's surface and plays a crucial role in planetary resilience and the provision of vital ecosystem services.[1] The ocean produces half the oxygen we breathe, absorbs over a quarter of global carbon dioxide,[2] and contributes to freshwater renewal.[3] Entire countries and numerous communities depend on the ocean for food, work, livelihoods, culture and spirituality.[4] Over-exploitation and multiple competing uses, sea

1 International Council for Science, *A Guide to SDG Interactions from Science to Implementation* 177.

2 See World Wildlife Fund, 'WWF Comments on Seaspiracy' (31 March 2021) <https://wwf.panda.org/wwf_news/?1919466/WWF-comments-on-Seaspiracy> accessed 12 April 2021.

3 Mathew R Fisher (ed) *Environmental Biology* (Open Oregon Educational Services 2018) 204, 205.

4 See Martin R Stuchtey, Adrien Vincent, Andreas Merkl, Maximilian Bucher, Peter M Haugan, Jane Lubchenco and Mari Elka Pangestu, Ocean Solutions that Benefit

level rises, pollution, climate change, coastal erosion, deoxygenation and ocean acidification, however, are pushing ocean ecosystems towards a tipping point[5] and have seriously impacted on local communities. In general, the status of the marine space – including oceans and rivers – and its resources have been deteriorating over the past century, compromising the services they provide.

The effects of all these issues have been well documented; the fact that those most exposed to these negative impacts are local coastal and marine communities has also been well documented.[6] Indeed, negative externalities on the marine space are a threat to the well-being of local communities, especially in the Global South, risking their ability to meet their social, environmental and economic needs and risking – for many of them, indigenous communities in particular – their age-old resilience.

As One Ocean Hub posits, current solutions to these challenges are disconnected across sectors and levels, and from those most affected by ocean degradation.[7]

This disconnection exists in two important respects relating to this study, namely public international law versus private international law, and powerful actors like states and their citizens or multinational companies versus local communities, the latter being within the remit of private international law. There has been much analysis from the point of view of public international law of the problems of marine space. What is less analysed is the relative utility of private international justice in that regard, especially in the context of local communities. For example, fishing communities around the world will face a dire situation with only 7 per cent of global fish stock not affected by the degradation of the marine environment. It is convenient to talk about the role of governments and non state actors in rolling back this menace. It is convenient to also talk about approaching the courts to hold harmful actors responsible. However, he remedial mechanisms in local legal systems may not have developed to a point that will allow local communities to seek remedy. In addition, the legal relations in many countries, especially developing countries, may be mired in asymmetric relations between the actors. In effect, it becomes necessary to

People, Nature and the Economy (High Level Panel for Sustainable Ocean Economy 2020) 2,71 and 76 <https://oceanpanel.org/ocean-action/files/full-report-ocean-solutions-eng.pdf> accessed 17 July 2021.

5 Patricia Birnie, Alan Boyle and Catherine Redgwell (eds), *International Law and the Environment* (OUP 2009) 381. See also Dirk Werle, Paul R Boudreau, Mary R Brooks, Michael J A Butler, Anthony Charles, Scott Coffen-Smout, David Griffiths, Ian McAllister, Moira L McConnell, Ian Porter, Susan J Rolston, and Peter G Wells, 'Looking Ahead: Ocean Governance Challenges in the Twenty-First Century' in *The Future of Ocean Governance and Capacity Development* (Brill/Nijhoff 2019).

6 United Nations, *The Second World Ocean Assessment* vol II, 2021) 150, 217, 229 and 261 <https://www.un.org/regularprocess/sites/www.un.org.regularprocess/files/2011859-e-woa-ii-vol-ii.pdf> accessed 13 July 2021.

7 One Ocean Hub <https://oneoceanhub.org/> accessed 11 February 2020.

explore how local communities may take up the issue *vide* private litigation at transboundary level. When they do so, it raises issues of jurisdiction and forum as there must be a connecting factor(s) linking the forum where a case is brought to the case itself.[8] In any event, the opportunity to institute such a case does not detract from the fact that local justice ought to be the first port of call.

This chapter explores the potential of private international law to deal with existing disconnections (with a focus on transnational justice) in law in a way that places local communities, who are most reliant upon the oceans, in a position to challenge infractions that affect them on the marine space. This will enable the communities to deal with issues between more powerful commercial marine players (for example the mining industry) and themselves, as the less powerful actors who are a repository of largely overlooked values of the ocean's deep cultural role, function in the carbon cycle and potential in medical innovation. It will also put them in a position to harness and share equitably environmental and socioeconomic outcomes from the sustainable use of the ocean.

2. AN OVERVIEW OF SDG 14

The importance of sustainable development for marine and ocean resources was articulated at the Johannesburg Summit on Sustainable Development.[9] SDG 14 takes this further and aims to 'conserve and sustainably use the world's oceans, seas and marine resources.' SDG 14 focuses on human interactions with the marine space.[10] It is underpinned by targets addressing conservation and sustainable use of the oceans, seas and marine resources, including coastal zones, and targets referring to capacity-building and ocean governance as well as those addressing marine pollution.

---

8 This may include domicile, residence, creation of contract, breach of contract or situation of property. See Christopher Forsyth, *Private International Law* (Juta 2012) 169, 205. For corporations see specifically 208–216.

9 Muhammad T Ladan, *Materials and Cases on Public International Law* (Ahmadu Bello University Press 2007) 167. The World Summit on Sustainable Development (Johannesburg Summit 2002) was held in Johannesburg, South Africa on 26 August – 4 September 2002. At the summit, states, non-governmental organisations (NGOs), the private sector and other groups converged to focus the world's attention on and stimulate action to tackle difficult challenges, including improving the lives of people and communities, as well as ensuring sustainable utilisation of the world's natural resources. See World Summit on Sustainable Development (WSSD)- Johannesburg Summit <https://sustainabledevelopment.un.org/milesstones/wssd and Earth Summit 2002> and <http://www.earthsummit2002.org/> both accessed 13 July 2021.

10 The International Institute of Environment and Development (IIED) put it this way: 'SDG 14 – Life below water – focuses on our oceans, estuaries, rivers and watersheds, and the human systems that intersect with them.' See Emilie Beauchamp and Dorothy Lucks (eds), *MEL Handbook for SDG 14: Conserve and sustainably use the oceans, seas and marine resources for sustainable development* (IIED 2019) 8.

One of the greatest challenges facing people in local coastal communities is marine pollution. Indeed, the ecological damage caused by oil spillage has become a major concern of international law.[11] An example is the Deep Water Horizon oil spill, which is regarded as the largest oil spill in history.[12] Pollution of the marine environment means the introduction by man, directly or indirectly, of substances or energy into the marine environment, including estuaries, which results or is likely to result in such deleterious effects as harm to living resources and marine life, hazards to human health, hindrance to marine activities, including fishing and other legitimate uses of the sea, impairment of quality for use of sea water and reduction of amenities.[13] A report by the Intergovernmental Platform on Biodiversity and Ecosystem Services (IPBES) warns that human actions continue to pose an existential threat to biodiversity on land and water, with 40 per cent of seas and 50 per cent of other water bodies around the world being severely degraded.[14] According to the report, a million species will become extinct within decades. This finding exposes a phenomenon that definitely poses a threat to the realisation of SDG 14 relating to the protection of lives under water, all more so when, according to the report, 400 million tons of waste is dumped into water bodies yearly. Such pollution emanates from both land and offshore sources and may include mining and mining-related activities of big companies on the marine space and shipping traffic.[15]

It is not too late to make a difference, but only if concerted efforts are made, from the local to the global level.[16] One effort in that direction is the instrumentality of transnational remedial action with the aid of private international law, the nature and relevance of which is the focus of next section.

11 John Dugard, *International Law: A South African Perspective* (4th ed, Juta 2016) 283.

12 On 20 April 2010, the Deepwater Horizon oil rig exploded in the Gulf of Mexico, killing 11 people and injuring many more. It caused hundreds of millions of barrels of oil to pour into the Gulf, extending many miles offshore. This catastrophe not only changed the lives of the families of the dead and injured and the communities who experienced the economic and social disruption of the spill – it challenged the survival of the ecosystem of the ninth largest water body in the world. The oil spill extended 50 miles offshore from Louisiana in the Gulf of Mexico. The oil spill also triggered several civil actions. See US National Response Team On Scene Coordinator Report Deepwater Horizon Oil Spill (2011) 1.

13 Article 1(4) of the United Convention on the Law of the Sea (1982).

14 Intergovernmental Panel on Biodiversity and Ecosystem Global Assessment, Paris (6 May 2019) <https://ipbes.net/global-assessment> accessed 13 July 2021.

15 For example, no less than 600,000 tons of crude oil are released into the Mediterranean Sea yearly; what is more, no less than 80 per cent of the urban waste discharged into it is untreated, in addition to agricultural overspills containing phosphates, nitrates and pesticides. See Paul Rose and Anne Laking, *Oceans: Exploring the Hidden Depths of the Underwater World* (University of California Press Los Angeles 2019) 44.

16 ibid.

Therefore, SDG 14 and its targets are aimed at sustainable practices in the course of exploiting marine resources and set out a programmatic action plan to ensure a productive and resilient marine space.[17] They help tap into the marine space with its enormous direct and indirect impact on society as a source of food, a source of resources, a repository of oxygen and a natural climatic regulator acting as some kind of ecological thermoset in terms of climate/weather stabilisation and rainfall patterns. This in itself underscores the importance of SDG 14 and its aim of seeking to sustainably conserve the ocean and use the ocean, seas and marine resources for sustainable development. This is no doubt a very important goal. The proven importance of the ocean and the scientific information above about its uses strengthen legal actions by affected, interested or concerned persons seeking relief from actions, or inaction, that degrade the marine space.[18]

However, in spite of its importance, SDG 14 has been described as the least reported- on goal of all the SDGs, and even worse, in terms of attention and allocated resources, it has been characterised as one of the lowest-priority goals.[19] Indeed, the goal ranks third-to-last when it comes to SDG philanthropic funding and financing.[20] The picture becomes even grimmer when one takes into consideration a survey of global business leaders which revealed that they consider it the second-least significant of the SDGs.[21] This is a call for concern considering the record of business leaders on the marine space in terms of sustainable development.

SDG 14 is predicated on the premise that enormous sustainable development potential lies in the balance between conservation and use of marine resources.

---

17 See Camilo Mora, Derek P Tittensor, Sina Adl, Alastair G B Simpson and Boris Worm, 'How many species are there on Earth and in the ocean?' (2011) 9(8) PLoS Biology e1001127.

18 See for example cases such as *In re Exxon Valdez Litigation*, 767 F. Supp. 1509 (D. Alaska, 1991); see further Keum J Park, 'Judicial Utilization of Scientific Evidence in Complex Environmental Torts: Redefining Litigation Driven Research' (2011) 7(2) Fordham Environmental Law Review 483.

19 Gerald G Singh, Andrés M Cisneros-Montemayor, Wilf Swartz, William Cheung, J Adam Guy, Tiff-Annie Kenny, Chris J McOwen, Rebecca Asch, Jan Laurens Geffert, Colette C C Wabnitz, Rashid Sumaila, Quentin Hanich and Yoshitaka Ota, 'A rapid assessment of co-benefits and trade-offs among Sustainable Development Goals' (2018) 93 Marine Policy 223.

20 ibid.

21 United Nations Global Compact, *Global Opportunity Report 2017* (2017) <www.unglobalcompact.org/docs/publications/Global_Opportunity_Report_2017_SM.pdf> cited in Emilie Beauchamp and Dorothy Lucks (eds), *MEL Handbook for* SDG 14*: Conserve and sustainably use the oceans, seas and marine resources for sustainable development* (IIED 2019).

2.1. SDG 14 TARGETS

For SDG 14, there are 10 targets matched with 10 indicators. The 10 targets are: reducing marine pollution; protecting and restoring ecosystems;[22] reducing ocean acidification;[23] ensuring sustainable fishing;[24] conserving coastal and marine areas;[25] ending subsidies contributing to overfishing; increasing economic benefits from sustainable use of marine resources; increasing scientific knowledge, research and technology for ocean health; supporting small-scale fishers; and implementing and enforcing international sea law.

All these targets address issues that are connected to one another and to other SDGs and have tremendous impact on local communities around the world. In terms of the targets' connection to one another,[26] an example of this is the connection between the target to reduce marine pollution (Target 14.1) and other targets such as restoring and protecting the ecosystem (Target 14.2), reducing ocean acidification (Target 14.3), conserving coastal and marine areas (Target 14.5), and ensuring sustainable fishing (Targets 14.4 and 14.7). Marine pollution affects the economic, social and cultural lives of local communities, destroys the ecosystem and may cause ocean acidification. In turn, the effects of acidification extend up to the food chain to affect economic activities such as fisheries, aquaculture and tourism.[27]

---

22 Globally, some 20 per cent of coral reefs, 19 per cent of mangroves and 29 per cent of seagrass habitat have been lost over about the last century. To preserve these and other critical coastal habitats, management of marine areas needs to apply ecosystem-based approaches using area-based tools such as marine protected areas, integrated coastal management, marine spatial planning and the large marine ecosystem approach. See <https://www.oceanactionhub.org/sdg-14-targets-context-and-indicators> accessed 11 June 2021.

23 This means the worldwide reduction in the pH of seawater as a consequence of the absorption of large amounts of carbon dioxide by the oceans. See John P Raffery, 'Ocean acidification' <https://www.britannica.com/science/ocean-acidification> accessed 1 December 2020.

24 This is intended to effectively regulate harvesting and end overfishing, illegal, unreported and unregulated fishing and destructive fishing practices and implement science-based management plans in order to restore fish stocks in the shortest time feasible, at least to levels that can produce maximum sustainable yield. See <https://www.globalgoals.org/14-life-below-water> published 26 October 2020, accessed 30 November 2020.

25 This requires that by 2020 nations 'conserve at least 10 per cent of coastal and marine areas, consistent with national and international law and based on the best available scientific information.'

26 As is the case with the SDGs, interconnectedness was also a major feature of their predecessors, the Millennium Development Goals. See Tajudeen Sanni, 'The Millennium Development Goal Relating to Environmental Sustainability: An Examination of the Legal Regimes in Uganda and Nigeria' (2012) 1(1) African Multidisciplinary Journal 127, 131.

27 <https://www.coastadapt.com.au/ocean-acidification-and-its-effects> accessed 2 November 2020.

However, in spite of their enormous promise, SDG 14 and its targets do not adequately anticipate future challenges arising from new technologies, with their attendant effects on local communities. For instance, the targets focus on existing industries, with few references to new and emerging technologies, such as blue carbon and bio-prospecting, that are intended to be used to explore oceans in order to develop new products for commercial purposes and which may cause tremendous harm. An important issue in this regard is the complication arising from activities carried out in the so-called 'areas beyond national jurisdiction' that may affect the environmental well-being and economic activities of persons and communities in areas within national jurisdiction.[28]

2.2. SDG 14, OTHER SDGs AND LOCAL COMMUNITIES

In terms of the connections between SDG 14 and the other SDGs, SDG 1 on eradication of poverty is a good example, considering the fact that the ocean is an important source of livelihoods for many around the world. Thus, protecting the ocean would, for example, help in securing the livelihoods of small-scale fishers in local communities. It would also help in securing the health of local communities who depend on the marine space, thereby helping to meet another goal, SDG 3, which is about ensuring the health and well-being of all. Furthermore, the capacity of local communities to secure and protect their marine space through private legal action has links with SDG 16, which aims to 'promote peaceful and inclusive societies for sustainable development, provide access to justice for all and build effective, accountable and inclusive institutions at all levels.'[29] Ensuring inclusiveness of and access to justice for local communities is quite important considering the vulnerability of these communities as peoples on the edge. In principle, the term 'indigenous and local communities' is used in recognition of communities that have a long association with the lands and waters that they have traditionally lived on or used.[30] In the context of this study, it is important to note that no less than three billion people who live in coastal communities have an even more intimate connection with the marine space compared to the rest of the world, as they depend on it for their livelihoods, for food and as a haven of culture.[31] In recognition of this, a number

---

28 World Wildlife Fund, 'Fishing for proteins: how marine fisheries impact on global food security up to 2050: A global prognosis' (2016) <www.fishforward.eu/wp-content/uploads/2017/01/20> accessed 14 June 2021.

29 UN SDGs <https://sdgs.un.org/goals/goal16> accessed 2 November 2020.

30 United Nations Environmental Programme, 'Convention on Biological Diversity: Who are local communities?', UN Doc UNEP/CBD/WS-CB/LAC/1/INF/5 (16 November 2006) 1.

31 Sylvia Michele Diez, Pawan Patil, John Morton, Diego J Rodriguez, Alessandra Vanzella, David Robin, Thomas Maes, Christopher Corbin, *Marine Pollution in the Caribbean: Not a Minute to Waste* (World Bank Group 2019) 19.

of countries have enacted legislation to deal with (sustainable) development challenges facing communities that depend on the sea.[32] Such legislation may be relied on in private actions, including transnational legal challenges to negative actions of multinational companies and other private entities on the marine space. Such private legal actions can be strengthened by provisions in national and international human rights instruments that lend legal support to SDG 14 and its targets.[33]

3. REALISATION OF SDG 14 THROUGH PRIVATE INTERNATIONAL LAW

The utility of private international law has been seen in such aspects as transnational maritime claims (for example those on maritime arrest),[34] lien and the oil pollution liability and compensation regimes. Thus the relationship *inter se* between SDG 14, which deals with life under water, on the one hand, and private international law on the other may take different forms and dimensions.

The chapter focuses on one aspect, namely the capacity of private actors, especially local communities, to take legal action, particularly at the transboundary level, in search of justice for actions or inaction by big actors such as multinational companies that run afoul of SDG 14 and cause these communities or the marine spaces to which they are connected some disadvantage or harm.

Progress on SDG 14 requires that the full arsenal of (international) law and policy – both private and public – be deployed to ensure equity for these most deprived and vulnerable communities, including by way of putting in

32 See for example Ghana's Coastal Development Act 961 of 2017 and Kenya Coast Development Authority Act No 6 of 1989 (revised as Cap 449 of 2012).

33 See for example Danish Institute for Human Rights, *Human Rights Guide to Sustainable Development*, SDG 14 <https://sdg.humanrights.dk/en/targets2?goal[]=74> accessed 30 May 2021. For example, that site dwells on the utility, for each SDG target, of such instruments as the International Covenant on Civil and Political Rights, the International Covenant on Economic, Social and Cultural Rights, the United Nations Declaration on the Rights of Indigenous Peoples, the African Charter on Human and Peoples' Rights, and the Regional Agreement on Access to Information, Public Participation and Justice in Environmental Matters in Latin America and the Caribbean – a number of the instruments listed here recognise both individual and communal rights. See also Office of the High Commissioner for Human Rights, *Human Rights and 2030 Agenda for Sustainable Development* <https://www.ohchr.org/en/issues/SDGS/pages/the2030agenda.aspx> accessed 21 May 2021. Cf also national laws of many countries; examples include provisions on the right to a clean and healthy environment, as in the Kenya Constitution 2010 (Arts 42, 69 and 70) and the South African Constitution 1996 (Art 24), etc.

34 See generally for example Verónica Ruiz Abou-Nigm, *The Arrest of Ships in Private International Law* (OUP 2011).

place proper mechanisms for remedial actions. However, it is worth reiterating that private international law has been explored to a lesser extent than public international law in the fulfilment of SDG 14 and the previous Millennium Development Goals relating to environmental sustainability. The need to explore the potential of private international law becomes all the more imperative considering the power asymmetry between most of those actors whose actions cause harm and the local people. This point is all the more glaring where big multinational companies are involved; indeed, some multinational companies are known to be even more powerful than governments in many countries in the Global South. This is one of the reasons why many of these multinational companies have not been held to account in their host countries. Another likely reason is that parts of the oceans are extraterritorial and therefore outside of national regulation.

Yet another reason lies in the limitations created by provisions in the relevant environmental or marine legislation, for example in terms of the requirement of *locus standi*, which may hamper the capacity of communities or the non-governmental organisations that are better placed to represent them. *Locus standi* is the right of an individual, group of individuals or states to bring an action before a court and to participate in judicial proceedings.[35] It is accorded to an individual or group when they are able demonstrate that the law or act in question infringes their legal rights or at least that it will cause a sufficient degree of harm to their particular interest. In public international law, it is primarily states that mostly have *locus standi* before international tribunals for civil actions, with a limited right recognised for international organisations, and sometimes individuals.[36]

As for the law of the sea, there are different means through which parties may resolve disputes relating to violations.[37] It may be through the International Tribunal for the Law of the Sea (ITLOS), the International Court of Justice (ICJ), an arbitral tribunal or a special arbitral tribunal.

In as much as reparations,[38] restitution[39] and compensation[40] are available remedies for an aggrieved party for internationally wrongful acts in those or other fora, such claims are only admissible when brought in accordance with the applicable rule relating to the nationality of claims,[41] which would affect

35 <https://www.lawyr.it/index.php/dictionary/867-locus-standi> accessed 11 January 2021.

36 ibid.

37 See for example Art 287 UNCLOS.

38 Art 34 of the Draft Articles on Responsibility of States for Internationally Wrongful Acts (2001).

39 ibid Art 35.

40 ibid Art 36.

41 ibid Art 44.

the *locus standi* of the local community where an international instrument restricts instituting such actions to states, as is in the case in many international instruments.[42]

3.1. INTERNATIONAL MARINE INSTRUMENTS AND PRIVATE ACTION

Indeed, there are a plethora of international law instruments whose objectives are to protect the marine environment but which, in effect, are limited if applied in this context, as the primary responsibility and liability essentially lies with states in all or many provisions of such instruments, particularly those dealing with the protection of marine environment.[43] In contrast, there is also a string of other international instruments that primarily provide for private civil liability.[44] In the context of the former, the example of the 1982 United Nations Convention on Law of the Sea (UNCLOS) may be given, which was described by Agenda 21 as providing 'the international basis upon which to pursue the protection and sustainable development of the marine environment and its resources'.[45] It is regarded in some quarters as the Constitution of the Sea – a description that has faced criticisms on a number of counts, without necessarily detracting from the enormous legal contributions this revolutionary instrument has made to law of the sea jurisprudence.

Certainly one can add another point to the criticism of UNCLOS as the Constitution of the Sea: it does not adequately capture the condition of the local communities, including indigenous peoples, particularly in terms of inclusion

---

42 Almost two decades ago now, a top scholar of international bemoaned the lack of political will on the parts of states to expand options for environmental actions that may help tackle this kind of problem: Philippe Sands, 'International Environmental Litigation and Its Future' (1999) 32(5) University of Richmond Law Review Volume 1641.

43 Examples include the Convention for the Prevention of Pollution from Ships (1978), the Convention on the Control of Transboundary Movement of Hazardous Waste and their Disposal (1989), the UN Agreement Relating to the Conservation and Management of Straddling Fish Stocks and Migratory Fish Stocks (1995), among others. It must be noted that domestication of these and other international treaties (such as those referred to in the footnote immediately below) by states by means of national legislation may give a boost to private action for violations of the marine space, including at transnational levels.

44 Some relevant international instruments – many of which will be briefly discussed below – include the International Convention on Civil Liability for Oil Pollution Damage (1992); the International Convention on Oil Pollution Preparedness, Response and Cooperation (1990), the International Convention on the Establishment of an International Fund for Compensation for Oil Pollution Damage (1992), and Vienna Convention on Civil Liability for Nuclear Damage (1996).

44 See Agenda 21 of the 1992 Rio Conference Report.

45 ibid.

and participation, as well as in terms of remedial mechanisms for harms they may suffer on the marine space. That is what a typical constitution would do. UNCLOS, by contrast, mostly refers to states and state organisations, and does not directly make ample provision for local communities. Nevertheless, it does establish ITLOS, with limited access for private actors.[46] The Statute of the Tribunal also allows non-state entities to have standing before the court in any case provided for in Part XI of UNCLOS and 'in any case submitted pursuant to any other agreement conferring jurisdiction on the Tribunal which is accepted by all parties to that case'.[47] Part XI of UNCLOS deals with exploration and exploitation of the Area which,[48] in terms of UNCLOS, may also be carried out by non-state entities and for this reason the latter are given access to the Tribunal's Seabed Dispute Chamber.[49]

This kind of access of private actors to international tribunals has made some scholars to reconsider the rigid boundaries between private and public international law.[50] While ITLOS is essentially a public international law body, its jurisdiction over private entities may contribute to the jurisprudence of private international law.[51]

As for the second case where ITLOS has jurisdiction, i.e. 'in any case submitted pursuant to any other agreement conferring jurisdiction on the Tribunal which is accepted by all parties to that case', this may encompass 'any agreement', including agreements that involve such subjects of municipal law as claims against a private entity by another private entity invoking a dispute resolution term that grants jurisdiction to the Tribunal.[52]

However, both instances are still restricted in terms of access for private victims. Firstly, actions under Part XI are limited to private parties that are part of an international agreement relating to mining activities in the Area. In the

46 See Art 291 UNCLOS.

47 Arts 20, 21 Statute of International Tribunal for the Law of the Sea.

48 Art 1(1) of UNCLOS defines 'Area' to mean 'the sea bed and ocean floor and subsoil thereof, beyond the limits of national jurisdiction'. It is also called the 'international sea bed area. See further Patrick Vrancken, 'Overview of the International Law of the Sea' in Patrick Vrancken and Martine Tsamenyi (eds) *The Law of the Sea: The African Union and its Member States* (Juta 2017) 20–22.

49 See Arts 186, 187 and 188 UNCLOS.

50 See for example Diego P Fernández Arroyo and Makane Moïse Mbengue, 'Public and Private International Law in International Courts and Tribunals: Evidence of an Inescapable Interaction' (2018) 56(4) Colombia Journal of Transnational Law 797, 801.

51 This is comparable to how international tribunals dealing with investment arbitration and commercial issues have helped to nurture the development of private international law. See for example Stephanie De Dycker, 'Private International Law Disputes before the International Court of Justice' (2010) 1(2) Journal of International Dispute Settlement 475.

52 See Philippe Gautier, 'Two Aspects of ITLOS Proceedings: Non State Parties and Costs of Bringing Claims' in Harry N Schreiber and Jin-Hyun Park (eds), *Regions, Institutions and Law of the Sea. Studies in Ocean Governance* (Martinus Nijhoff 2003) 75.

second instance, access is also restricted to parties – for example two private entities – that have entered into an agreement conferring jurisdiction on the Tribunal. Another indication of the limitations on access to the Tribunal for private parties is the Tribunal's rejection of a request for participation by two non-governmental organisations – Greenpeace International and the World Wide Fund for Nature – in advisory proceedings, even as *amici curiae*.[53]

Hence one of the targets of SDG 14, which relies on UNCLOS (and other international instruments) for the realisation of this goal, will need to be considered in this context as far as private legal action is concerned.[54] The target in question is Target 14.c, which seeks to 'enhance the conservation and sustainable use of oceans and their resources by implementing international law as reflected in UNCLOS, which provides the legal framework for the conservation and sustainable use of oceans and their resources, as recalled in paragraph 158 of The Future We Want'.[55]

In this regard, the provision in UNCLOS that requires further development of the liability regime for marine pollution provides a window of opportunity for the protection and sustainable use of the marine space.[56] That provision implies that there has been a number of instruments providing for liability for marine pollution and that there is a need to develop them further. These liability regimes contain provisions that allow private persons who are victims of oil pollution to hold ship owners liable for damage caused by oil pollution. They constitute examples of the instruments which primarily provide for private civil liability mentioned above.

---

53 See responsibilities and obligations of states sponsoring persons and entities with respect to activities in the Area 9 Request for Advisory Opinion submitted to the seabed Disputes Chamber), Advisory Opinion (1 February 2011).

54 Under Art 194(1) UNCLOS, states have to 'take, individually or jointly as appropriate, all measures consistent with this Convention that are necessary to prevent, reduce and control pollution of the marine environment from those and any other sources, deploying the best practicable means at their disposal and in accordance with their capabilities, and they shall endeavour to harmonize their policies in this connection'. Similarly, as per Art 194(2), states have the obligation to 'take all measures necessary to ensure that activities under their jurisdiction or control are so conducted as not to cause damage by pollution to other states and their environment, and that pollution arising from incidents or activities under their jurisdiction or control does not spread beyond the areas where they exercise sovereign rights in accordance with this Convention.' Other international instruments that protect the marine space from pollution include the Convention on the High Seas (1958), the International Convention for the Protection of Pollution from Ships (1973) and its Protocol of 1978, the International Convention relating to Intervention on the High Seas in Cases of Oil Pollution Casualties (1969), among others, all of which direct states to take steps to prevent pollution of the seas.

55 <https://www.un.org/development/desa/disabilities/envision2030-goal14.html> accessed 8 September 2020.

56 See Art 304 UNCLOS. See also Principle 13 Rio Declaration. Principle 10 requires the provision of 'effective access to judicial and administrative proceeding, including redress and remedy'.

In that category is the 1969 Convention on Civil Liability for Oil Pollution Damage, which imposed strict liability on the owner of the ship, now replaced by a 1992 Protocol which has further extended the marine area covered to the exclusive economic zone.[57] The Convention makes the owner of the ship strictly liable for pollution damage caused by a discharge from the ship.[58] The ship owner is liable, even in the absence of any fault, for any damage by pollution caused by the oil, although liability can normally be limited up to an amount established according to the tonnage of the ship. This amount is guaranteed by his liability insurance, which is compulsory.

Taking the liability regime further is the 1971 International Convention on the Establishment of an International Fund for Compensation for Oil Pollution Damage, now superseded by the 1992 Protocol mentioned above and terminated by a 2000 Protocol.[59] It aimed at making up the compensation for pollution damage to private persons where the compensation provided under the 1969 Civil Liability Convention was inadequate.[60] The Convention created the IOPC Fund, which provided supplementary compensation when the amount payable by the ship owner and his insurer was insufficient to cover all of the damage.[61] It allowed any person or company that had suffered pollution damage caused by oil transported by ship in a state party to the IOPC Fund to claim compensation from the ship owner, their insurers and the Fund. Individuals, businesses and local communities had standing for private action under it. The 1992 Protocol increased the amount of compensation available. Although the 2000 Protocol terminated the Convention, a 2003 Protocol created a supplementary Compensation Fund to the 1992 Protocol. There is also the Bunker Convention, which provides for effective compensation for

---

57 Art 3 Protocol to the Convention on Civil Liability for Oil Pollution Damage (1992). Art 55 of UNCLOS defines 'Exclusive Economic Zone' as 'an area beyond and adjacent to the territorial sea subject to the specific legal regime established under this part'. Section 57 of UNCLOS states 'the zone shall not extend beyond 200 nautical miles from the baseline from which the territorial sea is measured'. For further elucidation on Exclusive Economic Zone in general, and in the context of the domestic laws of a particular country, see Patrick Vrancken *South Africa and the Law of the Sea* (Martinus Nijhof 2011) 177, 178 and 179. See also Patrick Vrancken, 'The 2050 Africa's Integrated Maritime Strategy: The Combined Exclusive Maritime Zone of Africa as an instrument of sustainable development of the African Large Marine Ecosystems' (2020) 36 Environmental Development 1, para 2, available <www.elsevier.com/locate/envdev> accessed 15 July 2021.

58 Art 3 of the Convention on Civil Liability for Oil Pollution Damage (1969). See also Art 4 of the Protocol to the Convention.

59 See generally International Maritime Organization, 'Liability and Compensation' <https://www.imo.org/en/OurWork/Legal/Pages/LiabilityAndCompensation.aspx> accessed 22 April 2021. The 1971 Convention ceased in 2002.

60 See Art 2 of the International Convention on the Establishment of an International Fund for Compensation for Oil Pollution Damage (1971).

61 ibid.

persons who have suffered from damage arising from oil spills from ships' bunkers.[62]

While those regimes cover only oil pollution, there is the Convention on Liability for Noxious and Hazardous Substances, which covers pollution damage caused by hazardous and noxious substances, and provides for compensation to be paid in the event of accidents at sea involving hazardous and noxious substances, such as chemicals.[63] It covers not only pollution damage but also the risks of fire and explosion, including loss of life or personal injury and loss of or damage to property.

Similar to all the above in terms of private liability and action is the Nairobi International Convention on the Removal of Wrecks of 2007, which holds ship owners financially liable by mandating them to take out insurance or provide other financial security to cover the costs of wreck removal.

Another relevant instrument is the 1992 Convention on Biodiversity (CBD), which is also at the heart of the international legal and policy framework on SDG 14. The objective of CBD includes the conservation of biological diversity and the sustainable use of marine resources. A CBD-related instrument requires parties to ensure the full and effective participation of indigenous and local communities, at all relevant levels, particularly in employing and deploying the traditional value systems, practices and innovations of local communities and indigenous people that are relevant for sustainable use of biodiversity.[64] In this case, the instrument at least recognises the presence of the traditional communities and provides a basis for them not only to work together with other stakeholders in the sustainable development of the marine space but also to seek remedies in the event of infractions. Barring this generic provision on participation, however, which only has instrumental value for legal action, this instrument does not also include specific mechanisms that aid private actions to tackle infractions regarding the marine space at a transboundary level.

Instruments like the CBD have no functional value for private international actions in the context in question. They are relevant insofar as public international

---

62 See Arts 2, 3 of the International Convention on Civil Liability for Bunker Oil Pollution Damage (2001).

63 This Convention and its 2010 Protocol are not yet in force. See <https://www.imo.org/en/About/Conventions/Pages/International-Convention-on-Liability-and-Compensation-for-Damage-in-Connection-with-the-Carriage-of-Hazardous-and-Noxious-.aspx> accessed 30 May 2021.

64 Target 20 of the Aichi Biodiversity Targets for 2011–2020, with 20 targets. See Secretariat of the CBD <https://www.cbd.int/sp/targets/> last assessed 8 September 2020. For further explanation on the emphasis in the CBD instruments on local communities, see Elisa Morgera 'Fair and Equitable Benefit-Sharing at the Cross-Roads of the Human Right to Science and International Biodiversity Law' (2015) 4 Laws 804, 807; Elisa Morgera 'Justice, Equity and Benefit-Sharing under the Nagoya Protocol to the Convention on Biological Diversity' (2015) 24(1) Italian Yearbook of International Law Online 113, 114.

law instruments are an important source of private international law,[65] and insofar as they help to galvanise governments into enacting relevant, detailed national instruments that make instituting private actions easier. Such national instruments are also a source of private international law.

Certainly, interaction between public international law instruments and private international law is quite useful in the context of developing the norms required for strengthening private international law actions. When this is coupled with the increasing importance of non-state or transnational law on the national and international planes, the tight and strict divide between public law and private law further loosens in various ways and a plurality of new norms that can help strengthen transnational private actions in this regard have emerged and are being observed.[66]

In view of the above scenario, exploring the potential of private international law for a full and effective regime of responsibility, accountability and liability to achieve sustainable development becomes even all the more imperative. Where environmental damage is caused by private entities, restricting international liability for the damage to state actors hampers robust responses to a number of ecological damage-related and environmental problems in general. Thus, one positive measure has been the possibility of expanding responsibility for environmental damage to include private actors, including multinational companies. Multinational companies are being sued across borders in national and regional courts, thus contributing to environmental jurisprudence.[67] There have a good number of such cases around the world. One issue with these

65 The recent Dutch case of *Urgenda v the State of the Netherlands* (20 December 2019), in which a Dutch NGO had sued the Dutch government under Dutch civil tort law for not meeting its climate change goals provides good example in this regard. The Court referred to the UNFCCC (Rio Climate Change Treaty), and ruled that this treaty, although binding upon states only, so that it did not create rights the plaintiff NGO could directly invoke, nevertheless did have a 'reflex effect' upon the state's duty of care under Dutch civil tort law. The Court thus posited that 'this duty should be interpreted so as to avoid a conflict with the State's international obligations.' See further <https://elaw.org/nl.urgenda.15> accessed 30 May 2021. Based on this case and its 'reflex effect' reasoning, another Dutch NGO and private individuals have sued the Shell company in tort for its contribution to global warming. This case also has a private international law dimension, since the individual plaintiffs include foreigners based outside of the Netherlands.

66 Yuko Nishitani, 'Party Autonomy in Contemporary Private International Law – The Hague Principles on Choice of Law and East Asia' (2016) 59 Japanese Yearbook of International Law 300.

67 A common one is cross-border climate litigation, based on civil tort law. An example is the case of *Luciano Lliuya v RWE AG*, Case No 2 O 285/15 Essen Regional Court which involves a Peruvian farmer Saul Lliuya (in fact acting for his local community) against the German energy company RWE for RWE's CO2 emission contribution to the melting of the glacier behind Lliuya's village in Peru. That melting, the Court was told, had given rise to a serious threat of Palcacocha, a glacial lake located above Huaraz, facing a substantial volumetric increase since 1975, which has accelerated since 2003.

cases is the challenge of enforcing judgments. Another is that cases may sometimes be dismissed on technicalities, which frustrates the fight to achieve SDG 14.

3.2. SOME ILLUSTRATIVE CASES

Aguida v Texaco illustrates these two challenges perfectly.[68] In the case,[69] the plaintiff brought a representative suit before the United States Court of Appeals, Second Circuit, on behalf of a community in the Republic of Ecuador against a US-based company alleging that the defendant's oil operation activities polluted the rainforest and rivers in Ecuador and Peru. The choice of forum was based on the fact that the defendant's activities were designed, controlled, conceived and directed through its operations in the United States. The claimants sought monetary damages on the basis of negligence, public and private nuisance, strict liability, medical monitoring, trespass, civil conspiracy and violation of the US Alien Tort Claims Act.

In the trial court, the matter was dismissed for reasons of *forum non conveniens* and the failure to join the Republic of Ecuador and PetroEcuador on the premise that they were indispensable parties because their absence would make it impossible for the court to order the extensive equitable relief sought by the plaintiffs. In the first appeal, court vacated the dismissal and remanded for reconsideration. It stated that the *forum non conveniens* dismissal was inappropriate.

The Court of Appeals, however, dismissed the matter, inter alia on the principle of *forum non conveniens*. This is a doctrine applied mostly in common law judicial systems, which allows courts that have jurisdiction over a case to stay or dismiss the case upon determining that the case may be heard more appropriately in another court.[70]

The court dismissed the suit based on public and private interest factors that favoured Ecuador as a forum over the United States, where proceedings had been instituted. These factors included the ease of access to sources of evidence, such as medical and property records, given that all the plaintiffs resided in Ecuador and Peru, as well as the aim of avoiding the application of foreign law and the difficulty for New York court to have the documents for the 55,000 class members translated.

68 This case involves rivers, which are also covered by SDG 14, especially for the purpose of targets relating to fisheries.

69 303 F.3d 470.

70 See generally Ronald A Brand, 'Forum non Conveniens' in R Wolfrum (ed), *The Max Planck Encyclopedia of Public International Law* (OUP 2014, online edition).

The *Aguida v Texaco* case exemplifies a number of challenges that are faced by local communities in prosecuting cases against multinational companies. First are what may be termed private interest factors, which include the ease of access to sources of evidence, as noted above, as well as the availability of processes to compel unwilling witnesses to attend, and the costs of ensuring attendance of willing witnesses, the possibility of visiting the locus, if visiting would be appropriate to the action and any other issues that may affect the trial of a case in an easy, expeditious and inexpensive manner.[71] All of these pose challenges for local communities, as they are usually faced with financial difficulties, and may find it challenging to cover the transportation costs for witnesses to attend the trial. Equally, some witnesses may refuse to go to court and testify.

Second is the effect of public interest factors, including administrative difficulties associated with high caseloads, the administrative costs of court, and the interest in having local controversies decided at home and in avoiding difficult problems relating to conflict of laws and the application of foreign laws.[72]

A third factor is the limitation of actions. Local communities equally face this problem because they are often not acquainted with the international and national laws governing limitation. This includes limitation in filing suits and appealing judgments before international tribunals and courts.[73]

A fourth issue concerns the application of the doctrine of international comity, a foundational doctrine of private international law.[74] Courts, according to this doctrine, should apply foreign law or limit domestic jurisdiction out of respect for foreign sovereignty.[75] In terms of the doctrine, courts are required to strike a balance between competing public and private interests in a manner that takes into account any conflict between the public policies of the domestic and foreign states.[76] Authorities disagree as to whether comity is a rule of natural law, custom, treaty or domestic law.[77] Indeed, there is no agreement that comity is a rule of law at all.[78] The doctrine of comity poses a challenge to private international law in helping to fulfil SDG 14 because it is always difficult to find

71 For similar challenges normally encountered by victims and litigants in a private transnational action, see generally Iman Prihandono, 'Barriers to transnational human rights litigation against transnational corporations (TNCs): The need for cooperation between home and host countries' (2011) 3(7) Journal of Law and Conflict Resolution 89–103, available online at <http://www.academicjournals.org/JLCR> accessed 28 July 2021.

72 ibid.

73 ibid, para 34.

74 John Kuhn Bleimaier, 'The Doctrine of Comity in Private International Law: The Doctrine of Comity in Private International Law' (1979) 24(4) The Catholic Lawyer 327.

75 See generally Mark Janis, *An Introduction to International Law* (Little Brown & Co Law & Business 2003) 331, 339.

76 Joel R Paul, 'The Transformation of International Comity' (2008) 71 Law and Contemporary Problems 19–38 1.

77 ibid 20.

78 ibid.

a balance in the conflict between the public policies of the domestic and foreign sovereign states.

A fifth issue is the challenge associated with application of the principle of *forum non conveniens*, as explained earlier.

The aftermath of the *Aguida v Texaco* case illustrates another challenge mentioned above, namely enforcement of judgment. When the case was heard in Ecuador, the Court ruled that the local communities had to be compensated; however, enforcement of this ruling was challenging in countries where Chevron had assets (to recover compensation, for example), due in part to the influence of the company.[79]

Similarly, in *Wiwa v Shell Petroleum Development Company*,[80] the challenges of private international law in protecting marine space were exemplified. In this case, the defendants had polluted the local water supply and agricultural land upon which the livelihood of the plaintiff was based. The defendant and the government of Nigeria colluded and caused the arrest of the Ogoni 9, a group of activists who were hanged after a trial before a Nigerian special military tribunal. The case was brought by the Center for Constitutional Rights on behalf of the relatives of murdered activists who were fighting for human rights and environmental justice in Nigeria. Although the matter was settled through arbitration, the case is notable for the fact that the Nigerian government collaborated with a multinational company in violating the rights of individuals. It illustrates how many states frustrate the local communities in their attempts to get justice and typifies how the failure to monitor the activities of companies and hold them responsible for infractions may pose a challenge to the fulfilment of SDG 14.

The above cases offer a number of lessons, including in terms of the challenges associated with transboundary private environmental actions. This includes the place of scientific research and the importance of empowering local communities. Moreover, given that many of these cases are litigated in the Global North, where many of the companies come from, this indicates not only the importance of relevant legal and judicial reform in countries in Global South, but also the need for international rule of law so that big companies can be judicially held accountable anywhere, without further negative consequences for local communities and their countries.

Of relevance in this regard is the recent judgment of The Hague Court of Appeals delivered on 29 January 2021 in suits instituted by four Nigerian farmers. The case concerned massive oil spills in three Nigerian village communities in

---

[79] See further Carmen Otero Garcia-Castrillon, 'International Litigation Trends in Environmental Liability: A European Union-United States Comparative Perspective' (2011) 7(3) Journal of Private International Law 551, 552.

[80] *Wiwa v Royal Dutch Petroleum Co*, No 96 Civ 8386, 2002 WL 319887, at *20–21 (S.D.N.Y), decided 14 September 2000.

Goi, Oruma and Ikot Ada Udo which affected farmlands and water bodies.[81] The plaintiffs wanted the Court to hold Shell Nigeria and its parent body (Royal Dutch Shell, RDS) responsible for the oil spills and their effects, the latter on the basis that it had failed to exercise its duty of care to prevent and mitigate oil spills by its Nigerian subsidiary. The Court relied on *Lungowe v Vedanta*[82] and *Chandler v Cape plc*[83] and held that RDS owed the victims a duty of care to prevent the oil spill. The Court directed the defendants to commence purification of the water sources in and near Oruma within two weeks of notification of the judgment and to complete this purification within one month of commencement. Shell was directed to pay a penalty to the plaintiffs, and to pay €100,000 or another amount to be determined each time Shell acts in contravention of the directive on remediation of the soil and water sources in the affected communities.

It has been asserted that this case was the first time the parent body of a subsidiary was held liable for the infractions of its subsidiary abroad.[84] This is quite significant. Also significant is the use of scientific grounds in establishing SPDC's connection to the oil spill, reinforcing the importance of the SDG target about scientific research.[85] As far as the case is concerned, three important issues should be noted. Firstly, the Court based its jurisdiction in respect of the parent company Royal Dutch Shell on the Brussels I Regulation, and in respect of SPDC on Article 7(1) of the Dutch Code of Civil Procedure, which also determined how the Court conducted the proceedings. Regarding the substantive issues of the case, the Court applied Nigerian law, supplemented by English case law precedents which, the Court found, have persuasive authority under Nigerian law.

The Court held that in causing and not properly responding to the oil spill, thereby contaminating the agricultural land and fishponds of the plaintiffs and the local community, SPDC violated their right to a clean environment as enshrined in Articles 20, 33, and 34 of the Nigerian Constitution and Article 24 of the African Charter on Human and People's Rights. The Court made a pragmatic interpretation of the Nigerian law in the context of the

81 <https://uitspraken.rechtspraak.nl/inziendocument?id=ECLI:NL:GHDHA:2021:132> accessed 20 February 2021. See also 'International parent company responsibility: Shell and oil spills in Nigeria', *Loyens Loeff* (2 February 2021) <https://www.loyensloeff.com/en/en/news/news-articles/international-parent-company-responsibility-shell-and-oil-spills-in-nigeria-n21572/> accessed 20 February 2021.

82 [2019] UKSC 20.

83 [2012] EWCA (Civ) 525.

84 Wubeshet Tiruneh, 'Holding the Parent Company Liable for Human Rights Abuses Committed Abroad: The Case of the Four Nigerian Farmers and Milieudefensie v. Shell', *EJIL:Talk* (19 February 2021) <https://www.ejiltalk.org/holding-the-parent-company-liable-for-human-rights-abuses-committed-abroad-the-case-of-the-four-nigerian-farmers-and-milieudefensie-v-shell/> accessed 20 February 2021.

85 Target 14.7(a).

regional African human rights instruments to which Nigeria is a party. It did so because the Nigerian Constitution defines section 20 of the Constitution, which obligates the state to protect the land, water and atmosphere of Nigeria, as being non-justiciable, a point of law that contributes to the legal difficulties faced by victims of environmental infractions in terms of instituting cases against the state and other actors affiliated with the state. Nigeria is a party to the African Charter on Human and People's Rights and is bound to respect its provisions on environmental protection, especially in view of having domesticated this instrument. This leads to the second point, namely the importance of taking a human rights approach in transnational litigation on protecting the environment in general, and marine space in particular, for the benefit of local communities and their vulnerable members.

Third, it is also noteworthy that, as mentioned above, the Court had earlier held, in an interim judgment that it had international jurisdiction to hear the case, both in respect of Shell Nigeria and its parent body. Thus, the case also contributed to the jurisprudence on choice of law and jurisdiction in a transnational environmental context and offers a lesson on how transnational private actions may help protect the marine space.

4. PROPOSALS FOR REFORM

The principles of private international law (for example the principle of comity) should be reinterpreted or reviewed in the light of the SDGs, with sustainable development given due recognition as an international and transnational policy that has wide acceptance among countries of the world. Better – although more ambitious – would be to consider sustainable development to be a principle of both private and public international law, as it now has wide acceptance in the law and policy of most countries around the world, as demonstrated at the beginning of this chapter. All of this would mean that when a private action is instituted to protect the marine space, especially when it affects vulnerable groups such as local communities and their members, the national policy on the basis of which domestic courts assume jurisdiction should be viewed through the prism of sustainable development as an overarching principle of law.

Choice of law should be made on that basis, with a legal interpretation that best coheres with the principle of sustainable development. In appropriate cases, the 'better law' would be one that promotes or better promotes sustainable development. This latter approach will also inform the judicial process for the enforcement of foreign judgments against powerful private actors. Similarly, it will drive the possible abolition of the doctrine of *forum non conveniens*. To achieve this and for the purpose of transnational private actions concerning protection of the marine space, private international law would need to be reconceptualised as a system of international norms operationalised by national courts rather than merely a corpus of national laws dealing with foreign elements, at least for the purpose of offering much-needed protection to ward off negative anthropogenic impact on the sea and those who depend on it for livelihoods and culture. The international norms on the basis of which this would be done include the norms concerning respect for and protection of human rights, including the rights to (sustainable) development, to cultural identity and to a clean and healthy environment.

Doing all of this could have a revolutionary impact on all aspects of private international law, but would be particularly necessary at least for the purposes of responding to the emergencies associated with the perilous state of the marine space and its impact on members of local communities.

There have been calls for universal adoption of a global treaty to ensure accountability of multinational companies. Such a treaty would be more effective if this proposal were embedded in it. Enacting a model law christened the 'Model Law on Transnational Private Actions in Environmental and Marine Action', with similar provisions to be adopted by countries at the national, regional and global levels, will also be of help in this regard. It is further proposed that further development of liability and compensation regimes, as required by UNCLOS, should extend to other areas outside the exclusive economic zone to include the so-called 'areas beyond national jurisdiction'. These are quite ambitious measures, but they are no less ambitious than SDG 14 – or the SDGs as a whole – considering the level of challenges they aim at tackling, as comprehensively highlighted in this chapter.

5. CONCLUSION

The chapter has explored the potential of private international law in transnational legal actions to protect the marine space with the aim of realising SDG 14. As we have seen, local communities and/or individuals still face many legal, social, political and economic challenges in instituting such private suits; hence, most local communities give up their rights to sue over such matters, which negatively affects the realisation of SDG 14 in terms of conserving marine waters and their resources and protecting the communities that depend on them. If there is one significant takeaway on this issue, it is the impact of the emerging norms of private environmental action on the international legal architecture that allows transnational legal actions.

SDG 15: LIFE ON LAND

Drossos STAMBOULAKIS and Jay SANDERSON*

Goal 15: Protect, restore and promote sustainable use of terrestrial ecosystems, sustainably manage forests, combat desertification, and halt and reverse land degradation and halt biodiversity loss

15.1 By 2020, ensure the conservation, restoration and sustainable use of terrestrial and inland freshwater ecosystems and their services, in particular forests, wetlands, mountains and drylands, in line with obligations under international agreements

15.2 By 2020, promote the implementation of sustainable management of all types of forests, halt deforestation, restore degraded forests and substantially increase afforestation and reforestation globally

15.3 By 2030, combat desertification, restore degraded land and soil, including land affected by desertification, drought and floods, and strive to achieve a land degradation-neutral world

15.4 By 2030, ensure the conservation of mountain ecosystems, including their biodiversity, in order to enhance their capacity to provide benefits that are essential for sustainable development

15.5 Take urgent and significant action to reduce the degradation of natural habitats, halt the loss of biodiversity and, by 2020, protect and prevent the extinction of threatened species

15.6 Promote fair and equitable sharing of the benefits arising from the utilization of genetic resources and promote appropriate access to such resources, as internationally agreed

15.7 Take urgent action to end poaching and trafficking of protected species of flora and fauna and address both demand and supply of illegal wildlife products

15.8 By 2020, introduce measures to prevent the introduction and significantly reduce the impact of invasive alien species on land and water ecosystems and control or eradicate the priority species

---

* Email: Drossos.Stamboulakis@monash.edu; jsander4@usc.edu.au. We thank Anna Beckers for her helpful comments and suggestions. The editors and participants at the workshop held online in September 2020 also provided useful contextual and textual recommendations. Finally, we express our appreciation to the organisers of this project on the Sustainable Development Goals and Private International Law: they have been patient, adaptable and indefatigable during a challenging time.

15.9	By 2020, integrate ecosystem and biodiversity values into national and local planning, development processes, poverty reduction strategies and accounts
15.a	Mobilize and significantly increase financial resources from all sources to conserve and sustainably use biodiversity and ecosystems
15.b	Mobilize significant resources from all sources and at all levels to finance sustainable forest management and provide adequate incentives to developing countries to advance such management, including for conservation and reforestation
15.c	Enhance global support for efforts to combat poaching and trafficking of protected species, including by increasing the capacity of local communities to pursue sustainable livelihood opportunities

1. INTRODUCTION

The key question addressed in this chapter is whether private international law can assist in achieving Sustainable Development Goal 15 (SDG 15), particularly in protecting and sustainably managing terrestrial ecosystems, forests and biodiversity. In answering this question, we consider the global governance role that private international law can – and perhaps ought to – play in facilitating and incentivising private action geared at environmental protection and sustainability. This exploration has become increasingly important given the apparent paradox between the well-documented and ongoing decline of environmental markers (e.g. biodiversity and deforestation) globally,[1] despite the widespread global reach and support for the pro-sustainability and environmental protection values embedded in SDG 15.

This chapter has three substantive sections. Section 2 sets out the aims, targets and public international law grounding of SDG 15, as well as the case for engaging the private sector. Section 3 considers the relationships or intersections between private international law and SDG 15. We explore these through an analysis of regulatory approaches that support private litigation for environmental harm, and the increasing use of voluntary (trade-based) measures that aim to achieve sustainability *through* (rather than despite) trade and development. We turn finally, in section 4, to consider whether and how private international law might better facilitate private action in achieving SDG 15. We explore the environmental governance aspirations of private international law, as well as canvass a range of ways in which private international law can be adapted to do so. We conclude by highlighting not only that this is possible, but that taking greater account of the pressing environmental and sustainability concerns embodied in SDG 15 can be consistent with the normative basis of private international law.

2. UNPACKING SDG 15

The reach of SDG 15 is deceptively modest, as disclosed by its short title: 'Life on Land'. It focuses on the steps and methods states must take to protect, conserve and encourage the sustainable use of various terrestrial environments, spanning a number of complex environmental issues, including managing forests, combating desertification, and halting land degradation and biodiversity loss. Despite SDG 15's broad remit, progress towards it, like towards other SDGs, has been slow, and perhaps even retreating. As the

---

1 For example, the Intergovernmental Science-Policy Platform on Biodiversity and Ecosystem Services (IPBES) Report highlights that declining biodiversity is sustained by a paradigm in which economic activity trumps conservation, and that biodiversity continues to decline at alarming rates: 'Global Assessment Report on Biodiversity and Ecosystem Services | IPBES' <https://www.ipbes.net/global-assessment-report-biodiversity-ecosystem-services> accessed 1 November 2019.

United Nations Economic and Social Council noted, in a report reviewing the progress of the SDGs:[2]

> [T]he 2020 targets of Sustainable Development Goal 15 are unlikely to be met, land degradation continues, biodiversity loss is occurring at an alarming rate, and invasive species and the illicit poaching and trafficking of wildlife continue to thwart efforts to protect and restore vital ecosystems and species.

The United Nations Sustainable Development Goals Report 2020 also notes that despite 'valiant' efforts to turn the tide, including in sustainable forest management, more protected areas and progress in implementing biodiversity protection:[3]

> Conservation of terrestrial ecosystems is not trending towards sustainability. Forest areas continue to decline at an alarming rate, protected areas are not concentrated in sites known for their biological diversity, and species remain threatened with extinction. Moreover, surging wildlife crime, land use changes such as deforestation, and habitat encroachment are primary pathways of transmission for emerging infectious diseases, including COVID-19, threatening public health and the world economy.

The finding that achieving SDG 15 is a long way off is reinforced in other scientific and environmental literature. For example, the 2019 Intergovernmental Science-Policy Platform on Biodiversity and Ecosystem Services (IPBES) Report highlights the continuing decline of biodiversity globally at unprecedented rates, and the devastating effects this is having on local and indigenous communities.[4] The Report also confirms that declines in biodiversity mean that most international societal and environmental goals – such as those embodied in the Aichi Biodiversity Targets and the 2030 Agenda for the Sustainable Development Goals – will not be achieved. At the same time as this backwards progress on environmental goals globally, both states and private firms are increasingly focused on and formalising commitments to the environment and sustainability generally, particularly to concepts embedded in SDG 15.

Before considering the measures taken to pursue SDG 15, it is useful to break the goal into its constituent parts. SDG 15 is comprised of nine targets, and three means of implementation, set out immediately before this chapter. We consider

---

2 United Nations Economic and Social Council, 'Special Edition: Progress towards the Sustainable Development Goals: Report of the Secretary-General' (8 May 2019).

3 Nigel Dudley et al. 'Protected areas and the sustainable development goals' (2017) 23.2 Parks 9-12.

4 Intergovernmental Science-Policy Platform on Biodiversity and Ecosystem Services (IPBES), 'Global Assessment Report on Biodiversity and Ecosystem Services | IPBES' <https://www.ipbes.net/global-assessment-report-biodiversity-ecosystem-services> accessed 1 November 2019.

each in turn. Importantly, we see that SDG 15 targets are expressed strongly as obligations to 'conserve', 'restore' or 'protect' critical environments from further damage, and also to improve the overall governance and sustainable use of natural resources and ecosystems.[5] While the focus of this chapter is on private international law's impact on achieving SDG 15, it is necessary to begin with the way in which public international law informs and sustains SDG 15. This is because, as the following section explores, the SDGs were formulated primarily with public international law definitions and objectives in mind.

2.1. SDG 15's ENVIRONMENTAL (PUBLIC INTERNATIONAL) LAW GROUNDING

Both environmental law and SDG 15 share a commitment to the concept of sustainable development, and SDG 15's targets map on to, and are designed primarily around, the demarcation of environmental issues seen in a series of widely adopted public international law instruments (primarily treaties). For example, SDG 15's targets stem from and reinforce the obligations in key sustainable development treaties with respect to:

- '[c]onservation, restoration and sustainable use of terrestrial and inland freshwater ecosystems and their services' (Target 15.1, stemming from the Ramsar Convention (Wetlands)),[6] which is to occur 'in line with obligations under international agreements';
- combating desertification (Target 15.3, stemming from the Convention to Combat Desertification);[7]
- biodiversity (Target 15.5, stemming from the Convention on Biological Diversity);[8] and
- conservation of or trade in protected species (Target 15.7, stemming from the Convention on International Trade in Endangered Species of Wild Fauna and Flora).[9]

---

5 Measuring achievement of the targets is done by a series of indicators that sit beneath each target. This is itself subject to detailed analysis and varies over time. For example, the indicators under Targets 15.a and 15.b have recently been amended by the 2020 Comprehensive Review Proposals Submitted to the 51st session of the United Nations Statistical Commission.

6 Convention on Wetlands of International Importance Especially as Waterfowl Habitat (adopted 2 February 1971, entered into force 21 December 1975) 996 UNTS 245 (Ramsar Convention).

7 Convention to Combat Desertification in Those Countries Experiencing Serious Drought and/or Desertification, Particularly in Africa (adopted 14 October 1994, entered into force 26 December 1996) 1954 UNTS 3.

8 Convention on Biological Diversity (adopted 5 June 1992, entered into force 29 December 1993) 1760 UNTS 79 (CBD).

9 Convention on International Trade in Endangered Species of Wild Fauna and Flora (adopted 3 March 1973, entered into force 1 July 1975) 993 UNTS 243 (CITES).

Each of these targets – and the treaties that underlie them – attempts to give context and meaning to the way in which development should occur within the bounds and parameters of sustainable action, in a particular sector or domain (biodiversity, trade in endangered species, etc.). Because there is no way to set a bright line as to acceptable levels of development and sustainability in general – particularly as these obligations in public international law span a diversity of legal instruments and employ a 'vast array' of legal standards and principles – sustainable development can best be conceived of as a form of 'evolutive norm'.[10] In other words, it is a guiding or aspirational principle that aims to mediate competing concerns of intergenerational and intragenerational equity: balancing the need to preserve and conserve the terrestrial environment for future generations, rather than exhausting it for present development (intergenerational), with allowing for and equitably distributing proceeds of development, either within communities, across legal units (usually within a country), or globally (intragenerational).[11] Hence, SDG 15's targets – which draw heavily on environmental treaty obligations – share a commitment to realising a form of sustainable development.

The precise formulation of language in SDG 15's targets often also draws directly from public international law treaties or commonly understood meanings of key terms used by treaty secretariats (or arms of the United Nations). For example, the concept of 'sustainable use' features heavily in the SDGs generally, and specifically in SDG 15.[12] This term is defined in Article 2 of the Convention on Biological Diversity (CBD) as:

> the use of components of biological diversity in a way and at a rate that does not lead to the long-term decline of biological diversity, thereby maintaining its potential to meet the needs and aspirations of present and future generations.

This commitment to 'sustainable use' is also seen in the operation of the Convention on International Trade in Endangered Species of Wild Fauna and Flora (CITES). Although the Convention was signed in 1973–17 years before the Rio Earth Summit, where the 'sustainable use' term of art came to prominence – the CITES Secretariat and Conference of Parties to the Convention alike have subsequently adopted the concept as informing understanding of the obligations contained in the CITES. For example, regularly stressing the need for

10 See, generally, Virginie Barral, 'Sustainable Development in International Law: Nature and Operation of an Evolutive Legal Norm' (2012) 23 European Journal of International Law 377.

11 ibid 380–381.

12 This is seen in the debate and final form of the SDGs as a whole, and specifically in SDG 15 (in its overall chapeau), in Target 15.1, and means of implementation Target 15.a). This point is made by Andrew, in considering the trade-related aspects of SDG 15: Dale Andrew, 'Trade and Sustainable Development Goal (SDG) 15: Promoting "Life on Land" through Mandatory and Voluntary Approaches' (2017) 700 ADBI Working Paper Series, 5.

'legal and sustainable use' to support the Convention's role in 'regulating for legal, sustainable and traceable trade in wildlife'.[13] Further, Target 15.6 ('promote fair and equitable sharing of benefits') replicates a key goal in biodiversity conservation in precisely the same terms as the CBD and the subsequently agreed Nagoya Protocol.[14] Consequently, these shared terminologies and understandings inform the operation of SDG 15.

Despite close links, there remains a significant conceptual difference between the approach in SDG 15 and environmental law instruments. In particular, SDG 15 does not require deference to developmental interests to the same extent as environmental law instruments. SDG 15 is, foremost, a series of aspirational targets aimed at extending conservation and protection of environments beyond present levels. In this sense, it focuses much more heavily on the sustainable component of sustainable development. For example, SDG 15's goals not only reinforce and build on the objectives of environmental law instruments (as discussed above), but also set bold ambitions. This is seen in the high-level language of the targets employed in SDG 15: to '*ensure* … conservation, restoration and sustainable use', to '*promote*', to '*combat* desertification', and to '*take* … urgent and significant action'. By contrast, environmental law instruments defer to development to a greater extent: often leaving the definition of key indicators and terms to their specific socio-environmental contexts; operating via a series of obligations of means; and devolving responsibility to states to develop *national* strategies and plans in a fashion 'appropriate' for each implementing state.[15] This represents a significant deference to national development priorities, and hence a degree of latitude in employing environmental protection measures.[16]

---

13 A point made in ibid 6. The reference to sustainable use permeates many CITES documents, such as the *CITES Strategic Vision: 2008–2020*, and key resolutions like the *Sustainable use of biodiversity: Addis Ababa Principles and Guidelines*.

14 Conference of the Parties to the Convention on Biological Diversity, Report of the Sixth Meeting of the Conference of the Parties to the Convention on Biological Diversity (2010) UNEP/CBD/COP/10/27, [103] and Annex (Decision X/1, Annex, 89–109) (Nagoya Protocol on Access to Genetic Resources and the Fair and Equitable Sharing of Benefits Arising from their Utilization to the Convention on Biological Diversity) (Nagoya Protocol).

15 For example, in the context of biodiversity protection, the provisions of the CBD have been criticised, as the measures are potentially so vague as to lose meaning, based on allowing states latitude to act in an essentially unrestricted fashion. This is seen in the language of 'as far as possible and as appropriate' which presages almost every instrumental obligation in the CBD. See, further, Drossos Stamboulakis and Jay Sanderson, 'Certifying Biodiversity: The Union for Ethical BioTrade and the Search for Ethical Sourcing' (2020) 32 Journal of Environmental Law 503, 507–509.

16 Nonetheless, sustainability and environmental protection still serve as a primary rule in hundreds of environmental treaties, shaping their interpretation, implementation and application by judges and governments alike. Cf Vaughan Lowe, 'Sustainable Development and Unsustainable Arguments' in Alan Boyle and David Freestone (eds), *International Law and Sustainable Development: Past Achievements and Future Challenges* (OUP 1999), as explored in Virginie Barral, 'Sustainable Development in International Law: Nature and Operation of an Evolutive Legal Norm' (2012) 23 European Journal of International Law 377, 388 et seq.

Perhaps representing the strong pro-sustainability focus of SDG 15, the primary response to implementing it has been via large-scale public programmes driven by states and developmental organisations.[17] Yet, given the lacunae that arise because public international law instruments focus on states as their subject, SDG 15 has increasingly been interpreted to offer support for directly encouraging pro-social and pro-environmental conduct of *private* actors.

2.2. TRADE AND ENGAGING PRIVATE ACTORS IN THE IMPLEMENTATION OF SDG 15

Private actors are increasingly being encouraged to play a role in achieving SDG 15. In this conception, public and private actors or mechanisms are not styled as alternatives; rather they suggest a relationship of complementarity in which one reinforces the other in the pursuit of global governance goals (notably in this context, sustainability and environmental protection with respect to 'life on land').[18] The need for greater private-sector engagement derives from the text of SDG 15 itself, and from wider developments by the United Nations, civil society and the business community. Perhaps the most germane drivers from within SDG 15 are its three means of implementation. They read as follows:

> Means of implementation
>
> 15.a. Mobilize and significantly increase financial resources from all sources to conserve and sustainably use biodiversity and ecosystems
>
> 15.b. Mobilize significant resources from all sources and at all levels to finance sustainable forest management and provide adequate incentives to developing countries to advance such management, including for conservation and reforestation
>
> 15.c. Enhance global support for efforts to combat poaching and trafficking of protected species, including by increasing the capacity of local communities to pursue sustainable livelihood opportunities

As Dale Andrew notes, all of these means of implementation are 'trade-relevant'.[19] In other words, they call for policy interventions that promote and encourage private sector dealings in a manner consistent with the goals of SDG 15.

---

[17] A number of these are explored in the context of biodiversity in Peter Bridgewater et al, 'Implementing SDG 15: Can Large-Scale Public Programs Help Deliver Biodiversity Conservation, Restoration and Management, While Assisting Human Development?' (2015) 39 Natural Resources Forum 214.

[18] Fabrizio Cafaggi, 'The Many Features of Transnational Private Rule-Making: Unexplored Relationships between Custom, Jura Mercatorum and Global Private Regulation' (2014) 36 University of Pennsylvania Journal of International Law 875.

[19] Dale Andrew, 'Trade and Sustainable Development Goal (SDG) 15: Promoting "Life on Land" through Mandatory and Voluntary Approaches' 3.

This approach to the implementation of SDG 15 foregrounds the idea that while the primary responsibility for achieving SDG 15 rests with states, pursuit of sustainability goals requires extending legal obligations to private actors. Thus, SDG 15's push to promote greater engagement with conservation and sustainable use and management can also be conceived of as expanding the traditional public international law demarcation of state responsibility. This reflects a polycentric view of governance: premised upon a mix of private and public obligation, collaboration, and interaction.[20]

This form of polycentric governance has long been championed in sector-specific terrestrial environmental protection approaches. In particular, in the field of forestry, widely adopted standards and certification measures have increasingly highlighted the importance of the market, and other non-state authorities, in achieving sustainable outcomes.[21] As Cashore, Auld and Newsom put it, in a book entitled *Governing Through Markets*, the diverse range of institutions and actors who aim to promote sustainable development in the forestry sector can be described as:[22]

> 'non-state market-driven' governance systems because rule-making clout does not come from traditional Westphalian state-centered sovereign authority but rather from companies along the market's supply chain, who make their own individual evaluations as to whether to comply to the rules and procedures of these private governance systems. Environmental groups and other non-governmental organizations (NGOs) attempt to influence company evaluations through economic carrots (the promise of market access or potential price premiums) and sticks (public and market campaigns aimed at pressuring companies to support certification).

This shift to a consideration of market impacts and the role of civil society and certification has also occurred in other environmental fields. For example, in an article that explores the role of private actors certifying products sourced from biodiversity, we concluded that '[private] biodiversity schemes assist in identifying and improving biodiversity practices in countries where companies source natural ingredients (often in circumstances of weak domestic biodiversity protection)'.[23] Other contributions around biodiversity have also begun to

---

20 See, for a recent review of differing perspectives on global governance, Rakhyun E Kim, 'Is Global Governance Fragmented, Polycentric, or Complex? The State of the Art of the Network Approach' (2020) 22 International Studies Review 903.

21 This conception of a polycentric mode of governance in forestry – premised on market incentives – dates back at least decades. See, for example, Ronnie D Lipschutz, 'Why Is There No International Forestry Law: An Examination of International Forestry Regulation, Both Public and Private' (2000) 19 Journal of Environmental Law 153.

22 Benjamin William Cashore et al, *Governing Through Markets: Forest Certification and the Emergence of Non-State Authority* (Yale University Press 2004) 4.

23 Drossos Stamboulakis and Jay Sanderson, 'Certifying Biodiversity: The Union for Ethical BioTrade and the Search for Ethical Sourcing' (2020) 32 Journal of Environmental Law 503, 526.

directly analyse how the space reserved for private contracts to aid access and benefit-sharing for genetic resources sourced from biodiversity means that private international law has a governance role to play.[24] This reflects the broader idea of achieving terrestrial environmental goals, such as those contained in SDG 15, via a more fulsome understanding of the 'transnational regulatory space':[25] that is, a space in which the dual nature of public/private initiatives and responsibilities are increasingly important and acknowledged, and the governance role of both private and public international law explored.

What we are witnessing now is a broader focus on private contributions to sustainability action across all domains. This has been promoted strongly by civil society and intergovernmental organisations, perhaps most prominently in January 2020 with the United Nations Secretary-General formally launching priorities for the 'Decade of Action', a plan aimed at delivering the SDGs by 2030.[26] Reflecting the trade-related means of implementation, private action features heavily in this plan, including the need to facilitate pro-sustainability financing and trade, engage local and global partners to pursue sustainability goals, and further mobilise private actors (including both firms and civil society) to push for greater corporate engagement and adherence to the sustainability goals of the SDGs.[27]

Efforts to engage the private sector also extend directly to terrestrial environmental concerns, the focus of SDG 15. Perhaps most notable is the SDG Compass, a joint initiative of the Global Reporting Initiative, the UN Global Compact and the World Business Council for Sustainable Development. The Compass is designed to 'support companies in aligning their strategies with the SDGs and, in measuring and managing their contribution [to achieving the SDGs]',[28] provides a series of practical measures – ranging from understanding

---

24 Elisa Morgera and Lorna Gillies, 'Realising the Objectives of Public International Environmental Law through Private Contracts: The Need for a Dialogue with Private International Law Scholars' in Verónica Ruiz Abou-Nigm et al (eds), *Linkages and Boundaries in Private and Public International Law* (Hart Publishing 2018); Henning Grosse Ruse-Khan, 'The Private International Law of Access and Benefit-Sharing Contracts' in Carlos Correa and Xavier Seuba (eds), *Intellectual Property and Development: Understanding the Interfaces: Liber amicorum Pedro Roffe* (Springer 2019).

25 Fabrizio Cafaggi, 'The Many Features of Transnational Private Rule-Making: Unexplored Relationships between Custom, Jura Mercatorum and Global Private Regulation' (2014) 36 University of Pennsylvania Journal of International Law 875.

26 United Nations Secretary-General, 'Remarks to the General Assembly on the Secretary-General's Priorities for 2020' (22 January 2020) <https://www.un.org/sg/en/content/sg/speeches/2020-01-22/remarks-general-assembly-priorities-for-2020> accessed 27 July 2020.

27 United Nations Sustainable Development, 'Decade of Action' <https://www.un.org/sustainabledevelopment/decade-of-action/> accessed 27 July 2020.

28 'SDG Compass – A Guide for Business Action to Advance the Sustainable Development Goals' <https://sdgcompass.org/> accessed 24 July 2020.

the SDGs, to defining company priorities, setting goals, integrating sustainable practices into core business, and reporting and communicating on SDG performance. For example, the Compass recommends engaging a diverse range of stakeholders (with proper concern for marginalised and vulnerable groups) in any decision-making that has sustainability impacts, and mapping high-impact areas along the value chain to each of the SDGs. Under SDG 15, this requires a scrutiny of sourcing practices that may have an adverse impact on sustainability (such as sourcing from endangered biodiversity) and searching for alternatives.

The key question that remains unanswered under this conception of private action to support SDG 15 is whether this engagement is merely supposed to be a matter for the normative power of sub-legal corporate social responsibility (CSR), or ought to be supported by the operation of procedural law, such as private international law.[29] What is clear, however, is that SDG 15 is increasingly being theorised and operationalised as extending to private actors. It is this conception – rather than SDG 15's primary embodiment in or intersection with state obligations – that we use to analyse the potential of private international law in achieving SDG 15.

3. PRIVATE INTERNATIONAL LAW AND SDG 15's CONCERNS

Given that modern supply chains are interconnected globally, and there are pressing problems presented by production as a driver of environmental damage, there is a regular intersection of private international law rules with sustainability concerns. This is because environmental harms do not stop at legal boundaries, and, most relevantly from a commercial perspective, many transnational legal structures or economic organisations of companies, subsidiaries or supply chain relationships span multiple jurisdictions. As Jonas Ebbesson suggests:[30]

> From a justice perspective, the main concern is whether the locals – i.e. those affected in the state of the activity/harm – may make the transnational corporation responsible, so as to prevent or remedy harm, through legal proceedings outside that state, for example in the home state of the parent company. If no such opportunities

---

29 The potential trade-off between the normative power of CSR actions and legal enforcement avenues is one of the primary concerns of scholars considering the intersection of sustainability and private law. See, for example, Anna Beckers and Mark T Kawakami, 'Why Domestic Enforcement of Private Regulation Is (Not) the Answer: Making and Questioning the Case of Corporate Social Responsibility Codes' (2017) 24 Indiana Journal of Global Legal Studies 1.

30 Jonas Ebbesson, 'Piercing the State Veil in Pursuit of Environmental Justice' in Jonas Ebbesson and Phoebe Okowa (eds), *Environmental Law and Justice in Context* (CUP 2009) 270–271.

are available, or if international law so prevents, transnational corporations can benefit from inadequate national institutions and laws, and abuse jurisdictional borders so as to avoid taking appropriate measures to prevent, restore or compensate for harm.

In this section, rather than mapping private international law rules comprehensively, we focus on two situations where private international law rules significantly impact transnational corporations' responsibility for environmental matters. The first situation is where private international law rules operate to either support or limit private parties' cause of actions (usually in tort or delict) to achieve an injunction or damages against a firm that has caused damage to the environment. Traditionally these cases are brought in developed jurisdictions for harm that has occurred elsewhere – usually in places with relatively lax environmental regulation.[31] States, through their rules of private international law, can facilitate the use or extension of environmental protection obligations to private entities, such as corporations. The second situation involves market-based forms of environmental governance, usually underpinned by some sort of certification measure that is marketable to consumers. Private law, including private international law, plays a significant role here in holding firms that *choose* to legally commit themselves to higher environmental or sustainability standards than are otherwise legally required to those standards. In both cases, civil litigation is a way of enforcing environmental standards.

3.1. A REGULATORY APPROACH: PRIVATE ENFORCEMENT OF TORT-BASED ENVIRONMENTAL ACTIONS

Private international law's intersection with terrestrial environment concerns is seen most directly in the governance or regulatory role it plays in facilitating (or limiting) environmental actions against transnational corporations based on rights as civil tort/delict claims under the Alien Tort Statute (ATS) in the United States,[32] under European private international law, including within EU instruments,[33] and, recently, liability for breaches of duty of care in the English common law of negligence.[34] The private international law aspects of environmental actions, and intersections with the corporate form, under the

31 Geert van Calster, *European Private International Law* (2nd ed, Hart Publishing 2016) 357.

32 This ATS provision was originally a provision of the Judiciary Act 1789 (US) and is now recorded in federal code: 28 U.S.C. §1350. The ATS is also often referred to as the Alien Tort Claims Act.

33 The Brussels I Regulation offers a starting point from its general ground of jurisdiction (Art 4(1), read in conjunction with Art 63(1)), which will also be applicable. Also of note, and discussed below, is the specific environmental choice-of-law rule of Art 7 Rome II.

34 Discussed further below, but coming to prominence in the United Kingdom in the case of *Vedanta Resources plc and Another v Lungowe and Others* [2019] UKSC 20 (Supreme Court).

ATS and the EU approach have been extensively canvassed – and critiqued – elsewhere.[35] For this reason, we provide only a brief sketch of these approaches, and instead focus attention on the ways that extant private international rules intersect with environmental matters. We also note that, despite significant efforts to achieve environmental-inspired harmonised private international law rules, which we set out in section 4.2.2, these do not form a part of the global private international law landscape, as no such agreement has been successful.

3.1.1. *Jurisdiction*

The question of jurisdiction is the first hurdle that plaintiffs in transnational civil litigation for environmental actions face. The primary legal difficulty usually arises here due to the corporate form – as plaintiffs often seek to litigate against parent corporations in relatively more developed jurisdictions, rather than subsidiaries often located in jurisdictions with relatively lax environmental standards. This presents an initial hurdle for private environmental action, as rules of jurisdiction generally require a nexus based on some link to the state in question, for example via the location of the corporate headquarters or domicile, or marketing into that jurisdiction, such that the law of that state can be used as a 'jack for regulatory performance abroad'.[36] We consider how issues of jurisdiction for environmental actions based on tort have been handled within American and European private international law.

3.1.1.1. United States

Much scholarly attention has focused on the potential of using the ATS to hold transnational corporations to account for subsidiaries' conduct, including with respect to environmental harms.[37] The discussion arises as the ATS allows US district courts subject-matter jurisdiction over actions 'by an alien [non-US national] for a tort only, committed in violation of the law of nations or a treaty of the United States'. Thus, on its face, the ATS potentially allows foreign litigants to

---

35 See, for example, Geert van Calster, *European Private International Law* (2nd ed, Hart Publishing 2016) 357, 357–374. See also Hans van Loon, 'Principles and Building Blocks for a Global Legal Framework for Transnational Civil Litigation in Environmental Matters' (2018) 23 Uniform Law Review 298.

36 Geert van Calster, 'Environmental Law and Private International Law' in Emma Lees and Jorge E Viñuales (eds), *The Oxford Handbook of Comparative Environmental Law* (OUP 2019) 1141.

37 See, for example, the authorities and cases discussed in: Kathleen Jawger, 'Environmental Claims under the Alien Tort Statute' (2010) 28 Berkeley Journal of International Law 519. See also: Tony Kupersmith, 'Cutting to the Chase: Corporate Liability for Environmental Harm under the Alien Tort Statute, Kiobel, and Congress Note' (2012–2013) 37 William and Mary Environmental Law and Policy Review 885, 906–914.

bring suit for environmental harm suffered in breach of customary international law (or deriving from a treaty the US is a party to), even for conduct occurring outside the United States, and against foreign companies that are based outside of the country. However, no environmental ATS cases have been successful, and the prospects of these actions succeeding is limited.

This is the case, first, because case law developments in the United States in and since *Kiobel*[38] was decided by the Supreme Court have 'most likely eliminated' the avenue of pursuing actions for conduct outside the United States, by foreign plaintiffs against foreign companies based outside of the United States.[39] The rationale for this stems from the oft-cited extract of Chief Judge Jacobs sitting on the United States Second Circuit Court of Appeals in *Kiobel*, which emphasised that attempting to use the US courts to bring transnational corporations of other countries to account would lead to 'the very opposite of the universal consensus that sustains customary international law'.[40] Overcoming previous decisions that had taken an expansive view of general jurisdiction, the majority of the Supreme Court preferred a view that ATS claims must 'touch and concern the territory of the United States … with sufficient force to displace the presumption against extraterritorial application'.[41] The minority – who supported the outcome but disagreed with the reasoning – did not find a presumption against application, but held that jurisdiction under the ATS required a stronger connection to American interests, namely that the tort occurs in America, the defendant is an American national, or the defendant's conduct 'substantially and adversely affects an important American national interest'.[42] This was reinforced by the 2014 case of *Daimler AG v Bauman*,[43] where the Supreme Court unambiguously held that the ATS does not override the need for personal jurisdiction over a foreign corporate defendant. Absent evidence such as incorporation in the relevant jurisdiction (California), any pleaded links were not so '"continuous and systematic" as to render [the corporate defendant or its subsidiaries] essentially at home in the forum State'.[44] To put a further nail in the coffin, the Supreme Court in *Jesner et al v Arab Bank*[45] held that liability under the ATS does not

---

38 US Supreme Court, 17 April 2013, *Kiobel et al v Royal Dutch Petroleum Co et al*, 569 US (2013).

39 Hans van Loon, 'Principles and Building Blocks for a Global Legal Framework for Transnational Civil Litigation in Environmental Matters' (2018) 23 Uniform Law Review 298, 306.

40 *Kiobel v Royal Dutch Petroleum Co*, 642 F.3d 268 (2d Cir. 2011) 270.

41 *Kiobel et al v Royal Dutch Petroleum Co et al*, 569 US (2013), 4–6, 15 (Roberts CJ delivered the opinion of the Court, in which Scalia, Kennedy, Thomas and Alito JJ joined).

42 *Kiobel et al v Royal Dutch Petroleum Co et al*, 569 US (2013), 14–15 (Breyer J, with whom Ginsburg, Sotomayor and Kagan JJ agreed).

43 US Supreme Court, 14 January 2014, *Daimler AG v Bauman, et al*, 134 S. Ct. 746 (2014).

44 134 S. Ct. 746 (2014), 8 (per Ginsburg J).

45 US Supreme Court, 24 April 2018, *Jesner et al v Arab Bank* 584 US ___ (2018) (per Kennedy J, with whom Roberts CJ and Thomas, Alito and Gorsuch JJ joined for the relevant parts).

extend to foreign *corporate* defendants (as distinct from natural persons or states under international law). For these reasons, the ATS offers little succour for plaintiffs pursuing environmental actions for conduct that occurs outside the United States, against foreign companies that are commercially active in – but based outside – the country.[46]

The second reason why environmental actions under the ATS have faced little prospect of success is because, in the views of US courts, environmental norms 'have not sufficiently crystallized' into the law of nations (customary international law).[47] The rights or norms relied upon in ATS broadly arise in three categories: combating cross-border pollution, the right to sustainable development and the rights to life, health and the environment. No claims based on these rights have been successful to date, based largely on criticisms of their 'vague and amorphous' nature, or their lack of a 'specific, universal and obligatory' character.[48] For example, in *Flores v Southern Peru Copper*, the plaintiff's ATS action against a corporate defendant for mining operations that were alleged to have caused environmental and health harms was dismissed as it could not be established that 'high levels of environmental pollution … violate well-established, universally recognized norms of international law'.[49]

Kiobel itself is a further example of this difficulty. The case can broadly be described as environmental, as it involves a collective action by Nigerian nationals ('aliens' in the ATS terminology), against two large petroleum holding companies, and their joint subsidiary, in the context of poor environmental outcomes in oil exploration and production. However, what was pleaded in the ATS claim was that the law of nations was violated based on the subsequent suppression of protests against the environmental harms.[50] Notably, the fact of the environmental harm itself was not argued, likely because of the difficulties in demonstrating that environmental harms are sufficiently definite and certain to form part of the law of nations.

Nonetheless, as the environmental protection values in SDG 15 continue to be adopted by both states and the private sector, the more likely these norms are

---

See also, *Nestle USA, Inc v DOE et al*, 593 US ___ (2021), where an ATS claim based on forced labour failed due to the lack of sufficient connection between the offending conduct and the corporate entity pursued in the United States.

46 Hans van Loon, 'Principles and Building Blocks for a Global Legal Framework for Transnational Civil Litigation in Environmental Matters' (2018) 23 Uniform Law Review 298, 306–310.

47 Tony Kupersmith, 'Cutting to the Chase: Corporate Liability for Environmental Harm under the Alien Tort Statute, Kiobel, and Congress Note' (2012–2013) 37 William and Mary Environmental Law and Policy Review 885, 906.

48 Kupersmith cites a range of ATS authorities that support this characterisation: ibid 907–911.

49 253 F. Supp. 2d 510, 512, 525 (S.D.N.Y. 2002), cited in ibid 910.

50 The claims at first instance were summarised in the Supreme Court judgment as being based upon: (1) extrajudicial killings; (2) crimes against humanity; (3) torture and cruel treatment; (4) arbitrary arrest and detention; (5) violations of the rights to life, liberty, security, and association; (6) forced exile; and (7) property destruction.

to be treated as sufficiently definite and certain to support private environmental actions. This is true both in the context of ATS claims (mediated through customary international law and human rights law), but also more broadly for other private international law responses. As Atapattu notes, sustainable development norms stemming from both binding and non-binding instruments permeate customary international law, and the SDGs can serve as clear criteria for measuring and achieving sustainability outcomes.[51]

3.1.1.2. European Private International Law

Since the restrictive view of the US Supreme Court on jurisdiction under the ATS has emerged, the EU has been said to be the most promising arena for litigants deriving jurisdiction against companies based in the EU.[52] Claiming jurisdiction in these circumstances is relatively uncontroversial, as under the Brussels I Regulation, an acceptable basis of jurisdiction is the defendant's corporate or registered seat – its domicile – in any EU Member State.[53] As van Calster notes, however, the challenge is often that the ability to sue a parent company (domiciled in the EU) does not simplify bringing actions against any subsidiary companies (domiciled outside the EU).[54] As against companies outside the EU, national private international law rules apply (Art 6 Brussels Regulation). These can range from flexible rules based on the plaintiff's nationality (seen most notably in France), through to some form of minimum contact with the jurisdiction (in limited cases of *forum necessitatis*).[55]

Perhaps most recently, another potential avenue for parent company liability for environmental harm may be said to arise under the common law of tort, as expounded in recent decisions in both the Netherlands and the United Kingdom. In February 2021, the Supreme Court in the United Kingdom handed down judgment in *Okpabi*,[56] overturning the Court of Appeal's decision limiting parent

---

51 Sumudu Atapattu, 'From Our Common Future to Sustainable Development Goals: Evolution of Sustainable Development under International Law' (2018–2019) 36 Wisconsin International Law Journal 215, 235; Sumudu Atapattu, *Emerging Principles of International Environmental Law* (Brill 2007).

52 Hans van Loon, 'Principles and Building Blocks for a Global Legal Framework for Transnational Civil Litigation in Environmental Matters' (2018) 23 Uniform Law Review 298, 310–313.

53 Art 4(1), read in conjunction with Art 63(1).

54 Van Cals Geert van Calster, 'Environmental Law and Private International Law' in Emma Lees and Jorge E Viñuales (eds), *The Oxford Handbook of Comparative Environmental Law* (OUP 2019) 1149. Van Calster explores the approach within the EU, both under Brussels I, and in national laws within Europe.

55 Noting that these circumstances are heavily limited. See, further, Stephanie Redfield, 'Searching for Justice: The Use of Forum Necessitatis' (2013–2014) 45 Georgetown Journal of International Law 893.

56 *Okpabi and Others v Royal Dutch Shell plc and Another* [2021] UKSC 3 (Supreme Court).

company liability, and reaffirming its findings in the 2019 case of *Vedanta*.[57] In that case, Lord Briggs (with whom the Court agreed) set out the principles by which parent company liability could be established, noting that '[e]verything depends on the extent to which, and the way in which, the parent availed itself of the opportunity to take over, intervene in, control, supervise or advise the management of the relevant operations (including land use) of the subsidiary'.[58]

Notably, both cases involved liability for a foreign-based parent company for the environmental harms of their subsidiaries. *Vedanta* was an action bought by Zambian nationals for waste said to be negligently discharged from a copper mine that polluted the environment and caused personal injury and property damage. The mine operator was run by the Zambian subsidiary with a UK-incorporated parent company. The parent–subsidiary liability in *Okpabi*[59] was similar, although occurring in Nigeria, with significant environmental harm flowing from oil spills. The Supreme Court summarised the appellants' case as follows:

> 7. The appellants' case against RDS [the parent company] is that it owed them a common law duty of care because, as pleaded, it exercised significant control over material aspects of SPDC's [the subsidiary] operations and/or assumed responsibility for SPDC's operations, including by the promulgation and imposition of mandatory health, safety and environmental policies, standards and manuals which allegedly failed to protect the appellants against the risk of foreseeable harm arising from SPDC's operations. It is agreed that the issue of governing law should be approached on the basis that the laws of England and Wales and the law of Nigeria are materially the same.
>
> 8. In addition to the claims against RDS, the appellants allege that SPDC is also liable for damage caused by those oil spills under various Nigerian statutory and common law causes of action.

After reviewing the evidence, the Supreme Court was satisfied that the appellants had put forth at least an arguable case in relation to evidence of RDS's control, direction and oversight of the pollution and environmental compliance, and the operation of the oil infrastructure, of its Nigerian subsidiary. Evidence relied upon included the degree of monitoring, the promulgation of standards, and the degree of shared responsibility (or overall control) of RDS over its subsidiary with respect to environmental issues.[60] Notably, this is not a decision on the merits, as the finding of the Supreme Court relates only to a jurisdictional challenge – which only requires a determination of whether there is a 'real issue to be tried', rather than a final determination on the matter. On this basis, the matter was remitted back to the lower court for determination.

---

57 *Vedanta Resources plc and Another v Lungowe and Others* [2019] UKSC 20 (Supreme Court).

58 ibid [49].

59 *Okpabi and Others v Royal Dutch Shell plc and Another* [2021] UKSC 3 (Supreme Court).

60 The evidence relied upon by the appellants is set out at [29]–[37].

Going further than the approach in *Okpabi*, on 29 January 2021, the Hague Court of Appeal, in *Milieudefensie v Shell*,[61] delivered a judgment on the merits in favour of the plaintiffs. The original basis for jurisdiction was the fact that RDS was incorporated in the Netherlands, and hence Dutch courts accepted jurisdiction based on the Brussels I Regulation Recast. This had led to a ground-breaking decision on jurisdiction in 2013,[62] based on the foreseeability that *both* relevant entities in the Shell Group – as in *Okpabi*, the parent company (RDS) and its daughter (SPDC) – had that they might face proceedings in the Netherlands regarding liability for the oil spills. The Hague Court of Appeal, explicitly following the approach to jurisdiction set out in *Vedanta* – as the applicable law was Nigeria, a common law jurisdiction that is likely to find UK Supreme Court decisions persuasive – found on the merits against both parties of the Shell Group.[63] This decision is the first case where a parent company was found to owe a duty of care, at common law, to claimants residing in a third state: namely, individuals in communities negatively impacted by the environmental harm of the Shell Group.[64]

These approaches demonstrate that although rules of adjudicatory jurisdiction are not designed in a context-sensitive way to reflect environmental concerns, there may still be limited avenues to pursue transnational environmental actions based on tort.

3.1.1.3. *Forum Non Conveniens*

One final note of caution in common law jurisdictions, however, is the further concern that the confluence of strict jurisdictional rules (requiring a substantial link to the forum) and the discretionary ability to decline jurisdiction based on *forum non conveniens* grounds often operate together to relegate plaintiffs' claims to the place where the harm occurred: usually a jurisdiction with less rigorous environmental regulation or enforcement.[65] *Forum non conveniens*

---

61 Hague Court of Appeal, 29 January 2021 (ECLI:NL:GHDHA:2021:132). We are indebted to Dr Roorda for the detailed summary of the judgment in English: Lucas Roorda, 'Wading through the (Polluted) Mud: The Hague Court of Appeals Rules on Shell in Nigeria', *RightsasUsual* (2 February 2021) <https://rightsasusual.com/?p=1388> accessed 23 April 2021.

62 As discussed in Evelyne Schmid, 'A Glass at Least Half Full: The Dutch Court Ruling on Akpan v Royal Dutch Shell/Shell Nigeria', *RightsasUsual* (26 February 2013) <https://rightsasusual.com/?p=265> accessed 23 April 2021.

63 References to *Vedanta* can be seen at [3.28]–[3.33] of the 2021 judgment.

64 A point made in the blog post of Lucas Roorda, 'Wading through the (Polluted) Mud: The Hague Court of Appeals Rules on Shell in Nigeria', *RightsasUsual* (2 February 2021), who also stresses that although the decision is by an EU Member State, the decision is limited to the common law, as the applicable law is the common law of Nigeria.

65 These comments have been made in the context of considering transnational environmental litigation and the intersections of private international law in Hans van Loon, 'Principles and Building Blocks for a Global Legal Framework for Transnational Civil Litigation in Environmental Matters' (2018) 23 Uniform Law Review 298, 309.

relates to a finding that the forum where the proceedings are brought is not the ideal forum to resolve the claim; thus even if the court has jurisdiction to hear the dispute, it retains a discretion to decline jurisdiction on the basis that another more convenient forum to settle the claim exists. In the context of the United States, this confluence has been described as one of the 'procedural hurdles' to an ATS claim succeeding.[66]

The difficulties in declining jurisdiction in this way are illustrated most clearly through the infamous Chevron–Ecuador dispute.[67] The case was originally brought as a class action in 1993, by Ecuadorian plaintiffs against Texaco in the Southern District of New York, the place where the corporate defendant, Texaco, was incorporated (domiciled).[68] Like many of the transnational environmental actions discussed in the immediately preceding section, the dispute concerned a subsidiary of Texaco and the way its oil-drilling activities caused significant environmental harm (via an oil spill). Chevron later acquired Texaco, and continued to defend proceedings. Chevron asked the Court to decline jurisdiction based on international comity, respect for Ecuador's sovereign interests (its ability enact laws and policies in relation to matters of the environment, land, development, and any regulation thereof), and based on findings about the integrity of the Ecuadorian judicial system.[69]

The Court determining jurisdiction agreed with Chevron, and declined jurisdiction on the basis that the claim should be brought before courts in Ecuador. The plaintiffs did so, and the Ecuadorian court found in their favour, obliging Chevron to pay damages for the harm caused to the environment. In a somewhat paradoxical fashion, Chevron – the party that had originally argued that Ecuador was an appropriate and capable forum for resolving the dispute, as the basis for the finding of *forum non conveniens*, against the objections of the plaintiffs who argued that justice could not be done there – then succeeded in

---

66 Kathleen Jawger, 'Environmental Claims under the Alien Tort Statute' (2010) 28 Berkeley Journal of International Law 519, 525.

67 There are significant differences in the *forum non conveniens* approach across common law jurisdictions. For the purposes of this chapter, however, we focus only this exemplar of practice in the United States. For a comparative overview of the doctrine across jurisdictions, see James Fawcett, *Declining Jurisdiction in Private International Law* (1st ed, Clarendon Press 1995).

68 Our brief history of the dispute draws heavily and relies on the extensive source material presented in Howard M Erichson, 'The Chevron-Ecuador Dispute, Forum Non Conveniens, and the Problem of Ex Ante Inadequacy' (2013) 1 Stanford Journal of Complex Litigation 417; Laura Carballo Piñeiro, 'Access to Justice and Parallel Litigation: From Solitaire to Team Play' in Horatia Muir Watt et al (eds), *Global Private International Law: Adjudication without Frontiers* (Edward Elgar Publishing 2019) 66.

69 Howard M Erichson, 'The Chevron-Ecuador Dispute, Forum Non Conveniens, and the Problem of Ex Ante Inadequacy' (2013) 1 Stanford Journal of Complex Litigation 417, 418–422.

challenging the resulting judgment on the basis of the failings of the Ecuadorian court.[70] As Erichson notes, these concerns stem from the difficulty of the task the original court faces in determining, *ex ante*, if the other forum is likely to be adequate.[71]

Ultimately, what the Chevron–Ecuador dispute highlights is the potentially problematic connections between the decision to decline jurisdiction and procedures for recognition and enforcement in environmental matters. This has been described as a 'transnational access-to-justice gap', at least in the context of the common law of the United States, as a plaintiff may be denied access to a court in the first instance (due to a declination of jurisdiction on *forum non conveniens* grounds), and then be unable to enforce the judgment of the foreign court that the original court deferred jurisdiction to.[72]

3.1.2. Applicable Law

Applicable law is one of the only areas where specific environment-derived private international rules have been adopted. The leading approach to applicable law questions, from an environmental perspective, is seen in Article 7 of the Rome II Regulation in the European Union. Article 7 provides that:[73]

> The law applicable to a non-contractual obligation arising out of environmental damage or damage sustained by persons or property as a result of such damage shall be the law determined pursuant to Article 4(1), unless the person seeking compensation for damage chooses to base his or her claim on the law of the country in which the event giving rise to the damage occurred.

Article 7 thus supplements Rome II's standard or usual basis of *lex loci damni* – contained within Article 4(1) – that the applicable law is to be the law of the place where the damage occurs. The approach in Article 4(1) contrasts with the traditional choice-of-law rule for tort in most states, premised upon the traditional *lex loci delicti* response – applying the law of the place where the

---

70 As the judgment was subject to procedural deficiencies, and the proceedings tainted by corruption, Chevron received an order in a United States court for a stay and injunction against enforcement of this judgment and subsequently the State of Ecuador was made liable for significant damages: see, further, for a reflection of the litigation and arbitration proceedings and strategies employed, Damira Khatam, 'Chevron and Ecuador Proceedings: A Primer on Transnational Litigation Strategies' (2017) 53 Stanford Journal of International Law 249.

71 Howard M Erichson, 'The Chevron-Ecuador Dispute, Forum Non Conveniens, and the Problem of Ex Ante Inadequacy' (2013) 1 Stanford Journal of Complex Litigation 417, 423.

72 Christopher A Whytock and Cassandra Burke Robertson, 'Forum Non Conveniens and Enforcement of Foreign Judgments' (2011) 111 Columbia Law Review 1444, 1472–1481.

73 Regulation (EC) No 864/2007 of the European Parliament and of the Council of 11 July 2007 on the law applicable to non-contractual obligations (Rome II) [2007] OJ L 199/40.

plaintiff suffered the wrong.[74] Indeed, recital 15 of the Rome II Regulation highlights that the law of the place where the plaintiff suffered the wrong 'is the basic solution for non-contractual obligations in virtually all the Member States'. Even so, cognisant of the uncertainty this approach may engender with indirect harms (a real issue in environmental contexts), Article 4(1) instead premises the applicable law on a connection with the country in which the damage occurs. In addition, the rationale for a supplementary Article 7, applicable in cases of environmental damage, as put forward in the Explanatory Memorandum presented by the Commission of the European Communities, is that:[75]

> European or even international harmonisation is particularly important here as so many environmental disasters have an international dimension. But the instruments adopted so far deal primarily with questions of substantive law or international jurisdiction rather than with harmonisation of the conflict rules. And they address only selected types of cross-border pollution. In spite of this gradual approximation of the substantive law, not only in the Community, major differences subsist – for example in determining the damage giving rise to compensation, limitation periods, indemnity and insurance rules, the right of associations to bring actions and the amounts of compensation. The question of the applicable law has thus lost none of its importance.
>
> Analysis of the current conflict rules shows that the solutions vary widely. The lex fori and the law of the place where the dangerous activity is exercised play a certain role, particularly in the international Conventions, but the most commonly applied solution is the law of the place where the loss is sustained (France, United Kingdom, Netherlands, Spain, Japan, Switzerland, Romania, Turkey, Quebec) or one of the variants of the principle of the law that is most favourable to the victim (Germany, Austria, Italy, Czech Republic, Yugoslavia, Estonia, Turkey, Nordic Convention of 1974 on the protection of the environment, Convention between Germany and Austria of 19 December 1967 concerning nuisances generated by the operation of Salzburg airport in Germany). The Hague Conference has also put an international convention on cross-border environmental damage on its work programme, and preparatory work seems to be moving towards a major role for the place where the damage is sustained, though the merits of the principle of favouring the victim are acknowledged [the 1993 Convention, discussed in section 4 below].

What this extract reveals are the ongoing concerns – not just in the EU, but globally – with respect to the significant differences in private international law

---

74 See, from the perspective of the United States, Jack L Goldsmith and Alan O Sykes, 'Lex Loci Delictus and Global Economic Welfare: Spinozzi v ITT Sheraton Corp' (2007) 120 Harvard Law Review 1137.

75 Commission of the European Communities, 'Proposal of the European Parliament and the Council on the Law Applicable to non-Contractual Obligations ("Rome II")', COM(2003) 427 final, 18–19.

responses to the applicable law in cases of environmental harm. Indeed, the fact that national laws often differ in nature, scope, evidentiary approach and effect stands in stark contrast to the ostensibly universal values contained in SDG 15. It has been argued that these differences, and the lack of responsivity of most private international law rules to environmental concerns, 'foster and accentuate' the need for context-sensitive conflicts rules.[76] That is precisely what Article 7 is. Indeed, Article 7 was created because, in the words of the Commission:

> The basic connection to the law of the place where the damage was sustained is in conformity with recent objectives of environmental protection policy, which tends to support strict liability. The solution is also conducive to a policy of prevention, obliging operators established in countries with a low level of protection to abide by the higher levels of protection in neighbouring countries, which removes the incentive for an operator to opt for low-protection countries. The rule thus contributes to raising the general level of environmental protection.

Article 7 is explored in a comprehensive manner by Andrew Dickinson,[77] but for present purposes it suffices to note that this approach of environmental protection is central. This is reaffirmed in the recitals to Rome II. Recital 25 indicates that there 'should be a high level of protection based on the precautionary principle', and that 'the principle that the polluter pays, fully justifies the use of the principle of discriminating in favour of the person sustaining the damage'. Recital 24 also provides a broad definition of environmental damage as 'meaning adverse change in a natural resource' or 'impairment of a function performed by that resource' or 'impairment of the variability among living organisms', meaning that Article 7 is applicable to a wide array of environmental harms.

Taking a step back, Article 7 of Rome II represents a broader approach that private international law rules can take to offer procedural flexibility to assist in achieving substantive justice: via allowing for some form of the favourability principle (*Günstigkeitsprinzip*).[78] That is, where several legal approaches or norms are potentially applicable – e.g. potentially overlapping claims to the applicable law – the approach more favourable to the person concerned is to be applied (usually at their election). In cases of environmental damage, this will usually be the individuals or local communities who have been impacted. Although it is still comparatively rare for national law statute to provide a special private international law rule for environmental matters, this favourability approach is

---

76 Christophe Bernasconi, 'Civil Liability Resulting from Transfrontier Environmental Damage: A Case for the Hague Conference?' (1999) 12 Hague Yearbook of International Law 35, 38.

77 Andrew Dickinson, *The Rome II Regulation: The Law Applicable to Non-Contractual Obligations* (OUP 2010) Art 7 ('Environmental Damage').

78 André Duczek, 'Environmental Damage and the Rome II Regulation (Rom II – VO Und Umweltschädigung – Ein Überblick)' (SSRN Scholarly Paper, 8 December 2009).

also adopted in the private international law of particular jurisdictions.[79] While offering a choice of applicable law to a plaintiff in cases that involve environmental harm is far from a panacea, it does demonstrate that rules of applicable law can be adapted, in a fashion that is sensitive to environmental concerns, to take on a consideration of the 'planetary dimension of environmental protection'.[80]

3.1.3. Recognition and Enforcement

Last, but by no means least, are recognition and enforcement rules. We focus here on the significant global harmonisation efforts undertaken over many decades, resulting in the two key instruments on recognition and enforcement: the 2005 Convention on Choice of Court Agreements,[81] and the 2019 Judgments Convention.[82] The expressed rationale for harmonisation of recognition and enforcement is in improving the ability of private international law to 'promote access to justice and reduce costs and risks associated with cross-border dealings'.[83] The resultant certainty and predictability is beneficial as it opens avenues for greater, more efficient trade in goods and services (a development narrative). Additionally, harmonisation is grounded on improving plaintiffs' practical access to justice, promoting predictability, and allowing litigants more informed (and potentially greater) choice of where to bring proceedings.[84] Consequently, harmonisation efforts have largely focused on working through private rights and their pursuit, primarily by delineating the accepted territorial and personal bases for exercising jurisdiction, and for giving effect to a resulting decision, in a harmonised and predictable way. This addresses the broadly political question of when one court will defer to another on well-established jurisdictional grounds, or by giving effect to their decisions. It does not aim, however, for example, to play a substantive role in the 'fair' allocation of jurisdiction, or to promote choice-of-law rules or recognition and enforcement approaches that

79 See, for example, Art 138 of the Swiss Federal Law on Private International Law, which provides: 'Claims resulting from harmful emissions coming from an immovable property are governed, at the choice of the injured party, by the law of the State in which the real property is located or by the law of the State in which the result was produced'.

80 Horatia Muir Watt, 'Private International Law Beyond the Schism' (2011) 2 Transnational Legal Theory 347, 388. Yet even in this context Watt notes the reluctance of conflicts lawyers to move beyond any conception that the purpose of the choice-of-law methodology is other than to aid individual victims, falling far short of a true standard of environmental protection.

81 Hague Conference, Convention on Choice of Court Agreements (opened 30 June 2005, entered into force 1 October 2015).

82 Hague Conference, Convention of 2 July 2019 on the Recognition and Enforcement of Foreign Judgments in Civil and Commercial Matters (opened 2 July 2019, not in force).

83 Hague Conference, 'Judgments Convention: Revised Preliminary Explanatory Report' (Preliminary Document, May 2018) [5].

84 ibid [7]–[11].

aim to ensure that claims stemming from cross-border environment harms are ventilated.[85]

The key emphasis to note in this section is that private international law harmonisation is, almost without exception, not geared towards addressing substantive justice concerns, nor driven by concerns of global environmental governance. Despite this, any framework that facilitates recognition and enforcement of judgments may narrow the access-to-justice 'gap' that may be created if foreign judgments on environmental matters are not given effect.[86] For example, both instruments would be broadly apposite in facilitating holding private disputants liable in instances where they have voluntarily accepted such liability under contract (the 'win-win' scenario, discussed in section 3.2). If this contract included an exclusive choice of forum, the Choice of Court Agreements Convention provides a basis for recognition and enforcement; and, in default of such a choice, a judgment on a contractual obligation remains enforceable under Article 5(1)(g) of the Judgments Convention.

However, neither instrument is designed to play an environmental governance role, for instance in facilitating private enforcement of environmental matters. For example, for a judgment that finds tortious liability against a corporation for environmental damage to be recognisable under the 2019 Judgments Convention, the judgment essentially must have been rendered in a state where the corporation against whom this is sought is habitually resident (Art 5(1)(a)), or, alternatively, at the place where 'the act or omission directly causing [the] harm occurred' (Art 5(1)(j)). The element of directness required in the latter formulation rules out recognising and enforcing judgments that relate to indirect and cumulative forms of environmental damage, without a direct link between the act or omission and the harm suffered in the rendering state. Notably, this departs from an earlier draft of the 2019 Convention, which more broadly provided for a judgment to be recognised and enforced if the original action in tort or delict was brought in either the place where the act or omission occurred, or where the injury arose.[87] This lack of recognition and enforcement support is compounded by the fact that even in these cases, courts may – under their national jurisdictional rules – still refuse to take jurisdiction on the basis of *forum non conveniens* grounds, further limiting the Convention's effectiveness in facilitating cross-border environmental litigation.[88]

---

85 This stands in stark contrast to the environmental-law-inspired recognition and enforcement provisions highlighted in section 4.2.2 below, which narrow the bases for refusing to give effect to a judgment in matters of environmental harm.

86 Particularly in conjunction with respective *forum non conveniens* rules, discussed further at section 3.1.1.3 above.

87 Hague Conference, Preliminary Draft Convention on Jurisdiction and Foreign Judgments in Civil and Commercial Matters (Preliminary Document, August 2000) Art 10.

88 Explored at section 3.1.3 above, and noted in Hans van Loon, 'Principles and Building Blocks for a Global Legal Framework for Transnational Civil Litigation in Environmental Matters' (2018) 23 Uniform Law Review 298, 315.

3.2. A MARKET APPROACH: 'WIN-WIN'?

Outside of a regulatory or governance perspective, conceptions of private action contributing to sustainability goals usually centre around what can glibly be described as 'win-win' situations.[89] That is, where both the environment *and* the corporate bottom line benefit from pro-environmental action. In this instance, private international law rules operate primarily in a facilitative capacity to enable trade and development.[90] That is, private international law rules are context insensitive (i.e. to whether the substance of the dispute involves significant environmental harm), and only have room to operate within the space parties have already legally committed themselves to (e.g. via a sustainability clause in a contract). Where this is the case, private law will largely respect or defer to private choices, and support private action that attempts to give effect to this form of private ordering. For example, supporting the choice of contracting parties to bind themselves to contract, including to choice-of-jurisdiction or choice-of-law clauses. This is commonly seen in contracts with foreign investors, even when the subject matter concerns the terrestrial environment. In large part, this is due to the widespread imprimatur that national legal systems give to private parties to enforce voluntarily agreed commitments through their legal systems.[91] This is demonstrated through facilitative jurisdictional rules allowing for selection of forum, choice of law, and the increasingly widespread support for recognition and enforcement of both foreign arbitral awards and judgments rendered under a jurisdictional head based on such autonomy.[92]

Despite deference to the power of private parties, private law has increasingly been theorised as playing a critical regulatory role. This is not a mere thought experiment. Indeed, the contribution of private action and law to sustainability goals is so great that it has been described as a form of 'hybrid' transnational regulation.[93] The primary legal form that supports private action towards

---

89 The language of 'win–win' is sourced primarily from trade facilitation efforts. See, for example, the edited collection Matthias Helble and Ben Shepherd (eds), *Win-Win: How International Trade Can Help Meet the Sustainable Development Goals* (Asian Development Bank Institute 2018).

90 Ralf Michaels, 'The Dual Privatisation of Law in Globalisation (Note on Kasky v Nike)' in Horatia Muir Watt et al (eds), *Global Private International Law: Adjudication without Frontiers* (Edward Elgar Publishing 2019).

91 Despite differences in implementation and approach, most states provide for, and facilitate, private action derived from party autonomy. See, for a discussion of this idea in international commercial contracts, Marta Pertegás and Brooke Marshall, 'Party Autonomy and Its Limits: Convergence Through the New Hague Principles on Choice of Law in International Commercial Contracts' (2014) 39 Brooklyn Journal of International Law 975.

92 The extent of support for party autonomy as a guiding principle in private international law, and its theoretical and historical development, are explored comprehensively in Alex Mills, *Party Autonomy in Private International Law* (CUP 2018).

93 Kasey McCall-Smith and Andreas Rühmkorf, 'From International Law to National Law: The Opportunities and Limits of Contractual CSR Supply Chain Governance' in Vibe Ulfbeck

sustainability is sustainability clauses in contracts. These are widespread in contemporary commercial contracts, particularly along sourcing supply chains. They usually are a way for brand owners or retailers to exercise a degree of control or persuasion over the (outsourced) process of sourcing. They allow for this by obliging a contractor to, for example, either avoid or to take steps to avoid engaging in some form of unsustainable or environmentally harmful practice. Because they are creatures of contract, their precise scope, nature and content differ significantly. Examples of obligations that are commonly employed include obligations to avoid corrupt practices (e.g. bribery, fraud) or labour or human rights abuses (e.g. employing child labour or slavery), or, more relevantly for this chapter, to limit or prevent unsustainable sourcing (e.g. sourcing that negatively impacts on biodiversity or leads to environmental degradation). Increasingly, sustainability clauses are also being employed – often via chains of contract, or accepting liability for subsidiaries or sourcing partners' conduct – to regulate beyond the direct contracting parties; serving in many instances 'as [de facto] regulatory instruments of entire transnational supply chains'.[94]

When such sustainability action is driven by private actors, this is usually seen as a manifestation of corporate social responsibility (CSR). However, rather than having solely normative force, scholars at the intersection of CSR and sustainability have made both the positive and normative case that CSR commitments can and should have legal force. For example, Anna Beckers exhaustively explores the way in which CSR codes can, and in many instances do, serve as a form of global self-regulation, supported by national private law and private enforcement.[95] However, the fundamental normative question that remains unanswered is the extent to which achieving a more effective legal sanction may act to diminish CSR norms by 'crowding out' pro-social voluntary behaviour in favour of sustainability and environmental protection.[96] These issues remain hotly contested.[97] For the purposes of this chapter, however, it

et al (eds), *Law and Responsible Supply Chain Management: Contract and Tort Interplay and Overlap* (Routledge 2019) 36. See also Kasey McCall-Smith and Andreas Rühmkorf, 'Reconciling Human Rights and Supply Chain Management through Corporate Social Responsibility' in Verónica Ruiz Abou-Nigm et al (eds), *Linkages and Boundaries in Private and Public International Law* (Hart Publishing 2018).

94 Paul Verbruggen, 'Regulatory Governance by Contract: The Rise of Regulatory Standards in Commercial Contracts' (2014) 35 Recht der Werkelijkheid 79.

95 Anna Beckers, *Enforcing Corporate Social Responsibility Codes: On Global Self-Regulation and National Private Law* (Hart Publishing 2015).

96 Mark T Kawakami, 'Pitfalls of Over-Legalization: When the Law Crowds Out and Spills Over' (2017) 24 Indiana Journal of Global Legal Studies 147.

97 See, for an overview of a 2017 edited collection on the role of domestic enforcement in CSR codes, Anna Beckers and Mark T Kawakami, 'Why Domestic Enforcement of Private Regulation Is (Not) the Answer: Making and Questioning the Case of Corporate Social Responsibility Codes' (2017) 24 Indiana Journal of Global Legal Studies 1.

is not necessary to weigh in on this debate, as we focus on the role of private international law supporting *voluntary* environmental or sustainability commitments (rather than attempting to elevate potentially sub-legal normative CSR commitments). That is, unlike the emerging theorisation of private law's role in assisting to 'harden' otherwise imprecise or legally ambiguous forms of CSR,[98] voluntary obligations towards sustainability and the environment are creatures of party autonomy and can be incorporated in contract. So-called sustainability clauses purport to extend the contractors' obligations beyond the immediate objects of the contracted performance (and the direct interests of the contractors), and instead to the benefit of third parties or the environment.[99]

These contractual sustainability commitments often derive from private regulatory standards, such as environmental standards developed and adopted by private bodies.[100] There are hundreds of these schemes, with two of the most prominent being the Forest Stewardship Council (FSC) (sustainable forestry) and Fairtrade (sustainable and equitable sourcing) certifications.[101] These schemes, in turn, draw heavily for support on civil society action, and are usually buttressed by certification measures that can be publicly communicated, for example in the forms of logos or marks that are supplier- or consumer-facing. The resulting standards tend to compel private actors not only to meet commitments seen in environmental law treaties, and hence also in SDG 15 (see the discussion of overlap in section 2, above), but to go further in their aspirations.[102] As these standards are 'frequently driven by the changes in global value chains and in international trade',[103] they offer a more flexible mechanism to address evolving – and often worsening – terrestrial environmental concerns. Indeed, some

98 See, for example, Jan Eijsbouts, 'Corporate Codes as Private Co-Regulatory Instruments in Corporate Governance and Responsibility and Their Enforcement' (2017) 24 Indiana Journal of Global Legal Studies 181, 185.

99 Mitkidis provides a wide-ranging study and exploration of the nature of these clauses, which she refers to as 'sustainability contractual clauses' in Katerina Peterkova Mitkidis, *Sustainability Clauses in International Business Contracts* (Eleven International Publishing 2015).

100 Spencer Henson and John Humphrey, 'Understanding the Complexities of Private Standards in Global Agri-Food Chains as They Impact Developing Countries' (2010) 46(9) The Journal of Development Studies 1628.

101 For a comparative overview of the complex role of governance in both of these certification fields see Hannah Murphy-Gregory and Fred Gale, 'Governing the Governors: The Global Metagovernance of Fair Trade and Sustainable Forestry Production' (2019) 47 Politics & Policy 569.

102 We explore the use of such standards in the context of efforts to tie together private and public biodiversity endeavours in Drossos Stamboulakis and Jay Sanderson, 'Certifying Biodiversity: The Union for Ethical BioTrade and the Search for Ethical Sourcing' (2020) 32 Journal of Environmental Law 503.

103 Fabrizio Cafaggi, 'The Many Features of Transnational Private Rule-Making: Unexplored Relationships between Custom, Jura Mercatorum and Global Private Regulation' (2014) 36 University of Pennsylvania Journal of International Law 875, 878.

scholars have argued that this 'contractualisation' of sustainability means that contract law can, and should, be employed to assist in fulfilment of sustainable development goals.[104]

This is premised on the view that greater legal enforcement options, grounded in contract law and supported by facilitative private international law rules, may supplement or relieve some of the burden from the primary compliance mechanism of CSR. This is because CSR is largely premised upon fickle extralegal reputational 'sanction', operating only via threat of civil society action, or avoiding the imposition of greater regulation or a reduction in consumer demand.[105] It must be recalled, however, that contractual obligations to act (or refrain from acting) arise only from firms choosing to self-regulate.[106] Compliance and enforcement is driven largely by private action, with only minimal support from other mandatory regulation that may intercede, for example liability stemming from intellectual property law (e.g. in the improper use of a certification that relates to environmental standards), as well as liability for false and misleading behaviour or statements (e.g. in promoting a product as sustainable where it is not), including via market and consumer protection statutes. For this reason, a range of regulatory initiatives have arisen around promoting the goals contained in such standards, including promoting sustainability goals through procurement,[107] as well as mandatory national reporting laws that also have a sustainability or human rights focus.[108]

At its highest, the 'win-win' approach suggests that sustainability goals can be met through – rather than despite – trade and development. This relies on the idea that there are, or might be developed, markets in environmentally friendly (or 'ethically sourced') products and services, based on the willingness of consumers to seek out and pay a price premium for them; or, at the very least, that consumers will avoid products that are sourced in a way that is harmful to the environment. This mode of analysis dovetails with literature

---

104 Cristina Poncibò, 'The Contractualisation of Environmental Sustainability' (2016) 12 European Review of Contract Law 335.

105 Kenneth W Abbott and Duncan Snidal, 'Taking Responsive Regulation Transnational: Strategies for International Organizations' (2013) 7 Regulation & Governance 95, 98.

106 Kirton and Trebilcock, reviewing a series of edited chapters that consider the use of voluntary standards in a range of different fields, consider that this voluntary participation 'in the construction, operation, and continuation' of schemes is perhaps the critical differentiator between 'soft' and 'hard' regimes: Michael J Trebilcock and John J Kirton, 'Introduction: Hard Choices and Soft Law in Sustainable Global Governance' in John J Kirton and Michael J Trebilcock (eds), *Hard Choices, Soft Law: Voluntary Standards in Global Trade, Environment and Social Governance* (Routledge 2017) 9.

107 Marta Andrecka and Katerina Peterkova Mitkidis, 'Sustainability Requirements in EU Public and Private Procurement – A Right or an Obligation' (2017) 1 Nordic Journal of Commercial Law 55.

108 Seen in regulatory efforts to expand corporate disclosure, transparency and reporting requirements, for example in the Modern Slavery Acts in the UK and Australia.

that highlights private international law's role in trade facilitation,[109] and also reflects a broader discourse in environmental law towards balancing sustainability with acceptable levels of development.[110] This can be seen, for example, in the United Nations Conference on Trade and Development's (UNCTAD) attempts to promote private-sector engagement with sustainable development via an UNCTAD initiative referred to as the BioTrade Initiative (BTI). BioTrade is an aspirational definition, aimed at promoting 'activities of collection, production, transformation, and commercialisation of goods and services derived from native biodiversity under the criteria of environmental, social and economic sustainability'.[111] In other words, BioTrade is aimed not just at balancing development and sustainability, but at actively harnessing market forces to encourage innovation and commercialisation that makes progress towards environmental and sustainability concerns. This diverges from earlier conceptions of production and trade as an extractive and intrinsically harmful 'driving force' for the depletion of natural resources, environments and ecosystems.[112]

Despite the potential to contribute to terrestrial environmental concerns, private sustainability action remains subject to significant legitimacy issues.[113] One of the longstanding concerns is that sustainability clauses and schemes may primarily be used to reflect marketing messages, rather than setting or achieving more challenging ethical imperatives with respective to environmental concerns.[114] This is particularly challenging if there is little to compel or encourage the active monitoring of, compliance with and enforcement of these commitments.[115] Additionally, standards that most sustainability clauses are

109 See, for example, Ronald A Brand, 'Recognition of Foreign Judgments as a Trade Law Issue: The Economics of Private International Law' in Jagdeep Bhandari and Alan Sykes (eds), *Economic Dimensions in International Law: Comparative and Empirical Perspectives* (CUP 1998).

110 As set out at section 2.1 above.

111 This is the definition offered by UNCTAD as part of its BioTrade Initiative, explored further at section 2.1.

112 Dale Andrew, 'Trade and Sustainable Development Goal (SDG) 15: Promoting "Life on Land" through Mandatory and Voluntary Approaches', 4.

113 For a comprehensive discussion of legitimacy – and the various forms it can take in polycentric regulatory regimes – see Julia Black, 'Constructing and Contesting Legitimacy and Accountability in Polycentric Regulatory Regimes' (2008) 2 Regulation & Governance 137, 138.

114 Notable attempts have been made to determine firms' contributions to sustainability through supply chains – but these practices are 'limited in scope', and they only address a very small subset of sustainability challenges (primarily centring around pre-existing legal obligations such as with respect to labour rights): Tannis Thorlakson et al, 'Companies' Contribution to Sustainability through Global Supply Chains' (27 February 2018) 115 Proceedings of the National Academy of Sciences of the United States of America 2072, 2072–2076.

115 Katerina Peterkova Mitkidis, *Sustainability Clauses in International Business Contracts* (Eleven International Publishing 2015). However, it is clear that such contracts still may have significant value as they operate as a mechanism by which legal norms relating to the environment may

based on need to be rigorous enough to support claims about their legitimacy, but, at the same time, they also need to be 'attractive' to private industry, which is largely attributed to the scheme's potential value in creating value via market differentiation.[116] Less-than-rigorous private sustainability commitments may act to 'coopt, disactivate, or otherwise keep at bay' other regulatory regimes at either the national or international level,[117] and hence may limit the achievement of the environmental goals embodied in SDG 15.

4. A MORE SUSTAINABLE FOOTING FOR PRIVATE INTERNATIONAL LAW?

As section 3 has demonstrated, private international law can – and does by necessity – play a governance role in disputes that cross legal boundaries and have detrimental environmental effects. However, its lack of global governance aspiration has long been criticised.[118] This is because of private international law's traditional emphasis on procedural neutrality, primary anchoring to territorial units such as the state, and focus on the micro (individual and private rights), resulting in a form of 'tunnel-blindness'.[119] Going further, Horatia Muir Watt, commenting on an edited collection of views on the relationship between private international law and governance, concludes that private international law 'leaves unchecked the exercise of informal power beyond the state', and hence 'fails to do the job it is formally designed to do'.[120] Private international law's formal nature is also limiting, as it[121]

> [carries] with it into the transnational arena a set of assumptions borrowed from the liberal theory of state without any correlated concerted protection of the common good[;] it also ensures the legal promotion of such informal power in the name of private autonomy.

circulate: see, further, Natasha Affolder, 'Looking for Law in Unusual Places: Cross-Border Diffusion of Environmental Norms' (2018) 7 Transnational Environmental Law 425.

116 This concept has itself been criticised, as it is suggested that certain issues will necessarily be 'overlooked or excluded' where they cannot be readily codified or measured, or where standards 'leave unquestioned such rights as the freedom to trade, to invest and divest and to defer to market mechanisms as the arbiter of fair price' – in other words, reflecting market-based constraints: see, further, Mick Blowfield, 'Ethical Supply Chains in the Cocoa, Coffee and Tea Industries' [2003] Greener Management International 15, 22.

117 Horatia Muir Watt, 'Private International Law Beyond the Schism' (2011) 2 Transnational Legal Theory 347, 407.

118 See, for a thorough indictment – particularly as compared to public international law – Horatia Muir Watt, 'Private International Law Beyond the Schism' (2011) 2 Transnational Legal Theory 347.

119 ibid 387.

120 Horatia Muir Watt and Diego P Fernández Arroyo (eds), *Private International Law and Global Governance* (OUP 2014) 343.

121 ibid.

Simultaneously, outside of the European Union's approach in Article 7 Rome II Regulation, there has been a failure of political will to agree to private international law approaches that respond to environmental concerns. Instead, party autonomy serves as the dominant paradigm underpinning much of private international law doctrine. As Agatha Brandão de Oliveira and Lucia Bíziková note, this has been the case since at least the 1970s, when forum selection clauses came to be much more accepted in the United States, and subsequently, globally:[122]

> The Bremen v. Zapata Off-Shore Co. 407 U.S. 1 (1972) ('The Bremen') is a landmark case in the construction of contemporary private international law. By allowing contractual choice of jurisdiction, the United States Supreme Court opened the era of party autonomy in international commercial relations. The Bremen was arguably the first legal stone in the framing and facilitating of private globalised trade relations and, correlatively, a symptom of a disembedded economy. It questions the essence of 'legal borders' and sets the tone for later challenges to the very notion of jurisdictional limits, while simultaneously heralding the age of private economic governance through contract.

However, primary reliance on party autonomy as an organising principle for the distribution of legal authority does not sit easily with a broader global governance push premised upon protection of communal and public concerns such as sustainability and the environment (as embodied in SDG 15). Because of this, it is argued that an acute 'crisis' faces private international law in the context of globalisation of production – including with respect to environmental and sustainability impacts.[123] As we have seen from section 3, some private international law rules have been modified or adapted to meet terrestrial environmental concerns. In this section, we go further and highlight how private international law rules may be further developed to respond to the pressing global environmental issues embedded in SDG 15.

4.1. ENVIRONMENTAL GOVERNANCE ASPIRATIONS OF PRIVATE INTERNATIONAL LAW

In the face of environmental crisis, we argue that it is both 'proper' and desirable for private international law's governance role to be informed by SDG 15's

122 Agatha Brandão Oliveira and Lucia Bíziková, 'Forum Selection Clauses in a Brave New World: Opting out of Parochialism?' in Horatia Muir Watt et al (eds), *Global Private International Law: Adjudication without Frontiers* (Edward Elgar Publishing 2019) 24.

123 Horatia Muir Watt, 'Jurisprudence Without Confines: Private International Law as Global Legal Pluralism' (2016) 5 Cambridge International Law Journal 388, 392.

universal values.[124] As section 2 explored, SDG 15 places a particular emphasis on the sustainability component of the 'sustainable development' term: calling for concerted action to conserve, protect and ensure the continued viability of all kinds of terrestrial environments. Widespread global support for these SDG 15 values endorses an increasingly overwhelming normative case for greater private action in achieving terrestrial environmental goals. As we noted in section 3, this involves a combination of both state-based regulatory action and private market-based approaches premised upon[125]

> integrated corporate responsibility for sustainable development that applies to companies' own operations and to all of their business relationships, including those throughout their value chain … [offering] broad support for a new global normativity that forms a background for ongoing and future developments in transnational private litigation in environmental matters.

If the environmental protection values in SDG 15 are taken seriously as a matter of state policy, this suggests that 'developed' countries with strong regulatory environments ought to design their procedural laws in a manner which may, where appropriate, extend to covering the impacts of corporate behaviour outside their territory.[126] In recent years, there has been significant development on this front, so much so that in 2018, van Loon noted an 'emerging normative paradigm shift' towards facilitating cross-border civil litigation in environmental matters.[127] This shift is further witnessed in the recent ground-breaking judgments of *Okpabi* and *Milieudefensie*, which reinforce the idea that there may be an avenue (within the common law, at least) for holding transnational companies to account for environmental harms, even when such harms arise primarily through a subsidiary domiciled in a third country.[128]

Facilitating private action with respect to sustainability and the environment, in this way, can be seen as states working towards fulfilling obligations deriving from environmental law treaties. In the context of protection of the terrestrial

124 Ralf Michaels, 'Private International Law and the Question of Universal Values' in Franco Ferrari and Diego P Fernández Arroyo (eds), *Private International Law: Contemporary Challenges and Continuing Relevance* (Edward Elgar Publishing 2019) 168.

125 Hans van Loon, 'Principles and Building Blocks for a Global Legal Framework for Transnational Civil Litigation in Environmental Matters' (2018) 23 Uniform Law Review 298, 302–303.

126 This is particularly the case where transnational corporations operate, either directly or via subsidiaries or sub-contractors, in jurisdictions with relatively lax environmental standards: Geert van Calster, *European Private International Law* (2nd ed, Hart Publishing 2016) 357.

127 Hans van Loon, 'Principles and Building Blocks for a Global Legal Framework for Transnational Civil Litigation in Environmental Matters' (2018) 23 Uniform Law Review 298, 313.

128 These judgments are discussed further at section 3.1.1.2 above.

environment, these state obligations are seen most prominently with respect to biodiversity protection under the Convention on Biological Diversity and its accompanying Nagoya Protocol, which include a range of obligations for states to 'encourage' non-state participants and mechanisms that promote biodiversity conservation and access and benefit-sharing.[129] Additionally, various longstanding Declarations have stressed the need for states to develop both national and international law on liability for environmental damage.[130] Such action may also reflect the idea that states ought to be accountable for violations of international law and laws by corporations that are within their 'sphere of influence'.[131] As Muir Watt puts it:[132]

> In support of this idea, the economic tie between the corporation and the state of its seat or incorporation would seem to imply that the latter benefits from fiscal returns on corporate activity in trade and investment abroad. As a corollary, therefore, the home state can be seen to owe a duty of care to the local community of the host state and its environment, under which it is responsible for the harmful effects of the foreign conduct of the revenue-generating corporation.

A further driver for an expanded environmental governance role for private international law stems from its necessary intersection with rights-based discourses. Treaties that deal with the terrestrial environment, such as those set out in section 2, offer little succour here, as they are almost exclusively designed and intended to regulate the conduct of states. Obligations that are cast within them represent a pathway for state obligation, rather than leading to rights enforceable by individuals.[133] Instead, the primary source of privately enforceable rights implicated in environmental law matters arise via human

---

129 See, further, Drossos Stamboulakis and Jay Sanderson, 'Certifying Biodiversity: The Union for Ethical BioTrade and the Search for Ethical Sourcing' (2020) 32 Journal of Environmental Law 503, 508–509.

130 See, for example, Principle 22 of the Stockholm Declaration (Declaration of the United Nations Conference on the Human Environment, Stockholm, 16 June 1972) and Principle 13 of the Rio Declaration on Environment and Development (Rio de Janeiro, 14 June 1992).

131 The sphere of influence concept, as noted in the Preamble to the UN Global Compact, also encourages private sector actors to 'embrace, support and enact, within their sphere of influence, a set of core values in the areas of human rights, labour standards, the environment, and anti-corruption'. See, for a further exposition of the sphere of influence concept, John Ruggie, 'Report of the Special Representative of the Secretary-General on the Issue of Human Rights and Transnational Corporations and other Business Enterprises: Clarifying the Concepts of "Sphere of influence" and "Complicity"', UN Doc A/HRC/8/16 (15 May 2008).

132 Horatia Muir Watt, 'Private International Law Beyond the Schism' (2011) 2 Transnational Legal Theory 347, 399–400.

133 A notable exception is the Vienna Convention on Civil Liability for Nuclear Damage (adopted 21 May 1963, entry into force 12 November 1977), which places directly and exclusive liability on nuclear operators, as well as extending private international law including both jurisdiction and recognition and enforcement.

rights law[134] and, arguably, parts of customary international law.[135] These rights can either derive directly from international and regional instruments, or from national law (often in the elevated form of constitutions or charters). The European Union leads the field here. Rights embodied in European Union instruments, such as the right to life and to family life, have been widely applied by EU judicial organs to a range of environmental issues including pollution and access to environmental information, and encouraging governments to tackle environmental degradation.[136]

As Muir Watt argues, it might be supposed that private international law would be the body of law to respond to such transnational issues, particularly as there is a significant degree of overlap between rights, and the use of choice-of-law principles to govern cross-border private law relationships.[137] However, private international law's lack of governance aspirations means that it might simply be 'paralysed', 'sidelined' or 'brushed aside' by the mandatory operation of rights norms.[138] Muir Watt gives the example of the non-discrimination rights in the European Union, which, in some instances, mandatorily impose the protection of other rights, such as the right to privacy, 'irrespective of the national legal regime applicable under the forum state's conflict of laws rules'.[139] The consequence is that private international law rules may simply by bypassed,[140] even where they are tailored to meet environmental concerns (as occurs in Article 7 of the Rome II Regulation).

4.2. INTEGRATING SUSTAINABILITY CONCERNS: CONTEXT-ORIENTED RULES

In this section we set out a range of ways in which private international law could better integrate sustainability concerns. These range from tweaks to

134 See, for a detailed exploration of whether (and how) international law might recognise norms relating or extending to corporate liability, William S Dodge, 'Corporate Liability Under Customary International Law' (2012) 43 Georgetown Journal of International Law 1045.

135 These are explored, through a private international law lens, in Geert van Calster, *European Private International Law* (2nd ed, Hart Publishing 2016) 357, 1142 et seq and Hans van Loon, 'Principles and Building Blocks for a Global Legal Framework for Transnational Civil Litigation in Environmental Matters' (2018) 23 Uniform Law Review 298, 303–306.

136 See, for an overview, European Court of Human Rights, 'Factsheet – Environment and the ECHR' (December 2020) <https://www.echr.coe.int/documents/fs_environment_eng.pdf> accessed 20 January 2021.

137 See, generally, Horatia Muir Watt, 'Private International Law Beyond the Schism' (2011) 2 Transnational Legal Theory 347.

138 ibid 395–396, 403.

139 ibid 396.

140 ibid.

existing national law approaches, through to more ambitious calls, such as for regional or global harmonisation. We do not take a position on any of these approaches, other than to note that such possibilities exist and are worthy of further consideration, as they are likely to assist in addressing the terrestrial environmental concerns captured in SDG 15.

4.2.1. National and Regional Approaches

In addition to the approaches to jurisdiction and applicable law set out at section 3 above, several novel private international law rules have been espoused that aim to shift private international law rules to a normative basis that responds to environmental concerns. Hans van Loon has set much of the groundwork for considering these rules, via exploring what he terms a series of 'building blocks' of unified private international law rules that harmonise procedural aspects of cross-border civil litigation in environmental matters.[141] These structural components are largely built on minor tweaks to existing doctrine – including a call for broad definitions of domicile (or habitual residence) for non-natural persons; exclusion of *forum non conveniens* when under the jurisdiction of courts in the state of the defendant's domicile (as occurs in Brussels I); and allowing a plaintiff the choice to sue in the state where damage occurs or where the event giving rise to the damage occurs.[142] These proposals are related to sustainability and SDG 15 in the sense that they could provide a more facilitative approach to private actions against corporate defendants who engage in environmental harms.

More radical proposals have also been put forward, such as moving beyond private rights-based conceptions and remapping the idea of state versus non-state responsibility to be based on nexus or proportionality.[143] This means that rather than dogmatically applying existing rules of jurisdiction, the legal focus should instead shift to a single test of nexus: that is, providing for legal responsibility for an entity that exercises political and economic power and subsequently violates human rights (for example, the right to life or the right to a sustainable environment). Other suggestions, deriving from outside private international law, have also been proposed. Geert van Calster for example, draws on EU competition law for inspiration, and suggests it may be possible to craft some form of rebuttable presumption that the conduct of a subsidiary may be

---

141 Hans van Loon, 'Principles and Building Blocks for a Global Legal Framework for Transnational Civil Litigation in Environmental Matters' (2018) 23 Uniform Law Review 298.

142 ibid 316. And similar calls for reform to the applicable law, or the recognition and enforcement approaches as set out in the context of the 1993 Convention, at section 4.2.2 below.

143 This is an idea that arises in a human rights context, but is explored through a private international law lens in Horatia Muir Watt, 'Private International Law Beyond the Schism' (2011) 2 Transnational Legal Theory 347, 405.

imputed to a parent holding company in instances of environmental harm.[144] This would go a long way towards simplifying the challenging evidentiary task – explored closely in *Vedanta, Okpabi* and *Milieudefensie* – that plaintiffs face in demonstrating the control or supervision of the parent company, so that it may face liability for environmental harms due to a duty of care arising in tort.

Further examples of regional initiatives are seen in the EU's continual law reform process in sustainability initiatives, usually in a manner that is grounded in fundamental rights. Most recently, in a February 2021 report, the Committee on Legal Affairs of the European Parliament recommended an extension of the *forum necessitatis* rule within the EU into the Brussels I and Rome II Regulations.[145] These amendments were removed from the final resolution before it was adopted by the European Parliament;[146] however, it is still useful to consider them as they represent a novel approach to private international law and human rights (and, as discussed in section 4.1, human rights are often employed as a means of protecting environmental concerns). With respect to jurisdiction, the report suggests a new Article 26a in the Brussels I Regulation that would grant EU Member State courts a discretion to hear, 'on an exceptional basis', a case 'if the right to a fair trial or the right to access to justice so requires', if the following circumstances exist:

> (a) if proceedings cannot reasonably be brought or conducted or would be impossible in a third State with which the dispute is closely related; or (b) if a judgment given on the claim in a third State would not be entitled to recognition and enforcement in the Member State of the court seised under the law of that State and such recognition and enforcement is necessary to ensure that the rights of the claimant are satisfied; and the dispute has a sufficient connection with the Member State of the court seised.

Had it been passed, this amendment would have represented a ground-breaking approach to jurisdiction in private international law. This is because it opens up an alternative or additional forum in which civil actions can be brought, where it is difficult to bring proceedings or achieve justice. In addition to the proposed Article 26a in Brussels I, a new Article 6a was also proposed for applicable law under the Rome II Regulation, allowing the plaintiff an expanded choice of the applicable law in 'business-related civil claims for human rights', to include 'the law of the country in which the parent company has its domicile', and if that

---

144 Geert van Calster, *European Private International Law* (2nd ed, Hart Publishing 2016) 371–372.

145 European Parliament (Committee on Legal Affairs), 'Report: with recommendations to the Commission on corporate due diligence and corporate accountability', A9-0018/2021 (11 February 2021).

146 European Parliament, 'European Parliament resolution of 10 March 2021 with recommendations to the Commission on corporate due diligence and corporate accountability', 2020/2129(INL) (2021).

is not in a Member State, 'the law of the country where it operates'. It is clear, as van Calster noted in a contemporaneous blog post, that aspects of these amendments need refining to be workable.[147] For example, an initial difficulty arises under this applicable law extension because the amendments extend only to human, rather than environmental, rights (but it is unclear what law is to apply if a right is both a human right and an environmental right, or if both are pleaded in the same action).

Despite potential drafting issues, and their ultimate failure to be progress to legislative status, these proposed amendments evidence the increasing consideration of how private international law rules can better integrate sustainability concerns. Doing so would better facilitate the pursuit of environmental actions, and hence the pursuit of sustainability and SDG 15, particularly in the context of the 'transnational access-to-justice gaps' (set out in section 3.1.1.3).

4.2.2. Environmental-Law-Inspired Harmonised Private International Law Rules

One of the most significant and longstanding attempts to integrate sustainability issues into private international law arises in the context of attempts to provide a more favourable path to litigants seeking to pursue civil liability claims against private actors for environmental damage. Much of this work occurred in the mid to late 1990s, under the auspices of the Hague Conference of Private International Law (HCCH), as supported by a colloquium hosted in conjunction with the University of Osnabrück in April 1994.[148] This resulted in advanced multilateral efforts to intertwine both substantive and procedural responses to environmental issues: the Council of Europe's 1993 Convention on Civil Liability for Damage Resulting from Activities Dangerous to the Environment.[149] Although the Convention never came into force, it still demonstrates how private international law rules can be adapted to accommodate environmental goals, particularly at the multilateral level.

---

147 See, further, comments in relation to both proposed amendments: Geert van Calster, 'First Analysis of the European Parliament's Draft Proposal to Amend Brussels Ia and Rome II with a View to Corporate Human Rights Due Diligence', *GAVC law – Geert van Calster* (16 April 2021) <https://gavclaw.com/tag/forum-necessitatis/> accessed 23 April 2021; Thalia Kruger, 'European Parliament Resolution on Corporate Due Diligence and Corporate Accountability', *Conflict of Laws* (14 April 2021) <https://conflictoflaws.net/2021/european-parliament-resolution-on-corporate-due-diligence-and-corporate-accountability/> accessed 24 April 2021.

148 See, further, references in Hans van Loon, 'Principles and Building Blocks for a Global Legal Framework for Transnational Civil Litigation in Environmental Matters' (2018) 23 Uniform Law Review 298, 314, n 66.

149 Convention on Civil Liability for Damage Resulting from Activities Dangerous to the Environment (1993).

The Convention's primary objective was to create a practical avenue to 'ensure adequate compensation for damage resulting from activities dangerous to the environment and provide for means of prevention and reinstatement' (Art 1). To do so, it sets out both substantive rules on liability, and makes provision for private international law harmonisation. Notably, Article 19 ('Jurisdiction') allows the plaintiff choice with respect to where an action can be brought. This allows actions for compensation under this Convention to be brought, at the election of the plaintiff, where the damage was suffered, where the dangerous activity was conducted, or where the defendant has its habitual residence. This approach offers more flexibility than traditional jurisdictional exercises by national courts; however, it is introduced in a principled fashion, as the Convention does not go so far as to provide for wholesale extraterritorial reach without any connection to the state.[150]

Article 23 ('Recognition and enforcement') of the Civil Liability Convention also demonstrates how private international law rules can facilitate recognition and enforcement of foreign judgments that have an environmental dimension.[151] The traditional grounds for refusing recognition are narrowed for judgments that satisfy the jurisdictional test in Article 19, to three broad grounds: where contrary to public policy in the enforcing state; where a judgment was given in default (and the defendant not served in sufficient time to enable it to make a defence); and where the decision is irreconcilable with a decision already given in a dispute between the same parties. As soon as any decision is recognised in this fashion – and so long as it is enforceable in the state of origin – it is to be enforceable in every contracting state, once the formalities for enforcement are satisfied. Article 23(2) clarifies that it impermissible to reopen the merits of the case as part of the formalities required for this enforcement process. This may go some way to narrowing any 'transnational access-to-justice gaps', as set out in section 3.1.1.3.

Despite the potential in the Convention's private international law approach, more than 25 years later, it has not come into force, and there does not seem to be any prospect of this now occurring. The reasons for this are many, yet, relevantly for our purposes, unlikely linked to its private international law aspirations. No doubt, part of the Convention's failure stems from its ambitiousness in relation to its substantive law reach, diverging markedly from (and extending well beyond) existing national law civil liability approaches, and offering particularly

---

150 Noting that there have been calls for a rethinking of jurisdiction in international law, including in private international law: Alex Mills, 'Rethinking Jurisdiction in International Law' (2014) 84 British Yearbook of International Law 187, 200–209.

151 Albeit one that is subordinate to other private international law instruments in force between states: Art 24 clarifies that where a treaty establishing rules of jurisdiction or providing recognition and enforcement already exists between two or more states, the provisions of that treaty replace the corresponding provisions in the 1993 Convention.

wide and perhaps ill-defined breadth and scope in relation to definitions of key terms such as 'dangerous activity' and the 'environment'.[152] However, as Daniel suggests, its weak prospects of coming into force may also stem from inadequate attention to liability and insurance issues (as it provides for uncapped liability), and the existence of sectoral liability treaties and ongoing EU harmonisation work removing the underlying impetus – all leading to the 'general feeling that it is too vague and broad to be acceptable to States'.[153] That may be true, but the impetus towards sustainability has only strengthened since that time. For the purposes of this chapter at least, the key takeaway is that there are a range of concrete, discrete and feasible amendments to private international law rules that may better accommodate or integrate sustainability concerns.

5. CONCLUSION

In this chapter, we set out to explore the interactions between SDG 15 and private international law, and to determine whether private international law rules can (and indeed should) be modified to reflect pressing global environmental and sustainability concerns. What becomes readily apparent is that traditional private international law approaches offer little integration of sustainability concerns. Accommodating these concerns requires a reconceptualisation of private international law: highlighting its potential global governance role in promoting or facilitating private action geared at environmental protection and sustainability, rather than its apparently neutral basis, commonly undergirded in a trade context by deference to party autonomy. It is our hope that SDG 15's widely agreed sustainability and environmental protection goals – particularly with respect to protecting and conserving life on land and the sustainable use of various interrelated ecosystems – might provoke a discussion of how private international law rules can or might be reconfigured, and ultimately interpreted and applied.

Although this chapter has taken some initial steps in connecting private international law with SDG 15 and the values embedded within it,[154] the pressing

---

152 For example, the term 'dangerous activity' includes all organisms that pose a significant risk for man, the environment or property (Art 2(1)); and 'environment' extends to natural resources, but also cultural heritage, and 'the characteristic aspects of the landscape' (Art 2(10)). This is broader than the definition given to 'environmental damage' under Art 7 of the Rome II Regulation: see section 3.1.1.2 above.

153 Daniel explores a number of these in: Anne Daniel, 'Civil Liability Regimes as a Complement to Multilateral Environmental Agreements: Sound International Policy or False Comfort?' (2003) 12 Review of European Community and International Environmental Law 225, 227.

154 Responding to the injunction to tie private international law doctrine and reform to key global governance debates: a goal expressed by Robert Wai in his seminal 2001 article on the regulatory function of private international law. Robert Wai, 'Transnational Liftoff and

question that remains is precisely how, and to what extent, this should occur. It is not necessarily the case that private international law need be radically reshaped. Indeed, one of the discipline's core strengths is its legitimacy, founded upon technical, doctrinal responses. So, for example, value conflicts are resolved 'as if' they were not value conflicts – a necessary step 'in order to make them resoluble'.[155] As Michaels notes:[156]

> the irresoluble conflict between different sets of nonuniversal values … makes a technical response necessary. Private international law cannot share in the same evaluation criteria like substantive law without losing its legitimacy. It is only through technique that private international law can do what it is meant to do. (footnotes omitted)

Modifying private international law rules to accommodate the concerns of SDG 15 does not require abandoning the doctrinal or technical basis of private international law. Even relatively minor changes to existing private international law rules – for example, allowing a potential plaintiff greater choice in which law applies – can introduce a degree of sensitivity to the environmental context. Indeed, arguments have been mounted that the apparent 'apolitical' or 'neutral' approach of private international law is a fiction worth abandoning.[157] This is because irrespective of whether private international law sidesteps or ignores environmental and sustainability issues by omission or by design, doing so still represents a value judgment. As Michaels notes, within private international law, 'value judgments are always made from a specific perspective that is not universal', meaning that 'its values are as non-universal as those of substantive law'.[158] Indeed, there can be no value-neutral approach that ignores conflicts in values, particularly not in the furious and frequent collisions between sustainability and development.

Although there is no ready answer, contemplation of environmental issues requires private international law scholars to grapple with the uneasy question

---

Juridical Touchdown: The Regulatory Function of Private International Law in an Era of Globalization' (2001–2002) 40 Columbia Journal of Transnational Law 209, 212–213.

155 Ralf Michaels, 'Private International Law and the Question of Universal Values' in Franco Ferrari and Diego P Fernández Arroyo (eds), *Private International Law: Contemporary Challenges and Continuing Relevance* (Edward Elgar Publishing 2019) 168, 176.

156 ibid 175.

157 See, inter alia, Verónica Ruiz Abou-Nigm, 'Unlocking Private International Law's Potential in Global (Migration) Governance' in Franco Ferrari and Diego P Fernández Arroyo (eds), *Private International Law: Contemporary Challenges and Continuing Relevance* (Edward Elgar Publishing 2019) 207.

158 Ralf Michaels, 'Private International Law and the Question of Universal Values' in Franco Ferrari and Diego P Fernández Arroyo (eds), *Private International Law: Contemporary Challenges and Continuing Relevance* (Edward Elgar Publishing 2019) 168, 173. Michaels continues: 'But they then represent an outside influence only.'

that environmental law and governance scholars have long worried at. That is: to what extent are competing and potentially conflicting values of sustainability or environmental protection able to be balanced by development? This deceptively simple question implicates the nuanced balancing act that public international law has for many decades contended with when considering the reach of state responsibility towards various forms of sustainability and environmental commitments. Modifying private international law, so that it takes seriously the concerns embodied in SDG 15, will enable it to contribute to ongoing efforts to fully define and give content to concepts of sustainable development and use more broadly. It is likely private international law can offer a mediating influence in this respect, employing the disciplining power of doctrine and technique to – via civil actions and private remedies – assist in 'domesticating' potential conflicts and working towards more sustainable development.

SDG 16: PEACE, JUSTICE AND STRONG INSTITUTIONS

Sabine CORNELOUP and Jinske VERHELLEN

Goal 16: Promote peaceful and inclusive societies for sustainable development, provide access to justice for all and build effective, accountable and inclusive institutions at all levels

16.1	Significantly reduce all forms of violence and related death rates everywhere
16.2	End abuse, exploitation, trafficking and all forms of violence against and torture of children
16.3	Promote the rule of law at the national and international levels and ensure equal access to justice for all
16.4	By 2030, significantly reduce illicit financial and arms flows, strengthen the recovery and return of stolen assets and combat all forms of organized crime
16.5	Substantially reduce corruption and bribery in all their forms
16.6	Develop effective, accountable and transparent institutions at all levels
16.7	Ensure responsive, inclusive, participatory and representative decision-making at all levels
16.8	Broaden and strengthen the participation of developing countries in the institutions of global governance
16.9	By 2030, provide legal identity for all, including birth registration
16.10	Ensure public access to information and protect fundamental freedoms, in accordance with national legislation and international agreements
16.a	Strengthen relevant national institutions, including through international cooperation, for building capacity at all levels, in particular in developing countries, to prevent violence and combat terrorism and crime
16.b	Promote and enforce non-discriminatory laws and policies for sustainable development

1. INTRODUCTION

This chapter focuses on Target 16.9 of the Sustainable Development Goals (SDGs), which states: 'By 2030, provide legal identity for all, including birth registration.' It is a tentative attempt to explore the reciprocal influences between private international law and this SDG target.

In section 2, Target 16.9 is briefly positioned within the context of SDG 16 as a whole, before being presented in itself, as well as in the context of global migration, which also brings other SDGs into the picture and highlights the link to private international law. Section 2 ends with an overview of some initiatives that have been undertaken, within the United Nations agencies and in collaboration with the private sector, to support SDG Target 16.9.

In section 3, existing private international law instruments, methods and techniques on legal identity and their relevance in a migration context are assessed. A survey of international conventions and EU regulations on private international law will reveal that none of the existing instruments plays a prominent role, if any, in a migration context. At the national level, existing private international law methods and techniques on legal identity are assessed from the perspective of states of destination or states of transit as only then a cross-border element arises activating private international law. The use of the terms 'states of destination', 'states of transit' and 'states of origin' reflects a focus on Global South to Global North migration. We are adopting a European perspective and must draw attention to the limits such an approach inevitably entails.

Section 4 is an attempt to somehow overcome this limitation by also including the perspective of states of origin in the Global South. It addresses the question whether the evolving new global framework in line with SDG Target 16.9 could improve the situation in the states of origin by promoting and implementing birth registration and consequently spur new thinking on legal identity matters in private international law.

2. SDG TARGET 16.9 IN CONTEXT

2.1. LEGAL IDENTITY WITHIN SDG 16 AS A WHOLE

SDG 16 ('Peace, Justice and Strong Institutions') aims to promote peaceful and inclusive societies for sustainable development, provide access to justice for all and build effective, accountable and inclusive institutions at all levels. Very comprehensive in its definition, SDG 16 relies on 12 specific targets, and its implementation is measured by 23 indicators.

Among the different targets, many interdependences and interrelations exist. Target 16.3 on the rule of law and access to justice is particularly cross-cutting.

As it is fundamental to most of the chapters of this book, it is addressed from the perspective of the specific SDGs developed there.

Similarly, Target 16.9 on legal identity is key to advance other targets, within SDG 16 and beyond. The general goal of 'justice' and the specific targets of 'the rule of law' and 'access to justice' (Target 16.3), the protection of fundamental freedoms (Target 16.10) and the enforcement of non-discriminatory laws and policies (Target 16.b) cannot be addressed without providing legal identity for all. Legal identity is the gateway to the world of law and justice. Birth registration plays a primary role in ensuring individual rights and access to justice.

Likewise, there is an interdependence between the Targets 16.2 and 16.9. The target of ending child trafficking and all forms of violence against children is difficult to achieve when the victims of trafficking and violence do not have a legal identity/existence.

In turn, Target 16.9 cannot be reached without the possibility of relying on 'strong institutions' and the further development of effective, accountable and transparent institutions (Target 16.6) responsible for the registration, certification and acceptance of basic characteristics of an individual's identity. As many developing countries currently do not meet the objective of providing legal identity for all, their participation in international organisations must be strengthened (Target 16.8).[1]

Moreover, Target 16.9 is not only the vital foundation of SDG 16, but – as pointed out by the UN Legal Identity Expert Group[2] – 'legal identity is widely acknowledged to be catalytic for achieving at least ten of the Sustainable Development Goals (SDGs). Data generated from civil registration and population registers support the measurement of over 60 SDG indicators.'[3]

Hence, there are ample reasons to focus on the specific, but fundamental and wide-ranging, SDG Target 16.9.

2.2. LEGAL IDENTITY IN TARGET 16.9

According to the United Nations Legal Identity Agenda, SDG Target 16.9 'is key to advance the 2030 Agenda commitment to leave no one behind'.[4]

SDG Target 16.9 holds great promise: the promise of really implementing the fundamental right of everyone to be recognised as a person before the law. This fundamental right to a legal identity, as enshrined in Article 6 of the Universal

1 See *infra* section 4.1.

2 See *infra* section 2.4.

3 UN Legal Identity Expert Group, 'United Nations Strategy for Legal Identity for All', para 5 <https://unstats.un.org/legal-identity-agenda/documents/UN-Strategy-for-LIA.pdf> accessed 15 April 2021.

4 'United Nations Legal Identity Agenda' <https://unstats.un.org/legal-identity-agenda> accessed 15 April 2021.

Declaration on Human Rights and Article 16 of the International Covenant on Civil and Political Rights, is a prerequisite for exercising all other rights.

Providing legal identity for all presupposes an official trace of this identity, starting with registration at the time of birth. This is reflected in the current United Nations Operational Definition of the concept of legal identity[5] as:

> the basic characteristics of an individual's identity, e.g. name, sex, place and date of birth conferred through registration and the issuance of a certificate by an authorized civil registration authority following the occurrence of birth. In the absence of birth registration, legal identity may be conferred by a legally-recognized identification authority. This system should be linked to the civil registration system to ensure a holistic approach to legal identity from birth to death. Legal identity is retired by the issuance of a death certificate by the civil registration authority upon registration of death.[6]

Without registration of their legal identity people are invisible in the eyes of the law: '[f]or people to count, they must first be counted.'[7]

Birth registration is a fundamental right, recognised by Article 24(2) of the International Covenant on Civil and Political Rights and Article 7 of the Convention on the Rights of the Child. For SDG Target 16.9, one concrete indicator has been formulated: 'Proportion of children under 5 years of age whose births have been registered with a civil authority, by age.' Birth registration is often seen as the first right of the child, as it is the gateway to legal identity, the port of entry into the world of law. Through birth registration, the child's legal existence and identity is established, which is a prerequisite for exercising all other rights. Without birth registration, children may be denied basic rights, such as health, education and social welfare.[8] They are more vulnerable to violence and exploitation, for instance when proof of age is needed to help prevent child labour and child marriage. A birth certificate can also help protect children against family separation, trafficking, illegal adoption and the risk of statelessness.[9] Yet UNICEF recalls that the births of one quarter of children under the age of five worldwide (or 166 million children) have never been

---

5 ibid.

6 UN Legal Identity Expert Group, 'United Nations Strategy for Legal Identity for All' <https://unstats.un.org/legal-identity-agenda/documents/UN-Strategy-for-LIA.pdf> accessed 15 April 2021.

7 Plan International, 'Birth registration' <https://plan-international.org/early-childhood/birth-registration> accessed 15 April 2021.

8 UN Committee on the Rights of the Child, General Comment No 7 (early childhood), UN Doc CRC/C/GC/7/Rev (20 September 2006) para 25.

9 UN Committee on the Protection of the Rights of All Migrant Workers and Members of Their Families, Joint General Comment No 4 (2017) of the Committee on the Protection of the Rights of All Migrant Workers and Members of Their Families and No 23 (2017) of the Committee on the Rights of the Child on State obligations regarding the human rights of children in the context of international migration in countries of origin, transit, destination and return, UN Doc CMW/C/GC/4-CRC/C/GC/23 (16 November 2017) para 20.

officially recorded.[10] Fewer than half (46 per cent) of all children under the age of five in sub-Saharan Africa have had their births registered.[11]

Legal identity is much broader than birth registration only. It covers all aspects of one's personal status: age, name, gender, marital status, etc. Article 7 of the Convention on the Rights of the Child, for instance, links birth registration to the right from birth to a name and a nationality. Often, several aspects of personal status are interrelated. For instance, in some countries parents will have to present a marriage certificate before a birth certificate for their child can be issued, or a mother may face gender discrimination when she tries to register her child if she does not have a marriage certificate.[12] Therefore, promoting SDG Target 16.9 requires new governance practices which include 'ensuring the proper and universal registration of the occurrence of all vital events (births, deaths, marriages, divorces ...), issuance of certificates that serve as legal tenders and introduce the lifetime legal identity of the individual and the production of comprehensive, regular and reliable vital statistics based on universal civil registration of vital events'.[13] Concerned by the fact that the coverage of civil registration is not universal and complete in all countries of the world, the 2030 Agenda for Sustainable Development set as indicator 17.19.2: 'proportion of countries that have achieved 100 per cent birth registration and 80 per cent death registration'.

Legal identity requires not only the registration of all major life events, but also their certification. UNICEF reports on the large gap between the number of children whose births are reported as registered and those who actually have a birth certificate.[14] According to Plan International, globally, an estimated one billion people cannot officially prove their identity and 47 per cent of those are children without a birth certificate.[15] There is still a huge discrepancy between

---

10 See UNICEF, 'Birth registration' (June 2020) <https://data.unicef.org/topic/child-protection/birth-registration> accessed 15 April 2021. See also UN Department of Economic and Social Affairs, 'Goal 16' <https://sustainabledevelopment.un.org/sdg16> accessed 15 April 2021; UN Economic and Social Council, 'Special edition: progress towards the Sustainable Development Goals. Report of the Secretary-General' (8 May 2019) UN Doc E/2019/68, para 37: '*Even if many regions have reached universal or near universal birth registration, globally the average is just 73 per cent.*'

11 See UN Department of Economic and Social Affairs, 'Goal 16' <https://sustainabledevelopment.un.org/sdg16> accessed 15 April 2021.

12 UNICEF, 'What is birth registration and why does it matter?' <www.unicef.org/stories/what-birth-registration-and-why-does-it-matter> accessed 15 April 2021.

13 UN Legal Identity Expert Group, 'United Nations Strategy for Legal Identity for All' para 6 <https://unstats.un.org/legal-identity-agenda/documents/UN-Strategy-for-LIA.pdf> accessed 15 April 2021.

14 Of the roughly 508 million children under the age of five who are registered worldwide, about 70 million lack proof of registration in the form of a birth certificate, See UNICEF, 'Birth Registration for Every Child by 2030: Are we on track?' <https://data.unicef.org/resources/birth-registration-for-every-child-by-2030> accessed 15 April 2021.

15 Plan International, 'Birth registration' <https://plan-international.org/early-childhood/birth-registration> accessed 15 April 2021.

legal identity and proof of legal identity.[16] The right to be recognised as a person before the law often remains meaningless when the person concerned has no documentary evidence (civil registry certificate, identity card and/or passport) or, as we will discuss in section 3, when this proof of legal identity is questioned.

2.3. LEGAL IDENTITY IN A MIGRATION CONTEXT: THE ROLE OF PRIVATE INTERNATIONAL LAW

At the global (read: United Nations) level there is currently a political will to address legal identity issues from a human rights perspective, including in a migration context. The 2030 Agenda for Sustainable Development, and more specifically SDG Target 10.7, includes migration in its global framework. International migration requires international cooperation 'to ensure safe, orderly and regular migration, involving full respect for human rights and the humane treatment of migrants regardless of migration status, of refugees and of displaced persons'.[17]

SDG 16 also has a clear link with migration, as shown by the SDGs Report 2019:

> Realizing the goal of peaceful, just and inclusive societies is still a long way off. … In 2018, the number of people fleeing war, persecution and conflict exceeded 70 million, the highest level that the United Nations High Commissioner for Refugees has seen in almost 70 years. All are particularly vulnerable to various forms of abuse, including trafficking, violence and non-inclusive decision-making. Ensuring that they receive adequate protection is paramount to achieving the goal of inclusive societies and sustainable development.[18]

The latest figures for 2019 are even worse, and according to the UNHCR forced displacement nowadays is not only vastly more widespread but is simply no longer a short-term and temporary phenomenon.[19]

---

16 The latter is defined by the UN Legal Identity Expert Group as 'a credential, such as birth certificate, identity card or digital identity credential that is recognized as proof of legal identity under national law and in accordance with emerging international norms and principles'; see UN Legal Identity Expert Group, 'United Nations Strategy for Legal Identity for All' para 15 <https://unstats.un.org/legal-identity-agenda/documents/UN-Strategy-for-LIA.pdf> accessed 15 April 2021.

17 UNGS Res 70/1, UN Doc A/RES/70/1 (25 September 2015) para 29.

18 See UN, 'The Sustainable Development Goals Report 2019' (2019) <https://unstats.un.org/sdgs/report/2019> accessed 15 April 2021.

19 UNHCR, 'Global Trends. Forced displacement in 2019' <www.unhcr.org/globaltrends2019/> accessed 15 April 2021: 79.5 million forcibly displaced persons worldwide, the highest number ever reported by the UNHCR.

SDG Target 16.9 should be read together with the UN Global Compact on Refugees[20] and the UN Global Compact for Migration.[21] The Global Compact on Refugees (para 82) refers to civil and birth registration as a major tool for protection. While it does not necessarily lead to conferral of nationality, birth registration helps establish legal identity and prevent the risk of statelessness. Timely access to civil and birth registration and documentation should be facilitated for refugees and stateless persons. States are primarily responsible for providing proof of legal identity to refugees and stateless persons, but may be supported by UNHCR.[22] The Global Compact for Migration (Objective 4, para 20) commits 'to fulfil the right of all individuals to a legal identity by providing all … nationals with proof of nationality and relevant documentation, allowing national and local authorities to ascertain a migrant's legal identity' and 'to ensure … that migrants are issued adequate documentation and civil registry documents, such as birth, marriage and death certificates, at all stages of migration, as a means to empower migrants to effectively exercise their human rights'.

Providing (proof of) legal identity for all gives rise to private law issues. For instance, is an Afghan youngster an unaccompanied minor? Is a marriage a child marriage? How can a Pakistani couple prove their religious Ahmadi marriage? How does a Syrian man prove that a child is his when the child was born in a Turkish refugee camp and there is no birth certificate? In a migration context, these private law issues are inherently cross-border ones, which bring us to the field of private international law. The cross-border circulation and acceptance of documents that record the legal identity of people traditionally belongs to the field of private international law, which strives for as much cross-border continuity of people's legal identity as possible. For many refugees and migrants, this fundamental private international law objective is currently not being achieved, due to the lack of reliable documentary evidence. Refugees and migrants often face huge challenges in proving their legal identity.[23] Civil registry systems may be destroyed by war or simply not exist, and even where they do exist, people may, for various reasons – be it geographic distance, or the absence or corruption of official authorities – be unable to contact official authorities at the moment of birth, marriage or death. However, even where an

---

20 The resolution on the Office of the United Nations High Commissioner for Refugees which affirms the global compact on refugees was adopted by the General Assembly on 17 December 2018, UN Doc A/RES/73/151, Final Draft (June 2018) <www.unhcr.org/events/conferences/5b3295167/official-version-final-draft-global-compact-refugees.html> accessed 15 April 2021.

21 Adopted on 10 December 2018: UN, 'Global compact for migration' <https://refugeesmigrants.un.org/migration-compact> accessed on 15 April 2021.

22 UN, 'Implementation of the United Nations Legal Identity Agenda: United Nations Country Team Operational Guidelines', para 66 <https://unstats.un.org/legal-identity-agenda/documents/UNCT_Guidelines.pdf> accessed 15 April 2021.

23 See more in detail Jinske Verhellen, 'Cross-Border Portability of Refugees' Personal Status' (2018) 31 Journal of Refugee Studies 427.

institutional framework for universal birth registration is in place, officials may refuse to register the birth of migrant children, whether the parent's migratory situation is regular or not.[24] Moreover, those fleeing from war, persecution or poverty may leave documents behind or lose them during their journey (because they are confiscated by smugglers, for instance).

States of destination for migrants usually are accustomed to, and sometimes obsessed with, dates and documents. By contrast, in many countries of origin, people do not need official identity documents for their daily life. Sometimes they do not know their exact age. Major family life events, such as marriage, succession or the passing on of family names to children, are organised according to customary practices, without public authorities being directly involved. When an official document is required for access to specific services and activities, like education (in particular for the participation in national exams) or healthcare, documents such as the Afghan *tazkera*, for instance, despite being easily falsified, are considered sufficient. As will be discussed later, this reality in many States of origin does not correspond to the fundamental assumptions on which private international law relies. The post-colonial heritage sometimes strengthens that gap. In some post-colonial states, indeed, people perceive civil registration systems, which generally were built by the colonial state, as a symbol of survival of colonial domination, and therefore are reluctant to register major life events.

The purpose of this chapter is to bring the private side of legal identity into focus, or the objective of guaranteeing cross-border continuity of personal and family status, which can be considered 'an emerging human rights imperative in itself'.[25]

As will become clear in section 3, the current focus on combating irregular migration, as well as on police and security considerations, risks depriving SDG Target 16.9 of its very purpose by diverting attention from the rights and needs of human beings. Therefore, we will adopt a private law perspective as this implies a focus on migrants as individuals rather than on the state's interests.[26] States often focus on ideas of burden-sharing and fraud prevention. They manage international migration from a very distant and even statistical perspective (flows of people and figures), whereas consideration of the interests

---

24 See UN Committee on the Protection of the Rights of All Migrant Workers and Members of Their Families, Joint General Comment No 4 (2017) of the Committee on the Protection of the Rights of All Migrant Workers and Members of Their Families and No 23 (2017) of the Committee on the Rights of the Child on State obligations regarding the human rights of children in the context of international migration in countries of origin, transit, destination and return', UN Doc CMW/C/GC/4-CRC/C/GC/23 (16 November 2017) para 20.

25 Hans van Loon, 'The present and prospective contribution of global private international law unification to global legal ordering' in Franco Ferrari and Diego P Fernández Arroyo (eds), *Private International Law. Contemporary Challenges and Continuing Relevance* (Edward Elgar Publishing 2019) 228.

26 Sabine Corneloup, 'Can Private International Law Contribute to Global Migration Governance' in Horatia Muir Watt and Diego P Fernández Arroyo (eds), *Private International Law and Global Governance* (OUP 2014) 302.

of migrants and their family members requires a more engaged approach. Such a private law perspective does not necessarily mean that public law is taboo. Legal identity is a complex notion at the crossroads of public and private law: '[t]he need to contribute to the development of the global commons cannot stop at the boundaries of private or public law.'[27]

2.4. OVERVIEW AND ASSESSMENT OF IMPLEMENTATION INITIATIVES

Since the adoption of the SDGs, a significant number of initiatives have already been undertaken to support Target 16.9. The following overview will show their strong ambitions, as well as the concerns some of them are raising.

2.4.1. Developments within the United Nations: UN Legal Identity Agenda

As the issue of legal identity for all is of paramount importance in terms of fulfilling the SDG Agenda, the UN Legal Identity Expert Group (UN LIEG) was established in September 2018.[28] The substantive focus of the UN LIEG is an emphasis on building legal identity systems founded on civil registration from birth to death, and with a human rights approach.[29] In December 2019 the UN LIEG transitioned into the United Nations Legal Identity Task Force. This Task Force has to convene all United Nations agencies whose mandate is directly or indirectly linked with the holistic approach to legal identity. On civil registration (birth, death, marriage, divorce, adoption), for instance, these are UNICEF, the World Health Organization (WHO), the UN High Commissioner for Refugees (UNHCR), the International Organization for Migration (IOM), the UN Population Fund, and the UN Entity for Gender Equality and the Empowerment of Women. The Task Force also needs to involve other organisations outside the United Nations, such as the World Bank, the African, Asian and Inter-American Development Bank, and Plan International.[30]

---

27 Verónica Ruiz Abou-Nigm, 'Unlocking private international law's potential in global (migration) governance' in Franco Ferrari and Diego P Fernández Arroyo (eds), *Private International Law. Contemporary Challenges and Continuing Relevance* (Edward Elgar Publishing 2019) 208.

28 The LIEG is co-chaired by the Department of Economic and Social Affairs of the UN Secretariat (DESA), the UN Development Programme (UNDP) and the UN Children's Fund (UNICEF).

29 UN Legal Identity Expert Group, 'United Nations Strategy for Legal Identity for All' <https://unstats.un.org/legal-identity-agenda/documents/UN-Strategy-for-LIA.pdf> accessed 15 April 2021. See also <https://unstats.un.org/legal-identity-agenda/LIEG> accessed 15 April 2021.

30 UN, 'Implementation of the United Nations Legal Identity Agenda: United Nations Country Team Operational Guidelines' paras 184–186 <https://unstats.un.org/legal-identity-agenda/documents/UNCT_Guidelines.pdf> accessed 15 April 2021.

Within this UN LIEG framework, the United Nations Legal Identity Agenda (UN LIA) 2020–2030 has been defined. The UN LIA calls on all Member States to ensure universal civil registration of all vital events, rendered into regular, reliable and comprehensive vital statistics, and resulting in legal identity for all.[31] A recent UN report on the implementation of the UN LIA refers to the role of several UN agencies in the field of birth registration, such as UNICEF, the UNHCR, the IOM, the WHO and the UN Population Fund.[32]

A recent report by UNICEF shows that 'investments to increase birth registration levels have begun to yield results. But it also shows that much more effort is needed to reach the goal of universal birth registration and to improve civil registries to the point where such gains are irreversible'.[33] Hence, UNICEF calls for further actions.[34]

The UNHCR supports states in the registration of refugees and facilitates access to civil registration and documentation for refugees and stateless persons. While it does not necessarily lead to conferral of nationality, birth registration helps establish legal identity and prevent the risk of statelessness. The UNHCR's Global Action Plan to End Statelessness 2014–2024 contains actions that explicitly refer to the importance of legal identity for the prevention of statelessness.[35]

Implementing SDG Target 16.9 also includes special procedures for migrants. The IOM is primarily concerned with migrants located in other countries

---

31 ibid para 8.

32 ibid paras 153–174.

33 UNICEF, 'Birth Registration for Every Child by 2030: Are we on track?' 34 <https://data.unicef.org/resources/birth-registration-for-every-child-by-2030> accessed 15 April 2021.

34 UNICEF calls for five actions to protect all children, starting from birth. First, every child should be provided with a certificate following birth registration. Second, all parents, regardless of gender, should be empowered to register their children at birth. Third, birth registration should be linked to social services (health, social protection and education). The WHO and UNICEF emphasise, for instance, the cooperation between civil registration and health systems. They encourage the notification of births and deaths directly to civil registrars. Fourth, investments in safe and innovative technological solutions is needed to facilitate birth registration. Technology can be used to obtain timely, accurate and permanent records. For example, the use of mobile communications technologies, including cell phones, can help reach unregistered children by minimising the distance and related travel costs for remote populations. Fifth, communities should be engaged to demand birth registration for every child. To create effective, sustainable change, community members – particularly parents and community leaders – must understand how and why birth registration benefits their families. See UNICEF, 'Birth Registration for Every Child by 2030: Are we on track?' 35 <https://data.unicef.org/resources/birth-registration-for-every-child-by-2030> accessed 15 April 2021; UNICEF and Inter-American Development Bank, *Towards Universal Birth Registration. A Systemic Approach to the Application of ICT* (2015).

35 See UNHCR, 'Global Action Plan to End Statelessness: 2014–2024' <www.unhcr.org/ibelong/global-action-plan-2014-2024> accessed 15 April 2021: Action 7 urges states to ensure birth registration for the prevention of statelessness and sets out how states can implement this action including through procedures for late and delayed birth registration and campaigns to register older children and adults. Action 8 calls on states to issue nationality documentation to those who are entitled to it, ensuring that procedures to obtain such documentation are accessible, affordable and implemented in a non-discriminatory way.

without documentation. In order to assist migrants in obtaining civil status documents, which are critical for obtaining travel documentation, the IOM often works closely with consular authorities. The IOM also assists migrants with registering their children at birth. It has been looking into possibilities to develop more activities allowing for birth registration of children of migrants, through facilitation of access to consular authorities.

In addition, the UN Global Compact for Migration (Objective 4) mentions seven different and ambitious actions to realise the objective to fulfil the right to a legal identity by providing everyone with proper civil registry documents as a means to empower migrants to effectively exercise their human rights.

All these action plans within the framework of the United Nations are ambitious. They reflect the pursuit of universal birth registration, including the actual issuance of a birth certificate to all – and this not only at the time of birth, but also at later points in time. These action plans, however, also raise concerns. Initiatives implementing SDG Target 16.9 often focus on registration and certification of vital life events according to a public/administrative law understanding of legal identity. The civil registration apparatus is often considered from the angle of collecting statistical data. Comprehensive vital statistics are indeed of crucial importance for governments and UN agencies in order not only to implement SDG Target 16.9, but also to monitor public funding for several other SDGs. However, the essential objective of civil registration involves more than statistics. Above all, it provides individuals with the legal confirmation of a vital life event and the issuance of a legal document. As said above, this official trace of a person's existence is the entry point to the exercise of human rights, in the state of origin but also in a migration context.

2.4.2. Public–Private Partnerships

Several SDGs' implementation initiatives rely on public-–private partnerships. Such collaboration with the private sector includes both not-for-profit and profit-making entities.

Several initiatives of Plan International, for instance, illustrate this collaboration with not-for-profit organisations. With regard to SDG Target 16.9, Plan International emphasises innovations in birth registration. Through its 'Count Every Child' initiative, Plan International has helped register '40 million children and influenced laws in 10 countries so 153 million more can enjoy the right to a birth certificate'.[36] Plan is searching for innovative ways to increase birth registration rates and extend registration to the most marginalised.

---

36 See Plan International, 'Birth registration' <https://plan-international.org/early-childhood/birth-registration> accessed 15 April 2021.

It stresses the potential of technology to transform birth registration.[37] In order to improve civil registration services and to raise awareness in communities about the importance of getting children's births registered, Plan International has called for partnering with a range of stakeholders, such as governments, UN agencies, the private sector, academic institutions, civil society organisations and NGOs ('partner for impact').

In its report 'Innovations in Birth Registration' (2017), Plan International provides guidelines to help define solutions to the most challenging birth registration contexts. It also gives illustrations of birth registration innovations around the world. For instance, in El Salvador, Guatemala, Honduras and Paraguay, the Organization of American States (OAS), together with the civil registries, health ministries and hospital boards, developed a system of effective hospital-based birth registration. Having registration offices in hospitals represents a permanent response to birth registration in the Americas.[38] For Indonesia, the report refers to the problem that parents are required to show proof of their marriage to be able to obtain a birth certificate for their child that includes the father and mother's name. As a result, many children remained unregistered. The report describes the cooperation between the office of religious affairs (issuing marriage certificates), the religious courts (legalising marriage certificates) and the civil registry offices (issuing birth certificates) through a mobile legal identity service offered at the community level.[39] In Sierra Leone, due to the Ebola outbreak, the majority of children did not have their births registered. Cooperation between Sierra Leone's Ministry of Health and Sanitation, the WHO, UNICEF and Plan International led to mass birth registration and immunisation services, providing both services in one single movement.[40]

Public–private partnerships for the implementation of SDG Target 16.9 also include collaborations with the private, profit-making industry. Some initiatives are dedicated to the civil registration of vital events. For instance, in Burkina Faso, the government concluded a partnership with iCivil,[41] a company which developed a mobile technology to facilitate birth registration, particularly in

37 To give one example, in Kenya (Kwale County), a hybrid smart paper technology was piloted in 2018 in an effort to improve maternal and child healthcare as well as birth registration. Children are registered electronically. As a result, health workers stop using the existing manual system. See Plan International, 'Technology improves birth registration and health services' <https://plan-international.org/case-studies/new-technology-improves-birth-registration-and-health-services> accessed 15 April 2021.

38 Plan International and Accenture, *Innovations in Birth Registration* (16 October 2017) 24 <https://plan-international.org/publications/innovations-birth-registration> accessed 15 April 2021.

39 ibid 14.

40 ibid 16.

41 See for further information, <https://icivil.org> accessed 15 April 2021.

rural areas where birth registration rates remain low. The technology is based on a digital bracelet for new-born babies, combined with a mobile phone app, through which the health professionals transfer the information to the government's iCivil server. The registration details are then forwarded to the national birth registry. The digital bracelet is kept by the parents and can be used to obtain official documents, as well as to complete the registration if all the required information had not been provided by the parents at birth. Such flexibility allows cultural or religious traditions to be taken into consideration, for instance with respect to the choice of the child's name, which may be made only at a later stage. The contractual model iCivil is proposing is based on a licensing agreement with the government. The concept takes sustainable development into consideration, even beyond SDG Target 16.9, as it promotes a 'made in Africa' solution, based on economic and social inclusion and the respect for local traditions.

However, this is not the most widespread form of collaboration with private businesses. The private industry seems predominantly engaged in the security side of legal identity. Businesses producing identity documents and biometric identification systems are increasingly involved in government policies. African states, with the assistance of the IOM, the EU or other organisations, contract with foreign companies specialising in civil status and biometric identification systems, in order to produce biometric ID and voter cards and to build comprehensive identification databases. In particular, following the Valetta Summit of 2015, where the EU decided to cooperate with countries of origin of migrants to address the absence of identification documents, several African countries contracted, with the help of the EU Trust Fund for Africa, with private or semi-public security companies in order to set up biometric-based identification systems and documents. At present, it is not completely clear whether the strong interest of states in such identity management systems based on biometric identifiers is overtaking civil registration systems, or whether the former are being developed to support the latter. In any case, it has become clear that the financial assistance of the EU Trust Fund for Africa is increasingly tied to the EU's desire to stop irregular migration and to conclude agreements with countries of origin for the return of their nationals.[42] It must be acknowledged that the current international and European call for the strengthening of civil registration systems is not completely free from a post-colonial perspective. Although the best interest of the people directly concerned is obviously the main drive, another motivation behind that call lies in the political priority of

---

42 Tuuli Raty and Raphael Shilhav, 'The EU Trust Fund for Africa: Trapped between aid policy and migration politics', Oxfam Briefing Paper (January 2020) <https://oxfamilibrary.openrepository.com/bitstream/handle/10546/620936/bp-eu-trust-fund-africa-migration-politics-300120-en.pdf> accessed 15 April 2021.

Western states to combat irregular migration (often from former colonies) based on forged documents. Some of these projects are promoted as contributions to SDG 16, which is highly debatable because they tend to turn legal identity into a security rather than a human rights issue, which makes them far removed from the rights-based focus of SDG Target 16.9.[43]

One example of these projects is Civipol, a private company operating as the technical cooperation operator of the French Ministry of the Interior. In the field of identity, it provides expertise at all stages of civil registry and identity technology. In Senegal, for instance, Civipol worked on a technical assistance project which aimed to strengthen the civil registration system and create a biometric national identity register, including a fingerprint database of the whole population.[44] The project was funded by the EU Emergency Trust Fund for Africa in the Sahel region and Lake Chad area. Critics point out that, in reality, these kinds of projects seek to identify irregular migrants in order to enable states of destination to return them to their country of origin.[45] Despite this, they are promoted as a contribution to SDG 16.

Another example, Idemia (previously OT-Morpho), is a private company that produces biometric ID technologies. It has signed a contract with Mauritania, among others, for an integrated system combining citizen identification, production of biometric ID documents and border control.[46] In its border control component, the system, which is based on facial and digital recognition, aims at improving the management of migration flows, as well as the fight against terrorism and other forms of criminality. Legal identity is addressed through the lens of security and identity control.

These examples illustrate that there is a wide range of public–private partnerships in the field of legal identity and that some of them raise concerns from the perspective of sustainability and development. In particular, many public–private partnerships do not comply with good governance principles. Rather than taking into consideration local actors and traditions in an integrative approach, they often further the expansion of the Western security industry. Moreover, rather than enabling the populations to exercise their rights, they

---

43 In that sense, see also Mark Akkerman, 'Expanding the fortress. The policies, the profiteers and the people shaped by EU's border externalisation programme' (Transnational Institute and Stop Wapenhandel, May 2018).

44 Civipol, 'Senegal: Technical Assistance To Strengthen The Civil Registration System And The Creation Of A Biometric National Identity Register' <www.civipol.fr/en/print/pdf/node/160> accessed 15 April 2021.

45 Mark Akkerman, 'Expanding the fortress. The policies, the profiteers and the people shaped by EU's border externalisation programme' (Transnational Institute and Stop Wapenhandel, May 2018), 78–79.

46 See Nathalie Jullien, 'Morpho participe au renouvellement du système d'état civil mauritanien' <www.safran-group.com/fr/media/20100906_morpho-participe-au-renouvellement-du-systeme-detat-civil-mauritanien> accessed 15 April 2021.

build on immigration policy-based biases. Finally, sustainability also implies longevity,[47] which can only be ensured by the state through a state-owned civil registration system. There is no assurance that foreign and/or private funding is sustainable. Therefore, it is doubtful whether the right to legal identity for all can be sufficiently protected in the current operations of transferring the actual registration in the countries of origin from the public civil registry authorities to private or semi-public companies.

3. SURVEY OF EXISTING PRIVATE INTERNATIONAL LAW METHODS AND TECHNIQUES ON LEGAL IDENTITY

3.1. LEGAL IDENTITY IN INTERNATIONAL CONVENTIONS AND EU REGULATIONS ON PRIVATE INTERNATIONAL LAW

3.1.1. European Union

The 2016 EU Regulation on the circulation of public documents[48] provides a simplified circulation system for public documents issued by the authorities of a Member State that have to be presented to the authorities of another Member State. It builds on the principle of mutual trust and the assumption that equivalent legal guarantees exist in all EU Member States. The scope of the Regulation comprises civil status documents concerning birth, a person being alive, death, name, marriage, divorce, registered partnership, parenthood, adoption, domicile and/or residence, and nationality. For such public documents, the formalities required for their cross-border circulation are simplified: no legalisation or similar formality is necessary. Regrettably, its scope of application is extremely narrow. The Regulation only provides for the recognition of the *instrumentum*, not of the *negotium* those public documents contain.[49] It is not a Regulation on the recognition of personal status itself, but on the recognition of the public document attesting these civil status events. Moreover, it governs the

47 Term borrowed from Nico Schrijver, 'The evolution of sustainable development in international law: inception, meaning and status' (2007) 329 Collected Courses of The Hague Academy of International Law 217, 369.

48 Regulation (EU) No 2016/1191 of the European Parliament and of the Council of 6 July 2016 on promoting the free movement of citizens by simplifying the requirements for presenting certain public documents in the European Union and amending Regulation (EU) No 1024/2012 [2016] OJ L 200/1.

49 According to Art 2(4), the Regulation does not apply to the recognition of legal effects relating to the content of public documents.

circulation of such public documents only within the European Union.[50] And finally, it presupposes the existence of reliable public documents attesting the civil status of a person, whereas SDG Target 16.9 mainly deals with situations where (reliable) public documents do not yet exist.

In a global migration context, the Regulation nevertheless plays a certain role, especially for civil status events that occurred in an EU state of transit. For instance, children born in a refugee camp in Greece, who have their birth registered there, benefit from the Regulation when presenting their Greek birth certificate in Belgium or France. Moreover, the Regulation has potential for future policy developments. Indeed, one possible form of action could lie in the development of registration capacities in EU countries of first arrival of migrants, with a view not only to addressing vital events occurring there, but also to providing supplementary solutions for migrants born in a third country and lacking adequate civil status documents.[51]

3.1.2. *International Commission on Civil Status*

The International Commission on Civil Status (ICCS) aims at facilitating international cooperation in civil status matters. At first sight, it appears to be a highly relevant intergovernmental organisation for the implementation of SDG Target 16.9. Unfortunately, only a small – and constantly decreasing – number of states are party to it, which limits, if not annihilates, its actual contribution.[52] Moreover, states of origin of migrants are often not party to the ICCS, and even between European states, several potentially interesting conventions never entered into force due to the lack of ratification.

Some matters covered by the work of the ICCS are of importance for SDG Target 16.9, such as the 1985 Convention on the international cooperation in the matter of administrative assistance to refugees. It was designed to complement the 1951 Geneva Convention relating to the status of refugees. According to Article 25 of the Geneva Convention, the authorities of the state in whose territory the refugee is residing shall deliver such documents or certifications as would normally be delivered by the national authorities to whom the refugee

50 According to Art 2(3) a, the Regulation does not apply to public documents issued by the authorities of a third country; since 1 January 2021 the Regulation no longer applies to the UK, which has thus become such 'a third country'.

51 See also GEDIP, 'Declaration on the Legal Status of Applicants for International Protection from Third Countries to the European Union' (September 2015) <www.gedip-egpil.eu/documents/gedip-documents-25bis.htm> accessed 15 April 2021.

52 See Sabine Corneloup, 'Sur le Groupe européen de droit international privé: Recommandation concernant le maintien et le développement de la coopération internationale en matière d'état civil, adoptée le 14 septembre 2019 à Katowice' (2019) 4 Revue critique de droit international privé 1109; Hans van Loon, 'Requiem or Transformation? Perspectives for the CIEC/ICCS and its work' (2018–2019) 20 Yearbook of Private International Law 73.

can no longer have recourse. These documents replace the official instrument issued by the national authorities, and they shall be given credence in the absence of proof to the contrary. The 1985 ICCS Convention provides for international administrative cooperation in order to determine the identity and civil status of refugees. More precisely, the state in which the refugee resides and which is responsible for the application of Article 25 of the Geneva Convention can contact a state in which the refugee has previously resided, in order to obtain information on the identity and civil status under which the refugee was admitted to or registered in that state.[53] The 1985 Convention furthermore exempts documents emanating from the state of origin from any legalisation or equivalent formality.[54]

Other ICCS conventions, such as the 1997 Convention on the international exchange of information relating to civil status, or the 1999 Convention on the issue of a certificate of nationality, could also be of paramount importance for the legal identity of migrants. They facilitate the cooperation between national authorities, including civil registrars, in particular for the collection of information relating to identity and civil status. Regarding the evidential weight granted to foreign civil status documents, these conventions rely on the principle that public documents drawn up in conformity with the convention are recognised and shall be accepted as correct, unless and until the contrary is proved.[55] Furthermore, there is also the successful 1976 Convention on the issue of multilingual extracts from civil status records, which imposes an obligation on contracting states to issue multilingual extracts from records concerning birth, marriage or death, with no need for legalisation or any other formality. This Convention on the promotion of the circulation of civil status documents, together with the more modern 2014 Convention on the issue of multilingual and coded extracts and certificates from civil status records, served as a model for the abovementioned 2016 EU Regulation.

As with the public documents Regulation, the main concern is that all these ICCS conventions presuppose the existence of reliable civil status documents. Moreover, these conventions can only apply between contracting states and therefore depend on the number of ratifications and thus on the political will of states, which is fading even among European countries.

3.1.3. Hague Conference on Private International Law

In its Strategic Plan 2019–2022, the Hague Conference on Private International Law stresses that its work, which aims to improve global governance and to

53 Art 1(1) Convention on International Cooperation in the Matter of Administrative Assistance to refugees (adopted 3 September 1985).

54 Art 8 of the 1985 Convention.

55 See Arts 4 and 5 of the Convention on the issue of a certificate of nationality (adopted 14 September 1999).

strengthen the rule of law, may be connected to the UN SDGs in general.[56] Efforts are currently being made by the Permanent Bureau to promote further cooperation with the United Nations. To that end, an information document on 'The HCCH and the United Nations Sustainable Development Goals' was prepared for the Council on General Affairs and Policy of March 2020.[57] In terms of content, this document refers, on the one hand, to SDG 16, with a particular focus on the rule of law and access to justice and, on the other hand, to SDG 17, which aims to strengthen means of implementation and revitalise the global partnership for sustainable development.[58] So far, however, no initiative for further action has been taken with respect to issues concerning the legal identity and civil status documents of migrants. Nevertheless, some existing conventions are linked to it, or provide interesting methodologies or techniques which could be further developed with respect to SDG Target 16.9.

In particular, the 1961 Apostille Convention facilitates the circulation of public documents among states parties through the replacement of the long and costly legalisation process with the issuance of a single apostille certificate. The Convention has become one of the most widely applied multilateral treaties in the area of legal cooperation.[59]

According to the 1978 Convention on the celebration and the recognition of the validity of marriages, a marriage validly celebrated in one contracting state is recognised in all other contracting states. It thereby allows the cross-border mobility of spouses without exposing them to the risk of loss of their marital status. Where a marriage certificate has been issued by a competent authority, the marriage shall be presumed to be valid, until otherwise established. In theory, this could be relevant, for instance, for family reunification of migrants, allowing them to prove the existence and validity of their marriage, but the Convention only entered into force between Australia, Luxembourg and the Netherlands.[60]

The 1996 Convention on the protection of children deals with parental responsibility under both private and public law. It does not apply to matters

---

56 Hague Conference on Private International Law, 'Strategic Plan 2019–2022' (2019) 5 <www.hcch.net/en/governance/strategic-plan1> accessed 15 April 2021.

57 Permanent Bureau of the Hague Conference on Private International Law, 'The HCCH and the United Nations Sustainable Development Goals' (January 2020) <https://assets.hcch.net/docs/b5770a41-afef-4118-a2a9-39f939d4d832.pdf> accessed 16 April 2021.

58 The document of January 2020 was not further elaborated in the Council on General Affairs and Policy, 'Conclusions and Decisions adopted by the Council on General Affairs and Policy' (3–6 March 2020) <https://assets.hcch.net/docs/70458042-f771-4e94-9c56-df3257a1e5ff.pdf> accessed 16 April 2021. The Council just 'noted the report of the PB in relation to … the United Nations Sustainable Development Goals (SDGs), in particular SDG 16, to further the Strategic Priorities of the HCCH': para 56.

59 See <www.hcch.net/en/instruments/conventions/specialised-sections/apostille> accessed 16 April 2021.

60 See <www.hcch.net/en/instruments/conventions/status-table/?cid=88> accessed 16 April 2021.

of civil status, nor to decisions on the right of asylum and on immigration.[61] However, issues of parental responsibility or measures for the protection of children are not excluded from its scope of application for the mere fact that they arise in a context of asylum or immigration.[62] According to the explanatory report of Paul Lagarde, the exclusion applies to decisions which derive from the sovereign power of states. Therefore, only decisions granting or denying asylum or residence permits are excluded, whereas the protection and representation of children who are applying for asylum or for a residence permit fall within the scope of the Convention.[63] This refers to the traditional 'public law taboo', which is an important challenge for SDG Target 16.9, to which we will return in section 4.

In order to facilitate the cross-border proof of the capacity in which a person is entitled to act on behalf of a child and of the powers conferred upon him or her, a certificate can be requested from the authorities of the state where a protective measure has been taken or where the child is habitually resident.[64] The capacity and powers indicated in the certificate are presumed to be vested in that person, in the absence of proof to the contrary. This mechanism constitutes an efficient tool allowing foreign authorities to easily ascertain the capacity and powers of parents and other caregivers. Its extension to legal identity would significantly contribute to SDG Target 16.9.

More generally, the Convention provides a practical mechanism for cross-border cooperation to protect children, mainly through central authorities to be designated by each contracting state. The potential of this private international law instrument and the role of these central authorities for the protection of unaccompanied refugee children is currently under-exploited.[65] The central authorities of EU Member States do not yet cooperate, for instance, to gather information on the backgrounds of refugee and migrant children or to see if family members can be located or to exchange information in the event a

---

61 Convention on Jurisdiction, Applicable Law, Recognition, Enforcement and Co-operation in Respect of Parental Responsibility and Measures for the Protection of Children (adopted 19 October 1996), Art 4(j).

62 See our Study for the European Parliament (JURI Committee): Sabine Corneloup and Fabienne Jault-Seseke (coord) 'Children on the move: A private international law perspective' (June 2017, PE 583.158, with Bettina Heiderhoff, Costanza Honorati, Thalia Kruger, Caroline Rupp, Hans van Loon, Jinske Verhellen) para 1.1.

63 Paul Lagarde, 'Explanatory Report on the 1996 Hague Child Protection Convention' in *Proceedings of the Eighteenth Session* (vol II 1996) para 36.

64 Art 40 of the 1996 Convention on the Protection of Children.

65 See our two Studies for the European Parliament (JURI Committee): Sabine Corneloup and Fabienne Jault-Seseke (coord), 'Children on the move: A Private international law perspective' (June 2017, PE 583.158, with Bettina Heiderhoff, Costanza Honorati, Thalia Kruger, Caroline Rupp, Hans van Loon, Jinske Verhellen); Sabine Corneloup, Fabienne Jault-Seseke and Jinske Verhellen (coord), 'Private international law in a context of increasing international mobility: Challenges and potential' (June 2017, PE 583.157, with Bettina Heiderhoff, Costanza Honorati, Thalia Kruger, Caroline Rupp, Hans van Loon).

guardian is appointed. At present, the central authorities of EU Member States tend to give priority to their national asylum counterparts that are in charge of the implementation of the Dublin Regulation.[66]

Furthermore, there is the 1993 Hague Convention on International Child Adoption. Although this Convention does not deal with legal identity itself, identity is central to the matching mechanism. Moreover, it contains a provision concerning the identity of the child's biological parents. The authorities of the child's country of origin shall ensure that such information, if held by them, is preserved and that the child has access to it, insofar as is permitted by its law.[67] Moreover, the Convention also deals with the migratory status of the child in the country of the prospective adoptive parents. Cooperation between the central authorities of the state of origin of the child and the state of residence of the adoptive parents ensures that the adoption can only take place once it has been determined that the child is authorised to enter and reside permanently in the receiving state.[68]

3.2. LEGAL IDENTITY AT THE NATIONAL PRIVATE INTERNATIONAL LAW LEVEL

3.2.1. Private International Law Assumptions and Objectives

This is not the place for an in-depth presentation of the objectives and assumptions of private international law.[69] However, it is worthwhile to recall that, concerning personal and family status, the fundamental objective is to guarantee the permanence of legal identity and to avoid limping situations, in which the personal or family identity of an individual is considered lawful and valid in one legal order, but not in another. Cross-border mobility in general, and migration in particular, must not lead to a loss of the legal (personal and family)

---

66 Regulation (EU) No 604/2013 of the European Parliament and of the Council of 26 June 2013 establishing the criteria and mechanisms for determining the Member State responsible for examining an application for international protection lodged in one of the Member States by a third-country national or a stateless person (recast) [2013] OJ L 180/31.

67 Convention on Protection of Children and Co-operation in Respect of Intercountry Adoption (adopted 29 May 1993), Arts 16(1)(a) and 30.

68 Arts 17(d) and 18 of the 1993 Hague Convention.

69 See recently, among others, Ralf Michaels, 'Private International Law and the Question of Universal Values' in Franco Ferrari and Diego P Fernández Arroyo (eds), *Private International Law. Contemporary Challenges and Continuing Relevance* (Edward Elgar Publishing 2019) 148; Horatia Muir Watt, 'Discours sur les méthodes du droit international privé (Des formes juridiques de l'inter-altérité)' (2018) 389 Collected Courses of the Hague Academy of International Law 9; Yves Lequette, 'Les mutations du droit international privé : vers un changement de paradigme?' (2016) 387 Collected Courses of the Hague Academy of International Law 9.

identity of the person. The achievement of this objective requires a prima facie attitude of openness towards foreign legal orders, which is not made conditional upon the content of their laws.

However, one must also keep in mind that, historically, private international law rules were conceived on the assumption that the conflicts between national legal orders involve equal, like-minded and similarly developed states on both sides. Thereby, traditional private international law rules address legal identity from the perspective of the cultural background of Western industrialised states. With respect to (the proof of) legal identity, that approach results in attaching high value to dates and documents and in taking a reliable public civil registry for personal status events for granted, which objectively is not the situation worldwide. A gap exists between the assumptions of private international law and the actual nature of the conflicts between legal orders in matters relating to personal status on a global level.

When that gap between private international law assumptions and the global reality becomes too wide, and in addition restrictive migration policies interfere, private international law methods and techniques are deemed (even if only implicitly) inappropriate and are either adapted or not applied in practice.

3.2.2. Private International Law Methods and Techniques

In a cross-border situation, the legal identity of a person can give rise to several questions that fall into different private international law categories. According to the European tradition, legal identity belongs to the category of personal status. Within the matter of personal status, several conflict rules coexist under national private international law, requiring that each issue linked to legal identity be characterised, in order to identify the corresponding conflict rule. In this respect, a fundamental distinction is made between the validity of a legal relationship, on the one hand (section 3.2.2.2), and the proof thereof, on the other hand (section 3.2.2.3). Usually, the difficulties that arise when the migration status of the person is not at stake relate to the existence and validity of the legal situation. In practice, the proof of that status rarely is the main difficulty. By contrast, in situations where the migration status of a person depends on his or her personal and family identity, proof becomes the most important hurdle.[70] Below, parentage and marriage will serve as examples to illustrate how national private international law methods and techniques in two European countries operate in migration-independent situations, as well as in migration-related situations. But first, a broader perspective is taken in order to shed some light on

70 See more generally on the recognition, in a migration context, of personal status acquired abroad our Study for the European Parliament (JURI Committee): Sabine Corneloup, Fabienne Jault-Seseke and Jinske Verhellen (coord) 'Private international law in a context of increasing international mobility: Challenges and potential' (June 2017, PE 583.157, with Bettina Heiderhoff, Costanza Honorati, Thalia Kruger, Caroline Rupp, Hans van Loon).

the causes, explaining that validity and proof do not have the same importance for the two kinds of situations (section 3.2.2.1).

3.2.2.1. The Rise of Evidentiary Issues in Migration-Related Situations

The explanation behind the major difference between migration-related and migration-independent situations lies in the law, namely in the international and European law on human rights and refugee protection. Indeed, paradoxically, human rights and the right to asylum are a major cause of the importance the evidence of legal identity has gained over the past decades. This is of course not to say that human rights and refugee law should be criticised. However, it is important to acknowledge that these rights protected under international and European law may, in practice, have unintended side-effects. Analysing, among others, the categories of residence permits issued by France to non-European migrants between 2005 and 2017, the French sociologist François Héran stresses the significant proportion of rights-based migration, perceived as *migration subie*, compared to labour migration, often called *migration choisie*.[71] In 2017, of a total of 240,000 residence permits issued by French authorities, only 25,000 were labour-related, whereas 88,000 residence permits were issued to non-EU family members of French citizens and of foreign citizens legally residing in France. This family-based migration is a result of the recognition, under migration law, of the fundamental right to family life as enshrined in particular in Article 8 of the European Convention on Human Rights and Article 7 of the EU Charter of Fundamental Rights. In addition, 36,000 residence permits were issued to refugees and for health reasons, as a consequence of international and European refugee law (the principle of non-refoulement) and fundamental rights, which brings the total of rights-based migration to more than 50 per cent of the residence permits issued to non-EU migrants.[72]

In the political context that has dominated the migration policies of several states of destination over recent decades, governments wishing to reduce the number of migrants on their territory realised that they will have little impact on those rights-based residence permits so long as they do not want to denounce their international and European commitments. A legally valid marriage or parent–child relationship creates rights. Likewise, a specific nationality and

---

[71] François Héran, *Avec l'immigration – Mesurer, débattre, agir* (La Découverte 2017); see also his lectures on 'Migrations et sociétés' at the Collège de France, and in particular the 2018–2019 course on 'Pourquoi migrer?' <www.college-de-france.fr/site/francois-heran/course-2017-2018.htm> accessed 16 April 2021.

[72] Figures of the French Ministry of Interior, AGDREF Database (Application de gestion des dossiers des ressortissants étrangers en France), quoted by François Héran in his lectures of 10 January 2019 at the Collège de France (see previous footnote). Another important category of non-EU beneficiaries of residence permits are students (79,000 residence permits in 2017).

region of origin may entitle a refugee to international protection.[73] The only way not to recognise such rights is to challenge the existence of the legal relationship at their very source. Challenging the evidence of legal identity becomes one of the main legal levers for authorities wishing to reduce the numbers of migrants. Hence, even if the widespread suspicion of fraud is partly well founded, given the significance and reality of all kinds of irregularities, it is also a strategy to avoid the obligation to issue a residence permit to a migrant who would be entitled to it. For instance, the family of a migrant who holds a residence permit is entitled to family reunification on the grounds of parentage and marriage. Where the validity of the family relationship is not questionable in itself, the fundamental right to family life obliges the state to grant the family reunification, unless it is argued that there is insufficient evidence of the existence of the marriage or the parent–child relationship.

With this difference between migration-related and migration-independent situations in mind, the *summa divisio* between validity and proof of personal and family status will now be further explored.

3.2.2.2. Validity of the Legal Situation of a Person

3.2.2.2.1. General Private International Law Methods and Techniques

To take an example, if the succession rights of a child depend on the validity of the parent–child relationship between the child and the deceased, two different methods are applied in private international law depending on how parentage is established. Parentage by law or by recognition of paternity is addressed through choice-of-law rules, whereas parentage established by judgment is subject to rules on the recognition of foreign judgments. Both methods contain a public policy exception and both methods may require techniques of transposition and adaptation, if the foreign legal concept is unknown in the forum.

Regarding parentage by law or by recognition of paternity, first of all, the connecting factor used by the choice-of-law rule may differ from one country to another (nationality, domicile, habitual residence), but the overall methods and techniques are the same. For instance, parentage by law is governed in French private international law by the law of the state of the mother's nationality.[74] Recognition of paternity or maternity is valid, according to French private international law, if it complies either with the law of the state of the man's or

[73] In particular, with respect to subsidiary protection under Art 15(c) of the Qualification Directive 2011/95/EU of the European Parliament and of the Council of 13 December 2011 on standards for the qualification of third-country nationals or stateless persons as beneficiaries of international protection, for a uniform status for refugees or for persons eligible for subsidiary protection, and for the content of the protection granted (recast) [2011] OJ L 337/9.

[74] Art 311-14 of the French Civil Code.

woman's nationality, or with the law of the state of the child's nationality.[75] In Belgium, both parentage by law and recognition of paternity or maternity are governed by the law of the state of nationality of the person whose maternity or paternity is at stake.[76]

If the choice-of-law rule designates a foreign law the application of which would lead to a result which is manifestly incompatible with the fundamental principles of the forum, that law shall not be applied (public policy exception). In migration-independent as well as in migration-related situations, it is likely, for instance, that a foreign law that prohibits establishing legal paternity if the father and the mother are not married would be declared incompatible with the public policy of these European states.[77]

Secondly, if parentage is established by way of a foreign court decision, the permanence of personal status is achieved through the private international law rules on the recognition of foreign judgments. In several countries, those private international law rules are characterised by their openness and flexibility. The smooth recognition of judgments expresses private international law's fundamental objective to facilitate cross-border continuity and to avoid 'limping' situations. Of the requirements that may differ from one state to another, a common ground for refusal of recognition is the manifest incompatibility of the decision with the public policy of the requested state. In this context, public policy is understood in a very narrow sense, since the legal situation was created by a court decision in a foreign country.

In order to coordinate the coexistence of different legal orders in an individual case, private international law techniques such as transposition and adaptation fine-tune the mechanics of the general conflicts methodology. For instance, a foreign decision on the adoption of a child may require transposition into the categories of the forum distinguishing between full and simple adoptions depending on whether pre-existing legal parent–child ties are severed.[78] In a migration context, this can become relevant as regards migrants' access to the nationality of the state of residence, when nationality law provides simplified rules for full adoptions.[79] Another well-known example is the Muslim institution

---

75 Art 311-17 of the French Civil Code.

76 Art 62 of the Belgian Code of Private International Law.

77 At least, this has been the consistent position of the French Cour de cassation since Cass civ 1, 10 February 1993, no 89-21997. For a discussion on Belgian case law, see Hélène Englert and Jinske Verhellen, 'L'application du droit marocain de la famille en Belgique 2004–2015' in Marie-Claire Foblets (ed), *Le Code marocain de la famille en Europe. Bilan de dix ans d'application* (LGDJ/la Charte 2016) 327–330; Patrick Wautelet, *Relations Internationales. L'actualité vue par la pratique* (Anthemis 2010) 132–137; Patrick Wautelet, 'Ordre public international et filiation hors mariage' (2008) 19 Revue de Jurisprudence de Liège, Mons et Bruxelles 822, 835.

78 See, for instance, Arts 370-4 and 370-5 of the French Civil Code.

79 See for instance in France, Art 20 (full adoptions) and Art 21 combined with Art 21-12 (simple adoptions) of the Civil Code.

of *kafala*, which shall not be transposed into parentage because the institution has been specifically established as an alternative to adoption, which is prohibited by several Muslim countries. The relationship between the *kafils* and the *makful* cannot trigger the application of rules which are premised on the existence of a parent–child relationship. This holds true under civil law, as well as under migration law. The Court of Justice of the European Union has decided, with respect to entry and residence rights according to the Citizens Directive 2004/38, that a child placed under the Algerian *kafala* system is not a 'direct descendant' of a citizen of the Union, but falls under the category of 'other family members'.[80]

In general, these private international law rules potentially guarantee the cross-border continuity and permanence of the personal and family status of migrants. It is the proof of parentage or marriage that gives rise to difficulties (see section 3.2.2.3), whereas problems are relatively rare at the level of validity, with the notable exception however of sham marriages and sham recognition of paternity or maternity.

3.2.2.2.2. Fraud-Related Provisions on Sham Legal Relationships

Visa or residence permits, or access to nationality, may be denied where authorities suspect misuse of the right to family reunification. For instance, paternity established abroad is not recognised, because the acknowledgment or adoption of a child is seen as a way of evading nationality or migration law. Recognition is not refused on the ground that there would be validity problems in terms of the applicable foreign law, but because of suspicion of fraud.

Sham legal relationships can be addressed through traditional private international law techniques, such as the public policy exception, which may apply within the choice-of-law reasoning, or obstacles to the recognition of a foreign judgment.[81] In addition to these traditional techniques, in several European countries recent legislative changes to substantive law have given a larger role to the law of the forum. This predominance of states' own national law is justified by the concern of avoiding fraudulent situations, such as marriages of convenience,[82] sham adoptions[83] or sham recognitions of children.[84]

In Belgium, the recent legislation on sham acknowledgements of children[85] adds another layer by explicitly muting the abovementioned choice-of-law rules

---

80 Case C-129/18 *SM v Entry Clearance Officer, UK Visa section* [2019] ECLI:EU:C:2019:248. See also, ECHR *Chbihi Loudoudi v Belgium* App no 52265/10 (16 December 2014); ECHR *Harroudj v France* App no 43631/09 (4 October 2012).

81 See for a recent illustration in France with respect to a foreign adoption: Cass civ. 1, 15 January 2020, no 18-24261, requiring the motivations of the adoptant to be assessed.

82 See, for instance, Art 146*bis* of the Belgian Civil Code.

83 See, for instance, Art 365-2 of the Belgian Civil Code.

84 See, for instance, Art 330/1 of the Belgian Civil Code.

85 Act of 19 September 2017, *Moniteur belge* 4 October 2017.

and introducing a mandatory rule.[86] Belgian substantive law must be applied each time the establishment of parentage results in a residence permit for at least one of the parties, even if, on the basis of the choice-of-law rules, the applicable law is not Belgian law. Under French law, a marriage celebrated by a French spouse in a foreign country is subject to specific formalities aiming at ascertaining the genuine consent of the spouses. Among others, the spouses are interviewed in order to prevent or sanction sham marriages.[87] Moreover, the requirement of consent to marriage, according to French civil law, applies as an overriding mandatory provision even to the spouse who holds a foreign nationality.[88] This allows a sham marriage to be declared null and void, even if genuine consent is not required for the marriage to be valid according to the law of the spouse's nationality.

Hence, for migration-related situations, specific internationally mandatory provisions on the consent to marry, the recognition of a child, etc. provide derogating solutions. The general private international law assessment, characterised by openness towards foreign legal orders, is no longer deemed necessary or relevant.

3.2.2.3. Proof of the Legal Situation of a Person

The primary means of proof for facts and acts related to personal and family status are civil status documents, such as birth, marriage and death certificates issued by the authorities that are responsible for civil status registration in the country where these facts and acts took place. Private international law provides rules for the recognition of such civil status documents in a cross-border context. The submission of a document, however, is a significant challenge for many migrants and the very hurdle SDG Target 16.9 addresses.

In the current political context, when it comes to evidence, there is a big difference between migration-independent and migration-related situations. Below both situations will be compared for civil status acts (section 3.2.2.3.1), supplementary judgments (section 3.2.2.3.2) and age assessment and DNA procedures (section 3.2.2.3.3).

3.2.2.3.1. Foreign Civil Status Acts

According to private international law characterisations, the admissibility of modes of proof is governed by the *lex fori*. This law also determines the probative value of each means of proof. However, the modes admitted by the *lex loci*

86 Circular of 21 March 2018, *Moniteur belge* 26 March 2018.

87 Art 171-2 Civil Code. Sabine Corneloup, 'Maîtrise de l'immigration et célébration du mariage' in *Mélanges en l'honneur de Paul Lagarde* (Dalloz 2005) 207.

88 Art 202-1 French Civil Code.

actus are often accepted as well, especially with a view to protecting legitimate expectations of the parties. Exceptionally, in some areas, such as parentage, where the link between proof and substance is particularly strong, the private international law classification results in *lex causae* being designated, rather than the *lex fori*.[89] For example, according to Article 47 of the French Civil Code, full faith must in principle be given to acts of civil status made in a foreign country and drawn up in the forms in use in that country.[90] This is not a traditional choice-of-law rule but a substantive provision, into which a choice-of-law reasoning is incorporated as a precondition. The form of the act is governed by the *lex loci actus* and, according to the principle of *auctor regit actum*, foreign public authorities operate according to the law of their own states. Article 47 defines the legal effects of those documents, and in particular their probative value. The rule works perfectly well in migration-independent situations, when for instance an Australian child claims succession rights in France on the basis of an Australian birth certificate establishing the existence of a parent–child relationship with the deceased. If the foreign birth certificate is legalised/apostilled,[91] full faith will be given in France to this civil status document established by an Australian authority in conformity with Australian law.

However, Article 47 not only creates a presumption of probative value but also defines the limits thereof, by providing that full faith is not given when other records or documents retained, external evidence, or elements drawn from the act itself establish, after all useful verifications if necessary, that the act is irregular or forged, or that the facts declared therein do not square with the truth. These limits were introduced into Article 47 by legislative acts of 2003 and 2006, the main subjects of which were immigration, access to nationality and the scrutiny of the validity of marriages celebrated abroad. The political motivation of the legislators was to fight against documentary fraud in a migration context. Today, an attitude of suspicion of fraud has taken hold of nearly all public authorities.

---

89 See for parentage Cass, 24 May 2018, no 16-21163 in France. Or giving the choice between the *lex causae* and the *lex loci actus*, see Art 63 of the Belgian Code of Private International Law.

90 See, inter alia, Christine Bidaud, 'La transcription des actes de l'état civil étrangers sur les registres français: Cesser de déformer et enfin réformer …' (2020) 2 Revue critique de droit internationale privé 247; Sabine Corneloup, 'L'article 47 du Code civil et le droit international privé' (2020) 20 Revue de droit d'Assas 101; Christine Bidaud, 'Preuve de la nationalité et actes de l'état civil étrangers' in Amélie Dionisi-Peyrusse et al (eds), *La nationalité : enjeux et perspectives* (Institut Universitaire Varenne 2019) 299; Aurore Camuzat, 'La force probante des actes de l'état civil étrangers' in Hugues Fulchiron (ed), *La circulation des personnes et de leur statut dans un monde globalisé* (LexisNexis, Perspectives 2019) 311.

91 See the Hague Convention Abolishing the Requirement of Legalisation for Foreign Public Documents (adopted 5 October 1961), to which 118 states are parties, including France and Australia. No probative value is recognised if the requirement of legalisation or apostille is not met. For a recent re-affirmation of that principle, see Cass, 16 October 2019, no 19-16353. This is to be criticised because the foreign certificate could at least have an '*effet de fait*' and serve as a de facto presumption, to be completed by other means of proof.

A consultation on Legifrance[92] of the decisions rendered by the French *Cour de cassation* in 2019 gives an idea of the typical factual background of the cases falling under Article 47 in migration-related situations: the French authorities generally claim that the civil status documents presented by the person concerned are irregular or forged, and the latter has no alternative reliable means of proof of his legal identity in his or her possession. Migrants from countries whose civil status certificates are notoriously unreliable are today facing systematic suspicion of fraud in Europe. In migration-independent situations, by contrast, these limits are rarely applied, with the notable exception of surrogate motherhood.

3.2.2.3.2. Supplementary Judgments

In some countries, it is possible to have recourse to supplementary judgments if civil status documents are missing or not authentic. Most widely known are the declaratory judgments in lieu of birth certificates. Such judgments are generally rendered in the country where the fact or act relating civil status took place. Such procedures for missing birth certificates and, by extension, also for late or delayed birth registration could support the implementation of SDG Target 16.9.

According to private international law rules on the recognition of foreign judgments, these supplementary judgments are to be recognised like any other foreign judgment. In different European states, such as France and Belgium, which take a liberal approach even to decisions from non-EU states, this alternative means of proof of legal identity raises no major difficulty, as long as the situation is migration-independent. By contrast, in migration-related situations, the suspicion of fraud affects supplementary judgments in the same way as it affects civil status certificates. The judgment is not recognised if its authenticity is doubtful or, more generally, if the state of origin of the judgment is blacklisted. Here again, in practice, the (real or alleged) unreliability of a foreign legal system results in the general rules and methods of private international law being set aside.

3.2.2.3.3. Age Assessment and DNA Testing

Another example is age assessment procedures for migrant children. In general, the proof of the age of a child is rarely, if ever, an issue with which private international law has to deal. In migration-independent situations, difficulties arise only with respect to the actual implementation of the rules on parental responsibility and international child protection. The actual applicability of those rules is not questioned, whereas in migration-related situations the opposite is true. Indeed, migrant children in general, and unaccompanied migrant children in particular, benefit from more favourable derogating

92 <www.legifrance.gouv.fr/> accessed 16 April 2021.

provisions under migration and asylum law. As most unaccompanied minors are between 15 and 17 years old, doubts may exist regarding their age. Here again, fraud is (often systematically) suspected. Many European states have developed specific age assessment procedures, based on interviews with the child and/or medical examinations and bone tests.[93] According to EU asylum law, minority is presumed when, after exploring all the age assessment methods available, it is not possible to determine the child's age with sufficient certainty.[94] In practice, however, the presumption is not effectively applied in all Member States, since authorities tend to easily conclude that the child is over the age of majority. Numerous court decisions and decisions of administrative authorities bear witness to that attitude. Instead of focusing on access to protection as a minor, the boy or the girl will be scrutinised as a possible liar about his or her age. In this context, private international law methods and techniques are simply deactivated. Even if the child has documentary proof of his or her minority and the private international law rules on the recognition of civil status acts should apply, other invasive (medical) age assessment procedures often take over. There is no principle of giving the benefit of the doubt to the child.[95]

The same can be said about family reunification files in which migration authorities in the states of destination resort to genetic paternity/maternity tests even though this is not in accordance with the rules on parentage in their substantive family law (for instance because a man can acknowledge a child even in the absence of biological affiliation) or even if the persons concerned present civil status documents (e.g. late or delayed declaration of birth by means of a supplementary judgment).

---

93 For a comparative overview, see our Studies for the European Parliament (JURI Committee): Sabine Corneloup, Fabienne Jault-Seseke and Jinske Verhellen (coord), 'Private international law in a context of increasing international mobility: Challenges and potential' (June 2017, PE 583.157, with Bettina Heiderhoff, Costanza Honorati, Thalia Kruger, Caroline Rupp, Hans van Loon), para 1.2.1.4; Sabine Corneloup and Fabienne Jault-Seseke (coord), 'Children on the move: A Private international law perspective' (June 2017, PE 583.158, with Bettina Heiderhoff, Costanza Honorati, Thalia Kruger, Caroline Rupp, Hans van Loon, Jinske Verhellen), para 3.3.

94 Art 25(5) of the Procedures Directive 2013/32/EU of the European Parliament and of the Council of 26 June 2013 on common procedures for granting and withdrawing international protection [2013] OJ L 180/60.

95 As recommended in UN Committee on the Protection of the Rights of All Migrant Workers and Members of Their Families, 'Joint General Comment No 4 (2017) of the Committee on the Protection of the Rights of All Migrant Workers and Members of Their Families and No 23 (2017) of the Committee on the Rights of the Child on State obligations regarding the human rights of children in the context of international migration in countries of origin, transit, destination and return', UN Doc CMW/C/GC/4-CRC/C/GC/23 (16 November 2017) para 4. See also EASO, 'EASO Practical Guide on Age Assessment' (2018) 22–25 <www.easo.europa.eu/news-events/easo-publishes-practical-guide-age-assessment> accessed 16 April 2021; UNHCR and UNICEF, 'The Way Forward to Strengthened Policies and Practices for Unaccompanied and Separated Children in Europe' (10 July 2017) 9.

4. POTENTIAL OF THE SDG FRAMEWORK TO SPUR NEW THINKING ON LEGAL IDENTITY IN PRIVATE INTERNATIONAL LAW

The previous section does not leave much room for optimism. Private international law, or the private side of legal identity in a migratory context, seems to have been set aside.

At the global level, the abovementioned initiatives seem to signal that there is political will to address legal identity issues from a human rights perspective. These initiatives – even if some are liable to criticism – lead to more birth registration and certification. This evolving new framework under SDG Target 16.9 impacts on international migration too: more births are registered in the states of origin, and more migrants have access to reliable civil status documents, which can be presented to obtain passports and visas, to evidence family ties in the context of family reunification procedures, or to prove one's age as unaccompanied minor. In this emerging scenario, states of destination will have no choice but to take those civil status documents into account, otherwise they will be calling to question the SDG Target 16.9 implementation initiatives themselves.

In this new context of more and better civil registration, the potential of private international law instruments could be unlocked in several ways: (1) by overcoming the public/private law divide in order to effectively address legal identity issues in the current migration context; (2) by revitalising and building on international conventions and EU regulations on private international law; and (3) by disconnecting migration policies from legal identity issues.

4.1. OVERCOMING THE PUBLIC/PRIVATE LAW DIVIDE IN ORDER TO EFFECTIVELY ADDRESS LEGAL IDENTITY

With regard to SDG Target 16.9, the UN Legal Identity Task Force cooperates with organisations outside the UN whose mandate is directly or indirectly linked with the holistic approach to legal identity. This could be a concrete gateway for the Hague Conference to take initiatives – in line with its Strategic Plan 2019–2022 – to cooperate with the United Nations and its Legal Identity Agenda 2020–2030. Currently none of the Hague conventions directly address cross-border issues of legal identity, even though it is a central, personal status matter to which several conventions are closely linked. In the context of the new global framework, the fact that legal identity is widely acknowledged to be catalytic for achieving several SDGs should be an incentive to take initiatives.

Taking initiatives with respect to legal identity issues in a migration context would entail the Hague Conference, and by extension private international law in general, overcoming the public law taboo. To date, the Hague Conference has pushed aside issues directly or indirectly related to international migration, arguing among others that they involve public law aspects.[96] However, one of the very purposes of the SDGs is precisely to adopt an integrative approach that reaches beyond disciplinary boundaries. How can legal, social, economic and environmental considerations be integrated, if, within the legal sphere alone, it is not even possible to overcome the public/private law divide? In international law, scholars are increasingly questioning the lines of that divide, which have become blurred over the past decades.[97] Private international law has been confined to 'a purely ancillary function beyond (or beneath) the international political sphere', from which it has to find a way out, in order to participate 'in the politics of international law' and to 'ensure that interests beyond the state – of which some require tethering while others strive for recognition – work towards the planetary good'.[98] This is precisely what is called for to achieve SDG Target 16.9.

As discussed in section 3, several private international law methods and techniques codified in Hague conventions, despite not directly addressing legal identity, have the potential to provide solutions to problems related to international migration, if they were transposed to cross-border recognition of family ties in the context of family reunification or to cross-border cooperation in the field of protection of migrant and refugee children. That potential can only be unlocked if the Member States of the Hague Conference recognise that legal identity (too) is a private law matter and agree to initiate legislative projects in this area, despite the public law implications it has in the context of international migration.

In particular, improved operation of civil registration systems in states of origin, as a consequence of the implementation of SDG Target 16.9, will generate the need for more cooperation between states. Private international law lends itself pre-eminently to such international cooperation and the Hague Conference is very well placed to take initiatives, as it has states of origin, states of transit and states of destination among its Member States. Such initiatives could also support the implementation of SDG Target 16.8 on broadening and strengthening the participation of developing countries in the institutions of global governance. The Hague Conference has longstanding experience with methods and tools of cooperation, in which 'central authorities' play a prominent role. For instance, in

96 For instance, with regard to unaccompanied and separated children: Permanent Bureau of the Hague Conference on Private International Law, 'The application of the 1996 Child Protection Convention to unaccompanied and separated children' (February 2020) <https://assets.hcch.net/docs/64150323-9f1a-4f32-83a8-81558ea75e60.pdf> accessed 16 April 2021.

97 See the collection of foundational texts assembled by Horatia Muir Watt (ed), *Private International Law and Public Law* (2 volumes, Edward Elgar Publishing 2015).

98 Horatia Muir Watt, 'Private International Law Beyond the Schism' (2011) 2 Transnational Legal Theory 347 (the quotes are from pages 355 and 427).

the case of suspicion of fraud or the lack of any official documents, cooperation between central authorities of the concerned states should be set up, and the authorities of the state of origin should collaborate in investigations and the taking of evidence.[99] However, the experience of the Hague Conference has also shown that cooperation mechanisms are only effective if the central authorities are properly equipped, which presupposes sufficient financial support from their governments. Consequently, any initiative in this respect must include measures designed to support countries in the Global South.

4.2. REVITALISING AND BUILDING ON INTERNATIONAL CONVENTIONS AND EU REGULATIONS

In the light of the new global framework, a possible revitalisation of the conventions adopted by the ICCS deserves serious consideration. As described in section 3, several of the ICCS conventions presuppose the existence of reliable civil status documents. Implementing SDG Target 16.9 precisely meets this prerequisite. Implementing the goal of universal civil registration of all vital life events could revive the ICCS conventions. The very basis for the practical operation of these conventions would then be in place. The evolving new global framework under SDG Target 16.9 could possibly lead to more interest in these conventions and potentially to more ratifications and accessions. Hans van Loon describes the potential relevance of the ICCS conventions in the relations between the current (although decreasing) states parties and other states in Latin America, the Caribbean, the Middle East and Africa, and he goes on to say that 'if ICCS conventions were in force on a global scale, they would support the respect of the right to identity of migrants, and the interoperability of civil registry systems between States of origin (and return), transit States and States of destination'.[100]

A possible initiative for the Hague Conference could build on another recommendation previously formulated by Hans van Loon, namely to include the ICCS conventions when reviewing the practical operation of the Hague conventions: 'Given their complementary role in relation to the Hague Children's Conventions, relevant ICCS Conventions could usefully be included in the agendas of Special Commission meetings on the practical operation of these instruments.'[101] Unlike the Hague conventions, the ICCS conventions

99 Sabine Corneloup, 'Can Private International Law Contribute to Global Migration Governance?', in Horatia Muir Watt and Diego Fernández Arroyo (eds), *Private International Law and Global Governance* (OUP 2014), 316–317.

100 Hans van Loon, 'Requiem or transformation? Perspectives for the CIEC/ICCS and its work', (2018–19) 20 Yearbook of Private International Law 73, 83–84.

101 ibid 91.

deal with a variety of topics relating to legal identity and civil status. However little ratified, the Hague Conference could explicitly support the use of these ICCS conventions and thus put the issue of civil status and legal identity more prominently on its agenda.

Furthermore, it would also be in the spirit of the global SDGs framework to build on the 2016 EU Regulation on the circulation of public documents in order for the Regulation to reach its full potential in a migration context. This Regulation guarantees the circulation of civil status documents between Member States. For migrants lacking reliable documents, the EU could consider possible ways to respond to that lack by developing alternatives in the Member State of first arrival. Reliable documents issued there could then circulate with the migrant across the EU in line with the 2016 Regulation.

4.3. DISCONNECTING MIGRATION POLICIES FROM LEGAL IDENTITY ISSUES

In the ideal world of this new global framework in line with SDG Target 16.9, states of destination will be less and less able to challenge the existence and proof of legal identity as a strategy to refuse residence permits or nationality. In migration-related situations, the discussion might shift from evidence to content, from proof to validity. Consequently, existing private international law methods and techniques might regain their role and legal identity issues could be approached in a different way.

However, such a scenario is not yet likely, as we believe that the context of suspicion of fraud is not about to disappear soon. Nevertheless, states will have to adjust their strategy as the implementation of SDG Target 16.9 will leave less room for questioning the evidence and existence of legal identity. Continued practice based on suspicion of fraud will then impact on what Héran calls rights-based migration[102] and thus on states' international and European human rights commitments. It is unlikely that states will be willing to officially denounce those human rights commitments in order to limit rights-based migration. At the same time, it is also unlikely that states will abandon their restrictive migration policies, once the strategy based on the questioning of evidence is no longer available to the same extent as today. In the current European context, no crystal ball is needed to predict that states will increasingly have recourse to externalisation policies. By preventing migrants from approaching their territories, states can partially deactivate European human rights commitments,

---

[102] See François Héran, *Avec l'immigration – Mesurer, débattre, agir* (La Découverte 2017); see also his lectures on 'Migrations et sociétés' at the Collège de France, and in particular the 2018–2019 course on 'Pourquoi migrer?' <www.college-de-france.fr/site/francois-heran/course-2017-2018.htm> accessed 16 April 2021.

as the recent decision of the European Court of Human Rights in *M.N. and Others v Belgium* illustrates.[103] In relation to Belgium's refusal to issue a humanitarian visa to a Syrian refugee family who submitted their visa application at the Belgian embassy in Lebanon, the Court ruled on the extraterritorial reach of the ECHR and the territorial delimitation of states' obligations. It concluded by declaring the case inadmissible because Belgium had no jurisdiction over the applicants. Convention rights only apply to persons who find themselves within the jurisdiction of the states parties to the Convention, and, save in exceptional circumstances, jurisdiction is primarily territorial. In a configuration of this kind, private international law does not come into play.

Consequently, SDG Target 16.9 undeniably has the potential to improve the legal situation of migrants, if combined with private international law methods and techniques, by disconnecting migration policies from legal identity issues. If migrants can prove their legal identity, they are empowered to exercise their rights. However, one has to be realistic. As long as the migration policies remain the same, Western states will find other strategies to limit legal access to residence permits and nationality.

5. CONCLUSION

The overview in section 3 revealed that, at present, existing private international law conventions and regulations do not have much practical impact, whether because they have not entered into force, do not apply in the relation between states of origin and states of destination of migrants, or do not really address legal identity issues. Moreover, the comparison between migration-independent and migration-related situations from the perspective of proof of legal identity made clear that private international law methods and techniques are not applied in the same way in the two kinds of situations. The current migration context leads to an 'inconvenient truth': one of the fundamental private international law objectives is cross-border continuity and harmony, but because states in the Global North pursue their own specific migration policies rather than seeking cross-border solutions, migration often leads to a discontinuity and even destruction of legal identity and a violation of the right to be recognised as a person before the law. As long as a direct link exists between the migratory status and the civil status of a person and as long as national authorities are guided, with respect to the proof of legal identity, by the suspicion of fraud, private international rules are likely to remain ineffective.

Yet these current deficiencies should not make us lose sight of the potential of private international law. The more comprehensive approach of SDG Target 16.9

---

[103] ECHR *M.N. and Others v Belgium* App no 3599/18 (5 May 2020).

indeed creates a new and challenging context. We have formulated three possible avenues through which private international law instruments and methodologies could become more relevant in terms of achieving the substantive targets of SDG 16: (1) by overcoming the public/private law divide in order to effectively address legal identity issues in the current migration context; (2) by revitalising and building on existing international conventions and EU regulations on private international law; and (3) by disconnecting migration policies from legal identity issues. In addition, SDG Target 16.9 should go even further. Where it uses birth 'registration' as an indicator, it weakens its ambition: what is birth registration worth if one cannot take it along when crossing borders? Although under a lot of pressure, private international law has something to offer here. Private international law does not operate with indicators that only measure numbers of registrations. It has the potential to guarantee that legal identity is of real value across borders and thus a means to empower migrants to exercise their rights.

SDG 17: PARTNERSHIP FOR THE GOALS

Fabricio B. Pasquot Polido*

Goal 17: Strengthen the means of implementation and revitalize the global partnership for sustainable development

Finance

17.1 Strengthen domestic resource mobilization, including through international support to developing countries, to improve domestic capacity for tax and other revenue collection

17.2 Developed countries to implement fully their official development assistance commitments, including the commitment by many developed countries to achieve the target of 0.7 per cent of ODA/GNI to developing countries and 0.15 to 0.20 per cent of ODA/GNI to least developed countries; ODA providers are encouraged to consider setting a target to provide at least 0.20 per cent of ODA/GNI to least developed countries

17.3 Mobilize additional financial resources for developing countries from multiple sources

17.4 Assist developing countries in attaining long-term debt sustainability through coordinated policies aimed at fostering debt financing, debt relief and debt restructuring, as appropriate, and address the external debt of highly indebted poor countries to reduce debt distress

17.5 Adopt and implement investment promotion regimes for least developed countries

Technology

17.6 Enhance North-South, South-South and triangular regional and international cooperation on and access to science, technology and innovation and enhance knowledge sharing on mutually agreed terms, including through improved coordination among existing mechanisms, in particular at the United Nations level, and through a global technology facilitation mechanism

* E-mail: fpolido@ufmg.br.

17.7 Promote the development, transfer, dissemination and diffusion of environmentally sound technologies to developing countries on favourable terms, including on concessional and preferential terms, as mutually agreed

17.8 Fully operationalize the technology bank and science, technology and innovation capacity-building mechanism for least developed countries by 2017 and enhance the use of enabling technology, in particular information and communications technology

Capacity-building

17.9 Enhance international support for implementing effective and targeted capacity-building in developing countries to support national plans to implement all the sustainable development goals, including through North-South, South-South and triangular cooperation

Trade

17.10 Promote a universal, rules-based, open, non-discriminatory and equitable multilateral trading system under the World Trade Organization, including through the conclusion of negotiations under its Doha Development Agenda

17.11 Significantly increase the exports of developing countries, in particular with a view to doubling the least developed countries' share of global exports by 2020

17.12 Realize timely implementation of duty-free and quota-free market access on a lasting basis for all least developed countries, consistent with World Trade Organization decisions, including by ensuring that preferential rules of origin applicable to imports from least developed countries are transparent and simple, and contribute to facilitating market access

Systemic issues

Policy and institutional coherence

17.13 Enhance global macroeconomic stability, including through policy coordination and policy coherence

17.14 Enhance policy coherence for sustainable development

17.15 Respect each country's policy space and leadership to establish and implement policies for poverty eradication and sustainable development

Multi-stakeholder partnerships

17.16 Enhance the global partnership for sustainable development, complemented by multi-stakeholder partnerships that mobilize and share knowledge, expertise, technology and financial resources, to support the achievement of the sustainable development goals in all countries, in particular developing countries

17.17 Encourage and promote effective public, public-private and civil society partnerships, building on the experience and resourcing strategies of partnerships

Data, monitoring and accountability

17.18 By 2020, enhance capacity-building support to developing countries, including for least developed countries and small island developing States, to increase significantly the availability of high-quality, timely and reliable data disaggregated by income, gender, age, race, ethnicity, migratory status, disability, geographic location and other characteristics relevant in national contexts

17.19 By 2030, build on existing initiatives to develop measurements of progress on sustainable development that complement gross domestic product, and support statistical capacity-building in developing countries

1. INTRODUCTION

The existing interplay between multi-stakeholder partnerships and private international law offers relevant examples of how transformative and innovative partnering initiatives can shape the implementation of Sustainable Development Goal 17 (SDG 17) within the prospective development of the 2030 Agenda. This chapter offers a preliminary overview of SDG 17, its fundamental policy, the main structures and processes associated with innovative and transformative multi-stakeholder partnerships at global level, and experiences offered by private international law institutions and their constituents. The analysis covers the current discussion on the dual dimension of SDG 17 on sustainability and development and its intertwining with existing private international law instruments and doctrines. In addition, the relevance of such instruments and doctrines to the implementation of SDG 17 is explored in the chapter, in particular with regard to technological development.

Targets 17.6, 17.7 and 17.8, together with 17.16 and 17.17, are examined to reveal the opportunities and concrete outcomes related to the articulation between private international law and multi-stakeholder partnerships, in particular the designing and implementation of global technology facilitation mechanisms and cooperation frameworks from the standpoint of transformative multi-stakeholder partnerships. This aspect has been evidenced by the increasing use of enabling technologies and development of collaborative solutions in a range of relevant areas of private international law, with direct involvement of states, international organisations, NGOs, industry and academia. International cooperation regimes in cross-border civil and commercial matters are becoming increasingly influenced by technological developments. They provide fertile ground for the proposed intersectional analysis in this chapter, with examples of the specific application of private international law, SDG 17 and its tech-development-related targets. Furthermore, reform proposals are formulated with a view to reviewing policies and implementation of existing domestic laws and treaty provisions in the field of private international law.

The main aspirational ideal is to capture the core rationale of SDG 17 and its targets related to technological development (e.g. technology facilitation mechanisms, environmentally sound technologies and use of enabling technologies) and combine them with a range of solutions. They cover the review of ongoing cooperation (judicial and administrative) frameworks and post-conventional mechanisms administrated by most international organisations active in the field of private international law; the designing of indexes and aggregated rankings to measure distinct degrees of inclusiveness, transformative potential and sustainable technological development, in particular with regard to multi-stakeholder partnerships linking private international law to SDG 17; and likewise the commitment of private international law stakeholders to building up and implementing new partnering initiatives based on sustainable (technology) development targets.

2. OVERVIEW OF SDG 17

Considered a successor of Millennium Development Goal 8, SDG 17 is the most instrumental goal of the 2030 Agenda, as it supports the overall implementation of all of the SDGs.[1] The instrumental role played by global multi-stakeholder partnerships in SDG 17 has been highlighted as central to the achievement of the 17 Goals by UN Member States, particularly in developing countries. As to a broader dimension of the 2030 Agenda and UN Law, SDG 17 refers to

1 See for instance N Cooper and D French, 'SDG 17: partnerships for the Goals – cooperation within the context of a voluntarist framework' in D French and L Kotzé, *Sustainable Development Goals: Law, Theory and Implementation* (Edward Elgar Publishing 2018) 271 (noting that the former MDG 8, in seeking to establish a 'Global Partnership for Development', had an influence on the conception of SDG 17 in the new 2030 Agenda).

the universal commitment of Member States to foster and ensure the 'means of implementation and revitalisation of global partnership for sustainable development'.[2] During the progress made by the Open Working Group (OWG) prior to the final adoption of the 2030 Agenda, the proposed targets were arranged into distinct thematic lines within SDG 17: trade, finance, technology, capacity-building, policy and institutional coherence, multi-stakeholder partnerships, and data, monitoring and accountability.[3] The big picture for delegates was to keep the discussions guided by the need to raise 'living standards for all, beginning with the poorest, while keeping global burden on food systems, biodiversity, climate and natural resources in check'.[4] The final wording of SDG 17 was expressly drafted to emphasise the demands on the mobilisation and sharing of knowledge, expertise, technology and financial resources.

Another aspect deserves attention in terms of the policy shaping of SDG 17: it is placed at the centre of the governance dimension of Agenda 2030, which highlights the role of multi-stakeholder partnerships in enhancing cooperative and collaborative frameworks at transnational, regional and domestic levels.[5] The focus on multi-stakeholder partnerships could be understood also by looking at the articulation between three analytical dimensions of SDG 17 ('subjective', 'relational' and 'procedural'). Furthermore, several ramifications and intersections with different legal fields, such as human rights law, development law, public and administrative law, corporate and financial law, trade law and also private international law are identified in SDG 17. For example, existing international instruments (treaties, protocols, conventions), contracts and public-private partnerships used to formalise and instrumentalise 'global partnerships' are legal experiments being covered by an array of areas of law. They go beyond a strict public/private law divide or a narrow approach to the regulatory role played by SDG 17.

SDG 17 relies on the dual dimension of sustainable development at international and domestic levels. In this sense, the designing of global partnerships itself shall contemplate complementary intersectional goals, such as poverty eradication, health, education, food security and nutrition. SDG 17

---

2 D Wallace, 'The UN regime and sustainable development: Agenda 2030' in C Karlsson and D Silander (eds), *Implementing Sustainable Development Goals in Europe* (Edward Elgar Publishing 2020) 23.

3 M Kamau, P Chasek and D O'Connor, *Transforming multilateral diplomacy: The inside story of the sustainable development goals* (Routledge, 2018) 132 et seq.

4 M Kamau, P Chasek and D O'Connor, *Transforming multilateral diplomacy: The inside story of the sustainable development goals* (Routledge, 2018) ch 8.

5 D Wallace, 'The UN regime and sustainable development: Agenda 2030' in C Karlsson and D Silander (eds), *Implementing Sustainable Development Goals in Europe* (Edward Elgar Publishing 2020) 23. The other three dimensions related to the 17 SDGs are the social, economic and environmental dimensions.

provides for a flexible and open category of 'multi-stakeholder partnership', which includes any cooperative, collaborative and transactional arrangements between a range of actors and stakeholders.[6]

The debate on multi-stakeholder partnerships is not new. It recalls the concrete application of Article 71 of the UN Charter, which deals with the consultative status of non-governmental organisations with the UN Economic and Social Council.[7] Article 71 also provides the UN operation itself with a legal solid framework for the involvement of foundations, business associations and individual private-sector companies with the Organization's existing tasks and mandates related to global policy issues.

There are many examples of this, the United Nations Global Compact being one of the most remarkable. It is the largest voluntary corporate sustainability initiative worldwide, which has grown to over 12,000 corporate participants based in 160 countries (both developing and developed) since its launch by former Secretary-General Kofi Annan in 2000.[8] The Global Compact's network-based governance framework reinforces the initiative's multi-stakeholder and public–private aspect and enables governance to be shared between governments, businesses and civil society organisations. It also allows the establishment and operation of entities that engage participants and stakeholders at the global and local levels in both decision-making and advisory processes.[9] Further examples could be given in line with the existing international practice on multi-stakeholder

---

6 Broadly speaking, such actors are those involved in public, public–private and civil society partnerships. See E T Bristol-Alagbariya, 'Sustainable Development: A Soft Law Concept Transforming SD-Oriented Initiatives of the UN System into Hard Law Instruments in UN Member-States and Promoting Partnerships around the Globe' (2020) 94 Journal of Law, Policy and Globalization 40.

7 F Dodds, *Multi-stakeholder partnerships: Making them work for the Post-2015 Development Agenda* (United Nations 2016) 3 <https://www.un.org/en/ecosoc/newfunct/pdf15/2015partnerships_background_note.pdf> accessed 30 June 2021.

8 The Global Compact was established in line with its UN General Assembly mandate to 'promote responsible business practices and UN values among the global business community and the UN System' and calls on companies across the globe to voluntarily align their operations and strategies with 10 universally accepted principles in the areas of human rights, labour, environment and anti-corruption, and to take action in support of SDG goals. See <https://www.unglobalcompact.org/> accessed 30 June 2021.

9 Multi-stakeholder partnerships, such as the Global Compact, have been successful in bringing each partner's core competences and experiences into the daily operation of the network-based governance framework. For example, they help partners to build synergies and co-generate impactful outputs for sustainable development. In essence, multi-stakeholder partnerships contributed to renewing the methods of work of the United Nations system, in particular after the 1990s and the progressive realisation of the internationally agreed development goals, which began with the Millennium Development Goals. See F Dodds, *Multi-stakeholder partnerships: Making them work for the Post-2015 Development Agenda* (United Nations 2016) <https://www.un.org/en/ecosoc/newfunct/pdf15/2015partnerships_background_note.pdf> accessed 30 June 2021.

partnerships, such as the Global Alliance for Vaccines and Immunisation (GAVI Alliance),[10] the Global Polio Eradication Initiative,[11] the Renewable Energy and Energy Efficiency Partnership,[12] and the Forest Stewardship Council.[13]

This initial overview of existing cooperative frameworks established by the UN Global Compact leads to the 'subjective' dimension of SDG 17, which focuses on parties involved in different kind of partnerships that are aimed at fostering and enhancing the means for achieving the SDGs. National and international entities are relevant for this initial sketch. Global multi-stakeholder partnerships encompass local communities, the private sector – such as global corporations and multinational companies – international and non-governmental organisations, civil society organisations, governmental bodies or agencies, and further bilateral, regional or transregional organisations and networks.[14] From a regional as well as geopolitical perspective, SDG 17 thus enables such multi-stakeholder partnerships to be openly and flexibly conceived so as to include entities that exist and are based in different countries, allowing a combination of both South–South and North–South networks. Likewise, multi-stakeholder partnerships aimed at achieving SDG 17 can be based on the structuring and operation of public–private sector partnerships between host governments of developing countries, governments of developed countries, development aid agencies, global corporations and multinational companies.[15] The 'subjective dimension' of SDG 17 is therefore strongly focused on the roles of relevant

---

10 Gavi is a global partnership mainly focusing on strengthening primary health care (PHC). Its main partners are the World Health Organization, UNICEF, the World Bank and the Bill & Melinda Gates Foundation. During COVID-19 pandemic, Gavi has been quite active in leading COVAX, which is considered a pillar of the Access to COVID-19 Tools (ACT) accelerator. By means of the so-called COVAX Facility, Gavi promotes a global risk-sharing mechanism for pooled procurement and equitable distribution of COVID-19 vaccines. See <https://www.gavi.org/> accessed 30 June 2021.

11 <https://polioeradication.org/> accessed 30 June 2021.

12 <https://www.reeep.org/> accessed 30 June 2021.

13 <https://fsc.org/en> accessed 30 June 2021.

14 See N Kanie et al, 'Global Governance through goal setting' in N Kanie and F Biermann (eds), *Governing through goals: Sustainable development goals as governance innovation* (MIT Press 2017) 1; E T Bristol-Alagbariya, 'Sustainable Development: A Soft Law Concept Transforming SD-Oriented Initiatives of the UN System into Hard Law Instruments in UN Member-States and Promoting Partnerships around the Globe' (2020) 94 Journal of Law, Policy and Globalization 40, 41.

15 The recently adopted 10 Principles of the United Nations Global Compact highlighted the intersections of SDG 17 with the human rights agenda, as the focus on companies operating at transnational level ('Businesses should support and respect the protection of internationally proclaimed human rights; and make sure that they are not complicit in human rights abuses'). Although it is not expressly stated in the Principles, it should be noted that global corporations participating in multi-stakeholder partnerships would be directly covered by existing international human rights obligations. This aspect also recalls a more prominent role for private international law methodologies and policymaking in shaping the interfaces between private international law and human rights.

actors engaged in international collaborative arrangements emerging from those multi-stakeholder partnerships.

Secondly, a 'relational' dimension of SDG 17 concerns both the structure and operation of the multi-stakeholder partnerships at the global level. Such partnerships encompass the variety of contractual collaborations between state actors and non-state actors with domestic and global reach, and platforms consisting of various forms of sustainable development-related plans, policies and programmes (including public–private partnerships) in developing countries.[16] In addition, the structure and operation of multi-stakeholder partnerships can be based on a pool of cross-border contractual transactions anchored in sustainable development-oriented collaborations. Such transactions go beyond cooperative schemes that are often set up within the framework of the United Nations system and other international organisations, or those which are established as outputs or deliverables of UN conferences. SDG 17-related partnerships aim at fostering and enhancing sustainable development in a holistic fashion and at facilitating dissemination of new supportive technologies, as well as national initiatives to attract investments and resources devoted to the implementation of the existing SDGs.[17]

Finally, a 'procedural' dimension of SDG 17 seeks to articulate the appropriate means both to implement the SDGs and to develop SDG-related practices from the standpoint of transnational and national processes underlying public–private-sector governance. When discussing SDG 17 and multi-stakeholder partnerships, the literature refers to similar processes already used in the field of government social responsibility, corporate social responsibility, and Good Governance, accountability and transparency.[18]

The starting point, however, came with the UN Global Compact, referred to above, which was launched by the United Nations in 2000.[19] The Global Compact puts a strong emphasis on the role of multi-stakeholder partnerships

---

16 E T Bristol-Alagbariya, 'Sustainable Development: A Soft Law Concept Transforming SD-Oriented Initiatives of the UN System into Hard Law Instruments in UN Member-States and Promoting Partnerships around the Globe' (2020) 94 Journal of Law, Policy and Globalization, 40.

17 ibid 47.

18 See for instance N Jägers, 'Sustainable development goals and the business and human rights discourse: ships passing in the night?' (2020) 42 Human Rights Quarterly 145; E T Bristol-Alagbariya, 'Sustainable Development: A Soft Law Concept Transforming SD-Oriented Initiatives of the UN System into Hard Law Instruments in UN Member-States and Promoting Partnerships around the Globe' (2020) 94 Journal of Law, Policy and Globalization 40.

19 The UN Global Compact preceded Agenda 2030 as such and it subsequently encompassed SDGs 1, 5, 13, 16 and 17. For a further description, see the information available at: <https://www.unglobalcompact.org/what-is-gc> accessed 30 June 2021.

for the overall implementation of the SDGs within the framework of both the UN system and domestic systems.[20] Furthermore, it seeks to create a global policy-oriented initiative to bring the public and private sectors closer to the tasks of concretely implementing the SDGs and fostering a transnational movement of companies and stakeholders adopting best practices. These practices focus on plans of action and activities that align with human rights, labour, environment and anti-corruption principles, as well as strategic actions to advance the SDGs, through collaboration and innovation towards sustainable development.[21] For example, the Global Compact promotes so-called engagement frameworks for Human Rights & Labour,[22] an Anti-Corruption Call to Action[23] and Climate Change.[24]

The procedural dimension of SDG 17 equally refers to the strategic outputs resulting from processes of implementing the SDGs themselves. Following the main principles of the Global Compact and the core issues covered by Agenda 2030 within the UN system, multi-stakeholder partnerships are best driven by the SDGs insofar as they are able to serve the purposes and principles embodied in the UN Charter and offer concrete contributions to the full realisation of the SDGs.[25] In addition, they should be undertaken in a manner that preserves the integrity, impartiality and independence of the United Nations. Multi-stakeholder partnerships encompass a range of compliance goals established by the UN Guiding Principles on Business and Human Rights,[26] the core labour standards and fundamental conventions adopted by the International

20 F Dodds, *Multi-stakeholder partnerships: Making them work for the Post-2015 Development Agenda* (United Nations 2016) 3 <https://www.un.org/en/ecosoc/newfunct/pdf15/2015partnerships_background_note.pdf> accessed 30 June 2021, 3–4.

21 Bristol-Alagbariya, 'The UN Global Compact as a Soft Law Business Regulatory Mechanism Advancing Corporate Responsibility Towards Business Sustainability and Sustainable Development Worldwide' (2020) 94 Journal of Law, Policy and Globalization 28.

22 <https://www.unglobalcompact.org/engage-locally/manage/engagement/human-rights-and-labour> accessed 30 June 2021.

23 <https://www.unglobalcompact.org/take-action/action/anti-corruption-call-to-action> accessed 30 June 2021. A similar initiative has been undertaken under other frameworks, such as the Global Anti-Corruption Consortium (GACC), which was established in 2016 to accelerate the global fight against corruption by mingling hard-hitting investigative journalism and expert civil society advocacy with government actions. See <https://www.occrp.org/en/gacc/> accessed 30 June 2021.

24 <https://www.unglobalcompact.org/what-is-gc/our-work/environment/climate> accessed 30 June 2021.

25 F Dodds, *Multi-stakeholder partnerships: Making them work for the Post-2015 Development Agenda* (United Nations 2016) 3 <https://www.un.org/en/ecosoc/newfunct/pdf15/2015partnerships_background_note.pdf> accessed 30 June 2021, 11.

26 UNHRC, 'Guiding Principles on Business and Human Rights: Implementing the United Nations "Protect, Respect and Remedy" Framework', UN Doc A/HRC/17/31 (21 March 2011) <https://www.ohchr.org/documents/publications/guidingprinciplesbusinesshr_en.pdf> accessed 30 June 2021.

Labour Organization,[27] United Nations social and environmental standards,[28] the Guidelines on Cooperation between the United Nations and the Business Sector,[29] and the UN Global Compact principles.[30]

The following main remarks can be made at this stage. Multi-stakeholder partnerships under SDG 17 allow a choice of flexible transnational structures and contractual arrangements to promote broadly almost all the goals in Agenda 2030.[31] Technically, it should be noted that there are no apparent formal constraints capable of limiting the scope and frameworks of SDG 17-related partnerships and their application to further partnerships entered into by and between state and non-state actors in the field of private international law. Hence, private international law institutions and cooperation networks will benefit from SDG 17 partnerships.

For example, the ongoing work carried out by the Hague Conference of Private International Law (HCCH), the Organization of American States (OAS), the United Nations Commission on International Trade Law (UNCITRAL), the International Institute for the Unification of Private Law (UNIDROIT) and cooperation schemes established with Member States and non-state actors could be reviewed in order to expressly incorporate most of the core features of multi-stakeholder partnerships. Likewise, the agenda and future work of those institutions could be formulated based on the evolving global principles of sustainable development, such as those promoted by the UN Global Compact and relevant to partnership initiatives which have a transformative and innovative character.

Under the 2000 UN Guidelines on Cooperation, as revised in 2015, any arrangements between national and transnational partnerships can be recognised

---

27 <https://www.ilo.org/global/standards/lang--en/index.htm> accessed 30 June 2021.

28 UNDP, Social and Environmental Standards (SES), as reviewed and effective on 1 January 2021 <https://www.undp.org/content/undp/en/home/librarypage/operations1/undp-social-and-environmental-standards.html> accessed 30 June 2021.

29 Guidelines on a Principle-based Approach to the Cooperation between the United Nations and the Business Sector (2015). According to the request made by UN General Assembly Resolution A/RES/68/234, the Guidelines, first issued in 2000 and reissued in 2009, were revised in 2015.

30 For a comment on the relationship between the Global Compact and multi-stakeholder partnerships, see F Dodds, *Multi-stakeholder partnerships: Making them work for the Post-2015 Development Agenda* (United Nations 2016) 3 <https://www.un.org/en/ecosoc/newfunct/pdf15/2015partnerships_background_note.pdf> accessed 30 June 2021, 11–12.

31 For purposes of the analysis proposed by this chapter, a multi-stakeholder partnership is understood in accordance with the definition in the Guidelines on a Principle-based Approach to the Cooperation between the United Nations and the Business Sector: 'An ongoing collaborative relationship between or among organisations from different stakeholder types aligning their interests around a common vision, combining their complementary resources and competencies and sharing risk, to maximise value creation towards the Sustainable Development Goals and deliver benefit to each of the partners'.

and entered into by and between state and non-state actors.[32] Participation and collective contribution seem to be definite features of multi-stakeholder partnerships designed under SDG 17.[33] As also remarked on in the literature, multi-stakeholder partnerships envisage primarily the sustainable allocation, dissemination and use of specific resources under SDG 17: (1) technology development; (2) financial resources; and (3) capacity-building.[34] Such partnerships suggest that cross-border transactions between public and private entities are not purely dependent on contractual and property rights over those resources and/or over resources crossing borders. Such a feature is particularly sensitive when partnerships involve cross-border flow of goods, services, technologies, information and knowledge. Rather, the overall approach to the dual dimension of sustainability and development involves intersectionality with cross-cutting issues, such as investment, trade, macroeconomic stability, policy coherence and the culture of sustainable development itself.[35]

It could also be argued that the current need for a growing number of sustainable development-oriented arrangements formalising multi-stakeholder partnerships across the globe could pave the way for a desirable review of international obligations and general principles in international law.[36] Further, they reinforce a holistic approach to international cooperation toward SDG 17-oriented partnerships and collaborative agreements. The practices of state and non-state actors, as well as the operation of multi-stakeholder partnerships,

---

32 See for example M Schäferhoff, S Campe and C Kaan, 'Transnational public–private partnerships in international relations: Making sense of concepts, research frameworks, and results' (2009) 11 International Studies Review 451.

33 See for example the selected cases draw up by the Commonwealth Secretariat, 'Means of Implementation – SDG 17: Enhancing the Contribution of Sport to the Sustainable Development Goals' (Commonwealth Secretariat 2017) <https://www.sportanddev.org/sites/default/files/downloads/enhancing_the_contribution_of_sport_to_the_sustainable_development_goals_.pdf> accessed 30 June 2021 ('Aligned with these considerations, relationships between governments and various private, and civil society organisations, including sport federations, can be configured in different ways to contribute collectively to sustainable development'); see also E T Bristol-Alagbariya, 'Sustainable Development: A Soft Law Concept Transforming SD-Oriented Initiatives of the UN System into Hard Law Instruments in UN Member-States and Promoting Partnerships around the Globe' (2020) 94 Journal of Law, Policy and Globalization 40, 49 (referring to specific cases related to transnational projects potentially involved in SDG 17, in particular with regard to global corporations and civil society organisations).

34 For instance, V P Nanda, 'The Journey from the Millennium Development Goals to the Sustainable Development Goals' (2016) 44 Denver Journal of International Law and Policy 389.

35 A Falzarano, 'Agenda 2030 tra Sviluppo Sostenibile e cultura della sostenibilità: una lettura sociologica' (2020) 5 Culture e Studi del Sociale 143.

36 See for example, C R Fernandez Liesa, 'Sustainable Development Goals and Changes of International Law' (2016) 32 Anuario Espanol de Derecho Internacional 49.

should aim at ensuring 'the wellbeing of humans and overall nature, towards a fairer, kinder, more just, sustainable and peaceful existence' on Earth.[37]

As explored above, the three dimensions – subjective, relational and procedural – involving SDG 17 and multi-stakeholder partnerships and their fields of operation reveal the diversity of profiles equally generated in terms of global involvement of state and non-state actors in cross-border private matters. This potentially contributes to a closer dialogue between private international law institutions and the 2030 Agenda.

As a methodological reference, the 2020 SDG Partnership Guidebook helps to emphasise the role of 'partnering' as a critical approach to measuring the impact of the SDGs by looking at three 'layers' that cut across the 16 SDGs (healthy environment, thriving society and prosperous economy).[38] SDG 17, for its part, constitutes the main axis crossing those layers. 'Tools', 'guidance' and 'accelerators' are significant pieces of the overall engine of multi-stakeholder partnerships, from their initial structuring and the choice of the appropriate form of collaboration to their subsequent operation and the review stage. Partnering also includes further concerns such as trust, power imbalances, the frustrations and challenges of working across different organisational cultures, and the potential added value to multi-stakeholder partnerships as a whole.[39]

According to the Guidebook, partnership design should consider the concepts of the collaborative advantage and additional impact resulting from partnerships.[40] The 10 collaborative advantages and partnership differences (indicated as the 'Partnership delta' or 'ΔP') for traditional partnerships are

---

37 E T Bristol-Alagbariya, 'Sustainable Development: A Soft Law Concept Transforming SD-Oriented Initiatives of the UN System into Hard Law Instruments in UN Member-States and Promoting Partnerships around the Globe' (2020) 94 Journal of Law, Policy and Globalization 40, 42.

38 D Stibbe and D Prescott, *The SDG Partnership Guidebook: A practical guide to building high-impact multi-stakeholder partnerships for the Sustainable Development Goals* (UNDESA/The Partnering Initiative 2020) <https://thepartneringinitiative.org/publications/toolbook-series/the-sdg-partnerships-guidebook/> accessed 30 June 2021. The study is an outcome of the 2030 Agenda Partnership Accelerator, a collaborative initiative undertaken by United Nations Department of Economic and Social Affairs (UNDESA) and the Partnering Initiative, in collaboration with the United Nations Office for Partnerships (UNOP), the UN Global Compact, and the UN Development Coordination Office. The initiative seeks to help to accelerate and scale up effective partnerships in support of the SDGs.

39 D Stibbe and D Prescott, *The SDG Partnership Guidebook: A practical guide to building high-impact multi-stakeholder partnerships for the Sustainable Development Goals* (UNDESA/The Partnering Initiative 2020) <https://thepartneringinitiative.org/publications/toolbook-series/the-sdg-partnerships-guidebook/> accessed 30 June 2021, 6.

40 ibid 33–34 (under 'Collaborative Advantage', 'partnership facilitates the combining or aligning of multiple different resources from different sectors into levers that together have the power to transform a system'; 'Partnership Delta is the ongoing value generated by the new system in comparison with the old (for example, the transformation from an unsustainable to a sustainable palm oil value chain results in the saving of millions of acres of virgin forest which would otherwise have been destroyed over time)').

described as: complementarity, collective legitimacy and knowledge standards, innovation, critical mass, holism, shared learning, reduced risk, synergy, scale, and connection. The Guidebook offers a number of examples of existing multi-stakeholder partnerships that have been considered to be conducive to the realisation of SDGs overall,[41] for instance: Banking on Change, in East Africa;[42] the Accord on Fire and Building Safety, in Bangladesh;[43] GSK and Save the Children;[44] the NCD Alliance;[45] Marine Protected Areas;[46] End Violence against Children;[47] and the SDG Partnership Platform in Kenya.[48]

Since global partnering, cooperative schemes and multi-stakeholder arrangements are deemed to be central to the analysis proposed in this chapter, the SDG Guidebook provides a practical understanding of how and to what extent existing multi-stakeholder partnerships contribute to concrete achievement of SDGs. Reports on cases and experiences also provide a possible approach to the three dimensions of SDG 17-oriented multi-stakeholder partnerships, as explained above (subjective, relational and procedural). Such cases and experiences are capable of demonstrating the potential connections between multi-stakeholder partnerships and technology development, technical assistance and capacity-building.[49] However, some criticism can be raised regarding the risks of deep voluntarism in shaping multi-stakeholder partnerships. In most cases, cooperation is not seen as a general obligation capable of significantly maintaining or restoring international development affairs.[50]

---

41 ibid 33–34.

42 See Plan UK and CARE International UK, 'Banking on Change: Breaking the Barriers to Financial Inclusion' (April 2013) <https://insights.careinternational.org.uk/media/k2/attachments/Banking_on_Change_Breaking_Barriers__April2013.pdf> accessed 30 June 2021.

43 <https://bangladeshaccord.org/> accessed 30 June 2021.

44 <https://www.gsk.com/media/2756/save-the-children-partnership-progress-brochure.pdf> accessed 30 June 2021.

45 < https://ncdalliance.org/> accessed 30 June 2021.

46 <https://www.iucn.org/theme/marine-and-polar/our-work/marine-protected-areas> accessed 30 June 2021.

47 <https://www.end-violence.org/> accessed 30 June 2021.

48 <https://kenya.un.org/en/15284-sdg-partnership-platform> accessed 30 June 2021.

49 See F Dodds, *Multi-stakeholder partnerships: Making them work for the Post-2015 Development Agenda* (United Nations 2016) 3 <https://www.un.org/en/ecosoc/newfunct/pdf15/2015partnerships_background_note.pdf> accessed 30 June 2021, 12.

50 Critically, see N Cooper and D French, 'SDG 17: partnerships for the Goals – cooperation within the context of a voluntarist framework' in D French and L Kotzé, *Sustainable Development Goals: Law, Theory and Implementation* (Edward Elgar Publishing 2018) 271. The authors ask the question of how far both the formulation and implementation of partnerships would reflect the existence of a 'putative international duty to cooperate in development affairs'. From an international legal perspective, that question explains likewise the mistrust in relation to deep voluntarism in committing states and non-states actors to cooperate.

Existing and emerging cases dealing with the design and implementation of multi-stakeholder partnerships in SDG 17 thus may help private international law institutions to (re)think and (re)formulate initiatives at the global, regional and domestic levels.[51] New collaborative action and partnerships in private international law, as further explored in this chapter, can build trust and social capital for technology-based cooperation networks and schemes (for example in cross-border family, commercial and financial matters and expected roles of digitisation). Furthermore, new transnational collaborative actions in the field of private international law may deliver additional impact for SDG 17 itself, as an important reference for advancing the 2030 Agenda.

For those purposes, the existing law-making, cooperative and enforcement structures in the field of private international law should be sufficiently open to contemplating new forms of multi-stakeholder partnerships. The next section discusses the potential intersectional issues from the standpoint of existing private international law instruments and doctrines relevant for SDG 17.

3. EXISTING PRIVATE INTERNATIONAL LAW INSTRUMENTS AND DOCTRINES RELEVANT TO SDG 17

Several existing private international law instruments and doctrines are aligned with the general purpose of SDG 17, in particular with cooperative frameworks and cross-border arrangements and the transnational collaborative approach for multi-stakeholder partnerships. As noted in the previous section, the design and implementation of SDG 17 by UN Member States and the increasing role of multi-stakeholder partnerships are not dependent on purely contractual and proprietary schemes for goods, services and technology broadly speaking. Rather, the dual dimension of the SDGs in the 2030 Agenda requires a common approach for allocation, dissemination and use of financial and technological resources and capacity-building, so that the operation of sustainable

---

51 Besides the SDG Partnership Guidebook, a very illustrative account on emerging cases is provided by B Gray and J Purdy, *Collaborating for Our Future: Multistakeholder Partnerships for Solving Complex Problems* (OUP 2018) ch 4. SDG-driven cases are helpful to unpack the opportunities, challenges, processes, steps, outputs, outcomes and impact of multi-stakeholder partnerships in a concrete fashion, being subject to monitoring and review. On the other hand, a holistic view of multi-stakeholder partnerships could be contested through the recognition of both 'appropriation and tactical polyvalence' still surrounding the development discourse in the UN 2030 Agenda. On this debate, see A Ziai, *Development discourse and global history: From colonialism to the sustainable development goals* (Routledge 2016). Due to its limited scope, this chapter will not discuss policy and normative arguments related to SDG 17 in detail.

development-driven partnerships happens in a collaborative and transformative fashion. Having in mind the global reach of SDG 17 and its linkage with regional and national legal systems, private international law instruments and doctrines could be taken as being conducive to the implementation and effective operation of SDG 17-related multi-stakeholder partnerships.

For example, the current regime for cooperation (judicial and administrative) in cross-border family matters put in place by the 2007 Hague Convention on the International Recovery of Child Support and Other Forms of Family Maintenance[52] was mainly designed to overcome the concrete obstacles raised by the shortcomings and complexity of the pre-existing regime. This was based, on the one hand, on the 1958 and 1973 Hague Conventions dealing with the recognition and enforcement of child support and family maintenance decisions,[53] and, on the other, the 1956 United Nations Convention on the Recovery Abroad of Maintenance,[54] which dealt with administrative cooperation on those matters. In addition to the recognition of overarching principles applicable to cross-border family matters (e.g. the best interests of the child, and an adequate standard of living for the child's physical, mental, spiritual, moral and social development),[55] the 2007 Child Support Convention took a holistic approach for cooperation guided both by expected 'deliverables' in terms of cross-border proceedings and effective results[56] and the benefits accruing from new technologies shaping cooperation. Here, the deliberate combination of the proper allocation of resources, procedures and use of new enabling technologies pre-defines what the contracting states refer to as a 'comprehensive system of co-operation' for ensuring the 'effective international recovery of child support and other forms of family maintenance'.[57]

The Convention's international cooperation model was based on the idea of flexibility and availability of applications for the establishment of maintenance obligations. It was conceived to be flexible enough to continuously evolve and

---

52 Convention of 23 November 2007 on the International Recovery of Child Support and Other Forms of Family Maintenance. Full text available at: <https://www.hcch.net/en/instruments/conventions/full-text/?cid=131> accessed 30 June 2021.

53 See the Hague Convention of 15 April 1958 on the Recognition and Enforcement of Decisions Relating to Maintenance Obligations towards Children, and the Hague Convention of 2 October 1973 on the Recognition and Enforcement of Decisions Relating to Maintenance Obligations.

54 Convention of 20 June 1956 on the Recovery Abroad of Maintenance New York, 268 UNTS 3 and 649 UNTS 330.

55 See for instance Arts 3 and 27 of the United Nations Convention on the Rights of the Child of 20 November 1989.

56 See for instance the Preamble to the 2007 Hague Child Support Convention ('procedures which produce results and are accessible, prompt, efficient, cost-effective, responsive and fair').

57 See Art 1(a) of the 2007 Hague Child Support Convention.

capture the new opportunities created by 'further advances in technology'.[58] The Convention strengthens the cooperation of central authorities, as well as the involvement and close participation of contracting states in the post-conventional phase, begun by with the entry into force of the 2007 Child Support Convention. That model was preceded by the 1980, 1993 and 1996 Hague Children's Conventions and was technically built upon the experiences with the HCCH's procedural conventions (the 1965 Service Convention, 1970 Evidence Convention and 1980 Access to Justice Convention).

A very distinctive feature of Hague conventions, also found in the 2007 Child Support Convention, is the set of specific provisions related to the roles and functions of central authorities, including the general obligation for central authorities to seek 'possible solutions which arise in the application of the Convention' (Art 5). This obligation is not simply a procedural duty in cross-border family proceedings. Rather, it is a compromise rule which gives room to further multi-stakeholder engagement, such as inter-cooperative networks of diplomatic bodies, judges, judicial officers, specialist law firms and civil society organisations dealing with cross-border family matters.[59] In addition to the greater access to procedures and assistance for obtaining support achieved by the 2007 Child Support Convention, there is another aspect to this Convention that is relevant to the SDG 17's dual dimension. The instrument takes into account the differing capabilities of developed and developing countries by offering a more (Art 15) and a less (Art 16) generous system for providing legal assistance, and, likewise, a more (Art 23) and a less (Art 24) sophisticated system for recognition and enforcement.[60]

Two elements are incremental to the global regime of facilitated circulation of foreign acts and judgments relating to cross-border family matters. The first is directly associated with an integrated and improved system for recognition and enforcement of decisions and administrative cooperation. While taking into account differing capabilities between developed and developing countries, as explained above, the 2007 Child Support Convention goes further than its predecessors in respect of both procedures and assistance for obtaining child and family support, and the obligation of contracting states to make effective 'enforcement measures' available in their internal laws (Art 34). Another element – building on the practice established under preceding modern Hague Children's

58 Preamble, para 4 of the 2007 Hague Child Support Convention.

59 In addition, further provisions of the 2007 Convention refer to the expected practice coming from the central authorities, such as the use of amicable methods of dispute resolution (mediation, conciliation or similar processes) aimed at obtaining voluntary payment of maintenance (Art 6(2)(d)).

60 See further H van Loon, 'The present and prospective contribution of global private international law unification to global legal ordering' in F Ferrari and D Fernández Arroyo (eds.), *Private International Law: Contemporary Challenges and Continuing Relevance* (Edward Elgar Publishing 2019) 221.

Conventions – is the review of the practical operation of the 2007 Child Support Convention, which is a twofold process comprising the regular establishment of a Special Commission by the HCCH to review the Convention's operation and to encourage the development of good practices under the Convention, and the obligation of contracting states to cooperate with the HCCH's secretariat in the gathering of information, including statistics and case law on the Convention's operation in practice (Art 54).

The Organization of American States (OAS) also provides another concrete example in terms of private international law policymaking and instruments that could be useful for SDG 17. The current OAS Secured Financing Project[61] has been anchored in the premises and recognition of the regulatory complexities involving secured transaction reforms within OAS Member States and the need for consistency with existing initiatives at the multilateral and domestic levels (in areas such as cross-border insolvency and bankruptcy). The project expressly refers to 'international collaboration' to reinforce the presence and involvement of several organisations, such as UNCITRAL, the HCCH, UNIDROIT, the International Finance Corporation (IFC) of the World Bank Group and the American Association of Private International Law (ASADIP). The movement also reflects mutual understandings of a particular private international law-related sector, while at the same time recognising the distinct policy trends and governance regimes of those organisations, in a sort of neo-federalism of international institutions. The neo-federalist approach to international institutions is a sign of the recent development of constitutional-driven international legal standards. It captures the increasingly converging governance roles of state and non-state actors in shaping particular substantive and procedural areas of law and regulation, while at the same time recognising 'unity in diversity'.[62] Hence, this approach is likely to be complementary to the proposed linkage between private international law and SDG 17.

The OAS practice on transnational collaboration is a good example to use to explain the increasing involvement of interest groups in private international law policymaking, which is adaptable to the openness of regulatory schemes covering multi-stakeholder partnerships in SDG 17. The Organization expressly recognises the roles of distinct non-state actors in shaping reforms of secured

61 See the official information on the OAS website: <http://www.oas.org/en/sla/dil/secured_transactions_background_importance.asp> accessed 30 June 2021.

62 For a distinct perspective, see the developments and outcomes of the Project on Neo-Federalism, available at: <https://www.federalism.eu/projects/overview/> access accessed 30 June 2021. The project is perhaps still modest in relation to the actual roles and engagement of stakeholders from industry, civil society organisations and academia in shaping neo-federalist models (apart from states and international intergovernmental organisations, like the UN and its specialised agencies), but recognises the inability of contemporary international and constitutional theory to deal with 'non-sovereign subjects'.

transactions regimes, reinforcing capacity-building and collective legitimacy.[63] A similar approach can be extended to the inclusivity, diversity, transparency and representation of major international institutions involved in private international law normative developments, such as the HCCH, UNIDROIT and UNCITRAL, and their abilities to effectively partner with industry, the private sector, NGOs and academia. Furthermore, there are examples ranging from the 'loose, uncommitted' participation of stakeholders as observers in HCCH Special Commission meetings to much more concrete 'partnering' initiatives at global and regional level. Amongst those examples the partnership between UNCITRAL, ASADIP and several Latin American universities for the dissemination of knowledge and promotion of UNCITRAL instruments in Latin America and the Caribbean could be noted.[64]

Another possible analysis of the interplay between SDG 17 and private international law relates to the ability of existing doctrines to capture the needs and potential of the dual dimension of sustainability and development in cross-border collaboration and the operation in practice of multi-stakeholder partnerships. One example is reflected in part by the private international law scholarship covering the renewed debate on transnational law[65] and international collaboration law.[66] The other example deals with the possible contributions of regulatory competition models, cooperative frameworks and the (re)conciliation of laws. All of them can be understood as important components of the regulatory (prescriptive) jurisdiction debate in private international law.

The major proponents of a redesigned role for transnational law and international collaboration law resort to distinct theoretical frameworks and formulations but with common practical results. The global movement of resources and human beings has become more and more dependent on

63 According to OAS, there is a legitimate policymaking role played by a variety of stakeholders transforming secured transactions regimes: 'these are organizations that have developed legal texts that can serve as guides or models for Member States engaged in reforms of secured transactions regimes and related matters. … Our collaborative work extends beyond participation and input at events to other activities, such as sharing data, ideas and good practices and ways to address gaps in country data, capacity-building and institutional architecture – gaps that OAS Members States need to fill in order to implement resilient and functional secured transactions regimes'. See the information available on the OAS website: <http://www.oas.org/en/sla/dil/secured_transactions_international_collaboration.asp> accessed 30 June 2021.

64 See the information available at: <https://uncitral.un.org/en/events/2020-uncitral-latin-america-and-caribbean-day> and <http://www.asadip.org/v2/?p=6582> accessed 30 June 2021.

65 R Michaels, 'After the Backlash: A New PRIDE for Transnational Law' in P Zumbansen (ed), *The Many Lives of Transnational Law: Critical Engagements with Jessup's Bold Proposal* (CUP 2020); R Michaels, 'Does Brexit spell the death of transnational law?' (2016) 17 German Law Journal 51.

66 See for instance, C Kessedjian and F Latty, *Le droit international collaboratif* (Pedone 2016).

transnational rules and institutions. There is a strong link between transnational processes, collaborative models and their openness to the horizontal formulation of legal rules and decision-making structures. For example, Michaels' major submissions on PRIDE elements in transnational law[67] pave the way to approach multi-stakeholder partnerships as transnational legal experiments.

It could also be argued that the potential dialogues between transnational law and global redistribution of natural resources may replace the formalist and liberal approach to private international law rules applicable to cross-border transactions, in particular those related to technology, trade and finance.[68] In this sense, transnational collaborative actions in the field of private international law will be able to deliver incremental output and additional impact relating to the SDG 17 itself. Transformative partnering is also about upgrading the existing work and operation of private international law institutions, strengthening trust and social capital for cross-border technology-based cooperation, particularly where the expected roles of digitisation are conceived of and concretely performed by cooperation networks and schemes.

These views also help to understand how some of the flexibility and openness of SDG 17 can be attributed to the transnational aspect of multi-stakeholder partnerships. In line with the contextual background of the adoption of the SDGs, both the participation and involvement of relevant actors in SDG 17 multi-stakeholder partnerships appear to be influential for a practical account of private international law initiatives. Participation and involvement may also evidence how legitimate authority becomes a conceptual and normative issue shaping transnational legal experiments. As remarked on by the literature, existing state-centric accounts of authority usually do not explain the presence of multiple legitimate authorities over the same subjects (here, one could highlight the authentic 'plurality of legitimate authority'[69] vested in global multi-stakeholder partnerships).

Private international law-related doctrines focusing on collaboration and, to a certain extent, legal pluralism also appear to play an important role

---

67 According to R Michaels, 'After the Backlash: A New PRIDE for Transnational Law' in P Zumbansen (ed), *The Many Lives of Transnational Law: Critical Engagements with Jessup's Bold Proposal* (CUP 2020), PRIDE comprises the following elements: politicisation of law, redistribution as challenge, inclusion of outsiders (including opponents), democratisation of law-making and adjudication, instead of exaggerated trust in experts or seemingly natural consequences, and energisation and emotion to counter the emotionality of opponents.

68 See for instance T Keijser, 'Transnational commercial law and natural resources' (2018) 23 Uniform Law Review 172 (discussing the original targets of commercial law as to facilitation of economic growth and monetary/short-term profits, and the overall conceptual conflicts related to natural resources as assets and their regulatory framework).

69 See N Roughan, *Authorities: conflicts, cooperation, and transnational legal theory* (OUP 2013). The author's account of shared and interdependent legitimate authority between states, regional and international bodies, transnational orders and sub-state governments support the view of the concurrent and converging multiple authorities on the establishment and operation of multi-stakeholder partnerships.

in the design and implementation of global multi-stakeholder partnerships for the purposes of SDG 17. Kessedjian proposes an original formulation for approaching international law and methods of application of legal rules based on cooperation. Legal pluralism, in turn, represents an instrument of collaboration, particularly due to the participation of civil society organisation in both law-making and decision-making processes.[70]

Collaboration is thus the pivotal concept for understanding how legal experiments circulate at global level. In this sense, a critical approach is further explored by Riles, who contends that collaboration could be perceived as a modality of comparative law and legal anthropology, as well as a 'wider template for social and political life'.[71] The involvement of distinct states, organisations, groups and communities in multi-stakeholder partnerships determines the extent to which zones of influence are defined in law-making and decision-making processes associated with SDG 17.[72] Here, a collaborative approach is useful for avoiding a battle of forms and narratives related to the design, regulation and implementation of global multi-stakeholder partnerships, as collaboration is the ultimate aim of partnering.

Private international law and comparative legal scholarship also offers a contribution to SDG 17, in particular the 'conciliation of laws' approach.[73] Joint instruments and regulations resulting from the dialogue and convergences between legal patterns and legal systems are appropriate tools for strengthening the dual dimension of sustainability and development in global partnering initiatives operating under SDG 17. Conciliation of laws matches the underlying public–private transnational regulatory goals related to the cross-cutting issues

---

70 The trade/finance and technology interfaces in multi-stakeholder partnerships also benefit from the participation of public policy specialists, groups of experts, interest groups and professional groups, including the influence over law-making and decision-making processes in developing countries: C Kessedjian and F Latty, *Le droit international collaboratif* (Pedone 2016), 13.

71 See A Riles, 'From comparison to collaboration: Experiments with a new scholarly and political reform' (2015) 78 Law & Contemporary Problems 147.

72 One could provide a range of situations where states, organisations and individuals will participate and be involved in multi-stakeholder partnerships, since most of them would be initially conceived as a kick-off project; the implementation phase would also not be deprived of the presence and participation of 'pressure groups', a term also used by Catherine Kessedijan when she discusses, for instance, the actual involvement of organisations and networks in decision-making processes pertaining to the regulation of cross-border e-commerce, such as the Internet Law and Policy Forum and the Global Business Dialogue on Electronic Commerce. Such involvement contributes to the creation of rules sufficiently 'adaptable' to the current cyber/tech-related activities, in particular 'self-regulation, accountability, convergence, protection of online users, jurisdiction, content of websites'. See C Kessedjian and F Latty, *Le droit international collaboratif* (Pedone 2016), 13–15.

73 See mainly H P Glenn, 'Conciliation of Laws in the NAFTA Countries' (2000) 60 Louisiana Law Review 1103; H P Glenn, 'Harmony of Laws in the Americas' (2013) 34 The University of Miami Inter-American Law Review 223.

affecting the operation and implementation of multi-stakeholder partnerships, for example financial schemes, trade, macroeconomic stability, technology, data flows, policy coherence and the culture of sustainable development. Inter- and multi-jurisdictional projects rely on minimum commitments related to harmonisation of legal systems.[74]

Although 'choice of law', 'choice of forum' and recognition of judgments cannot be easily detached from their distinctive 'competitive regulatory' components,[75] it is also true that policy choices as regards formal and informal harmonisation of laws may serve as catalysts for the strategic selection and production of standards, principles, rules and guidance, all of them inspired by a compromise with diversity. Due to the strong appeal of sustainable development goals, multi-stakeholder partnerships capture the essence of harmonisation processes, and to a greater degree, conciliation of laws.[76]

4. SPECIFIC APPLICATION OF PRIVATE INTERNATIONAL LAW, SDG 17 AND NEW TECHNOLOGIES

Targets 17.6, 17.7 and 17.8 refer to technological development; establishment of global technology facilitation mechanisms; transfer, dissemination and diffusion of environmentally sound technologies; science, technology and innovation capacity-building; and use of enabling technology, in particular information and communication technologies (ICT). Existing and prospective initiatives based on the intersection between private international law and multi-stakeholder partnerships may also be relevant for the achievement of those tech-related targets in SDG 17. As explained in section 3, the development of Hague Conventions on administrative and judicial cooperation provides a model for increasing direct cross-border cooperation of central authorities and, as exemplified by the 2007 Hague Child Support Convention, for increasing involvement of the contracting states in the post-Convention stage of the implementation and application of the instrument in practice, which does not exclude the

---

74 See for instance M Mantovani, 'Contractual Obligations as a Tool for International Transfers of Personal Data under the GDPR' (2020) <https://ssrn.com/abstract=3522426> or <http://dx.doi.org/10.2139/ssrn.3522426> accessed 30 June 2021.

75 F J Garcimartin, 'Regulatory competition: a private international law approach' (1999) 8 European Journal of Law and Economics 251; H Muir Watt, 'Choice of Law in Integrated and Interconnected Markets: A Matter of Political Economy' (2002) 9 Columbia Journal of European Law 383, 386–387 (referring to the 'reversal of perspectives' based on the contemporary economic analysis, the main prevailing point of which turns on the assumption that 'diversity is a source of disorder to be smoothed out wherever possible' and 'superseded by the conviction that competition between national legislators is basically salutary').

76 H P Glenn, 'Harmony of Laws in the Americas' (2013) 34 The University of Miami Inter-American Law Review 223; H P Glenn 'Sustainable diversity in law' (2011) 3 Hague Journal on the Rule of Law 39.

involvement of further stakeholders. The ultimate objective of providing fast and straightforward cooperation is best achieved with an emphasis on transformative partnering.

Gradually, the general reinforced HCCH administrative and judicial cooperation framework will be facilitated by the growing use of digitisation and smart technologies, new applications of intensive data and cross-border secured data transfer, as well as the enhancement of enabling technology in ICT. The effective interplay between new technologies and global administrative and judicial cooperation generates additional gains for the daily practice of HCCH, in particular with regard to the existing regimes set up by the procedural and legal cooperation conventions in force. For example, one could remark on the ongoing HCCH initiatives and projects undertaken in connection with the International Network of Judges, direct judicial communication and the desired development of a cross-border family mediation framework, as detailed in the HCCH Specialised Section on Child Abduction.[77]

The UNCITRAL insolvency cooperation initiative is also illustrative of the specific application of private international law, SDG 17 and new technologies, insofar as it may provide improved coordination between existing mechanisms, in particular at the UN level, and through a global technology facilitation mechanism. Article 27(b) of the 1997 UNCITRAL Model Law on Cross-border Insolvency ('Communication of information by any means considered appropriate by the court')[78] anticipated most of the concerns related to social distancing like those faced during COVID-19 pandemic. The cross-border insolvency cooperation framework relies on the supportive development of new technologies to reduce delays, facilitate face-to-face contact and encourage the use of methods of direct communication, such as videoconferencing. Access to ICT for court-to-court communication processes, in turn, rely on mere physical access through available hardware and software and use of videoconferencing. Rather, access to ICT should be strongly allied to the equitable treatment of stakeholders in their distinct levels of digital knowledge, digital capacities and digital literacy when engaging in court-to-court and direct communications.[79]

---

77 <https://www.hcch.net/en/instruments/conventions/specialised-sections/child-abduction> accessed 30 June 2021.

78 See UNCITRAL Practice Guide on Cross-Border Insolvency Cooperation (2010) 1–19 <https://uncitral.un.org/sites/uncitral.un.org/files/media-documents/uncitral/en/practice_guide_ebook_eng.pdf> accessed 30 June 2021. The UNCITRAL Model Law was adopted by the Commission in 1997. As stated in its Preamble, it focuses on the legislative framework needed to facilitate cooperation and coordination in cross-border insolvency.

79 A good overview of the topic and the distinct perspectives coming from governments is provided by the UNCITRAL Draft Notes on cooperation, communication and coordination in cross-border insolvency proceedings, United Nations Commission on International Trade Law, Thirty-sixth Session, New York, 18–22 May 2009 <https://undocs.org/en/A/CN.9/WG.V/WP.86/Add.1> accessed 30 June 2021.

In addition, technology development associated with cross-border proceedings and cooperation frameworks both requires and promotes the use of new technological innovations and digitisation techniques. Most of the new ICT, digital technologies and innovative solutions in artificial intelligence (AI), big data and cloud computing are designed and owned by global corporations and large innovative research institutes across the globe. This is to say that benefits accruing from global multi-stakeholder partnerships in the field of private international law and digital international cooperation will increasingly depend on the integration of new participants. The current practice in those fields ranges from, for instance, the issuance, registration and circulation of electronic apostilles, via the Electronic Apostille Programme (e-APP),[80] to legally more challenging cases such as the use of enabling technology to facilitate and improve regulatory schemes for e-service of documents[81] and the taking of evidence through video-link.[82]

Interestingly, all these innovations to facilitate the use of digitisation techniques have been initiated on the basis of existing multilateral treaties, such as the 1961 Hague Apostille Convention, the 1965 Hague Service Convention and the 1970 Hague Evidence Convention, and their implementation in practice. Without amending the text of these conventions in any way, the members of the HCCH and the states parties to the conventions have accepted that an evolutive interpretation of these conventions allows, and indeed requires, the use of electronic means.[83] Indeed, the 2003 HCCH Special Commission on the practical operation of the Apostille, Evidence and Service Conventions stressed that:

> the Apostille, Evidence and Service Conventions operate in an environment which is subject to important technical developments. Although this evolution could not be foreseen at the time of the adoption of the three Conventions, the [Special Commission] underlined that modern technologies are an integral part of today's

80 The e-APP was launched in 2006 to support the electronic issuance and verification of apostilles at global level and refers to the 1961 Convention Abolishing the Requirement of Legalisation for Foreign Public Documents. Information on the Apostille Section is available at: <https://www.hcch.net/en/instruments/conventions/specialised-sections/apostille> accessed 30 June 2021.

81 See HCCH, *Practical Handbook on the Operation of the Service Convention* (2016) Annex 8, 167–201. <https://www.hcch.net/en/publications-and-studies/details4/?pid=2728> accessed 30 June 2021.

82 See HCCH Evidence Section, in particular 'Taking of evidence by video-link' and the *Guide to Good Practice of the 1970 Evidence Convention*. Available at: <https://www.hcch.net/en/instruments/conventions/specialised-sections/evidence> accessed 30 June 2021.

83 For a theoretical discussion of the implications of technology and context in treaty interpretation, see U Linderfalk, *On the interpretation of treaties: the modern international law as expressed in the 1969 Vienna Convention on the Law of Treaties* (Springer 2007) 131 (commenting on Art 31(3) of Vienna Convention and 'subsequent practice' of contracting parties in the application of the Treaty).

> society and their usage a matter of fact. In this respect, the SC noted that the spirit and letter of the Conventions do not constitute an obstacle to the usage of modern technology and that their application and operation can be further improved by relying on such technologies. The Workshop held prior to the SC (i.e., on 27 October 2003) clearly revealed the means, possibilities and advantages of using modern technologies in subject matters falling within the scope of the Conventions.[84]

Multi-stakeholder partnerships have proven vital for the implementation of HCCH Conventions, especially those that establish direct communication and cooperation channels between the administrative authorities and courts of contracting states. Since the 1990s, the HCCH has been a pioneer in providing such implementation assistance for its Legal Cooperation and Children's Conventions, through diagnostic visits and the delivery of advice, consultation and judicial seminars, first on a country-by-country basis and gradually through regional initiatives. These activities were funded through partnerships with HCCH members. Since 2007, these initiatives were put on a more secure footing, through the establishment, as an integral part of the Secretariat, of the International Centre for Judicial Studies and Technical Assistance,[85] funded through supplementary contributions from the members. The Centre enabled the development of technical assistance, capacity-building and judicial training, with the support of UNICEF and NGOs such as Terre des Hommes, Defence for Children and others.

The most elaborate of these assistance programmes, which continues to run today, is the Intercountry Adoption Technical Assistance Programme (ICATAP), which relates to the Hague Intercountry Adoption Convention. This programme has included the provision of (1) legal assistance towards the signature and ratification of the Convention; (2) legal assistance with developing and reviewing national implementing legislation and related regulations; (3) advice on the creation and functions of central authorities and other competent authorities; and (4) training and other operational assistance for authorities and other relevant actors. Following two successful pilot programmes in Guatemala and Cambodia, a large number of other countries – some encouraged by the UN Committee on the Rights of the Child in its recommendations to states parties to the UN Convention on the Rights of the Child – requested and obtained assistance through the ICATAP. Many countries in Asia, Africa, Europe

---

84 See Conclusions and Recommendations of the Special Commission, held from 28 October to 4 November 2003, para 4.

85 See HCCH, The Hague Conference International Centre for Judicial Studies and Technical Assistance, 'The Intercountry Adoption Technical Assistance Programme (ICATAP)', document drawn up by the Permanent Bureau (November 2009) <https://assets.hcch.net/docs/c955e159-53a1-4aea-89b6-c8b09b1c3f55.pdf> accessed 30 June 2021. See also 'News from the Hague Conference on Private International Law' (2011) 16 Uniform Law Review 993.

and the Americas have received assistance under the ICATAP.[86] Technical assistance under ICATAP was provided even if the state concerned was not a HCCH Member, following which many such states sought membership to the organisation.[87] In other words, non-Member States would be encouraged to join HCCH while taking part in such technical assistance framework.

As explored above, multi-stakeholder partnerships in the field of private international law have turned out to be good examples of potential cases for integration and incorporation of new technologies into pre-existing transnational cooperation schemes. This leads to a partial conclusion that the design and implementation of global technology facilitation mechanisms or even the delivery of science, technology and innovation capacity-building programmes in private international law are indeed conducive to SDG 17 compliance in its targets related to technology. Here, one should notice a sound interplay between current and prospective multi-stakeholder partnerships and the enhancement of technology-oriented international legal (judicial and administrative) cooperation in the interests of both private international law and SDG 17.

5. REFORM PROPOSALS

Multi-stakeholder partnerships in the field of private international law can benefit from the experience already consolidated at the global and domestic levels and be integrated more effectively with SDG 17, in particular Targets 17.6, 17.7 and 17.8. In areas where private international law could benefit from new technologies (facilitation mechanisms, environmentally sound technologies and enabling technologies), relevant instruments and partnerships could be scrutinised under the requirements of multi-stakeholder involvement and collaborative actions. This can be done in line with the UN Global Compact principles, the converging roles of state and non-state actors in law-making and decision-making, innovative transnational legal experiments (like joint regulations and principles), and a compromise with a pragmatic goal of 'conciliation of laws'.

---

86 These countries include Azerbaijan, Benin, Cape Verde, Chile, Colombia, Croatia, the Democratic Republic of Congo, Côte d'Ivoire, Ethiopia, Ghana, Haiti, Honduras, Kazakhstan, Kenya, the Republic of Korea, Kyrgyzstan, Lesotho, Madagascar, Malawi, Mauritius, Mozambique, Nepal, Nicaragua, Niger, Paraguay, Serbia, Togo, Vietnam, Ukraine and Zambia.

87 The ICATAP can thus be considered a remarkable example of a multi-stakeholder partnership involving relevant state and non-state actors with a common objective of providing assistance to states which are planning ratification of, or accession to, the Hague 1993 Intercountry Adoption Convention, or which have ratified or acceded to the Convention but need assistance with implementing it. See further the Annual Reports of the Hague Conference 2007–2020 <https://www.hcch.net/en/publications-and-studies/publications2/annual-report> accessed 30 June 2020.

Relevant roles for transformative and innovative partnering in private international law may be further explored under the methodological assessment proposed by the 2020 SDG Partnership Guidebook.[88] As remarked in this chapter, SDG 17 multi-stakeholder partnerships operate based on the initial structuring phase, the choice of the appropriate form of collaboration, as well as the implementation and review phases. The procedural dimension of SDG 17 includes other concerns, such as trust, power imbalances, the frustrations and challenges of working across different organisational cultures, and potential added value for multi-stakeholder partnerships,[89] which is also applicable to cooperation frameworks existing in connection with international instruments adopted by members of the HCCH, UNCITRAL, UNIDROIT and OAS. Reforms could be guided by SDG 17 assessment tests that are applicable to existing instruments and global collaborative frameworks, for example partnerships involving international institutions and relevant stakeholders active in the private international law area, such as described in sections 3 and 4. Designing focused global indexes or aggregated rankings on the practical operation of a specific international instrument or of a multi-stakeholder partnership in the field of private international law could be useful in assessing the distinct degrees of inclusiveness, transformative potential and sustainable technology development in ongoing partnership initiatives.

For example, such experiments could be designed with the proactive involvement of local governments, international organisations, industry, civil society and academia, with the purpose of measuring not only the success and effectiveness of a particular instrument or partnership in private international law,[90] but also how SDG 17-compliant the operation and outcomes of such instrument and partnership have been. SDG 17 compliance levels would comprise the ability of such instruments and partnerships to foster social, economic and environmental change and innovation in partnering, as well as inclusiveness and success in developing standards, principles, rules and guidance inspired by respect for diversity. In addition, SDG 17 compliance levels would ideally take into consideration the outcomes of multi-stakeholder partnerships in fostering sustainable allocation, dissemination and use of technological and financial resources, and capacity-building programmes.

Another aspect concerns a 'convertible' feature of existing legal (judicial and administrative) cooperation regimes in private international law. Such regimes

---

88 D Stibbe and D Prescott, *The SDG Partnership Guidebook: A practical guide to building high-impact multi-stakeholder partnerships for the Sustainable Development Goals* (UNDESA/The Partnering Initiative 2020) <https://thepartneringinitiative.org/publications/toolbook-series/the-sdg-partnerships-guidebook/> accessed 30 June 2021, 33 et seq.

89 ibid 6.

90 Number of members/adherents, responses to individual or mutual requests, frequency of application of an instrument or assistance by partnership members, decisions made using legal grounds based on the instruments, etc.

could be redesigned in multi-stakeholder partnering initiatives based on a sustainable technology-oriented goal. This means that existing multi-stakeholder partnerships created to promote policies and cooperation frameworks in the field of private international law can be redesigned through the lens of the dual dimension of SDG 17 and its main tech-related targets.

Target 17.7, for instance, seeks the promotion of 'development, transfer, dissemination and diffusion of environmentally sound technologies to developing countries on favourable terms, including on concessional and preferential terms, as mutually agreed'.[91] This target would require existing multi-stakeholder partnerships and the practical administration and operation of treaties and conventions in the field of private international law to be conducive to the dissemination and use of 'environmentally sound technologies'.[92] Environmentally sound technologies are techniques and technologies capable of reducing environmental damage through processes and materials that generate fewer potentially damaging substances, recover such substances from emissions prior to discharge, or utilise and recycle waste products.[93]

Targets 17.6 and 17.8, in turn, may offer innovative solutions for improving policy and legislative designs involving multi-stakeholder partnerships within international legal (judicial and administrative) cooperation frameworks and their supporting roles for the dissemination and use of new digital technologies. Innovative enabling technologies would expedite and enhance direct court-to-court communication, operation of central authorities, service of documents, the exchange of information on foreign law applicable to proceedings, and the obtaining of evidence.

This is all to say that the current design and operation of cooperation frameworks, such as those involved in cross-border civil and commercial matters, including transnational litigation (HCCH, OAS, UNCITRAL), could not be conceived without a main concern being the diffusion of enabling technologies and facilitation mechanisms. The existing cooperation frameworks should be

---

91 See also Target 17.7 developments under the SDG Indicators Metadata Repository <https://unstats.un.org/sdgs/metadata/?Text=&Goal=17&Target=> accessed 30 June 2021.

92 It should be noted that Agenda 21, adopted by UN Member States at the 1992 Conference on Environment and Development, introduced the term in several chapters, its goals and means of implementation. See Report of the United Nations Conference on Environment and Development, Rio de Janeiro, 3–14 June 1992 <https://sustainabledevelopment.un.org/content/documents/Agenda21.pdf> accessed 30 June 2021. Chapter 34 of Agenda 21, in particular, emphasises the recommendations for 'transfer of environmentally sound technology, cooperation and capacity-building', which is directly linked to Target 17.7 of the SDGs consolidated in Agenda 2030. Such interactions have been critically discussed by M Muchie, 'Old wine in new bottles: a critical exploration of the UN's conceptions and mechanisms for the transfer of environmentally sound technologies to industry' (2000) 22 Technology in Society 201.

93 See *Glossary of Environment Statistics*, Studies in Methods, Series F, N.67 (United Nations 1997).

reformulated or reviewed in order to fine-tune them in view of these targets. Targets 17.6 and 17.8 are inherently connected with the transformative potential of multi-stakeholder partnerships active in the field of ICT and digitisation. That is why to a great extent such targets were designed to highlight the sustainability-supporting role of new technologies in reducing delays, facilitating face-to-face contact and encouraging the use of methods of direct communication between stakeholders.

The 'inclusiveness' aspect of transformative sustainable multi-stakeholder partnerships based on SDG 17 also reveals an important implicit target, which is not found in Targets 17.6, 17.7 and 17.8. This implicit target refers to the equitable access to the internet and ICT and adequate digital literacy on the part of the different stakeholders involved. This occurs for example in partnerships relevant to cross-border proceedings and international legal cooperation. If this observation is made from a broader perspective, equitable access to ICT and digital literacy may be a decisive component of the achievement of the goal of access to justice (laid down in SDG 16) in cooperative frameworks and, overall, in private international law.[94]

6. RESULTS AND CONCLUSION

This has chapter sought to explain how private international law instruments and doctrines are supportive of and supported by SDG 17. Here, the interplay between SDG 17 and private international law is based on diversity of methods and cooperative frameworks, whereby multi-stakeholder partnerships are set up in a collaborative, transformative and sustainable fashion. As discussed earlier, several concrete examples showcase that synergy. The HCCH approach, reinforcing the cooperation regime in cross-border family matters with the adoption of the 2007 Child Support Convention, was guided by both expected deliverables and effective results[95] in terms of assistance, transnational proceedings and benefits accruing from new technologies that shape legal (judicial and administrative) cooperation.

---

94 This is precisely why adequate access to ICT for court-to-court communication processes or convening hearings could not be reduced, for example, to global indicators on availability of ICT tools and physical access through computers, smartphones, use of videoconferencing and digital platforms. SDGm17 and its corresponding technology-related targets require multi-stakeholder partnerships to be sympathetic to a commitment to fostering digital knowledge, digital capacities and digital literacy in transformative outputs dealing with court-to-court, direct communication and further dealings in cross-border litigation.

95 See for instance the Preamble to the 2007 Hague Child Support Convention ('procedures which produce results and are accessible, prompt, efficient, cost-effective, responsive and fair').

The applicability of SDG 17 and its technology-related targets to private international law policies and institutions has led to common goals defined by the combination of adequate allocation of resources and procedures to the increasing use of new enabling technologies by stakeholders. Such combination promotes what a variety of stakeholders would expect from a global cooperation framework in cross-border civil and commercial matters: a system of cooperation that is comprehensive enough to make advances in that field and sustainable enough to further stimulate stakeholders to overcome challenges posed by SDG 17.

The 2007 Child Support Convention was expressly designed to be flexible enough to continuously evolve, in such a way as to engage in solutions benefiting from technological development, which is also a vital component of SDG 17. To a great extent, the flexibility, inclusiveness and openness of the HCCH cross-border administrative and judicial cooperation model, with the involvement and participation of diverse stakeholders, is in a sense unique. It enables a distinctive set of multi-stakeholder dialogues and partnering schemes, allowing diplomatic bodies, governments, national and regional courts and central authorities to engage with industry, civil society organisations and academia.

As explored in this chapter, technology facilitation schemes, environmentally sound technologies and use of enabling ICT would offer new opportunities for existing multi-stakeholder partnerships, such as those involved in the regulatory and policy affairs of the main organisations devoted to global private international law. The HCCH, OAS, UNCITRAL, UNIDROIT and ASADIP, as well as governments, their specialised departments and ministries of foreign affairs, industry organisations and other NGOs, will benefit from the conceptual frameworks and concrete cases offered by SDG 17 and multi-stakeholder partnerships on an ongoing basis.

Based on the research findings supporting this chapter, the desired intersection between private international law, SDG 17 and its specific Targets 17.6, 17.7 and 17.8 is the catalyst for the design of new multi-stakeholder partnerships or for an operational review of existing ones. Some partnerships are still open for reformulation and new experiments, such as technology facilitation schemes designed for cooperation frameworks in private international law. Such technology facilitation schemes will serve the main goal of improving direct communication and the roles of central authorities and law enforcement authorities in the course of cross-border proceedings, in addition to the close involvement of further stakeholders in the post-conventional phase and legislative projects relating to the operation of treaties and conventions in the field of private international law. One could also remark on the fact that the dissemination of environmentally sound technologies and the development of new enabling technologies by multi-stakeholder partnerships support tasks relating to the drafting and implementation of general principles, guidelines and best practices associated with private international law and SDG 17.

Partnerships in legislative and regulatory sectors in private international law and SDG 17 may promote joint regulations based on the distinct contributions and experiences of stakeholders across the globe. In this sense, such legislative outcomes would represent novel transnational legal experiments and the concrete achievement of the goal related to the 'conciliation of laws', as proposed earlier in this chapter.

The recent publication of the Legal Guide to Uniform Instruments in the Area of International Commercial Contracts, with a Focus on Sales,[96] a joint publication of UNCITRAL, UNIDROIT and the HCCH, offers an excellent illustration of how cooperation between organisations, enabled by technology and with input from the academic world, can lead to a user-friendly resource. The Guide illustrates how the instruments on contracts and sales prepared by these organisations interact to achieve the shared goals of predictability and flexibility.

In line with the overall implementation of the 2030 Agenda, private international law policies and practices should be continuously formulated with a focus on the dual dimension of the 2030 Agenda. In the case of Targets 17.6, 17.7 and 17.8, cooperation (judicial and administrative) regimes in cross-border civil and commercial matters should prioritise designing of multi-stakeholder partnerships in a collaborative and transformative fashion and ones which support technological development. The development and use of enabling technologies in cooperation frameworks established under UNCITRAL and the HCCH, for example, still have room for further improvement in terms of properly allocating and disseminating technological resources and sharing such resources with other private international law institutions. This includes the operation of sustainable development-driven partnerships within regional and domestic systems, based on the premises of new technology facilitation regimes.

In turn, the dual dimension of SDG 17, the operation of multi-stakeholder partnerships relevant to private international law and the use of enabling technologies are conducive to the gradual approach on implementation of the SDGs in the 2030 Agenda. This feature, as evidenced by the provisions of the HCCH 2007 Child Support Convention relating to legal assistance and enforcement of decisions, and HCCH practices such as the assistance given to emerging states under the ICATAP, is also based on the differing capabilities of industrialised and emerging economies as both promoters and recipients of technical assistance in substantive and procedural issues related to private international law.

Regional and domestic experiences, such as those observed in relation to the OAS Member States, local governments, organisations, academia and

---

96 <https://www.unidroit.org/instruments/commercial-contracts/tripartite-legal-guide> accessed 30 June 2021.

existing collaborative projects, offer examples of how private international law policies and instruments are conducive to the achievement of the main goals of transnational collaboration and multi-stakeholder participation. In this sense, such experiences are characterised by a bottom-up formulation, since they mostly originated from domestic practices. The main goals of transnational collaboration may be further improved by multi-stakeholder partnerships thanks to the increasing use of new technologies (for example, the current practices based on mutual assistance, e-practices and e-learning projects developed by UNCITRAL, the HCCH, ASADIP and stakeholders at the domestic level).

ABOUT THE EDITORS AND PROJECT COORDINATOR

Editors

Ralf Michaels, LL.M. (Cambridge), Dr. iur. (Passau), MAE, is Director at the Max Planck Institute for Comparative and International Private Law, Hamburg, Germany, Chair in Global Law at Queen Mary University London, UK and Professor of Law at Hamburg University, Germany.

Verónica Ruiz Abou-Nigm, LL.M (Edin.), Ph.D. (Edin.), Dr. en Derecho (UCU), is Senior Lecturer in International Private Law at Edinburgh Law School, UK.

Hans van Loon, LL.M., Dr h.c., is a Member of the *Institut de droit international* and former Secretary General of the Hague Conference on Private International Law.

Project Coordinator

Samuel Zeh is Research Associate and doctoral student at the Max Planck Institute for Comparative and International Private Law, Hamburg, Germany.

www.ingramcontent.com/pod-product-compliance
Ingram Content Group UK Ltd.
Pitfield, Milton Keynes, MK11 3LW, UK
UKHW051918100926
8556IPUK00021B/1237

9 781839 701665